New Religions

New Religions
A Guide
New Religious Movements, Sects and Alternative Spiritualities

Edited by Christopher Partridge

OXFORD
UNIVERSITY PRESS

OXFORD
UNIVERSITY PRESS

This edition first published in 2004 in the United States
of America by Oxford University Press, Inc., 198 Madison
Avenue, New York, NY 10016

www.oup.com

Library of Congress Cataloging-in-Publication Data is
available

First published in Great Britain in 2004 by Lion
Publishing

Copyright 2004 Lion Publishing

Text Acknowledgments
The scripture quotations contained herein are from The
New Revised Standard Version of the Bible, Anglicized
Edition, copyright © 1989, 1995 by the Division of
Christian Education of the National Council of the
Churches of Christ in the United States of America,
and are used by permission. All rights reserved.

Picture Acknowledgments
Please see page p. 446.

Previous page: *Cao Dai worship in the Holy See
Temple in Tay Ninh province, Vietnam.*

Below: *Brides holding pictures of their betrothed at
a mass wedding of the Unification Church.*

Contents

How to Use This Book

1. The articles have been chronologically ordered. With the exception of the 'feature articles', entries are ordered according to the date (or approximate date) when the new religion, sect or alternative spirituality was founded. A list of the articles can be found at the beginning of the book: see the 'Detailed Contents and Chronology'.

2. At the beginning of each section there is an overview of the relevant dominant religious tradition(s). For example, at the beginning of the section 'New Religions, Sects and Alternative Spiritualities with Roots in Christianity', there is a simple introduction to Christianity. The volume can be used without reference to these introductions, but individual new religions often refer to the histories, beliefs and practices of a major world religion, and thus a basic understanding of the latter is important. The introductions provide necessary basic background information.

3. Cross-references are indicated with an asterisk. Prior to a word on which there is a separate article there is an asterisk. Hence, *Elan Vital indicates that there is a separate article on Elan Vital. This article can be located using the index. A term is cross-referenced *only* the first time it appears in an article. Subsequent appearances in the same article will not include an asterisk.

4. The comprehensive index at the back of the volume can be used to locate particular groups, movements, beliefs, practices and individuals. When you have found the word you want, while it may be tempting simply to read only the paragraph in which it appears, you are encouraged to read the whole article. The major reference to each new religion, sect or alternative spirituality is highlighted in bold.

5. Also included at the back of the volume is a select bibliography. An extensive bibliography can be found on the publisher's website (see address on page 4). This bibliography is not exhaustive (an exhaustive bibliography would run into several volumes), but rather includes key books and articles recommended by the authors. Some of these are *secondary texts* (written by 'outsiders', i.e. those who are not members of the particular group) and some are *primary texts* (written by 'insiders', i.e. members of the particular group). Using both will help the reader to gain an accurate, critical understanding. Also included in the bibliography are *primary* websites and websites on which *secondary* material can be found. While not all religions and sects have active websites, and although websites do change and close over time, every effort was made to include as many useful and up-to-date websites as possible.

Detailed Contents and Chronology

Foreword

It has become a truism in religious studies that we in the West now live in a condition of extreme religious pluralism. While the traditional Christian churches still command the allegiance of the largest percentage of the religious segment of the population, they no longer command exclusive hegemony over the religious life of the West. In most Western countries, worshipping communities representing the full spectrum of the world's religions can now be found. This shift, which has become so evident in the past few decades, has made it almost impossible for any, apart from those few specialists in new religions, to possess knowledge of more than a small number of the many religious/spiritual alternatives now presenting themselves for the public's approval. Hence the need for and the function of this book.

In the pages that follow, readers will find a handy map of the major religious and spiritual groups functioning in the world today. The general editor, Christopher Partridge, has been assisted in his compilation by a number of capable scholars, each of whom possesses special knowledge of individual new religions. He has assembled the material into a user-friendly handbook that will open up the world of modern spiritualities, especially to those who are in need of a relatively objective third-party look at what may seem unfamiliar territory, the domain of some fringe and even bizarre ideas and practices.

Of course, the overall smooth process of the emergence of the world of religious alternatives has been disturbed and distorted by several incidents of violence and illegal activity in which a few have been involved. Thus, an additional role served by this guide is consumer protection. With so many unfamiliar religious groups operating in society, many of whom are actively recruiting new members, one looks for a way to double-check initial perceptions of what on first contact may be an attractive spiritual option for the religious seekers among us.

Getting a handle on new religions

With so many new and very different religions, one searches for a means of ordering what at first appears to be a very chaotic world. Several insights may assist that process. Firstly, it is helpful to remember that the 'new' in new religions most often refers to the seeker rather than the religion itself. That is to say, *most new religions are presenting old religions in a new context and to a new audience.* The majority of new religions are simply fresh variations on older religions now blossoming in places they would not have been found even several decades ago. A great number, if not a majority, of the new religions are Eastern and Middle Eastern religions that have been transplanted to the West in the decades since the Second World War. Since 1945, there have been large-scale migrations of people from countries that are dominantly Hindu or Buddhist or Islamic. In addition, Daoist, Radhasoami, Shintoist, Jainist, Sikh and Zoroastrian leaders have also migrated to the West, where they have built communities of support. The newness in most of the groups that have originated elsewhere is in the eye of the beholder, who most likely has never seen anything like it before.

Secondly, in spite of the Christian dominance through the last millennia, *an alternative religious tradition has continued to exist in the West and has flowered since the 16th century.* It goes under various names, most popularly occultism, but is now usually referred to as Western esotericism. Esotericism experienced a rebirth in the 17th century through *Rosicrucianism, and has subsequently given birth to *Freemasonry, ceremonial magic traditions (for example, the *Hermetic Order of the Golden Dawn), *Spiritualism, Theosophy (see the

*Theosophical Society), *Wicca and, most recently, the New Age. Esotericism remains one of the most understudied of religious phenomena, religious scholars eschewing a subject that has been so despised in many quarters. It is also the case that many esoteric groups have often found protection from those who would persecute them by redefining themselves as 'non-religious'. However, esotericism is best understood as a genuine religious phenomenon, and its groups, generously represented in the text that follows, are best seen as representatives of a singular religious tradition.

Thirdly, having acknowledged the role of the older religious traditions as the home of most new religions, we also must recognize some newness about the new religions themselves: *new religions are the products of the continual changes all religions are simultaneously undergoing in their effort to remain relevant to their time and place and the people they serve.* Religions are not static entities; they are always undergoing transformation as the faith is passed to each new generation. In a rapidly changing culture, such as that characterizing the modern West, we should not find it surprising that around the fringes of the older religious bodies, new religions are constantly born. Such new religions attempt to hold back the process of change and perpetuate an older way of life (some forms of *Fundamentalism), champion particular teachings believed once, abandoned or forgotten (*Celtic Spirituality, the *Worldwide Church of God), or incorporate new teachings into the tradition (the *Nation of Islam, *Prosperity Spirituality). Others strike out in different directions in bold attempts to find a fresh sense of the Divine.

Newness in new religions may come from the founding of a new organization, the emergence of prophets presenting fresh spiritual visions, or the creation of new religious syntheses. In the 1940s, visionaries proposed a new religious metaphor – flying saucers. In the 1950s, a British teacher, Gerald Gardner, suggested the creation of a new religion by combining remaining fragments of pre-Christian cultures, esoteric teachings and a healthy addition of religious imagination. The resulting religion became known as Wicca.

More often than not, new religions in the modern world come from the mixing of religious traditions. At one end of the spectrum is the very eclectic *Family Federation for World Peace and Unification (Unification Church), which draws material from a variety of faiths found in post-war Korea. The new *African independent churches mix the Christianity introduced by 19th-century Christian missions with insights and practices drawn from traditional African religions, while at the same time critiquing both their parents. Many of the newer Eastern and Middle Eastern groups emerged in response to the imposition of Christianity by colonial authorities.

Most new religions emerge within a previously existing religious context, a context which initially nurtured it and from which it draws basic insights. However, a minority of new religions have developed as the products of innovative women and men and present themselves as genuinely new phenomena even after the roots of their teachings have been explored. Such is the case with many groups born from the teachings of a new prophet – the *Nation of Islam, the *Meher Baba Movement, *Yiguandao and the *Church of Scientology. Some of these, like Scientology, are unique enough to challenge our very definitions of religion, and others cause us to continually re-examine the boundaries of the religious life. (A few new religions even challenge the imagination of the most knowledgeable students of the varieties of religious experience – *Thee Church ov MOO and *Jasmuheen and the Breatharians, to name a couple – and cause us to long for a more orderly world in which to do our work.)

But what's so special about new religions?

In the last few decades, new religions have become an item of intense interest and scrutiny by not just religious scholars but a range of professionals from psychiatrists to police and legal authorities. Given the fact that most of them are small and relatively ephemeral, and the fact that few will play a significant role in the future of society as a whole, why have so many become concerned about them? Without being anywhere near exhaustive, we can provide a few observations.

New religions have been among the most visible products of the changes pushing Western culture into the 21st century. The forces altering and weakening the traditional secular structures in Western society have challenged religious institutions just as they have all the others. In the face of the new religions, these institutions have moved to conserve, protect, defend and revive their own religious life. While many of these attempts have been very successful, some institutions have proved ineffective in maintaining the support of the once faithful. New religions arise to challenge the insufficiencies of the older religious communities. The ferment they cause at the edge of familiar religion reverberates through those whose own religious ideals are firmly rooted in tradition.

New religions thus become the target of religious polemicists who freely challenge their spiritual credentials. New religions are, in many cases, religions still in the process of becoming. They change rapidly and mature slowly. They experiment with new forms of religious organization, offer differing moral perspectives, and explore different possibilities for salvation and enlightenment. As experiments fail, they can quickly drop options and adopt new ones. Their whole programme opens them to critiques by their more experienced competitors.

While challenging older religious structures, new religions are also viewed by many as destructive of the very fabric of society. And it is certainly the case that the emergence of religious pluralism challenges the ability of a nation to see itself as representative of a common religious culture in more than a vague historical sense. For those who wish to see specific religious values permeating society, commonly held religious teachings supported by governmental agencies, and a religious-based morality enforced by law, the emergence of so many divergent religious competitors is extremely threatening and demoralizing.

New religions extend the choices available to anyone seeking to resolve a spiritual crisis. Just as people now have an immense number of choices in other realms, from what clothes they will wear to what music they prefer, they now also have a choice of the religious teachings that most make sense of their life. The real choice was to accept or reject one dominating form of religion or unbelief, but today there is a plethora of choice. Thousands of religious groups now exist that embody one of a host of the differing metaphysical descriptions of the human condition. And in them people may not only choose their religion but choose the level at which they wish to practise, from a dedicated full-time religious existence to occasional attendance at a religious service.

Having so many religions competing for the public allegiance changes the function that religion can serve in the society. In particular, religion's ability to serve as the primary correlate of national identity is now extremely limited. Society's members no longer grow up knowing a common set of religious texts or acknowledging a common set of religious symbols. The resulting space inhabited by so many 'unknown' religious communities in the larger secular community creates a new reason for anxiety, which in turn calls forth groups concerned about the potential for danger posed by the new religions in our midst.

However, no fact so calls our attention to new religions as the fact that some religions have betrayed the implied trust placed in them. Society has expectations of any group that would describe itself as spiritual or religious. However different new religions might be, we expect them to be supportive of the social good, we might expect their leaders to integrate a moral consciousness into society as a whole, and we might expect them to be generally attentive of their members and society's happiness and welfare. Amid hundreds of new unfamiliar religions, the occasion of one that fails to live up to expectations causes the status of all to be called into question.

The most well known of the new religions are those that have betrayed both their members and society with dramatic incidents of violence – for example, the *Peoples Temple, *Aum Shinrikyô, the *Order of the Solar Temple and *Heaven's Gate. Others, in challenging traditional moral codes in the larger society, have found both religious and secular authorities striking out against the various alternatives to limiting sexual relations to married heterosexual couples – polygamy, adulterous intragroup relationships or free love.

Almost by definition, new religions are dissenters, offering different paths from those that dominate in society. And, while it is most regrettable that a few have adopted courses that have proved destructive of life and morality (though such destructive courses have by no means been limited to the new religions), it is also the case that new religions also exist as a healthy sign within the religious community, a sign that staid religious patterns are constantly under scrutiny, that the structures of the religious life that tend to become fossilized are continually being examined for signs of decay, and that the adequacy of theologies are constantly being put to the test.

If the study of modern religious pluralism has taught us anything, it is the fact that religious homogeneity in a society can in the long run only be maintained by the power of the state. The lack of religious ferment in a society is a sign that some people in the society are expending enormous amounts of energy to suppress the freedoms of other members. The existence of religious freedoms means that some will choose differently. The existence of a wide spectrum of forms of religious life in a society, even while a single form may be the dominant or majority one, appears to be the state of the society that is truly free.

It is popular to ask the following question: Why do people join new religions? Such an enquiry remains an important one. Apart from the conditions that allow the posing of alternatives (legal provisions concerning religious freedom), it is of continuing interest as to why people adopt them. However, it may be more important in the long run to pose other questions that will help us to come to some understanding as to why some countries and cultures persist in rejecting contemporary trends towards honouring human choices about the spiritual/religious life.

A step in participating in these enquiries concerning the viability and worth of new religions, however, requires some basic knowledge about them. As a reader, you now have a viable tool before you to begin to acquire that basic set of information. The facts are so interesting that you may wish to read straight through. Or you may find yourself dipping into the content occasionally as a question about different groups comes to the fore. Either way, you will find this book an invaluable guide.

DR J. GORDON MELTON
FOUNDER/DIRECTOR OF THE INSTITUTE
FOR THE STUDY OF AMERICAN RELIGION
SANTA BARBARA, CALIFORNIA
JANUARY 2003

Introduction

Christopher Partridge

Religions are never static, as they are always, to a greater or lesser extent, in the process of evolution. They are ways of life that shape, and are shaped by, their contexts. Consequently, throughout religious history and within every culture, there have been reform movements, revivals and novel developments; new emphases emerge, mystical ideas evolve, fundamentalisms resurge and old forms of religion die out. In other words, new religions, sects and alternative spiritualities have always been part of the flow of religious history. As individuals and religious communities face new challenges as a result of, for example, travelling to new countries and cultures or even as a consequence of reflecting on the uncertainties and questions raised by the approaching milestones of history – such as the *fin de siècle* (end of a century) or, more significantly, the turn of a millennium – subtle social and psychological pressures seem to be exerted, which can lead to new, sometimes dramatic, religious developments. Again, when religions and cultures meet the result is often the emergence of new lines of enquiry, some of which seek interreligious integration and others of which resist dialogue and explore avenues of 'fundamentalist' opposition. Throughout the world there are numerous examples of movements that have appeared as the result of the merging of religious traditions (syncretism) or as the result of resistance to 'foreign' or 'heretical' traditions. In Melanesia, for example, the impact of European trade, Western government and Christian missions has led to the emergence of many new movements. Some of these have been and still are essentially Christian movements, while others are a mixture of Christian and indigenous religious traditions, and others are prophetic indigenous movements that resist the impact of foreign religions and cultures.

Who joins new religions, sects and alternative spiritualities?

There are, of course, numerous distinctive new religions, sects and alternative spiritualities, many different types of people who find them persuasive and attractive, and a variety of reasons why they do so. Many of those who joined Melanesian *cargo cults, for example, did so because, in Melanesian culture, power and authority is invested with religious significance. It was believed that the adoption of certain Christian beliefs and practices would allow access to the power and prosperity Europeans enjoyed. Many of those who joined David Koresh's *Branch Davidians or Jim Jones's *Peoples Temple were black and working class, but, generally speaking, westerners who join new religions tend to be white, middle class and well educated. While adults from across the age range join new religions and adopt alternative spiritualities, they are more often than not at the younger end of the spectrum (i.e. in their twenties and thirties). Many of these join from outside the group, but there are increasing numbers of individuals who have been born into new religions and who have grown up in homes where alternative spirituality is an accepted way of life.

The contemporary rise of new religions, sects and alternative spiritualities

While the existence of new religions is not a new phenomenon, arguably it is the case that the last hundred years or so, and particularly the last fifty years, have seen an unprecedented proliferation of new religions, sects and alternative spiritualities. One of the key changes underlying this unprecedented growth is the emergence of religiously plural societies. That is to say, increasingly societies are multicultural and multi-religious. For various reasons, people, sometimes whole communities, have travelled from the countries in which they were born to settle

in other countries and cultures. This has led to a situation in which many people in the world live in a religiously plural society. Again, not only do modern methods of travel mean that the world's cultures are only a few hours away, but, thanks to radio, television and increased literacy, information about other cultures and religious communities is disseminated widely and rapidly. As a result, people in the modern world are increasingly aware of, influenced by and challenged by the teachings and the very existence of other religions and cultures. Of course, religious pluralism is actually nothing new, in that there has always been religious diversity in the world and it has always been difficult for even the most isolated of tribal groups to remain ignorant of the fact that other people exist who hold different beliefs from their own. However, the point is that, while this is true, the 20th century witnessed an unprecedented exposure to and, consequently, a *greater understanding* of the beliefs of others. Whereas in countries such as India religious pluralism has always been a fact of life, this has not been the case in the West. At the beginning of the 20th century, the majority of westerners would have known very little about non-Christian faiths and probably regarded non-Christians as deluded and backward. Generally speaking this is not the case today. Not only are people much more tolerant of and interested in the religious beliefs of others, but, in some cases, they adopt those beliefs in preference to the dominant beliefs in their own culture.

It is not surprising that, within this religiously plural context, people should start not only to look away from traditional religious providers such as the Christian church, but also to experiment with spirituality – even pick and mix from a range

Pope John Paul II and representatives of the world's religions attend a Day of Prayer for Peace, in Assisi, Italy, 2002.

of spiritualities. Hence, while Christianity has gone into decline in the West, other religions – including smaller movements such as the *Jehovah's Witnesses and the *Church of Jesus Christ of Latter-Day Saints – and many alternative spiritualities, such as Paganism, are experiencing growth, often substantial growth. (Indeed, Paganism is regularly reported as being Britain's fastest-growing religious tradition.) As J. Gordon Melton (a leading scholar and chronicler of new religious movements) has noted, 'during the 20th century, the West experienced a phenomenon it has not encountered since the reign of Constantine: the growth of and significant visible presence of non-Christian and non-orthodox Christian bodies competing for the religious allegiance of the public. This growth of so many alternatives religiously is forcing a new situation on the West in which the still dominant Christian religion must share its centuries-old hegemony in a new pluralistic religious environment.' With very few exceptions, if you were to carry out a survey of the beliefs of people living within a five-mile radius of where you are now, you would come across a multitude of diverse beliefs and practices, many of which will be new and eclectic. As well as the alternative religious groups, which can trace their origins directly back to one of the major world religions, there has been a proliferation of groups and movements that draw inspiration from a variety of religious sources. For example, a range of New Age philosophies, practitioners and treatments can be found throughout Western culture.

What are new religions, sects and alternative spiritualities?

How are 'new religions', 'sects' and 'alternative spiritualities' distinguished from each other? This is a relatively complex question about which more than a few books and essays have been written.

NEW RELIGIONS

In this book, the term 'new religions' carries essentially the same meaning as the terms 'new religious movements' (NRMs), 'fringe religions' and 'alternative religions', all of which have been used in scholarly literature on the subject. My decision against using these terms is primarily a matter of personal preference. However, my decision against using another popular term – 'cults' – was taken because of the particularly negative baggage that often attaches to it. In actual fact, the term 'cult' is often usefully used within sociological literature to indicate a type of religion that is considered deviant by society and is individualistic, in the sense that the emphasis is on the final authority of the individual, rather than on the authority of a particular charismatic leader or sacred text. Individuals – not the church, the guru, the Bible or some other external religious authority – choose their own spiritual path and decide for themselves what is true and useful. In this sense, 'cultic religion' is similar to what is described below as 'alternative spirituality'. However, because the media and many Christian observers have been guilty of indiscriminately using the term 'cult' pejoratively to refer to groups and movements they consider to be heretical, dangerous or even demonic, the term has become unhelpful and offensive. Also, because many popular books on new religions have been explicitly 'anti-cult' books and, moreover, have often been misleading in their treatment of such groups, it seemed wise to avoid the term altogether. This is *not* an 'anti-cult' book, but rather an objective, judgement-free guide for those who want, for whatever reason, reliable information about a range of new religions, sects and alternative spiritualities.

ALTERNATIVE SPIRITUALITIES

The term 'alternative spirituality' has been included because not all the articles in this volume discuss beliefs and practices that can be described as 'religious'. Arguably, one of the more significant developments in particularly Western religious adherence is the emergence of private, non-institutional forms of belief and practice. The sacred persists, but increasingly it does so in non-traditional forms. There is, as the sociologist Grace Davie has argued, 'believing without belonging'. More specifically, it can be argued that much of this believing without belonging should be defined as 'spirituality' rather than 'religion'. There is in the West, for example, a move away from traditional forms of belief, which have developed within religious institutions, towards forms of belief that focus on the self, on nature or simply on 'life'. While there may be particular traditional teachings that are valued by the individual seeker, or particular groups to which the individual belongs, generally speaking there is a suspicion of traditional authorities, sacred texts, churches and hierarchies of power. There is a move away from a 'religion' that focuses on things that are considered to be external to the self (God, the Bible, the church) to 'spirituality' – that which focuses on 'the self' and is personal and interior. Hence, while there are, of course, 'spiritualities' within the world religions, particularly 'mystical' movements, which focus on the individual's inner experience of the divine, 'alternative spiritualities' are not necessarily allied to any particular religious tradition. The individual may draw inspiration from, for example, the writings of the Christian mystics, or the Buddhist scriptures, or Sufi (Islamic mystical) texts, but these sources of inspiration are not viewed as external authorities in the same way that the Bible is viewed as an authority in Christianity or the Qur'an within Islam. In pursuance of an alternative spirituality the individual might reflect on the teachings of Jesus, Daoist ideas or even the spiritual significance of dolphins or UFOs, they might take hallucinogenic drugs or follow a course of meditation, but, whatever they do, they will follow a personally tailored path that focuses on 'the self' and which can

usefully be distinguished from what would normally be regarded as 'a religion'.

While the term 'spirituality' in this volume often has a particular reference to the 'turn to the self', it is also used of religious reflection that, strictly speaking, refers to more than this. For example, much contemporary *feminist and eco-feminist spirituality cannot be considered as principally a 'turn to the self' and, indeed, is often developed within a particular religious tradition. Hence, when the term 'spirituality' is used of such developments it is used in a broader, less precise way, which merges with what might be understood as a 'soft definition' of religion. Indeed, in contemporary Christian thought, the term 'spirituality' is notoriously vague and often seems to mean simply 'being spiritual' or 'being religious' – as opposed, I suppose, to being profane. That said, the Christian spiritualities discussed in this volume seek to overturn the distinction between the spiritual and the non-spiritual and understand spirituality to be a quest for full humanity that embraces the whole of the created order. Perhaps spirituality can be understood as a path that, while focusing on the self, seeks to extend to all life and certainly beyond the bounds of institutional religion. It is important to say that, while some would argue that institutional religion stifles true spirituality, many today within particular religious traditions understand spirituality to be at the heart of all true religion.

SECTS

The term 'sect' is perhaps equally important. Whereas many of the articles in this volume deal with relatively novel groups which, while having their roots in a particular religion or religious tradition, have now broken away and formed new religions, there are also groups which, while they are new developments, are not 'cults', 'new religions' or 'spiritualities' but 'sects' that sometimes have explicitly traditional, orthodox beliefs. Indeed, sects typically claim to be the defenders of true and vital faith in the face of a church or a religion that has become 'lukewarm' and barely distinguishable from the surrounding society and culture. Hence, sects tend to be revivalist, enthusiastic and 'fundamentalist', and can often be identified by their understandings of truth and authority and by their notions of separateness and distinctiveness as sacred communities. They are voluntary organizations that require members to fulfil certain, usually strict, criteria (e.g. tangible evidence of conversion, and acceptance of particular doctrines and codes of ethics) and to achieve levels of commitment well beyond those found in non-sectarian religion. In other words, they have a strong sense of self-identity with clear 'insider-outsider' boundaries (i.e. beliefs, practices and ways of life that clearly identify who is 'in' and who is 'out'). This is supported by an exclusivist theology and an elitist understanding of the sect as the sole possessor of religious truth. Consequently, it is separated from both 'the world' (wider society) and also the dominant orthodoxy. Sometimes, failure to fulfil doctrinal and ethical requirements can lead to shunning and even expulsion. For example, the sociologist Bryan Wilson, who has studied the *Exclusive Brethren, notes the following:

When there is persistent wrongdoing or false teaching, the local assembly becomes concerned, and if the case cannot be resolved by rebuke, then an unrepentant individual is said to be 'shut up', a term used to indicate that he is not admitted to the Brethren's meetings and, in particular, to the meeting for the 'breaking of bread'. One who fails to repent is then 'withdrawn from' or 'put out', and any brother who fails to dissociate himself from the unrepentant himself becomes subject to the same form of censure. Little as such measures might be appreciated by outsiders, they are well understood by those who have committed themselves to the fellowship as something unfortunate but essential to the maintenance of its purity.

To summarize, the chief characteristics of sectarian religion are a strong emphasis on individual commitment to the sect's doctrines and codes of morality, a focused sense of self-identity, and clear purity-pollution boundaries (e.g. an obligation to maintain purity and avoid pollution by eating the right food, or refusing blood transfusions, or avoiding social interaction with non-members).

Having said that, obviously not all sects are the same. They do not, for example, all demand the same levels of commitment from their members, or the same degrees of separation from the wider society. Wilson distinguishes four sub-types of Christian sects: conversionist, Adventist/revolutionist, introversionist/pietist and Gnostic. Sect types are determined by 'the response of the sect to the values and relationships prevailing in society'.

The conversionist *sects seek to alter men, and thereby to alter the world; the response is free-will optimism. The* Adventist *sects predict drastic alteration of the world, and seek to prepare for the new dispensation – a pessimistic determinism. The* introversionists *reject the world's values and replace them with higher inner values, for the realization of which inner resources are cultivated. The* Gnostic *sects accept in large measure the world's goals but seek a new and esoteric means to achieve these ends – a wishful mysticism.*

Moreover, over time, as sects become established institutions, they become 'cooler' and can even be accepted as denominations. For example, while Pentecostalism is now an orthodox, mainstream Protestant denomination, early in the 20th century it was a breakaway movement: a 'sect'. Similarly, from a sociological perspective, Methodism, now an important denomination, was once, strictly speaking, a sect. Today, an orthodox Christian group such as the *Jesus Fellowship (also known as the Jesus Army), while not a 'new religion' or an 'alternative spirituality', can be included in a volume such as this because its distinctive practice and separateness mark it out as being sectarian.

As the above discussion indicates, defining new religious movements, sects, alternative spiritualities and 'cults' is not straightforward. Groups once considered sects can become denominations and churches. Loosely organized spiritualities can become organized movements. Certainly, while the distinctions are useful when analysing new religions, one should avoid treating them as discrete boxes. Such typologies are simply blunt tools used to aid understanding and analysis.

How new is new?

What religions should be considered *new*? Again, this is another complex issue about which there is a lack of consensus in the scholarly community. Certainly some of the groups discussed in this volume date back over 100 years – some even date back many centuries. Hence, it can be difficult to see in what sense they can be considered *new*, and thus why they are included in this volume.

While there are several definitions of 'new' in this context, the editor's definition of a *new* religion, sect or alternative spirituality, is as follows: a religion, sect or alternative spirituality that emerged or *rose to prominence* during the 20th century. Whereas the *Muttappan Teyyam in India, for example, is many centuries old, it is only since the 1950s that it has become popular and spread rapidly. It is a 'new' religion in the sense that it rose to prominence within the last century. This is also true of some *Japanese new religions. While this definition of 'new' is fairly broad in comparison to some scholarly definitions, it seems to do the job more adequately than narrower definitions. For example, some scholars would like to limit the definition to those religions that have emerged since 1945 (i.e. since the end of the Second World War) or, indeed, even later (i.e. since 1960). And it has to be said that, because there has been a flowering of new religions in the West after 1945, this volume has prioritized post-1945 developments. However, to draw the line at 1945 (or later) seems a little arbitrary

and limiting in that it excludes new movements that one would expect to see in this volume. For example, the Jehovah's Witnesses, the Church of Jesus Christ of Latter-Day Saints, *Christian Science and the *Theosophical Society were all founded prior to 1900, but rose to prominence during the 20th century before 1945. Other significant recognizably new groups such as *Sôka Gakkai, were founded in the 20th century, but again prior to 1945. To adopt the post-1945 definition and yet to include religions, sects and alternative spiritualities such as these would require some unnecessary qualification of the word 'new'. Moreover, when one considers the long histories of the principal religious traditions in which many of these movements have their roots, it is difficult to describe them as anything other than new.

Not only did it seem practical to cast the net more widely and take in the whole of the 20th century, but it also seemed important to include a few groups that were founded over a century ago and which have subsequently gone into decline. These groups are crucial for an adequate understanding of the rise of other significant contemporary new religions and alternative spiritualities. For example, while the *New Church, *Rosicrucianism, *Freemasonry and indeed the whole Western esoteric tradition are hardly *new* developments, it seemed important to include entries on them in this volume because their influence can be found in a host of recent occult and New Age religions and spiritualities.

It is perhaps worth noting that, to some extent, the post-1945/Second 'World' War and post-1960 definitions of 'new' also betray a certain Western bias in the study of new religions. Indeed, some scholars will not only limit their definitions of new to post-1945 or post-1960, but will also explicitly limit their definitions to groups within the West, or to groups that have had an impact upon the West. In the words of Elizabeth Arweck, a scholar of new religions, 'the important point about NRMs is that they are movements which have come to prominence in North America and Europe since the Second World War'. She continues, 'It can be said that a significant number of NRMs spread from the United States to Britain, and from there to Continental Europe. Although some had been founded or started in other countries before coming to the United States, it is in the United States where they came to prominence.' While this is clearly true of a large number of new religions, sects and alternative spiritualities, the problem is that many movements not only have their origins in the non-Western world, but also have their centre of gravity there. Indeed, movements such as *Falun Gong, the Muttappan Teyyam and *Candomblé, while having followers in North America and Europe, are by no means Western movements. Indeed, some notable movements, such as *cargo cults, have virtually no presence in North America and Europe. Hence, while it is true that many of the largest international groups have settled and grown in the West, it is important that the study of new religions resists parochialism.

Families of new religions, sects and alternative spiritualities

Academics are, as ever, keen to create categories and to construct typologies so that some order can be given to the great variety of new religions, sects and alternative spiritualities. For example, in *The Cult Experience*, J. Gordon Melton and Robert Moore grouped new religions into eight 'families', each of which represents 'a common thought world, lifestyle and heritage':

■ *The Latter-Day Saint family* are 'held together by a shared belief in the revelations of Joseph Smith Jr', the founder of Mormonism.

■ *The communal family* is made up of alternative religions that emphasize communal living.

■ *The metaphysical family* draws on ideas developed within the 19th-century New Thought movement in the United States. Essentially, this family denies the reality of evil and emphasizes the power of the mind over matter and personal health. A person, it is believed, can determine their own health, wealth and happiness by correct thinking and attitude.

■ *The psychic-spiritualist family*, the largest of the families, focuses on psychic phenomena, the paranormal and the occult. Drawing on *Spiritualism, revelations are, it is believed, communicated through mediums or channels. The family includes a range of groups from theosophy to New Age organizations, and from UFO religions to some forms of *psychedelic spirituality.

■ *The ancient wisdom family* consists of groups (many of which overlap somewhat with the previous family) that believe humans are in a position to access powerful, occult knowledge from the ancient past. Such groups will often emphasize truths that have been passed down within secret traditions, and will stress the importance of ancient cultures, particularly those of Egypt and the mythological Atlantis (which many within the occult/New Age subculture believe to have been a real, ancient, technologically advanced civilization).

■ *The magical family* overlaps somewhat with the previous two families, in that, again, there is an emphasis on ancient wisdom and the paranormal. However, groups within this family seek to harness natural and supernatural forces and contact spiritual entities by means of ritual magic. Typical of this family would be the *Hermetic Order of the Golden Dawn, *Ordo Templi Orientis, some Satanist organizations and, more recently, the *Servants of the Light. Melton also included in this family, Pagan traditions such as *Druidry and *Wicca/witchcraft.

■ *The Eastern family*, as the name suggests, draws inspiration from 'Eastern religions' (e.g. Buddhism, Hinduism, Daoism and Sikhism). Often these groups have a single teacher (guru) who will tutor them in certain techniques, disciplines (e.g. yoga and meditation) and philosophies. Typical members of this family of new religions are *ISKCON (the International Society for Krishna Consciousness) and the *Osho movement (founded by Bhagwan Shree Rajneesh).

■ *The Middle Eastern family* consists of those religions, sects and spiritualities that have their roots in faiths (often the mystical traditions of these faiths) with origins in the Middle East (most notably, Judaism, Christianity and Islam). This family includes new religions such as *Meshihistim, the *Nation of Islam, the *Sufi Movement and the *Meher Baba movement.

Another once-popular way to classify new religions was developed by the sociologist of religion, Roy Wallis. In *The Elementary Forms of Religious Life* (1984), he argued that new religions could be quite easily categorized under the following broad headings: world-affirming, world-renouncing and world-accommodating. In other words, religious movements can be classified according to their relationship with society. *World-affirming* religions accept many of the values, goals and aspirations of society, but believe that they can offer a more effective route to attaining such goals and provide a better model of such values. For example, those within the *human potential movement do not want to distance themselves from the world, but rather want to be more successful and happier within it. It is not the material world that is fundamentally flawed, but rather the individual's relationship with and understanding of themselves within the world that needs to be developed. Hence, in this sense, such groups can be seen as 'world-affirming'. Wallis cites movements such

as *Transcendental Meditation, *est* (*Landmark Forum) and the *Church of Scientology as being typically world-affirming.

Many groups, of course, clearly do not view the world in this way, believing it to be corrupting and detrimental to spiritual growth. Such groups are what many people would associate with the term 'cult'. These religions and sects are *world-renouncing*: as members seek to step outside society and away from the influence of the world they may even distance themselves from their families and friends. Such groups typically require total commitment, absolute obedience and sometimes even celibacy. Moreover, theologically, because there is often an enormous emphasis on the 'sinfulness' of the present age, there is sometimes an equal emphasis on imminent, apocalyptic divine intervention, which will bring 'the age' to an end. Typical of such groups are David Koresh's Branch Davidians (many of whom tragically died in the fire at Waco in February 1993), the *Family Federation for World Peace and Unification (Unification Church), and the Children of God (now known as *The Family). In extreme cases (which are thankfully rare) the renunciation of the world can lead to mass suicide. This is what happened in November 1978 when over 900 members of Jim Jones's Peoples Temple committed suicide in Jonestown, Guyana.

Finally, situated between these two groups are *world-accommodating* movements which, while not entirely rejecting the world, do claim that humanity has, so to speak, 'backslidden'; we are not living as God intended, so there is a need to recommit oneself to the spiritual life and to increase one's devotion. However, while Wallis identifies movements such as neo-Pentecostalism and charismatic Christianity as being 'world-accommodating', strictly speaking, such a view applies to most major religious traditions.

Wallis's last category highlights a problem with the typology, namely that it is rather too broad and sweeping. As noted above, most traditional religious believers who simply attend the local church, mosque, temple or synagogue once a week consider the world to be in some sense flawed, but do not want to separate themselves from it. Moreover, while the world-accommodating category is clearly problematic, in that most religions could be included, the other categories have similar problems. Should we include, for example, Buddhist monasteries and Roman Catholic religious communities in the world-renouncing category? Moreover, this way of categorizing new religions fails to take adequate account of the complex beliefs that many new movements hold. Some groups may be a complex mixture of two or more categories. There may be certain tendencies, such as a trend towards fundamentalism, that could lead normally world-affirming or world-accommodating groups to hold world-renouncing ideas without becoming world-renouncing groups. While Wallis's model does allow for movement between groups, it doesn't allow for the complexity of beliefs that are sometimes held.

Does this mean that a more sophisticated and closely defined typology such as that of Melton and Moore is preferable? Again, there are pros and cons. Yes, the 'family' model is better because it is more sensitive to complex beliefs. It is not a model based on a group's relationship to society, but rather a model based on the principal beliefs held by new religions. However, it also has problems in that, because there are so many new beliefs, and because many new religions pick and mix from a variety of sources, there is often considerable overlap between categories, and there is always going to be a need for further categories in order to accommodate the great variety of new religions, sects and alternative spiritualities. For example, on the one hand, not only do some forms of Wicca seem to be influenced by Eastern thought, but they could easily be placed within the psychic-spiritualist family, the ancient wisdom family or the

magical family. On the other hand, there are some groups, such as Scientology, that are difficult to fit comfortably into any of the boxes provided by Melton and Moore. Apart from these problems, it seems unbalanced to allocate a separate category to Latter-Day Saint groups. While there are numerous groups related to Mormonism, this category clearly reflects a further problem with the model: it is overly determined by American new religions. Larger groups elsewhere in the world, such as new African religions or Japanese new religious movements, may not be so easily categorized.

Guide to new religions, sects and alternative spiritualities

Bearing in mind the above problems, it seemed sensible to categorize entries according to religious traditions. While this volume could have simply ordered the entries alphabetically or chronologically, in the final analysis it seemed more helpful to provide some categorization. Unfortunately, even the preferred method – categorizing new religions, sects and alternative spiritualities according to the religions in which they have their roots – was not always easy and uncontroversial. While determining the religious origins of some groups is straightforward, others are far more difficult, in that some will deny having roots in any particular religious tradition and others will have roots in more than one. Having said that, when tracing the religious *roots* of founders, groups or spiritualities, it is often fairly clear which particular religions have been initially important, even if they have grown away from those religions in subsequent years. However, there are other new religions, spiritualities and 'psycho-spiritual therapies' that do not have roots in any particular religion, but are principally (if not always solely) rooted in modern Western culture, such as Scientology and *transpersonal psychologies. While all typologies and attempts at categorization are problematic and while some entries in the volume have been particularly difficult to place, it is hoped that the structure of the volume will be a help to the reader, rather than an unnecessary and distracting hindrance.

The reader will also note that the articles have not been listed alphabetically. In order to provide a sense of their place in history, the new religions, sects and alternative spiritualities have been chronologically ordered. That is to say, with the exception of the feature articles, the entries have been ordered according to the date, or approximate date, when they were founded.

As to the volume as a whole, while there are many reliable and authoritative reference books on the major world faiths, this is not the case for new religions, sects and alternative spiritualities. Although there are far more reference books than there once were, there is a need for an accessible, reliable reference tool for interested non-specialists. To fulfil this need, the articles are written clearly and for the non-specialist. The contributors represent the best in contemporary scholarship from around the world and each article is a reliable and informed treatment of its subject. As noted above, this is not an 'anti-cult' (nor, indeed, 'pro-cult') volume, but rather a judgement-free survey of new religions, sects and alternative spiritualities.

While the volume provides overviews of the principal new religions, sects and alternative spiritualities, and also many minor and even obscure groups, it is not comprehensive. Some years ago, Harold Turner estimated that there were 10,000 new religions and movements among the tribal peoples alone. Eileen Barker has estimated a further 2,000 exist in Europe, and a similar number can be found in the United States. Susumu Shimazono has suggested that there are probably a few thousand in Japan. Given that some of these figures are increasing all the time, a comprehensive volume would need to be both very large and also constantly updated. Having

said that, this volume is more comprehensive than most. Indeed, it would be difficult to find such accessible and informed treatments of some of the groups and ideas dealt with in this volume in any other reference work. Moreover, because very short dictionary articles can often be more misleading than helpful, many of the articles are longer than one would normally find in such a reference work. Some may be significantly longer because they discuss numerically large groups. Some may be longer because they introduce particularly influential religions and spiritualities. Others may be longer because they describe spiritualities and religions that are felt to be of particular interest to the majority of readers. There are also several feature articles dealing with groups of new religions (e.g. Japanese new religions, *African neo-traditional religions and *Ufology and UFO-related movements), key themes (e.g. *apocalypticism and millenarianism, *postmodern spirituality and feminist and eco-feminist spirituality), and particular beliefs and practices popular in contemporary new religion (e.g. *astrology and *tarot). There is also an introduction to each section outlining the principal beliefs and practices of the religious traditions in which the particular new religions, sects and alternative spiritualities have their roots.

New Religions, Sects and Alternative Spiritualities with Roots in **Christianity**

The Crucifixion of Christ *by an anonymous Spanish artist (c. 1405–1407).*

CHRISTIANITY

Christopher Partridge

Christians are the followers of Jesus Christ, a Jew born in Palestine during the reign of the Roman Emperor Augustus (27 BCE–14 CE). Every form of Christianity, in one way or another, claims the authority of Jesus Christ. Much of what is known of Jesus is found in the Gospels (Matthew, Mark, Luke and John), the first four books of the New Testament. These are central to the Christian scriptures (the Bible), the authority of which is accepted by all the principal Christian traditions. The Bible is made up of two collections of writings: the Old Testament (or Hebrew Bible/the Jewish scriptures) and the New Testament. The Old Testament is written in Hebrew and the New Testament in Greek. Added to these collections, the Roman Catholic Church also accepts the authority of a number of other writings collectively known as the Apocrypha.

Central to the Gospel narratives and the message of the New Testament as a whole is Jesus' death and resurrection, in which, it is believed, God acted decisively for the salvation of the world: 'For God so loved the world that he gave his only Son, so that everyone who believes in him may not perish but may have eternal life. Indeed, God did not send the Son into the world to condemn the world, but in order that the world might be saved through him' (John 3:16–17). For many Christians the Old Testament points forward to this 'Christ event' and the New Testament looks back to it. From the early chapters of Genesis, which speak of creation, the significance of humanity, and the entry of sin into the world, to the final book of the Bible, the book of Revelation, which looks forward to the climax of human history and the ultimate victory of God over sin and the forces of evil, Christians think in terms of a 'salvation history'. Jesus is the centre of this salvation history and the key to its significance.

For Christians, salvation is always linked to the life, death and resurrection of Jesus Christ. Although increasing numbers of theologians in the modern period have developed exemplarist or subjective understandings of salvation – in which Christ demonstrates something about the nature of God, or provides a great example for humanity to follow – traditionally Christ did more than reveal something to humans. Rather, on the cross he actually did something for humanity, something without which salvation would not be possible. In other words, in some way, Christ acted as a 'substitute' for humans enslaved by sin and subject to death. As God, he did something we could not do: he faced sin and death head on, overcame them, and came out the other side. Hence, the resurrection speaks of salvation: it testifies that the sin and evil that separates humanity from God has been finally dealt with, and it promises eternal life. Death – 'the final enemy' – has been overcome. In Christ, a new form of life is now possible.

For the early Christians, Jesus' resurrection also indicated that God's rule had been inaugurated on earth. Consequently, the New Testament is, even in the face of death, dominated by the theme of hope. As a result of the resurrection, something new and decisive has happened in human history, something that has implications for 'the end-times'. Quite simply, for the early Christians, the resurrection ushered in the last days. Around this belief several other important teachings cluster, some of which have been central to the theologies of apocalyptic new religions (see *Apocalypticism and Millenarianism). They can be summarized as follows:

■ Jesus Christ will return again in power and glory to bring an end to history as we now know it (often simply referred to as 'the second coming'): 'For the Lord himself, with a cry of command, with the archangel's call and with the sound of God's trumpet, will descend from heaven, and the dead in Christ will rise first.

Then we who are alive, who are left, will be caught up in the clouds together with them to meet the Lord in the air; and so we will be with the Lord for ever' (1 Thessalonians 4:16–17).

■ These verses also indicate that the resurrection not only says a great deal about the significance of Jesus, but, as noted above, it is also the foundation of the believer's future hope, in that the believer will share in that resurrection. Just as Jesus was resurrected, so believers, too, will experience resurrection: 'Christ has been raised from the dead, the first fruits of those who have died. For since death came through a human being, the resurrection of the dead has also come through a human being; for as all die in Adam, so all will be made alive in Christ. But each in his own order: Christ the first fruits, then at his coming those who belong to Christ. Then comes the end, when he hands over the kingdom to God the Father, after he has destroyed every ruler and every authority and power' (1 Corinthians 15:20–24).

■ These verses mention a further complex area of Christian belief about the end-times, a belief which, again, often appears in new religious thought, namely 'the kingdom of God'. There has been much debate as to whether the kingdom of God has been fully realized in the coming of Jesus, or is a rule of God that has begun to have an effect in history, but awaits full realization, or is a future rule that will apocalyptically break into human history. But, whatever the interpretation, the kingdom of God is central to Christian theology.

Bearing the above in mind, it is not surprising that, for the first Christians, the resurrection of Jesus also testified to his status as Messiah, the redeemer promised to Israel many years before. Indeed, the term 'Christ' is a title designating Jesus as 'the Anointed One' or 'the Messiah'.

The rise and spread of Christianity

The first five centuries of the Christian church saw many debates, controversies and 'heresies'. As a result of these, church councils (meetings of bishops) formulated creeds or statements of belief that set forth the parameters of orthodoxy. (Heresy often precedes orthodoxy, in that it forces the church to state what it considers to be correct belief.) For example, the Nicene Creed of 325 CE stated that there is only one God (monotheism) and this God should be understood as a Trinity, namely Father, Son (Jesus Christ) and Holy Spirit (now operative within the church and within individual Christians). However, Father, Son and Spirit should not be understood as three modes or manifestations of God (modalism), and nor should they be understood as three separate divinities (tritheism), but should rather be understood as three persons (*hypostases* in the Greek) sharing a single divine substance (*homoousios*), each being fully God. Hence, God is correctly understood as a Tri-unity. This, of course, raised further questions. For example, if Jesus is divine – 'of one substance (*homoousios*) with the Father' – does this mean that he was not *fully* human? Perhaps he only *seemed* to be fully human (docetism). Not at all. A further council held at Chalcedon in 451 CE insisted that, without thinking of him as some strange hybrid being or a being with a split personality, Jesus should be understood as having two 'natures' in a single unified person, a fully human nature and also a fully divine nature.

Initially a sect of Judaism, Christianity first organized itself in Jerusalem. However, although Jewish Christianity was dominant at first, within 20 years it had moved out into the Gentile (non-Jewish) world, spreading rapidly westward into Europe and Africa, and eastward into Asia. While Christianity's initial expansion was within a unified Roman empire, certain political changes within the empire had a lasting effect on the church. Because the empire was becoming too large to manage, the Emperor Diocletian effectively divided it in two in the late 3rd century. The Eastern half, which included Greece, Asia Minor, Palestine and Egypt, was predominantly Greek-speaking. The Western half, which included the rest of North Africa, Britain, Gaul, Spain and Italy, spoke Latin. This division had immense cultural and religious implications. In the west, Christianity converted the 'barbarian' invaders and survived the fall of the Western empire in 476 CE. In the east, the empire survived as the Christian state of Byzantium until 1453 CE, when Islamic invasions brought it to an end. Although the Greek-speaking east and the Latin-speaking west had begun to drift apart many centuries before, by the 11th century the church in the east and the church in the west had formally separated and had become distinct traditions with different theology and liturgy. They also differed in their understandings of the church's hierarchy

and the church's relationship with the state (Orthodoxy was more closely identified with the state than the church in the west).

The Reformation

All the main branches of Christianity subscribe to the final authority of the Bible and are united in their principal beliefs. There are, however, different branches of the Christian church, each with their own particular interpretations and practices. The principal Christian groupings are Roman Catholicism, Orthodoxy and Protestantism.

In the west, Roman Christianity invested increasing authority in the bishop of Rome, the pope. This authority, along with the authority of the church and the priesthood was questioned during the 16th-century Reformation, and the church again split into two. Protestantism was born. There were several key developments, largely as a result of the theological work of Martin Luther (1483–1546) and John Calvin (1509–64).

■ The Bible was declared to be the sole authority for church teaching. The phrase *sola scriptura* (by scripture alone) expressed the principal concern of the Reformers. Of course, this development had certain consequences, the most important of which were a new emphasis on the teaching and preaching of the Bible and consequently on the production of biblical commentaries, and the rejection or diminution of any beliefs that could not be shown to be grounded in the Bible.

■ There was an insistence that salvation is solely the result of the grace of God through personal faith in Christ. Summed up in the slogan *sola fide* (by faith alone), this doctrine stressed the inability of humans to contribute anything to their knowledge of God or their salvation. This was linked to a doctrine of election, which argued that God in his love graciously chose humans for salvation without regard for any good works they might do. The chosen were saved, not because of their merits, but solely because of the work of Christ. Moreover, the fact that a believer had faith was also attributed to the grace of God and, as such, provided some assurance that a person was indeed one of the elect.

A celebration of Mass in the Roman Catholic Church, where the sacraments are central to spiritual life.

◼️ Although the debates concerning the sacraments (e.g. Communion/ Eucharist and Baptism) are complex, and although the different parties of the Reformation had distinct understandings of the nature and purpose of them, generally speaking, there was a move away from the sacramentalism of Roman Christianity to an emphasis on the centrality of the pulpit and the preached Word. Moreover, the Reformers saw the sacraments as visible reminders of God's promises, which God lovingly provided to strengthen faith, and not as channels of grace and salvation.

◼️ Because we are justified by faith alone, the church should not be understood as the intermediary between God and humanity. A church, as far as Luther was concerned, is not principally about an ordained priesthood, but rather simply about the preaching of the gospel. A church is a community of believers in which the gospel is preached. If the true gospel of justification by faith alone is not preached to the congregation, then there is no church. Although Calvin and the later Reformers developed this understanding into a more systematic theology of the church, they fundamentally agreed that the marks of the true church were the faithful preaching of the gospel and the correct administering of the sacraments. These theological and political developments resulted in the formation of 'Protestant Christianity' which has, consequently, often understood itself over against Roman Catholicism.

Although, at the time of the Reformation, Protestantism was divided into two basic parties, the Lutheran (following Martin Luther) and the Reformed (following John Calvin), soon a third wing of 'radical Reformers' emerged: the Anabaptists (re-baptizers). 'The Anabaptists' was the nickname given to a range of 16th-century sects who baptized adult believers, rather than infants, as a mark of church membership. They were also distinguished by their emphasis on new birth and discipleship in the power of the Holy Spirit, their establishment of believers' churches free from state control, their commitment to economic sharing, and their vision of restoring New Testament Christianity. Seen as revolutionaries and often heretics, they were severely persecuted by Reformers throughout Europe. However, believing suffering to be a mark of the true church, this served to strengthen their commitment.

Since the Reformation, numerous 'sects' and 'denominations' have formed, each with their own distinctive emphases. Indeed, arguably, denominations begin life as sects. As sects evolve and become established, they grow into large, mainstream denominations with a global presence (e.g. the Methodist Church and the Baptist Church, each of which have since fragmented). Other groups, of course, such as the Cowherdians or the Muggletonians, Christian sects which sprang up in 17th-century England, never attracted more than a few hundred followers and eventually died out. The principal modern Protestant denominations are Lutherans, Presbyterians, Anglicans, Methodists, Baptists, Free Churches and Pentecostals.

Although there are many differences between the various branches of Christianity, perhaps the main difference is that regarding the understanding of authority.

◼️ For Roman Catholicism, focusing on the pope, the human head of the church (Christ is the true head), the following are key: the institutional church, the sacraments, tradition (i.e. the church's teaching and practice, which has been handed down) and the Bible.

◼️ For Eastern Orthodoxy, tradition (principally the creeds and the writings of the early church theologians), liturgy and the Bible are central.

◼️ For the reasons outlined above, Protestantism tends to attribute far greater authority to scripture than to tradition and has a less hierarchical understanding of the church.

■ Added to this, it is worth mentioning Pentecostalism and charismatic Christianity (the fastest-growing manifestation of the faith within the world today). The latter transcends denominational boundaries and, although essentially Protestant, can also be found within Roman Catholicism. This type of Christianity, while insisting on the authority of the Bible, places great emphasis on the believer's immediate experience of the Holy Spirit and the miraculous.

Christianity today

With over 2 billion Christians (i.e. over 32 per cent of the world's population), Christianity is currently the largest of the world's religions. While Christianity is in decline in the West, this is not so in other areas of the world. Indeed, the last century has seen it spread rapidly across the globe. In particular, Africa, and some parts of Asia and Latin America, have seen phenomenal growth. This growth has meant that it has come into contact with many other religions and cultures, which has, in turn, led to reactions against Christianity, conversion to Christianity, or the absorption of Christianity into indigenous belief systems. This has often resulted in the emergence of new indigenous religions or new syncretistic Christian religions. It is hard to avoid the fact that, in the contemporary world, there are many new forms of religion and spirituality that are Christian, derived from Christianity, or the result of reactions to Christian expansion.

Christian new religions are not, however, a new phenomenon. The history of Christianity is littered with new religions, sects and alternative spiritualities, from Gnostic Christianity and Montanism in the early church, to the Cathari (the pure) and the Hussites in the medieval period, to later groups, such as the Muggletonians, Southcottians, Quakers, Ranters, Irvingites, Shakers and *Christadelphians. Some have become major branches of the Christian church, while others, such as the *Church of Jesus Christ of Latter-Day Saints (Mormonism), the *Jehovah's Witnesses and *Christian Science, have become large, international alternative expressions of Christianity, even though they are not recognized by the older churches.

The New Church
Robert A. Gilbert

The New Church, sometimes called the Church of the New Jerusalem (and often, but erroneously, termed Swedenborgianism) was founded at East Cheap in London in 1787, to perpetuate and propagate the doctrines of the Swedish scientist and visionary, Emanuel Swedenborg (1688–1772). Swedenborg, who was a devout churchman and the son of a Lutheran bishop, wanted his ideas to be taken up by the established churches and had no intention of founding a new body. He maintained, however, that the second coming

Portrait of Emanuel Swedenborg by Pehr Kraft.

of Christ had taken place in the heavens in 1757, and his followers felt that this should be mirrored by instituting a new church on earth.

In its early years, the church grew slowly, suffering from the schisms that seem inevitable in all churches offering novel doctrines, but within 20 years it had become firmly established, its greatest strength in England, then and now, being in the north-west. The ministry of the New Church is derived from the ordained Methodist ministers who comprised its first clergy, while church government is congregational, each individual society of the New Church appointing representatives to the annual general conference. In the United States, where the New Church was established in 1792, it has been governed since 1817 by a General Convention, although there is a separate body, the General Church of the New Jerusalem, that holds a more exalted view of Swedenborg's writings and is episcopal in its government. Numerically the New Church is declining, with a current membership of 1,300 in Britain, approximately 6,000 in the United States, and some 25,000 elsewhere, the majority being in Africa.

Distinctive Swedenborgian doctrines concern the nature of God and his relationship with man, the interpretation of scripture, and the future life of man. Swedenborg held an unusual view of the Trinity, maintaining that there is one God and that the Trinity is not of persons but of aspects of the divine nature. God took on human form in Christ, his humanity being glorified through his constant resistance to temptation and his conquest of the powers of evil, thus ensuring the redemption of man.

For Swedenborg, God is also present in the Word: the inspired sacred scriptures. These have both a literal meaning and an internal, spiritual sense, which was revealed to Swedenborg during the last 30 years of his life. This internal sense is not found fully, however, in some of the books of the Old Testament or in Acts and the Letters, and thus, for Swedenborg, these are excluded from the biblical Word. Specific interpretation of the internal sense depends on the doctrine of 'correspondence' between things of the material world and those of the spiritual world; much of Swedenborg's expository writing is designed to elucidate these correspondences.

The function of the Word is to guide humanity in a knowledge of God and of God's will in respect of human conduct. Men and women have free will and by their choice of action will determine their eternal spiritual home. Salvation has been made possible by Christ's work of redemption, but it can be attained only by freely choosing to believe in God and to live according to his will. Thus, for the Swedenborgian, salvation is attained not by faith alone, but by a combination of faith and works.

The Church of Jesus Christ of Latter-Day Saints (Mormonism)
Douglas J. Davies

The Church of Jesus Christ of Latter-Day Saints, or Mormonism as the movement is popularly called, was founded in 1830 by Joseph Smith Jr (1805–44) in New York State, United States, as the Church of Christ. It became the Church of the Latter-Day Saints in 1834 and assumed its present title in 1838. By the beginning of the 21st century it had some 11 million members, more than half of them outside the United States.

Latter-Day Saints describe their church as a restoration movement: God has restored the teachings, practices and organization previously withdrawn from the earth shortly after the time of Christ as a result of human disobedience. Indeed, obedience and disobedience play key roles throughout the church's thought. In 1823, the teenage Joseph Smith Jr found previously hidden metallic records, often called 'the golden plates', telling the history of peoples who migrated to North America from the Holy Land at the time of the Old Testament prophets. Their divisions and disobedience led to divine displeasure, disputes and to self-destruction documented by Mormon (survived only by his son Moroni, who hid Mormon's account). Smith translated the text using special objects found with the plates and, with the secretarial help of Oliver Cowdery, *The Book of Mormon* was published in 1830. All this followed Smith's desire to know which church to join. God cautioned him against joining any existing church and told him to wait for future guidance which, in a series of angelic visits, led to the founding of the new church.

Smith was an inspiring leader and many joined his community of faith, but while in prison in 1844 he was killed by an unruly mob opposed to his religious views, an event Latter-Day Saints viewed as martyrdom. A brief competition for leadership between Sidney Rigdon and Brigham Young witnessed Young's triumph, with Rigdon forming his own Church of Christ on 6 April 1845, the 15th anniversary of the formation of the original Church of Jesus Christ of Latter-Day Saints. After local opposition, Brigham led the Latter-Day Saints westwards until they finally arrived in the Great Salt Lake Valley, Utah, in July 1847. Not all followed as some believed that leadership should have passed to Smith's son. This group formed the Reorganized Church of Jesus Christ of Latter Day Saints in 1860, with its headquarters and temple at Independence, Missouri. Ongoing revelations from its prophet resulted, for example, in the ordination of women in 1985. This branch is far more in line with mainstream Christian belief and in 2001 was renamed the Community of Christ.

In Utah, the original Church of Jesus Christ of Latter-Day Saints prepared for Christ's second coming, demonstrating its continuity and discontinuity with traditional Christianity. Alongside many Protestants, Latter-Day Saints were Adventist (believing in the return of Jesus), and millenarian (he would rule for a thousand years with his Saints). But, crucially, Christ would appear in the United States.

Only church members who live a morally acceptable life are allowed to enter the temple in Salt Lake City.

Zion, the site of divine rule, was American; the rest of the world was defined as 'evil Babylon', from which converts should flee in response to the message of the missionaries who were sent to many parts of Europe as well as to other parts of the United States. Just as the *Book of Mormon* recentred the ancient history of the prophets, so it refocused contemporary events. Unlike groups who had to disband or thoroughly revise their doctrine when Christ did not come, five factors saved the Latter-Day Saints from crushing disappointment: there was no single date for the end; new temple rituals were developed to focus religious energy; a significant majority survived the prophet's death; European converts brought fresh blood; and a new territory and leadership challenged them to survive.

In theological and practical terms, Mormonism underwent two major phases represented, firstly, in the *Book of Mormon* and, secondly, in the *Doctrine and Covenants*. The former's description of ancient periods resembles biblical accounts of God's striving with his disobedient people yet promising future salvation. It covers traditional Christian theological debates, but sets them in the past. The *Doctrine and Covenants*, dealing with contemporary issues through new revelations on practical church organization, behaviour and doctrine, is almost a kind of contemporary Acts of the Apostles (the fifth book of the New Testament, describing the early church). In both the *Doctrine and Covenants* and other addresses, Smith developed ideas absent from the *Book of Mormon* and altered church life in quite distinctive ways. Early church teachings were familiar to many Christians, but were given a distinctive American focus. Many early Latter-Day Saints were alienated by developments from the 1840s on as new patterns of doctrine and ritual developed.

Some believe the transition occurred as a result of Smith's brief yet deep experience of *Freemasonry. Some left the movement because it was not what they had first believed, but others saw the developments as part of Mormonism's progressive revelation. At the heart of this doctrinal development lay three major features: priesthood, afterlife and family. In Mormonism, these three are intimately combined in a unique way.

The priesthood is divided into two levels. Boys progress through the three grades of deacon, teacher and priest within the Aaronic order (between the ages of about 12 to 19), before becoming an elder within the Melchizedek priesthood. Subsequently, elders may become a high priest. Priesthood applies only to males, for women share in priesthood through their husband; all women are expected

Latter-Day Saints at the Missionary Training Center in Provo, Utah. Over 60,000 missionaries are currently working for the church.

to marry and produce children in a family group, the unit of salvation. But salvation has a distinctive meaning. Practically everyone, Latter-Day Saint or not, will be saved, in the sense that when humanity is resurrected and faces divine judgement each will gain the reward due for the endeavour achieved in life. Saints believe that the suffering and death of Jesus, in an act of atonement, removed the original sin that came to people through Adam's Fall, enabling individuals to set about a life of dedicated living, obedient to the divine commandments made clear to them, especially in certain temple rituals. Three levels of heaven, the terrestrial, telestial and celestial, each with their own internal subdivisions, allow for salvation in respect of the quality of one's earthly life, but the celestial is only attainable by married Melchizedek priests, their wives and families united through special temple ceremonies. Latter-Day Saints speak of this higher form of salvation as 'exaltation'.

When Smith introduced the idea of polygamy or plural marriage (abandoned at the end of the 19th century) a decade or so after the church was founded, he did so as part of a doctrinal belief in a conquest of death that was possible as a result of the rites of endowment, which became part of the developing temple activity. Today, individuals who are living a morally acceptable life, pay a tithe to the church, and support the divine basis of its leadership are given permission to attend the temple, which is closed to others. There they are ritually washed and anointed, introduced to the core teachings of the church and enter into vows that establish a covenant between them and the divine. This gives power to gain exalted status after the resurrection and is often referred to as 'the keys', a phrase symbolizing this control of after-death forces. The belief that men and women who are united in a temple marriage are 'sealed' for all eternity and not simply 'until death do us part' as in any ordinary church, is fundamental to Mormonism. Within their eternal union the Latter-Day Saint couple

continue a journey from the soul's pre-existence with God before this life, through earthly life and into their own divine identity, something Latter-Day Saints call 'the plan of salvation'. The conquest of death through the power of the Melchizedek priesthood, the union of a family and the eternal path to divine status stand together as the foundation truths and practices of Mormonism, called by Latter-Day Saints the 'Laws and Ordinances of the Gospel'. This explains why Latter-Day Saints study family trees, as genealogy provides the documentary basis for conducting temple rites on behalf of those who are dead and who never belonged to the church. Living Latter-Day Saints may be baptized and married on behalf of the dead who are in the other world of spirits and must decide for themselves if they wish to avail themselves of the rites conducted on their behalf. Nothing is 'forced' on the dead, for the Mormon principle of 'agency', of self-decision and action, applies as much to the dead as to the living.

The prophet, as church leader, is taken from the 12 apostles, who are followed by 'the Seventy'. Local leaders serve for limited periods while maintaining full-time secular jobs. All offices involve a leader with two counsellors, each expected to seek divine guidance for their task or church 'calling'. Many men and women serve as missionaries for approximately two years before college or marriage and often find that this strengthens their 'testimony' or sense of the truthfulness of this church and its prophetic origin.

The Exclusive Brethren
Nigel Scotland

The roots of Exclusive Brethrenism are traceable to John Nelson Darby (1800–82), the youngest son of John Darby of Leap Castle, Kings County, Ireland. His grandfather was Admiral Lord Nelson. Darby studied law at Trinity College, Dublin, and was called to the

Bar in 1822. On being 'converted' he took orders in the Anglican Church of Ireland, becoming Curate of Calany, a remote parish in County Wicklow. In 1827, during a period of convalescence, Darby came into contact with a group of discontented upper-class evangelicals who were experimenting with informal 'breaking of bread' (communion) services in Dublin. Among their number were Edward Cronin (d. 1882), Anthony Norris Groves (1795–1853), a dentist, and John Gifford Bellett (1794–1864), a lawyer. Darby met with these and other individuals and the group expanded into what became the first Brethren assembly.

Darby did not return to his parish, becoming instead the dominant figure of this select circle. He was an inveterate traveller and early on visited both Cambridge and Oxford. Meetings were established in many places, including London and Bristol. It was, however, at Plymouth in 1847 that the split occurred that resulted in the formation of the Exclusives.

Portrait of John Nelson Darby.

Here Benjamin Newton (1807–99), a former Church of England clergyman and leader of the newly formed Brethren assembly, taught what Brethren later termed 'the tainted Christ', in which he maintained that Jesus had, like the rest of the human race, been born under the curse of God until the time of his baptism in the River Jordan. Most of those who sat under Newton's teaching soon acknowledged its error, as indeed did Newton himself. Darby, however, maintained that those who had listened to Newton were 'tainted'. When some of their number went to the Bethesda Assembly in Bristol and were allowed to break bread, Darby called on the leaders to exclude them, even though there was no evidence that any of them had accepted Newton's teaching. They declined and instead issued *The Letter of the Ten* in June 1848, which committed Bethesda to the original Brethren position of keeping the communion table 'open' to all who share the historic biblical Christian faith. In response, Darby issued his celebrated *Bethesda Circular* later the same year in which he maintained that to associate with evil 'is opening the door to the infection of the abominable evil'.

From 1849 onwards, the 'Exclusives' emerged as a separate group and expanded into Europe, the United States and Canada as Darby travelled and preached. Darby divided biblical history into seven periods, which included the pre-millennial second coming of Christ. His scheme was taken up by a number of mid-19th century American evangelists and popularized at prophetic Bible conferences, which met annually after 1876. From this base, dispensationalism, as his scheme was called, found its way into most of the Protestant denominations. When Darby died in 1882, the movement continued to be controlled by a series of dominant leaders: James Butler Stoney (1814–97), Frederick Raven (1837–1903), James Taylor Sr (1870–1953) and James Taylor Jr (1896–1970). Each of these individuals extended Darby's teaching of separation from evil to avoid contamination. James Taylor Sr, who was by all accounts a godly man, stressed the need to 'withdraw from evil' and asserted that 'salvation was in the church', that is, the assembly. It was his son, James Taylor Jr (Big Jim), who brought the movement into disrepute by his extreme teaching and disreputable personal behaviour. He introduced the doctrine of 'separate tables', which required that no one was allowed to sit at table with any of their own family over 12 years of age if they did not break bread in the assembly. This was later extended to not eating food prepared by an unbeliever. Under Big Jim's regime, other strictures were introduced. Exclusive Brethren children were not allowed to socialize with other children or take part in religious education or after-school activities. In 1961, all members were prohibited from going to university or college and young people had to leave their courses. Soon after, a ban was placed on membership of any public body, such as trade unions, and all occupations that required professional validation, such as medicine or pharmacy. The power Big Jim exerted eventually brought about his downfall as he became engrossed in money making, gripped by alcohol and obsessed with women and sex. After a meeting in Aberdeen in August 1970, Taylor was found in bed with one of his women followers. Taylor later tried to pass the event off as a test to see which of his followers were truly committed to him. The scandal, which hit the national press, resulted in the loss of about 8,000 members over the next two years. Since Taylor's time, a number of smaller Exclusive breakaway groups have been formed. Most have taken the name of their faction leaders, such as Frost and Renton. One group, the Croham Hall Brethren, took their name from Croham Hall in Croydon, England, where they originated. The main group are still sometimes

Big Jim Taylor brought the Exclusives into disrepute in the 1970s.

known as the 'Jims' in deference to Taylor.

Since the 1970s, Exclusivism has continued in much the same vein under James Symington (1914–87), a North Dakota pig farmer, and John Hales (1922–2002), a chartered accountant who was based in Sydney, Australia. His son, Bruce David Hales, succeeded him as 'universal leader' and 'elect vessel'. In recent years, rules have tightened and members cannot live in a semi-detached house or share a common wall with another business whose owner is not in fellowship. Cats, dogs and domestic pets cannot be kept, and radios, televisions and computers are banned. Failure to comply with such regulations results in the individual concerned being 'withdrawn from', which means no brother or sister will eat or speak with the offender for the set period of punishment. Their worship meetings centre on a simple 'breaking of bread service' usually held at 6 a.m. with everyone, including infants, partaking of the elements. On these occasions a Bible passage is read and discussed by the Brothers who are present; women are not allowed to speak. In addition, there are other 'fellowship meetings', Bible-study gatherings and three-day conferences. Membership is reckoned by those who have recently left to be about 27,000 worldwide. The Exclusive Brethren are a tightly knit and highly intensive religious organization who exercise a strong control over every aspect of the lives of their members.

The Christadelphians
Nigel Scotland

The Christadelphians are a Bible-based lay movement whose members, roughly speaking, follow the teachings of the movement's founder, Dr John Thomas (1805–71). The name 'Christadelphian' was chosen by Thomas in 1865 and means quite simply 'Brethren in Christ'. Thomas was born at Hoxton Square in London and studied medicine.

Early in 1832 his father, who was at one point minister at an independent Congregational church, was seized with the American emigration fever and John decided to go too, partly because of his intense dislike for what he termed 'the priest-ridden society of England'. After a traumatic Atlantic crossing, the formerly agnostic Thomas attached himself to the Campbellites, an extreme Baptist group who followed the teachings of Alexander Campbell (1788–1868) and sought to recover 1st-century Christianity. Thomas was baptized by one of their number by the light of the moon in the Miami Ship Canal, which led to the jibe that he had been 'moonstruck'.

Thomas remained in association with the Campbellites until 1847, when he came to the view that 'we are saved by hope' (Romans 8:24) and that this hope is the coming of the Lord in power and great glory to set up a heavenly kingdom on earth, beginning at Jerusalem. This kingdom would not be 'beyond the skies', rather it 'would be in the Holy Land, when it shall be constituted a heavenly paradise'. Having reached this opinion, Thomas asked to be baptized again with the words: 'Upon confession of your faith in the things concerning the kingdom of God and the name of Jesus Christ, I baptize you in the name of the Father, Son and Holy Spirit.' Following this step of obedience, Thomas published a lengthy confession, which included a further section on this future hope. Thomas maintained that this kingdom would be ruled by Jesus, to whom all nations will be politically and ecclesiastically obedient.

Thomas found some initial support among the Campbellites in Baltimore and Buffalo, but his hearers in New York could not come to terms with the idea of the restoration of the Jews. In June 1848, he returned to England and was well received in Nottingham and had further speaking engagements in Derby, Birmingham and Plymouth. He was particularly successful in Scotland. After a highly acclaimed campaign in Edinburgh he returned to London, where he wrote *Elpis Israel: An Exposition of the Kingdom of God*. This success in the British Isles is generally taken as marking the beginning of the movement. In 1862, he made a second journey to England and visited perhaps as many as 15 major towns and cities. During this time he met with Robert Roberts (1839–98), who he appointed to succeed him as overall leader. Roberts was an able speaker and writer who published a series of lectures under the title *Christendom Astray*.

Christadelphian assemblies, known by the Greek word *ecclesia*, continued to grow in both England and the United States. Roberts travelled extensively in the United States, Australia and New Zealand. In 1872–73, Robert Roberts' own ecclesia in Birmingham drew up the *Birmingham Statement of Faith*, which was gradually adopted as a doctrinal basis by Christadelphian ecclesias all over the world, although in the United States unamended and amended groups have existed since a rift in the 1880s.

Christadelphians regard God as a person, but reject the doctrine of the Trinity. They take the view that Jesus was not eternal – he came into existence at the incarnation – and died as a 'representative' rather than as a 'substitute' for the sins of the human race. Salvation for the Christadelphian is essentially a progressive journey, which will be completed in the millennium or 1,000-year end-time period. There are two basic requirements: obedience to the teachings of Jesus and immersion baptism on profession of faith in the future coming kingdom. Roberts and more recent Christadelphian writers believe the gifts of the Holy Spirit have been withdrawn.

Christadelphians maintain high standards of behaviour and, generally speaking, withdraw from places and activities that are considered to be 'of the world'. In more recent years, there has, however, been a growing acceptance of entertainment and television. Certain occupations are closed to members because of the Christadelphians' non-violent stance, including the police force, politics and the military. Marriage with a non-Christadelphian is not acceptable and leads to disfellowshipping. There are 300 ecclesias and 20,000 members in Britain, the major centre of the faith, and another 550 congregations worldwide, including Africa, Australia, New Zealand, the United States, Southeast Asia and Europe.

Christian Science
Nigel Scotland

The origins of Christian Science are traceable to an American woman, Mary Baker Eddy (1821–1910), who bore this name following her marriage to Asa Gilbert Eddy on New Year's Day, 1877. Her parents, Mark and Abigail Baker, were devoted members of a Calvinistic Meeting House at White Rock Hill, New Hampshire. At the age of 16, Mary was admitted into membership of her parents' Congregational Church at Sanbornton Bridge, New Hampshire. Mary's first marriage to George Glover, though happy, was short. Her husband died of yellow fever after only six months, and she subsequently had a son, George. The years that followed were a period of extended sickness and pain, compounded by the harsh and unfaithful treatment she received at the hands of her second husband, Daniel Patterson, whom she married in 1853. They were permanently separated in 1866, and Mary subsequently obtained a divorce in 1873 on grounds of desertion.

During her second marriage, Mary encountered Phineas Quimby (d. 1865), whose remarkable healings were widely reported in the press. Quimby's system was based on creating wholesome moral attitudes in his patients. Under his treatment, Mary made rapid progress, and despite having had severe 'spinal inflammation', in less than a week she was able to climb the 182 steps to the Dome of the City Hall. However, the freedom Mary experienced under Quimby's treatment was short-lived, and she suffered a relapse. In February 1866, she fell on ice at a street corner in Lynn, Massachusetts, and appeared to have suffered some form of spinal dislocation, as well as severe internal injuries. While lying flat on her back, Mary read the account of Jesus raising the palsied man in Matthew 9. Quite suddenly, she was filled with the sense that God was the only life, and she was instantaneously healed.

Shortly after her healing, Mary began to write out some simple principles, based on what she had learned through her experience. In the summer of 1868, she began to offer classes in order to share the method of spiritual healing she was discovering. She produced *Science and Health with a Key to the Scriptures* in 1875, in order to better inform her students. Fundamental to Christian Science is the understanding that God is Spirit – and that

Portrait of Mary Baker Eddy.

Spirit is Truth, Life and Love. All that God creates reflects this spiritual substance, and is pure, perfect and completely harmonious. Mary saw this as the Truth that healed the sick, the compassionate spiritual Love that Jesus expressed in his healing ministry.

Just as she felt Jesus had done, so Mary encouraged her students not to be impressed by physical or material evidence, but to turn instead to the spiritual identity of the individual. In her terms, the material was unreal, invalid, in error – the result of wrong (unspiritual) thinking. In *Science and Health* she explains that the Bible is an inspired and reliable guide to health, and that the one loving and all-powerful God is ever present, always taking care of his beloved children, who are created in his image and likeness. Prayer or metaphysical work is key to Christian Science treatment. Mary knew that to heal the sick, she had first to free her own thinking of any material sense of disease, weakness or vulnerability. Critics of Christian Science can struggle with these ideas, mistakenly supposing that it is a matter of blind faith or will power. Rather, to the Christian Scientist, treatment is an act of grace, a childlike trust in the healing power of the divine Principle, God, revealing what he knows of us.

Mary has not been without her critics, some of whom have contended that *Science and Health* contained plagiarisms from Phineas Quimby and Francis Lieber. She was undoubtedly influenced by Quimby, but the links with Lieber are harder to sustain and not acknowledged by many Christian Scientists. In July 1876, Mary established the Christian Scientist Association for her students and practitioners. By 1877, however, she had come to the view that some sort of organization was necessary, and this led her to establish The First Church of Christ, Scientist, Boston, in 1879, and two years later, the Massachusetts Metaphysical College, which was closed in 1889. The church is also known as 'The Mother Church', and it is the international headquarters of Christian Science. The Bible and *Science and Health* together are the ordained pastor of branches of The Church of Christ, Scientist, throughout 80 countries. As a sermon, Mary instigated the weekly Bible lesson published in *Christian Science Quarterly*, which is read by lay-readers. She described this as 'uncontaminated by human hypothesis and divinely authorized'.

Christian Scientists believe God is 'All-in-all' and think of God in terms of Principle rather than as a person. They reject the idea of God as three persons in one, but accept the Trinity, defined as 'three in one – the same in essence, though multiform in office: God the Father-Mother; Christ the spiritual idea of sonship; divine Science or the Holy Comforter.' They regard sin and evil as having no objective reality. There are 2,000 churches in 80 countries, 120 of which are in the UK. Estimates of world membership are between 350,000 and 450,000.

The Jehovah's Witnesses
Nigel Scotland

The early development of the Jehovah's Witnesses is closely linked with the life and teaching of the first four leaders and presidents of the movement. The first of these, Charles Taze Russell (1852–1916), was the son of a Pittsburgh draper in the United States. Born in the town of Allegheny, he entered into partnership with his father and managed a chain of clothing stores. Russell reacted against the Congregational Church, of which he was a member, but was brought back to faith in Christ as a result of a sermon on the second coming. Excited by what he had heard, Russell developed a deep interest in Adventism and began to gather a study group around him in Pittsburgh. The beliefs of Russell's circle differed from those of the Adventists in one important respect: Jesus' second coming would be spiritual and invisible rather than physical.

In 1879, Russell established a journal

Charles Taze Russell, the first leader of the Jehovah's Witnesses.

under the title *Zion's Watchtower and Herald of Christ's Presence*. This swiftly led to the formation of congregations all over the United States. In 1881, he constituted his following as Zion's Watchtower Tract Society, with himself as manager. As a major part of this strategy Russell began a seven-volume work, later entitled *Studies in the Scriptures*. In 1879, Russell married Maria Frances Ackerly, a well-educated woman who had been one of his Bible students. They divorced in 1913 on account of his 'domination and improper conduct in relation to women', according to Mrs Russell. However, little evidence of immorality or cruelty was brought to light.

Like the Campbellites, Millerites, Adventists and others, Russell predicted the date of Christ's return. His first chosen date of 1874 failed to materialize and was advanced to 1878. Disappointment inevitably

followed and Russell began to teach that Jesus had in fact returned in 1874, but invisibly, and that the elect would be taken to heaven in 1914.

Russell's successors in the leadership of the movement each made a significant contribution. Joseph Franklin Rutherford (1869–1942), who succeeded Russell in 1916, had been the movement's legal officer. For a brief period he served as a substitute judge, which caused him to be known in the movement as 'Judge' Rutherford. Rutherford was a fertile author who, despite a punishing schedule of travel and speaking engagements, averaged a book a year. In 1920, he published his most celebrated volume, *Millions Now Living Will Never Die*. Rutherford moved away from 1874 and even 1914 and maintained that 1925 was the time when the rule of God would be established on earth.

Rutherford made sure the movement would be under much tighter control than formerly. In 1922 he took the step of requiring that the *Watchtower* should be studied in both congregational groups as well as individually. As an aid to members, questions to be discussed were also printed. To the present time, the *Watchtower* carries the text for Sunday Bible study in Kingdom Halls, as their meeting places are known, throughout the world. It was also during Rutherford's presidency in 1931 that the name 'Jehovah's Witnesses' was first adopted.

Rutherford was succeeded by Nathan Knorr (1905–77). Under his presidency a number of significant doctrinal books were produced, including *Let God Be True* (1946), which ran to more than 17 million copies. In 1961, the New World Translation of the Bible was published, which is used by all Jehovah's Witnesses. Other versions are regarded as secondary. A major blow in Knorr's presidency was the failure of the prediction that the world would end in 1975, which had been predicted in the 8 October 1966 issue of *Awake*. The organization acknowledged their error in the *Watchtower* of 15 March 1980.

The Jehovah's Witnesses are under the direction of their governing body, which consists of 11 men and a president. It is regarded as a theocracy or the means through which Jehovah God carries out his kingdom work on earth. They decide all matters of doctrine and public policy. They also have oversight of all writing, including books, tracts and, above all, the *Watchtower*. Jehovah's Witnesses currently work in more than 230 countries and these are arranged into branches, which are directly accountable to the governing body.

Witnesses believe in one God, whom they call 'Jehovah'. They reject the doctrine of the Trinity, seeing Jesus as 'a mighty one but not almighty as Jehovah God is'. Jesus is seen as 'the first of Jehovah God's creations' (Colossians 1:15). The Holy Spirit is not regarded as a person but rather as 'God's active force' that enables God's people to live for him. The great future hope to which all Witnesses look forward will only be realized after the cataclysmic end-time battle known as 'Armageddon'. At the conclusion of this conflict, faithful Witnesses will enjoy God's promised salvation. There will be two categories of the saved: the 'little flock' or 144,000 and the 'great company' or other sheep to whom Jesus referred in John 10:16.

Jehovah's Witnesses aim to spend whatever time they can going from door to door seeking to share their faith and distributing the *Watchtower*. For many, this is about ten hours a month. They are called 'publishers', and numbered 6,350,564 in 2000. In addition there are 'pioneers' who are able to make a greater commitment and may spend as many as 50 hours a month sharing their faith. There are other adherents who worship at Kingdom Halls and who attend the annual Memorial service. Only those who feel they are part of the 'little flock' are permitted to take the bread and wine at the annual Memorial Communion. In 2002, only 8,661 partook of

the sacrament out of a total worldwide attendance of 15,597,746. Witnesses are often best known for their rejection of blood transfusions. What is less well known is their high stress on the importance of family life and discipline. They do not bear arms; they stand aloof from politics and take no part in elections. They do not celebrate birthdays, the festivals of Christmas and Easter, or New Year's Day, May Day and Mother's Day because of their possible association with 'pagan gods'.

The Unity School of Christianity
George D. Chryssides

Originally founded as Unity in 1891, and incorporated in the United States in 1903 as the Unity School of Practical Christianity, the organization acquired its present name in 1914, and has its headquarters in Unity Village, Missouri. Part of the New Thought movement, it was founded by Charles Fillmore (1854–1948) and his wife Myrtle (1845–1931). The Fillmores were students of Emma Curtis Hopkins, who was at one time an associate of Mary Baker Eddy, the founder of *Christian Science.

The Unity School of Christianity emphasizes 'mind cure', believing that human illness can be relieved by exercising mind over matter. Myrtle Fillmore claimed to have been cured of tuberculosis in 1886 after listening to a New Thought lecture, and using the affirmation 'I am a child of God and therefore I do not inherit sickness' for two years. The Unity School makes much use of healing, affirmations and prayer; absent healing is also practised for some 2 million requests that are received annually. The Unity School teaches that poverty and misfortune can also be dealt with by these techniques, as well as sickness.

The Unity School is non-credal, claiming to bring together ideas from a variety of religious traditions. It emphasizes training rather than worship, and is not a church. However, the Association of Unity Churches was founded in 1966 in Unity Village and links some 400 churches founded by Unity students. Estimates of membership varied from 75,000 to 1,000,000 in 1998.

The New Apostolic Church
Tim Grass

Although its centre of gravity has traditionally been German-speaking Europe, the New Apostolic Church is strongly represented in many countries of the British Commonwealth. Its headquarters is located in Zürich, and its buildings may be recognized by the distinctive logo of a cross superimposed on a sun rising over the sea.

The movement has its roots in the Catholic Apostolic Church, founded in England during the 1830s. The Catholic Apostolic Church claimed to represent the end-time restoration of God's perfect order for the church, headed by 12 apostles as counterparts to the 12 New Testament apostles. This movement never achieved a large following in Britain, but became quite strong in Protestant areas of Germany. When some of the apostles died, tension arose between those who believed that no steps should be taken to ensure the continuance of the apostleship and those (in Germany) who believed that new apostles could be called through prophecy. In the early 1860s, when an elder from Königsberg accepted such a call, the Catholic Apostolic Church excommunicated those involved and their supporters, precipitating a schism.

The new movement gradually took shape through division and theological clarification over subsequent decades, adopting the name 'New Apostolic Church' in 1906. It developed a centralized structure, which placed a 'Chief Apostle' at the top who was viewed as Christ's representative. He is the channel through whom God speaks to his people and his words possess equal authority with those of the New Testament apostles.

The Bible (including the Apocrypha) is regarded as the Word of God, but needs authoritative interpretation by living apostles. Under the Chief Apostle, who normally serves for life, the church is divided into geographical districts, each with a well-defined hierarchy of apostles and other ministers, the lower levels of which serve without pay.

The New Apostolic Church accepts the doctrines of the Apostles' Creed, and of Christ's sacrifice on the cross, but stresses certain distinctive beliefs and practices. It celebrates three sacraments, baptism (of infants), Holy Communion (communicants receive a wafer with three drops of wine on it) and 'sealing' (by the laying on of an apostle's hands), which conveys the gift of the Holy Spirit. These may be performed on behalf of the departed. Because sealing and submission to the apostles are seen as essential for entry into God's kingdom, other churches are understood to be unable to offer salvation. Although there are indications of recent interest in ecumenical contact, the New Apostolic Church still regards itself as the exclusive continuation of the apostolic church of the New Testament. Its members await Christ's return, when the faithful will be taken up to heaven as part of the 144,000 (mentioned in the book of Revelation) who will share in the first resurrection. After a time of tribulation, all who have ever lived will be offered the opportunity to respond to Christ during his millennial reign.

Under Chief Apostle J.G. Bischoff (1871–1960), the New Apostolic Church in Germany gave unstinting support to Nazism, a manifestation of the movement's political conservatism, which enjoined support for whatever government was in power. In 1951, Bischoff declared that God had revealed to him that Christ would return during his lifetime. In spite of the failure of his prediction, which led to a number of members leaving, the

☞ *continued on page 52*

AFRICAN INDEPENDENT CHURCHES

Richard Hoskins

There are over 8,000 new religious movements in Africa, many of which may be called 'African independent churches' (AICs). These are found almost entirely in Africa south of the Sahara. To the north, Islam predominates and while there are also Islamic new religious movements this article focuses on AICs.

Terms

The term 'African independent churches' has been the source of some debate. In this article we make a distinction between AICs and new religious movements. The former is used for broadly Christian and Christian-derived movements; the latter for others who, by their own admission, do not claim to be Christian. However, this at once raises a profound problem in any study of African religions, for the boundaries between religious traditions in Africa are notoriously blurred. And, while this may also be true in other parts of the world, Africans display a particular 'magpie quality': an ability to borrow what seems to work from a variety of sources. This can be frustrating for the purist observer who wants

clear boundaries, and who does not like apparently contradictory truth-claims being mixed together. This is not something abstract: examine the *Nazareth Baptist Church (Shembe) of South Africa and it would be possible to apply any number of labels from 'Christian' through 'Zulu-Zionist' to 'neo-traditional' – none of which would necessarily be completely correct. It is important to resist the temptation to rush into categorization.

Further discussion on the term 'African independent churches' centres specifically around the word 'independent'. Some scholars prefer other terms, normally using the same initials (AIC), including 'indigenous', 'initiated' or 'instituted'. It is worth noting that, long before the term 'African independent churches' came into being, some scholars were preferring to speak of 'native separatist churches' in order to describe the phenomena of these movements. A scholar called Bengt Sundkler then suggested that the term 'native' might be offensive to blacks in South Africa, and so suggested 'Bantu independent churches'. Most scholars since then have retained the last two words, but changed 'Bantu', both because this was being used just as offensively by the ruling white population in

South Africa under apartheid and because it did not embrace all the churches in Africa (there are many non-Bantu peoples in Africa). Instead, the term 'independent' has been adopted. Some scholars, however, prefer to use the term 'African indigenous churches'. They point out that 'independent' refers to a church that has separated from another, and that this does not therefore apply to all churches being studied. 'Initiated' or 'instituted' are attempts to recognize the particular origins within Africa.

A different attempt at categorization has been applied by B.W. Jules-Rosette. In this scheme there are, firstly, indigenous or independent churches. These began with the initiative of African leaders and now represent about 15 per cent of all Christianity in sub-Saharan Africa. They are characterized by their own doctrines and organizations. Secondly, she suggests that there are separatist churches, by which she means churches that broke away from the original mission churches. Thirdly, there are neo-traditional movements, such as the Nazareth Baptist Church of South Africa.

Although questions about

A worshipper holds a crucifix made in traditional Dogon style.

the use of terms are close to the heart of the issue regarding how we are to understand and categorize these movements, it needs to be borne in mind that there are great dangers in making any religious categories too rigid. Some movements may have roots and influences from more than one category. Terms have also often been applied in order to prove either the truth or falsehood of a given movement in Africa. No terms are entirely satisfactory.

History

In the early centuries of the Christian church, Christianity spread along the North African coast and down into Ethiopia. But, after the advance of Islam across North Africa from the 6th century onwards, Christianity was largely wiped out from the continent for the best part of a thousand years, with the exception of Ethiopia and Egypt. As trade routes around the African coasts emerged from the 14th century and the 15th century onwards, so Christianity travelled slowly with European travellers. But it was not until the 19th century that a serious expansion of Christianity into Africa took place with missionaries and mission societies. Usually the missionaries tried to repeat European patterns in the churches they founded in

Africa. But, in reaction to this, by the end of the 19th century many African Christians had begun to form their own 'independent' congregations. The AICs were born. Some of the new AICs consciously drew their inspiration from the Zionist movement of Illinois in the United States and later Pentecostal movements in North America and Europe. But many sought, above all, to be authentically African.

Distribution

Africa is a huge continent of some 800 million people. The modern countries are the result of decisions by colonial powers to carve up the continent, and these boundaries often cut straight through geographical areas inhabited by indigenous peoples, a classic example being the division of the ancient BaKongo people into three nation states – Angola, the Democratic Republic of Congo (formerly Zaire), and the People's Republic of Congo. Travel is also notoriously difficult in parts of Africa, so that many villages to this day remain relatively isolated from other parts of their countries, and certainly from the continent as a whole. These factors are very important, because a numerically insignificant AIC in one part of Africa may be the single most dominant and important force if you happen

to be living there. For example, if home is Nyanza Province of western Kenya the Legio Maria movement will be prominent: yet its total numbers are in the tens of thousands, and few others may have heard of it. Locally focused studies, therefore, remain of great significance.

Nevertheless, there are some very large AICs that have broken across tribal and national boundaries, of which the biggest are the Kimbanguists (see *Kimbanguism) with up to 10 million members worldwide; the various Aladura churches, including the *Celestial Church of Christ, with perhaps 10 million members; the Nazareth Baptist Church with up to 4 million followers; and the *Zion Christian Church with up to 6 million members. There are, however, a vast number of smaller AICs, among them the Sweet Heart Church of the Clouds (Umutima Uwalowa wa Makumbi) of Zambia; the Harrist Church of the Ivory Coast; the Oruuano Church and the Church of Africa in Namibia; the Church of Moshoeshoe in Lesotho; the Church of Christ in Africa, Johera and the Legio Maria movement in Kenya. The reality is that the list is seemingly endless; new AICs are born every day in Africa, and existing ones constantly evolve.

It is also very important to remember that AICs, and movements deriving from them, are now to be found throughout the world in almost every country. Further adaptations often occur in the countries outside Africa. Remarkable examples of such adaptation can be seen among the Yoruba-derived religions in South America and the West Indies, such as *Kardecism.

Characteristics

Given the great diversity of AICs, characterizing them is fraught with danger. AICs display almost infinite variety. But, is it possible to point to distinctive characteristics of AICs? The answer is, in one sense, 'no'. One church's poison is another's food and drink. To take a very simple example, the Nazareth Baptist Church and the Kimbanguists share many similar features. And yet, in the former men are required not to use a razor on their faces, while in the latter beards are forbidden. What makes the exercise of studying these churches more complex is that most AICs use the Bible to justify respective beliefs and practices. In other words, the same texts are used in different ways by different groups in different settings.

Nevertheless, there are certain features which *may* be found in several AICs, and

some of the most important of these are as follows.

PLACE

Home is very important for Africans, not only as a place where the living dwell, but also where the spirits of the departed inhabit. Even when people move to the cities, they retain a strong spiritual attachment to their traditional home or village. Some of the AICs meet a point of need, which can help account for their phenomenal success. The amaNazarites (Shembe) are a good case in point here. To a people who had lost their land, Shembe provided a sense of place and belonging. The Zulus lost their empire to white control, and the Native Land Act of 1913 displaced many thousands of families from their ancestral communal lands. There was widespread despair, with the removal of families and livestock, and the killing of herds. One of Isaiah Shembe's hymns in this regard goes as follows:

Our land (our people) are
*   scattered*
Our homesteads are abandoned
We are like widows and orphans
Thou Lord of the sabbath why
hast thou deserted us?
Without you we have no
*   saviour.*

It was because of this sense of displacement that Isaiah Shembe also bought land at a

small place north of Durban called Ekuphakameni, meaning 'exalted place'. Ekuphakameni thus became a focus, a sacred site for a displaced and dispossessed people. One of their songs says:

All generations of heaven
They will rejoice through you at
*   Ekuphakameni*
When they enter through the
*   gates*
May they come to praise
*   Jehovah.*

The amaNazarites also have a second sacred centre further to the north, a mountain called Nhlangakazi, which Isaiah Shembe called the Holy Mountain.

A similar sense of place exists among the Kimbanguists, focused on N'Kamba. Before Simon Kimbangu's ministry began, N'Kamba was a tiny village, no more than a few huts, in a remote part of the lower Congo. But it was destined to become one of Africa's great centres of pilgrimage. As the movement expanded, thousands of Kimbanguist faithful carried stones for the building of the temple several miles up to the holy hill. The resultant temple can seat 37,000 people, a capacity that is exceeded at least twice a year. But, here again, the significance is about more than numbers and impressive building projects. For the

Kimbanguists, like the amaNazarites, their holy place is one where there is an encounter between humans and God. This feature may be found in many AICs, where a holy place is established as the point at which God and humans meet. Even the most hardened observer is likely to be impressed by a remarkable sense of peace at both Ekuphakameni and N'Kamba.

This point about 'place' links with the concept of Zionism, found in a great many AICs. In this context, Zionism is meant as the literal acceptance of parts of the Old Testament, especially the belief that, just as God came down among humans in the temple on Mount Zion in Jerusalem, so today God comes down to meet with people in the sites and special places of some AICs. This also relates to a strong sense in many AICs that the future reign of God is to be found here and now. When the faithful gather, they experience the presence of God among them; the kingdom of God in the present. This is the context in which many AICs pray for healing – something that attracts many Africans.

PERSECUTION

Many AICs sprang up out of a time of persecution and suffering. The importance of this root should not be underestimated in any study

of AICs, and is a feature common to some of the most significant AICs. The Aladura churches, which began with the teaching in 1925 of Josiah O. Oshitelu in Nigeria, arose out of a period of intense suffering from the worldwide flu epidemic, bubonic plague and persecution of the new movement. The Kimbanguists, likewise, emerged from a period of extreme suffering: the same flu epidemic and the construction of a railroad from Kinshasa to the Congo coast, in which many

hundreds of Africans died. The persecution of Simon Kimbangu himself – his arrest in 1921, death sentence (later commuted to flogging), enforced exile away from his wife and children – and the mass deportations of Kimbanguists by the Belgians, rank among the most serious human rights atrocities of the 20th century, with little evidence of remorse on the part of the colonial powers. From this crucible of suffering

has emerged one of the most remarkable of the AICs. The amaNazarites must also be understood from the perspective of the loss of the Zulu empire. In all these cases, a great African prophet stood up and began to speak to the people in their own language and addressed their needs.

HOLY GROUND AND OTHER CUSTOMS

Given the variety in AICs it is very difficult to speak of common practices. Nevertheless, it is true that there are some practices that

Hymns are sung during an open-air service. Many AICs have their own hymns and songs.

are shared across many AICs. A good example of this is the removal of footwear when on 'holy ground'. Kimbanguists, amaNazarites and many others remove shoes when entering places of worship. In the case of Kimbanguists, socks may still be worn. In the case of the amaNazarites, it usually means being barefoot.

The wearing of special robes is very common in AICs. Often these will be white, as they are in the many Aladura churches, and the amaNazarites. Sometimes other colours are worn. For the Kimbanguists the sacred colours are green and white: green for hope and white for purity.

Some, but not all, AICs practise baptism. This is often in the name of the Christian Trinity, but may also include, or be entirely in, the name of the movement's leader or founder: the amaNazarites are a notable example of the latter. Communion, or the Eucharist, is practised in a number of AICs, but, once again, in by no means all. The Kimbanguists brought communion in very late to their movement. Some accused them of doing so only to win over members of the World Council of Churches to whom they had applied for membership. Even then, it is celebrated only three times a year, and using local produce (*tschikwanga* or manioc roots and wild honey mead) rather than European-style bread and wine.

AIC services vary enormously. Some AICs have been heavily influenced by the distinctive type of Pentecostalism originating in the Azusa Street Revival in Los Angeles in the United States from 1906 onwards. These churches, among them the Zion Christian Church, have some features in common with 'classic Pentecostalism'. Others have been influenced by the more recent worldwide charismatic revival movement in Christianity. But other AICs seemingly defy such simplistic threads, and the observer must be very wary before assuming that all AICs are of a certain worship style. The first-time observer of a Kimbanguist service, for example, is often surprised at the formal liturgical structure and worship. Many AICs have their own hymns and songs. These are nearly always in the local languages of the movement's origins or the place to which it has settled. More often than not, these have not been formally set down, but belong to a tremendous well of oral tradition. This presents a particular challenge to students of AICs, for the work of collating and understanding this information is often undervalued and overlooked. This is all the more ironic when one considers that some of the most important teachings about a particular AIC may be found embedded in these songs (a fine example of this is in the Kimbanguist church in which there are thousands of undocumented songs in Kikongo about Simon Kimbangu's life, ministry and role in the church).

Most AICs use the Christian Bible, consisting of the Old Testament (Jewish Hebrew scriptures) and New Testament. Some AICs supplement this with stories relating to key figures in their own movement – often the founder. In some AICs (notably the amaNazarites) the Old Testament is emphasized, particularly the commandments.

Relatively strict moral codes are very common in AICs, as is the banning of smoking, alcohol and drugs. In many AICs, women are required to cover their heads and to dress modestly (usually this means they are to wear skirts or dresses rather than trousers). Polygamy (the taking of more than one wife) is tolerated by some AICs (Zion Christian Church) but banned in others (Kimbanguism). Most AICs officially disapprove of the use of traditional diviners (sometimes misleadingly and unhelpfully termed 'witch doctors' by missionaries and some anthropologists). The official stance of most AICs is that their believers should consult God alone for healing. This often reflects what is technically called a dualistic view of the universe. This simply means the belief that the universe is starkly divided between good and evil forces; that there is a battle on between these forces; and that to consult a diviner would be to tap into the forces of evil, not good. Nevertheless, what is stated officially and what takes place in practice is not always the same, and there is plenty of evidence of AIC members throughout Africa using traditional diviners for healing.

LEADERSHIP AND AUTHORITY
Leadership is very important in most AICs, and this is a similarity with 'traditional' African life. In many AICs, the founder of the movement has been succeeded by a member of his (or occasionally her) own family – usually the son. Notable examples of such 'successions' have occurred in the Nazareth Baptist Church, *Brotherhood of the Cross and Star and Kimbanguism. While some AICs might not be comfortable with too close a comparison to traditional 'tribal' chiefdom, there is no doubt that in many AICs this is very close to the leadership pattern. Genuflection (bowing the knee) is very common before leaders of AICs. In both the amaNazarites and the Kimbanguists, for example, it would be unthinkable to enter the presence of the respective spiritual chief without kneeling. This is not to be confused with worship of these leaders. Rather, it

reflects the strong sense of veneration of the elder. AIC leaders are people to be venerated and revered. They may be a manifestation of God on earth. But certainly they are viewed as 'set aside', representatives of all the people before God. They stand, therefore, between two worlds, the world of everyday human affairs, and the spirit world in its many forms. It is very common for followers to pay homage to these leaders.

AIC beliefs
The place of Christ and the Christian Trinity in AICs has sometimes been controversial. The reason for this usually centres around the position of the particular movement's leader or founder. Followers revere and venerate their leaders. But they may also think of them as having a saving aspect. Most AIC leaders will shy away from stating something like this so starkly. But among many AIC members one can hear the founder being referred to in terms that approach a salvation quality. For some non-African Christian observers this can be a threat to their understanding of the 'uniqueness' of Christ. Here a recognition of African inclusiveness is important. For most Africans an 'either/or' approach is unnecessary and they are happy to accept both the unique place of Christ *and*

the special place of their own leader, to whom they will often give a special title, such as prophet, special envoy, universal teacher or chief.

And yet many of the themes by which we have looked at AICs come to a head around beliefs, and especially the thorny one as to just how Christian they are. The Nazareth Baptist Church (Shembe) makes an interesting case study in this regard. Talk to many other Christian leaders in South Africa today, and one can hear considerable suspicion towards the amaNazarites. A key issue here then must be to listen to how the AICs view themselves. With Shembe this provides interesting lessons. Certainly, many of the believers describe themselves as Christians. But members of other churches in South Africa are more hesitant. For some they are simply 'non-Christian'. For scholars this has also been a hotly contested debate. G.C. Oosthuizen thought that the amaNazarites were an African movement distinct from Christianity. Bengt Sundkler and Absalom Vilikazi argued that Shembe provides an authentic form of Zulu Christianity. This latter view is one that many Christian scholars have found very attractive when studying African Christianity. Aware of the cultural dressing of the Western Christianity brought by the European missionaries, they have often longed to see 'authentically African' expressions of Christianity – and they found what they saw as ready examples in the AICs. One of the problems with this approach, however, has been that it can smack of yet one more example of Western scholars telling Africans what, and who, they are. Londa iNsiKayakho, who led a smaller branch of the amaNazarites after the death of Johannes Galilee Shembe, stressed that the amaNazarites were an African religion in their own right, and rejected notions of Shembe as an 'African Christianity'. But the main body of the church, which followed Amos Shembe and, since 1996, Vimbembi, has kept open ties with Christianity. Certainly, for many of his followers Isaiah Shembe is for the Zulus what Moses was for the ancient Israelites. He is often referred to as *iNkosi*, the Zulu word for king; this concept of divinity and living ancestry is closer than that of the distant creator God, *Nkulunkulu*.

A similar situation arises when we look at possibly the largest of the AICs, Kimbanguism. Two highly controversial moves have recently made the position of the Kimbanguists within the World Council of Churches, which they had joined in 1969, come under the spotlight. The first of these

came in 1999 when the then leader of the Kimbanguists, Papa Dialungana, who was the only surviving son of Simon Kimbangu, decided to move the date of Christmas from 25 December to 25 May, which happened to be the date of his own birthday. The second arose when, in April 2000, Dialungana announced through his spokesmen to the world that he is 'Christ Returned'. Kimbanguists justify such moves on a number of grounds. They point out that the dating of Christmas to 25 December is a conventional date, made when the then Roman emperor adopted a pagan festival to re-use for the date of Christ's birth. Most importantly in the context of other AICs, they claim that this new date of 25 May has been revealed to them by God the Holy Spirit through prayer. That sense of immediate contact with God is one that pervades AICs – a belief that God can, and does, speak today to those who seek him. As for the announcement that Dialungana was 'Christ Returned', they claim that biblical texts point to this, and that, again, it is something revealed to them by God. Dialungana himself died in August 2001 and was succeeded by his son, Kiangani Simon Kimbangu.

It remains to be seen in what direction the

Kimbanguists will now go. They may seek to remain within the World Council of Churches, and in so doing ensure their teachings remain within the boundaries of perceived acceptability to other Christian churches, or they may strike off on their own. Likewise, the question may be asked if Shembe is a Christian movement or a wholly new form of Zulu religion. These are questions we can apply across the spectrum of AICs: in short, are all AICs 'Christian'? Much depends on how one defines both African religion and Christianity. Recognizing that there is no 'pure' form of culture-free Christianity, whether it be in Africa or Europe or elsewhere, may provide the most helpful starting point from which to assess the AICs.

movement has continued to expand. It now numbers about 10 million members, with a presence in most countries. Much of the higher leadership remains German-speaking, although most of the membership is now found in Africa and the Indian subcontinent.

Evangelism is carried out primarily through personal contact, and members are encouraged to invite others to services. The strong sense of community and spiritual security attracts many, as does the successful appearance of the church, which conveys the impression of sober prosperity and good taste in the architecture of its buildings and the high quality of its orchestral and choral music. Worship is fairly similar to that of traditional Protestantism. Preaching tends to be devotional rather than expository, and majors on the unique blessings available to members through the apostles. Hymnody is of a similar character, and many 19th-century revivalist items are used.

Although a full programme of activities is provided for various age groups in the local congregation, the New Apostolic Church faces the challenge of maintaining the commitment of its members. That this is proving difficult in countries where it has long been established is evident in the fact that, in recent years, Sunday afternoon or evening services have been dropped.

A number of groups have broken away from the New Apostolic Church, but few are of any size, apart from the Old Apostolic Church, which numbers at least 250,000 members in South Africa.

Nazareth Baptist Church members climb up Nhlangakazi mountain to praise God and honour Isaiah Shembe, who died on the mountain in 1935.

The Nazareth Baptist Church (Shembe)
Richard Hoskins

As a young man in the 1900s, a Zulu named Isaiah Shembe (d. 1935) believed he was receiving a series of revelations from God, which he referred to repeatedly in later sermons. Following these callings, Shembe left

his four wives and home village and became an itinerant preacher and healer. He went through local catechism and was ordained a minister in the African Native Baptist Church. But he eventually left that church because he felt that the Jewish sabbath, not the Christian Sunday, was the correct day for worship.

In 1911, Shembe founded the *iBandla lama-Nazaretha* or Nazareth Baptist Church (sometimes simply called the amaNazarites or Shembe). He travelled throughout Natal healing, casting out demons and preaching about God as revealed to him in his readings of the Bible, dreams and visions. For him the sabbath commandment was the essential law; it symbolized the ancient Israelite orientation

Ekuphakameni (meaning 'exalted place'), just north of Durban. The second is a holy mountain further to the north called Nhlangakazi.

When Isaiah Shembe died in 1935 he was buried in a mausoleum at Ekuphakameni. His son, Johannes Galilee Shembe, then became leader. After his death in 1975 a split occurred in the movement, with a smaller branch under Londa iNsiKayakho, and the main movement under Amos Shembe, son of Isaiah Shembe. Amos was succeeded on his death in 1996 by his son, Vimbembi, the current leader of the church.

The church continues many of the practices set down by the founder, Isaiah Shembe. Baptism takes place throughout the year, by full immersion, and is performed in the name of the prophet Shembe. Males and females are baptized separately. A Shembe believer should only marry another Zulu, illustrating how closely tied the movement is to culture. Of great note is the special Shembe dancing, known as *mingiko*, through which followers communicate with God. It involves a number of slow steps made to the sound of long trumpets. Although drawing on both Zulu and Old Testament influences, this dance is quite unique to Shembe. There are annual festivals in July (at Ekuphakameni) and January (at Nhlangakazi).

The Nazareth Baptist Church is flourishing and claims to have some 4 million members. However, some scholars think the true figure may be closer to 1 million.

of his church and so distinguished it from European Christianity. Other laws and rituals from the Old Testament were followed. For example, Shembe removed his shoes when preaching. He also taught his disciples not to eat pork, prayed in the name of Jehovah, brought in a Feast of Tabernacles in January, and instituted a modified Zulu First Fruits festival in place of Christmas. Similarly, he reinstated male circumcision (an ancient Zulu custom), allowed polygamy, and taught that all Old Testament references to Nazarites in fact referred to his church.

It is important to recognize that many Zulus were displaced through colonialism, and that the Native Land Act of 1913 left many thousands of families isolated from their ancestral homes. For a people without a land, Shembe gave hope. In particular, his new church viewed two places as of special significance. The first of these is

Oneness Pentecostalism
Allan Anderson

Oneness Pentecostalism is not a homogenous movement, as there are several varieties and at least 90 denominations. It emerged as an alternative to the Trinitarian doctrine and baptismal practice of early 'classical' Pentecostalism. One of the most fundamental and acrimonious of the divisions that soon emerged in North American Pentecostalism erupted when a type of Unitarianism arose called the 'New Issue', 'Jesus' Name' or 'Oneness' by its proponents, and 'Jesus Only' by its opponents. In a Los Angeles camp meeting in 1913, Canadian evangelist Robert McAlister began to preach about baptism 'in the name of Jesus Christ' (Acts 2:38), which he said was the common practice of the early church, rather than the triune formula (Matthew 28:19). This new teaching not only resulted in calls for re-baptism, but also developed into a 'theology of the name of God', leading ultimately to what became known as the 'Oneness' doctrine of God. Baptism was 'in the name of Jesus' because Jesus was the 'name' of God, whereas 'Father, Son and Holy Spirit' were different titles for the singular name of Jesus Christ. Early leaders in the Oneness movement included Frank Ewart (1876–1947), Glenn Cook (1867–1948), Garfield T. Haywood (1880–1931) and Howard Goss (1883–1964). Ewart, a Pentecostal pastor in Los Angeles, was credited with first formulating the distinctive Oneness theology on the nature and the name of God to accompany the new baptismal practice. This he first announced in a public sermon in 1914, when he and Cook re-baptized each other. The new doctrine spread through evangelistic meetings and, in Indianapolis, Cook baptized the prominent black preacher Haywood, together with 465 members of his congregation.

The 'New Issue' became a schism in the ranks of 'Finished Work' (Baptistic) Pentecostals, especially in the Assemblies of God (AOG). Goss, a disciple of Pentecostal pioneer Charles Parham, was one of the organizing founders of the AOG in 1914. The AOG was split on this 'New Issue' in 1916, when 156 ministers, including Goss, Ewart and Haywood, were barred from membership over the doctrine of the Trinity, which became a condition for membership. The AOG emerged thereafter as a tightly structured, centralized denomination with a 'Statement of Fundamental Truths' affirming the Trinity. The split also meant that the AOG lost its black membership and became an all-white denomination, especially with the departure of Haywood, the only prominent black leader associated with the AOG. The AOG's stand for 'orthodoxy' at this time was to ease their later acceptance by evangelicals. Oneness Pentecostalism, in contrast, was destined to remain isolated from the rest of Pentecostalism and Christianity in general, particularly through its practice of re-baptism and rejection of Trinitarian beliefs.

In January 1917, an organization called the General Assembly of Apostolic Assemblies was formed, and it joined Haywood's Pentecostal Assemblies of the World (PAW) in 1918. This remained a racially integrated church until 1924, after which most of the whites withdrew and the PAW adopted episcopal government, with Haywood as presiding bishop. After an abortive attempt to unite under the umbrella of the newly formed Pentecostal Church of Jesus Christ (PCJC) in 1931, the PAW has since been predominantly an African-American church. The United Pentecostal Church (UPC) is now the largest Oneness group in North America, a white denomination formed in 1945 from a union of the PCJC and the Pentecostal Church, Incorporated. Howard Goss was the first general superintendent of the UPC. Included in the UPC were those who believed that baptism in the name of Jesus and baptism in the Spirit with the sign of speaking in tongues constituted the new birth. There are also a large number of smaller organizations, usually having the name 'Apostolic' in their names, many of which formed a loose association called the Apostolic World Christian Fellowship in 1971. Oneness Pentecostals are found all over the world and may account for 25 per cent of all 'classical' Pentecostals. The UPC operates in over 100 nations. In Canada, the Apostolic Church of Pentecost is a Calvinistic Oneness

☞ continued on page 56

NGUNZISM

Richard Hoskins

Ngunzism refers to a varied group of healers and 'spiritual' leaders in the Democratic Republic of the Congo in central Africa, who have no formal religious affiliation, but who exert great influence on people's lives. Ngunzist activity usually involves the entrance into a heightened spiritual state, which may be trance-like, and the ability to heal and perform miracles in God's name.

The word *ngunza* comes from the Kikongo word meaning 'prophet'. The translators of the Kikongo Bible translated the word for prophet used in the Old Testament as *ngunza*. In traditional Congolese society, the *ngunza* used to speak in the name of the tribal chief. This is a different role from the traditional healers, known as *nganga*, although the two roles have sometimes been confused by observers of African religions.

The Ngunzist movement has been linked with *Kimbanguism. Shortly before the arrest and imprisonment of Simon Kimbangu there was a rise in Ngunzist activity, which spread further shortly afterwards. This was partly because of the great number of legendary stories associated with Kimbangu himself. All sorts of miracle stories grew,

and, after his death, many believed that Kimbangu would return as the *ntotila* (a mythological figure) in richly laden ships to re-establish the ancient Kingdom of the Kongo. He would drive the whites into the sea and establish black rule for the black people. The belief persists to this day. Some Ngunzists offered their healing for payment, which is contrary to Kimbangu's teaching. When Zaire (as it came to be called) gained independence the Ngunzists played a part in hunting out white missionaries. Prophetic offshoots from Kimbangu's ministry quickly emerged, many of whom have become known under the umbrella term Ngunzists, and some of these appear to have urged refusal to pay colonial taxes. Erroneously, some even began to identify Kimbangu with such activities.

Today, Ngunzists are often called *trembleurs* because of their ecstatic shaking (rather like the origin of the term Quakers). Many of the Ngunzists crossed the Congo River and linked up with breakaway groups in the former French Congo associated with a movement called Animicalism under André Matswa. Another large movement began under Simon Mpadi during the Second World War and the Mpadistes, known as the Mission des Noires or Mission

of the Blacks, still exists today, though it is much smaller. A further movement sprang up around a man called Simeon Toko (1918–84) who, because of his extraordinary powers, was accused by some missionaries of using black magic.

Marie-Louise Martin, who was one of the delegates supporting the entry of the Kimbanguists into the World Council of Churches, was adamant that Ngunzism and Kimbanguism are separate. Others have been less convinced. However, there is also a lot of blurring among other religious groups within the Congo. It is important to point out that so-called Ngunzist behaviour, including trembling and ecstatic states induced through repetitious rhythmical drumming, can be seen in many African churches, including Roman Catholic and Protestant ones.

denomination. Most, if not all, of the black British Apostolic groups are Oneness in doctrine, with roots in the Caribbean. The largest Chinese Pentecostal church, the True Jesus Church, is Oneness in doctrine, but also observes the sabbath. Several Oneness groups, including the UPC and the PAW, practise footwashing.

The essence of Oneness teaching as it has developed is a rejection of the traditional Christian concept of 'separate but equal' Persons in the Trinity. Oneness Pentecostals hold that Jesus is the revelation of God the Father, and that the Spirit proceeds from the Father (Jesus). Unlike the traditional idea that Jesus is the human name of Christ, in Oneness teaching Jesus is the New Testament name of God, and this name reveals his true nature. The one God of the Old Testament reveals his immanence in the incarnation of Jesus, and his transcendence in the presence of the Spirit. God has now permanently taken up his abode in the human body of the Son. The Spirit indwells Jesus in fullness as God (the Father) incarnate, and thus an attempt is made to resolve the intricacies of Trinitarian theology. Oneness Pentecostals charge that Trinitarians have embraced tritheism, because they assume that Trinitarians believe in three separate and distinct 'Persons' in the Godhead. Instead, Oneness teaching affirms that Jesus is fully God and not one divine being out of three. They prefer to refer to Father, Son and Spirit as three 'manifestations' of God, all of which are present in the manifestation of each one. It follows that they also reject the traditional Christian teaching of the eternal Sonship of Christ, and that Oneness teaching on the dual nature of Christ tends towards a separation of the divine and the human. A prominent part of Oneness Pentecostalism teaches a three-stage view of salvation based on Acts 2:38: repentance, baptism in the name of Jesus Christ and the gift of the Spirit accompanied by speaking in tongues are all essential to salvation.

Iglesia ni Cristo
Tim Grass

The Iglesia ni Cristo ('Church of Christ', but not to be confused with other groups bearing this name) was founded in the Philippines by Felix Manalo (1886–1963) during a period of resurgent Filipino nationalism, and its organization and ethos reflect aspects of Filipino culture. Now working in over 70 countries, estimates of its membership vary from 3 to 10 million. It is growing rapidly, and is now the largest religious group in the Philippines, apart from Roman Catholicism. Yet, it is little known because of its almost entirely Filipino membership and its reluctance to allow research by outsiders.

The movement teaches that the true church disappeared from the early centuries until Iglesia ni Cristo was founded in 1914, and that Manalo was God's final messenger to humanity. It rejects the doctrines of the Trinity and the divinity of Christ, and much of its vigorous outreach focuses on debating and disproving these doctrines in order to win members from Catholic and Evangelical churches. Salvation comes though faith, baptism, joining the church and doing good works.

The Bible is regarded as God's word, but it requires authoritative interpretation. To ensure unity of belief, every minister follows the same sermon outline in the Sunday service. Highly centralized and strongly authoritarian, the church is headed by Manalo's son Erano as 'Executive Minister'. A high degree of commitment and loyalty is expected, and thus the church has been able to build many striking places of worship and to establish itself in Filipino society through health care, education and broadcasting. The practice of voting en bloc in elections as directed by the leadership has also made it a significant political force in the Philippines.

Kimbanguism

Richard Hoskins

Kimbanguism originated in the Democratic Republic of the Congo (formerly Zaire), and has now spread to many countries in Africa and beyond. It is probably the largest *African independent church (AIC), with up to 10 million members worldwide. The movement takes its name from the founder, Simon Kimbangu.

Kimbangu was born in 1887 at N'Kamba, a small and isolated village in the Lower Congo, some 200 miles from the capital, Kinshasa. He grew up in the church of the British Baptist Missionary Society. But, in 1918, Kimbangu believed he received a call from God to go and look after his people, for God was telling him that the Europeans had been unfaithful to the call of Christ. On 6 April 1921, Kimbangu began his ministry of

The temple at N'Kamba was consecrated in 1981, 60 years after Simon Kimbangu performed his first healing miracle here, in his home village.

healing, and extraordinary scenes followed, with vast numbers flocking to N'Kamba to hear his message and to be healed. Kimbangu healed in the name of Jesus Christ, and stood up against local sorcerers. But the large numbers pouring into N'Kamba were too much for the Belgian colonial power, who feared a political uprising. A state of emergency was declared and, in September 1921, Kimbangu was arrested, flogged, and sent into exile in Lubumbashi, 1,500 miles from his home. He died in solitary confinement on 12 October 1951.

Between his deportation and death, Kimbangu never again saw his wife and three sons. But this is not quite how Kimbanguists themselves view events. For them, Kimbangu has made many miraculous appearances. They do not think of these as solely visions and dreams (although Kimbangu is said to appear to them in these ways, too), but as actual appearances in the flesh. He is said to come to believers and to give them advice and instruction.

The persecution of Kimbanguists was severe. Wherever they were found

throughout the Congo there were deportations to other areas, so that the oft-quoted figure of 37,000 deportations of heads of families (meaning at least 100,000 people in total) between 1921 and 1959 is quite possible. During those years, Kimbangu's wife, Muilu Marie (b. 1885), effectively helped run the movement. Following her death in 1959, the third son, Joseph Diangienda (1918–92), was appointed spiritual head, something Kimbangu had instructed shortly before being deported.

Diangienda's leadership was an important period for the Kimbanguists. It was a time of expansion and conscious unification. Diangienda himself travelled widely around the Congo and beyond. In addition, he presided over the vital decision of the Kimbanguist movement to become a church within the World Council of Churches – something which took place on 16 August 1969. They are now officially known as 'The Church of Jesus Christ on Earth through his Special Envoy Simon Kimbangu'.

Kimbanguist practices are an interesting blend of different influences. Main church services take place on Sundays. Prayers are held officially five times a day, though in practice the morning and evening prayers are the most well attended. Sometimes prayer meetings are held through the night, and days of fasting are also announced from time to time. Bigamy, smoking, drugs, alcohol, the eating of pork, sleeping naked, and trading on Sundays are all forbidden. The traditional African practices of wailing at the time of a death and dancing are also forbidden. Among positive obligations, Kimbanguists have to pray and read the Bible regularly. Shoes are removed before entering places of worship because they should not be worn on holy ground. All women are required to cover their heads and dress modestly. Kimbanguists prefer the colours of green and white, and most of their churches, and indeed the believers themselves, are decked

out in these two colours. Green is said to represent hope, and white purity. Kimbanguists have their own alphabet, a language known as Mandombe, which they believe has been given to them miraculously by Kimbangu.

Sunday services usually fill the whole day – for it is a day set aside for the Lord. There is a formal structure, and set order, to the services. Highlights include the many choirs, sermon (which sometimes lasts an hour or more), parades and the special social collection. The parades are a remarkable sight, with groups of Kimbanguists marching in regimented style past the most senior person present. At N'Kamba this is the spiritual head himself. A colour (flag) is similarly trooped past.

Music plays a major part in Kimbanguist life. From the outset, some of Kimbangu's teachings were set down in song, usually in the Kikongo language. During prayers, some of these songs will be sung unaccompanied. The choirs also have a prominent role in the services, as do the flute players and bands.

Services close with major social collections, for which there are often specific projects set by the leaders of the church. These include the running of a hospital in Kinshasa, and medical dispensaries elsewhere. Major building programmes, of which the temple at N'Kamba is the most famous example, have taken place for many years. The 37,000-capacity temple was built with the help of ordinary believers, many of whom literally carried rocks and stones several miles to the site on the hill at N'Kamba. The village itself, known by believers as N'Kamba New Jerusalem, has a regular number of visitors. Many of them go to bathe in a site where they believe there is holy water: this water, and the very soil from N'Kamba, is taken elsewhere for healing. A more recent major project has been the building of a substantial number of luxury apartments near N'Kamba called Kendolo.

These apartments have been built in response to a prophecy that many of those of African descent who live in the United States will return to Africa – specifically to N'Kamba.

The role and place of Kimbangu and his successors has sparked some controversy. At first Kimbangu was said to be a prophet. But it was clear that for many believers, Kimbangu was something more than this. Eventually the church has described Kimbangu as the Holy Spirit made flesh and, as such, as the special envoy of Christ. Diangienda was succeeded by another of Kimbangu's sons, Papa Diulangana (b. 1916), who was a controversial figure. He announced that he was Christ returned, but also moved the date of Christmas to 25 May, which happened to be his own birthday. Dialungana died on 16 August 2001 and was succeeded by the eldest surviving male grandchild of Kimbangu and son of Diulangana: Kiangani Simon Kimbangu.

The Zion Christian Church
Richard Hoskins

The Zion Christian Church (ZCC) is South Africa's largest and fastest-growing church, with a membership estimated at somewhere between 2 and 6 million in around 4,000 parishes.

The ZCC was created in 1924 just after the Anglo-Boer war by Engenas Barnabas Lekganyane (b. c. 1885–1948). Like Isaiah Shembe (see the *Nazareth Baptist Church), he was a rural worker. Based in the Northern Province, Lekganyane was brought up in the churches of Scottish Presbyterian missionaries. He preached a message that included the healing power of God. When he died he was succeeded as spiritual head, after a brief power struggle, by his son Edward Lekganyane.

Among ZCC practices, alcohol, smoking and (like *Kimbanguism and the Nazareth Baptist Church) the eating of pork are forbidden. Uniforms are worn, traditional dances are used as an expression of faith and members give tithes. All forms of violence are forbidden by the ZCC, and 'peace' is the greeting ZCC members first give to one another when they meet. The ZCC attempts to place the spiritual realm above the earthly. However, this approach has not always endeared them to others in South Africa, where to take a non-violent stance during the apartheid years of white control over the majority black population was not viewed positively. Some anti-apartheid hardliners even went so far as to attack ZCC members.

The ZCC believes in the healing power of God. This places them at odds with traditional Zulu healers, whether *inyangas* (traditional healers) or *sangomas* (diviners). Prophets are very important in the church, as the instruments of God's healing power. In many ways they mirror the traditional role of the *iSangoma* in that they will discern the cause of a person's ailment. As with some other *African independent churches, holy water, or other symbolic objects, may be used in healing. During church services it is common for people to be filled with the Holy Spirit and to prophesy. Sometimes prophets may 'name and shame' the practices of people in such public services, even accusing people of witchcraft. For the neutral observer, such practices might be seen as a powerful means by which control through fear is exerted over church members. Most frequently, however, the role of the prophet is simply to discern the cause of an illness, and then to provide a means of healing. Sometimes the latter is very close to the work of an *iSangoma*. Often, for example, a prophet will attach a healing medicine, using holy water or some other object (a practice known as *mohau*, meaning grace), to the afflicted person. Other blessed objects may include walking sticks, pieces of cloth, or string worn on the body. A piece of blue cloth (known as *khutane*) is often worn by members under their garments as a protective device against assaults and lightning, and pieces of blessed copper wire are used on doorposts or gateposts for a similar purpose. While these are dedicated to the name of Christ, the similarity with the methods of African traditional healers is marked. Certainly, the ZCC also has great respect for traditional African beliefs and practices.

For many new members, it is the Africanness of the church that is attractive. The church continues to grow fast. At least 10 per cent of the black population of South Africa are ZCC members. The Easter celebrations of the ZCC are vast, with some 1 million members coming together at Zion City in the Northern Province for a festival lasting several days.

A colourful celebration of the Zion Christian Church.

The Church of the Lord (Aladura)

Richard Hoskins

The Yoruba word 'Aladura' means 'church of the Lord' and, in practice, this refers to a large number of closely related, but independent, churches coming from West Africa.

The Aladura movements began when, in 1925, a catechist of the Church Missionary Society (CMS) in Nigeria called Josiah O. Oshitelu had a series of visions. He began to see a great 'eye' of God, something he found

disturbing. He attempted to use traditional medicines to ward off these recurrent visions and then, when these did not seem to work, turned to a Christian healer called Samuel Shomoye. The latter told Oshitelu not to use traditional healers and that he was chosen by God. Shomoye prayed over Oshitelu and bathed him in consecrated water. Thereafter, Oshitelu began to receive revelations from God. He believed that he received a special holy script, new religious symbols, and new names for God (Kadujah and Taroja). He also felt God prohibiting him from eating pork. When his views became known, he was thrown out of the CMS church, and spent two years praying and fasting.

Oshitelu founded his own church by 1927, something he believed God was telling him to do. He taught his followers to focus on faith in God, fervent prayer and fasting. He found a ready audience. Like Simon Kimbangu (the founder of *Kimbanguism) in the Congo, Oshitelu's message came at a time of great need and hardship. Not only was Yoruba culture under threat from the missionary churches, but there was also a severe economic crisis and both the worldwide flu epidemic and the bubonic plague had swept through the area, causing widespread suffering and distress. Oshitelu said that these hardships derived from God. If the source was God, so the reasoning ran, it was to God that the people should turn, not the traditional healers. The church that derives from Oshitelu has spread to many countries, among them Ghana, Liberia, Sierra Leone, the United States and Britain (especially New York and London respectively).

Under a prophet-healer, Joseph Babalola (1906–59), great expansion occurred. One Aladura church that flourished under this impetus was the Christ Apostolic Church, which now has several hundred thousand members. Other major branches are the *Celestial Church of Christ and the Society of the Cherubim and the Seraphim, founded in 1925–26 by Moses Orimolade Tunolashe and Christina Abiodun Akinsowon. Tunolashe had prayed over a teenage girl who was in a trance state and she recovered. Initially the Cherubim and Seraphim society (named when angels appeared to them in a vision) was formed to complement existing churches. But soon Tunolashe himself became a figure of authority with his own following who addressed him as 'Baba Aladura'(Father of Prayer).

The Aladura churches retain belief in evil forces and sorcery, but believe that God is greater than these. Through specific rituals and prayers it is possible to overcome evil. In these activities the adherent engages the forces of good from beyond the grave (God, Christ, the Holy Spirit) against the forces of evil waging war against the saints on earth.

Rastafarianism
Christopher Partridge

Originating in the 1930s as a black liberation movement in the ghettos of Kingston, Jamaica, Rastafarianism can be found throughout the Caribbean, Western Europe, North America and, in smaller numbers, in certain parts of Africa, Australia and New Zealand, where the Maori have been particularly receptive. However, the movement has grown most rapidly and has had its greatest cultural impact in Jamaica and Britain.

It is not surprising that many Africans who were forcibly transported to the Caribbean, the Americas and Europe by white slave traders longed to return to their homeland. Over time, this longing had a sacralizing effect, in the sense that, as in Rastafarian theology, Africa came to be understood in terms of a sacred, promised land of peace and goodness. This in turn led to the emergence of Back-to-Africa movements from the late 18th century onwards.

One of the first key figures in the Back-to-Africa movement was the black Christian clergyman Edward Wilmot Blyden (1832–1912). Acutely aware of the problems caused for Africans by Western society and the great cultural and historical riches of Africa, he sought to inspire pride in Africa and blackness. Like the Rastafarians, he also claimed that Western Christianity had hindered the development of the African personality.

Following Blyden, one of the greatest influences on Rastafarianism (and indeed Islamic movements such as the *Nation of Islam) was the Jamaican, Marcus Garvey (1887–1940), the leader of the first genuine large-scale black movement in the United States and Europe. Central to Garvey's teaching and to his militant Universal Negro Improvement Association was the return of Africans to Africa, the only place, he believed, where black people would feel at home and be respected as a race. Africans should be proud of their blackness, return to their homeland, lay the foundations for a new superior African civilization, correct the prejudiced white histories of Africa, and worship a black God 'through the spectacles of Ethiopia'. Although physical repatriation did not take place, and although Garveyism eventually died out in the 1920s, Garvey did succeed in focusing the minds of Africans on these issues, which were to become central to the emerging new Rastafarian movement.

It was widely believed that Garvey had made the following prophecy: 'Look to Africa for the crowning of a black king; he shall be the redeemer.' In November 1930, Ras (meaning 'prince') Tafari (meaning 'creator') Makonnen (1891–1975), the great grandson of King Saheka Selassie of Shoa, was crowned Negus of Ethiopia. Declaring himself to be in the line of King Solomon and taking the name Haile Selassie I (Might of the Trinity), as well as 'King of Kings' and 'Lion of the Tribe of Judah', it is not surprising that, when he was crowned in St George's Cathedral in Addis Ababa in front of representatives from

many nations, those who had been inspired by Garvey's teaching saw more than the accession of another Ethiopian ruler. In Haile Selassie I/Ras Tafari many saw the Messiah, Christ returned, the fulfilment of biblical prophecy, God incarnate. This was particularly taught by Leonard Howell, a well-travelled Jamaican with mystical leanings, who came to believe that Ras Tafari had been prophesied in the Bible (e.g. Revelation 5:5; 19:16) and would lead Africans out of white society and back to the promised land of Ethiopia (often used as a synonym for Africa). Howell openly identified with Selassie's armed resistance to Italian invaders, and, after reading an article in a newspaper about the militia force established by Selassie (the Niyabingi Order of Ethiopia), he coined the term *nyabinghi* as a Rastafarian rallying cry.

Although initially a very small Jamaican movement, in the 1950s Rastafarianism began to grow rapidly, particularly among the poor and disaffected, who were inspired by its teachings regarding black superiority, the destruction of white oppressors and the soon return of Africans to the promised land of peace and justice. Indeed, Rastafarianism is a millennial religious movement that teaches the apocalyptic end of the present era, the judgement of Babylon (oppressive white society and religion), and the dawning of a new age of peace and love.

While there are several branches of Rastafarianism, in the West (particularly in Britain) perhaps the most important is the 'Twelve Tribes of Israel' (founded in 1968 by Vernon Carrington), the most visible expression of Rastafarianism.

Although the Bible is important in Rastafarianism, in the final analysis biblical authority must submit to the authority of 'the self'. Biblical truths and their correct

Some Rastafarians smoke 'ganga'. They believe it to be a source of spiritual inspiration.

interpretation must be personally verified by privately 'head resting' (meditating) with Jah and/or by communally 'reasoning' at 'groundings' (religious discussion sessions). Suspicious of much biblical interpretation, particularly that of traditional Christianity, they seek only the guidance of Jah and thus will not accept any doctrine until it has been internally validated. This, it is claimed, leads to spiritual 'knowledge' rather than simply 'belief'. Moreover, trust in the judgement of 'the self' is supported by a strong immanentist theology, which understands the divine to be *within* 'the self'; to 'know' the will of Jah and to know 'truth' one must turn within.

In accordance with Numbers 6, and recalling Samson's strength, many Rastas take the Nazirite vow and do not cut their hair. The consequent 'dreadlocks' are believed to resemble the mane of the lion. This is significant, not only because Ras Tafari is 'the Lion of the Tribe of Judah', but also because the lion symbolizes strength, vitality, superiority and royalty. Along with this spectrum of meaning, as with fashion in many subcultures, dreadlocks are also a symbolic way of confronting and standing apart from society.

One of the most controversial Rastafarian religious practices is the sacramental smoking of 'ganga' (marijuana). Although not all Rastas smoke ganga, there are a great many who do take 'the chalice' (large pipe) or 'spliff' (long cigarette). Drawing on biblical passages such as Revelation 22:2 ('And the leaves of the tree of life are for the healing of the nations'), they argue that not only does it have biblical support, but also that it is good for physical and spiritual healing. It not only relaxes, but, in a similar way to proponents of *psychedelic spirituality, they claim that 'the herb' is a source of inspiration, in that its use makes one more receptive to the divine within.

Ganga smoking is also in accordance with the Rastafarian concern to live naturally: to live in obedience to the laws of nature (central to Rastafarian ethics). Many devout Rastas will

thus only eat organic food, much of which they seek to grow themselves. Indeed, not only are many Rastas vegetarian, but many observe strict dietary rules, which require, for example, abstinence from pork, alcohol, and food which has come from an unknown source.

The Worldwide Church of God
Richard Kyle

The Worldwide Church of God was founded in 1933 as the Radio Church of God by Herbert W. Armstrong (1892–1986). Though the Worldwide Church of God traces its roots to the Adventist movement, its beliefs and practices reflect a mixture of Seventh-day Adventism, *Jehovah's Witnesses, Judaism, Mormonism (the beliefs of the *Church of Jesus Christ of Latter-Day Saints) and British Israelism.

Armstrong, a former advertising man, applied his talents for merchandising to religion. In the 1930s he began his radio broadcasts and published a magazine, which has subsequently been called *The Plain Truth*. Prior to the Second World War the movement grew slowly, but in the next two decades it experienced spectacular growth. Armstrong opened several colleges, the circulation of *The Plain Truth* expanded dramatically, the radio broadcasts spread to Europe, and a television ministry was added in the 1960s – allowing Garner Ted Armstrong, the son of the founder, to come into many homes.

Beginning in 1972, the church entered a period of intense controversy that did not abate until the mid-1980s. End-time predictions failed to materialize, and internal disputes developed. Garner Ted left to found the Church of God International. Following this, Herbert Armstrong (who had condemned the remarriage of divorced people) divorced his wife and remarried. But, by the mid-1980s, the church recovered from these problems only to have Herbert Armstrong die. Joseph Tkach (1927–95) became the new leader and he took the church more in the direction of conventional Christian beliefs. About 50 splinter groups rejected this new direction and have remained largely faithful to Armstrong's teachings.

Theologically, the Worldwide Church of God draws much from Adventism and British Israelism. It observes Old Testament dietary practices and festivals and rigidly maintains the sabbath. It regards the English-speaking peoples as the literal descendants of the ten lost tribes of Israel. It deviates from traditional Christianity in that it is non-Trinitarian and rejects many Christian holidays. However, in recent years under the new leadership the church has modified a number of these beliefs – now accepting such traditional Christian beliefs as Christ's divinity and humanity, his bodily resurrection, and salvation by grace alone. The church is currently led by Joseph Tkach Jr and has about 40,000 constituents.

Worshippers in the Celestial Church of Christ celebrate at a harvest festival.

The Celestial Church of Christ (Aladura)

Richard Hoskins

The Celestial Church of Christ (CCC) was founded by Samuel Oshoffa (1909–85). As with several other Aladura churches, Oshoffa believed he received a call from God. In his case this occurred in a forest (traditionally a place of magical forces in Africa) during a solar eclipse, and the story runs that Oshoffa then became lost in the forest for several months, though according to his followers this was for exactly 40 days and 40 nights. Oshoffa felt called to preach, heal and raise the dead. He went to Porto Novo in the Republic of Benin (then called Dahomey) and in 1947 founded the CCC.

The Bible is vital in the life of the CCC. For its members, there are no practices except those they can derive from the Bible. CCC services are a mixture of influences. Ritual symbols are extremely important, as is prayer. Believers pray for the guidance of the Holy Spirit, and see their churches as heavenly places on earth. Such places are last refuges from the world. Visions, trances and prophecies

☞ *continued on page 70*

COMMUNAL GROUPS

George D. Chryssides

Living in spiritual communities has been a feature of all the traditional world religions, although, understandably, it has tended to be more common in the 'world-renouncing' variety. It has been practised from ancient times to the present day: Buddhism and Jainism have typically portrayed the monastic life as the ideal; members of Hindu groups often live within an ashram; Jewish community living was practised by the Essenes and the Dead Sea sect (and there are a few present-day religious kibbutzim); Islam has given rise to Sufi communities; and, within Christianity, Eastern Orthodoxy and Roman Catholicism offer monastic living. Christian Protestantism, with its work ethic, has tended to emphasize living within the world. However, some controversial new groups that have emerged from a Protestant background have included the Unification Church (the *Family Federation for World Peace and Unification), the *Branch Davidians, the *Peoples Temple and the *Jesus Fellowship (also known as the Jesus Army). Some Protestant groups have emulated the early Christians' practice of communal living and sharing possessions (Acts 2:44).

Early developments in communal living

J. Gordon Melton identifies three periods of spiritual communal group living: the period up to 1860, 1860–1960 and 1960 to the present. The communal movement gained some momentum in Europe during the period of the Protestant Reformation, particularly among the Anabaptists – those who believed in the re-baptism of believers. Of particular note were the Taborites, led by Jan Zizka, who separated themselves from conventional society so that the world could not enforce its norms, and expected an imminent end to human affairs. The 16th-century Bohemian Taborites shared property in common.

One noteworthy experiment in communal living was the Kingdom of the Saints, established in Münster from 1534 to 1536. It was from this short-lived group that the Hutterites and the Mennonites emerged. These groups were named after their respective leaders Jacob Hutter (d. 1536) and Menno Simons (1496–1561); they were apocalyptic, and required communal ownership of goods. The Mennonite movement grew in Holland during the 17th and 18th centuries; in the 19th and 20th centuries persecution forced Mennonites to emigrate to the United States and Canada.

Of the Mennonite groups, the best known are the

Amish boys. The Amish preserve the dress and lifestyle of their founders.

Amish. Founded by Jacob Ammann (c. 1644–c. 1725), the Amish retain the dress and lifestyle of the period in which they were established. They principally engage in farming, rejecting recent technological innovations, such as tractors, automobiles and even electricity. They reside principally in Ohio, Pennsylvania and Indiana, and now attract a growing tourist industry.

Early modern communal groups

The mid-19th century (the beginning of Melton's second period) saw the rise of other communal groups. The best known of these is probably the *Church of Jesus Christ of Latter-Day Saints, more popularly known as the Mormons. Originating in New York State, its founder-members lived conventional lifestyles. However, persecution, culminating in the murder of founder-leader Joseph Smith Jr in 1844, caused Brigham Young to lead over 30,000 followers to the west, arriving at the Great Salt Valley, Utah, where they established themselves in their own territory. Currently Latter-Day Saints constitute some 51 per cent of the population of Utah.

Less well known is the Oneida Community of Perfectionists, led by John Humphrey Noyes (1811–86). The community originated in Putney, Vermont, but official opposition caused them to establish their own community in Oneida, New York, in 1841. Noyes taught that each male was married to the entire female community, and each month was assigned an exclusive female partner. Ten years later, a second Oneida community was set up in Wallingford, Connecticut. These attempts at communal living were short-lived, and – for reasons that are unclear – the movement was disbanded in 1881.

One significant revival of the Hutterite movement in Melton's second period is the Bruderhof (also known as the Hutterian Brethren, or Hutterian Society of Brothers), founded by Eberhard Arnold (1883–1935) and his wife Emmy. Arnold wrote and lectured on theology, and discovered to his surprise that the Hutterites were still in existence. After visiting every Hutterite commune in the United States and Canada, Arnold returned to Germany to set up his own *hof* (community), with its emphasis on sharing possessions in common. After suffering persecution from the Nazis from 1937, the Bruderhof emigrated to Paraguay, and from there to the United States, establishing a *hof* in 1954. At the time of writing six *hofs* existed in the United States and two in Britain.

Twentieth-century communal groups

In the study of new religious movements, the term 'communal groups' principally refers to Melton's third period, especially to groups that stemmed from the *Jesus movement of the 1960s, whose members were typically hippie converts to Protestant fundamentalism. However, several groups originating in this period are not of this variety: for example the Unification Church, *ISKCON (the International Society for Krishna Consciousness) and other Eastern guru-led organizations, as well as neo-Pagan and New Age communities, such as Tim Zell's *Church of All Worlds and the *Findhorn Foundation in Scotland.

The Jesus movement consisted largely of ex-hippies, originally known as Jesus People, Jesus Freaks or Jesus Children. They had typically been on drugs: some movements legitimated them, while others offered rehabilitation. The group's lifestyle and means of propagating the gospel message were unconventional: for example, Moses David (David Berg), founder-leader of the Children of God (now called *The Family), devised a comic series called

True Comix as a means of disseminating his teachings.

The Calvary Chapel, in Costa Mesa, California, led by Chuck Smith from 1965, pioneered the Jesus movement by inaugurating an outreach to hippie communities. Its fame grew rapidly, and some 600 other chapels were soon established. Duane Pederson pioneered Jesus People International in 1969, and Jim Palosaari established the Milwaukee Jesus People, which became the Jesus People United States in 1972. Also in 1972, the Messianic Communities of New England were set up by Gene and Marsha Spriggs.

Influential communal groups

The best known of the communal groups are The Farm, the Church of Jesus Christ at Armageddon, Alamo Christian Ministries, The Family, Shiloh and the *Synanon Church.

THE FARM

The Farm was established by Stephen Gaskin (b. 1936), once a professor at San Francisco State College. In 1966, Gaskin began a series of lectures on 'cultural ferment', which proved so popular that he was persuaded to go on tour country-wide. Followers came with him in a convoy of buses, and eventually

acquired a 1,000-acre site in Summertown, Tennessee, where they established their first community.

The Farm was non-credal, but was committed to non-violence, respect for life, vegetarianism, natural childbirth and healing. Being part of the psychedelic revolution, Gaskin encouraged free love, as well as the use of 'sacred drugs', principally peyote, marijuana and psilocybin mushrooms. This led to the prosecution and subsequent imprisonment of Gaskin and others. The group reconsidered its policy on drugs, which they then totally prohibited, together with alcohol and caffeine.

THE CHURCH OF JESUS CHRIST AT ARMAGEDDON

Another communal group that appears to have sanctioned drug-taking – principally cannabis – is the Church of Jesus Christ at Armageddon, also known as Love Israel the spiritual name of its founder-leader, Paul Erdmann (b. 1940). All members assume the name of a virtue as their forename, together with 'Israel' as their surname, underlining the notion of a communal family membership. Communal ownership is practised. The church gained notoriety in 1972, when two of its members died as a result of sniffing toluene.

ALAMO CHRISTIAN MINISTRIES

In contrast, the Alamo Christian Ministries was set up with the purpose of rehabilitating drug addicts. Originally incorporated as the Christian Foundation in 1969, it was founded by Tony (born Bernard Lazar Hoffman) and Susan Alamo (born Edith Opal Horn; 1928–82). The first community was set up in Dyer, Arkansas, where it established a tabernacle, a school and a small publishing concern, as well as small businesses to generate income. It subsequently moved to Alma, and has assumed various names, including the Alamo Christian Foundation, Holy Alamo Christian Church Consecrated and the Music Square Church. The organization is fundamentalist, relying on the King James translation of the Bible, and Pentecostalist – unusual for a Protestant community group. The Alamo organization has strict views on sexual morality, being opposed to homosexuality, abortion and promiscuity. It gained notoriety in the early 1990s when Tony Alamo was convicted of tax violations and served a prison sentence from 1994 to 1998. The movement remains small, attracting a following somewhere between 200 and 750.

THE FAMILY

The Family is possibly the best known of the communal

groups. It was originally founded in 1967 in California by David Brandt Berg (1919–94), known to his followers as Moses David. Known initially for its 'sackcloth vigils', for which its members donned dark robes and proclaimed end-time prophecies, the movement expanded to become a worldwide movement that now claims around 9,000 full-time members.

SHILOH

Although now defunct, Shiloh is worthy of mention as part of the Jesus movement. It was founded in 1968, being then called the House of Miracles, a commune in Oregon. Founder-leader John J. Higgins Jr (b. 1939) had been a drug addict, but converted to Christianity. The movement experienced rapid growth until 1978, when Higgins was accused of authoritarianism and dismissed. Many of the 163 centres were unable to survive his departure, while a few struggled on until the mid-1980s. The organization was formally disbanded in 1988. After being ousted from Shiloh, Higgins became a pastor in the Calvary Chapel, where the Jesus movement began its rise.

THE SYNANON CHURCH

Although the Synanon Church slightly anticipates the Jesus movement, being founded in 1958, Synanon is also worthy of mention as an example of a communal group. Set up by Charles Dederich (1914–97) as the Synanon Foundation in Santa Monica, California, the organization grew to 15,000 members at its peak in the 1970s. It was not originally founded as a religious organization; indeed many of its several communities did not regard themselves as having any particular religious affiliation. However, in 1974 it declared itself to be a religion, and assumed the name of Synanon Church in 1980. Unlike the groups that stemmed from the Jesus movement, Synanon drew on a variety of traditions, including Buddhism, Daoism and Western mystical teachers, such as Ralph Waldo Emerson. A number of court cases in the 1970s, including an accusation of conspiracy to murder, put the organization under a cloud, and caused membership to decline markedly, finally disbanding in 1991.

With the passage of time, there appears to have been a decline in community living. In some organizations, such as the Farm, membership has dwindled, and in some cases – such as Shiloh and Synanon – the movement has been disbanded altogether. As members have grown older, community living has proved less convenient: restricted accommodation is inconducive to family life, and members have often sought careers or more conventional employment. One response to this situation is for the communal groups to devise various categories of membership. The Family, for example, distinguishes between 'charter members', who are full time (the majority), and 'fellow members'. The Unification Church has a three-tier membership, consisting of full-time, 'home church' and 'associate member'. ISKCON, likewise, has a core membership living in ISKCON temples, but the vast majority of members live at home and follow an otherwise conventional lifestyle.

take place, and special services to exorcize evil spirits are not uncommon. Before services begin, prayers and incense fill the church. Candles are lit as symbols of the heavenly presence. Once the service is underway, crosses are placed across the doorways, mainly to prevent people from coming in and out during the service, but also as a symbol to show evil cannot enter. Members coming into this 'sacred space' wear white gowns as symbols of purity, leave their shoes outside the church, and sprinkle their heads with holy water for purification. This water symbolizes both life and power. Shaking is not uncommon in services. Four guardian angels (Michael, Gabriel, Uriel and Raphael) are said to enter the church through the front doors, move down the aisle, and hover above the altar. These angels have special powers over the forces of evil. People go forth from the services with prayers for God's protection, and openness to his guidance.

As well as its homeland of Benin, the CCC is a major force in Nigeria, to which it spread in 1950 and where it now has nearly 2,000 parishes (branches). It has also spread through other parts of the world, with another 350 parishes outside Nigeria, and a worldwide membership estimated by scholars at several million.

The Brotherhood of the Cross and Star
Richard Hoskins

The Brotherhood of the Cross and Star (BCS) originated in Nigeria with Olumba Olumba Obu (b. 1918). It claims to be a 'brotherhood' rather than a church, and embraces those from all faiths, particularly Islam.

After its emergence in the 1950s, the BCS grew rapidly in the 1960s. It played a role in the reconciliation process in Nigeria following the Biafran conflict. At its heart is the teaching of Obu that people should love one another. Followers consider Obu to be the sole spiritual head of the universe, the 'Universal Teacher' and the 'Spirit of Love' in human form. From the world headquarters in Calabar, Nigeria, the ageing Obu still gives out words of wisdom to the faithful. Members believe that the Universal Teacher will bring the world to a greater understanding of the truth. This involves living in the practical reality of 'brotherhood love'. This is the original way laid down by Jesus, 'the man from Nazareth' who was put to death for revealing this love to the world – a message Obu continues to teach the world.

Like many new religious movements in Africa, BCS is a mixture of different influences. Members recognize a holy day (Thursday), wear white robes, remove shoes in places of worship (which they call 'bethels') and use the Bible extensively in life and worship. They also practise fasting and a ritual bowing (or sometimes knocking) of the head. Smoking and alcohol are forbidden, and faith, rather than medicine, should be used to cure illness. The BCS sees itself as open to everyone, regardless of their creed, colour, class, age or gender. Because Obu believes that humans derive from animals, he advocates vegetarianism. Nature is also part of the brotherhood with humanity, and thus should be respected and looked after.

The two symbols of the cross and star are indicative of how the movement sees itself. The cross is viewed as a prime example of self-sacrificial suffering love. But the cross also represents something in the past. For the BCS it is also important to look to the future, hence the symbol of the star – the morning star of the book of Revelation in the Christian New Testament, whose presence in the person of Christ is believed to be with us now, but who also anticipates a glorious and heavenly future.

The BCS believes there are three stages to God's revelation in the world. The first stage was Judaism (the Age of God the Father), the second, Christianity (the Age of God the

Son), and the third is taking place now (the Age of the Spirit). This is to be an age of reconciliation, a time when old religious divisions, both in the church and between religions, break down. As such, the BCS sees itself as a universal spiritual movement.

The BCS now has some 2 million followers in many countries. In Africa it is mainly to be found in Nigeria and Ghana. In Europe there is a significant presence in Britain, France, Germany and the Ukraine. There are also members in the United States, the West Indies and India.

The Family Federation for World Peace and Unification (Unification Church)
Sarah Lewis

The Family Federation for World Peace and Unification (FFWPU) is the new name for the Holy Spirit Association for the Unification of World Christianity (HSAUWC), which was more commonly known as the Unification Church and more popularly known as the Moonies. The Unification Church was founded in Seoul, in 1954, by Sun Myung Moon (b. 1920). Unificationism has always highlighted the importance of the family unit within society, and an increasing emphasis over the course of the last few years on the importance of the family is reflected in the new name chosen for the movement. To limit confusion, the group will here be referred to as the Unification movement or Unificationism.

The events that would eventually lead to the formation of the Unification movement began in 1936. Moon states that Jesus appeared to him in Easter of that year and told him that he, Moon, was to complete the mission that Jesus had begun but had not been able to complete due to his premature death. The years following this meeting saw Moon embracing his mission, after a period of uncertainty, and developing his ideas through various means.

Unificationist theology is based largely on highlighting parallels between the Old Testament and the New Testament, in the belief that if we study these parallels we will discover what is going to happen in our own age. The result of this study forms the 'Completed Testament' or *Divine Principle* that outlines the beliefs of the Unification movement.

Unification theology has been heavily influenced by the indigenous religions of Korea (Buddhism, Confucianism, Daoism and *Shamanism) and also by Korean Christianity, and finds a place within a wide scheme of religious development and growth in post-1950s Korea (after freedom from Japanese rule and the Korean War). The Unification Church was one of several new religious movements that emerged in Korea during the 1950s, and these movements had many common beliefs and aims. When the beliefs of the Unification movement are placed in the context of the general syncretic religious climate of Korea, the influence of indigenous religions becomes evident and explains some of the beliefs of Unificationism that are less familiar in a Western context.

In Unification thought, God is an invisible essence composed of dual characteristics – spirit and energy – and all existence is generated by these. God created Adam and Eve as the first human ancestors in the Garden of Eden, projecting them out of himself, and reflecting his dual characteristics. However, the premature joining of Adam and Eve through a sexual relationship led to the Fall of humanity away from God's hands and into Satan's, and that is where it has remained. The first ancestors should have married, centred on God's love and produced perfect children, thus creating the True Family, and establishing God's kingdom of heaven on earth.

With the belief that the kingdom of heaven would have been created in this way, it follows that the role of the Second Adam (Jesus) would be the same. According to Unificationism, Jesus should have married a perfect Eve and had perfect children, thus creating God's kingdom of heaven and fulfilling the divine plan. When Jesus was crucified, God realized that he would have to create a Third Adam, a new Messiah, known in Unificationism as the Lord of the Second Advent, to complete the mission.

Although Moon only declared his messiahship publicly in 1992, and nowhere in *Divine Principle* is it stated that Moon is the Messiah, he would certainly have been seen by most of his followers as fulfilling the messianic role. Theologically, the Messiah is a couple, and therefore the messiahship should be shared between Moon and his wife, Hak Ja Han, yet Moon remains the central figure. Since the declaration of Moon's messiahship, however, the emphasis has

Twenty-two thousand couples gather in New York's Madison Square Garden for the Blessing Ceremony that lies at the heart of Unificationism. Reverend Sun Myung Moon and his wife preside over the mass wedding.

shifted to the ability of members themselves to become messiahs and little is now said about Moon's own messiahship. Similarly, all Unificationist couples may now become True Parents, and this is not restricted to Moon and Hak Ja Han.

The Blessing Ceremony, or mass wedding, stands at the core of Unificationism as each member should ideally be blessed if they are to enter God's kingdom of heaven. Through the blessing, Moon believes that he is creating a new heavenly family tradition – the True Family, led by the True Parents – and this is an attempt to heal the broken relationships that have arisen throughout history.

There are several different levels of membership, from people who work full time at the core and accept all teachings, to those who do not accept the teachings of the group, but who offer their support to the many organizations founded by the movement and the general aims of the movement. Members do not withdraw from wider society. Those who do not work full time for the movement are to be found in all types of employment and the children of Unificationists are not educated separately from the children of non-Unificationists. With increasingly less

emphasis on theological issues, such as the messiahship of Moon, members are increasingly involved in missionary activity, showing support for the promotion of interfaith dialogue and world peace.

The Unification movement has been active in promoting interreligious dialogue and world peace through organizations such as the Professors World Peace Academy (PWPA), the Women's Federation for World Peace (WFWP), the Interreligious and International Federation for World Peace (IIFWP) and the International Religious Foundation (IRF). One of the main aims of these organizations has been to encourage people of different faiths to meet and find harmony in their beliefs.

Along with the change in name and increasing emphasis on the role of the family has been the opening of the blessing to non-members. People who support the wider aims of the movement, but who do not necessarily adhere to the main body of its theology, are now welcome to show their support through being blessed by Moon and Hak Ja Han.

Early Unificationism undertook a great deal of missionary activity, taking Unificationism across the globe, concentrating initially on Japan, then the United States and Britain. More recent expansion has been in Eastern Europe and South America. Much of the attraction of the Unification movement has been the idea that members themselves are helping to create the kingdom of heaven. The kingdom of heaven will be established when everyone joins the movement and the work of individual members is therefore vital in the creation of the kingdom of heaven on earth.

The Way International
Richard Kyle

The Way International had its origin in the early ministries of Victor Paul Wierwille (1916–85). He founded the organization in 1942 as 'Vesper Chimes', a radio ministry aimed at college students. Wierwille was serving as the pastor of an Evangelical Reformed Church in Ohio, United States. The name was changed several times, first to the 'Chimes Hour' and then, in 1947, to the 'Chimes Hour Youth Caravan'. The name 'The Way' was assumed in 1955 and in 1974 the present name, The Way International, was adopted.

The Way grew steadily during the 1960s, recruiting largely from the youth counter-culture and the *Jesus movement. That said, some in the Jesus movement regarded Wierwille as a heretic. The organization and its facilities expanded and, in 1971, it hosted the first national Rock of Ages Festival, aimed at youth culture. The Way considers itself to be a biblical research, teaching and household fellowship ministry. It does not build or own any church buildings but holds its meetings in homes.

Theologically, The Way draws its beliefs from an unusual combination of dispensationalism, Arianism and Pentecostalism. It separates history into nine periods of 'divine administration', with the current 'period of grace' beginning at Pentecost. The Way resembles the early Christian heresy of Arianism in that, while it affirms Christ's status as Son of God and Saviour, it denies his full divinity, and therefore also denies the Trinitarian orthodoxy of Western Christianity. This position is argued by Wierwille in his book *Jesus Christ is Not God* (1975). Orthodox Trinitarianism is further undermined by the belief that the Holy Spirit is not a 'person' but a divine power. That said, the Spirit is important and there is an emphasis on receiving the fullness of the Holy Spirit, which may be evident in the manifestations of the gifts of the Spirit. The Way also affirms the inerrancy of the Bible.

The Way is organized on the model of a tree. The international headquarters in Knoxville, Ohio (the roots), feeds all its

☞ *continued on page 77*

THE ANTI-CULT MOVEMENT

George D. Chryssides

The anti-cult movement is often distinguished from the counter-cult movement, the latter consisting principally of mainstream Christians who seek to publish rebuttals of the teachings of new religious movements (NRMs), purporting to demonstrate their unorthodox nature. Such opposition can be traced back to the early parts of the 20th century, when William C. Irvine published his *Timely Warnings* (1917), later reissued as *Heresies Exposed* (1955). This approach was dominant until the 1970s, and targeted older NRMs such as the *Jehovah's Witnesses, the *Church of Jesus Christ of Latter-Day Saints, *Christian Science and Moral Re-Armament.

Origins of the modern anti-cult movement

The new wave of NRMs in the late 1960s and early 1970s gave rise to a different response. With the onset of secularization, the public became less interested in theological critiques and more concerned about societal problems. Principal concerns included psychological manipulation ('brainwashing'), total commitment, unquestioning obedience to the leader, sub-standard living conditions with long working hours, and sleep and food deprivation. The mass deaths at the *Peoples Temple in Jonestown, Guyana, in 1978, added considerable fuel to the anti-cult movement.

The present-day anti-cult movement can be traced back to Ted Patrick, who began work as a deprogrammer in 1972, and whose activities are described in his autobiographical book, *Let Our Children Go!* Deprogramming involves forcible physical abduction, after which members are subjected to isolation and faith-breaking tactics. The deprogramming movement reached its height in the 1980s in the United States and in Europe, but is now rare. As deprogramming is illegal, several deprogrammers received custodial sentences for their activities. Most anti-cult organizations now confine their activities to consciousness-raising, political campaigning and warning potential converts. 'Exit counselling' tends to replace deprogramming: this involves counselling and persuasion, rather than physical intervention.

Major anti-cult groups

Initially, anti-cult groups targeted specific NRMs, but cult-specific groups tended either to widen their focus or become defunct. Patrick's original organization, FREECOG, was focused on the Children of God (now known as *The Family), but widened, becoming the Citizens' Freedom Foundation, and later the Cult Awareness Network (CAN). Although CAN claimed not to practise deprogramming, there is good evidence that several leaders were involved in the practice. The *Church of Scientology conducted a long-standing campaign against CAN, and, following a series of lawsuits, CAN became bankrupt in 1996, whereupon the Church of Scientology liaised with other interest groups to purchase its assets and hotline number. Scientologists are now responsible for CAN's operation.

The American Family Foundation (AFF) is less activist than the old-style CAN. AFF was founded in 1987 by psychiatrist John Clarke. It focuses on research and education, although it relies essentially upon the opinions of a small number of American psychiatrists, such as Margaret Thaler Singer, who subscribe to the 'brainwashing theory' – a theory not endorsed by the majority of professionals in the field. AFF publishes *The Cult Observer*, the *Cultic Studies Journal* and the internet journal *Cultic Studies Review*.

Also prominent on the American anti-cult scene is

the Freedom of Mind Resource Center, run by Steven Hassan. Hassan was formerly a member of the Unification Church (now the *Family Federation for World Peace and Unification), from which he disengaged in 1976. Hassan qualified as a 'mental health counsellor' in 1985, and offers professional counselling to his clients, as well as information and publication. He has authored a number of books, the best known of which is *Combatting Cult Mind Control* (1988). Hassan does not advocate deprogramming, although he admits to participating in 'about a dozen involuntary interventions' shortly after leaving the Unification Church.

In Britain, the most prominent cult-monitoring group is Family Action Information and Resource (FAIR). This organization was founded in 1976 by Paul Rose, a member of parliament for Manchester. Rose had received a number of complaints about the Unification Church from anxious parents, and decided to form an organization, although his own involvement was short-lived. Other British anti-cult organizations include the Cult Information Centre, established by Ian Haworth in 1987, and Catalyst, which offers exit counselling from a Christian perspective and is run by Graham Baldwin, a Pentecostalist.

In France, the principal anti-cult group is UNADFI (National Association for the Defence of the Family and the Individual). FECRIS (European Federation of Centres for Research and Sectarianism), founded in 1994, covers Europe more widely, having representatives from ten European countries.

Christian counter-cult groups

Notwithstanding the rise of secular anti-cult groups, a number of Christian evangelical counter-cult organizations have emerged in recent years. The largest is the Christian Research Institute, founded in 1960 by Walter Martin, and currently headed by Hank Hanegraaff. Also prominent is the Spiritual Counterfeits Project (SPC) founded in Berkeley, California, in 1973. Ironically, SPC stemmed from the Berkeley Christian Coalition, which in turn derived from Jack Sparks' Christian World Liberation Front, part of the *Jesus movement. Other Christian counter-cult groups include the Dialog Centre in Denmark, founded in 1973 by Johannes Aagaard, and the Reachout Trust in England, established in 1981. Reachout originally targeted Jehovah's Witnesses and subsequently members of the Church of Jesus Christ of Latter-Day Saints, both of which remain its primary focus, but its compass includes a wide variety of NRMs, as well as other major world religions. Christian critique of NRMs continues in counter-cult publications, and prominent Christian counter-cultists include Ronald Enroth, Edmond C. Gruss, Bob Larson, Josh McDowell and Don Stewart.

The anti-cult movement tends to gain recognition principally from the media, while counter-cultists' credence seldom goes beyond that of their faith community. Although Britain and the United States have allowed religious freedom to extend to NRMs that act within the law, there can be little doubt that the anti-cult movement was instrumental in persuading the French and Belgian authorities to restrict severely the activities of NRMs. Although influential, the anti-cult movement's generally negative view of NRMs is unsupported by most academic studies, which it tends to ignore. While mainstream Christians, like most of the public, tend to endorse the anti-cult movement's view of 'cults', the churches are wary of officially endorsing their views, fearing that repressive legislation might also affect mainstream religious organizations.

members through national organizations (the trunk), regional bodies (the limbs) and finally through individual groups (the twigs). It also propagates its teachings through *The Way Magazine* (first published in 1954) and enquirers are introduced to the movement through 'Power for Abundant Living' courses (started by Wierwille in 1953).

Although it is difficult to assess membership figures, estimates of which are between 10,000 and 100,000, it has declined since the 1980s. There are several reasons for this decline, including changes in counterculture, the death of Wierwille and various internal difficulties. The movement is currently led by L. Craig Martindale (b. 1948).

The Peoples Temple
John A. Saliba

Founded by James (Jim) Warren Jones (1931–78), the Peoples Temple, often referred to as Jonestown (the commune he founded in Guyana), will be remembered for its tragic end in a mass suicide/murder of over 900 men, women and children. It became a paradigm of an 'evil cult' and can certainly be considered to be one of the most tragic events in the history of religion in the 20th century.

Jones was born in east central Indiana, United States, on 13 May 1931. He was attracted to the socialist and communist ideals of the Marxist revolution. At first he was attached to the Methodist Church, which he left as it excluded African-Americans from membership. In late 1954 he moved to Indianapolis where, in April 1955, he founded a church called 'Wings of Deliverance', a name that was soon changed to the 'Peoples Temple'. By 1960, the Peoples Temple became affiliated with the Christian Church (Disciples of Christ), which ordained Jones in spite of his lack of formal theological training. Jones gradually assumed a prophetic role; he preached racial equality and harmony as well

as an apocalyptic end of the world through race war, genocide and nuclear war. He maintained that he was the manifestation of the Christ principle and that he had the power to heal. Controversy over his radical theology led to the movement of the Peoples Temple to Ukiah in northern California in 1965. By 1972, a second Peoples Temple was established in San Francisco.

In 1977, the United States Internal Revenue Service denied the tax-exemption

The aftermath of the mass suicide known as the Jonestown Massacre of 1978. Bodies lie strewn around a vat containing a drink laced with cyanide.

Peoples Temple leader Jim Jones. Many theories have been put forward to explain the catastrophic demise of his movement.

status of the Temple. This, along with the external and internal conflicts brought about by his teachings and practices, led Jones to move the Temple to a remote area in Guyana. Here its members lived in a tightly controlled communal society where the practice of catharsis, which involved public confession and punishment for transgressing the rules of the commune, was introduced. The concerns of the defectors and the relatives of those who remained members instigated an investigation by Congress led by Leo Ryan. Eventually, Ryan flew to Guyana to investigate. Four days later, on 18 November 1978, Ryan and three others were killed by a commune member. What Jones called a 'revolutionary suicide', an event the commune had practised, followed the

same night. Children and then adults swallowed cordial mixed with poison and tranquillizers. Jones apparently committed suicide by shooting himself.

Many attempts have been made to understand the nature of the Peoples Temple and to provide reasons for its catastrophic demise. Many psychiatrists see Jim Jones as a mentally ill person suffering from a host of emotional disturbances, including paranoia, megalomania and/or sadomasochism. Others see him as an antinomian personality and an irrational psychopath. The fanaticism of the group is interpreted as a form of infantile regression and narcissism. Sociologists and anthropologists find such theories unsatisfactory. While all admit that, towards the end, Jones, who was heavily addicted to drugs, was instrumental in leading his followers to destruction, it has been suggested that Jonestown might be better understood as an utopian and millenarian society where suicide and murder were the final strategy when the idealistic goals of the movement failed to materialize (see *Apocalyticism and Millenarianism). The conflicts Jones had with the outside world and the isolation of the experimental commune are key factors that contributed to the Peoples Temple's self-destruction. The sociology of knowledge, the systems theory and the mobilization theory have all been employed to throw light on a religious/political movement that will probably continue to baffle interpreters for quite a while.

The Branch Davidians
James R. Lewis

The Branch Davidians, a descendant of an earlier group that had splintered from the Seventh-day Adventist Church, made international headlines as the result of a confrontation, siege and tragic fire that took place outside of Waco, Texas, in 1993. The Branch Davidian sect is one of several organizations that derive from the Davidian Seventh-day Adventists (originally referred to as the Shepherd's Rod) founded by the Bulgarian immigrant Victor Houteff (b. 1885) in 1930. The Shepherd's Rod moved to Texas in 1935 and established the original Mount Carmel Center near Waco.

Following Victor Houteff's death in 1955, leadership of the group passed to his wife Florence. Florence Houteff prophesied that on 22 April 1959, God would directly intervene in human history. When Florence Houteff's prophecy failed to manifest, there was widespread disillusionment. Many of her former followers joined a splinter group, the Branch Davidian Seventh-day Adventists, which had been founded by Benjamin Roden following the death of Victor Houteff.

In 1962, Florence Houteff stunned her few remaining followers with the announcement that her teachings contained errors and dissolved the Davidian Seventh-day Adventists. Within a short time, Roden won the loyalty of most of the remaining Davidians and gained legal control over the remaining 77 acres of the Mount Carmel property.

Benjamin Roden's wife Lois began having spiritual visions in 1977. She first announced that the Holy Spirit was in fact female and then elaborated on this vision, asserting that God is both male and female and that at the second coming the Messiah would assume female form. Later she founded a magazine, *Shekinah*, as a vehicle for her theological views.

In 1978, Benjamin Roden died and Lois Roden quickly laid claim to the leadership. However, a substantial proportion of members defected because of political infighting and Lois's controversial theological doctrines. The Rodens' son, George Roden, was determined to regain what he believed to be his rightful position as leader. He unsuccessfully appealed to Mount Carmel residents and also to the courts. The feud between mother and son became so bitter that Lois Roden finally obtained a court order barring George from the Mount Carmel property.

In the late 1970s, Vernon Howell was a young man attending the Seventh-day Adventist Church in Tyler, Texas (the church his mother attended). Howell learned of the Branch Davidians from a Seventh-day Adventist friend and began working as a handyman at Mount Carmel in 1981. He became a favourite of 67-year-old Lois Roden. Rumours began circulating that the two were lovers. The relationship elevated Howell's

A woman at the ceremonies marking the third anniversary of the burning of the Branch Davidian Compound at Mount Carmel, Dallas. Her T-shirt bears an image of David Koresh.

status with the group and Lois Roden gained an ally in her struggle with her son. Vernon Howell and George Roden competed for power, both claiming divine inspiration and revelations.

Lois Roden attempted to resolve the power struggle between her son and Vernon Howell by naming Howell as her successor and inviting Branch Davidian adherents to come to Mount Carmel to listen to his teachings and prophecies. Converts point to Howell's biblical knowledge more than any other single factor in explaining their own attraction to the Branch Davidians. Following Lois Roden's death in 1986, the feud between George Roden and Vernon Howell intensified. Howell was eventually victorious.

The Branch Davidians recruited both nationally and internationally, travelling to Hawaii, Canada, England, Israel and Australia. Efforts at street recruiting had been unsuccessful, so the recruitment campaigns continued to target current or former Seventh-day Adventists. Branch Davidians were willing to disrupt church services to gain a hearing for their messages. Those converted were usually ostracized or 'disfellowshipped' by the Seventh-day Adventist Church. The recruitment campaigns yielded several dozen converts and created an international, interracial community of about 100 at Mount Carmel.

In 1987, Howell began taking 'spiritual wives' from among the young, unmarried women in the group. He later expanded these relationships to include the wives of male Branch Davidian adherents. Some members felt unable to go along with his demands in this area and left the group. Howell enunciated this controversial 'New Light doctrine' in 1989. He asserted that, as a messiah, he became the perfect mate of all the female adherents. Part of his mission was to create a new lineage of God's children from his own seed. These children would ultimately rule the world. The New Light doctrine made all female Branch Davidians spiritual wives to Howell, who

claimed that male adherents would be united with their perfect mates in heaven.

In 1990, Howell legally adopted the name 'David Koresh'. The word 'Koresh' is Hebrew for Cyrus, the Persian king who defeated the Babylonians 500 years before the birth of Jesus. In biblical language, Koresh is a (rather than the) 'messiah', one appointed to carry out a special mission for God. By taking the first name 'David', he claimed a spiritual link to the biblical King David. By 1992, Koresh increasingly concluded that the apocalypse would occur in the United States rather than Israel, and the group began adopting a survivalist outlook, stockpiling large amounts of food, weapons, ammunition and fuel. Koresh renamed the Mount Carmel community 'Ranch Apocalypse'.

The Branch Davidians retained a biblical base for their teachings, but the Bible was supplemented, and in certain respects supplanted, by revelations of the living prophet. They observed a Saturday sabbath and eschewed meat, alcohol, caffeine and tobacco. They rejected ostentatious dress and grooming, birthday celebrations and television viewing. Koresh taught that Christ had died only for those who lived prior to his crucifixion. Koresh's mission was to permit the salvation of all subsequent generations. In contrast to Christ, who was sinless and therefore an impossible role model, Koresh was a 'sinful messiah'. Koresh taught that human sinfulness does not prevent humans from attaining salvation. Koresh informed his followers that Armageddon would begin in the United States with an attack on the Branch Davidians.

On 28 February 1993, a force of 76 agents of the Bureau of Alcohol, Tobacco and Firearms raided the Branch Davidian community. The raid turned into a shoot-out between federal agents and Branch Davidians. The resulting stand-off became a 51-day siege that ended on 19 April when federal agents launched a new attack on the Davidian

☞ continued on page 85

CELTIC CHRISTIAN SPIRITUALITY

Ian Bradley

Celtic Christianity provides one of the most appealing products in the booming contemporary consumer market for accessible spirituality. Books retelling the stories of 5th- and 6th-century saints or providing anthologies of prayers and poems in the Celtic tradition jostle for space with tapes and compact discs of Celtic chant and Celtic mood music on the shelves of 'body, mind and spirit' shops as well as Christian bookstores. Miniature reproductions of Irish high-standing crosses and prayer cards decorated with the motifs found on ancient illuminated manuscripts are on prominent display in visitor centres and tourist gift shops.

Its appeal is also manifested at a less commercial level in the growing popularity of pilgrimages to Celtic holy sites, workshops, quiet days and retreats. Celtic prayers and liturgies have been enthusiastically taken up by many churches and a number of communities have been established in recent years with rules of life based on those drawn up in Celtic monasteries.

The modern appeal of Celtic spirituality extends across both the theological and denominational spectrum, and well beyond the company of Christian believers. New Agers, feminists and ecologists, as well as liberal, evangelical and charismatic Christians identify with its ethos and message and call for a recovery of its key principles.

To some extent this appeal is part of the more general enthusiasm for all things Celtic that has made *Riverdance* a hit musical, put Gaelic pop groups into the music charts and stimulated a widespread popular interest in the archaeology and mythology of Celtic Britain and Ireland. It also clearly ties in with the recrudescence of Irish, Scottish and Welsh nationalism in the context of weakening loyalty to the concept of an English-dominated Britain. The particular appeal of Celtic Christian spirituality also taps into a long-standing fascination with the exotic nature of 'the other' (in this case, the spirituality of the marginalized Celtic fringe perceived as existing on the edge of and in contrast to the predominant and more prosaic Anglo-Saxon culture) and a desire to find a purer, simpler and more free-ranging expression of the faith at a time when there is increasing impatience with the hierarchy, organizational complexity and narrow inflexibility of institutional churches.

The Celts and Celtic Christianity

The word 'Celtic' derives from the term *Keltoi*, which the ancient Greeks applied to those who lived north of the Alps, and so were beyond the pale of classical civilization. From the time of this first usage it has carried exotic connotations and suggested 'otherness' and has been used more by outsiders than by Celts themselves. The term was taken up in scholarly circles to denote a group of European peoples whose languages conform to a broad category or family. There is some dispute as to whether we can, in fact, legitimately talk about the Celts as a distinct ethnic rather than simply linguistic grouping. Their origins are generally seen as lying in the area around the Black Sea in roughly 1000 BCE. During the next 500 years or so they spread south as far as the Pyrenees, north to the Rhine and west to Ireland, possibly migrating because of climatic changes. Much of continental Europe was effectively colonized and occupied by the Celts when the Roman empire took hold.

Despite this pan-European pedigree, the term 'Celtic Christianity' nearly always applies only to the native Christian practices, beliefs and customs of the British Isles (and occasionally Brittany) in the period between the departure of the Romans at the beginning of the 5th century and the arrival of the Normans in the middle of the 11th century. This 650-year period hardly presents a homogeneous Christian culture. The indigenous 'Celtic' peoples were themselves divided between the Gaelic-speaking Irish (confusingly called *Scoti* by the Romans and ultimately giving their name to Scotland to which they emigrated in increasing numbers), the *Cymri* or British found in south-west Scotland, north-west England and Wales, and the elusive and mysterious Picts of highland and eastern Scotland. Much of England was invaded by the Jutes, Saxons and Angles from northern Europe who arrived as pagans but often became enthusiastic converts to Christianity. Native 'Celtic' Christianity undoubtedly owed much to the legacy of the Romans and incorporated Romano-British Christianity as well as drawing on strong links with the eastern Mediterranean and Continental Europe.

The Celtic saints

If both the geographical and ethnic complexion of Celtic Christian spirituality is more diverse and confusing than its nomenclature suggests, then so also is its temporal location. While the focus is often on the lives and

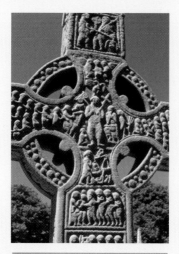

A 9th-century Celtic high cross.

supposed writings of the saints who flourished in Celtic Christianity's 'golden age' from the 6th to the 8th centuries, the prayers and poems found in anthologies often come from much later sources, notably the great collection of Hebridean chants and lays collected in the late 19th century by Alexander Carmichael, the *Carmina Gadelica*. For many of its devotees, indeed, Celtic Christian spirituality is a kind of seamless tradition that runs from the poems emanating from hermits' cells at the time of Columba to the writings of modern Welsh and Irish bards.

Although much later material is often interpolated and incorporated within the tradition, the lives and stories of the saints who flourished in the 7th and 8th centuries give Celtic Christian

spirituality its main foundation and provide one of the main sources of its distinctive appeal. It is through encountering Ninian, Patrick, Columba, Brigit, David, Aidan, Cuthbert and a whole host of other apparently almost superhuman holy men and women that many people gain their first taste of Celtic Christianity. Texts such as Adamnan's *Life of Columba*, Patrick's *Confession* and famous Breastplate poem and Bede's *Life of Cuthbert* provide important source material for both academic study and popular appreciation of the subject.

Fascination with and idolization of the Celtic saints of the 6th and 7th centuries is by no means a modern phenomenon. As early as the mid-8th century the Venerable Bede, writing the first history of the English-speaking peoples in his monastery at Jarrow in Northumbria, was looking fondly back to the golden age of Aidan and Cuthbert, whose purity and simplicity he compared with the corrupt and cynical ways of the churchmen of his own time. Bede was the first in a long line of English writers to propagate the myth of a pure and primeval Celtic church, distinguished by a special spiritual quality. His highly coloured account of the debate between proponents of 'Roman' and 'Celtic' Christianity at the Synod of Whitby in 664 was seized on and amplified by later historians and propagandists who turned it into a set-piece confrontation between a hierarchical, authoritarian church and a gentler and more anarchic Christian tradition.

Medieval chroniclers further propagated the romantic and exotic character of Celtic Christianity (though they did not yet call it that) by weaving connections between the Irish and British saints and legendary figures such as Arthur and Merlin. Hagiographical spin doctors, often working to promote the territorial or political claims of a particular monastery or church centre, produced ever more fanciful accounts of the exploits and miracles of their saintly founders. Pre-Christian legends were fused with Christian themes to produce epic stories like the Brendan Voyage. Connections were made with the Grail legend and with Glastonbury, which William of Malmesbury identified as the site of the first Christian church in Britain, set up by Joseph of Arimathea in 63 CE on the express orders of the apostle Philip. His suggestion that Patrick had come over from Ireland to serve as its first abbot and that it had also been visited by Brigit, David and Aidan established Glastonbury's status as the epicentre of Celtic Christian spirituality 700 years before it became the New Age capital of Britain.

Modern trends in Celtic Christianity

The historians and apologists of the Reformation period were the first to talk about 'Celtic Christianity' and contrast it with Roman Christianity. The notion of Celtic spirituality was given a further boost with the 18th-century interest in Druids and the development of a syncretistic agenda, which portrayed Celtic Christianity as being much closer than other inculturations of the Christian faith to the values of primal religions. Nineteenth-century romanticism, and particularly the Celtic twilight movement associated with the Irish poet W.B. Yeats, further blurred the boundaries between its pagan and Christian elements and enhanced the misty and esoteric aspects of Celtic spirituality. Late Victorian antiquarians like Carmichael in the Scottish Highlands and islands and Douglas Hyde in Ireland contributed to the image of the 'spiritual Gael' by producing anthologies of Gaelic poems and incantations in translation.

Perhaps the most influential 20th-century proponent of Celtic Christian spirituality was George Macleod who, in 1938, launched his project to establish a religious community on Iona in conscious imitation of Columba. As well as authentically recreating some of the practices of Celtic Christianity, such as the penitential early morning dips in the sea, he also assiduously promoted its romance and spirituality, describing Iona as 'a thin place' where heaven and earth were particularly close, and emphasizing the Celtic church's attachment to the more mystical fourth Gospel.

The current revival of interest and enthusiasm in Celtic Christianity, which began in the 1960s with the publication of a clutch of paperback anthologies of material from the *Carmina Gadelica* and other collections, is thus simply the latest expression of a long love affair that has gone on for more than 1,300 years. Perhaps the main ways in which it differs from earlier revivals are the strong North American interest and the way in which the looser term 'Celtic spirituality' has come to eclipse the more specific 'Celtic Christianity'. Both trends are exemplified in the enthusiasm of the American monk, Thomas Merton, who noted shortly before his death in 1968 that a whole new world had opened up as he read about Celtic monks, hermits, lyric poets, pilgrims and sea travellers.

The first modern use of the phrase 'Celtic spirituality' that I can trace is in *Paths to Spirituality*, a book written in 1972 by John Macquarrie, the distinguished Scottish theologian who held chairs in New York and Oxford. In a highly influential passage, he presented it as a counter-model to the culture of secular materialism, which characterizes contemporary Western society, and identified at its heart an intense sense of the presence of God in which transcendence was combined with immanence.

This dimension of immanence undoubtedly accounts for part of the contemporary appeal of Celtic Christian spirituality. For its adherents it provides a creation-centred version of Christianity in which God can be encountered in a flower, a river or a mountain as well as through biblical revelation and the church's sacraments. It also provides an obvious area of overlap and convergence between Christian spirituality and a broader and more pantheistic Celtic spirituality. As in the many other earlier revivals, people are also attracted to Celtic Christianity because it seems to offer a purer, freer and less hierarchical and dogma-ridden faith than they find in the institutional churches. It also

appeals to feminists and environmentalists, although there is in truth little evidence that at least in its golden age it was notably feminine or eco-friendly.

Iona remains a Mecca for modern seekers after Celtic Christian spirituality. Many pilgrim-tourists are now also visiting Lindisfarne, or Holy Island, off the Northumbrian coast where Aidan established his monastery and where David Adam, the author of a series of highly popular anthologies of Celtic-style prayers, is rector. Lindisfarne is also the base for the Community of Aidan and Hilda, a dispersed community following a lifestyle consciously modelled on Celtic monastic practices, whose founder and guardian, Ray Simpson, is another key figure in the current revival.

Interest in Celtic spirituality has moved significantly over recent years from being largely confined to liberal and catholic Christians to a much wider constituency that takes in many charismatics and evangelicals. Charismatics, in particular, have identified with the encounters with demons and angels and the signs and wonders that feature so prominently in the lives of the Celtic saints. Several of the leaders of the burgeoning house church movement in Britain have recently adopted what they take to be Celtic models and themes, notably

the monastic character of the church and the emphasis on blessings and miracles.

So far, in Britain at least, there has been little attempt to create new Celtic churches although there is a small Celtic Orthodox Church, which has outposts in Glastonbury, York, Edinburgh and Aberdeen. In the United States, such churches have been established, some of which come under the umbrella of the Celtic Christian Communion, which has its own presiding archbishop based in Springfield, Oregon, who is also Abbot in the Church of the Culdees.

Interest in Celtic Christian spirituality spans traditional churches and the much more free-ranging world of new religious movements. It is invigorating the liturgical life of many mainstream denominations, which use Celtic-style prayers and music. On the fringes of the church, it provides a meeting point for Christians and New Agers, while its exotic and esoteric aspects continue to appeal to romantics, seekers and dreamers, as they have done for well over a thousand years.

complex. Agents of the federal government used military equipment to batter holes in buildings through which they injected noxious gas in an attempt to force the Davidians outside. A fire ignited in the buildings and over 80 members died. The surviving Branch Davidians for the most part continue to adhere to their faith.

The Jesus Movement
Duncan MacLaren

The Jesus movement refers to a diverse range of Christian groups that sprang up in the major cities of the west coast of the United States in the late 1960s in the wake of the counter-culture. They were also known as Jesus Freaks or Jesus People, the former title based on the fact that many adherents were former 'speed freaks' or drug addicts. Typically, these groups rejected middle-class American values and retained the language, dress and musical style of the counter-culture they emerged from. However, since their beliefs and values were informed by fundamentalist Christianity, they also rejected the prevalent permissive mores regarding sex and drugs, and proclaimed an alternative solution to social ills.

The genealogy of the movement is obscure. One significant beginning, however, can be traced to the conversion of former drug addict, Ted Wise, in 1966. In 1967, he began street witnessing in the Haight-Ashbury district of San Francisco and established a coffee house ministry among the hippies, called 'The Living Room'. After 18 months, Wise moved to Novato, and started one of the earliest Jesus communes,

'Jesus Freaks' attend a rally in Philadelphia.

the House of Acts. Wise's early converts were significant: Steve Heefner and Jim Doop went on to lead communes run by Victor Wierwille's sect, *The Way International. Lonnie Frisbee, an art student, established the House of Miracles commune in Santa Ana, and subsequently became the influential youth pastor of Calvary Chapel. Another significant ministry in San Francisco was the Christian World Liberation Front, established on the Berkeley campus by Dr Jack Sparks, who consciously adopted the style of the counter-culture. His organization was aimed at students rather than street people, and was engaged in teaching, food distribution, hospitality and the production of the newspaper *Right On*. This had the most intellectual content of all the 60 or so Jesus papers that grew up with the movement.

If the movement began in San Francisco, its epicentre lay in Los Angeles. It coalesced around a cluster of charismatic figures, including Arthur Blessitt, a street evangelist, and Duane Pederson, a former conjurer. In 1969, Pederson began publishing the *Hollywood Free Paper* as an evangelistic tool. By 1971, circulation had reached over 400,000 monthly, and it was published in six other cities across the United States. Perhaps because of its wide circulation it was seen as the main paper of the Jesus movement, but it also received much criticism for its simplistic approach. One further figurehead of the movement was the foremost Christian rock musician, Larry Norman.

The Hollywood Boulevard also played host

to street witnesses from sectarian groups such as the Children of God (now called *The Family), founded by David Berg. Their time was divided between Bible study, witnessing and manual labour. A similarly strict sectarian group was the Christian Foundation, formed by Tony and Susan Alamo.

In addition to charismatic leaders and sectarian groups, the Jesus movement found expression in the so-called 'hip' churches. The most prominent of these was Calvary Chapel, located in the Santa Ana suburb of Los Angeles. In 1969, just 12 people met there for Bible study under its pastor, Chuck Smith. By 1971, over a thousand young people were meeting in a tent a block away, on four nights a week. Calvary was also notable for its mass baptisms in the sea, up to 1,000 being baptized in a single service. Other hip churches included Bethel Tabernacle at Redondo Beach. Unusually, it retained an older Pentecostal style, rejecting the language and music of the hip scene. One of the earliest hip churches was the Hollywood Presbyterian Church, which opened a coffee ministry, the Salt Company, and sponsored a successful touring musical group of the same name.

In addition to San Francisco and Los Angeles, the Jesus movement had an early beginning in Seattle, under Linda Meissner. Curiously, she too gained a following of street people who were converted and baptized in the Spirit independently of any contact with Blessitt or the Alamos in Hollywood. In 1969, she founded the Corps of the Jesus People's Army. A revival at Lincoln High School followed. The Catacombs, a ministry similar to the Salt Company, opened its doors to around 2,000 people a week. Communes were founded, and the first edition of the newspaper *Agape* was published.

The very diversity of the Jesus movement makes it hard to generalize about beliefs and practices. However, there were some common emphases. These can best be understood in relation to the two ideological streams that

converged in the Jesus movement – one, counter-cultural, the other, Christian fundamentalist. Some of the emphases of the counter-culture were retained, including a striving for authenticity; an openness to emotional and religious experience; a view of subjectivity as the key to reality; an ethic of love; the communal ideal; and a negative attitude to the intellect, materialism and the established churches. Other emphases were transposed, including the radical left's critique of social ills, which the Jesus People domesticated into a narrow focus on individual sin. What mattered was not the war in Vietnam, but the war within the soul. Likewise, the counter-culture's utopian vision of social revolution was transposed into the Jesus People's utopian vision of the imminent apocalypse, fuelled to a large extent by Hal Lindsay's bestseller *The Late Great Planet Earth*, and by the wider cultural crisis of the 1960s. Under this pressure, social reform was eclipsed by the urgency for personal conversions. Still other emphases were rejected altogether, such as permissive sexual practices and drug use.

It is significant that most of the movement was comprised of young people between the ages of 15 and 24. As they matured, many of the movement's emphases mellowed, and many of its adherents joined the mainstream churches they once criticized. As the counter-culture petered out in the mid-1970s, the cultural basis for the Jesus People receded. Today, the movement is scarcely visible, but its impact within American Christianity has undoubtedly been profound.

The Family (Children of God)
Richard Kyle

Formerly known as the Children of God, and later as the Family of Love, the Family, as they are currently known, arose out of the *Jesus movement in the 1960s. Because of doctrinal deviations, it split from the larger movement.

The Children of God (COG) began in 1968 in California under the leadership of David Brandt Berg (1919–94), an evangelical minister associated with the Christian Missionary Alliance Church. In 1969, Berg claimed to have received a revelation that California would sink into the sea as the result of an earthquake. Consequently, he and his followers wandered through the south-west for eight months. They acquired the name Children of God and Berg became known as Mo, Moses or Moses David.

By 1970, the COG had settled in several locations in Texas (where Berg led the Texas Soul Clinic Ranch, a religious community with 200 members by 1971) and California, becoming a national organization that practised a disciplined communal existence. But as a result of their desire to reach the world's population and to avoid hostilities they decentralized. The COG dispersed around the United States in some 40 colonies of no more than a dozen people. Berg continued to lead the COG, but delegated some authority. He also began directing the evolving doctrine of 'the scattered flock' by means of letters, which came to be known as 'Mo-letters'.

Firmly convinced of the coming downfall of the United States, by the early 1970s Berg and many of his followers had left the country. Though they believed the whole world would soon end, they were obsessed with the total downfall of the United States in particular. Thus they moved in small groups to Europe, Asia, Africa, South America and Australia. By the mid-1970s, few COG members remained in the United States and Berg set up his headquarters in London.

As time progressed, the COG strayed progressively further from traditional Christian beliefs, although retaining the gospel message at their heart. The COG began with the holiness perspective of the Christian Missionary Alliance, to which it added a fervent belief in the end of the world, the need to abandon worldly structures (churches, governments, economic systems), communalism and the coming Jesus revolution. Berg's disciples observed a strict community discipline, which involved isolation from external contacts, lack of privacy, relinquishing of possessions, and forsaking unbelieving spouses. Paid work was

Children of God members worship at their headquarters in Los Angeles in 1971.

forbidden, and only the King James version of the Bible was allowed to be read. Their extensive use of the gift of prophecy and other aspects of charismatic Christianity are features of their daily life, yet what most sets them apart has been their interpretation of the 'law of love', that the essence of the teachings of Jesus are to love God and love our neighbours, and that these are the only moral laws needed. Most controversial was the practice of 'flirty fishing'. Berg ordered the female members to use their feminine assets and to become 'hookers for Jesus'. This practice continued until 1987, and was abandoned partly because of the emerging AIDS epidemic. Berg came to see himself more as a prophet, and his prophecies (which increasingly were seen as coming from disembodied spirits) assumed the dominant role in moulding the group's ideas.

The future of the Family is uncertain after the death of Berg, as the group catered to the radical mindset so prevalent in the youth culture of the late 1960s and early 1970s, which is out of step with the early 21st century. In 1995, the Family adopted a written constitution defining the rights and rules of membership, such as the autonomy of individual Family members. There are now around 9,000 full-time Family members living in around 100 countries worldwide. The Family remains a millennial group, expecting the imminent return of Christ and the commencement of his 1,000-year reign. Their work has diversified to include more traditional evangelism and a host of humanitarian aid projects.

The Holy Order of MANS
Christopher Partridge

Founded in 1968 in San Francisco by Earl W. Blighton (also known as Father Paul; d. 1974), the Holy Order of MANS, which originally appealed to the hippie community, drew inspiration from both modern Western esoteric spirituality and Eastern Orthodox Christianity.

The inspiration of Orthodoxy was evident in the two monastic orders related to the group, the Immaculate Heart Sisters of Mary and the Brown Brothers of the Holy Light. Indeed, these suborders were not simply meditative, esoteric groups, but sought to practically contribute to the wider community through voluntary social work (e.g. helping in hospitals).

While traditional Orthodoxy clearly appealed to Blighton, the Holy Order of MANS was essentially a New Age group with an interest in Western esotericism. The acronym 'MANS' reflects both these sources of inspiration: *mysterion* (mystery), *agape* (divine love), *nous* (mind) and *sophia* (wisdom). Indeed, Blighton himself had links with *Freemasonry, *Spiritualism and the Ancient and Mystical Order Rosae Crucis (AMORC). In the Holy Order's secretive 'Temple Services', angelic beings were invoked and protective medallions distributed to help members resist negative spiritual influences.

According to Blighton, the Holy Order of MANS had appeared just as humanity was about to enter a new golden age of spiritual awareness. Its crucial role in human history was to prepare the human race and to teach essential esoteric ideas. Many of these ideas are set out in a book Blighton co-authored with his wife Ruth, *The Golden Force*.

In 1974, Blighton unexpectedly died. His successor, Andrew Rossi, took over during a time of significant growth, growth that was to continue under his leadership. By 1977, the group had around 3,000 active members. However, sensitive to the group being labelled a 'cult' in the late 1970s (principally as a result of the publicity following the suicide of over 900 members of Jim Jones's *Peoples Temple in 1978), Rossi sought to stress the Christian beliefs and practices within the movement. This was more than mere lip service, for it eventually led to his own conversion to Eastern Orthodoxy in the 1980s and to a theological shift within the movement away from esotericism to

Orthodox theology. In May 1988, all members were baptized, the name Holy Order of MANS was dropped, and the group became the Christ the Savior Brotherhood.

The move from the Holy Order of MANS to the Christ the Savior Brotherhood is striking, in that the group shifted from what might be considered a fairly secretive esoteric organization to an explicitly Christian organization with an emphasis on mission to the American occult subculture. In 1990, after a leadership challenge, Rossi was succeeded by Father Podmoshensky and Metropolitan Pangratios ('Father' and 'Metropolitan' are titles within Orthodox Christianity). While the group has not yet been recognized as a legitimate Orthodox community, they are seeking unification with the Greek Orthodox Church. Those wishing to continue the traditional teaching of Blighton have formed breakaway groups, such as the Gnostic Order of Christ.

The Jesus Fellowship (Jesus Army)
William Kay

The Jesus Fellowship (also known as the Jesus Army) includes the New Creation Christian Community (NCCC). This community aspect is unusual in present-day Protestantism, and it is this, rather than any doctrinal innovation, that makes the Jesus Fellowship of particular interest.

The Jesus Fellowship originated from the effect of the charismatic renewal on a Baptist chapel in Bugbrooke near Northampton, England, in 1969. In its beginnings the emerging congregation included bikers, drug users and other members of the counter-culture and therefore paralleled aspects of the Californian *Jesus movement. At the same time it attracted radical Christians and seekers from all types of backgrounds.

From 1973, having been influenced by the story of the Church of the Redeemer in Houston, Texas, the congregation decided to embark on community living. Members purchased a large old house and shared possessions while embracing a simple lifestyle. Nuclear families (husband-wife and any children) were incorporated within the community without losing privacy or identity. Major expansion took place between 1976 and 1979 so that the communal lifestyle of the NCCC is now distributed in approximately 70 properties holding between 6 and 60 residents each. The NCCC comprises approximately a quarter of the Jesus Fellowship and the remaining three-quarters are drawn from connected congregations in all parts of Britain. It represents probably the largest and most long-standing charismatic community in Europe.

Over time a sophisticated and practical set of living patterns have been established. Married couples retain personal space while enjoying communal eating arrangements. Single people may make a commitment to celibacy. Openness to other members along with a willingness to accept help from each other so as to be consecrated to the service of God is expressed in a seven-point covenant pledge, which is also made by many other members of the church.

On commitment to the community (which takes place after a probationary period of between one and three years) members surrender their possessions for collective use but may reclaim them should they subsequently decide to leave. Those who do not wish to live within the community may remain covenant members while living in their own homes and earning money outside the community. In a sense they operate like Christians who attend a particularly close-knit Sunday congregation. There are also a variety of ways in which Christians may belong to the Jesus Fellowship with a looser commitment.

The community has founded a series of Christian businesses employing some 250 people. Profits from the businesses help fund the wider work of the Jesus Fellowship. Community houses are owned by a trust fund ultimately controlled by the members.

After criticism of what were seen as cultic aspects of the Jesus Fellowship in the mid-1980s, deliberate attempts were made to widen and loosen the organization. It still maintains a form of mutual accountability and specifically seeks to safeguard biblically based differentiation of gender roles. It is now again a member of the Evangelical Alliance and has good relationships with a wide range of evangelical and charismatic groups and networks.

The Jesus Army (which has similarities with the early Salvation Army) is the evangelistic expression of the Jesus Fellowship. The Army is noted for vibrant street evangelism, concern for marginalized and homeless people, for its vigorous and noisy praise and worship, its publication *Streetpaper* and its linkage with more than 40 other independent Christian churches in the Multiply Network. Rootless people who respond to the Jesus Army's communication of the gospel may find the Jesus Fellowship's community care especially attractive.

The Jesus Fellowship can be seen as part of the same wave of the Holy Spirit that brought the New Church movement (a charismatic house church movement beginning in the 1970s) into existence in Britain. It shares many characteristics of New Church doctrine and practice, including believers' baptism, belief in the Bible as the Word of God and an acceptance of charismatic gifts. It hosts national events and seminars and has a strong website presence.

The Word of Faith Movement

Allan Anderson

This movement is also known as 'positive confession' and the 'faith message', and by its detractors as the 'prosperity gospel' and 'health and wealth'. It is widely regarded to have originated in the early Pentecostal movement and particularly in the writings of Baptist pastor Essek W. Kenyon (1867–1948), who taught 'the positive confession of the Word of God' and a 'law of faith' working by predetermined divine principles. The development of the movement was stimulated by the teachings of Pentecostal healing evangelists like William Branham and Oral Roberts, contemporary popular televangelists, and the charismatic movement in North America. It is now a prominent teaching of charismatic and Pentecostal churches all over the world.

Its leading North American exponents have been Kenneth Hagin (b. 1917), widely regarded as the 'father' of the Word of Faith movement, Kenneth Copeland (b. 1937) and African-American Frederick Price (b. 1932), among many others. The teaching has been embraced by many Pentecostal and charismatic preachers in other parts of the world, and leading exponents include David (Paul) Yonggi Cho of Korea, Nigerian David Oyedepo and South African Ray McCauley. Links have been made with Norman Vincent Peale's teaching on 'Positive Thinking', with dualistic materialism and with the 19th-century 'New Thought' of Phineas Quimby and the *Christian Science of Mary Baker Eddy. That said, it is arguably more helpful to see this movement within the context of Pentecostalism and its healing emphasis.

Hagin received a 'revelation' in 1934 based on Mark 11:24, which resulted in his recovery from a heart ailment, and in 1937 became a Pentecostal pastor. His Rhema Bible Training Center, founded in Tulsa, Oklahoma in 1974, trained many thousands of disciples in the 'faith message' and made him very well known. Hagin's teachings are based on the books of Kenyon and emphasize the importance of the 'word of faith', a positive confession of one's faith in healing, despite the circumstances or symptoms. Copeland developed Hagin's teaching with a greater emphasis on financial

☞ *continued on page 94*

PROSPERITY SPIRITUALITY
William Kay

Prosperity teaching, because it is precise and carefully articulated, should be distinguished from the 'redemption lift' brought about by conversion to Christianity. Thus, those who were previously unreliable and undisciplined in their attitude to secular work become, after conversion, honest and disciplined. Whether as employees or as entrepreneurs they are capable of viewing their secular employment as being subsidiary to their religious vocation. Indeed, in Lutheran theology the magistrate serves God as authentically as the priest; this is one of the legacies of the Reformation. Consequently, the converted poor gradually become well-to-do, sometimes to the detriment of their religious fervour – that is, they prosper.

Origins
Prosperity spirituality is characterized by the doctrine that God desires Christians to be prosperous. The doctrine originates in the pages of the Pentateuch (the first five books of the Bible). For example, we read in the book of Deuteronomy, 'God will make you most prosperous in all the work of your hands' (Deuteronomy 30:9). In order to apply this teaching to contemporary Christians it is necessary to ignore major differences between the Old and New Testaments and to presume that the blessings promised to Israel in the days of Moses are transferable to the church. Such a theological transference is only possible if biblical texts warning of the persecution of the church – for example, 'we must go through many hardships to enter the kingdom of God' (Acts 14:22) – are set aside. Historically and psychologically there were, however, good reasons to do this.

When the Pentecostal movement emerged at the start of the 20th century, it tended to accept a dispensational eschatological scheme that envisaged the onset of great tribulation preceding the second coming of Christ. Even where such a scheme was modified to include the rapture (or snatching away) of the church prior to the worst of these dark events, such an outlook induced pessimism in Christians, even among those who were financially secure. Among the poor, its effects might produce morality or stoicism, but little hope in this life. The American dream, and the one that attracted immigrants at the start of the 20th century, was of a land of opportunity and plenty. It is no surprise therefore that, when prosperity teaching appeared in the late 1950s in the United States, many of its first converts were people who had grown up in the grinding poverty of the 1930s. Prosperity Christianity may therefore be interpreted as a psychological reaction to theological pessimism combined with a willingness to embrace the benefits of rampant American capitalism.

Development
The Oral Roberts Evangelistic Association published *God's Formula for Success and Prosperity* in 1956. The book is essentially a series of life histories or testimonies of individuals who, by maintaining Christian standards in business and by giving generously to Christian causes, have prospered. For example, in a chapter entitled 'God's banker', Lee Braxton explained how he entered into partnership with God and became rich. A chapter by Demos Shakarian tells of similar business triumphs and of the founding of the influential and prosperity-conscious Full Gospel Businessmen's Fellowship International. Roberts himself published *Miracle of Seed-Faith* in 1970

Oral Roberts preaching at the National Church Growth Conference at Heritage USA in 1987.

and printed over half a million copies in that year. The book specifies three key principles of 'seed-faith'. These are as follows: God is your source of supply, rather than your job or your business; 'Give that it may be given to you' (Luke 6:38), especially when giving is thought to be a form of planting seeds that will generate 'a harvest of plenty'; and expect a miracle by living with an attitude of trust and confidence in God.

The doctrine rapidly spread, particularly among charismatics and Pentecostals, to South Africa, Korea, Sweden and other parts of the world. Cynics might, and did, argue that the emphasis on giving was simply designed to fund the expensive ministry of Roberts and those who followed him. Both Roberts (b. 1918) and T.L. Osborn (b. 1923) became televangelists. This allowed them to appeal to huge audiences while, at the same time, they incurred huge costs to keep their programmes on the air. The danger was that the process became circular: evangelists appealed for money to support broadcasting, promised blessing to those who gave, and then issued further appeals in further broadcasts. Local churches were often ignored in the cycle of giving, a matter that was bound to lead to the resentment of ordinary ministers. But criticism did not have any impact on the televangelists, who felt they had been 'raised up' by God for special prominence and that their success was a guarantee that their doctrine was correct. The American pattern was emulated in other countries, where broadcasting regulations permitted it, and, where they did not, powerful preachers proclaimed the benefits of giving from the pulpit.

The prosperity message may be seen as a stimulant to church growth and evangelism where economies are liberal and the market is free. Where there is historic poverty, the message may be conjoined with movements for national work and discipline (as in Korea). Faith in this way becomes a powerful force in human affairs and its results are largely beneficial.

Variants

There have been other steps in the substructure of prosperity spirituality that are more likely to be associated with the *Word of Faith movement's proponents, Kenneth Hagin (b. 1917) or Kenneth Copeland (b. 1937), and to have developed in parallel with healing doctrines. It is said that human beings have rights that God is bound to respect. These rights were given to human beings at creation, forfeited to Satan at the Fall and regained through Christ. These rights are the basis for human prayer and are realized by faith. In their own self-description, Christians must 'positively confess' wealth even when they do not possess it. In prayer, Christians may command divine blessings as their words echo God's written promises and, in one formulation, God's words spoken by human beings are just as powerful as God's words spoken by God.

Contexts and critique

In the take-up and prevalence of these teachings, one should draw distinctions between the Pentecostal, charismatic and Faith movements. The first is expressed in a series of relatively recent denominations, the second is expressed as a style and theological emphasis in the older denominations, and the third is a free-standing set of networks, usually with broadcasting adjuncts. Typically the beliefs and practices of each of these three movements are different, even if there is blurring, borrowing and overlapping between them. In practice, however, the more organized Pentecostal denominations are likely to use their supervisory structures to counter the extremes of prosperity teaching and so to suppress its expression within their congregations.

Whatever the benefits to the church as a whole of increased motivation for financial giving and expectations that material conditions can be improved by faith, there have been doubts raised about the legitimacy of the whole doctrine. The most sustained criticisms of the prosperity movement have been along the following lines: in the case of Oral Roberts, the law-like results of giving so as to receive have been considered either morally suspect (is giving genuine in these circumstances?) or particularly suited to capitalist economies. More damningly, it would appear not to be supported by the traditions and practices of the early church. In the case of the Word of Faith movement's emphasis on prosperity there are three objections: God becomes obedient to human commands of faith, rather than remaining sovereign; the process of 'positive confession' is self-deceptive, since it encourages poor people to claim they are rich; and the poverty-bearing by Christ upon the cross (2 Corinthians 8:9) is misplaced and not properly parallel to his sin-bearing.

prosperity and formulated 'laws of prosperity' to be observed by those seeking health and wealth. Poverty is seen as a curse to be overcome through faith. Through 'faith-force', believers regain their rightful divine authority over their circumstances. One of the more controversial aspects of Copeland's teaching is that Christians are little 'Gods'. The Word of Faith movement teaches physical healing and material prosperity, usually through special revelation knowledge of a Bible passage (as distinct from 'sense knowledge') – a 'Rhema word' that is positively confessed as true. The teaching asserts that when Christians believe and confess this 'Rhema word' (taken from one of the New Testament Greek words for 'word') it becomes energizing and effective, resulting in receiving it from God. When people do not receive what they have confessed, it is usually because of a negative confession, unbelief or a failure to observe the divine laws. Some faith teachers reject the use of medicine as evidence of a weak faith, and overlook the role of suffering, persecution and poverty in the purposes of God.

Creation Spirituality
Bronislaw Szerszynski

Christianity, particularly as it was shaped by the apostle Paul, is a religion of anticipation, in that humanity is understood to be suspended in time between Christ's first and second coming, knowing that the world's restoration to its original wholeness and divine indwelling is assured but not yet completed. This suspension gives Christian time a certain evening quality; the present epoch is a time of looking forward and making do, suffused with ennui rather than enthusiasm. In this epoch certain things are not possible – Christians can look for signs, hope and anticipate, but cannot yet experience full communion with the divine.

In many ways, Christianity inherits this general orientation from Judaism, which took great pains to distinguish itself from the surrounding religions and cultures of the Middle East, which grounded their institutions in the divine and in nature. One can see this move in the great origin narrative of Genesis 1–11, in which the Fall from the Garden of Eden and the Flood are among many break points that ensure human institutions cannot be seen as traceable back to some act of God or gods. Even Israel's status as the 'chosen people' takes the form of their being bound in a covenant, a contract between two parties, rather than some essential bond dating back to creation.

But, by the same token, Genesis seems to say that neither can humanity find an easy solace in their co-creatureliness with nature. Not only are they given 'dominion' over the other creatures, but the Fall puts humanity at odds with nature's bounty, forcing Adam for the first time to labour and sweat. In the New Testament, too, the apostle Paul insists that the whole of creation 'groans', is disordered by the Fall, and is no longer in harmony with itself or with humanity.

It is against this background that Creation Spirituality needs to be understood, for if Christianity has in general been a religion of the evening, Creation Spirituality is one of the morning – not just the anticipated new morning when all will be transformed, but a perpetual morning in which, it is claimed, we have always dwelled. Initiated in California by Matthew Fox (b. 1940), Creation Spirituality combines mystical theology from the Christian spiritual tradition; rituals from indigenous cultures and neo-Paganism; cosmological ideas from modern science and New Age thought; and political values and forms of social organization from post-1960s social movements, such as the ecology and peace movements and radical feminism.

Fox had been ordained a Dominican priest in 1967, but after he started advancing the ideas and practices of Creation Spirituality the Vatican responded in 1988 by silencing him for a year, and then in 1993 expelled him from the Dominican order. In order to further promote his ideas Fox founded the Institute in Culture and Creation Spirituality in 1977, and later the University of Creation Spirituality, both in Oakland, California. With his many books and frequent lecture tours, Fox has propagated an international network of locally based Creation Spirituality groups.

For Fox, the dominant Christian worldview described above amounts to a heresy – a departure from Jesus' original teachings, and a great error in relation to the nature of the cosmos and our relationship to it as revealed both by spiritual experience and also by modern science. Fox blames this 'Fall/redemption' tradition largely on Augustine, and denounces it as dualistic, anti-emotional, anti-sensual, hierarchical and patriarchal. Against this, Fox points to an alternative, minority tradition of Creation Spirituality running through Christianity, citing figures such as Irenaeus of Lyons, the 12th-century mystic and polymath Hildegard of Bingen, Meister Eckhart and Teilhard de Chardin. Together with these Christian theologians and mystics, Fox draws upon non-Christian sources such as Native American cultures and past matriarchal societies to point to what he sees as a perennial current in human history, a life-affirming spirituality which celebrates the beauty and creativity of the natural world and of human individuals.

Fox sees the keystone of the Fall/redemption tradition as the doctrine of Original Sin – the idea that ever since the Fall, when the first humans disobeyed God, human beings have been born with an innate flaw that prevents them from naturally discerning the good. In anthropological or comparative religious terms, this doctrine can be seen as a particular expression of the notion, shared with many cultures, that the order of creation is not as it ought to be – that it has been disrupted by some

transgression in primordial time by an ancestor figure, so that the easy intercourse with the natural order, and the easy discernment of signs and meanings in the world, is but a distant mythic memory. Fox sees the adoption of the doctrine of Original Sin as the key break point, the moment at which the Christian tradition chose the path of Fall and redemption rather than that of Creation Spirituality. Against this, Fox posits the idea of Original Blessing, with a celebratory attitude to creation – human beings contain a spark of the divine, nature is to be regarded with awe and reverence, and the body and its pleasures are intrinsically good. Appreciation of this Original Blessing can be nurtured through spiritual exercises designed to guide the individual along the four paths of Creation Spirituality – the *via positiva* of celebration and praise, the *via negativa* of suffering and sacrifice, the *via creativa* of art and creativity, and the *via transformativa* of justice and compassion.

Three other key figures in the canon of Creation Spirituality are Neil Douglas-Klotz, Brian Swimme and Thomas Berry. The Sufi writer Douglas-Klotz reinterprets the sermons and prayers of Jesus as expressions of an indigenous Middle Eastern Creation Spirituality. In his books, Douglas-Klotz reconstructs a mystical, cosmic worldview that he sees as implicit in the original Aramaic language spoken by Jesus. It is largely through the work of Swimme and Berry that science feeds into the Creation Spirituality tradition. Contemporary scientific ideas, particularly drawing on cosmology, quantum physics and evolution, are marshalled into myths that seek to ground the human being in a picture of a cosmos full of emergent meaning and purpose.

Creation Spirituality speaks to many individuals in the Western world who want to find congenial spiritual resources within their own religious traditions, yet are disillusioned with the strictures of mainstream religion. It offers a threefold validation – in experience, science and tradition. Creation Spirituality radicalizes the Reformation notion of the 'priesthood of all believers', insisting that each individual is able to experience the divine, both within themselves and in nature. The narratives offered by contemporary cosmology and ecology offer a mythic grounding for spirituality in a seemingly independent, objective confirmation of cosmic interconnectedness for people no longer able to believe in the broken mythic time of Christianity's traditional metanarrative – one of creation, Fall, incarnation and end-time. And the attractive idea of a continuous current that runs through the history of religion and culture, connecting otherwise isolated individuals and cultures who have stumbled upon their own version of Creation Spirituality, offers a historic grounding for a religious phenomenon that is very at home at the beginning of the 21st century.

The International Churches of Christ

Nigel Scotland

The International Churches of Christ (ICOC) has its roots in the American Churches of Christ, which emerged from American Restorationism in the later 19th century and finally became a denomination in its own right in 1906. Beginning with a membership of 160,000 in that year, it reached 1.2 million in the 1990s.

In 1967, the Gainesville Church of Christ in Florida embarked on an evangelistic crusade among the students of Florida University under the title 'Campus Advance'. One of those who was powerfully impacted by the 'Soul Talk Bible Studies' was Kip McKean, who was converted in 1972. He had several jobs as campus minister with mainline Church of Christ congregations until 1979, when he was invited to take on the pastorate of the struggling Lexington Church of Christ, later called the Boston Church of Christ. Kip McKean developed a vision to set up 'pillar churches' in key world cities. By 1982, planters had gone out from Boston and established congregations in Chicago and New York City. By 1993, the movement had 130 congregations in different parts of the world. Much of this early growth was due to the fact that the mainline denominations, and the American Church of Christ in particular, were in a state of institutional decline. In the early 1980s, ICOC established pillar churches in a number of major world cities, including London, Birmingham and Sydney. In February 1994, the ICOC announced their six-year plan to establish a congregation in every nation in the world with a city of a population of over 100,000. By the end of 2000, that goal was accomplished with 407 congregations in 171 nations. Figures as of September 2002 show there are now 440 ICOC congregations worldwide, with an average Sunday attendance of 196,651.

ICOC beliefs are very largely in keeping with those of orthodox creedal Christianity. The key doctrinal difference is baptism. The ICOC asserts that for a baptism to be valid the candidate must be 'someone who has the desire and heart to become a committed disciple'. This is derived from a particular understanding of Matthew 28:19–20, in which Jesus gives the commission to 'go and make disciples, baptizing them in the name of the Father, the Son and the Holy Spirit'. This is taken to mean that baptism is an essential step in a person becoming a disciple. Bare faith or mere trust in Jesus for forgiveness is not sufficient for salvation. It is not counted for righteousness until the candidate obeys God by being baptized with the conscious knowledge that at the moment of baptism one is being saved. Thus, in the words of one of their key texts, 'the new life begins in baptism'.

ICOC is noted for its 'in your face'

evangelism and its teaching on biblical authority, control and submission. Members engage in aggressive forms of gospel proclamation, which in the early days included 'restauranting', 'tubing' and 'bussing', that is, buttonholing people wherever the opportunity arose. More controversial has been ICOC's top-down, authoritarian structure. Over recent years this has developed into an emphasis on strong relationships within the church, with a belief that part of discipleship is giving and accepting help from others. Within the ICOC this is done on a group basis as well as individually through discipleship partners. There is a strong emphasis on mature Christians helping the weaker brethren and encouraging them to develop a mature approach to biblical authority – to 'obey everything that Jesus commanded' (Matthew 28:20). 'Opening up your struggles' (sharing your hurts) is seen as a very important aspect of this process. In general, ICOC members are highly committed in terms of their time and financial giving. All are expected to tithe their income and, once a year on a special gift day, disciples are required to give 14 to 16 times their normal weekly tithe to help evangelize the poorer countries in the developing world. Most save during the course of the year for this. The ICOC is a vigorous conversionist movement that is making marked inroads among the young and students in some of the world's major cities, including those traditionally regarded as closed to Christianity.

The Embassy of Heaven Church

George D. Chryssides

Founded in 1987, by Pastor Paul Revere (formerly Craig Douglas Fleshman), this Christian organization is based in Stayton, Oregon. It holds that the Christian is a resident of the kingdom of heaven, and that this conflicts with membership of secular civil society.

The Embassy has several objections to state government. States are led by 'unregenerated men' (*sic*): being regenerated involves being 'born again' and having undergone 'water baptism'. States enact negative laws against malpractices, rather than giving positive injunctions to love God and one's neighbour. State laws also permit un-Christian practices such as the remarriage of divorcees and homosexuality. The state intrudes on religion by requiring planning permission for buildings, demanding incorporation, and imposing health and safety regulations: the Embassy sees this as 'alien jurisdiction' and refuses to comply. It even goes so far as to ban hygiene notices in its toilets.

The Embassy of Heaven issues its own official documents – identity cards, passports, driving licences and vehicle registrations – to be used in lieu of secular documents. Members are encouraged to avoid debt, to refuse to make voluntary court appearances and to gain employment where business licences are not required. Divorcees are urged to return to the spouses of their first marriage, since this is the only valid one in God's sight.

Unsurprisingly, Embassy members have fallen foul of the law and in some cases have been imprisoned, but they regard this as persecution for the sake of the gospel, as Jesus predicted. It is likely that members are restricted to the United States, but the group's lack of communication with outsiders makes numbers and distribution difficult to gauge.

GLOBAL NETWORK OF DIVERGENT MARIAN DEVOTION

Peter Jan Margry

From its earliest days, the Roman Catholic Church has given an important place to the veneration of the Virgin Mary, the Mother of Jesus. Marian devotion has become the most significant 'cult of saints' in the church. At certain times, Mary reveals herself to various Catholic Christians through visions and messages. In the early Middle Ages, a phenomenological tradition of apparitions began. Before the 1920s almost all the places where this occurred developed into shrines that have been acknowledged by the church. Sometimes these shrines became of international importance, such as Guadeloupe in Mexico, Lourdes in France, Knock in Ireland and Fatima in Portugal. The activity of this devotional circuit focuses on devotions and sites of approved apparitions, which take part in the mainstream Marian veneration of the Roman Catholic Church.

Since the 1940s there has been an exponential increase in the number of new apparitions of and messages from Mary, and also of other saints and of Christ, although they are less frequent. Sometimes it is claimed that statues and pictures weep, bleed or move. Most of the groups and shrines connected with these recent apparitions and private revelations are not acknowledged by the church and form a divergent or alternative devotional circuit. The Catholic Church has become increasingly wary of the boom in such private devotional activities, groups and organizations, especially because the number of people who can be reached by them is much greater than it would have been in the past. As such, it affects the position of the Catholic Church, its doctrines and religious practices.

Network structure

These alternative devotions are not shaped or governed by official ecclesiastical structures. Rather, they are grass-roots movements, the rituals and devotions of which are shaped informally by individual visionaries, particular religious leaders associated with the group and the ideas and practices of related groups of devotees. Although each of the apparitional groups are independent, they can be considered collectively in that they attract very similar types of visitors, who, generally speaking, can be understood as devotees and believers with conservative, traditionalist and even fundamentalist views.

Collectively, the individual shrines form a globally oriented network which, to a large extent, is 'controlled' by the devotees and their prayer groups. This network has absolutely no formal status or structure and no headquarters. In many ways, it functions in a similar way to the World Wide Web, in that literally millions of devotees are connected with one another in an open manner. They locate and communicate with each other in eclectic ways at constantly changing sacred sites. In this way they participate in the devotional life or group of each place, and at the same time create their own specific religious system with its own concentrated spirituality and rituality. In their own local settings they practise their religion, evangelize by distributing prints, folders of information and images, share ideas by word of mouth and actively participate in prayer groups.

Not only has there been an increase in the number of apparitions taking place, but there has also been a change in the type of people receiving the visions. Instead of young people receiving visions, revelations are increasingly reported by adults. Moreover, the nervousness of the church about such revelations, groups and movements stems from the fact that the recipients of visions and revelations not only spread messages related to their 'own' apparitions, but also interpret them in relation to their personal views about the church and the world, some of which conflict with formal church teaching. Indeed, the efforts of the church to control these individuals and groups has proved ineffective because the messages and interpretations can be quickly and widely distributed by adult visionaries, and also because, with or without the support of the media, adult visionaries have shown themselves to be particularly effective in establishing movements, prayer groups and organizations that publish and disseminate their messages.

In their local communities, large proportions of the individual devotees will belong to one or more prayer groups. Some of these groups are linked to a person (often the visionary) or a shrine; others are 'free' prayer groups. The thousands of prayer groups in Europe and northern America form the basic structure of the devotion network. They often play an important role in missionary 'world actions'. For example, prayer groups based in Amsterdam sent

individuals to other countries with dozens of copies of the painting of 'The Lady of All Nations', in order to increase devotion to her. Similarly, over the last few decades, hundreds of copies of the Rosa Mystica statue of Montichiari in Italy have been distributed around the world. Dozens of these have since become the nucleus of their own miraculous shrines. Many of these groups, such as the Bayside devotees in New York and their shrine of Our Lady of the Roses or the

Queen of Love followers around Schio, Italy, have their own websites.

While the network has no international umbrella organization, there are international publishers who tailor their book lists and magazines to these devotional interests. With the information they supply they also form important links among the various devotions. For example, the magazine *Maria Heute* (or the French *Stella Maris*) is a mouthpiece for various devotions.

Newly made copies of the Rosa Mystica statue are sanctified at the Marian shrine of Montichiari, Italy.

Although they have commercial motives, there are also strong, apologetic forces at work. For example, the editors prepare their own commentaries with well-substantiated, polemic support for revelations criticized by the church.

The devotional network is, to a large extent, independent of mainstream Roman Catholic Marian devotion. Having said that, there is a continual interaction with the institutional church. On the one hand, the Catholic Church ignores, discourages or impedes these devotions because of the perceived possible negative consequences for Roman Catholicism. On the other hand, there are also conservative forces within the church that wish to give elements of this 'authentic' voice of the people (as the voice of God) a stronger role, because of the indirect benefits for the 'threatened' modern church. For example, the Medjugorje movement (beginning in Bosnia-Herzegovina in 1981) is said to have produced many vocations for the priesthood. Such encouragement has, during the pontificate of John Paul II, led to the positive toleration of, or at least a level of acknowledgment of, some 'banned' sites of apparitions (such as the Lady of All Nations in Amsterdam and the Queen of Love at Schio).

Spiritual sources

The apparitions and messages received at Fatima in 1917 (and before that, the Rue du Bac visions in Paris in 1830 and those of La Salette in 1846) are still one of the most important sources of inspiration in the network's spirituality. Although Fatima was recognized by the church in 1930 as a place of pilgrimage and 'mainstream' Marian devotion, it still has a particular function as a standard-bearer for conservative and fundamentalist Marian movements, comprised of a number of Catholic groups and institutions that take their inspiration from the messages. The Fatima messages frequently reappear, either in their original form or interpreted, in the messages announced by contemporary visionaries. The importance of Fatima can also be seen in several conservative groups with large numbers of adherents, such as the Marian Movement of Priests, with about 100,000 members, the Legion of Mary, with 3 million, and the Blue Army of Our Lady of Fatima, which claims to have about 10 million adherents worldwide.

According to the organizations and devotees involved, the messages of Fatima should form the basis for a worldwide re-evangelization and missionary programme to save the 'degenerate' world and church from the ever-present Satan. Among the typical and central themes in the messages are penitence, prayer (particularly the rosary), conversion of all sinners, war, anti-Communism and anti-atheism. The constant activity of the Devil further points to the approaching, apocalyptic end-time and an ultimate separation of good and evil individuals, the saved and the unsaved.

The renewal within the Roman Catholic Church launched by the Second Vatican Council (1962–65) was an extra stimulus for the rise of unorthodox views within Marian messages. Since the Second Vatican Council, the interpretation of the Fatima messages has begun to take on a life of its own, and has increasingly begun to function as the model for new Marian apparitional groups and movements of alternative devotion. After the fall of Communism, this emerging network of groups and movements found new enemies, including apostasy, social degeneracy, abortion, homosexuality, euthanasia and the corruption of the church and its priests. This forms the 'classic' representation of the church-related range of thought and belief of the conservative devotees. Major unacknowledged and private shrines (e.g. Medjugorje, Amsterdam and Montichiari) generate their own spiritualities, which then influence other sites.

Another important issue in many recent apparitions is the question of the recognition of 'the fifth dogma'. Various visionaries claiming Marian apparitions promote the desirability of recognizing the position of Mary as co-redemptress (a saviour along with Christ). This dogma, which was particularly propagated in the Amsterdam apparitions (1945–59), is heavily contested both inside and outside the church. Mary revealed herself in Amsterdam as 'The Lady of All Nations', and introduced a prayer that, together with the desired spread of the rosary, was to realize the swift promulgation of a new, fifth dogma of Mary as 'Coredemptrix, Mediatrix, Advocate'. This view has now won worldwide support from Marian devotees who want to give Mary a place of her own in God's acts of salvation, something Fatima would also have supported.

In the 1990s, the 'Third Secret' of Fatima, which the visionary Lucia shared only with the pope, continued to be the inspiration for end-time prophecies and speculations of an apocalyptic nature about the further course of the world and the concrete beginning of the end-times. The fall of the Communist regimes, growing interest in the end of the world caused by the approach of the year 2000, and his own personal devotion to Fatima led Pope John Paul II to reveal the Third Secret in 2000. The content appeared less dramatic and apocalyptic than many had thought. The year 2000 having quietly passed, fundamentalist circles suggested that the message has not yet been fully revealed, and that the end of time will begin some years later. In this way, too, Fatima continues to be an important source of nourishment for groups within the network.

Medjugorje

Medjugorje is probably the most famous and most frequently visited shrine within the network. The authenticity of the apparitions that have taken place there since 1981 is one of the most contentious topics within modern Roman Catholicism. Since that year, six children have been receiving daily messages from Mary, who appears as the 'Queen of Peace'. From the beginning, the bishop of Mostar-Duvno had doubts about the authenticity of the apparitions and suspicions of manipulation by the Franciscans arose. Over the years, many influential persons in the Catholic Church, up to and including Pope John Paul II, have either spoken out about the movement or expressly refused to take a position on it. The whole subject is too politically problematic for many priests, there being enormous tensions between adherents who seem genuinely to 'see' Mary, those who consider such visions the work of Satan, others who suggest pious deception on the part of the visionaries and their advisors, and still others who assume a conspiracy involving the Franciscans and their conflicts with the local bishop. Whatever the case, three diocesan investigative committees have declared the apparitions and messages non-authentic, and in 1998 the Vatican itself also accepted that standpoint.

However, over against the negative position of the church hierarchy stands a massive following of believers who find considerable strength in the shrine and the series of messages associated with it. Since 1981, more than 35 million pilgrims, devotees and believers, including thousands of regular priests and hundreds of bishops, have visited the shrine. The majority were theologically conservative Catholics. However, because of the opposition of the ecclesiastical hierarchy, the movement exists in a problematic spiritual vacuum, and links have arisen with other unacknowledged apparitions and devotions around the world, such as the group of devotees associated with the Lady of All Nations in Amsterdam.

The spiritual and theological autonomy of unorthodox Marian devotion is further stimulated by a powerful relationship between the movement and Catholic charismatic renewal, another movement that can tend to disassociate itself from institutional ecclesiastical structures. For example, Catholic charismatic prayer groups associated with Medjugorje have been established and now function as models for similar groups elsewhere in the world. The intensive mission activities of the movements are supported by the world tours of visionaries and priests supportive of such Marian devotion. The worldwide establishment of Medjugorje prayer groups, foundations, committees and magazines, along with the creation of branch shrines, meets the demand for frequent, local devotion from the millions of devotees who find travel to Medjugorje difficult.

The massive growth of the network means that its future looks secure and its continued rejection by the Vatican is unlikely. Its position is further strengthened by a constant reference to the 'fruits' the movement has produced for the Catholic Church (e.g. conversions, vocations for the priesthood and healings). Indeed, history shows that when a certain critical mass is achieved, devotions are often officially recognized by the church.

Medjugorje is one of the hundreds of sacred sites around the world where visionaries or shrine guardians claim to receive the only correct or true apparitions or messages. A list of the principal devotional sites and shrines in the network should include Heede, Germany (established 1937), Kérizinen, France (1938), Amsterdam, the Netherlands (1945), Montichiari, Italy (1946), Marienfried, Germany (1946), Heroldsbach, Germany (1949), Necedah, Wisconsin, United States (1949), Eisenberg, Austria (1955), Garabandal, Spain (1961), San Damiano, Italy (1961), Wollongong, Australia (1968), Akita, Japan (1969), Bayside, New York, United States (1970), Tampa, Florida, United States (1973), Dorrego, Argentina (1975), Olawa, Poland (1981), Kibeho, Rwanda (1981), Medjugorje, Bosnia-Herzegovina (1981), Soufanieh, Syria (1982), Maasmechelen, Belgium (1982), Melleray, Ireland (1985), Schio, Italy (1985), Naju, South Korea (1986), Cuenca, Ecuador (1988), Conyers, Georgia, United States (1988), Manduria, Italy (1992), Paratico, Italy (1994), Valkenswaard, the Netherlands (1998), Marpingen, Germany (1999) and Seuca, Romania (2000).

New Religions, Sects and Alternative Spiritualities with Roots in **Judaism**

The Rabbi *by Reuven Rubin, 1964.*

JUDAISM
Christopher Partridge

Judaism is the religion of the Jewish people, who currently number around 15 million worldwide. While many Jews live in Israel (around 4.5 million), almost half of the Jewish population (around 7 million) live in the United States. Other major Jewish populations can be found in France (525,000), Canada (362,000), Britain (292,000), Argentina (206,000), the Ukraine (180,000), Brazil (100,000) and South Africa (95,000). However, it is important to understand that a great many Jews have little connection to Judaism as a religion. While many Jews want to maintain their Jewish identity, the majority are secular Jews with little interest in the beliefs and practices of Judaism. For example, less than a third of American Jews are members of one of the religious movements into which Judaism is divided.

Judaism, which has its roots in the ancient history of Israel and the Hebrew Bible (referred to by Christians as the Old Testament), developed into its present form in the period following the destruction of Jerusalem and the Temple in 70 CE. Hence, Judaism as we now know it developed not prior to Christianity but alongside it. For example, whereas in the Hebrew Bible religion centred around a sacrificial system, this was not the case after 70 CE, and nor could it be, as the Temple – the centre of religious life – had been destroyed. The Law of Moses functioned properly as the religious and civil law of an independent Jewish nation. After 135 CE, the nation no longer existed and only a minority of Jews remained. Consequently, the sacrificial system could not be carried out in the Temple, the laws could not be imposed and festivals could not be celebrated as national events.

After the destruction of the Temple, the local synagogue became the focal point for religious activity. (The term 'synagogue' originally referred to a 'congregation', but later came to refer to the building in which Jews congregated.) In particular, there was a shift from a religion focused on the Temple, to a religion focused on the home and the synagogue. Indeed, the family is the basic unit of Jewish ritual, in that, for example, key aspects of festivals, such as the Passover, will take place within the home. However, while the home was clearly the primary location for Jewish ritual for many centuries, in more recent times the synagogue has become more important as the focal point for community worship and religious instruction, largely as a result of the increasingly secular nature of Jewish homes.

As well as the increased significance of the home and the synagogue, the basis of the Judaism that emerged after 70 CE was the outlook of the Pharisees, who had been an influential minority group prior to 70 CE. It was out of Pharisaic circles that the post-70 CE rabbinic movement arose. While prior to 70 CE the term 'rabbi' was a form of respectful address, after 70 CE it was used in a more technical sense as the title for accredited Jewish religious teachers (or 'sages') who sometimes also exercised judicial functions.

Since 70 CE, although most Jews have not lived in Israel they have continued to feel a strong attachment to the 'promised land'. Synagogues were built facing Jerusalem and Jewish liturgy spoke of a longing to return; at each Passover Jews would exclaim 'Next year in Jerusalem', thereby expressing their hope that they might return in the coming year and celebrate the next Passover in Jerusalem. Daily prayers asked God to restore his people to Zion. (Zion is derived from an ancient Hebrew term, probably meaning 'fortress' or 'rock', and is used to refer to Jerusalem, or to the mount on which the Temple was built in Jerusalem.) During the 19th century, this led to a Zionist movement that developed plans for the Jewish colonization of Palestine. In particular, Theodore Herzl (1860–1904) developed a political programme that sought sovereign state rights over the territory. The famous British Balfour Declaration of 1917 supported this. After the Second World War and the horrors of the Holocaust (the murder of over 6 million Jews by the Nazis), the establishment of a Jewish State received the support of the United Nations. In 1948, the State of Israel was formed. Zionism, however, is still an active movement that encourages Jews to return to Israel. For Zionists, many of whom are not religious, the state of Israel is of supreme importance as the protector of the Jewish people and culture.

Foundations and beliefs

The principal source of Judaism is the Hebrew Bible, which contains 24 books, divided into three sections: the Torah (the first five books of the Bible, also known as the Pentateuch), *Neviim* (the Prophets) and *Ketuvim* (the Writings). Another very significant source of authority is the Jewish law – the *halakhah*. The *halakhah* is divided into two principal categories, the 'written Torah' and the 'oral Torah'. The written Torah is the Pentateuch which, it was believed, was delivered in written form to Moses on Mount Sinai. The oral Torah, a large collection of rabbinic discussions and commentaries on the Torah, includes the Mishnah (c. 200 CE), an important collection of Jewish legal material developed over a period of about 200 years, and the Babylonian Talmud (c. 700 CE), a collection of rabbinic traditions and reflections on Jewish life and law. The different streams of Orthodox and Conservative Judaism have emerged as a result of their different interpretations of the *halakhah*.

As to the beliefs of Judaism, while they are complex, a basic outline would include the following:

■ Monotheism (there is only one God) is a core belief strongly expressed in the proclamation of faith known as the *Shema*: 'Hear, O Israel, the Lord our God, the Lord is one.'

■ The world is not the product of chance, but the deliberate creation of God, who continues to maintain its existence moment by moment.

■ God is not made up of matter as humans are, but is spirit.

■ God is all-good, all-wise, all-knowing and all-powerful. Indeed, he is so far above humanity that an understanding of him is greatly limited.

■ God's will is primarily expressed in a natural moral law and also in the Torah.

■ To disobey God's law is sin.

■ After death, the individual is judged by God and rewarded or punished accordingly.

■ God is constantly active in the world, guiding and directing history and providing spiritual and material sustenance.

■ Judaism is the religion of the 'chosen people'. In choosing Abraham, God chose his descendants, the Jewish people: 'Now the Lord said to Abram, "Go from your country and your kindred and your father's house to the land that I will show you. I will make of you a great nation, and I will bless you, and make your name great, so that you will be a blessing… and in you all the families of the earth shall be blessed"' (Genesis 12:1–3). Hence, while God is understood to be the one true God, the God of all peoples, Judaism is the religion of those 'chosen' by the one true God – Judaism is an ethnic faith. Understood in terms of obligation, rather than simply privilege, Jews seek to preserve the worship of God and to be an example to the nations.

■ Fundamentally linked to this choice of the Jewish people is God's choice of a land, the land God promised to Abraham: 'The Lord appeared to Abram, and said, "To your

offspring I will give this land… for ever'"
(Genesis 12:7; 13:15). Consequently, the
'promised land' of Israel has always occupied
a prominent place in Jewish thinking.

■ While there are different notions of the
'Messiah', there is a widespread belief that
the Jewish people will be liberated by God in
a messianic age, the age in which a descendant
of King David will found a perfect and
peaceful society. David was the king of biblical
Israel (c. 1037–967 BCE), and is deeply
embedded in the Jewish consciousness. All
subsequent legitimate kings of Israel had to be

descended from David, and even the coming
Messiah, it is believed, will belong to the line
of David. David has thus become a symbol of
redemption within Judaism, and Jews still pray
for the house of David to be restored.

Divisions within Judaism

There are two broad families of Jews, namely
the Ashkenazim and the Sepharadim. *Ashkenaz*
is the Hebrew word for the country we now
know as Germany, and the Ashkenazim are
those Jews who have their modern origins in
a geographical area covering Germany and
northern France. Subsequent communities that

settled in Scandinavia and Eastern Europe usually belong to Ashkenazic Jewry. Their common language, known as Yiddish, was a mixture of Hebrew, High German and various local languages. *Sephard* is a term originally used of the Iberian peninsula; Sephardic Jews are descended from communities that settled in Spain and Portugal. As a result of a forced mass expulsion at the end of the 15th century, many Sephardic Jews fled east and settled in Italy, Turkey, Palestine and North Africa, while others moved north into Western Europe, particularly Holland, Germany and England. Eventually, fleeing persecution, substantial

numbers travelled to North America and Latin America (particularly Argentina and Brazil). The common language of Sephardic Jews is the Spanish-based Ladino. As might be expected, although these two families of world Jewry are united in their commitment to the survival and growth of Judaism, they do have their own distinctive customs, traditions and rituals.

In addition to this fundamental divide in contemporary world Jewry, there are various other divisions. As well as the non-religious traditions of political Zionism (some of which are anti-religious) and secular Jews, who may have only a tentative link with their faith, there are, arguably, six principal religious movements:

■ Reform Judaism, which is sometimes called Liberal or Progressive Judaism, began in early 19th-century Germany. As a movement that was seeking to respond to the concerns of the European Enlightenment, it was a self-consciously modernizing movement. It sought to adapt the rituals of Judaism and explain its basic beliefs in terms that took account of the new rational and liberal thinking emerging in the West. Some of its proponents wanted to remove what they understood to be archaic practices and superstitious beliefs in order to develop a Judaism for the modern age.

■ Ultra-Orthodox Judaism emerged in the early 19th century as an anti-reform movement. In Hungary, particularly, there was bitter rivalry between those who sought to hold on to traditional beliefs and those who sought reform. Rabbi Mosheh Sofer (1762–1839), an influential leader, argued that any deviation from traditional Jewish belief and practice was a direct violation of the will of God. He thus rejected any changes in the

The Western Wall (the only part of the Temple left standing following its destruction in 70 CE) is a holy site for Jews.

tradition and, indeed, any substantial accommodation with the wider culture. As a consequence, his followers and disciples distanced themselves from other Jews and, in a similar way to the Hasidic community, developed highly centralized separatist communities.

■ Orthodox Judaism (also called Modern or neo-Orthodox Judaism) came into being as a less extreme response to the innovations of Reform Judaism. While there is today no 'Orthodox movement' as such, in that Orthodoxy consists of a range of distinct groups, it is a term that can be usefully applied to those Jews who share the basic tenets of a tradition that emerged in mid-19th-century Germany, the leading figure of which was Samson Raphael Hirsch (1808–88). He and other Jewish leaders insisted on the unchanging authority of the Torah and *halakhah* and agreed with some of the concerns of Ultra-Orthodox Jews. Nevertheless, they felt the force of modernity and were keen for Jews to integrate into wider European society. Hence, Hirsch's position can be summed up in the following popular slogan, *Torah im derekh eretz* (Torah and the way of the world). In other words, while holding on to the authoritative tradition and refusing to compromise their heritage, Orthodox Jews sought to make the most of what modernity had to offer. This creative synthesis of Judaism and modernity is characteristic of much contemporary Orthodox Judaism. However, there are many today (sometimes termed *Haredim*) who, having become dissatisfied with fundamental features of modern culture, such as relativism and pluralism, are turning to right wing and separatist forms of Judaism.

■ Conservative or Mesorati Judaism arose in mid-19th-century Germany as yet another response to the challenge of European modernism. If Orthodoxy can be understood as steering a course between Ultra-Orthodoxy

and Reform Judaism, the Conservative movement can perhaps be seen as steering a course between Orthodoxy and Reform Judaism. Unhappy with the customs and the tradition-bound worship of Orthodoxy, but not willing to go as far as the reformers, some Jewish leaders nevertheless wanted to see Judaism carefully evolve into a religion for the modern age. They wanted to conserve traditional Judaism, but in a way that took more account of the modern context. Hence, for example, while they maintained the separate seating of men and women in the synagogue, they sanctioned the ordination of women as rabbis and the training of women as cantors. Again, they insisted on the authority of the Torah, but not that it was the actual Word of God. While Conservative Judaism can be found throughout the Jewish world, it is strongest in the United States. Outside the United States, the movement is generally known as the Mesorati movement (from a Hebrew word meaning 'traditional').

■ *Humanistic Judaism and *Reconstructionist Judaism are recent movements founded in the United States that represent a trend towards secularism.

■ Finally, while the Hasidic community might have been mentioned along with Ultra-Orthodoxy, because they are a distinct community, not least in their origins, they are listed separately. If asked to picture a religious Jew, the image that comes to the minds of most non-Jews will perhaps be that of members of this movement: long beards, long ear locks of hair and long black clothes. Hasidism emerged in 18th-century Poland, founded by Rabbi Israel ben Eliezer (c. 1700–60), the Ba'al Shem Tov (Man of Good Repute). A growing dissatisfaction with traditional Judaism, which had for many Jews simply become too dry and intellectual, led to the desire for something new. The Ba'al Shem Tov met this desire with a non-intellectual form of Judaism. He taught that personal devotion, prayer and a meaningful relationship with God were far more important to God than learning. Along with this emphasis on the mystical experience of God, Hasidic Judaism has also developed a strong opposition to modernity and has even been described as 'fundamentalist' in its approach. Moreover, as with the Ultra-Orthodox communities, it has maintained a distance from the wider culture. For example, in seeking to erect social boundaries adherents have adopted a distinctive dress, refuse to participate in secular education, and enforce very strict food rules.

The Lubavitch Movement
Shirley Lucass

Emerging from Jewish Hasidism, the Lubavitch movement was founded in the 18th century by Shne'ur Zalman of Lyady (known as the Rav of Lyady; 1745–1813). His descendants and followers moved to Lubavici in Russia, which became its main centre until 1916. Zalman, a student of Dov Baer, the Maggid of Meseritz, developed Chabad Hasidism, which not only forms the basis of the Lubavitch philosophy but has become synonymous with it.

'Chabad' is an acronym of *chokmah*, *binah* and *da'at* (wisdom, understanding and knowledge) – the higher *sefiroth*, representing the operations of the mind. In the *kabbalism of Isaac Luria, on which Rabbi Israel ben Eliezer, the Ba'al Shem Tov (c. 1700–60), based Hasidism, the ten *sefiroth*

Rabbi Menachem Mendel Schneerson listens to a Torah reading during morning prayer in Brooklyn, New York, in 1992.

are emanations of the Godhead. In the *sefiroth* the emotional processes occur as a result of the intellectual processes. Thus in Chabad philosophy, humanity, which is created in the image of God, should reflect this process: religious emotions should flow from the intellectual process of contemplating God and not the other way round. The distinction between different types of ecstasy is addressed in Dov Baer's *Kuntres ha-Hitpa'alut* (*The Tract on Ecstasy*). However, the principal text of the movement, written by Zalman, is the *Likkutei Amarim* (*Collected Sayings*, also known as the *Tanya*), which sets forth systematically the principles of Chabad. Although Chabad is considered to be more philosophical than the warmer, more intimate approach of the Ba'al Shem Tov's Hasidism, it is characterized not only by its emphasis on intellectual study, but also by its celebratory nature.

Since 1916, the two main centres of the Lubavitch movement have been Israel and the United States. Hasidic groups are often dynastic and the head of the American headquarters in New York, Rabbi (or *Rebbe*) Menachem Mendel Schneerson (1902–94), was the son-in-law of the previous rabbi, the sixth after Zalman. Particularly since the Second World War, Lubavitch has been considered a revivalist movement within Judaism. The Lubavitch movement regards the conversion of Jews to Torah-observant Judaism as a high priority in order that the return of the Messiah may be hastened. This is not just an external observance but, as the seventh rabbi explains, 'the Torah and *mitzvot* [commandments] must become an integral part of the individual and permeate his very essence'. *Simcha shel mitzvah* (joy in the performance of a commandment) as well as warmth and affection in dealing with others are the hallmarks of Hasidism. Also, prayer is more than petition, it is 'cleaving to God' – the relinquishment of the consciousness of separate existence (*Bittul ha-Yesh*). With the Lubavitch, the desire for the spiritual improvement of all Jews is coupled with concern for their material welfare encompassed in the doctrine *ahavas Yisroel*, the complete and unconditional love of fellow Jews. Despite the death of the seventh rabbi in 1994 (who was considered by some to be the Messiah; see *Meshihistim), and despite the fact that no successor has been chosen, the movement has continued to grow, with more than 1,400 institutions in 35 countries and over 200,000 members worldwide.

Reconstructionist Judaism
Dan Cohn-Sherbok

Unlike Reform and Conservative Judaism, Reconstructionist Judaism developed out of the thinking of an individual scholar. Born in Lithuania in 1881, Mordecai Kaplan had a traditional Jewish education in Vilna and came to New York City as a child in 1889. After graduating from the City College of New York and the Jewish Theological Seminary, he received a master's degree from Columbia University in 1902. He then became an associate minister of Rabbi Moses S. Margois at New York's Orthodox Kehilath Jeshurun (synagogue). Although officially Orthodox, Kaplan increasingly became disenchanted with traditional Jewish doctrine. In 1909, he was invited by the Cambridge scholar Solomon Schechter to direct the Teachers' Institute of the Seminary. The following year he became professor of homiletics at the Seminary's rabbinical school, where he taught philosophy of religion. Kaplan died in 1983.

According to some scholars,

Reconstructionism began as a movement in 1922 when Kaplan initiated a policy of 'reconstructing' Judaism to meet the demands of modern life; others trace its origin to the publication of his book *Judaism as a Civilization* in 1934. Kaplan himself contended that the movement emerged in 1935 when, as a result of publishing *Judaism as a Civilization*, he and others launched the *Reconstructionist* magazine. In any event, his book provided the foundation for Reconstructionist ideology.

According to Kaplan, God is not a supernatural being but the power that enables salvation. God, he argues, is the sum of all the animating, organizing forces and relationships that are forever making a cosmos out of chaos. In his view, the idea of God must be understood fundamentally in terms of its effect: 'We learn more about God when we say that love is divine than when we say God is love. A veritable transformation takes place… Divinity becomes relevant to authentic experience and therefore takes on a definiteness which is accompanied by an awareness of authenticity.' For Kaplan, God is a 'trans-natural', 'super-factual' and 'super-experiential' transcendence that does not infringe on the law of nature. Such a notion is far removed from the biblical and rabbinic concept of God as the creator and sustainer of the universe who chose the Jewish people and guides humanity to its final destiny.

Turning to the doctrine of revelation, Reconstructionism differs markedly from Orthodoxy. Adopting the findings of modern biblical scholars, who believe the Torah was written by different authors, Kaplan stressed that the Bible was not a record of God's dealings with his chosen people; rather it reflected the Jewish search for God. Reconstructionists thus do not regard Jewish law as holy and unchanging. In place of traditional language, Reconstructionists utilize the terms 'folkways' and 'customs' to designate traditional observances, expressions which reflect the fact that throughout history all

☞ *continued on page 116*

KABBALISM
Eric S. Christianson

Kabbalah (also spelled kabbala, kabala, cabala, cabbala, cabbalah, qabala, qabbala or qabbalah) literally means 'received' or 'what has been received' and designates a mainly esoteric body of Jewish mysticism. The word refers at once to a particular mystical experience and to the ascetic process of enabling aspirants to reach it. In recent times kabbalism has come to be acknowledged as one of the most important (if most hidden) movements to have shaped modern Judaism.

Distinctive features

Traditional kabbalism seeks the essence of God as opposed to his outward manifestations. God is hidden in his own self and cannot be discovered through the use of words, which by necessity fail to encapsulate God's being. God is essentially impersonal, even 'nothing'. In these respects kabbalism is a radical departure from the Jewish sources of scripture, Mishnah, Talmud and Midrash, which all return habitually to the personhood of the divine, even and especially the divine as named. At the same time, however, kabbalism embraces and enjoys a lively relationship with those traditions, particularly as expressed in *halakhah* (Jewish law) and *aggadah* (legend). Indeed, the ability and willingness of the kabbalists to embrace and transform these traditions enabled kabbalah to succeed where Jewish philosophy ultimately failed; that is, in providing a hugely popular Jewish worldview. *Aggadah*, for example, had always expressed itself in terms of the striving of Jewish existence *between* heaven and earth. In kabbalistic terms, every human incident has its *direct* effect on the heavenly realm, so much so that the realm of heaven subsumes that of earth. (In this respect kabbalism's closest kin in ancient Jewry is the apocalyptic literature, in which the heavenly realms symbolize their earthly counterparts, and in which the hero is able to crack the code that is constructed between them.) Words, then, while not sufficiently describing God, can symbolize the divine in a *corresponding* relationship.

Another feature that distinguishes kabbalah is its emphasis on inner mystical experience, particularly as achieved (or mediated) through prayer and (usually informal) liturgy. In the medieval period, when kabbalah presented a viable alternative to a more intellectual and academic (and perceptibly alienating) rabbinic Judaism, this emphasis was hugely influential, even indirectly on opposition movements. The path to communion was not perceived as accessed through any form of pure reason or logic, but through some faculty of the soul. Yet this was balanced with an extreme form of Gnosticism. Limited to small groups, at first the secret teachings were passed on orally, from master to pupil. The message was cryptic, sometimes concluding, 'This is sufficient for one who is enlightened' or 'I cannot expand on this, for thus have I been commanded.'

The most prominent model of inner mystical experience has been, and remains, the ten *sefiroth*. The *sefiroth*, in varying degrees and expressions, classify the mystical aspiration into ten symbolic areas of God's activity and existence. From the *keter*, the head (the crown of primordial Adam), down to the nether regions of *yesod* (phallus, life-force of the universe) and beyond to *malkhut* (kingdom, God's *shekinah*/presence), the *sefiroth* are mythological facets, mini-embodiments of God's being, each one acting as a staging post (from top to bottom) in the ascent (or descent) to the One. Once the aspirant has truly penetrated this system they can explore the *sefiroth* as a map of consciousness.

Historical roots

Although there are occasional instances of mysticism hinted at in the Hebrew scriptures (e.g. Moses and the burning bush), many scholars point to the early forms of Merkabah mysticism, modelled on Ezekiel's heightened encounter with God's chariot in Ezekiel 1 (*merkabah* is Hebrew for 'chariot'), which took root in 1st-century Palestine, as somehow defining the proper beginnings of kabbalah. Merkabah mysticism highlighted means of mediation (already present in apocalyptic literature) between God and men (specifically not women). Significantly, the destruction of the Temple in 70 CE intensified the mediatory aspects of this Jewish thinking and as such resulted in a heightened emphasis on inner experience, an experience that could be accessed *outside* the locus of the Temple. Such emphasis soon came to be replaced by the more academic, *halakhic* and discourse-orientated forms of Pharisaic Judaism that would define the Talmudic period that followed (roughly from the 2nd to the 7th centuries CE), particularly in diaspora Judaism. That said, some circles of Merkabah mystics managed to flourish in Palestine and Babylonia throughout the Talmudic and even post-Talmudic periods.

This movement produced two significant pre-kabbalistic texts: *Heikhalot Rabatti* (*The Greater Treatise on the Heavenly Palaces*) and *Sefer Yetzira* (*Book of Creation*), both of which celebrate the secrets of nature and the wonders of God's heavenly throne. The latter had the more long-lasting impact (it is still influential in modern kabbalah) and put forward two particularly potent ideas: the numerical value and significance of the Hebrew alphabet (to be developed by medieval exegetes as *gematria*) and the ten *sefiroth*. Gradually the *sefiroth* evolved into the central symbol system of kabbalah.

From the close of the classical rabbinic period (c. 650) until the emergence of some of the core texts of kabbalistic Judaism (c. 1150), Jewish life was profoundly influenced by Arabic-Islamic culture. A considerable portion of Jewry existed under mainly Islamic rule in this period and was duly influenced by its predilection for forms of Greek philosophy and Islamic mysticism. The latter emphasized a systematic progress of an ascetic path to the divine that would influence the spiritual drive of kabbalah. Such influence, combined with the still surviving streams of Merkabah mysticism, accounts for the emergence of several theosophical

ideologies in the south of France (c. 1150). The first significant text to emerge from that context is the *Sefer ha-bahir* (*Book of Brightness*). It was fragmentary, poorly written and ascribed to fictitious ancient sources. But these texts started to lend a systematic treatment to the 'tenets' of kabbalah, in particular the notion that the ethical life of Israel has a direct correspondence to cosmic harmony.

Not long after the appearance of the *Book of Brightness* emerged the school of Isaac the Blind, whose most prominent teacher was otherwise known as Isaac ben Abraham. His 'school' achieved a synthesis of ideas already present in the traditions of the books of *Creation* and *Brightness*, and this moment might properly be identified as the height of 'classical' kabbalah. The 'school' spread beyond France and into Spain, finding a spiritual home in Catalonia in the early 1200s. Here kabbalah flourished and some influential figures emerged, among them Nachmanides (Moses ben Nachman; c. 1195–1270). Nachmanides is a rare instance of a kabbalist who contributed significantly to more traditional rabbinic commentary (including *gematria*) as well as to kabbalah. On the whole, however, this was not welcomed by the various rabbinic authorities. Indeed the rabbinic critics latched onto a particular talmudic text for highlighting the dangers inherent in kabbalah. It reported the entry into *pardes* (literally 'orchard'; by extension the garden of God) of four rabbis. One glimpsed and died. Another glimpsed and went mad. A third became an apostate, and only one 'emerged in peace' (Babylonian Talmud, *Hagigah* 14b).

Until the expulsion of the Jews in 1492, kabbalah continued to develop in Spain. There the work of Moses ben Shem Tob de León marked a turning point in Jewish mysticism. Over a period of about 30 years, Moses de León produced a series of writings that he ascribed to a 2nd-century CE rabbi, Simeon bar Yochai. The collection came to be known as *Sefer ha-zohar* (*Book of Splendour*). Commonly known as the *Zohar*, few other texts have had a comparable influence on the development of Judaism. Through the *Zohar*, kabbalah gained clarity. In other words, the *Zohar* gave definition and focus to a range of scattered ideas about, among other things, the problem of evil and communion with *Ein Sof* (an epithet for God, meaning 'without end'), and disciplined such themes around the conceptual tool of the ten *sefiroth*. The *Ein Sof* cannot

be known except *within* the attributes of the *sefiroth*, for this is how God has chosen to reveal his self: 'The Holy One, blessed be he, has produced ten holy crowns above [the *sefiroth*], wherewith he crowns and invests himself. He is they and they are he, being linked together like the flame and the coal' (*Zohar*, Aharei Mot, III 70a). The bulk of the *Zohar* is in the form of a mystical midrash on the Torah, the first five books of Moses, and as such (ironically in light of rabbinic opponents) accords a high value to Torah and Talmud study. The *Zohar* would come to be a foundational text and general framework for all Jewish theosophies in the centuries ahead. (Some present-day Orthodox kabbalists, still zealously subscribing to the idea of Simeon bar Yochai's authorship, accord the *Zohar* as high a place as Torah in the religious life.)

Beyond the early influence of the *Zohar*, the most significant pre-modern expression of kabbalah emerged from Isaac ben Solomon Luria (1534–72) who proposed the most influential system of later kabbalism, which was also its most complex. As well as the *Zohar* itself, Luria studied the work of the greatest kabbalist of his time, Moses ben Jacob Cordovero of Safed (modern

Zefat in Israel, still a geographical focus for kabbalah). The fruit of Luria's study was communicated through apparently highly popular and dynamic teaching. Luria gathered around himself a school of discipleship, based in Safed, that evidenced deep devotion, asceticism and withdrawal from the world. Although Luria wrote very little, after his death his doctrines were recorded by his disciples and became known as the Lurianic kabbalah. The system focuses heavily on the relationship between the creation and subsequent degeneration of the world. The spiritual goal is thus *tikkun*, restoration of the created order as brought about through prayer and through mystical intentions involving secret combinations of words. The Lurianic tradition was to have a serious impact on subsequent movements in modern Hasidism, which have tended to reject the rigid asceticism of the former in favour of a more informal, story-orientated kabbalism.

Contemporary expressions

Partly due to the widespread popularity of Lurianic theology and (less so) ritual, as early as the late 15th century kabbalah was influencing Christian thinkers such as Giovanni Pico della Mirandola (1463–94) and

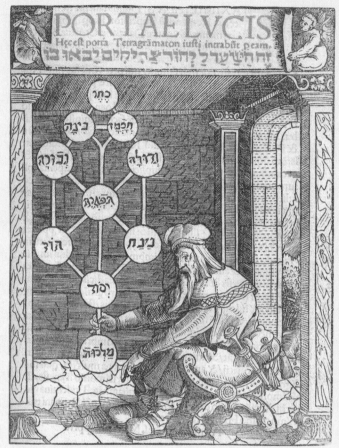

Earliest representation in print of the ten sefiroth, from a Latin translation of Joseph Gikatilla's Sha'arei Orah, *1516.*

insufficient. Among Scholem's most lasting achievements is his conclusive demonstration of the impact of the kabbalistic movements on the course of Jewish history. From his initial and subsequent work on the topic has emerged a whole academic discipline in its own right. But he was as likely as anyone to disapprove of some of the directions that interest in kabbalah has since taken. Rabbi Abraham Kook (1865–1935), a fervent Eastern European Zionist and mystic, was the most prominent kabbalist of his time and his writings are still influential on modern kabbalah.

Gilles of Viterbo (Egidio da Viterbo; c. 1465–1532) in Italy, and Johannes Reuchlin (1455–1522) in Germany. Some Christian kabbalists became quite well trained in its finer details and even suggested that the kabbalistic system could prove the divinity of Christ. In the late 19th and early 20th centuries the impact of kabbalah can be discerned in the works of such diverse figures as William Blake, Franz Kafka, Gottfried Leibniz, Jorge Luis Borges, Walter Benjamin and, more recently, Jacques

Derrida and Umberto Eco.

In recent years, kabbalah has undergone something of a revival, but in forms that would have been considered anathema by most devout classical adherents. Ironically, however, it was an academic, Gershom Scholem, professor of Jewish mysticism at the Hebrew University of Jerusalem, who was to herald its resurgence in the public consciousness. Before he published his seminal *Trends in Jewish Mysticism* (1941), attention given to kabbalah was sporadic and often

The type of 'kabbalah' that can be easily purveyed by searching the term on the internet, lays a great deal of emphasis on the gnostic and solution-orientated aspects of kabbalah. As one website puts it, 'the first rule of kabbalah is not to believe anything you read or hear. The whole idea of belief bears a residue of doubt. Knowing, on the other hand, leaves no trace of scepticism. The act of knowing means total certainty. Complete conviction. In your gut. In your heart. In your soul.'

Kabbalah has found a home among the 'rich and famous', including, apparently, Roseanne Barr, Naomi Campbell, Jeff Goldblum, Jerry Hall, Mick Jagger, Madonna and Elizabeth Taylor. For example, in January 2000, it was reported that Mick Jagger and Jerry Hall had turned to kabbalah in an attempt to rescue their relationship. Their spiritual advisor was Rabbi Eliyahu Yardeni, the brother of Hall's and also Madonna's kabbalah teacher, Rabbi Eitan Yardeni of the Los Angeles Kabbalah Learning Centre. (The Kabbalah Learning Centre, which has 39 centres around the world, was established in Jerusalem in 1928. The dean and director of the centre is the influential kabbalist, Rav Berg.) Unsurprisingly, some of the less rigorous forms of kabbalah have elicited strong condemnation from scholars and traditional (mainly Hasidic) practitioners of the subject. The words 'charlatans', 'lazy', 'obscurantist' and 'insubstantial' are frequently employed in their assessments. It is also worth noting, however, that some *mekubbalim* (people who actively study and practise kabbalah), are often sceptical of academic approaches to its study. One anecdote captures the tension nicely. Rabbi Abraham Chen once declared before a seminar of Gershom Scholem's students, 'A scholar of mysticism is like an accountant: He may know where all the treasure is, but he is not free to use it.' Whatever the value of its academic study or sometimes superficial adherence, it seems that kabbalah is likely to be a religious force in the world for some time to come.

Jerry Hall and Mick Jagger with Eliyahu Yardeni at a charity dinner in honour of the Kabbalah Centre in London. Kabbalah is proving increasingly popular with the rich and famous.

peoples have created their sacred events, holy days and religious objects.

In Kaplan's view, folkways and customs help to sustain the Jewish nation and enrich the spiritual life of Jewry. Yet Kaplan argued that such observances should be accepted voluntarily. In the modern world, there is no rôle for coercive authority. In this regard, Kaplan endorsed the concept of democratic decision-making in determining which laws are relevant for the community. For Kaplan, anachronistic laws as well as regulations that conflict with the highest ideals of Judaism have no place in a modern Code of Jewish Law unless meaning can be given to them. Further, Kaplan stressed the importance of formulating new customs to take the place of those that had ceased to give meaning to contemporary Jewish life.

Many of the ideas found in *Judaism as a Civilization* were reflected in the religious literature of the Reconstructionist movement. The *New Haggadah*, for example, applied Kaplan's theology to liturgical texts, subordinating miracles and plagues in the traditional *Haggadah* (Passover prayer book) to the narrative of Israel's redemption from Egypt and its contemporary significance. Again, the sabbath prayer book was designed for those who were dissatisfied with synagogue worship – its aim was to arouse emotion by eliminating theologically untenable passages and adding inspirational material drawn from tradition. This new prayer book deleted all references to the revelation of the Torah on Mount Sinai, the chosenness of Israel and the doctrine of a personal Messiah.

By the end of the 1960s, Reconstructionist Judaism had become a denomination – it had established a seminary to train Reconstructionist rabbis and had instituted a congregational structure. Regarding *halakhah* (Jewish law), the Reconstructionist Rabbinical Association issued a statement of its 1980 convention that placed authority in the Jewish people (as opposed to the rabbis) and created

a process whereby each congregation would be free to evolve its own customs. Three years later, the association produced guidelines on intermarriage, encouraging rabbis to welcome mixed couples (Jew and non-Jew), permit them to participate in Jewish synagogue life, and recognize their children as Jewish if raised as Jews. In addition, the association decreed that rabbis could sanctify an intermarriage as long as it was accompanied by a civil, rather than a religious, ceremony.

ALEPH: Alliance for Jewish Renewal
Shirley Lucass

The name B'nai Or (Sons or Children of Light) originated in the Dead Sea Scrolls and was taken up by Reb Zalman Schacter, who founded a movement called the B'nai Or in 1962. Reb Zalman was born in Poland in 1924, raised in Vienna and ordained at the Lubavitch *yeshiva* (Jewish university) in Brooklyn. He also has a degree in psychology from Boston University and a doctorate from the Hebrew Union College. The movement was originally conceived as semi-monastic (mirroring the Essene community, generally considered to be the source of the Dead Sea Scrolls). Reb Zalman envisioned a community that would be responsible for the preservation of the Hasidic teachings, which could be used to renew Jewish spirituality in the aftermath of the Holocaust. In effect it represented more of a spiritual path than a movement and was closer to Orthodox Judaism than the later Jewish Spiritual Movement, which developed out of it and which was influenced by *Reconstructionist Judaism. Although attracting Jews from all backgrounds, including Reform and Conservative Judaism, the B'nai Or nonetheless observed *halakhah* (Jewish law) in order that Orthodox Jews could also participate. Although the monastic community never eventuated, in its earlier period communal retreats would take place, with members dwelling in tents or cabins enjoying simple vegetarian (and hence kosher) food.

One of the features of the earlier B'nai Or was the rainbow-coloured *tallith* (prayer shawl), developed by Reb Zalman in response to a vision he had during the course of a meditation on creation. The colour, width and arrangement of each stripe of the *tallith* relates to a mystical sphere, that is the seven lower *sefiroth* of *kabbalism and also to the days of the creation myth of Genesis. The *sefiroth* (ten in all) are emanations of the Godhead in kabbalistic (Jewish mystical) philosophy. Hence the third stripe is green and represents the third day, when vegetation was created, and *tiferet* (beauty). Although B'nai Or was from the outset inclusivist, welcoming Jews from all different backgrounds and, in particular, women (even ordaining women) it took the further step of changing its name in 1985 from B'nai Or (Sons of Light) to P'nai Or (Faces of Light). The movement has continued to develop and since 1993 has been known as ALEPH: Alliance for Jewish Renewal. ALEPH is a network of affiliated groups based in North America that sponsors the Shalom Center and the Jewish Renewal Life Center. Current numbers of adherents are unknown.

In its early days, B'nai Or combined both traditional and contemporary Torah study and prayer with the hasidic practices of davening, storytelling and *hisboddidus* (solitary prayer in the woods), and as such has been described as neo-hasidic. Latterly, in its desire to update Jewish theology and spirituality, P'nai Or became more syncretistic, absorbing and utilizing the spirituality of other religions and spiritual paths as well as incorporating modern psychology and philosophy. Therefore, in addition to Hasidism and kabbalism, it encompasses elements from Sufism, Buddhism and Native American religion in order to achieve not only inner healing for the individual but to effect *tikkun olam* (the healing of the world).

Humanistic Judaism
Dan Cohn-Sherbok

Humanistic Judaism originated in 1965 when the Birmingham Temple in Detroit, Michigan, United States, began to publicize its philosophy of Judaism. In 1966, a special committee for Humanistic Judaism was organized at the Temple to share service and educational material with rabbis and laity throughout the country. The following year, a meeting of several leaders of the movement met in Detroit, issuing a statement affirming that Judaism should be governed by empirical reason and human needs; in addition, a new magazine, *Humanistic Judaism*, was founded. In 1969, the Society for Humanistic Judaism was founded in Detroit to provide a basis for cooperation among Humanistic Jews.

In 1986, a proclamation stating the ideology and aims of Humanistic Judaism was issued:

We believe in the value of human reason and in the reality of the world which reason discloses. The natural universe stands on its own, requiring no supernatural intervention. We believe in the value of human existence and in the power of human beings to solve their problems both individually and collectively. Life should be directed to the satisfaction of human needs. Every person is entitled to life, dignity and freedom. We believe in the value of Jewish identity and in the survival of the Jewish people. Jewish history is a human story.

In accordance with this philosophy of Judaism, a new conception of Jewish identity was advocated. In answer to the question 'Who is a Jew?', the International Federation of Secular Humanistic Jews (the major body of Humanistic Judaism) declared:

We... believe that the survival of the Jewish people depends on a broad view of Jewish identity. We welcome into the Jewish people all men and women who sincerely desire to share the Jewish experience regardless of their ancestry. We challenge the assumption that the Jews are primarily or exclusively a religious community and that religious convictions or behaviour are essential to full membership in the Jewish people.

According to Sherwin Wine, the major exponent of Humanistic Judaism, the traditional conception of Jewish history is mistaken. In his view, Abraham, Isaac and Jacob never existed. Furthermore, the Exodus account is a myth: 'There is no historical evidence to substantiate a massive Hebrew departure from the land of the Pharaohs. As far as we can surmise, the Hebrew occupation of the hill country on both sides of the Jordan was continuous. The 12 tribes never left their ancestral land, never endured 400 years of slavery, and never wandered the Sinai desert.' Moreover, Moses was not the leader of the Hebrews, nor did he compose the Torah. In this light, it is an error to regard the biblical account as authoritative; rather it is a human record of the history of the Israelite nation, the purpose of which is to reinforce the faith of the Jewish nation.

Like *Reconstructionist Judaism, Humanistic Judaism denies any form of supernatural belief. Instead, it regards religious belief as fundamentally psychological in origin. According to the *Guide to Humanistic Judaism*: 'The deity is the projection of the first and most intimate human experience, the dependence of the child on the parents. Patriarchy, monarchy and traditional religion go hand in hand. Just as the family requires a father-leader and the nation requires a father-king, so does the universe require a father-God.' Despite such common ground, however, Humanistic Judaism distances itself from Reconstructionism in its use of non-theistic language. Reconstructionist congregations continue to use the religious vocabulary of the past despite the changes that have been made to the liturgy. Humanistic Judaism, however, has jettisoned theistic language.

The word 'God' has thus been eliminated from 'worship'. Humanistic 'prayers' are thus radically different from those found in the traditional prayer book. A typical example of such liturgical change is found in the Passover *Haggadah*. In place of thanksgiving for God's deliverance, Humanistic Jews declare:

Tonight is a night of memories. Many years ago our fathers were slaves in the land of Egypt. In bitterness and in hardship they struggled to please their masters and win the precious opportunities of mere survival. Many died from the heat of work; others perished from the cold of despair. Through the agonies of oppression, they searched their hearts for one thing that would make life bearable. They searched for hope and found it. They dreamed of freedom and believed that one day it would be theirs. Tonight is a night of hope.

Like Jewish festivals, life-cycle events have also been reinterpreted in humanistic terms. Unlike traditional Judaism, for example, Humanistic Judaism does not promise eternal life. Instead it accepts the finality of death. According to the *Guide to Humanistic Judaism*, a Humanistic philosophy of death:

recognizes that, although death may be painful and tragic for those who survive and may be profoundly regretted, there is nothing in death to fear, any more than one fears sleeping. One may well be afraid of the pain that may precede death, as one may be afraid of, and would try to avoid, pain generally. But, in the absence of consciousness or feelings after death, there is no reason to fear death itself.

Humanistic Judaism thus offers an option for those who wish to identify with the Jewish community despite their rejection of the traditional understanding of God's nature and activity. Unlike Reconstructionist Judaism, with its emphasis on the observances of the past, Humanistic Judaism fosters a new approach. The Jewish heritage is relevant only insofar as it advances humanistic ideals. In addition, traditional definitions and principles are set aside in the quest to create a Judaism consonant with a scientific and pluralistic age. Secular in orientation, Humanistic Jews seek to create a world in which the Jewish people are dedicated to the betterment of all humankind.

The Havurot Movement
Shirley Lucass

Havurah can be translated as friendship, community or fellowship. *Havurot* are usually small groups of between 12 and 20 individuals or families (including children) who meet together to participate in and explore different aspects of Judaism, usually once a month in one of the members' homes. Modern *Havurot* emerged in the United States in the late 1960s as a response to the perceived impersonality of the larger synagogues and the lack of spirituality and community. This period also witnessed a general resurgence of Jewish pride and a desire to affirm Jewish identity in the wake of Israel's victory in the Six Day War (1967). Although some *Havurot* are independent, others are associated with a particular synagogue, but nonetheless run autonomously. The National *Havurah* committee was founded in 1973 and many *Havurot* are affiliated to a national network, which provides suggested structures for meetings as well as study material and listings of *Havurot* nationwide. The groups participate in a number of similar activities, but each group has its own emphasis. While the five main areas addressed are community, study, celebration, prayer and social action, most groups study the traditional Jewish texts, along with Jewish culture and history. Some *Havurot* have teaching input from a rabbi, but in many the study is lay led with each member making a contribution. *Havurot*

members also share life-cycle celebrations and often share sabbaths once or twice a month. As well as developing community projects, such as visiting the sick or elderly, the members also form a support network for one another.

Many *Havurot* are affiliated to *ALEPH: Alliance for Jewish Renewal formed in 1993 or the Jewish Reconstructionist Federation and therefore subscribe to the *Reconstructionist Judaism philosophy which grew out of the work of Mordecai Kaplan (1881–1983). Reconstructionist *Havurot*, therefore, encompass a wide range of beliefs and great emphasis is placed on participatory worship and on engaging the creativity and diversity of the individual members. Egalitarianism is a fundamental principle and differences in background, learning and observances are accommodated, although shared meals are vegetarian to cater for those members who require kosher food. Current numbers of adherents are not known, but the movement spread rapidly in the 1970s in the United States. Other groups are based in Britain, Australia and Israel.

Gush Emunim
Shirley Lucass

Gush Emunim (Bloc of the Faithful) is a Jewish religious nationalist movement, formally established in February 1974 in the wake of the Yom Kippur War. It views itself as a continuation of the Zionist dynamic and has encouraged and established many new Jewish settlements in the West Bank.

The spiritual mentor of the group was Rabbi Abraham Yitzchak Ha-Cohen Kook, who became the first Ashkenazi Chief Rabbi of Israel in 1921. His thinking was influenced by Hegel, Marx, *kabbalism and messianism. Following his death in 1935, his son Tzevi Yehudah Kook (Rav Kook; 1891–1982) continued his work. Rav Kook, influenced by his father's kabbalistic-messianic approach, viewed the present era from the founding of the Zionist movement as the beginning of the redemptive process in which both secular and orthodox Jews would play a part, with the State of Israel viewed as 'the first flowering' of that redemption. Members of Gush Emunim believe in the mystical unity of the Jewish people and the land of Israel and consequently that it is incumbent on every Jew to support the repossession of all of the land that falls within the borders outlined in Genesis 15 – the land given to Israel by God as part of his covenant with his people.

Political and world events are interpreted messianically. The influx of large numbers of Jews in the 1980s was viewed as the beginning of the ingathering of the exiles, heralding the imminent arrival of the Messiah. Similarly, the 'liberation' of Judea and Samaria during the Six Day War (1967) was understood as another stage in the process of messianic redemption. Consequently, any pressure to return these sites to Arab possession is resisted as contrary to God's will. While political difficulties are viewed as testing the readiness of the people to receive the Messiah, the establishment and continued existence of the State of Israel are believed to be divine sanctions of Zionism and the Gush Emunim.

The leadership of the Gush Emunim is principally derived from Rav Kook's Talmudic academy, the Merkaz haRav. Students of this establishment were greatly influenced by his teaching and in particular by his 'prophetic' speech on Independence Day, which it was believed 'came to fruition' in the events of the Six Day War. Those who attended this academy came predominantly from the B'nei Akiva youth movement (characterized by their 'knitted skullcaps', which differentiate them from the orthodox and secular members of Israeli society). Nonetheless, the Gush Emunim continue Rav Kook's policy of the integration of the

At the newly liberated Western Wall, soldiers of the Six Day War come to receive blessings and to pray.

secular and the orthodox and have established a number of 'mixed' settlements with settlers from a broad range of religious backgrounds. The Gush Emunim also support the system that allows Israeli recruits to spread the three years of conscription over six, alternating semesters at a religious academy with semesters in the army. Since the death of Rav Kook in 1982, the status of the Gush Emunim has been debated among its members; some believe it no longer exists in its original format, while others believe that its ideology continues through the Amanah, its settlement movement. In 1992, it was estimated that there were over 50 settlements and 100,000

part of the world and had resulted in Jews continuing to observe their religion strictly but with no great desire to celebrate joyfully. This movement, with its overtones of spiritual (if not physical) and messianic redemption elicited much support from the peasants, who rallied to the banner of what became known as Hasidism or pious living. It also attracted its critics, principally among scholarly circles, who were suspicious of Redemptionists and kabbalistic (mystical) groups (see *Kabbalism), and cited the potential dangers of false messiahs as a reason for their opposition. Of the many Hasidic 'courts' that arose following the lifetime of the Ba'al Shem Tov, a now leaderless Hasidic group called the *Lubavitch movement commands the greatest following.

The seventh 'Hasidic' rabbi (or *rebbe*) of the Lubavitch movement, Rabbi Menachem Mendel Schneerson (b. 1902), was installed as its leader in 1950. Under his leadership, the movement grew enormously. Since his death in 1994, a new, blatantly messianic trend has grown at fast pace within the movement. Many Lubavitch synagogues, schools and *yeshivot* (higher education institutions for the study of the Talmud) insist on the triple declaration of Schneerson's messianic majesty with the words '*Yechi Adoneynu, Moreynu Verabeynu, Melech HaMoshiach LeOlam Va'Ed*' (May our Master, Teacher and Rabbi, the King Messiah live for ever and ever).

Most Lubavitch are elusive as to their beliefs about the status of the deceased rabbi as the living king of Israel. Others are more explicit, and belong to circles that decorate their homes and traditional headgear with the 'Yechi' declaration and name their institutions to reflect this belief. Few in the Orthodox world have openly voiced opposition to the popular messianic trend within the Lubavitch movement, which continues to train, ordain and post scores of young rabbis in positions as congregational and communal spiritual

settlers in the movement, but it is difficult to extrapolate from this the numbers of committed supporters. Since 1994, the movement has been known as Emunim.

Meshihistim
Ariel Abel

Rabbi Israel ben Eliezer (c. 1700–60), better known as the Ba'al Shem Tov (Man of Good Repute), travelled through towns and villages in Poland with the express mission of lifting the spirits of the masses of unlearned Jewish peasants, telling them that they were no less worthy to God than the scholarly rabbis and the learned Talmudic students, and inspiring them to serve the creator with joy. The horror of the Cossack pogroms of 1648–49 was still fresh in the collective memory of Jews in that leaders throughout the mainstream Orthodox Jewish world.

At the time of writing this article, the position of the Chief Rabbinate of Great Britain and the Commonwealth is not to question the theological leanings of candidates for the ministry. In the United States and Israel, much awareness has been generated by an American Modern Orthodox rabbinic scholar, David Berger, following the publication of a work exposing the essentially heretical, even heathen approaches leading to the acceptance of the rabbi as a divine, omniscient and omnipotent being, Messiah even after death.

Although Judaism has long believed in the concept of messianic redemption, it rejects the notion that a Messiah is a spiritual being only. The most widely accepted codex of Jewish law in the last millennium spells out clearly that, should the candidate for Messiah fail to accomplish his mission during his lifetime, it is inadmissible to believe in a second coming. This dogma has distinguished Jewish loyalty to their religion from the acceptance of Christianity throughout the ages of persecution, but is being gradually eroded by a large core of an otherwise strictly ritually observant Jewish movement. These Lubavitch Messianists are referred to in Hebrew as 'Meshihistim'.

The implications of membership of a theologically heretical movement within Judaism include prohibitions on mixed marriages or mixed socializing. Meat slaughtered by the Meshihistim is declared to be non-kosher, and their wine is equated with a 'defiled beverage' or wine dedicated to idolatry. Their belief in a divine human being is defined in Judaism as foreign, idolatrous worship and, as such, excludes its adherents from the Jewish people, despite their otherwise strict observance of Jewish ritual. Consequently, Meshihistim becomes a contemporary sect.

New Religions, Sects and Alternative Spiritualities with Roots in **Islam**

A detail from the interior of the Dome of the Rock, Jerusalem.

ISLAM
Christopher Partridge

Islam is currently the fastest-growing world religion and, with over a billion followers, is the second largest (Christianity being the largest). The word 'islam' means recognition of and active submission to the will of Allah, the one and only God. A Muslim is one who acknowledges and obediently submits to Allah – submission leads to salvation. Indeed, ideally, all areas of life – personal, social and political – should submit to the divine will, as set forth in Islam's sacred book, the Qur'an.

Beliefs

Islam is founded on the guidance of Allah as this is recorded in the Qur'an, which Muslims believe to be the literal word of God as delivered by Allah to his special messenger, the prophet Muhammad (c. 570–632 CE). Hence, central to Islam is the following twofold confession, known as the *Shahadah*: *La ilaha illa Allah; Muhammad rasul Allah* (There is no god but God [Allah], and Muhammad is his prophet). The first thing to note about this confession is that there is only one God; Islam is rigorously monotheistic. Indeed, the greatest sin in Islam is *shirk*, the denial of the uniqueness of God by claiming that there are other coequal beings *associated* with God. There must be no worship of other gods and no idolatry. It is not enough simply to confess that God exists, but, as the *Shahadah* declares, there needs to be an equally forceful declaration that *only* God is God.

This enormous stress on monotheism needs to be understood in the context of the religious environment in which Muhammad was brought up. Muhammad was born in Mecca, the inhabitants of which worshipped a high God, Allah, along with other divinities, including three goddesses known as the 'Daughters of Allah'. It was this type of worship that offended Muhammad and which he wholly rejected in favour of the worship of only Allah. This shift to the worship of Allah alone is considered by Muslims to be the great achievement of Islam. That said, monotheism was not unknown to other religions. Both Christianity and Judaism are strictly monotheistic. Indeed, Islam not only recognizes the monotheistic roots of these faiths, but believes that Muhammad is the last and the greatest of a line of prophets ('the seal of the prophets') that began with Abraham, the first monotheist and thus the first Muslim (one who fully submits to God alone).

According to traditional accounts of Muhammad's life, his father Abdullah died prior to his birth and his mother Aminah died when he was six. After the death of his mother, his grandfather, a deeply religious man who made a living providing water for pilgrims, took care of Muhammad for two years until his own death. Muhammad then moved to the care of his uncle, Abu Talib, also a devoutly religious man. He lived a relatively meagre existence until about the age of 25, when he married his employer, Khadija, a wealthy widow. Then, around 15 years later (610 CE), he was visited by the angel Gabriel during a solitary retreat in the hills near Mecca. Gabriel told him that he was to be the messenger (*rasul*) of Allah. Although Muhammad initially experienced self-doubt, he eventually submitted and began preaching the message of Islam to his fellow Meccans. Muhammad continued receiving the revelations that now constitute the Qur'an until his death in 632 CE. (The word *qur'an* means recitation, thereby indicating its essentially oral nature. This is a message that is supposed to be recited and listened to.)

The completed Qur'an, which is a little shorter than the New Testament, contains 114 'suras' (chapters). After the first sura, called 'the Opening', which is only seven

---

The angel Gabriel is revealed to Muhammad – from the eighth sura of the Qur'an. Turkey, 1594–95.

verses long, the following suras are arranged in order of length. The second and longest sura has 286 verses and the shortest suras at the end of the Qur'an have only three verses. That the Qur'an is understood to be the *eternal* word of God is significant, in that the Qur'an is not understood to have come into being as a result of the revelations to Muhammad, but rather to have existed in eternity, prior to Muhammad. When Gabriel related the words of the Qur'an to Muhammad, he was revealing information that already existed, in that the qur'anic revelations are part of an eternal 'Mother of the Book' (Sura 13:39), also called 'the well-preserved tablet' (Sura 85:22). Hence, for Muslims the Qur'an is entirely trustworthy in all respects, an inerrant sacred text of divine origin. Indeed, it is considered to be a physical manifestation of the Divine. Although other prophets (notably Abraham, Moses, David and Jesus) have received revelations from God, they are now all considered to be corrupt. Only the Qur'an remains as the pure communication of God to humanity. Hence, if anyone wishes to know what God's will is, the nature of God, or the purpose of creation, only the Qur'an can be wholly trusted to provide it.

While the Qur'an is of supreme importance, because Muhammad was the chosen messenger he became a second source of spiritual authority, as the *Shahadah* indicates. Indeed, he is often understood to be the 'perfect man' who lived his life in a state of sinlessness. Consequently, everything he did and said is supremely significant, in that it is considered to be a direct manifestation of the will of God. The Sunna (Way of the Prophet), a multi-volume collection of anecdotes, stories, observations and collected memories, is understood to be a record of Muhammad's exemplary sayings and deeds. Each of these accounts is called a *hadith* (tradition). These, therefore, complement the Qur'an, in that, because Muhammad is the most reliable interpreter of the Qur'an, the collections

of *hadith* help the Muslim community towards a correct understanding.

There are five essential religious duties, known as the 'five pillars of Islam':

■ The *Shahadah* (the profession of faith noted above) is the sincere recitation of the twofold confession concerning God and his chosen messenger: 'There is no god but God [Allah], and Muhammad is his prophet.'

■ The *salat* (formal prayer) must be performed at prescribed hours, five times a day, while facing towards the holy city of Mecca, the focal point of community worship.

■ *Zakat* (the giving of alms), while regarded as worship, is a form of community welfare understood as the sharing of one's wealth out of gratitude for Allah's favour.

■ *Sawm* (fasting) is the religious requirement to abstain from food and drink from sunrise to sunset during Ramadan, the ninth month.

■ If at all possible, every Muslim should perform a pilgrimage (*hajj*) to Mecca. The proper time for the pilgrimage is a period of four days during the twelfth month of the Islamic year, which is lunar.

The Sunni and the Shia

There are two basic groups within Islam: Sunni Muslims and Shia Muslims. The overwhelming majority of Muslims (around 85–90 per cent) are Sunni. Sunnis are therefore considered to be mainstream Islam. Indeed, Sunnis consider Shia Muslims to be members of an unorthodox movement. The historical division between Sunni and Shia Muslims originates in a disagreement over who should succeed Muhammad. When he unexpectedly died, the majority of his followers recognized his companion, Abu Bakr, as the first Caliph. He in turn was followed by three successors. The four came to be referred to as 'the rightly guided Caliphs'. Muslims who accepted this line of succession also accorded the Sunna and *hadith* with great authority. Consequently, they were called Sunni (derived from Sunna). Other followers of Muhammad rejected this line of succession, claiming that, during his lifetime, Muhammad had designated his son-in-law, Ali (the fourth Caliph), to be his successor. These became known as the Party of Ali or *Shi'at 'Ali*. For Shia Muslims, authority resides in the divinely appointed leader of the community, the successor of Ali, the Imam. According to Shiite theology, Allah provides an Imam for each age, although sometimes the Imam is hidden. While the principal source of authority for both groups is the Qur'an, Shia Muslims deny that the Sunni collections of *hadith* are reliable. They are, it is claimed, biased reports designed to undermine the beliefs about the leadership of the Shia community. Consequently, Shiites have compiled their own Qur'anic commentaries. The Shia have since evolved into three main streams, the Imamis, the Zaidis and the Isma'ilis. The Shia, who number only about 40 million, can be found in Iran, the Lebanon, the Indian subcontinent, Yemen, Bahrain and Iraq. Of these, Shia Islam is most prominent in Iran, where it has been the official religion since the 16th century.

Sufism

Another particularly distinctive form of Islam, and one that has attracted great interest in the contemporary Western world, is Sufism or *tasawwuf*, often described as Islamic mysticism. (As is apparent from the articles in this section, many trends and movements within contemporary Islam that can be described as new religions or alternative spiritualities are Sufi in orientation.) From a very early period, mystical ideas began to be developed within Islam. Indeed, Sufism can be understood as a protest movement against a faith that was becoming strongly legalistic and emphasized

obedience to Allah, who was understood as transcendent and wholly other. Some Muslims, however, sought a more devotional, warm and closely personal spirituality. Sufi thinkers called for a life of loving devotion to God. Indeed, the goal within Sufism can be summed up as spiritual union with God through love.

Existing within both Sunni and Shiite Islam, Sufism is organized into *tariqas* (orders, or organized 'paths' of spiritual guidance). Since the 12th century, *tariqas* have become large, disciplined brotherhoods of mystics, each of which are led by a *pir* or *shaikh* (spiritual leader). The teachings of *shaikhs* were spread by their appointed representatives, the *khalifas* – who, in turn, would often set up their own spiritual centres. The different Sufi *shaikhs* and their *khalifas* taught their own particular methods by which a devotee could experience divine closeness and eventually attain union with Allah.

Most Sufism teaches that Allah and the devotee are separate. Just as one needs two human persons for a meaningful loving relationship, so, too, with the divine–human relationship if love and devotion are to be fostered. However, as with mystical paths in other religious traditions, some Sufis have developed understandings of the oneness of God and humanity. Some Sufi thinkers have gone so far as to speak of themselves as identical with God. For example, the important Sufi mystic al-Hallaj (c. 858–922), who was martyred for his controversial ideas, made the famous statement, '*ana'l-haqq*', which has been translated 'I am the Truth'. Although this might not seem too controversial, when one considers that one of the most cherished names for God in Sufism is *al-Haqq* (the Truth), the full force of the statement is apparent.

Islam today

Not only has Islam grown significantly in recent years, but it has also seen the emergence of an intellectual, devotional, ethnic and cultural diversity. For example, some reformists seek to create a form of Islam compatible with the modern Western world, while various revivalist movements view Western secularism and capitalism as a threat to Islamic cultural and religious identity. Yet others identify themselves with particular communities, such as the African-American

*Nation of Islam. Indeed, while Sufism has a growing influence, the most conspicuous trend within contemporary Islam is that commonly labelled 'fundamentalist' or 'Islamicist'. While the term 'fundamentalist' was coined in 1920 to describe a movement to defend the 'fundamental beliefs' of Protestant Christianity, it was later, in 1979, extended to the Iranian revolutionaries to describe their religiously inspired political activism. Since then, the term has been applied to numerous 'right wing' movements, including (in Islam)

Each year around 2 million Muslims make a pilgrimage to Mecca.

Hamas (Israel/Palestine), the Taliban (Afghanistan) and the Tablighi Jama'at (an international proselytizing movement), and it has been perceived as the underlying cause of numerous extreme activities, including suicide bombings, the Rushdie affair, and, most notably, the terrorist attacks on the twin towers of the World Trade Center and the Pentagon on 11 September 2001 (see *Fundamentalisms).

While, historically, Islam has been a religion of the non-Western world, it is today a global

faith, which is spreading throughout the West. This global presence has led to significant engagement with the modern world and to important new developments. Modernist thought within Islam, as David Waines points out,

> has sought in several ways to reduce customary male privilege within the family: by arguing that the Qur'an's true intent supported monogamous marriage, not polygamy; by raising the minimum age of marriage for young men and women and thereby abolishing child marriages; by restricting the male right of divorce and increasing the grounds upon which women may sue for termination of marriage and by adjustment to the traditional laws affecting the custody of children in the event of the dissolution of marriage. Profound structural changes in modern Muslim societies – among them the promotion of equal education for girls and boys and economic pressures forcing women into the job market, male migration in search of better work opportunities – have further eroded the age-old patriarchal edifice.

Moreover, although many new groups and movements within Islam maintain conservative attitudes and, particularly in the West, seek to distinguish themselves from the surrounding culture, there are developments, such as the *Haqqani Naqshbandis or Hazrat Inayat Khan's *Sufi Order of the West, that are far more accommodating and innovative.

The Halveti-Jerrahi Order of Dervishes
Ron Geaves

This Turkish Sufi order (also known as the Jerrahiyyah Order of Dervishes) has its origin in the life and teachings of Pir Nurreddin al-Jerrahi (1678–1721). Pir Nurreddin, the founder of the new *tariqa* (order), was appointed chief judge of Egypt under the Ottomans at the age of 19. However, his departure from Istanbul was delayed and during the delay he met a Sufi of the Jalwatiyyah Branch of the Khalwati Order, al-Hajj Ali Alauddin al-Khalwati Kostendili, who became his teacher. Pir Nurreddin remained in Istanbul under the tutelage of the Sufi master until the latter's death in 1704. At this time, Pir Nurreddin became the new *pir* (spiritual leader) at the age of 26. He established his own order opposite the Canfeda Hatun mosque in the Karagumruk district of Istanbul and the headquarters remains there to the present day.

In the late 1970s, the order was established in Spring Valley, New York, by Tosun Bayrak al-Jerrahi al-Halveti (b. 1926), an artist from Istanbul educated in the West who had returned to Turkey to rediscover traditional Sufi teachings. After initiation into the order, Tosun returned to the United States and established a Sufi centre (*dergah*). He is the *shaikh* (spiritual leader) for the United States, but the overall leadership of the order remains in Istanbul under Sefer Efendi, who occasionally visits the American offshoot. The order practises traditional Turkish Sufism, including *semeh* (circle dancing), *dhikr* (remembrance of Allah through chanting and music), *khalweh* (retreat), fasting, ritual cleanliness, vigils and silence.

Although initially attracting young American converts from the 1960s counter-culture, the order has increasingly become a centre for the immigrant and African-Caribbean Muslim population. Shaikh Tosun has been instrumental in translating several important texts of traditional Sufi literature. The order also has small branches in Britain, Italy, Spain, Canada, Argentina, Brazil and Peru. It has recently become involved in charitable relief work in the Balkans and other parts of the Muslim world.

The Haqqani Naqshbandis
Ron Geaves

The Haqqani Naqshbandis have their historical origins in Damascus and their cultural roots in the Ottoman empire. Although they trace their roots back through the Naqshbandi Order (*tariqa*) to the Indian branch, linking themselves to the great Indian master Shaikh Ahmad Sirhindi (d. 1625), they returned to the Middle East through the initiation of Murad ibn Ali al-Bukhari (d. 1720), who made Damascus his centre of activities, travelling extensively throughout the Middle East. By the 1880s, there were over 50 centres in Istanbul alone.

Historically, the Haqqani Naqshbandis would have remained a traditional Sufi order, and consequently of no interest to a book on new and alternative religions, if it had not been for the ground-breaking work of Shaikh Muhammad Nazim Adil al-Haqqani (b. 1922) in attracting non-Muslims from the counter-culture of North America, Britain and other parts of northern Europe. Shaikh Nazim began his missionary work in Europe after the death of his master, Shaikh Abdullah ad-Daghestani, in 1973, although he had already been active in his own home on the island of Cyprus. After 20 years of living with his master, undergoing numerous spiritual retreats and completing over 27 pilgrimages to Mecca, Shaikh Nazim began to visit London regularly, using the Cypriot Muslim community as a base for his activities. Some young Germans had already become his followers after meeting him in Damascus. It is to be assumed that this meeting with Western non-Muslims first triggered his desire to establish the teachings of Islam in the West through the vehicle of Sufism. In 1991, Shaikh Nazim visited the United States, where there are now over 30 centres dedicated to establishing the Haqqani Naqshbandis.

Shaikh Nazim never loses sight of the fact that he is a Muslim and therefore his first concern is to promote the final revelation of Allah to both Muslims and non-Muslims. However, his own considerable charisma and his roots in Islamic mystical practice have been significant contributions to his success in attracting converts. Shaikh Nazim also maintains a tolerant approach to the outer proscriptions of Islam, although he is himself scrupulous in their observance. In this way, he is different from many other Muslim missionaries, in that he relates to newcomers according to their understanding and never criticizes their current beliefs and practices. He does not insist that they become Muslims when joining the order, and, if they do, he allows them to develop according to their capacity and desire to embrace their new faith. Shaikh Nazim is very aware of the situation of many westerners seeking spirituality, the ethos of New Age spiritualities, and the belief that there is a common ground underlying and underpinning all forms of religious expression. His openness and tolerance to this viewpoint has enabled him to accept invitations to speak to several religious movements. He has stayed at Buddhist monasteries and been the guest of various Hindu-orientated spiritual movements in Britain.

In his speeches, Shaikh Nazim is often critical of conventional religious forms, either inside or outside Islam, arguing that, above all, a tradition must have access for its followers to the experience of the Divine Presence. Shaikh Nazim emphasizes religious experience over every other dimension of religion and teaches that religious leaders need to be able to connect their followers to an experience of the divine. It is Shaikh Nazim's charismatic presence, his willingness to visit the centres towards which young seekers have gravitated in their search for fulfilment, and his message – imbued with tolerant universalism and the focus on spiritual experience – that undoubtedly has made the Haqqani Naqshbandis a significant presence among Sufi movements teaching outside the Muslim world. The Haqqani Naqshbandis are one of the very few traditional Sufi orders that have been able to transcend particular ethnic groupings in the allegiance of their supporters and develop a base that is not restricted to a particular cultural following. This has been achieved in spite of strong dynastic roots in Damascus and a large number of followers of Turkish–Cypriot origin.

The success of the order has invited criticism from other traditional Sufi orders, especially those from the Indian subcontinent, who have also established themselves in the West, but have so far only been able to attract followers from within their own ethnic community. The criticism usually highlights Shaikh Nazim's tolerance and his acceptance of new recruits without necessarily establishing them in strict obedience to the requirements of Islam and the minutiae of everyday injunctions that can be found in orthodox interpretations of the religion.

The Bahá'í Faith
Mike McMullen

The Bahá'í Faith is the world's most recent 'world religion', claiming over 5 million followers worldwide. The Bahá'í Faith began in 19th-century Persia (modern-day Iran), and thus grows out of a Shiite Islamic context. Bahá'í history begins with the religious figure known as the Báb (which in Arabic means 'the gate'), born in 1819 as Siyyid 'Alí-Muhammad in Shíráz, Iran. A merchant by profession, in 1844 the Báb began teaching new religious ideas among the Muslim population, gathering many followers and angering the ruling mullahs (Islamic clergy). The Báb claimed to fulfil many of the expected prophecies of Islam, and saw as his chief mission to herald the coming of 'Him

Whom God Shall Make Manifest', a prophet of greater importance who would lead all of humankind into an era of peace. This prophet would be called Bahá'u'lláh, which in Arabic means 'The Glory of God'. The Báb was executed in 1850 by the Persian government to try to end this pioneering religious movement.

Mírzá Husayn-'Alí was born on 12 November 1817 into a noble family from Mázindarán, Iran. Initially a follower of the Báb, he was imprisoned in 1853 in Tehran, Iran, as part of the continuing persecution of Bábís (followers of the Báb). Bahá'í history records that in prison he had a religious vision revealing that he was 'Him Whom God Shall Make Manifest' as foretold by the Báb. As such, Bahá'ís believe that Bahá'u'lláh fulfils the expected prophesies of *all* the world's religious traditions at the same time: for example, Bahá'u'lláh is the fifth incarnation of the Buddha for Buddhists, the reincarnation of Krishna for Hindus, the Messiah for the Jews, the return of Christ for Christians, and so on. Thus, Bahá'u'lláh is the expected prophet of all the world's religions, whose teachings will finally usher in the long-awaited kingdom of God.

Bahá'u'lláh was released from prison after four months, was exiled to various locations throughout the Middle East, and began teaching his revolutionary and progressive message and attracting followers (including most Bábís, who accepted his claims). Finally, in 1868, Bahá'u'lláh and his followers were permanently exiled to 'Akká, Palestine, the prison-city of the Ottoman Empire (near present-day Haifa, Israel, the location of the Bahá'í World Centre).

While imprisoned and in exile, Bahá'u'lláh wrote nearly 15,000 documents – what Bahá'ís call 'Tablets', which range in length from a few pages to book-length treatises on government, philosophy, law, ethics, spiritual life and personal conduct. These partially comprise the canon of Bahá'í scripture. When Bahá'u'lláh died of natural causes in 1892, he left behind a growing movement, and a written will and testament that named his eldest son, 'Abdu'l-Bahá, as his successor and the authoritative interpreter of Bahá'í scripture. After 'Abdu'l-Bahá's death in 1921, Shoghi Effendi Rabbání, the great-grandson of Bahá'u'lláh, led the Bahá'í Faith until his death in 1957. Shortly thereafter, in 1963, the Universal House of Justice was elected by the Bahá'ís of the world, in accordance with the strictures delineated by Bahá'u'lláh's writings. The Universal House of Justice is the nine-member supreme governing body of the Bahá'í Faith. Bahá'ís believe that the Universal House of Justice receives guidance from God, is infallible and is the institutional foundation for the kingdom of God.

Three basic principles summarize the beliefs and ideology of the Bahá'í Faith: the oneness of God, the oneness of religion and the oneness of humanity. Bahá'ís believe that there is only one God, the creator and sustainer of all life. While invoked by many names, all persons of faith, according to Bahá'ís, are worshipping the same Divine Presence. All created things bear the sign of the Divine Reality, so that all creation mirrors, to varying degrees, the beauty and glory of God. God transcends the creation, but reveals himself through what Bahá'ís call 'Manifestations of God'. These Manifestations are the founders of the world's religions, all sent forth by the same one God to be the educators of humanity, teaching us about the nature of spiritual reality and how to treat one another and live with each other. The Manifestations have founded the various historic civilizations around the world, and include, but are not limited to, Abraham, Krishna, Buddha, Zoroaster, Moses, Jesus, Muhammad, the Báb, and most recently, Bahá'u'lláh. Bahá'ís believe that while Bahá'u'lláh is the *latest* Manifestation sent by God, he will not be the *last*.

A Bahá'í temple in Delhi.

The oneness of God is related to the second major principle of the Bahá'í Faith: the oneness of religion. In order to understand the universalizing goal of Bahá'í ideology and its promotion of global order and solidarity, one must understand the central ideological concept for Bahá'ís: progressive revelation. Bahá'ís' vision of global unity includes the claim that all of the world's major religions are only evolutionary stages in God's plan to educate and unify the whole planet – in effect, there is only one religion, but it is revealed by God in distinct historical stages. Bahá'ís claim that the *spiritual* truths of all religions are the same; religions appear to be in conflict due to their *social* laws, which differ because of the need throughout history for new moral and social codes to unify large segments of humanity. Differences in the social laws reflect the different requirements for social and moral solidarity of the age in which they were revealed. Bahá'u'lláh also condemns discrepancies in prophecy or conflict among religious ideologies as human-made misinterpretations.

Bahá'ís do admit, however, that there are differences in the content (but not the function) of the messages brought by the Manifestations of God. For Bahá'ís, there is a twofold function of religion: the spiritual education of individual souls and the social solidarity of humanity through various laws and institutions. Examples of *spiritual laws* governing Bahá'ís are laws that regulate daily prayer, fasting, sexual morality, abstinence from drugs and alcohol, and burial. Examples of Bahá'í *social laws* and principles that establish the foundation of a global civilization include laws surrounding marriage and divorce; the founding of a single auxiliary language that every person on the planet would learn; a world government that includes a global executive, legislature and court system; collective security and the reduction of the nations' armaments; the elimination of racism, sexism and prejudice;

the reduction in the extremes of wealth and poverty; and universal education.

The final key principle of Bahá'í belief is the oneness of humanity. Bahá'ís teach that all humanity is created by the same God, and we should see each other as members of one human family. A quote frequently cited by Bahá'ís comes from their scripture: 'The earth is but one country and mankind its citizens.' Bahá'ís claim that every religion was sent by God to unify and organize larger and larger collections of humanity, starting with the family, and expanding to include the clan, tribe and nation. The purpose of the Bahá'í Faith is to unify all of humanity into one family (considered the culmination of social evolution on this planet), which can only be done by eliminating racism and all other forms of prejudice (national, ethnic, religious, gender, etc.). Distinctive to this religious movement is the explicit manner in which Bahá'ís connect local race unity efforts and their global worldview, and their confidence that this hoped-for global civilization will be achieved. Bahá'ís declare that the elimination of all forms of prejudice is a fundamental requirement for achieving global unity and peace.

A Bahá'í's daily life is governed by the personal laws given to the Bahá'í community by Bahá'u'lláh, and include requirements such as daily prayer, fasting, study of Bahá'í scripture, monetary contributions to Bahá'í funds, and pilgrimage to the Bahá'í World Centre. The organizational participation of the average Bahá'í is dictated by the rituals of the Bahá'í calendar. Bahá'í theology states that whenever a new Manifestation of God appears to humanity, they bring with them a new calendar to institutionalize a new pattern of worship, festivals and holy day celebrations. In the future, Bahá'ís say, the Bahá'í calendar, which was first proposed by the Báb and sanctioned by Bahá'u'lláh, will become the accepted global standard for dividing the year. The last month in the 19-month Bahá'í year is the period of fasting, where Bahá'ís fast

from sunup to sundown (similar to the Muslim fast during Ramadan).

On the first day of each Bahá'í month, Bahá'ís gather for the Nineteen-day Feast, the central worship experience in the Bahá'í Faith, and which only Bahá'ís are allowed to attend. The Feast consists of three loosely structured parts: a devotional period, where the writings and prayers of the Báb, Bahá'u'lláh and/or 'Abdu'l-Bahá are read; an administrative period, where the chairperson of the local spiritual assembly leads community-wide consultation on important issues facing the community; and a social portion, involving fellowship and refreshments. Feasts are usually held in members' homes, although some communities own or rent a building designated as the 'Bahá'í Centre'. It is usually the 'host' or 'hostess' of the Feast who prepares the refreshments, and chooses the readings from the Bahá'í writings (since there are no clergy). This reinforces the 'democratic' nature of Bahá'í collective ritual, as individual community members are each given the chance to shape the devotional services.

The Shadhili-Akbari Sufi Order
Ron Geaves

Although the Shadhili-Akbari Sufi order is no longer found as a significant presence in the West, it remains very important for those interested in the history of Sufi presence outside of Muslim countries. The Shadhili-Akbari *tariqa* (order) was founded by Shaikh Abd al-Rahman at the end of the 19th century in Damascus, Syria. Shaikh Abd al-Rahman combined his own branch of the Shadhiliya, known as the Arabiyya, with the teachings of Ibn Arabi (sometimes called Shaikh al-Akbar), thus giving the new order its name.

The resulting synthesis produced an order much more concerned to promote Sufism as primordial universal mysticism than adherence to Islam. In 1904, Shaikh Abd

☞ *continued on page 138*

CONTEMPORARY SUFISM
Ron Geaves

Sufism can be simply defined as Islamic mysticism, and in this context one of the best and most succinct statements belongs to Reynold Nicholson, a scholar of Sufism: 'The transformation of the One transcendent God of Islam into One Real Being who dwells and works everywhere, and whose throne is not less, but more, in the human heart than in the heaven of heavens.' However, there is some difficulty in using this definition in regard to exploring, for example, Sufism in the West. Although many Western adherents to Sufi belief and practice would be happy with the self-definition of aspiring to be mystics, the dominant Muslim population who have settled in the West through economic or political migration and belong to the many Sufi *tariqas* (orders) would find the label problematic. Many Muslim Sufis do not consider themselves to be mystical in any sense, and a large number of the Western adherents define themselves as Sufis but do not consider themselves to be Muslims, even when belonging to eminent orders that remain rooted in Islam. Most Muslims regard Sufism as simply the inner dimension of Islam that must accompany the external domain –

discovered by observation of the shariah (Islamic law). Those who follow both the inner and the outer dimensions regard themselves as committed Muslims and may abjure the self-definition of 'Sufi' as distracting from their primary loyalty to Islam. On the other hand, Western adherents often avoid the outer manifestations of Islam completely, preferring to adopt a universal Sufism.

Types of Sufism
In order to categorize the range of practices that occur in the Muslim community I have chosen to adopt a sliding scale based on the relationship of religion and ethnicity as follows:

■ The organization of orders around ethnic groups: This category refers to various groups of Muslims who belong to orders that enable them to maintain strong ethnic boundaries through loyalty to a *shaikh* (spiritual leader), who shares their place of origin before migration. These will often be the type of order that focuses its attention upon a shrine cult maintained by family descendants of the original saint.

■ The emergence of separation from ethnicity: This category refers to *shaikhs*, leading a variety of orders, who have begun to challenge the relationship

between religious affiliation and ethnic background. Often these *shaikhs* will lead renewals or revitalization of an order in which the emergence of a charismatic saint brings a renewed focus on spirituality.

■ The transcendence of ethnicity: Whereas the success of the charismatic *shaikh* may not necessarily fully emerge from a distinct ethnic group, in some cases the fame of the *shaikh* has been able to transcend the region of origin and thereby develop transnational orders representing a diversity of ethnic groups and nationalities among the followers.

■ Universal Sufism: The emphasis is on the mystical element of Islam framed within a worldview of a universal mysticism drawing upon Hindu, Buddhist, Christian, Egyptian and Gnostic traditions. It removes the Muslim content, which is perceived as a cultural historic accretion to a universal and eternal message concerning the human relationship with the divine. This version of Sufism not only challenges the idea of ethnic loyalty, but removes Sufism from its location in Islam.

In some ways, all of these categories of Sufism can be regarded as alternative religions. Firstly, Sufism remains an alternative discourse in the world of contemporary Islam, challenging various forms of orthodoxy. Secondly, all of the categories exist in the Muslim community and therefore co-exist alongside other dominant worldviews. Thirdly, the last two categories have been able to draw recruits and converts from an alternative counter-culture.

The contemporary appeal of Sufism

Sufism continues to attract converts either to its universal form or into the fold of Islam itself through its particular manifestation of mysticism. A number of movements have been successful in promoting the teachings of Islam through the vehicle of Sufism and thus reach out beyond the confines

Sufi Muslims sway to the beat of religious songs during a ceremony marking the last days of the holy month of Ramadan.

of migrant communities to converts. Generally, converts in the West came from alternative counter-cultures at the end of the 1960s and increasingly into the 1970s. These were usually as a result of contact with Sufi orders in North Africa, South Asia, Turkey and Egypt by 'truth-seekers' who travelled worldwide to enlarge their experience and make contact with Eastern spirituality. The contact with Western converts, in turn, brought a number of Sufi *shaikhs* to the West to create outposts of their orders in northern Europe and North America. However, it is unusual for Sufi orders that arrived in the West through migration processes to make inroads into the new community, as the *shaikhs* and their followers tend to remain as a resource for the ethnic Muslim community where they originated. Many Western converts to Sufism are already experienced in spiritual and

physical self-discipline arising from their previous contact with Buddhism, Daoism or Hindu-based religious movements. However, contact with the above forms of Sufism also brings the practitioner into contact with Islam, which offers not only an inner experiential dimension, but also a comprehensive way of life that introduces a code of morality based upon a historical monotheistic revelation with exclusive truth claims. Islam, therefore, offers the convert both the certainty of historical revelation and the support of close-knit communities perceived to be a warm alternative to the breakdown of social institutions in the West. Sufism provides the internal dimension of mystical experience and the possibility of charismatic leadership.

Even in the first half of the 20th century, Western individuals were attracted to Sufism through the efforts of high-profile figures such as Idries Shah (1924–96) or Hazrat Inayat Khan (1882–1927) who came to Europe and North America to teach. Kim Knott, a scholar of contemporary religion, has correctly noted that the new religious movements of the 1960s and 1970s were preceded by an 'interest in alternative religious philosophies, psychotherapy, esotericism and spiritualism' that had

been developing in the previous 80 years – for example, the *Theosophical Society, the *School of Economic Science, the *Anthroposophical movement, and *Gurdjieff and Ouspensky groups. These movements were highly eclectic and lent themselves to the introduction of a different kind of Sufism that placed itself within an unfolding mystical revelation that drew upon Gnostic, neo-platonic, Christian, Buddhist and Hindu influences in addition to Islam.

There have always been Sufis who have departed from strict obedience to Islam's exoteric code of law but maintain a loose Muslim allegiance through birth and culture. Such figures have generally asserted that the primacy of their own individual experience of ecstasy or mystical union has provided a deeper and more personal connection to Allah that overrides the dictates of Muslim law (perceived to be a tool for the unenlightened masses to come closer to the Divine Presence). This alternative Sufism developed two main forms: the Qalandaris and the Malamatis. The Qalandaris, often associated with wandering dervishes or fakirs, focused on the individual experience of the ecstatic heart and, as individual wanderers, had little contact

with established orders. Many maintained celibacy, and in the context of the Indian subcontinent were little different from itinerant Hindu sadhus. The Malamatis, on the other hand, rejected all outer manifestations of religion, worked in normal professions and never displayed their spiritual experiences to people around them. The spiritual focus of the Malamati is not on union with God but loss of ego-consciousness. Both of these groups within Sufism have had a substantial influence on the development of universal Sufism in the West.

Hazrat Inayat Khan, the first Sufi to teach in the West outside the confines of Islam and founder of the *Sufi Movement and the *Sufi Order of the West, promoted a universal Sufism influenced by devotional Hindu traditions and the monism of the *Upanishads*. As a seeker he had been eclectic and drawn towards the renunciate fakirs loosely linked to the Chishti order in India and themselves part of the Qalandari tradition. However, the most significant figure in promoting an awareness of Sufism in the West has to be Idries Shah, a prolific author of over 35 books selling over 15 million copies. Although his tales of Mullah Nasruddin represented the ideal of the Qalandari, there is no doubt

that Idries Shah displayed all the characteristics of the Malamati form of Sufism. He was not inclined to rejection of the world or outer displays of Sufi identity but agreed with the Qalandari emphasis on experience and rejection of the dead wood of organized religion. Idries Shah taught that Sufis have been present in all cultures and that the Sufi truth lies at the heart of all religions. For Idries Shah, Sufism was above all a way to human self-fulfilment and development through ego-transformation. Idries Shah was able to move fluently into European society and was more at ease with the world of the dinner party than the cultural milieu of the rural Sufi.

Both Sufism within the fold of Islam and universal Sufism continue to attract Western seekers of an experiential truth. There is considerable movement between the two camps. Those who are attracted to Islam through Sufism may move back to universal Sufism, especially attracted to new developments such as the New Age, with its focus on holistic living, alternative healing and ecological themes. However, many devout Muslim converts may have begun their journey by being interested in the eclecticism of universal Sufism.

al-Rahman initiated John-Gustav Agueli (1869–1917), a painter and former member of the *Theosophical Society who had already converted to Islam after visiting Egypt. Agueli was made a *muqaddam* (given authority to initiate others into the order) with the name of Abd al-Hadi al-Maghrabi. Abd al-Hadi published journals in Cairo and Europe, vigorously promoting universal wisdom teaching as primordial Sufism.

In 1912, Abd al-Hadi met and initiated Rene Guenon (1886–1951), who took the name Shaikh Abd al-Wahid Yahya. Although Rene Guenon also believed in the perennial philosophy that asserts a common primordial esoteric core at the heart of all religions, he also taught that there is an outer form made up of laws and ritual practices that derive from and support the inner dimension. This enabled him to feel more sympathy for traditional Muslim forms and he migrated to Egypt in 1930 where he was initiated into the Hamadiyya, a more traditional branch of the Shadhiliya. Guenon married a Muslim, brought up his children in the faith and was held in high regard by his fellow Muslims in Egypt.

In the 1930s, Rene Guenon met Frithjof Schuon (Shaikh Isa Nur ad-Din) who was already a *muqaddam* in the Alawiya, a sub-branch of the Shadhiliya. Consequently, he was able to initiate individuals into the order and Guenon introduced him to over a hundred Europeans who were initiated into Sufism. The Shadhiliya Order and its sub-branches, the Alawiya and the Darqawiya, have continued throughout the 20th century as popular destinations for Western converts to Sufism.

The Sufi Movement (International Sufi Movement)
Ron Geaves

The Sufi Movement was the name given to the organization created in 1923 by Hazrat Inayat Khan (1882–1927) to replace the 'Sufi

Order' he created when he left India in 1910. It is claimed that Inayat Khan originally wanted his son, Vilayat Khan (b. 1916), to be appointed as his successor after his death. However, Vilayat Khan showed no interest in picking up the reins of his father's work until the 1960s, when he formed the *Sufi Order of the West. In the meantime, the Sufi Movement was taken over by Inayat Khan's brother and then by a cousin. In 1988, Hidayat Inayat Khan, another of Hazrat Inayat Khan's sons, was appointed the leader of the Sufi Movement with the title of Representative-General. Another prominent leader of the movement is Dr H.J. Witteveen, also known as Murshid Karimbakhsh, a Dutch citizen who was initiated into the movement in 1921. In his book, *Universal Sufism*, he provides a good introduction to the history and teachings of the movement. The headquarters of the Sufi Movement is based in The Hague, Holland.

The Sufi Movement is less inclined to the eclecticism of the New Age than the Sufi Order of the West and focuses its attention on five separate activities.

The Brotherhood/Sisterhood Activity exemplifies the central teaching that God is not found in sacred buildings but in the human heart. The ideal is to promote universal brotherhood and explores ideas that bring together Eastern and Western thought through lectures and discussion.

Universal Worship, open to anyone who wishes to participate, was developed by Inayat Khan in 1921 with the intention of introducing a form of worship that would respect all the world's founder-teachers and scriptures. Symbols are brought together from all the world's major religious traditions, various scriptures are read, prayers created by Inayat Khan are performed and blessings are given to all present.

The School of Inner Culture, or the Esoteric Activity, is the core activity of the movement, where the teachings of universal

Sufism as promoted by Inayat Khan are revealed to initiates. Inner Culture refers to the realization of the self and the movement requires initiates to take a *bayat* (an oath of loyalty) through a qualified guide or teacher. Progress along this esoteric path takes place through gradual introduction to the corpus of teachings left behind by Inayat Khan.

The traditional Chishti Sufi order, in which Inayat Khan had his roots, retains a strong tradition of healing, utilizing both spiritual power and herbs. The Sufi Movement has expanded these into an all-inclusive, holistic, alternative medical practice based upon the importance of mental equilibrium for physical well-being. The central philosophy behind these activities is that each human being contains the healing power of the divine within themselves.

Students are introduced to Symbology, a deeper understanding of the symbolic in daily life. This is taught by focusing on two ceremonies: Zirat and the Element Ritual. Zirat attempts to free the mind from unwanted thoughts that are an obstacle to the spiritual path. The Element Ritual is a form of dance choreographed by followers and claimed to be based on ancient Zoroastrian dances.

In 1997, the Sufi Movement created the Federation of the Sufi Message as an umbrella organization for Sufi orders that were united in their devotion to Inayat Khan and his teachings. The present members are the International Sufi Movement and the Sufi Islamia Ruhaniat Society. The Sufi Order International (formerly the Sufi Order of the West) has declined to participate.

The Nation of Islam
Theodore Gabriel

The organization known as the Nation of Islam is fundamentally an expression of the frustration felt by African-Americans after many decades of discrimination and oppression. Although slavery was abolished in 1865, African-Americans continued to suffer from discrimination, social ostracization and a lack of equal opportunities in the 20th century.

The movement was originated by a charismatic and enterprising individual, Wallace Dodd Ford (1877–1934), who later took the Arabic title 'Fard' (Righteousness) and the name 'Muhammad' to signify conversion to Islam. Fard Muhammad was not actually black, according to some scholars, but the child of a white and a Maori. A.I. Palmer opines that Fard Muhammad drew inspiration from the Moorish Science Temple, founded in 1913 by Timothy Drew, and The Universal Negro Improvement Association, founded in 1914 by Marcus Garvey.

Fard Muhammad incorporated ideas from Islam into his ideology, and the organization later came to be known as the Nation of Islam. The incorporation of Islam was most probably to distinguish the members from the white majority and its association with Christianity, and also because of the egalitarian ideals of Islam, in which emancipating slaves is considered to be a pious act.

In time, Fard Muhammad came to consider himself an incarnation of Allah and the creator of the world. He also presented himself to his followers as the Messiah of the Judeo-Christian tradition and the Mahdi of Islam. (The Mahdi is the title given to the 12th Imam of Ithna Ashari Shiism, who is believed to be still living [The Hidden Imam], and who is expected to come back at some undisclosed time.) Fard Muhammad designated a black worker, Elijah Poole (1898–1975), whom he renamed Elijah Muhammad, as his successor in 1931.

Elijah Muhammad enunciated a myth that depicted blacks as the original human beings created by Allah, and whites as the result of a genetic experiment conducted by a black scientist named Yacub. The whites would be

Malcolm X addresses a civil rights rally in 1963 in support of desegregation in Birmingham, Alabama.

leadership and steered the sect into Islamic orthodoxy under a new name – the American Muslim Mission. This led to a rift in the organization. Louis Farrakhan (b. 1933), a charismatic musician and orator, established a rival sect, called the Original Nation of Islam, based on Elijah Muhammad's teachings. Farrakhan, who organized a 'million man march' to Washington in 1995 to rival Dr Martin Luther King's 1963 march on the capital, attracts considerable media attention, though the majority of the members are with Warith Deen Muhammad. He deems himself to be the spokesperson and champion of African-Americans. In recent times, Warith Deen Muhammad is reported to have made friendly overtures to Farrakhan, as he believes Farrakhan is leading his organization closer to orthodox Islam. The Nation of Islam (as the two groups are collectively known) does not release membership figures, but it is estimated that there are from 25,000 to 100,000 adherents in the United States, Canada and Britain.

destroyed by blacks at the 'end of times', now imminent, a day interpreted as the judgement day of which Islam speaks. Blacks would then rule in a paradise set up by the Mahdi/Messiah.

One of the favourite disciples of Elijah Muhammad was Malcolm Little (1925–65), renamed Malcolm X. Many of the members of the Nation of Islam took X as their surname in order to reject their original surnames, which were those of the slave masters of their ancestors. Malcolm X became a spokesperson for the organization, but later on wanted to disassociate himself from the Nation of Islam, and to adopt more orthodox Islamic beliefs. This led to a rift in the organization and eventually to the murder of Malcolm X in 1965, allegedly by members of Elijah Muhammad's faction. After Elijah Muhammad's death in 1975, his son, Warith Deen Muhammad, took over the

Subud
Christopher Partridge

Subud was founded by Pak Subuh (meaning 'dawn'), born Muhammad Sukarno Sumohadiwidjojo (1901–87) in Indonesia to a Muslim family. In 1924 he had an experience that violently shook his body. Interpreting it spiritually, he referred to it as his first *latihan kejiwaan* ('spiritual exercise' or 'opening'). It was to be followed by several similar experiences between 1924 and 1928. When he was 32 he claimed to have received his culminating revelation, during which he had an out-of-body experience that took him beyond space and time to the 'living presences' of Moses, Jesus and Muhammad.

Keeping these experiences to himself for several years, he continued his everyday secular life. However, in 1932 he gave his first spiritual training session. The following year he resigned from secular employment and began spreading the *latihan*. Followers were encouraged to call him *Bapak* (father).

In 1954, Hussein Rofé, a Syrian Muslim who had been educated in Britain, travelled to Indonesia looking for 'the wisdom of the East'. He met Subuh and was 'opened'. He wrote an article for a British magazine on Subuh's teaching and travelled to Cyprus and Turkey to spread it. On returning to England, he took Subuh to 'Coombe Springs', a mansion in Kingston upon Thames, where John Bennett, a British Army interpreter who had for many years been a follower of Gurdjieff, was now teaching the Gurdjieffian system (known as 'the Work'; see *Gurdjieff and Ouspensky Groups). Bennett was very attracted to Subuh's teaching and eventually wrote one of the most significant texts of the movement, *Concerning Subud* (1958). As to Subuh's significance for those who follow his teachings, while, strictly speaking, he is not regarded as a prophet, guru or teacher (because only God is the teacher), he is understood to be an important spiritual guide.

As to the name Subud, unlikely as it may seem it is not derived from the name of the founder – the similarity is merely coincidental. In 1947, the early group of 300 members needed to be registered in Indonesia, so Subuh sought spiritual guidance and 'received' the word 'Subud', meaning, in Javanese, 'a perfect fit', 'fortunate' and 'worthwhile'. Bapak said that it could also be interpreted as meaning 'zero' and 'empty'. Along with this, Subuh pointed out that SU-BU-D was an acronym for the following words: *susila* (excellent character and right living), *buddhi* (the divine essence within an individual), and *dharma* (the potential ability to surrender completely to the will of God).

It is important to understand that, while Subud is sometimes understood to be Islamic (Subuh was born into a Muslim family), and while many followers will, for example, observe Ramadan, followers of Subud do not regard it as a religion, let alone an Islamic sect. Subud is understood to be simply a way of strengthening one's faith and spiritual practice, whatever faith or spiritual practice that might be. As Matthew Barry Sullivan, a follower of Subuh, points out: 'I am not a Muslim. I am a Christian, who has been a member of Subud since it first arrived in the West from Indonesia 36 years ago. Subud, moreover, is not a faith, nor is it a sect. It is not connected with any system of belief. It is an experience.' There is no creed, no necessary teachings, only the *latihan*, the Subud practice of standing and 'waiting to receive'. In fact, while these were generally understood to be particular periods of time, in 1977 the theory of the 'continuous *latihan*' was developed. The whole of one's life should be such that it is open to 'receiving'. Rejecting the occult, the magical, the paranormal and the fantastical, Subud seeks to cater for the spiritual needs of ordinary persons, whatever their personal religious beliefs.

The Subud International Association (which in 1998 reported 385 groups and 12,000 members) consists of a world council, nine zonal representatives and 18 international helpers. There are also national and regional bodies and local groups. That said, members insist that this is not a hierarchical structure and emphasize equality and 'common feeling'.

The Sufi Order of the West (Sufi Order International)
Ron Geaves

The earliest phase of Western interest in Sufism began with Hazrat Inayat Khan (1882–1927) who left India for Europe and the United States in 1910, where he founded the 'Sufi Order', which later grew into the *Sufi Movement and the Sufi Order of the

West. Inayat Khan had trained as a professional musician under the guidance of his grandfather, who had brought up his grandson with an attitude of tolerance towards all religions. The young Inayat Khan began to express a deep interest in religion and spirituality and sought the company of Indian holy men of all persuasions. However, he finally accepted the spiritual guidance of Shaikh Sayyid Muhammad Abu Hashim Madani of the Chishti Sufi order. After his master's death he continued to question and learn from various teachers from both Hindu and Muslim backgrounds. A Brahmin seer foretold that Inayat Khan's future would be in the West.

Inayat Khan taught an eclectic universal Sufism in which he asserted that true Sufism is above any individual religion and based on direct experience of inner truth. All world religions possess this inner kernel and everything else is cultural accretion. His teachings embody elements central to traditional Chishti Sufism and Advaita Vedanta (Hindu philosophical thought). Central to his teachings was his belief in the role of music in attuning the human soul to the divine unity pervading the universe.

In 1923, Inayat Khan founded the Sufi Movement, which was taken over by his brother on his death in 1927 and later inherited by a cousin. However, the movement was divided in two by the decision of Inayat Khan's son, Vilayat Khan (b. 1916), to pick up the reins of his father's work in the 1960s. The leadership of the Sufi Movement objected, despite the claim that Inayat Khan had originally wanted his son to succeed him. Vilayat Khan established the Sufi Order of the West to promote the inner teachings of his father. Initially, Vilayat Khan was followed by the original disciples of his father who had been recruited from primarily middle-class seekers, often with a background in the arts, but then began to attract large numbers from the counter-culture. The order now attracts considerable numbers of spiritual seekers and

has grown since the 1970s. It is well established in North America, Britain and western Europe and remains eclectic. The esoteric school for promoting the ideals and practices of universal mysticism remains at the heart of the order's work. Central to introducing students to the order's teachings is the Dance of Universal Peace created by Sam Lewis. The dance is accompanied by chants that often retain the Muslim origin of the order but are also likely to be drawn from other faiths. Initiates are introduced in stages to the works of Inayat Khan under the guidance of a self-selected guide, but they do not consider themselves to be Muslims. The major emphasis is on retreats but contemporary seekers are just as likely to find themselves involved with all-inclusive, holistic, alternative medical practices and spiritual psychotherapeutic systems that promote mental equilibrium rather than practices that have evolved out of traditional Islamic mysticism.

United Nuwaubian Nation of Moors
Theodore Gabriel

The United Nuwaubian Nation of Moors (or the Ansaru Allah Community – in Arabic, literally 'Helpers of God') is one of the numerous black new religious movements associated with Islam that have sprung up in the United States, such as the *Nation of Islam, the Black Sunnis and the Submitters Institute. The United Nuwaubian Nation of Moors is distinct from other groups because of its periodically shifting theologies and ideologies, and its claim to be an 'extraterrestrial religion'. Its founder, Dwight York (b. 1945), who is said to be a former convict arraigned in the 1960s for assault and possession of a dangerous weapon, calls himself 'The Lamb', which incidentally was the title assumed by David Koresh of the *Branch Davidians. In 1965 he converted to Islam in

Brooklyn and gathered several followers around him who dressed in exotic costumes and peddled their sectarian literature on the streets. The women were veiled and worked in publishing and mailing the sect's tracts.

At one stage, York assumed the name 'Rabboni Y'shua Baar El Hardy' and redefined his followers as Jewish and the title of the cult as the Nubian Hebrew Mission. They were characterized as the 'real Hebrews' as opposed to the 'so-called Jews of the cursed seed from Canaan'.

The United Nuwaubian Nation of Moors holds a concoction of beliefs, incorporating ideas from Islam, Judaism, *ufology, quantum physics and ancient Egyptian religion. The cult is also known as the Ansaru Allah Community, the Yamassee Native American Tribe, Sons of the Green Light, the Egyptian Church of Karast (Christ) and the Ancient and Mystic Order of Melchizedek. Dwight York goes by various names and titles, such as Imperial Grand Potentate Reverend Doctor Michael Z. York, Malachi York, Chief Black Eagle, Amun-Re (an Egyptian deity), Pharaoh Neter A'aferti Atum-Re and Nayya Malachizodoq-El. In 1993, York purchased a ranch in Eatonton, Putnam County, Georgia, erected exotic gates, and pyramids in the Egyptian style decorated with hieroglyphics and Egyptian figurines, and named the

The Nuwaubian complex outside Eatonton. A white pylon painted with Egyptian hieroglyphics marks the entrance to a 476-acre compound.

complex Tama Re (Egypt of the West). York claims he came from the planet Illyuwn in the 19th galaxy in a spaceship on 18 March 1970, and states that Bennett's comet, which was visible that year, was actually his spaceship. The Nuwaubians believe that at some point in the near future a spacecraft from Illyuwn will come and gather 144,000 Nuwaubians to be taken to the planet Rizq for rebirth.

Although mostly African-Americans, the Nuwaubians claim to be descendants of ancient Egyptians, who migrated to the North American continent prior to the continental drift, and call themselves Tahits or Tu'af, descendants of the ancestor Tah (meaning 'the opener').

The United Nuwaubian Nation of Moors does not claim to be a new religion. Members believe that by joining them a person will gain Nuwaubu – sound/right reasoning, the way the ancient Egyptian deities thought. The leader gives instruction on the successful way of living, how to enjoy good health, and how to gain an abundance of material wealth. Members are encouraged to develop mental faculties and the ability to influence others using Sykametre (Psychometry) and ESP (extrasensory perception).

The presence of the Nuwaubians has led to some concern in Putnam County, and they have come into conflict with local civil and police officials. Most of the disputes concern zoning violations and building codes. But the Nuwaubians claim sovereignty on the basis that they are an ancient Native American tribe, the Yamassee, and are therefore entitled to independence from the United States. In 1997 they are said to have issued their own passports, licence plates and currency. Some of the local residents allege racism, but the Nuwaubians hotly dispute this, pointing to the existence of whites and Asians among their ranks. However, the presence of armed guards and esoteric rites and celebrations have raised concerns. The Nuwaubians have now entered local elections and some fear they may take over Eatonton. They themselves discount these apprehensions and claim to be law-abiding and non-violent.

The Bawa Muhaiyaddeen Fellowship

Ron Geaves

The Bawa Muhaiyaddeen Fellowship was founded in 1971 in Philadelphia, Pennsylvania, United States. It was created through the inspiration of Bawa Muhaiyaddeen (d. 1986), affectionately known as 'Bawa' (father) by his followers. Bawa started out as a wandering celibate ascetic, equally at home with teaching in Muslim or Hindu idiom, as is commonly found at the level of popular religion in the subcontinent. Little is known of his early life and Bawa himself provides little insight into his life story other than stories of a cosmic nature describing his personal encounters with the divine.

It is known that he began teaching in Sri Lanka in the 1940s after being discovered by a small group of Hindus undertaking a pilgrimage. They found Bawa emerging from the jungle and asked him to become their teacher. Bawa established himself in the town of Jaffna, where he began to collect a Muslim following and established a mosque known as God's House. Bawa's teachings possess a monistic understanding of the Muslim doctrine of divine unity manifested within traditional Sufi (mystical) practices and interpretations of the Qur'an and Sunna. Bawa began to attract more orthodox Muslims, albeit from the Sufi spectrum of Islam, and slowly his teachings began to take on a more scriptural emphasis rather than focusing on the popular practices associated with rural Islam. At the same time, Bawa began to identify himself as the *qutb* (the highest possible manifestation of a Sufi master) of this age and the spiritual successor to Abd al-Qadir al-Jilani (d. 1176), the founder of the Qadiri Sufi *tariqa* (order). Al-Jilani is regarded

as the ultimate manifestation of the *qutb* by almost all Sufi orders, however, it is important to note that Bawa's claim to be al-Jilani's successor is not based on a traditional master–disciple chain to the original founder usually used to authenticate a Sufi lineage.

In 1971, Bawa agreed to come to the United States after being invited by a correspondent, and taught young 'spiritual seekers' in Philadelphia who had been part of the 1960s counter-culture. Very few realized that they were being introduced to Sufi beliefs and practices and it was five years before Bawa announced that 'this is Islam'. A more articulated expression of Islamic belief and practice began from 1976, when Bawa began to formalize *dhikr* (remembrance of Allah) and other traditional Muslim devotional practices associated with Sufi disciplines. Bawa also began to construct a mosque in the district. At the present time, the movement consists of around a thousand members and has developed links with the migrant Muslim communities, providing resources for Islamic education and accommodation for visiting representatives passing through from Muslim countries. The primary source of guidance for members remains Bawa's teachings and conduct. The Bawa Muhaiyaddeen Fellowship is important for the study of Sufism in the United States as it is a good example of how Muslim spiritual movements passed through a variety of stages: firstly catering for American converts and spiritual seekers and then increasingly beginning to serve the developing migrant communities from the Muslim world, thereby moving closer to orthodox Islam.

New
Religions,
Sects and
Alternative
Spiritualities
with Roots in
Zoroastrianism

The sacred fire and urn of Zoroastrianism.

ZOROASTRIANISM
Almut Hintze

Zoroastrianism, the religion of pre-Islamic Iran, derives its name from Zoroaster, the Greek form of the name of the prophet Zarathustra. Known of old as 'the Persian religion', Zoroastrianism is one of the world's most ancient, prophetic monotheistic faiths and one of Iran's great contributions to the history of religious thought. Deeply rooted in the prehistoric Indo-Iranian and, ultimately, Indo-European traditions, it shares a common heritage with the Vedic religion and Hinduism. There was much intellectual interaction between the Persians and the Greeks through whom Zoroastrianism is known in the West as 'the religion of the Magi'. In its long history it has influenced many of the world's major religions. From the mid-7th century CE, Zoroastrianism was gradually supplanted by Islam but lives on as the religion of minorities in Iran, India and elsewhere.

History
Zoroastrianism was inaugurated by the prophet and priest Zarathustra, who is believed to have lived in southern central Asia in the late 2nd millennium BCE. In his hymns, the *Gathas*, he claims to have had a vision, in which the god Ahura Mazda (Lord Wisdom) revealed the new teachings to him. An event decisive for the religion's success occurred when the ruler Kavi Vishtaspa became Zarathustra's follower and patron. As a result, Zoroastrianism spread rapidly through the lands under his control.

For over a thousand years, Zoroastrianism was the official religion of mighty empires under the Achaemenian (558–330 BCE), Parthian (247 BCE – 224 CE) and Sasanian (224–651 CE) dynasties, at times extending from the Indus River to Egypt and to the coastline and islands of Asia Minor. During this millennium of expansion, it was one of the most powerful and influential faiths in the world, although it was never adopted as a state religion outside the Iranian sphere of influence.

From the time Islam supplanted Zoroastrianism, its adherents have declined in number to such an extent that today only about 150,000 Zoroastrians are estimated to live around the globe. Between 10,000 and 30,000 (there are no precise figures) survive in Iran. Most of the others, however, live in India, particularly in Bombay and Gujarat, to which they emigrated in the 10th century in search of religious freedom.

In their second homeland, India, where they became known as Parsees (because they came from Persia), they have made a decisive contribution to the rise of Bombay as the subcontinent's commercial capital. Within Indian society, Zoroastrians occupy high-ranking positions both in the country's economy and in its politics. Having acquired wealth and power in India in the 18th and 19th centuries, they followed the expansion of their global trade interests and began to travel. In the 20th century they settled in growing numbers in the financial centres of the world. The largest community outside India or Iran is found in Great Britain and is focused on London. Other centres include Hong Kong, Nairobi, Toronto, various cities in Australia and, most importantly, the United States, especially Houston, Los Angeles, San Francisco and New York. Despite being dispersed around the globe, Zoroastrians today constitute influential minorities wherever they live. In general, they are highly educated members of the professional middle class and business community.

The distance from their ancient homelands coupled with life in different cultural contexts has had a variety of effects on the diaspora communities. Some of them maintain their old traditions and appear to be more conservative than those in India or Iran, while others adapt to the new environment and develop new traditions. From the 1880s, some groups of Indian Zoroastrians were attracted by the

*Theosophical Society and its Zoroastrianized form, *Ilm-e Khshnoom.

Sources

Knowledge of the teachings of Zoroastrianism is essentially based on the *Avesta*, composed in an old Iranian language, and the Pahlavi literature, written in Middle Persian. The *Avesta* is not just a single text, but a collection of hymns, liturgies, prayers, blessings and law books dating from different periods. The oldest and most venerable parts consist of 17 hymns (the *Gathas*), the *Yasna Haptanghaiti* (a liturgical prose text called 'the worship in seven parts') and two holy prayers. Both the *Avesta* and later Zoroastrian tradition refer to the *Gathas* as the work of Zarathustra. Moreover, in recent years, it has been argued convincingly that the *Yasna Haptanghaiti* was also composed by the prophet. If such is the case, these texts are more than 3,000 years old and are authentic documents attributable to the religion's founder. The *Avesta* has chiefly been transmitted by oral tradition. Only texts recited during Zoroastrian rituals have survived.

The Pahlavi literature was compiled from Avestan texts and oral traditions in the early Islamic period, when Zoroastrians were increasingly being reduced to a minority. Zoroastrian priests decided to collect such texts in order to preserve them from being forgotten. The Pahlavi accounts are usually more explicit and detailed and complement those of the *Avesta* in a valuable way.

Doctrine

Zoroastrian teaching provides a unique and fascinating view of life. One of its most salient features is the belief that both types of life – that is, the spiritual and the material – were created by God (Ahura Mazda), and that they were wholly good. Accordingly, the human body, which forms part of Ahura Mazda's material creation, is considered to be equally as good as the soul, which belongs to the spiritual creation. Thus, physical life is viewed as

positive, just like the natural world. This and a range of other doctrinal points appears to have been first formulated by Zarathustra. Perhaps the most central of such doctrines concerns the antagonism between good and evil, together with its eschatological resolution in evil's ultimate defeat and elimination.

The major points of Zoroastrian doctrine may best be identified by considering the Zoroastrian concept of cosmic history as laid out in the Avestan and Pahlavi texts. History is divided into three periods: 'Creation', 'Mixture' and 'Separation', the latter achieving its completion in 'Perfection', which is the eternally perfect state of creation at the end of time. The beginning is when Ohrmazd (the Middle Persian form of 'Ahura Mazda') created first spiritual life and then the material world, both in a perfect state. The end is marked by the restoration of that perfect world, brought about through the elimination of all evil.

Evil is conceived not as a god, but as an impersonal force unconnected with Ahura Mazda and antagonistic to him and his work. While Ahura Mazda's creation has both a spiritual and a physical existence, evil exists only on the spiritual plane. In-between the two extreme points on the timescale, the onslaught of Angra Mainyu (Evil Spirit) takes place. All evil in the physical world, including death, comes from that external source. However, it clings, so to speak in a parasitic manner, onto Ahura Mazda's good physical creations and tries to corrupt and eventually destroy them.

The state of 'Mixture' is perceived not only as a cosmic conflict between supernatural, spiritual forces, but also as a struggle in which human beings play a clearly defined role. We were created by Ahura Mazda to be his co-workers, friends, helpers and supporters in the struggle against evil. In contrast to the rest of the physical world – such as animals and plants – human beings are fit for this task because they are equipped with the intellectual facility of being able to distinguish between

A Zoroastrian harvest festival in Yazd City, Iran.

good and evil. Thanks to this gift, men and women have access to the spiritual world. On the spiritual plane, they can acquire either Ahura Mazda's own characteristics, which include truth, good mind and right-mindedness, or those of evil, such as deceit, evil mind and arrogance.

If people choose rightly and strive to acquire Ahura Mazda's spiritual creations (Bounteous Immortals, *Amesha Spentas*), they both fulfil the purpose for which they were created and become his friends and co-workers, and thus strengthen both him and his cause. However, they do have free choice, and may decide to become supporters of evil. Thus, as a result of their intellectual capacities, human beings have freedom to choose, and each person, 'man for man' as it says in the *Gathas*, must make up his or her own mind and decide whether or not to support Ahura Mazda. This 'choice' (*fravashi*), for which they are morally responsible, is what allows Zarathustra to distinguish between 'truthful' and 'deceitful' people. People of either sex (Zoroastrianism makes no distinction

between men and women as moral agents), are good or evil not by nature but by choice.

However, not only do people's choices have a bearing on whether or not they contribute towards Ahura Mazda's cosmic goal – the defeat and complete removal of evil – but their own destiny is also shaped by the fundamental decision they make at that stage. For when their physical life is over, their immortal soul will be united with the party they have chosen to join during their lifetime. Those who align themselves with evil will end up in the place where evil dwells, while the supporters of Ahura Mazda will be close to their lord in the 'House of Welcome' (the *Garo Demana*). Thus, after death, human beings will be judged on the stance they took with regard to Ahura Mazda's cosmic plan and on how they led their lives as a result.

After death, when the immortal soul is separated from the mortal body, the soul beholds its own inner outlook on life or 'vision' (*daena*), which has been shaped and cherished by each individual during his or her lifetime. Standing by the 'Bridge of the Separator' (*Cinwad* Bridge), the 'vision' appears as a beautiful maiden if the person was 'truthful', but as a hideous, stinking hag if they were 'deceitful'. If bad 'thoughts, words and deeds' outweigh the good ones, the soul, while crossing the bridge, falls off into the 'House of Darkness' where all evil dwells and where its retribution is 'bad life' until the final Perfection. In contrast, if the person was 'truthful', the soul crosses the bridge easily and joins Ahura Mazda in the 'House of Welcome'. In their respective places, the souls await the resurrection of their bodies and the perfection of the physical world.

At the end of time a 'World Saviour', who is presented as a posthumous son of Zarathustra and born of a virgin, will victoriously complete the struggle against evil in general, and death in particular, by resurrecting the bodies of the dead and reuniting them with their souls. There will be a great final battle between the forces of good and evil, and the latter will be completely defeated. The evil spirit, Angra Mainyu, will retreat powerless, and escape from Ahura Mazda's creation through the very hole he pierced in the sky when he first attacked. All resurrected bodies will be purified from evil in the ordeal of molten metal and then be united with their respective souls. From then on, the whole of creation will exist in perfection, as originally intended by its creator.

Influence on other world religions

During the millennium of expansion (c. 558 BCE to 651 CE), Zoroastrianism is believed to have influenced other world religions, in particular Christianity, but also Judaism, Buddhism and Islam. Jews lived under Persian rule from 538 BCE, when Cyrus, hailed in the book of Isaiah as God's 'Anointed' (or Messiah; Isaiah 45:1–4), liberated them from captivity and made Babylonia a province of the Persian empire. In Judaism, ideas akin to those of Zoroastrianism become prominent from the 2nd century BCE in the intertestamental literature and in the teachings of the group of Essenes at Qumran. In Christianity, ideas related to Zoroastrian teachings are those of free will and responsibility, religious equality of men and women, physical resurrection, individual and universal judgement, the Devil, heaven and hell, the second coming of the saviour, and a perfect world at the end of time.

Doctrinal parallels between Zoroastrianism and Islam can be found with regard to Islamic apocalyptic teachings and eschatology. A number of Shia teachings recall Zoroastrian ideas, in particular belief in the messianic figure of the Mahdi, the human saviour to come. Since the original Arabic practice was to pray only three times a day, the five periods of Muslim prayer probably originate from the five Zoroastrian watches.

By translating Buddhist texts into Chinese, Iranians (Parthians, Sogdians, Sakas and Bactrians) played an important part in the dissemination of Buddhism in the East. They were active in Chinese Turkestan, and it is likely that much of the influence of Iranians on Buddhist thought and culture was exerted there. It has even been suggested that Zoroastrianism had an impact on the teachings of Mahayana Buddhism.

Ritual

To the present day, Zoroastrians pray in the ancient Iranian language of the *Avesta*. It is because of the use of these ancient texts in ritual and prayer that they have survived to the present day – transmitted, in a predominantly oral tradition, by priests and laypeople who are trained from childhood to learn the sacred texts by heart.

The Zoroastrian community is divided into two major groups: the hereditary priesthood and the laity or *behdins* (those of the 'good religion'). The priests are called *mobad* or *ervad*, while a high priest has the title *dastur*. The primary duty of priests is to pray and perform rituals on behalf of the member of the community who has requested and paid for them.

The focus of all Zoroastrian rituals is the fire. During the oldest and highest of them, called Yasna 'worship', Ahura Mazda's heavenly fire comes down to the place of worship and merges with the ritual fire. The belief that Ahura Mazda is present in the ritual fire, which is considered to be his son and his most beautiful visible form, is the foundation of the central position taken by the fire. Zoroastrian places of worship are fire-temples, where a fire is kept burning continuously, fed by priests who live there while on duty. The holiest fire of the Parsees, known by the name Iranshah (king of Iran) has been burning for more than a thousand years. Since 1742, its home has been the fire-temple of Udvada (Gujarat). Inner rituals, such as the Yasna ceremony, must be performed inside a fire-temple. Laypersons may be present, but do not have to be. Outer rituals may be solemnized in any clean place, such as a Zoroastrian house. Priestly rituals are performed in order to worship Ahura Mazda and to strengthen his presence and that of his spiritual creations in the physical world.

The function of private prayer, in contrast, is to enable the individual followers of the religion to express their allegiance to Ahura Mazda and strengthen themselves in the struggle against evil. Laypeople have the religious obligation to say their prayers daily and to observe certain purity laws. This is why non-Zoroastrians are not admitted into fire-temples. Pollution, especially that resulting from contact with dead matter, is a product of evil and has to be avoided or at least contained. In order not to pollute the elements of earth, water or fire, Zoroastrians traditionally expose the bodies of their dead in constructions called 'Towers of Silence'.

Ethics and worldview

The teachings of Zoroastrianism constitute the backdrop and source of Zoroastrian cultural values and practices, such as love of education, striving for material wealth, equal religious status for men and women, and charitable works. Love of learning and education is deeply ingrained in Zoroastrians and has proved to be the basis for their economic success. Their mental outlook encourages critical self-awareness and scientific forms of reasoning. Deeply rooted in their doctrine is the Zoroastrians' uniquely positive attitude towards life. Joy, laughter and appreciation of all good things given by Ahura Mazda is not only a pleasure but a religious duty. It is virtuous to enjoy life, because it strengthens what is good, whereas it is bad to be sad, depressed or ill. Fasting and asceticism are not encouraged, neither is withdrawal from the world. A person should marry and have children. Observance of all these precepts produces good fighters for Ahura Mazda against evil. Although women are barred from entering the priesthood, in all other respects they have equal status to men, a phenomenon quite unique among ancient religions. Like men they are co-workers in the struggle against evil.

A good use of wealth, acquired with honesty, is an important part of Zoroastrian ethics. Charity is a way of fighting evil. Zoroastrians do so by providing housing for the poor and medical care in hospitals and elsewhere, by contributing towards the growth of their countries' economy, and by supporting education and the arts. These are some of the characteristics for which Zoroastrians are renowned today. The fact that the less prosperous members of the community are traditionally cared for by a charitable network providing education, housing and medical care inspired Mahatma Gandhi's famous saying: 'Parsee, thy name is charity.'

Parsee Theosophy
Almut Hintze

Naojote, the initiation of a Parsee child into the faith.

Theosophy (in Greek, 'wisdom of God') refers to systems of thought that aim to arrive at the truth underlying all religions and thus, ultimately, to God. By means of mystical and occult techniques, the human intellect is raised to levels that culminate in the experience of the divine in mystical unity. In general, theosophical ideas are found in various strands of human thought, such as neo-Platonism, Gnosticism, Manichaeism, Catharism, *Freemasonry, Anabaptism, *Kabbalism and Bahá'ísm (see the *Bahá'í Faith).

Modern Theosophy is usually associated with the *Theosophical Society, which was founded in New York in 1875 by Helena Petrovna Blavatsky (1831–91) and Henry Steel Olcott (1832–1907), the latter being its first president. In 1877, the society moved to

India, first to Benares and then, in 1879, to Bombay. When it arrived in Bombay, it attracted a considerable number of both Hindus and Parsees. On 14 February 1882, Olcott delivered a lecture in Bombay before more than 700 Parsees. The lecture was entitled 'The Spirit of the Zoroastrian Religion', and was published later that year. Olcott believed that dualism was at the heart of the Zoroastrian faith, and urged the Parsees to continue to pray in the ancient Avestan language (see *Zoroastrianism) and to preserve their rituals and traditions.

Parsee theosophists believe that the prophet Zarathustra and his successors transmitted their thoughts to posterity in the guise of an obscure language and an external ritual in which 'pyroelectricity' was created. By applying occult techniques, Parsees should seek the lost key of understanding, the true meaning of the *Gathas* (the 17 hymns of Zarathustra) and of their religion. At the same time, they should ignore the findings of philological and historical disciplines as practised by European scholars. Parsee theosophists regard Zarathustra as a divine being, greater even than theosophy's other hidden 'Masters of the Wisdom', and have created new symbolism-laden rites, which they practise in their own homes.

After Olcott's death in 1907, the Theosophical Society moved its centre to Adyar near Madras under its new president Annie Besant (1847–1933), the social reformer and founder of the Indian Home Rule League. At the same time, *Ilm-e Khshnoom started to absorb many Parsees formerly involved in theosophy. However, there are still followers of Parsee theosophy, even though it is not possible to estimate the numbers involved.

Mazdaznan
Christopher Partridge

The word 'Mazdaznan' is derived from the Zoroastrian deity, Ahura Mazda. The movement teaches that, over 9,000 years ago, Ainyahita, a female prophet living in Tibet, received revelations that are now the basic teachings of Mazdaznan. Indeed, it is believed that these teachings spread to many of the world's great civilizations and, although they have been altered over time, form the foundation of much human religious and philosophical thought. Following the revelations to Ainyahita, the next key point in religious history, according to Mazdaznan, came 3,000 years later when the prophet Zarathustra (Zoroaster) revived the vision of Ainyahita, and added further important practical teachings about, for example, hygiene. Again, these teachings, claim Mazdaznan, spread to and influenced the cultures of Israel, Greece,

India and China. Hence, their declarations state, among other things, that:

Mazdaznan is the Eternal Religion that stands behind all other religions, revealing the tie that binds finite Man to his Infinite God – Mazda – and is recognized by the world at large through its own recognized authorities as the 'religion behind all other religions', and as a 'complete system of education that has no equal'… Mazdaznan declares to be the oldest and most comprehensive system ever devised by man or revealed by God, embracing as it does every Essential Truth upon which are founded all systems of religion, philosophy, science and sociology – from that of Ainyahita to Zarathustra, Jesus to the Soshyants, from Ancient Thought to Modern Thought.

While many people rejected the teachings of Ainyahita and Zarathustra, a few faithful communities secretly living in the Himalayas passed them from one generation to the next. Periodically these communities send prophets and wise men to other cultures to inspire them and to encourage them to live according to Mazdaznan principles.

Mazdaznan claims to have a particularly close relationship with Christianity. Adherents of Mazdaznan believe that the wise men who visited the infant Jesus travelled from a Mazdaznan community and were priests of the order of Zarathustra. They not only brought gifts from the East, but also taught the holy family the ancient way of Mazdaznan, thereby laying the foundations for much later Christian thought. Hence, Mazdaznan has a particularly high view of Christ as the 'incarnation of love and wisdom', and as a teacher of righteousness and peace. Many Mazdaznan statements and affirmations are drawn from the New Testament.

As to the contemporary Mazdaznan movement, it is taught that a surviving Mazdaznan community located in the Kunlun mountain range decided that the time was right to send another messenger out into the world. This messenger was Rev. Dr Otoman Zar-Adusht Ha'nish (d. 1936). Alternatively, some sources suggest that he was the son of a Chicago grocer who had become interested in the metaphysical and theosophical thought popular at the time. However, it is claimed that he spent years travelling the world, particularly the East, before studying medicine at Oxford University. This was all preparation for his mission. He was now in a position to teach the truths revealed to Ainyahita and Zarathustra, and also the general wisdom of the East, by demonstrating their beneficial effects on the mind and the body. However, Mazdaznan teaches that, because his message was initially rejected in Europe, in 1880 he travelled to the United States and, in 1890, established the Mazdaznan Peace Center in Chicago.

Without commenting on the reliability and veracity of the Mazdaznan version of religious history presented above, it is clear that Mazdaznan was the first broadly 'Zoroastrian' group to be established in the United States. Mazdaznan seems to have been inaugurated in 1902 in New York and within its first decade it had spread to several other American cities, established headquarters in Chicago, started the publication of a periodical, *The Mazdaznan*, and, as a result of the tireless efforts of Ha'nish, established groups in Latin America and Europe. In 1916, the headquarters was moved to Los Angeles, finally moving to its present location in Encinitas, California, in the mid-1980s. It became remarkably popular in England during the inter-war years, being particularly well received in the northern towns and cities of Yorkshire and Lancashire. During the 1970s it seems to have experienced some growth in Mexico, Denmark, France, Belgium, Holland, Germany and Switzerland. Now known as the Mazdaznan Temple Association, it is currently overseen by an 'Elector', Alfonso Rodriguez Calderon.

Much of Ha'nish's teaching was concerned with self-improvement and bodily health. He taught a system of controlled breathing, vegetarianism, abstinence from alcohol, physical exercise and meditation, all of which, he claimed, would lead an individual to spiritual purity and to their full potential as a human being. The motto of his movement was 'breath of life' and the exercises included singing, humming and yoga-like techniques.

The contemporary Mazdaznan Temple Association teaches much the same system as that taught by its founder. The health element of Mazdaznan teaching is termed 'Life4Sys' (pronounced 'life forces') and the 'mystical' element is referred to as the 'Science of Life'. These two elements are then combined and given added spiritual direction in the 'Mazdaznan Religious Life'. Together, these related elements or programmes form the structure of Mazdaznan teaching, and together they are believed to improve the individual's health, emotional well-being, mind and spirituality. Mazdaznan claims to enable the individuals to become their own masters. Improvement is understood in terms of the strengthening of 12 'senses' (teaching about which is set out in Ha'nish's book *The Power of Breath*): four physical senses (sight, hearing, smell and taste); four emotional senses (touch, feeling, intuition and transmission of ideas); and four intellectual senses (spiritual discernment, telepathy, clairvoyance and realization).

There are several key interrelated teachings. The body (including mind, soul and spirit) is understood to be the Temple of God. Hence, through the practical application of the mystical teachings of Mazdaznan (the Science of Life), the Life4Sys programme focuses on improving this temple by means of breathing techniques, exercises to enhance the endocrine glandular system, and healthy diet. Mazdaznan also maintains that all faiths, creeds, beliefs and philosophies are valuable in so far as they stimulate the quest for the truth within: 'There is no greater

authority than God and no religion higher than truth.'

God is to be understood as 'our higher inner self', 'that part of us from which we cannot hide the truth, that tells us what is right or wrong, inspires us to think, speak and act our best, and gives us real and lasting strength in the moment we are weak... Not one man or woman is our saviour, but every man and woman is his or her own saviour.' Hence, the Mazdaznan religious life is one of listening to, and living according to 'the still, small voice' (the divine) *within*. Indeed, it is important to understand that 'anyone who strives to fulfil the will of God [to listen to the voice within] and who exhibits constructive behaviour, respect for life and performs daily caring acts is living in accordance with Mazdaznan principles and can be called Mazdaznan.' (Although there is no formal membership, those who explicitly support the Mazdaznan Temple Association are called 'Mazdaznan associates'.) We all come from the same divine source and, to some extent, are divine. This is clear in the following Mazdaznan affirmation: 'I am all in One individually and one in All collectively; I am present individually and omnipresent collectively; I am knowing individually and omniscient collectively; I am potent individually and omnipotent collectively; All is of God and God is All!' Pacifism and vegetarianism are required of Mazdaznan associates and peace and non-violence, practical love and charity, are central to the Mazdaznan way of life. The 'Mazdaznan Statement' includes the following: 'I must assist the needy, the afflicted, the distressed, the fallen, the neglected, the struggling, the perishing, and do so in a spirit of love, kindness and respect, bearing in mind that charity begins at home.'

The prophet Zoroaster who, according to Mazdaznan, revived the vision of Ainyahita.

Ilm-e Khshnoom

Almut Hintze

Ilm-e Khshnoom (in Persian, 'knowledge of gratification') is an occult Zoroastrian movement that was started in 1907 by a Parsee called Behramshah Shroff (1858–1927). Shroff was born to a poor priestly family from Bombay, India, and brought up in Surat, where he received only a basic education. After a quarrel with his mother, he left home and stayed with an uncle in Peshawar. According to legend, Shroff then joined a caravan of Iranians, who were outwardly Muslims but secretly Zoroastrians. They led Shroff to Mount Demavand in the north of Iran and showed him a secret cave system, called Firdos (in Persian, 'garden, paradise'), where a community of Zoroastrians lived, and he remained there for three years. Firdos was an agricultural paradise where the spiritual and material treasures of ancient Iran were preserved. Shroff was one of only three outsiders who have ever been allowed to enter Firdos.

During his years in Firdos, Shroff was enlightened by spiritual masters, called *Magi*, who had preserved all Zoroastrian scriptures and ceremonial utensils. By means of ecstatic techniques, they taught him astrology and Ayurvedic medicine, explained the true meaning of the *Avesta* (the sacred scriptures of *Zoroastrianism) and gave him esoteric wisdom, referred to by the Avestan word *khshnoom*. Shroff was said to have entered Firdos illiterate and with a stammer, but left it as a powerful orator and interpreter of Zoroastrian texts.

Between 1881 and 1891, Shroff toured India and met teachers of various religions, but remained silent about his experiences in Firdos until 1907, when a Zoroastrian priest noticed his enlightened interpretations of the ritual fire. Subsequently Shroff lectured in Bombay under the auspices of various organizations, including the Parsee Vegetarian and Temperance Society, the Anjuman Atash Bahram and the Theosophical Lodge.

Shroff's teaching appealed to Parsees because it stressed their links to Iran at a stage when the *Theosophical Society, under the leadership of Annie Besant, had been taken over by militant Hindus. The idea of direct mystical contact with spiritual powers in Iran attracted many Parsees to the movement, who felt that Western scholarship and the influence of Christianity and materialism threatened the religious life and identity of their community. The stress on rituals and performance of prayers in the ancient Avestan language appealed particularly to orthodox Parsees. In 1919, the Khshnoomists founded the Zoroastrian Radih Society. Shroff attempted to set up a fire-temple operating according to the Persian calendar, which is in agreement with the seasons. When this attempt failed in 1923, Shroff underwent a religious crisis.

Shroff's teachings included the concept of a single impersonal God, reincarnation, various planes of being and planetary lore. He stressed the importance of exactly performed rituals and adherence to purity laws, while disregarding textual and historical accuracy. Some of his esoteric ideas may be traced back, via theosophy, to the *Desatir*, a 16th-century Persian Sufi work containing the sayings of 14 successive prophets (published in India in 1818). Ilm-e Khshnoom has been characterized as a Zoroastrianized form of theosophy, as it shares with the latter ideas of reincarnation and vegetarianism, an emphasis on occult powers and vibrations, the value of traditional rituals and a devotional commitment to prayers in the ancient sacred language rather than in the vernacular. Shroff differed from the theosophists in attributing his inspiration not to hidden 'Masters of the Wisdom' in Tibet, but to a secret colony of spiritual Masters in an Iranian cave, with whom he claimed to be in regular direct communication.

An extensive Kshnoomist literature includes publications by F.S. Chiniwalla, a pupil and personal friend of Shroff, Adi F. Doctor and Meher Master-Moos, the founder of the Zoroastrian College at Sanjan (Gujarat). From 1981, she published English translations of Shroff's lectures on the origins of the cosmos. In accordance with his will, these lectures had been kept hidden in a trunk for 50 years after his death. Ilm-e Khshnoom was taken to America by Rev. Dr Otoman Zar-Adusht Ha'nish (d. 1936), who claimed to be one of the three outsiders to have visited Firdos (see *Mazdaznan).

New
Religions,
Sects and
Alternative
Spiritualities
with Roots in
Indian
Religions

Sculpture of Vishnu at
Perumal Temple in Singapore.

INDIAN RELIGIONS
Christopher Partridge

The principal Indian religions are Hinduism, Buddhism, Sikhism and Jainism. Of these, Hinduism is the principal indigenous religion of India. Buddhism and Jainism emerged as reform movements within early Hinduism. Sikhism, which has some roots in Hinduism (and Buddhism), originated in the 15th century as another major indigenous Indian religious tradition. What follows is a brief overview of the religions that have a significant presence in this volume, namely, Hinduism, Buddhism and Sikhism.

Hinduism
With over 800 million adherents worldwide, Hinduism is the third-largest religion. Calling itself *sanatana dharma* (the eternal religion), it claims to be the oldest religion in the world. Indeed, for many Hindus *sanatana dharma* is preferable to 'Hinduism', which has only recently been used by Hindus of themselves. The term 'Hinduism' is derived from a Persian term originally used simply to refer to those who lived on the far side of the River Indus.

Hinduism is not, strictly speaking, a single religion, but rather an umbrella term for a diverse collection of beliefs, practices and traditions that are rooted in the ancient Vedic scriptures and civilizations and date from roughly 2500 BCE. Beliefs differ from village to village, and vary considerably between the major regions. In modern India, Hindus worship in different ways, honour different deities (traditionally numbering 33 million), have different temples and sacred sites, observe different festivals and read a variety of sacred writings; they may believe in an ultimate God who is personal (e.g. *Brahma*) or they may not (e.g. *Brahman*); they may worship a single deity or a variety of deities. Beliefs range from the small movements, such as the *Muttappan Teyyam, to modern gurus, such as Satya Sai Baba (see the *Satya Sai Baba

Society), to complex and highly abstract philosophical systems, such as those of the philosophers Shankara and Radhakrishnan.

The belief in reincarnation is common to most forms of Hinduism, and to new religions influenced by Hindu thought. At death the body dies, but the soul (*atman*) lives on and adopts a new body. Like taking off a jacket and putting on a new one, the *atman* moves into a new body and a new life. *Samsara* is the continual process of birth and rebirth we all experience. Karma (Sanskrit for action/work) refers to the moral principle that a person's actions have consequences that extend to future lives. What you do in this life determines the 'suit' you will wear in the next. In essence it refers to a law of cause and effect by which the consequences of a person's actions are carried forward into the next life, the result of which is the determination of the character of that life (a person's position, health, etc.). If I have lived according to the principles of *dharma* (the moral and righteous life), I can look forward to my next life. On the other hand, if I have, for example, been cruel to others in this life, I will be the recipient of cruelty and misfortune in the next. However, the ultimate spiritual aim of Hindus is release from this cycle of *samsara*, from the continual round of birth and rebirth with all its disappointments, misery and struggles. This is *moksha* (liberation), the goal of the religious life.

From early on in Indian religious history, there was a belief that the individual *atman* had its origin in the universal *Brahman*. The *Brahman* is the source of the *atman*. Hence, *Brahman*, ultimate reality, the source of all that is – God – could be discovered by looking within oneself. In particular, the 9th-century thinker Shankara formulated a philosophy known as Advaita Vedanta, which argued that the human *atman* and *Brahman* are of the same substance. These ideas have greatly influenced much contemporary Western alternative spirituality.

Much Hindu religious thought and practice

is directed towards clearing karma, understanding the true nature of the *atman* and its relationship with *Brahman*, and enabling an individual to realize *moksha*. For example, there is evidence that from prehistoric times meditation has been practised in India, and, in particular, a group of disciplines collectively known as 'yoga' was developed to facilitate the transformation of consciousness. The term 'yoga' (related to the English term 'yoke') is often thought to mean 'unite', and refers to the realization of one's essential unity with the divine. Yoga is the means whereby a person controls the senses and the mind to such an extent (by regulating breathing and focusing) that the physical, limited self can be transcended and the individual's true identity realized. (This, too, has been very popular in the West.) It may also involve difficult exercises and postures. (These have been popular in the West simply as physical exercises.)

While it is the classical philosophy and the meditative disciplines of Hinduism that have been adopted most readily in the West, in India the worship of deities is far more popular. Stories of the exploits of gods and goddesses and devotion to these deities make up much of the religious practice of Hindus. Temples are full of posters, paintings and images (*murti*) depicting the deities and scenes from popular narratives. Again, typical of this form of worship is the recently popular Muttappan Teyyam and the warm devotion offered to Lord Krishna. Indeed, in the religious texts of popular Hinduism, the most famous of which is the *Bhagavadgita* (Song of the Lord), it is loving devotion to God (*bhakti*) that is recommended as the most effective path to the religious goal. While there are numerous religious texts within Hinduism, most Hindus

The Brahmins perform religious rituals and study sacred texts.

will regard the *Bhagavadgita*, a poem from the large Hindu epic, the *Mahabharata*, as the supreme expression of their faith. The *Bhagavadgita* consists of a dialogue that takes place on the eve of a great battle between two branches of the Kaurava family – the Kauravas proper and the Pandavas. The dialogue is between Arjuna, a warrior prince, and the Lord Krishna, an incarnation of the Supreme Being, Vishnu, disguised as Arjuna's charioteer. (Traditionally, Krishna is understood to be the eighth incarnation or avatar of the Hindu deity Vishnu.) Apart from the discussion of the role of the avatar, perhaps the most important religious emphasis in the *Bhagavadgita* is that on the nature of God. Apart from being the awe-inspiring, omnipotent, omniscient ruler of the cosmos, God desires to draw devotees into a warm, loving relationship with himself, regardless of their status in life, and is himself personal, gracious and loving: 'In any way that men love me, in that same way they find my love: for many are the paths of men, but they all in the end come to me' (*Bhagavadgita* 4:11).

Perhaps the most common form of *bhakti* devotion to Krishna in the West is *ISKCON (the International Society for Krishna Consciousness), often known simply as the Hare Krishna movement. Founded by A.C. Bhaktivedanta Swami Prabhupada in 1965, the movement gained popularity as a result of the involvement of George Harrison, who popularized the ISKCON mantra in his song 'My Sweet Lord'. Harrison has since been followed by other popular artists, such as Boy George, who have in turn produced their own songs celebrating Krishna devotion. ISKCON has successfully made the Hindu devotion to Krishna accessible to westerners. Hence, while

many within the New Age network have been influenced by the non-personal conception of the divine within *advaita* forms of Hinduism, others have been attracted by the intensely personal understanding of God found within the *bhakti* traditions of popular Hinduism.

Finally, the notion of 'caste' needs to be introduced. A term that is Portuguese in origin, caste usually describes what is referred to in India as *jati* (literally meaning 'birth'), the social status one inherits at birth. That is to say, one's *jati* is hereditary, in that a person belongs to the same *jati* as one's parents, who are also of the same *jati* because marriage outside one's *jati* group is traditionally forbidden and certainly discouraged. There are also numerous other social restrictions imposed by the caste system, including eating only within one's caste group (commensality). A *jati* is often identified with a particular occupation (there are *jati* associated with barbers, gardeners, potters etc.). Furthermore, it is important to understand that the caste system is fundamentally linked to notions of pollution and purity. From an early age, children are taught about pollution and purity regarding everything from bodily functions to food to particular *jati* (as some groups are polluting to others). Hence, for example, because all that is dead and all that comes out of the body is polluting, certain groups whose occupations necessarily deal with such matter, such as undertakers or barbers (dead hair), are considered polluting to other groups. (Indeed, all members of a caste group are polluted purely because of their association with that caste, regardless of whether they personally practise that occupation.) At the top of the caste hierarchy are the Brahmins, who perform religious rituals and study sacred texts. Many Brahmins, however, will pursue other career paths. Typically these include owning

The exteriors of Hindu temples are breathtaking in both their scale and decoration. This one is at Madurai, India.

restaurants (as all castes can be served by their hands without fear of pollution) and practising medicine (as all can be treated by them, again, without fear of pollution). At the other end of the caste spectrum are the Dalits or 'Untouchables', who are so-called because even to be touched by their shadow is polluting. Typically they will be involved in highly polluting occupations such as road sweeping and dealing with sewage. Although the caste hierarchy is no longer publicly acknowledged, and has been subjected to wide-ranging government legislation in India, it is hard to ignore the fact that caste is still important in some areas of Hindu social life, particularly marriage.

Buddhism

Buddhism has been particularly well received in the modern West. Certainly, its rapid growth in the West has contributed significantly to its status as the fourth-largest religion in the world, with over 357 million devotees.

Buddhism was founded by Siddhartha Gautama (c. 563–c. 483 BCE). His personal name was Siddhartha, his family name was Gautama, and the term 'Buddha', by which he is now known, roughly translates as 'enlightened one'. There are several stories of the religious quest of Prince Siddhartha or Gautama as he is more commonly known. For example, one popular story relates that, although he had been brought up surrounded by luxury in a pleasant royal court isolated from the world outside, when he was about 30 years of age he grew restless. Even though he was discouraged from straying out into the world by his protective father, he eventually made three excursions over three consecutive days. On each of the three days he had an encounter that caused him to reflect on the nature of life. He encountered an old man, bent, weak, supported by a stick and leaning against a wall; a man with leprosy, crippled with pain; and a corpse about to be consigned to the flames of a funeral pyre. Amazed and

shocked at these sights, his charioteer explained to him that not only were sights such as these common but that ageing, sickness and death are experienced by all people. Finally, a fourth excursion led to an encounter with a holy man with a shaven head, who, although dressed in rags, had a peaceful demeanour. This meeting inspired Gautama to adopt the life of a holy man. Hence, that night he left the pleasant surroundings and security of the royal court, left his beautiful wife and family, abandoned all his worldly ambitions and began his spiritual journey in search of enlightenment. (This renunciation of worldly possessions and family life is understood to be a symbolic precedent for the monasticism that has been a prominent feature of Buddhism.) Although his subsequent travels led him to various teachers, ideas, practices and extreme ascetic techniques, he was left unsatisfied and unenlightened. Finally, he sat under a tree – which has since, for obvious reasons, become known as the *Bodhi* (enlightened) tree – and determined not to move until he had attained a state of supreme enlightenment. Further accounts tell of his progression through levels of contemplation which, eventually, led to perfect enlightenment. At the age of 35 he was finally the Buddha.

Influenced by his earlier experiences, the Buddha taught that everything is subject to change and impermanence (*anicca*). Unlike Hinduism, for the Buddha even the 'self' or the 'soul' lacks permanence. Indeed, to think in terms of a 'self' at all is misleading. It is of course common to believe that, whatever else changes in one's life, there is some essential 'I-ness', some essential 'me' that does not change. The Buddha fundamentally questioned this belief. Everything is subject to change. There is no unchanging self. This doctrine of 'not-self' (*anatta*) is important. Although quite difficult to grasp, the teaching is essentially that there is no unchanging 'I' that experiences change in the world (in the sense that we often say 'I suffer' or 'I grow older'); everything changes and is conditioned by change. A person is understood to be a collection of complex and quickly changing physical and mental events and states. Of course, because one state influences the next, there is some pattern to the change and thus a continuity of personal characteristics. Thinking of life as a series of moments, we can see that, for example, a state of frustration can lead to a state of anger, which in turn leads to another possibly destructive state and so on. Moreover, because there is no full control over these changing states, many of which are influenced by forces wholly beyond our control, our life of impermanence is a frustrating one characterized by *dukkha* (which can be translated as 'suffering', 'illness' or, more generally, 'unsatisfactoriness'). Needless to say, the doctrine of the not-self has immense implications, not least for the teaching about reincarnation. Unlike Hinduism, there is no permanent self that travels from life to life burdened with the karma of previous lives. Rather, just as one psychological and physical state gives rise to the next in this life, so our attitudes and desires give rise to a reborn state of being in the next life. Hence, in Buddhism, karma is less about one's works and actions, and more about one's attitudes and desires. That is to say, that which ensures rebirth is not wrong action as such, but rather the desire for life. Only by quenching desire, relinquishing attachment to this life, removing the very belief that one is a self to be saved, can a person find release from the cycle of rebirth. Indeed, while Buddhists often explain *nibbana* (nirvana) – the goal of the spiritual quest – to be a state of *being without craving*, it originally meant 'blowing out', in the sense that one extinguishes the flames of desire, delusion (e.g. about the self) and craving.

Nirvana should not, therefore, be understood as a heaven or some state in which the self exists in bliss, for to attain nirvana means that, after death, there will be no more rebirth and that the series of states and events that makes up the individual simply ceases – the flame is extinguished. So, after death, what happens to the individuals who have destroyed their passions and purified their minds? Do they simply cease to exist? The Buddha offered no systematic treatment of the afterlife, believing that such questions were pointless and distracted from the spiritual quest in this life. Buddhism in this sense is very practical, in that the emphasis is on dealing with the problem of *dukkha*, rather than contemplating what happens when the problem is dealt with. Indeed, the question itself revealed the belief in a self that lives on after death and the desire to survive death, both of which were characteristic of unenlightened persons. That said, nirvana after death does indicate something. The problem is that this something is so incomparable to anything we know now that it is difficult to say what nirvana is. In a sense, nirvana is beyond existence, beyond anything we are currently familiar with.

Unfortunately, because people are ignorant of their current state and understand the self as essentially unchanging (an entity that may even continue into the afterlife), they become attached to the things of the world, which they fail to perceive as changing and impermanent. This teaching is set out in the Buddha's 'four noble truths', which form the core of Buddhism. They are 'noble' because they are true, because they are taught by a noble person and because, when understood, they produce noble persons. The four noble truths are as follows:

■ all forms of existence, particularly human life, are characterized by *dukkha*;

■ *dukkha* and rebirth are caused by desire and craving for the things of this world and for the survival of the self, whether in this world or the next;

■ the cessation of *dukkha* (i.e. nirvana) is only possible if such craving can be removed;

■ the way to remove craving and thereby to find release from *dukkha* is the noble eightfold path.

The noble eightfold path, the fourth of the Buddha's noble truths, prescribes the practical steps to be taken towards enlightenment. It is also known as 'the middle path', because it seeks to steer a course between strict asceticism and the excesses of sensuality. The path involves following the stages: right understanding; right directed thought or right intention; right speech; right action; right livelihood; right effort; right mindfulness; and right concentration. The first two, concerning wisdom, are essential for spiritual seekers, in that they need both to have a correct understanding of reality and also to direct their thought to that end. The following three relate to Buddhist morality, which is summed up in 'the five precepts' (or virtues). Seekers should refrain from:

■ harming living beings (including, of course, animals);

■ stealing (i.e. taking that which is not given);

■ misconduct concerning the pleasures of the senses (e.g. fornication, adultery);

■ false speech (e.g. lying, boasting, gossiping, causing offence);

■ the use of substances such as drugs and alcohol, as these tend to hinder awareness, and lead to loss of control and wrong thought.

Finally, the remaining three states of the noble eightfold path – right effort, right mindfulness and right concentration – are central to Buddhist practice. Cultivating meditative and

A seated Buddha sculpted on the Shanti Stupa in Kashmir.

psychic skills, they lead to contemplative states in which the mind is freed from distracting thoughts and images and able to concentrate (*samadhi*). This is typically done by sitting in a quiet place, as the Buddha had done under the *Bodhi* tree, and concentrating on a single object.

Since the time of the Buddha, various schools of Buddhism have evolved. Although the differences between them are often complex, there are essentially two broad

streams: a conservative stream, which wants to preserve the traditions, and a more liberal stream, which accepts innovation. Theravada Buddhism (*theravada* means 'the teaching of the elders'), a conservative tradition that seeks to preserve the original teaching of the Buddha, became firmly established in Ceylon (now Sri Lanka). Today, it is the dominant form of Buddhism in Sri Lanka, Burma, Thailand, Cambodia and Laos. Indeed, it was in Sri Lanka that the early Theravadan monks compiled and preserved the principal Buddhist scriptures, the *Tipitaka* – meaning 'three baskets' – which is written in Pali. Its practitioners claim that it is the purest form of Buddhism.

Mahayana Buddhism, the second stream, emerged in northern India later (around 1 CE) and is now commonly practised in China, Tibet, Mongolia, Nepal, Korea and Japan. Although Buddhism does not worship a creator God, Theravadan Buddhism being

explicitly non-theistic, the Mahayana school includes movements that do, to some extent, deify the Buddha. Central to Mahayana teaching is the doctrine of the 'bodhisattva' – a person who has achieved enlightenment can choose not to enter nirvana, but rather to voluntarily remain in the world in order to help lesser beings achieve an enlightened state. This is linked to another characteristic of the Mahayana tradition, namely the elevation of the virtue of compassion (which, unlike the Theravadan school, is equal to wisdom). Out of compassion for others, the bodhisattva postpones nirvana. Because all living beings are able to attain buddhahood, the bodhisattva seeks to assist them towards this goal.

Finally, it is worth noting a very popular form of Mahayana Buddhism, namely Pure Land Buddhism. Becoming particularly important in China and Japan, Pure Land Buddhism is characterized by devotion to the bodhisattva Amida (Amitabha, in Sanskrit) who, it is claimed in the sutras, vowed to lead all people to paradise, 'the Pure Land'. While the Pure Land is not nirvana, one can be sure to attain nirvana from the Pure Land. Central to Pure Land devotion is the chanting of Amida's name in a formula called *nembutsu*: 'Hail Amida Buddha' (*Namu Amida Butsu*). Indeed, Honen (1133–1212), a scholarly Japanese Buddhist priest whose ideas led to the founding of the Pure Land School (Jodoshu) in Japan, claimed that he was following an 'easy path', a path which emphasized only a sincere and simple faith in Amida. Liberation is not difficult or complex, and nor is it only for the few. Whether the devotee is a scholar or uneducated, only devotion to Amida and the practice of *nembutsu* will lead to rebirth in Amida's Pure Land.

Sikhism

Not only has Sikhism always been closely linked to its place of origin (the Punjab in north-west India) but the majority of Sikhs (around 13 million) still live there. In the rest of India there are around 2 million and outside India the largest number (around 500,000) live in Britain. Altogether, the total world population of Sikhs is about 16 million.

The founder, Guru Nanak (1469–1539), was born to Hindu parents in the Punjab near Lahore, which, at that time, had a powerful Islamic presence. This dual context of Islam and Hinduism is reflected in the origins of Sikhism. Unhappy with aspects of both Islam and Hinduism – particularly Hinduism's ritualism, use of images, bathing at places of pilgrimage, and notion of caste – Nanak, in common with much *bhakti* devotion, stressed inward loving devotion to the one God. Closeness to God is achieved through inner, devotional spirituality, not through ritualism and ceremony. Having had a direct experience of God, Nanak emerged saying 'there is no Hindu, there is no Muslim'. This signalled his mission to provide a third way, the Nanak *Panth* (Path of Nanak) – the community of Sikhs devoted to Nanak as their guru. This early group of disciples was drawn almost entirely from Hinduism. As well as gathering a group of disciples around him, Nanak wrote many beautiful, devotional hymns and set out the basic doctrines of what was to become Sikhism. Following Nanak there were nine further gurus, the last of which was Guru Gobind Singh (1666–1708). Sikhism prospered under this succession of gurus: the Sikh sacred city of Amritsar was founded, and the Sikh sacred text, the *Guru Granth Sahib* (also called the *Adi Granth*), was compiled. Hence, Sikhism is often referred to as the religion of the gurus. Indeed, the concept of guruship and discipleship is central to Sikhism; the word *sikh* means 'disciple' or one who learns from the guide/guru. The *Guru Granth Sahib* is understood as a guru, as is God, who is acknowledged as 'the true Guru' (*Sat-Guru*

A Sikh soldier in traditional dress, which includes a large talwar (*sword*).

and *Waheguru*): 'The true Guru is the bestower of life and lends support to all.' It is the truth of 'the true Guru' that the historical gurus and the *Guru Granth Sahib* communicate to humanity. Hence, the historical gurus are simply agents of the true Guru.

As indicated above, Sikhism is a monotheistic faith. The opening phrase (*mool mantra*) of the *Guru Granth Sahib* reads as follows:

There is one God, his name is truth eternal.
He is creator of all things, the all-pervading spirit.
Fearless and without hatred, timeless and
    formless.
Beyond birth and death, he is self-enlightened.
He is known by the Guru's grace.

Hence, within the *Guru Granth Sahib* there are statements that specifically criticize the worship of Hindu deities, insisting rather that God is one (*Ek Om*).

In 1699, in Anandpur, the final historical guru, Guru Gobind Singh, instituted the Sikh order, the Khalsa, which gave the Sikh community its outward identity. The Khalsa was essentially an elite community of devotees dedicated to the Guru. Entry into the Khalsa is by means of an initiation ceremony (*Amritsanskar*), which includes an initiatory baptism. An obligation of membership is also the addition of the titles *Singh* (Lion) to male names and *Kaur* (Princess) to female names. Finally, male initiates are obliged to wear 'the five Ks' as outward marks of Khalsa membership (although non-Khalsa Sikhs may also wear them in order to declare their commitment to Sikhism). The five Ks (*Panj Kakke*) are so called because, in Punjabi, they all begin with 'K':

■ *Kes* is uncut body hair. The hair of the head is usually gathered up within another symbol of Sikh identity, the turban. Concerning the wearing of a turban, although this is not one of the five Ks, all the gurus have traditionally

worn one and the Sikh Code of Discipline recommends the wearing of one.

■ The hair under the turban is gathered up and held under control with a topknot. This topknot is held in place by the second K, the *Kangha*, a comb.

■ The *Kirpan* is a ceremonial sword or dagger worn as part of the required dress.

■ Also worn as part of the ceremonial dress is a plain, steel bangle called a *Kara*.

■ Finally, the *Kachh*, a pair of shorts, is worn, usually as an undergarment in Western countries.

The Swaminarayan Movement
David Burnett

During the 18th century, foreign powers, including the British and French, were invading India and the country was in a state of social upheaval. Chapaiya was born in 1781 to a Brahmin family. It is claimed that from childhood he possessed miraculous powers. At the age of 11 he left home for a seven-year pilgrimage to the Himalayas, moving from temple to temple until in Loj, Gujarat, he met Ramanand Swami, who initiated him into the ascetic order and named him Sahajanand Swami. He was appointed leader of the order at the age of 21 after Ramanand died in 1802.

He then began his mission and became popularly known as Swaminarayan. His charismatic personality attracted many followers, who were soon numbered in the hundreds of thousands. This transformed the despised lower castes of Gujarat and put an end to animal sacrifice, female infanticide and suttee. The social impact upon the region was immense, and it is not surprising that many people considered him a god while he was still alive. He died in 1830 at the age of 49, but it is believed that he remains with his followers through a succession of sadhus.

The philosophical teaching of Swaminarayan is a qualified non-dualism, which holds that *Jiva, Ishwara, Maya, Aksharbrahman* and *Parabrahman* are five fundamental realities distinct from one another. *Parabrahman* is the highest reality, the supreme Godhead. *Aksharbrahman* is lower than *Parabrahman*, who incarnates himself to serve the supreme Lord. The highest manifestation of *Parabrahman* was the figure of Krishna who is an important object of devotion. *Maya* is the inert primordial substance from which the universe is formed, *Ishwara* is a cosmic self, and *Jiva* is the finite individual self. Liberation comes as a result of devotion to God through a spiritual guide.

An important aspect of devotion is the place of *murti* (images) as the focus of worship. These include the images of Radha and Krishna, Shiva and Parvati, as well as those of Swaminarayan and the saints of the movement. The *murti* are housed in temples (*mandirs*), ritual centres for the community. The teaching of Swaminarayan was not only preserved through the sadhus as he promised, but in the 212 sayings of the founder known as the *Shikshapatri*. These give details of how offerings should be made by members of various backgrounds.

Following the death of the guru in 1830, Gunatitanand (1785–1867) became the leader of the movement. He was succeeded by Bhagatji Maharaj (1829–1897), then on his death by Shastriji Maharaj (1865–1951), and then on his death by Yogiji Maharaj (1892–1971). The latter was the first of the gurus to travel overseas, and organized the building of *murtis* in East Africa and England. The community in Britain has built the beautiful *mandir* in Neasden, north London. Pramukh Swami Maharaj (b. 1921) became

The Shree Swaminarayan Mandir in Neasden, north London.

leader in 1971 and it is believed that through him Swaminarayan is currently manifesting himself in the world.

The Swaminarayan movement now numbers over 5 million, mainly among Gujarati-speaking people around the world. The Gujarati are known for their hard work, and this has resulted in economic wealth for the community. The movement is showing continued growth among Gujaratis in Europe and North America as well as India. In addition, a number of socially motivated groups have emerged from within the movement. The Bochasanwasi Shri Akshar Purushottam Swaminarayan Sanstha (BAPS) was established in 1907 by Swami Yagnapurushdas. It runs hospitals and schools for those in need. The International Swaminaraya Satsang Organization (ISSO) was established in 1978 by Shre Tejendraprasadji Acharaya Mahrajshri. It seeks to spread the teaching of the movement and has established temples in Europe and North America.

The Radhasoami Tradition
Gavin Flood

The Radhasoami Tradition is part of the north Indian devotional or *bhakti* movement known as the Sant Tradition, with over half a million active members throughout the world. There are a number of historically related Radhasoami branches, based mainly in India and the United States; all share certain common features, notably the goal of union with God, the centrality of the master or *sat* (true) guru, and meditation on inner sound.

The centre of Radhasoami teachings is the master. The tradition maintains that liberation or salvation from the endless cycle of reincarnation, driven by the power of action or karma, comes about through the master or guru, by whose power the disciple is liberated. The master is believed to be at one with the Lord (the transcendent source of the universe) and through the master the Lord bestows his grace. Specifically, at initiation the master is thought to take on the karma of the initiate and to connect the devotee's soul with the divine sound current (*shabd*) that flows through all things. Through repeating the secret names of God given at initiation, and through listening in meditation to the inner sound current, devotees seek to merge with the current, which conveys their souls back to God, the soul's true home. Devotees believe they will reach the goal after initiation through regular meditation, leading a life according to the Radhasoami precepts (a vegetarian diet, no adultery and no intoxicants), and attending meetings (*satsangs*) with other devotees. Radhasoami teachings offer an elaborate cosmology in which the material world is but one level of a vast universe. The path back to the Lord is a path back through the different regions of the hierarchical universe to the 'true world' (*sat lok*) or 'place of the Lord' (*radhasoami dham*). With initiation, past karma is eradicated and liberation will occur, if not within this lifetime, then within a limited number of lifetimes.

The focus on the master has meant that sometimes there have been competing claims to the master's mantle. Although Radhasoami teachings are found in the doctrines of the north Indian Sants, such as Kabir (15th

century), the modern tradition can be traced to Shiv Dayal Singh or Soamiji Maharaj (master 1850s–1878) in Agra. The name Radhasoami, the 'Lord of Radha', also indicates some influence from Krishna devotion (Radha is the consort of Krishna and a symbol of the soul). From Soamiji, two branches developed, one based at Agra, the other at Beas. In Agra, two disciples, Pratap Singh (master 1878–1911) and Rai Saligram (master 1878–98), established distinct lineages. In the Punjab, Jaimal Singh established the tradition at Beas, a village by the banks of the River Beas, where he founded the Radhasoami colony or *dera*. He passed the mastership on to Sawan Singh or the 'Great Master' (master 1903–48) with whom the teachings began to spread to the West. With Charan Singh (master 1951–90) the teachings spread further and the present master is Gurinder Singh (master 1990 to the present). Other lineages have also developed from the Beas branch. Although the teachings resemble Sikhism, and the masters use the Sikh holy book, the *Guru Granth Sahib*, in *satsangs*, orthodox Sikhs reject the Radhasoami guru as a living master.

Ramakrishna and the Ramakrishna Mission

David Burnett

Ramakrishna (1836–86) was born into a pious Brahmin family from a village some 65 miles north-west of Calcutta. He is said to have been conceived under miraculous circumstances and was initially named Gadadhar (Bearer of the Mace). He was his mother Chandra's second son, her first son Ramakumar having been born almost 30 years earlier. Although Gadadhar was encouraged to attend the local village school, he preferred to memorize the tales of the Hindu deities and began to experience ecstatic trances. His father died when he was still a child and Ramakumar became his second father. As the family was struggling financially, Ramakumar went to Calcutta to earn money. During this time, Gadadhar began to copy the manners of women and even dress in their clothes. Questions about his sexuality were raised throughout his life.

When Gadadhar was 16 his brother summoned him to Calcutta to assist him in his priestly duties. A wealthy widow by the name of Rani had a vision from Kali encouraging her to build a temple in Dakshineswar, Calcutta. Gadadhar was initiated into the cult of Kali, and it was at this time he became known as Ramakrishna. In 1856, Ramakumar suddenly died, and Ramakrishna was bereaved of his second father. It is said that he almost gave up eating food, slept little, and his relationship with the goddess became like that between a mother and child. Many people around him thought Ramakrishna was insane. Eventually his mother took him home, and, after some improvement, his mother arranged for him to marry a girl aged five. The marriage was duly performed in 1859, but the girl stayed with her parents until she was old enough to take her role as a wife; the marriage was never consummated.

On Ramakrishna's return to the temple in 1860, the 'divine madness' reappeared, and his unconventional behaviour reached new extremes. It was during this time that he started to explore new modes of religious experience, and was eager to learn from teachers of various sects. Under the guidance of Bhairavi Brahmani he studied tantra. In 1864, a monk named Jatadhari visited Dakshineswar, carrying with him a small metal image of the god Ram in the form of a boy in a metal cage. By constant worship of

Ramakrishna.

the image the monk had visions of Ram at play, like those of a child with an invisible imaginary friend.

Next to arrive was a naked Mussalman guru, who believed in a formless absolute devoid of duality and initiated Ramakrishna into Advaita Vedanta, the philosophical teaching of the ultimate reality as being *Brahman*, which is beyond description. In 1866, Ramakrishna began to adopt the mystic practices of Islam. Under the direction of his guru he dressed as a Muslim and chanted the name of Allah. He began praying five times a day to Mecca and neglected the Hindu deities, including Kali. Then, in 1874, he sought to learn about Christianity. Ramakrishna became increasingly well known in the region of Calcutta for the ease with which he could enter mystical states. He began to teach that all religions had at their core a common mystical experience of the divine.

He was convinced that many young men would come to him as disciples. The first to arrive came in 1879: Ram Chandra Datta, a young doctor, and his cousin, Manomohan Mita. A few months later, Surendranath Mitra came, and then from 1881 onward various students from local schools and colleges joined the group. These included Vivekananda who was to become famous for his presentation of the Advaita Vedanta at the Parliament of World Religions in Chicago. In 1882, Mahendranath Gupta, or 'M', the author of the *Gospel of Sri Ramakrishna*, also became a follower.

After Ramakrishna's death from cancer in 1886, his young disciples took the message of Ramakrishna to the world. The power of Ramakrishna was said to have passed into Vivekananda, who set up the Ramakrishna Mission in 1897. The mission has three major aims, the first of which is the training of monks, and for this purpose the Ramakrishna Math (order) was established in 1899. The second aim is the promotion of education and social action: it therefore runs many schools and colleges, organizes relief projects, and runs libraries as well as dispensaries and hospitals. The third aim is the promotion of Vedantic teaching. The core of the mission's teaching is pluralistic, with the belief that all religions lead to the same goal, which is God-realization. Christ is highly revered by the members, but only as a perfect ideal for humanity.

The headquarters of the mission is the Belur Math near Calcutta, which is largely controlled by the monks. It now has 131 branches in India and different parts of the world. The stated aim of the mission is the uplifting of the masses, educating women, rebuilding India and regenerating the world through Hindu spirituality. The mission has done much to revitalize Hinduism in the face of Christian evangelization, especially during the colonial period. Although the mission and its missionaries are modelled after Christian missionary practices it denounces religious conversion, and is against Christian missionary work in India. It has spread to have a global influence in the second half of the 20th century.

The Meher Baba Movement
Ron Geaves

Meher Baba was born Merwan Sheriar Irani in 1894 to a Parsee (Zoroastrian) family in Poona, India. He declared himself to be the avatar of this age and from 1925 maintained a vow of silence, communicating with his disciples by hand gestures and pointing to letters on an alphabet board. This vow of silence was undertaken to bring about a complete transformation of consciousness in the world through a release of divine love.

His personal biography claims that he met

an old woman named Hazrat Babajan, one of five perfect masters of the time, at the age of 19. She kissed him on the forehead and his cloud of ignorance fell away, leaving him with the knowledge that he was God incarnate. Meher Baba also visited Shirdi Sai Baba, Narayan Maharaj, Tajuddin Baba and Upasni Maharaj, who it is believed also acknowledged him as the avatar of the age. From 1921, he gathered a group of disciples around him who gave him the name Meher Baba, meaning 'compassionate father'. In 1923, they established an ashram (named Meherabad), complete with free hospital and a school. Meherabad remains important as the location of Meher Baba's tomb and is a place of pilgrimage for his followers worldwide.

After extensive tours of India, in 1931 Meher Baba travelled to the West on the first of his several visits to England, where he established the Meher Baba Association. He continued his travels to the United States and eventually, in 1952, established his home in the West in Myrtle Beach, South Carolina. Meher Baba did not see himself a teacher, but as a transformer of global consciousness through his presence in the world. In the final years of his life he went into seclusion, except for a few mass gatherings in which he gave his blessings to those who believed in him. In 1968, he declared that his work was complete and he died the following year.

His followers gather informally to share experiences of his love and continued guidance and some go on pilgrimage to the tomb-centre in Meherabad. They feel themselves to be guided in their spiritual journey to destroy the ego and to realize 'God' as their true selves. It is believed that Meher Baba continues to live in the hearts of all that believe in him. The message is eclectic and does not deny the essential truths contained at the heart of all world religions, but the influence of Hindu Vedantic philosophy and Persian Sufism is foremost in the spiritual worldview presented to the followers. The main centre of the movement's activities is at the 500-acre retreat centre at Myrtle Beach, which is visited by spiritual seekers from all over the world. Meher Baba also prophesied that his *samadhi* site (tomb) would become the most frequented place of pilgrimage in the world within 70 years of his death. It is also believed that, for 100 years from his death, entering the tomb site is the same as actually coming into his physical presence. Since Meher Baba provided no teachings above and beyond his actual presence in the world, there is a considerable degree of freedom for individual followers to express their spiritual journeys within the framework of universal mysticism and the eclecticism of the New Age under the umbrella of Meher Baba's divine presence and guidance.

The Self-Realization Fellowship
David Burnett

Mukunda Lal Ghosh (1893–1952) was born in Gorakhpur, India. As a child, he was said to stare at the photograph of Lahiri Mahasya, who was responsible for reviving the practice of kriya yoga. In his autobiography he tells of his first encounter with a swami, who seemed strangely familiar, and then on the following morning a divine voice announced 'Thy Master cometh today!' The swami was Sri Yukteswar, a renowned master of yoga and pupil of Lahiri Mahasya. The boy was given the name Yogananda and became his close disciple. After studying at Serampore College and graduating from Calcutta University in 1915, his father wanted him to work as a railway manager, but Yogananda refused and became a monk in the swami's order. Sri Yukteswar planned for Yogananda to travel to the West and spread the teaching of kriya yoga.

In 1920, Yogananda began his travels in the United States. Commencing at the Boston Congress as an Indian delegate, he was invited to speak at many more assemblies as his popularity increased. Having, in 1917, founded the Yogoda Satsanga in India, he established its Western headquarters in 1920 in Los Angeles. In 1925 he founded the Self-Realization Fellowship at the Los Angeles headquarters and in 1927 established a sister organization in Washington, the Self-Realization Church of All Religions (see the *Self-Revelation Church of Absolute Monism). Both these organizations worked together under the leadership of Yogananda. (The headquarters of the Yogoda Satsanga is in Dakshineswar, near Calcutta, and there are over 90 meditation centres, 21 educational institutions and several charities in the country.)

In 1935, Yogananda made his final visit to India, where Sri Yukteswar gave him the title 'Paramahansa' to signify his high spiritual status. Back in the United States, Yogananda wrote *Autobiography of a Yogi*, which was published in 1946. This book has become very important to the Self-Realization Fellowship, because it not only describes his extraordinary experiences but his life is seen as a supreme illustration of his teaching.

His teaching on kriya yoga claims to be a scientific technique of God-realization and achieving inner peace. When a devotee achieves inner peace they can then realize God and God's love. Yogananda taught that kriya yoga draws extra oxygen into the body's system, which is transformed into 'life currents' that reinvigorate the brain and the spinal centres. Thus, it enables one to become free from karma, and to halt the decay of mind and body. It is said that, after his death on 7 March 1952, Yogananda's body remained in his chamber for 20 days awaiting burial but showed no sign of decay. Followers of the Self-Realization Fellowship are taught various kriya yoga techniques and are asked to practise daily. However, they are not required to change their religious allegiance and are proud of their tolerance. They have recently established a gay section of the Self-Realization Fellowship.

Swami Rajarsi Janakananda (James J. Lynn) succeeded Yogananda, but he died only three years later. Sri Daya Mata (Faye Wright; b. 1914) became the leader/president of both the Self-Realization Fellowship and the Yogoda Satsanga Society of India in 1955, and she has continued to teach Yogananda's ideas and techniques. She has been a disciple of Yogananda from the time she first heard him speak in Salt Lake City in 1931 and is revered in the organization as *Sanghamata* (Mother of the Society). She is now regarded by devotees as 'Self-realized' (or 'God-realized') and, therefore, omnipresent, omniscient and omnipotent. The headquarters of the organization remains in Los Angeles, with 150 other centres in the United States and around 500 meditation centres worldwide.

The Self-Revelation Church of Absolute Monism
Christopher Partridge

The Self-Revelation Church of Absolute Monism has its origins in the Self-Realization Church of All Religions founded in 1927 by Paramahansa Yogananda (1893–1952; born Mukunda Lal Ghosh in Gorakhpur, India). Having being initiated in 1915 by his master, Sri Yukteswar, Yogananda founded the Yogoda Satsanga in India in 1917. (A *satsanga* is a sacred or divine fellowship; *yogoda* is a term coined by Yogananda meaning 'that which yoga imparts', i.e. 'self-realization'.) Following Sri Yukteswar, Yogananda traces his lineage back through Sri Yukteswar and Lahiri Mahasya to a guru called Babaji who taught a form of yoga known as kriya yoga. Yogananda believed that his particular mission was to teach kriya yoga to the West.

While the Self-Revelation Church of Absolute Monism claims its founder to be

Yogananda, arguably the most significant figure in the establishment of the church is Swami Premananda (1903–95). Originally known as Brahmachari Jotin, he was initiated by Yogananda in India in 1920. Shortly after Jotin's initiation, Yogananda set sail for America as a delegate to the International Congress of Religious Liberals held in Boston. He then established the Western headquarters of the Yogoda Satsanga in 1920 in Los Angeles. In 1925, he founded the *Self-Realization Fellowship at the Los Angeles headquarters and in 1927 established a sister organization in Washington, the Self-Realization Church of All Religions. Both these organizations worked together under the leadership of Yogananda. However, because of his enormous success in America, in 1928 he asked Bramachari Jotin to assist him and lead the work in Washington as the head of the Self-Realization Church of All Religions. In 1941, Jotin made further vows of commitment to Yogananda and became Swami Premananda.

It seems clear, however, that Jotin gradually began to seek independence from the Self-Realization Fellowship. On 23 October 1938, a group met for the first time in a chapel Jotin had established in Washington. Then, sometime after 1946, against the wishes of Yogananda, Premananda separated the church from the Self-Realization Fellowship. Although Yogananda appealed to Premananda to reunite the church and the Self-Realization Fellowship, Premananda did not. After the death of Yogananda, Premananda, who had never resigned from the Self-Realization Fellowship, was asked to resign. Eventually, at some time after this date, Premananda's independent organization became the Self-Revelation Church of Absolute Monism, and, on 23 November 1952, the Church's Golden Lotus Temple in Washington, designed by Premananda, was consecrated.

The current leader of the Self-Revelation Church of Absolute Monism is Srimati Kamala (b. 1945). Having studied philosophy, language and literature at university, she was initiated by Premananda in 1973, has served as a minister of the church since 1975, and was consecrated by Premananda as a Swami in 1978 (she is now known as Swami Kamalananda Giri).

A similar group linked to the Self-Revelation Church of Absolute Monism is the Divine Life Church of Absolute Oneness (based in Baltimore). Emerging out of the Yoga Society in Baltimore, this organization was established by Premananda in 1974, receiving the name Divine Life Church of Absolute Oneness in 1975. The current leader of this group is Swami Shankarananda (formerly assistant minister of the Self-Revelation Church of Absolute Monism in Washington).

The Self-Revelation Church of Absolute Monism and the Divine Life Church of Absolute Oneness believe Premananda to be in the lineage of kriya yoga gurus. This claim is rejected by the Self-Realization Fellowship.

Central to the philosophy and practice of kriya yoga are breath control, withdrawal of the senses, meditation, harmony with 'life energy', the belief in the divinity of the self, a recognition that the material world is actually *maya* (illusory), and the related belief that all reality is a divine oneness – absolute monism (absolute 'one-ism'). In Hindu philosophy, this belief is particularly associated with the doctrine of non-dualism (*advaita*) and the philosophy of Shankara (788–820), often regarded as India's greatest philosopher. It is this monist/non-dualist emphasis, which teaches that the self (*atman*) is identical with the absolute (*Brahman*/the Divine), that lies at the heart of the teaching of the Self-Revelation Church of Absolute Monism and the Divine Life Church of Absolute Oneness. According to the stated 'Ideal of the

Church', 'Every man is essentially divine. Man is the divine self. The ideal of human existence is the recognition of man's divine nature, otherwise called self-realization. When one realizes his true self, spirituality guides his daily life and conduct. Life guided by spiritual vision ensures inner contentment and world peace.' According to Premananda, 'Soul is inseparable from God as the ray is from the sun.' Through meditation one is able to come to a realization of the true nature of the self and, consequently, one is able to rise above the turmoil of bodily existence. 'We will,' says Kamala, 'inwardly become so free that nothing of the changing world of experience can diminish, betray, threaten or rule us.' Sometimes with reference to the teaching of Jesus, this understanding of the self as divine is explained in terms of the kingdom of God within us.

The Brahma Kumaris
Frank Whaling

The movement that later became known as the Brahma Kumaris began with the spiritual experiences vouchsafed to Mr Lekhraj, a respected diamond merchant living in Hyderabad, Sindh. In 1936, when these visions began, Sindh was part of India, but it later became part of Pakistan.

Lekhraj was a 60-year-old lay Hindu famed for his generosity and courtesy. He was married with a family. His visions changed his life, and he became the leader of a new movement until his death in 1969 at the age of 93.

Family, then friends, then others gravitated towards Lekhraj, who became known as Prajapita Brahma, and he sold his millionaire share of the diamond business and before long founded a Trust with 11 women as the trustees of the new movement forming around him. This was revolutionary in the India of the late 1930s and the movement is still led by women today, both at the top and in almost all of its branches around the world.

'Dada' Lekhraj had a strong sense that God, the Supreme Soul, had descended into him with a new and deep message for humanity, which was important not only for himself, but also for the wider world. His followers became known as the *Brahma Kumaris*, the pure daughters of Brahma, and over 300 people, including men, joined the early community.

Lekhraj gained the understanding that God lives in a world of light, a dimension beyond the physical, which is also the original home of all souls. Throughout the ages, God has inspired the revelation of great truths through special messengers and prophets, and he is now revealing new teachings in our current age. The present age, he taught, is unparalleled in spiritual potency and power. The Brahma Kumaris are sharing the message that it is up to each one of us to use this spiritually vibrant time to the full in order to create a better world. Lekhraj had visions of the degeneration and transformation of this world, of the Golden Age to follow and of God, all of which are crucial to the Brahma Kumaris worldview.

During this intermediate age, Lekhraj suggested, persons could live humbly, yet triumphantly, as forerunners of a new Golden Age of spiritual vibrancy and ecological beauty. In order to do this effectively, it was necessary to move from body consciousness to soul consciousness. This did not mean retreating from the world or demeaning the body. However, it did involve unselfishness, withdrawal from absorption in material pursuits, and the practice of celibacy. Positively, it involved the building-up of a strong spirituality centred upon the sense that each person is essentially a 'soul'. Thus outward features of gender, age, colour, race or appearance were superficial. People needed to be treated as souls, and this required the attributes of calmness, empathy, generosity,

The Dilwara Temple at Mount Abu, India. Mount Abu is the spiritual powerhouse of the Brahma Kumaris.

kindness, love, and so on. Underlying this was the need for a deep spirituality now directly available from God to those willing to receive the peace and love he was willing to bestow. This spiritual power emanating from God could satisfy the fullest needs of everyone and send them out in service to the rest of the world. The empowerment of women and the nurturing ethical qualities of women are stressed. Such, in brief, was the framework of knowledge and spirituality opened up by Lekhraj to those who gathered round him at that time.

Just after the partition of India and Pakistan, the community moved to Mount Abu in Rajasthan, India, where the headquarters remains to this day. A daily routine evolved, which is still largely in place, involving meditation from 4.00 to 4.45 a.m., the reading of a message (*murli*) from about 6.30 a.m., practical work during the day, and evening meditation and evening classes. Every Sunday afternoon, Brahma Kumaris meet to meditate for peace in the world. The movement has no scripture as such. However, the *murlis* read at the 6.30 a.m. meetings are slowly developing the nature of potential scriptures. The earlier ones, mediated by Lekhraj while he was alive, are now repeated in a five-year cycle. They are supplemented by later *murlis* received by Dadi Gulzar of Delhi in trance states, and these, too, are written down. The situation is thus ripe for the development of a Brahma Kumaris 'scripture'.

The many centres that arose around India were superintended by people, mainly women, who also worked. Mount Abu became a spiritual powerhouse and resource centre for the growing community, which was remarkable for its combination of superb administration and deep spirituality. Moreover, by this time, although Lekhraj remained the overall spiritual leader, the pragmatic day-to-day leadership of the community had been taken over by a gifted young woman, Mateshwari Saraswati (known as 'Mama'). The teachings of the Brahma Kumaris are universal and people of all faiths study at their university.

Mama died in 1965, and, in 1969, Lekhraj (now known fondly as Brahma Baba) also died. In theory, the passing of these great souls might have been catastrophic, but in practice, from 1969 onwards, further significant growth ensued. The present leader, Dadi Prakashmani, and other co-leaders took over, and the arrival of the gifted Dadi Janki in London in the early 1970s led to the setting up of centres in 84 countries outside India, in addition to the continuing spread in India. Although relatively small ('regular students' [i.e. members] now number around 600,000 in about 5,000 centres), the overseas students (especially the Western students) have had a universalizing and perhaps streamlining impact upon an originally very Indian movement.

Symbolic of this is the growing significance of their work attached to the United Nations. In 1983, the first of many Universal Peace Conferences was held at Mount Abu, which by now could accommodate 3,000 people. In 1984, Dadi Prakashmani was awarded the Peace Medal, and consultative status at the United Nations was given to the Brahma Kumaris, who have since coordinated major international projects, such as the 'Million Minutes for Peace' project in 1986, the 'Global Cooperation for a Better World' project from 1988, the 'Year of Interreligious Understanding and Cooperation' in 1993, and more recently are the main sponsors of a significant Values and Education project called Living Values: An Educational Program (LVEP). The building of Global Cooperation House in London and the purchase of the Nuneham Retreat Centre in Oxfordshire, England, in the 1990s have further stimulated overseas expansion.

Hao Hoa
David Burnett

A living Buddha known as 'The Healing Buddha of Tay An' made his first appearance on the mountain of Tat Son, Vietnam, in 1849 and founded *Buu Son Ky Huong* Buddhism. Ninety years later, in 1939, Huynh Phu So founded Hao Hoa in the Vietnamese village of that name with the aim of revitalizing this tradition of Buddhism. Although he was assassinated in 1947, the movement grew in the Mekong River delta, especially among peasant farmers.

Hao Hoa is a Pure Land form of Mahayana Buddhism that has retained ancestor veneration. They worship in the home with an altar consisting of Buddha statues, bells and gongs arranged on a brown cloth, symbolizing human harmony. Under that altar is another to honour the ancestors. Followers must worship the Buddha every morning and evening. Hao Hoa adherents are also encouraged to comply with the 'four great debts of gratitude': to ancestors and parents, to their country, to 'the three jewels' – Buddha, *dharma* (teachings of the Buddha) and *sangha* (community) – and to humanity.

The nationalistic character of the movement resulted in its rapid growth during the Japanese occupation. It opposed both the French colonialists and the Vietnamese nationalist movement of Ho Chi Minh. After

1954, it began armed opposition to the United States-backed government of Ngo Dinh Diem, and, although many Hao Hoa adherents joined the communist National Liberation Front, it remained an independent force. When the Vietnam War ended in April 1975, communist authorities began to confiscate Hao Hoa properties and banned many of their celebrations. The 5 million followers claimed by Hao Hoa have joined the growing opposition movement in collaboration with many Vietnamese living overseas.

The Church of the Shaiva Siddhanta

Gavin Flood

The Church of the Shaiva Siddhanta is a substantial worldwide movement that has developed from a Hindu tradition focusing on the god Shiva. A Shaiva is a devotee of Shiva. The movement was founded by the American master Satguru Shivaya Subramuniyaswami (d. 2001), known as Gurudeva, who brought the tradition to the West from Sri Lanka. Subramuniyaswami was initiated in 1949 by the Tamil-speaking Shaiva Yogaswami (1872–1964), who told his disciple to spread Shaivism in the United States. He thereupon founded the Shaiva Siddhanta Yoga Order and the Church of the Shaiva Siddhanta, which Subramuniyaswami then took to the United States. He founded a further institution, the Himalayan Academy, in 1957 and established a Hindu monastery on the Hawaiian island of Kauai in 1970. Here there is a community of approximately 30 monks, along with householder or family groups. The ordained monks or swamis follow a path of *brahmacarya* or celibacy and lead a life of meditation and service to the community. There are two Hindu temples on the 50-acre site.

The teachings of the church are based on the Tamil Shaiva Siddhanta tradition, mediated through Subramuniyaswami. The goal of life is 'enlightenment' by following the Shaiva path of service, devotion to God, and meditation or yoga, which is said to give direct knowledge and union with Shiva. Subramuniyaswami advocates non-violence and vegetarianism. Shaiva Siddhanta (the tradition of Shiva) originated in India, possibly in Kashmir, and particularly developed in the Tamil-speaking south, where it was established by the 11th century. Here the tradition reveres the revelation of Shiva – texts called the Shaiva tantras or *Agamas* – which cannot confidently be dated much before the 9th century. When the tradition became established in the south, its ritual systems were complemented by a more emotional devotion or *bhakti* expressed in the poetry of Tamil Shaiva saints, the Nayanars. In contrast to the monistic 'Kashmir' Shaivism, the teachings of the Shaiva Siddhanta are dualistic, maintaining an ontological distinction between the self, Shiva and the world. It is not clear that this dualism has entered the Church of the Shaiva Siddhanta, as the goal is the realization that 'All is Shiva', achieved through knowing 'thy Self by thyself'. This last teaching of Subramuniya's master could reveal some influence of Theravada Buddhism, as would be likely in Sri Lanka, and the Buddha's teaching of 'be a lamp unto yourselves'. But, in contrast to Buddhism, the Church of the Shaiva Siddhanta is a theistic tradition.

Subramuniyaswami had a high international profile. He was honoured in 1986 at the World Religious Parliament in New Delhi as one of five Hindu leaders outside India who promoted the 'eternal truth or law' or *sanatana dharma*. In 1993 he was elected to the President's Assembly at Chicago's centenary of the Parliament of World Religions. He also established the international newspaper *Hinduism Today*, which promotes Hinduism as a world religion and supports the 'Hindu renaissance'.

The Satya Sai Baba Society
David Burnett

Indian religion has been characterized by great gurus, and by far the most famous of contemporary miracle workers is Sai Baba (b. 1926). He is considered to be an incarnation of a previous guru, also known as Sai Baba. In order to distinguish between them, the first is called Shirdi Sai Baba (1838–1918), and the second Satya Sai Baba. Shirdi is also attributed with many miracles, and is said to continue to visit his devotees in dreams, giving them guidance and protection.

Satya Sai Baba was named at birth Satyanarayana Rajuin, meaning 'true all-pervading God'. Shortly after his birth, a cobra was found under his bed. As this snake is considered to be the symbol of Shiva, the child was associated with this deity. From an early age, Sai Baba began to compose religious songs and was said to be able to materialize objects out of thin air. When he was 14, he was stung by a scorpion and fell into a deep trance, and when he finally awoke he claimed to be the reincarnation of Shirdi Sai Baba. He returned to school and performed many notable miracles in front of the local community, though critics have queried their veracity. His fame spread rapidly and, in 1950, Sai Baba established an ashram in a village outside Puttaparthi in south India. Today, devotees come to experience 'Sai power', which not only manifests miracles, but also allows telepathy and spiritual surgery.

Sai Baba has given four important principles in his teaching. First is *satya* (truth), not in the sense of an ethical principle, but an understanding of the world. Ordinary mortals are said to be born in accordance with their karma, and should give

Satya Sai Baba at the ashram outside Puttaparthi in south India, where devotees come to experience 'Sai power'.

selfless service in order to achieve a better rebirth and, eventually, liberation. Certain holy figures, such as Sai Baba, are freed from their karma, and manifest themselves to dispense grace and perform miracles.

The second principle is *dharma* (duty). Sai Baba rejects caste, and teaches the equality of all regardless of caste, creed, race or gender. To gain liberation requires a combination of good deeds, wisdom and devotion. Most Sais are vegetarian, as they seek not to harm any living being. *Shanti* (peace) is the third principle. Sai Baba claims he can help humanity to attain peace in the sense of absence of war, and harmony with other people and the environment. Finally, *prema* (divine love) should be expressed to one's fellow human beings and especially to Sai Baba himself.

He has millions of followers in India and among Asian communities in Europe and North America, many of whom display his picture in their homes. The Satya Sai Baba Society has not had the same level of criticism as some groups, possibly because Sai Baba has fewer Western followers.

The Muttappan Teyyam
Theodore Gabriel

The Muttappan Teyyam (*Teyyam* is the ritual complex surrounding a deity) has its origins in Parassinikkadavu, a small township about 30 miles (50 km) to the east of Kannur city in northern Kerala. The cult, originally of tribal origins, is now widely popular and Muttappan temples have sprung up all over northern Kerala and even in other states, such as Vijayawada in Andhra Pradesh, Chennai in Tamil Nadu and Mumbai in Maharashtra. A Muttappan temple may soon be established in Singapore. Devotees numbering in their thousands include not only 'untouchable' caste groups (Dalits), the groups with whom the Muttappan deities were initially

The Muttappan duo of gods.

associated, but also caste Hindus.

The origins of the Muttappan Teyyam are lost in antiquity. However, because it is believed that the gods incarnated specifically to ameliorate the intense discrimination and the oppression of lower castes and untouchables by higher caste Hindus, and because the caste situation in Kerala deteriorated considerably after the eclipse of Buddhism in Kerala around the 10th century CE, it is, therefore, assumed that the birth of the Muttappan was in or shortly after this period. However, having said that, because it became really popular only in the 1950s, when transport facilities to Parassinikkadavu improved, and the power and charisma of the Muttappan came to the attention of other parts of Kerala, the Muttappan Teyyam can be considered to be a modern rather than a medieval phenomenon.

The 'Muttappan' (gem of a god) comprises two gods, the Valiya Muttappan and the Cheriya Muttappan (literally, the Big Muttappan and the Little Muttappan). The gods are of tribal origin and were probably originally heroic figures in the forested northern hill regions of Kerala. The legends associated with the gods state that a male baby was found on the banks of the River Vaveli by Padikkutti, the wife of a local ruler, the Ayyankara Tampuran, as an answer to the prayers of this childless couple. Brought up by the ruler and his wife with great affection, the Valiya Muttappan began to display from his childhood a fascination for the forest, and for meat and palm toddy, which brought him into confrontation with his parents, who were Brahmins and strict vegetarians and teetotallers. His passion for hunting took him often to the forests and among wild animals, of which he had no fear.

Eventually the estrangement of the Muttappan from his father grew so great that he decided to leave the palace. Anger seethed within him at the courtiers who had forced his father to chastise him and flames came from his eyes and burned up the palace and the surroundings. His mother implored him to cover up his eyes. Consequently, in Muttappan iconography the god appears in rituals permanently blindfolded. He left his parents for the forest, where his companions were tribal people, untouchables, low-caste Hindus and wild animals. He fought against local rulers and high-caste landlords and sought to emancipate the tribal people and untouchables from their oppression. In the forest, the Muttappan met a hermit with whom he engaged in a dance and who became his companion – the Cheriya Muttappan. The two appear in rituals together whenever the senior god, the Valiya Muttappan, is present (the *Tiruvappana*), but a shorter ritual can also be conducted (the *Vellatt*) in which only the junior deity features. Modern interpreters portray this

duo as Vishnu and Shiva, who incarnated in Kerala in order to ameliorate the iniquitous caste situation of the region.

The rituals of the Muttappan Teyyam belong to the genre known as the *Teyyam* (from the Sanskrit term *deivam*, meaning 'god'). In this category of ritual, elaborately painted and masked ritual specialists enact the roles of gods and goddesses. There are no images of deities in the temples where these rituals are enacted. By means of drumming and the chanting of devotional songs, the spirits of the deities are invoked into the ritual specialists, who thereon perform a vigorous dance, culminating in the circumambulation of the central shrine, where the spirits of the gods are believed to normally reside. Thereafter, the gods meet with the devotees, accept offerings of cash, offer solutions to their problems, and heal, comfort and bless them. Interestingly, the burgeoning popularity of the cult is said to be due to the effectiveness and accuracy of the predictions of the gods, their evident mystical knowledge, and the potency of their healing and blessing.

Ananda Marga
Frank Whaling

The name of this new religious movement is taken from the Sanskrit for 'way of bliss'. It was founded in 1955 by Prabhut Ranjan Sarkar, who was born in Jamalpur, India, in 1921 as the eldest son of a railway accounts clerk. As the leader of Ananda Marga, he became known as Anandamurti, and his followers call him 'Baba'. The movement established a presence in the West after 1970, but it has remained traditionally Hindu in provenance.

Ananda Marga has been relatively unusual among Hindu new religious movements in its dual stress upon social and political matters as well as upon spiritual development. Thus, on the one hand, the aim is realization and liberation of the self, and on the other hand the aim is service to humankind and social and political development.

Various general life disciplines are required, including bodily purity, a suitable diet, correct bodily posture, social service and meditation. Celibacy is favoured, but marriage is also accepted, providing it is for the purpose of procreation.

The meditation used is generally that associated with tantric yoga and its techniques. It is therefore aimed not merely at individual spiritual uplift, but also at arousing within a person a universal interest in the wider world and a deep concern for social justice. The ultimate aim is to be part of setting up a world government of enlightened individuals. Anandamurti had pretensions to being a political theorist; at one time he founded a political party and he also began, in 1964, the promotion of a model city named Anand Nagar.

In some quarters Anandamurti has established the reputation of being a miracle-worker. He is the head of a hierarchical leadership and has aroused within his followers a deep commitment to him, to the extent of devotees being willing to self-immolate during a time of trouble.

The movement has not lacked controversy. Seventeen members of Ananda Marga were killed by a Calcutta mob in 1982. Anandamurti was arrested in 1971 and imprisoned on suspicion of murder, but human rights supporters denounced the arrest and he was released in 1978 when Indira Gandhi fell from power. Three Australian members were convicted for attempting to murder a politician in the 1970s, but the sentences were later overturned. Apart from the Australian case, no other arrests or convictions have become known.

Ananda Marga is an unusual mixture of the spiritual, the social, the political, and a tinge of the revolutionary.

Transcendental Meditation
Christopher Partridge

Transcendental Meditation (TM) was founded by Maharishi Mahesh Yogi in 1957 and claims to be a modern form of the techniques taught in the Yoga Sutra – attributed to Patanjali (2nd century BCE) but probably compiled about 600 years later. Little is known about the early life of the Maharishi – there is even little certainty as to when he was born (possibly 1917). (The assumed title 'Maharishi' means 'Great Seer'.) After graduating in physics from Allahabad University in 1940, he studied for 13 years under Swami Brahmananda Saraswati (1869–1953), commonly known as 'Guru Dev'. After his death, the Maharishi went into seclusion for two years in Uttar Kashi, emerging as the leading teacher of TM in 1955. He published his first book in 1956, *The Beacon Light of the Himalayas*, and in 1958 founded the Spiritual Regeneration Movement in Madras to promote his teachings.

In 1959, the Spiritual Regeneration Movement acquired premises in Los Angeles, and in 1960 the Maharishi travelled to Britain to give a lecture in the Caxton Hall, London. He also founded the International Meditation Society in 1960. In 1961, the Maharishi began to train others as teachers of TM in order to increase the spread of the technique. In 1963, he published a key TM text, *Science of Being and Art of Living* and in 1965 he established the Students' International Meditation Society, which focused on spreading the TM technique to the student population in the West. However, the most significant factor for the spread of the movement came in 1967 when the Maharishi visited Britain again and inspired the popular musician George Harrison. Although Harrison later became far more interested in the Hare Krishnas (*ISKCON), his trip to India in 1968, followed by the rest of the Beatles and other celebrities, attracted international attention to the Maharishi and TM. Certainly many young people in the West who had become disillusioned with the psychedelic experience offered by drugs, and yet were still interested in Indian religion and altered states of consciousness, found the Maharishi's teaching liberating. The Maharishi International University was founded in 1968 in Iowa, United States, and in the following year he announced his 'World Plan' to create one teaching centre per million people, with one TM teacher per thousand people.

Although Maharishi originates from a Hindu background, was taught by a Hindu guru, and teaches techniques and mantras that have their origins in the Indian religious tradition, the Maharishi and his followers insist that TM is not 'a religion', but rather a scientific technique. Indeed, it is very fond of quoting scientific research which, it is argued, supports the claims of TM. Moreover, one need not be religious to practise TM: 'TM technique requires no belief or lifestyle change, is non-religious, is not time-consuming, and can be learned by anyone regardless of age or level of education.' One of the Maharishi's students, Peter Russell, describes the TM technique in the following way:

The TM technique allows the mind to settle down to a less excited state. The person experiences quieter and quieter levels of thinking till he or she arrives at a state of complete mental stillness. In this state, the attention is said to have gone beyond, or transcended, the everyday levels of thought – hence the description 'Transcendental Meditation'.

As the mind settles down the body follows suit, becoming more relaxed than during sleep. One does not however go to sleep: one remains fully conscious and is usually aware of all that is happening in the world around. It is not a state of unconsciousness or hypnotic trance: it is simply a state of mental and physical quiet with full inner wakefulness.

The famous meeting between the Beatles and the Maharishi in Bangor, Wales, in 1967.

To practise the TM technique takes about 20 minutes twice a day, once in the morning and again in the early evening. One simply sits down comfortably, closes the eyes and begins the mental practice. As a result the mind is allowed to settle down into a complete state of rest…

The technique does not involve sitting in any strange physical postures, any change of lifestyle, or the adoption of any philosophy.

Again, while there is a great deal of theoretical material that one can study, teachers insist that one can enjoy the effects of TM without believing it. Moreover, apart from the meditation period itself, one is not required to withdraw from one's affairs in the world. Indeed, TM is believed to increase effectiveness in the world. It is understood in terms of the reduction of stress and the charging of one's mental and physical batteries.

While the TM technique is straightforward and can be mastered in, usually, four days, generally speaking those interested will progress through the following steps: *the introductory lecture* (1 hour 30 minutes), during which the individual will be introduced to the possibilities and benefits TM makes available; *the preparatory lecture* (1 hour 30 minutes), during which basic information about the technique and the origins of TM are related; *a personal interview* (ten minutes) with a qualified teacher for those wishing to continue; *personal instruction* (2 hours) in the technique; and *verification and validation of experiences*. Following personal instruction, there are three 2-hour follow-up sessions, during which the teacher 'checks' the progress of the student, and provides further instruction in the technique and the development of higher states of consciousness.

Beginning in 1976, the 'TM-Sidhi programme' was developed as a natural extension of TM, intended to speed up an individual's progress towards enlightenment.

According to their literature, this programme develops 'higher levels of intelligence, learning ability, creativity and neurological efficiency'. An important aspect of the TM-Sidhi programme, sometimes controversially referred to as levitation, is 'yogic flying'. The body, it is claimed, 'lifts up and moves forward in short hops. Subjectively one experiences exhilaration, lightness, and bliss.' The upward lift is understood to be the outward manifestation of 'optimum coherence in brain functioning [which, in turn] creates perfect mind/body coordination. When yogic flying is practised in groups, this influence of coherence spreads throughout the environment, reducing negative tendencies and promoting positive, harmonious trends in the whole society.'

The claimed beneficial social effects of yogic flying have been vigorously promoted by the Natural Law Party, which was formed in the UK in 1992. According to TM, 'Natural Law is the intelligence and infinite organizing power that silently maintains and guides the evolution of everything in the universe. The activity of every grain of creation and of every level of Nature – from the tiniest sub-atomic particle to the vast galaxies – is governed by Natural Law with perfect efficiency so that everything in the universe functions with perfect precision and is in perfect coordination with everything else.' The Natural Law Party insists that only a Natural Law-based approach to politics and the encouragement of as many as possible to become yogic flyers will lead to a real reduction in crime, an end to war, ethical policies, etc. The party has contested many elections throughout the world, claiming 'to bring the light of science into politics' and to offer 'conflict-free politics and problem-free government'.

TM and the Natural Law Party seek to bring human life and consciousness in line with Natural Law. To be thus in tune with that which governs the universe, is to be truly

☞ *continued on page 187*

TANTRIC SPIRITUALITY
Elizabeth Puttick

For many centuries, the West has perceived sexuality and spirituality as incompatible opposites. This attitude can be traced back to a dualism found within Christian belief and sensibility. However, some other religions have a generally more positive attitude to the body. Tantra originated in India as a revolt against the caste-bound hierarchy of orthodox Hinduism; it was later developed by Buddhists, particularly in Tibet. Similar practices developed in Chinese Daoism. Tantra has mostly been an underground movement, as it has sometimes been actively suppressed, but at other times has been revered as an approach equal to yoga. It contains a wealth of practices and rituals, of which working with sexual energy is only one – but the one that has been seized upon with most interest by westerners.

Tantra is a spiritual methodology. Its approach is non-dualistic, or, to use the modern buzzword, 'holistic'. It believes that the higher is hidden in the lower, spirituality in sexuality. Therefore the lower should not be condemned, but transformed from poison into nectar, and it has developed a range of techniques to achieve this result. The aim of its techniques is to awaken the sexual energy, known as *kundalini*, but not allow it to be released through orgasm. Instead, practitioners are taught to direct this energy towards higher states of consciousness, which ultimately lead to enlightenment.

The Western approach to tantra
In the 1970s, some gurus of the new religions worked with tantric techniques and *kundalini* energy. The best known was Osho (formerly Bhagwan Shree Rajneesh) of the *Osho movement, sometimes known as the 'sex guru' on account of his beliefs about sexuality. However, his teachings were not simply a licence for 'free love' but a synthesis of psychology with tantra that made it accessible to westerners: 'People think that I teach sex. I am one of the persons who is teaching God. If I talk about sex there is a reason for it – I would like you to know it before it is too late. Know it totally, go into it headlong and be finished with it. Go into it meditatively, alert – that is the approach of tantra. If you know something well, you are free of it.' He developed a four-stage model of sexuality, culminating in an ecstatic meeting of male and female energies; this gave a natural experience of meditation, which could lead to enlightenment alone or in combination with other methods.

Nowadays, tantric spirituality has spread to the New Age and self-development movements. Most of the centres are located in the United States (approximately 125) and Germany (approximately 40), though there are also centres in most European countries, including Britain, and India, Australia, New Zealand and Russia. The largest and best-known centre, with eight offshoots worldwide, is the SkyDancing Institute. This was founded by Margo Anand, a disciple of Rajneesh (as are a number of other tantric teachers) and author of the best-selling book *The Art of Sexual Ecstasy*, who has trained many of the current tantric teachers. Another well-known teacher is Alan Lowen, who runs the Art of Being in Hawaii, which has a broader mission than sacred sex alone: 'The Art of Being is a human and warm-hearted way of learning to live consciously, lightly and lovingly. Its workshops and courses are all paths of awakening. They explore life's elemental themes, such as birth, death, sex, love, intimacy and being itself. And whatever the theme may be, they are ways to realize more and more of your human and spiritual potential.'

Most of the centres run

programmes of short courses, which can offer at most an introduction to the process; they import selected elements from tantra to enhance relationships, whereas in 'authentic' tantra the contents of the relationship are used in order to pursue and attain enlightenment. These courses have therefore been criticized as symptomatic of the widespread predilection for instant gratification and quick-fix techniques, encouraging a belief that it is possible to become an

---

A Tibetan Monk, adorned in symbols of tantric Buddhism, performs the Black Hat Dance. The dance commemorates the assassination (in 842) of the Tibetan King Langdarma, a persecutor of Buddhism.

accomplished 'tantrika' after one weekend workshop. In traditional tantra, sexuality is respected as a powerful force and practitioners spend many years training in these techniques, which require maximum dedication and discipline. It is therefore unsurprising that some Asian teachers take offence that Western tantra has been co-opted into the service of hedonistic materialism, and that the approach has become diluted and distorted in the process. On the other hand, it can be argued that Asian tantra is impoverished by its neglect of relationship skills. Neo-tantra emphasizes safe, responsible sex, commitment to one partner, intimacy and gender equality. While it is sometimes argued that these are not spiritual goals, the holistic philosophy of self-development postulates that spirituality needs to be grounded in the body, intimate relationship is a valid spiritual path, and emotional health is a precondition for the flowering of meditation.

Tantra and Paganism

Sacred sex practices are also found in Paganism. One of the main progenitors was the occultist Aleister Crowley (1875–1947), who developed a sex magick partly based on tantric texts in order to create altered states of consciousness. The other main source for Paganism is Goddess spirituality, which affirms the female body. In the words of Starhawk (Miriam Simos), one of the best-known Pagans: 'Sexuality is sacred because it is a sharing of energy, in passionate surrender to the power of the Goddess, immanent in our desire. In orgasm, we share in the force that moves the stars.'

The myth of the Sacred Marriage between king and priestess to ensure good harvests and control of the land is fundamental in Paganism, and its re-enactment is a recognition of the power of sex. It is the basis of the Great Rite: ritual sex between the high priest and priestess in Pagan rituals, including the third degree of initiation in Alexandrian *Wicca. However, the evidence suggests that it is more often symbolic than actual, unless the participants are already partners. Some witches compare it to tantra as a sacred ceremony to raise and release power, and channel it for the purposes of healing, consecration, creativity and inspiration.

On balance, despite criticisms of vulgarization, the teachings of tantric spirituality have played a major role in creating and promoting a body-positive spirituality that counteracts the misogynistic, life-negative attitudes often evident in the world religions.

content and at peace. That is to say, because violating Natural Law and living out of step with it leads to stress, frustration, sickness, crime, violence and general negativity in the world, only those who understand and who are in tune with Natural Law can provide significant personal and political help. To bring life into harmony with Natural Law is the solution to all life's problems and the aim of the Natural Law Party. When this eventually happens they will have 'created heaven on earth'.

ISKCON: The International Society for Krishna Consciousness (Hare Krishna Movement)
Malory Nye

Most members of ISKCON (the International Society for Krishna Consciousness) do not consider themselves to be part of a 'new religious movement'. For them, ISKCON is an international Hindu movement, with its roots in a religious tradition that goes back centuries in India. There is much justification in this claim, as the central figure for ISKCON is the 16th-century Indian religious figure Chaitanya (also known as Gouranga), a mystic and reformer who is considered by his followers to be a divine incarnation (avatar). The religious group that developed from Chaitanya – Gaudiya Vaishnavism – is a prominent and mainstream part of the religion of Bengal (the area of eastern India in which he lived). The history of Gaudiya Vaishnavism is, however, complicated by the fact that it was revised and reformed in the late 19th century, at the time of British colonial rule in India, under the spiritual leadership of an Indian civil servant called Bhaktivinod Thakur. Through Bhaktivinod Thakur, and his son and successor Bhaktisiddhanta Saraswati, the Chaitanya

movement was brought into the 20th century, with a new leadership and the creation of an organization called the Gaudiya Math – in a sense a 'church of Chaitanya'.

It is from Gaudiya Math that ISKCON is itself derived. In 1922, Bhaktisiddhanta Saraswati instructed a young man called Abhay Charan De (1896–1977) to travel to the West, to take the teachings of the movement to the English-speaking world. It was not until 1965 that Abhay Charan De was able to fulfil this instruction, when under his guru-name of A.C. Bhaktivedanta Swami Prabhupada (more informally known as Prabhupada), he made his way to the United States. Within a year of arrival in New York, Prabhupada had brought together a small group of local American followers, whom he was instructing in the rituals and philosophies of Gaudiya Vaishnavism, and legally incorporated this group as ISKCON. From New York, ISKCON spread to other parts of the United States, and on to Europe and across the globe. Unlike the Gaudiya Math, which was made up almost exclusively of Indian Hindus, ISKCON was an international organization with members from many ethnic and cultural backgrounds.

A well-known name for ISKCON is the 'Hare Krishna movement', which refers in particular to the central religious ideas of the group. As mentioned already, Chaitanya is considered to be an avatar, specifically an incarnation of the deity Krishna – and it is Krishna (through Chaitanya) that is at the heart of the ISKCON way of life. ISKCON is fiercely monotheistic and expects its devotees to live their lives rigorously focused on Krishna (who is called the 'Supreme Personality of Godhead') in order to achieve full 'Krishna consciousness', which will lead to the soul getting 'back to Godhead'. Achieving this is not simply a matter of believing in Krishna; it also requires substantial physical commitment – primarily

Devotees of Hare Krishna process through London in 1987.

through the chanting of the name of Krishna on a regular basis each day (through the 'Hare Krishna' chant, or *mahamantra*, which goes 'Hare Krishna, Hare Krishna, Krishna Krishna, Hare Hare; Hare Rama, Hare Rama, Rama Rama, Hare Hare'). This *mahamantra* is chanted in a rosary-style way on a string of 108 beads (called a *mala*) – a round of the mala involves saying the *mahamantra* 108 times, and a Krishna-conscious devotee should chant 16 rounds of the *mala* each day.

Further to this, a devotee should live by the four regulative principles: no violence, no gambling, no intoxicants and no illicit sex. Thus a vegetarian diet is required (since meat-eating entails animal slaughter), and all alcohol, tobacco, intoxicating drugs (including coffee, tea and chocolate) must be avoided. Extramarital sexual relations are forbidden, and even within marriage sex is

only permitted for the creation of Krishna-conscious children. This all adds up to a very austere religious and cultural lifestyle – focused on what devotees see as the spiritual world of Krishna overcoming the false consciousness of the material world of the body and its desires.

By far the most important event in the development of ISKCON was the death of Prabhupada in 1977. It came as no real surprise, since he was nearly 80 and had been ill for some time. Despite this, the transfer of power in ISKCON was a messy affair, particularly because the 11 gurus who became his successors were largely too inexperienced to assume their new responsibilities. Thus, within just ten years, seven out of these gurus 'fell from grace', through a combination of drug-taking, illegal arms and drug dealing, and heavy-handed management. Following a leadership reorganization in the late 1980s, the situation was brought back under control, but the result was a great deal of disenchantment for many devotees who had suffered under the young gurus, plus a very tarnished public image of ISKCON as a whole. The problem continues to the present, with a small but vocal group of dissenting ISKCON followers (often called 'ritviks') claiming that Prabhupada's succession has still not been resolved.

In the late 1990s, a further scandal hit the movement with the revelation that many of the children brought up in ISKCON in the 1970s and 1980s were subjected to a sustained regime of physical and sexual abuse by their teachers. ISKCON have reacted in a constructive way to these charges, and of course the problem of child abuse is not limited to this religious movement. But the levels of anger remain, and, in 2002, a multimillion-dollar lawsuit was initiated in the Texan courts, implicating not only specific individual abusers, but also ISKCON itself, as well as Prabhupada for having allowed the abuse to happen. This charge against Prabhupada – who remains at the heart of the movement 25 years after his death – has shocked many devotees and has polarized the movement still further.

ISKCON at the beginning of the 21st century is quite different from what it was in its first flush in the early 1970s. It is still a strongly missionary movement with an international focus. Although its North American centre is still important, its main base is in Mayapur, Bengal, highlighting the significance of its ties with India. Increasingly, in the United States and Britain, support for ISKCON comes from diasporic Hindus, who have been turning to ISKCON as an authentic expression of their ancestral religious traditions. Hence, the development of ISKCON has been to reconcile its status as a traditional Hindu Vaishnavite organization with an international missionary drive. The future is likely to see it retain both elements, but to be seen increasingly as a global Hindu organization.

Eckankar
James R. Lewis

Eckankar is a new religious movement founded by Paul Twitchell in California in 1965. It is currently an international organization headquartered in Minneapolis, Minnesota. Twitchell was a spiritual seeker who was involved in a variety of alternative religions – from L. Ron Hubbard's *Church of Scientology to Swami Premananda's *Self-Revelation Church of Absolute Monism – before starting Eckankar. He asserted that in 1956 he had experienced 'God-realization' when he was initiated by a group of spiritual masters, the Order of the Vairagi Masters. Twitchell was assigned the role of 971st Living Eck Master by these higher spiritual beings.

Soon after Twitchell established Eckankar, he moved its headquarters to Las Vegas, Nevada. He wrote several of the movement's key books, including *Eckankar: The Key to Secret Worlds* (1969), which served as an introductory text for many years. Twitchell and his organization gained widespread attention following the publication of Twitchell's biography, *In My Soul I Am Free*, written by the prominent metaphysical author Brad Steiger. Building on contemporaneous popular interest in astral projection, Eckankar's early teachings emphasized soul travel, and the organization billed itself as 'The Ancient Science of Soul Travel'. This self-designation was eventually dropped in favour of 'The Religion of the Light and Sound'. Eckankar still discusses soul travel in its teachings, emphasizing the spiritual experiences encountered in dreams as a basic form of soul travel.

Eckankar's vision of the human condition is related to the religions that originated on the South Asian subcontinent as well as to the worldview of the West's metaphysical-occult subculture. In common with these traditions, Eckankar accepts the notion that the individual soul is trapped by the passions and illusions of the material world, which is viewed as a realm of spiritual learning. Because of the related processes of reincarnation and karma, the death of the physical body does not free a person from further spiritual learning in the material world. Only through the practice of certain spiritual techniques – referred to in Eckankar as 'spiritual exercises' – can individuals liberate themselves from the cycle of death and rebirth.

The Temple of Eck, in Chanhassen, Minnesota.

Eckankar's basic cosmology and meditation techniques are closely related to the Sant Mat tradition, a north Indian spiritual lineage. The notion that God's Voice is light and sound is a core doctrine of this tradition. Rather like Western Gnosticism, the cosmos is pictured as a multi-level emanation in which human souls are trapped by passions and illusions, and the spiritual devotee needs to move through these levels and return to the divine source. A 'sound current' (a 'river of vibration'; alternatively pictured as a ray of light) from the higher levels – an emanation from the high God – flows down through all of the lower levels. A living master – referred to in Eckankar as the Mahanta or the Eck Master – links the devotee to this current at the time of initiation. Contemplating the sound current and the inner light (the visual aspect of the divine sound) with the Master's guidance allows the individual to follow the sound back to the source from which it emanated (the Supreme Being), resulting in spiritual liberation.

In the larger Sant Mat tradition, new splinter groups have often arisen out of disputes over who should be the new leader following the death of a guru. One of the more important splinter groups to arise out of the *Radhasoami Tradition, the largest Sant Mat organization, was Kirpal Singh's Ruhani Satsang, which was formed in the wake of the passing of the master, Sawan

Singh. Kirpal Singh's followers, in turn, splintered repeatedly into different groups following his death. Kirpal Singh was one of Paul Twitchell's teachers, and a number of outsiders have argued that Kirpal Singh is the source of Eckankar's 'sound current' practices. Twitchell died unexpectedly in 1971, and was succeeded by Darwin Gross. Gross in turn was succeeded by the present leader, Harold Klemp, the 973rd Living Eck Master.

Klemp felt led to move Eckankar's headquarters to Chanhassen, near Minneapolis, Minnesota, where the Temple of Eck was erected. The Temple opened its doors in 1990. Under Klemp's leadership, Eckankar has grown steadily. Eckankar publications are now authored primarily by Klemp, though Twitchell's writings are still published by the organization. Members of the movement are referred to as 'Eckists'. Although the core of the group is constituted by American Eckists, there are a significant number of European members (particularly in Germany). The fastest-growing segment of the movement is in the horn of Africa. Although Eckankar does not publish membership statistics, approximately 5,000 members attend its annual worldwide conference held in Minnesota every October. From these numbers, it can be inferred that Eckankar's active membership is upwards of 20,000 members or more.

The Osho Movement

Elizabeth Puttick

The Osho movement was the best-known and most fashionable new religion of the 1970s. At its height, seekers and other visitors from many fields of life, including well-known artists, writers and scientists, were drawn to the ashram in Poona, India. The movement fell into disrepute after its relocation to the United States, but has recovered somewhat in reputation if not numbers since then. Osho himself is now recognized as a major influence on contemporary alternative religion, on account of his holistic, body-positive teachings, particularly his innovative integration of Eastern meditation with Western psychotherapy.

Osho was born as Rajneesh Chandra Mohan (1931–90) in India, and became a professor of philosophy at Jabalpur University. After leaving academia to become a guru (1966), he attracted enormous crowds in Bombay with his fiery orations, particularly his controversial views on sex and politics, and soon began to draw local and Western followers. He changed his name to Bhagwan Shree Rajneesh in 1972, and soon after founded an ashram at Poona, which attracted seekers from all over the world. At this time there were around 250,000 members, of whom around 3,000 were permanently based in Poona, though present numbers have dropped to 15–20,000.

In 1981, Osho moved with the majority of his disciples to a ranch he called Rajneeshpuram, in Oregon, United States. Rajneeshpuram became famous partly on account of its fleet of 93 Rolls Royces. It was criticized as a glorified labour camp, where disciples worked for 12 hours a day or longer, enduring primitive conditions, including the harsh climate. However, the enterprise was envisioned by Osho as a grand experiment, which he called a 'Buddhafield': a safe, secluded community 'where only one thing is significant – how to become a Buddha… The possibility is that we can create one of the greatest and the most powerful Buddhafields ever created in the world, because never before was there such a search. We are on the threshold of something new – either humanity will die and disappear, or we will take a leap, and a new being will be formed.' The Poona ashram had been the prototype. Rajneeshpuram was founded as a 'New City for the New Man' with a utopian vision of greening the desert: work as meditation, leading to enlightenment. However, in 1985 the commune was disbanded after Osho was arrested and charged with a number of crimes, including tax evasion, embezzlement, wire-tapping and immigration offences. He was discharged but deported, and three of his chief administrators were arrested. He went back to Poona, changing his name to Osho and returning to the simplicity of his early teachings. The movement flourished, though on a smaller scale, and continues after his death, with meditation centres and communities in most countries.

Osho was against all doctrine and belief. Nevertheless, some clear themes emerge in his teaching, which is collected in hundreds of books and videotapes. The most important is that the aim of spiritual development is enlightenment. Osho claimed that he had become enlightened at the age of 21; he was believed by his disciples to be an enlightened master who could lead them towards enlightenment. This was the goal, and there was a plethora of practices to achieve it. The first step was to 'take *sannyas*': an initiation into discipleship based on the traditional Hindu final stage of life for men. Osho radically changed its meaning to a path open to all ages and both genders, with four conditions: a name change, wearing orange robes, wearing a mala with a locket of Osho's picture around the neck, and doing at least one daily meditation. The first three conditions were dropped after the return to Poona in

1986. Traditional *sannyas* is world-renouncing and ascetic, whereas Osho's 'neo-*sannyas*' was about life-affirmation; one of his mottoes was 'life, love, laughter'. The most controversial manifestation of this ideology was his tantric teaching on sexuality, which was criticized in India and in the West. He taught that sexuality is a gift to be enjoyed and celebrated, but also used as a path to enlightenment.

The master–disciple relationship is one of the most contentious issues in new religions, and there is confusion regarding its meaning. Osho was a guru in the traditional Hindu sense of a spiritual guide. He worked in various ways, providing an enormous range of meditations and therapies to release energy, which could then be channelled into sustained meditation. He also spoke daily on the mystical traditions of the world religions, using his philosophical and oratorical gifts to create a synthesis of essential spirituality that is widely acclaimed for its intellectual breadth and depth. But the most important part of the master–disciple relationship was *shaktipat*, a Sanskrit term akin to grace or charisma. Osho adapted the traditional Hindu ceremony of *darshan*, a meeting between master and disciple, into a highly intensified celebration with live music, singing and dancing, using female 'mediums' to generate ecstatic states in disciples. Many claimed to achieve altered states and glimpses of enlightenment in *darshan*, as well as through meditation. Since his death this ceremony, now renamed the Brotherhood of the White Rose, has become a daily ritual using *darshan* videotapes. There were criticisms regarding the abuse of power in this sensitive relationship, especially after the move to the United States, when the organization grew too large and top-heavy for personal contact between master and disciple. Opinion is divided as to how far Osho

was responsible for the demise of Rajneeshpuram, and many of his disciples left at this stage. However, many of those that stayed claimed that the experience was spiritually beneficial, even enjoyable.

Whereas traditional Hinduism believes that women are ignorant, impure, and both socially and spiritually inferior, Osho believed that women were spiritually superior and made better disciples. He claimed that the feminine virtues of intuition, receptivity and devotion made it easier for women to surrender to a guru and open to the subtle energies of meditation. Even male disciples were expected to develop their 'inner feminine' in order to progress spiritually. Although there were criticisms that such qualities were regressive, most women found it liberating to be offered

The Buddha Hall of the Osho ashram at Poona, India. Music, dancing and meditation are said to help practitioners achieve glimpses of enlightenment.

an alternative path to motherhood: 'A woman is not only capable of giving birth to children, she is also capable of giving birth to herself as a seeker of truth.' Osho believed that women were good administrators as well as devotees, and women have always held most of the leadership positions in this movement, which is unusual in any religion.

The Friends of the Western Buddhist Order

Robert Morrison

The Friends of the Western Buddhist Order (FWBO) is one of Britain's largest Buddhist movements, with 30 major centres in Britain and another 50 worldwide. It was founded in London in 1967 by Sangharakshita, an Englishman (Dennis Lingwood; b. 1925) who was ordained as a Theravada Buddhist monk in India in 1949. In 1968, Sangharakshita founded the Western Buddhist Order (WBO), which consists of members who have committed themselves formally to the ideals of Buddhism. At present there are around 1,000 members of the WBO, over half of whom live in Britain.

In 1950, while visiting the Himalayan border town of Kalimpong, Sangharakshita was asked by his teacher, Kashyap, to remain there and 'work for the good of Buddhism'. Sangharakshita remained based in Kalimpong until a visit to Britain in 1964, during which he decided he could do more good for Buddhism by returning to the West.

During his time in India, Sangharakshita studied with teachers from several Buddhist traditions, resulting in a broad, non-sectarian approach reflected in his teaching and writing. He regards Buddhism as a universal teaching that is as applicable to the modern West as it has been to the East. However, to make the transition from the East to the modern world, Sangharakshita considers it necessary to distinguish between Buddhism's core teachings and principles, and the various cultural forms in which these have been expressed in place and time. Sangharakshita considers these 'core teachings and principles' to underlie the Buddhist tradition as a whole. What the FWBO is can therefore be best understood as an attempt to express these teachings and principles in the modern world.

One expression of this attempt is that ordination into the WBO is described as 'neither monastic nor lay', but is based on 'going for refuge to the Buddha, *dharma* and *sangha*': commitment to the ideal (Buddhahood), teachings (*dharma*) and exemplars of community (*sangha*) drawn from the whole Buddhist tradition. Thus, members of the WBO follow a variety of lifestyles (some live with their families, others live a more monastic life) but all share a common commitment to the Buddhist path. Sangharakshita considers the traditional 'going for refuge' to be a unifying principle for the whole of Buddhism.

The FWBO sees its approach as pragmatic rather than eclectic. For example, FWBO centres teach just two basic meditation practices to newcomers. These are the Theravada practices of the mindfulness of breathing and the development of loving kindness (*mettabhavana*), which are considered the essential basis for all meditation. It stresses a balanced approach to Buddhist practice that emphasizes ethics, study, faith and devotion.

As well as selecting practices from within traditional Buddhism, the FWBO also seeks

to develop new modes of Buddhist practice. For example, it has developed structures that support a committed Buddhist lifestyle in modern society, particularly through communal living and team-based ethical forms of livelihood. Several hundred FWBO Buddhists today work together in such businesses. It also stresses the value of the arts, and the need for Buddhism to be expressed in the terms of Western culture.

Krishnamurti and the Krishnamurti Foundation
Kevin Tingay

The Krishnamurti Foundation exists to preserve and propagate the teachings of Jiddu Krishnamurti (1895–1986). His life falls into two distinct parts. The child of poor Brahmin parents, he lived near to the headquarters of the *Theosophical Society in Adyar, Madras

Jiddu Krishnamurti giving an open-air lecture at the Logan Estate near Bristol, Pennsylvania, in 1932.

his links with the Theosophical Society.

From that time until his death he devoted himself to lecturing and writing. He taught that no religion, no teacher, no organization could mediate the truth to seekers of the truth. He did, however, attract to himself a body of followers whose support permitted him to live the life of an independent spiritual teacher. He was instrumental in the establishment of schools in India, England and the United States, where his philosophy was embodied in the educational practice – encouraging the greatest possible freedom of intellectual exploration among students and staff. The administration of Krishnamurti's work was reorganized in 1968 as the Krishnamurti Foundation, with branches in India, the United States, Britain and several other countries. Since his death, the Krishnamurti Foundation has ensured that his writings continue to be available for future generations.

Auroville
David Burnett

Auroville was founded in 1968, in a rural area of Tamil Nadu, south India, just north of Pondicherry. At present, it is home to around 1,700 residents from more than 35 countries, and it is networked with some 20 surrounding villages. Auroville's aim is to become a town of 50,000 persons, where men and women of all countries can live in peace and harmony, rising above all creeds, politics and nationalities to achieve an actual human unity. Auroville seeks to promote sustainability on all levels, and it has gained international acclaim for its land-reclamation and reforestation work. More than 2,500 acres of marginal land have been transformed by soil and water conservation and the planting of over 2 million trees.

Auroville's underlying vision comes from the Indian scholar Sri Aurobindo

(now Chennai), India, where his father worked in an administrative capacity. The Theosophical Society's leader Annie Besant (1847–1933) and her associate C.W. Leadbeater perceived hitherto unnoticed spiritual potential in the child and arranged for him to receive a European-style education. In 1911, the Order of the Star in the East was founded by the theosophists to prepare for the coming of a 'world teacher'. Though technically not part of the Theosophical Society, the movement attracted wide support from its membership as well as from elsewhere. In the period from 1925 to 1929 Krishnamurti's teachings began to challenge the messianic expectations of the order's followers. In 1929 he dissolved the Order of the Star, as it had become, and severed all

(1872–1950), but it was his co-worker Mirra Richard (née Alfassa, 1878–1973) who founded Auroville and gave it its four-point Charter at the time of its inauguration. Alfassa, who became known as 'The Mother', originally came from France and claimed to have had various spiritual experiences as a child. She first visited Aurobindo in Pondicherry in 1914, and she rejoined him in 1920. During the following years, the number of disciples increased, and she became the supervisor of the Sri Aurobindo Ashram.

Aurobindo rose to prominence through the editorials he wrote for the Calcutta newspaper *Bande Mataram* between 1906 and 1908. He retired in 1910 to concentrate on yoga at

The Temple of the Mother (Matrimandir) at Auroville in India.

Pondicherry. Aurobindo taught that the universe is one eternal reality – the One Being and Consciousness. All beings are united in this, but divided through ignorance of their true 'Self'. It is possible by psychological discipline to remove this veil of separate consciousness and become aware of the true 'Self', the divinity within all. Through a gradual process of evolution this reality liberates itself from the material realm towards greater perfection. Life is the first step of this release of consciousness and mind is the second. The process awaits a release into something yet greater, a consciousness that is both spiritual and supramental and the dominant power in the conscious being. Only then will the divinity in things release itself entirely and it will be possible for life to manifest perfection. Aurobindo taught that the method of achieving this was through yogic

practice, in which the descent of the higher principle brings knowledge of the supramental.

Alfassa became the primary interpreter of Aurobindo's teaching after his death in 1950. The Mother and Aurobindo aimed to bring down upon the earth a new spiritual consciousness they called the Supramental. This is partly reflected in the building at the very centre of Auroville known as the Matrimandir (literally, Temple of the Mother, though it is not in fact a temple). The Matrimandir is a 100-foot-high elliptical sphere resting on four pillars, which represent Wisdom, Strength, Harmony and Perfection. It is considered to be like a large golden sphere that appears to be rising out of the earth, symbolizing the birth of a new consciousness.

The Mother was the undisputed spiritual and administrative head of the Sri Aurobindo Society, the original nurturing body behind the

Auroville project, but after her death in 1973, disagreements arose between the Society and the inhabitants of Auroville. On two occasions, in 1977 and 1978, acts of violence involving hired 'watchmen' led to police intervention. Finally, after an initial intervention by the Indian Government in 1980 to take control from the Sri Aurobindo Society, an Act of Parliament was passed in 1988 creating the Auroville Foundation. This body, comprising a largely Indian Governing Board, an International Advisory Council of eminent people from around the world, and the Residents Assembly (all adult Aurovillians), now oversees the development of the project in a spirit of mutual support and cooperation.

The 3HO Foundation (Healthy, Happy, Holy Organization)
Ron Geaves

The 3HO Foundation is the inspiration of Yogi Bhajan (b. 1929) who arrived in the United States in 1969 from the Punjab and began to teach kundalini yoga to young Americans, most of whom had a 1960s counter-culture background. He has established the headquarters of the movement in New Mexico. Kundalini yoga is an eclectic system that draws upon a large range of traditional Hindu and Buddhist systems and techniques. Meditation is advocated as leading to improved mental concentration and physical well-being and a general sense of happiness. However, there is little focus in the movement's advertising on a devotional or intimate relationship with the divine. Kundalini yoga or the 'yoga of awareness' is described as promoting strength, beauty, a consistent sense of well-being, heightened sensory awareness, enhanced intuition, improved relationships, creativity, a heightened spiritual sense and freedom from negative habit patterns. Yogi Bhajan also claims to be an enlightened initiate of tantra or Mahan tantra passed on to him in 1971 by Lama Lilan Po of Tibet. It is claimed that there is only one Mahan tantra at any given time and, through the authority of this status, Yogi Bhajan is able to teach white tantric yoga, a system of meditation comprising six to eight techniques incorporating posture, breath control, music, mental focusing and mantras. Until 1986, Yogi Bhajan travelled around the world presenting white tantric yoga courses, but these are now available on videotape.

The movement organizes a variety of activities, including summer camps for learning yoga; women's programmes that emphasize self-esteem, relationships and communication; children's camps for learning *dharma*; and camps for kundalini yoga teacher training. The language of the movement's publicity suggests a strong awareness of the themes of the New Age with a corresponding eclecticism, and a focus on physical and mental well-being based on inner equilibrium. Yogi Bhajan is even advertised as a teacher for the Age of Aquarius. The language and activities of the movement suggest the influence of the inner core of Californian seekers who have joined, rather than the Sikh origins of Yogi Bhajan.

However, it is in its relationship to Sikhism that the movement becomes of interest to scholars of religion. Yogi Bhajan is Sikh by background and maintains all the outer symbols of orthodox Khalsa Sikhs. He maintains contact with the Sikh communities in diaspora and at the religious centre of Sikhism in Amritsar. Among the movement's programme for summer camps can be found opportunities for promoting Sikhism more obviously geared to the diaspora Sikh community, for example, a Khalsa Ladies Camp in Vancouver and a Gatka Camp in France. Yogi Bhajan is sensitive to his position in the Sikh community and is described as 'the chief religious and administrative authority for the ministry of Sikh *dharma* in the western

hemisphere'. It is claimed that he has been given the title of Siri Singh Sahib by the Akal Takhat, the central governing body of orthodox Sikhism in Amritsar, for his missionary work in the Western world. There is no doubt that Yogi Bhajan has succeeded in converting a number of North Americans to Sikhism and these converts dominate the leadership of 3HO; however, the movement is keen to promote the fact that it is not necessary to become a Sikh in order to practise kundalini yoga. The Sikh converts are easily recognized by their white turbans and robes and other outer signs of Khalsa, such as long, uncut hair.

However, the relationship with orthodox Sikhism is not without its problems. Although many Sikhs are proud of Yogi Bhajan's attempts to introduce westerners to Sikh *dharma*, others do not believe that it is possible to be Sikh except by birth. This raises a number of interesting questions concerning Sikh identity and it is this issue which makes 3HO controversial. Yogi Bhajan would no doubt look to the spiritual origins of Sikhism and deny that the ten Gurus were concerned with ethnic or religious identity. In this assertion he would be correct, but contemporary Sikhs are more inclined to perceive their identity as ethnic, especially those living outside of India.

A more problematic criticism comes from the religious spectrum of orthodox Sikhism, whose representatives are concerned that Yogi Bhajan is promoting a version of Sikh *dharma* that does not conform to the teachings of the ten Sikh Gurus. The language of the *Guru Granth Sahib*, the sacred writings of the Sikhs believed to be the final and eternal Guru, resonates with an ecstatic relationship between the devotee and a formless but personal deity mediated by the teachings and example of the Gurus. Little of this language of ecstatic devotional union is replicated in the teachings of kundalini yoga, which tends to emphasize the material, mental and physical benefits of practice. The *Guru Granth Sahib* itself contains poems of the Gurus that would appear to be critical of tantric practices, yoga and special dietary restrictions, denying that such practices can assist in coming closer to the divine. One orthodox British Sikh organization has created a website listing specific quotes of the *Guru Granth Sahib* that would explicitly criticize the teachings of Yogi Bhajan. The website is entitled 'Reasons why Yogi Bhajan might not be a Sikh'.

Thus 3HO and Yogi Bhajan find themselves being criticized by both ethnically and religiously conservative Sikhs, while at the same time gaining the pride of a minority community for their efforts to promote Sikh *dharma* to non-Sikhs. This tension will remain at the heart of the movement and will only probably be resolved by Yogi Bhajan's continuing success as a teacher both in the Sikh and non-Sikh communities. However, as with other movements that represent both an ethnic/religious community and a non-ethnic spiritual truth-seeker contingent, problems are likely to continue as the two communities learn to coexist.

Mother Meera
Christopher Partridge

Mother Meera was born Kamala Reddy on 26 December 1960 in the village of Chandepalle in southern India. Although her family was not particularly religious, at the age of six she began going into trances ('the state of *samadhi*') and, it is claimed, having visions in which spiritual guides would meet her. At the age of 14, with the help of her uncle, she went to live at the Sri Aurobindo ashram in Pondicherry, but left for Europe in 1979. In 1982 she married a German, and settled in Germany in 1983. She currently lives in Thalheim, Germany.

According to her followers, 'the unique gift of Mother Meera to the world is to make available for the first time in the history of the earth the radical transformative Light of *Paramatman*, the Supreme Being. In this time of crisis and growing spiritual hunger, the Mother offers her children a direct transmission of Light that dissolves all barriers and changes the entire being. The Light can be received by all who are open, whether or not they have met the mother in the body.' She is understood to be an avatar (or incarnation) of the Divine Mother (who, it is claimed, has also made herself known as, for example, the Virgin Mary, Kali and Isis). Consequently, Mother Meera is revered as 'the sustaining soul and force of the universe' in human form who has the supernatural ability to heal, protect and spiritually transform.

Although her ideas are fundamentally Hindu, she claims to teach no specific doctrines, but only to enable spiritual transformation: 'I have come to say that all paths are as good as each other and all lead to the Divine, and that therefore the various believers should respect each other's ways... People who follow any path can come to me – I help them to remember the Divine, and give them peace and happiness when they are in trouble... The whole purpose of my work is in the calling down of the *Paramatman* Light and in helping people. For this I came – to open your hearts to the Light.' Central to devotion to Mother Meera is the receiving of this transforming divine light by means of *pranam* and *darshan*. During *pranam* she takes the individual's head in her hands and 'works on the deep aspect of the being'. She explains how she does this: 'On the back of the human being is a white line that runs from the toes to the head. In fact, two lines start from the toes, rise along the legs, join at the base of the spine and then become a single line reaching to the top of the head. This line is thinner than a hair, and has some knots in it here and there, which divine personalities help to undo. It is very delicate work and great care has to be taken to undo these knots, as there is danger for your life if the thread is broken. When I hold your head I am untying these knots.' During *darshan* (which is identified as the 'self-revelation of the deity to the devotee'), Mother Meera contemplatively looks into the eyes of the devotee knelt before her: 'I am looking into every corner of your being. I am looking at everything within you to see where I can help, where I can give healing power. At the same time, I am giving Light to every part of your being. I am opening every part of yourself to Light. When you are open you will feel and see this clearly.'

Sessions with Mother Meera (*darshans*) are free, last about two hours and are held four times a week. However, she does emphasize that it is not necessary to visit her, for she can communicate 'the Light' to persons without them actually being present.

Andrew Harvey's book *Hidden Journey* and Martin Goodman's *In Search of the Divine Mother* have been important in the promotion of Mother Meera in the West.

Sahaja Yoga
Elizabeth Puttick

Sahaja Yoga was founded in 1970 by Sri Mataji Nirmala Devi (b. 1923), known simply as Mataji or the Divine Mother. Although Mataji was born into a Protestant family in central India, and her husband is a high-ranking official in the United Nations, Sahaja Yoga is in many ways a traditional Hindu path. Mataji was originally a disciple of Osho (formerly Bhagwan Shree Rajneesh; see the *Osho Movement), but fell out with him and set up her own movement. Mataji teaches mainly in Britain and India, but has disciples worldwide and travels extensively. The movement claims approximately 20,000 members, half of whom are in India, with another 100,000 loosely associated.

Sahaja Yoga is unusual among new religious movements, and indeed all religions, in being founded and led by a woman, but the movement is not feminist or matriarchal, and women are encouraged to be meek, submissive and 'feminine' in imitation of traditional Indian wives. Leadership positions are held almost exclusively by men. There appears to be a fairly high turnover among the membership, which is not growing, but there have been no public scandals. However, there is some concern at the high level of commitment demanded by Mataji. There is also concern about separation of the children from their parents at the movement's school in India and the strictness of the discipline, although it is not compulsory for children to be educated there.

Sahaja means spontaneity, and the basis of Sahaja Yoga is spontaneous union with the divine. This is accomplished through kundalini yoga, which is claimed to awaken a powerful spiritual energy located at the base of the spine. With Mataji's help, *kundalini* can be awakened in anyone. When it happens, practitioners are said to feel a cool breeze on the palms of their hands and above their heads. The experience also produces deep peace and happiness, and leads to enlightenment when it reaches the top chakra (chakras are energy centres on the central nervous system). As they develop 'vibratory awareness', devotees can tell from feelings of coolness and heat and from discomfort in their own chakras where their own and other people's chakras are blocked and learn to heal themselves and others. They believe in deities who personify the qualities of the chakras. The ultimate aim, as with most yoga-based teachings, is self-realization.

As well as the symbolism of kundalini yoga, traditional imagery of the divine, drawn from Hindu and tantric sacred texts, is important in Sahaja Yoga. The *shakti* or original feminine principle of which Mataji herself claims to be an avatar is particularly important. As Laxmi, the wife of the God Vishnu, she is the model of the ideal wife upon which female disciples are expected to model themselves, and which Mataji herself is seen as exemplifying perfectly. As an enlightened guru and the avatar of the *shakti*, she also represents the divine feminine. Photographs of Mataji are also used as symbols in meditation. Devotion may also be expressed through the ancient Hindu ritual of pouring a 'nectar' of honey, ghee and other substances over Mataji's feet, which is kept and drunk.

Elan Vital
Ron Geaves

Elan Vital is the generic term used for a number of independent organizations around the world that promote the teachings of Prem Pal Singh Rawat (b. 1958), commonly known as Maharaji. It is an organizational structure rather than a movement and does not have any membership. Each organization is volunteer based and organizes itself according to the national, legal and cultural differences found in each place where Maharaji's teachings have found a foothold. At the present time this amounts to over 80 countries but the number of practitioners ranges from a handful in some places to tens of thousands in others, notably India.

Maharaji was originally known as Guru Maharaji and came to fame when he first visited Britain, Europe and the United States as a 13-year-old in 1971. His message and personal charisma spread rapidly among members of the 1960s counter-culture. In the early 1970s, Divine Light Mission, the movement made up of Maharaji's followers, was the fastest-growing group in North America and Britain. It is estimated that there were 50,000 followers in the United States alone.

Maharaji had originally taken on the role of master after his father's death in 1966. He was only eight years old but the position was not hereditary. It is stated that his father had chosen him as the person best suited to carry the teachings forward in an international arena as well as in India. Maharaji's childhood is full of accounts of how he would encourage his father's followers to practise the teachings and speak publicly at his father's events. However, Maharaji's young age meant that his mother and eldest brother effectively controlled Divine Light Mission in India. As Maharaji began to grow older and establish his teachings worldwide he increasingly desired to manifest his own vision of development and growth. This conflict resulted in a split between Maharaji and his family, ostensibly caused by his mother's inability to accept Maharaji's marriage to an American follower rather than the planned traditional arranged marriage.

Throughout the 1980s and up to the present, Maharaji has travelled around the world continuously meeting with interested people and inspiring those who practise his teachings. In the 1980s, Divine Light Mission was disbanded and Elan Vital was established to more effectively promote Maharaji's teachings in a way that was free from any particular religious or cultural association. Maharaji's teachings are not new but belong to an age-old wisdom tradition that is continuously renewed under the inspiration of a living master. Thus, although parallels to Maharaji's teachings are found among such figures as Guru Nanak (the founder of Sikhism), Kabir (a 15th-century north Indian Sant) and Rumi (1207–73; a Persian Sufi poet and founder of the Mevlevi brotherhood), they exist independently of any tradition and do not rely upon any requirement to be authenticated by scriptures or authorities sanctified by the past.

However, at the heart of Maharaji's teachings lies the simple message that the human quest for fulfilment can be resolved by turning inward to discover a constant source of contentment and joy within. This message is supported by four techniques, together known as Knowledge, which provide the practical application that allow the practitioner the possibility of the experience spoken about by Maharaji. Knowledge lies at the heart of Maharaji's message. He is insistent that it is not the product of any one culture or the property of any religious tradition and that it can be practised by anyone. Consequently, Maharaji asserts that he is not teaching a religion and there are no particular rituals, sacred days, pilgrimages, sacred places, doctrines, scriptures or specific dress codes, dietary requirements or any other dimension associated with a religious lifestyle. Those who practise Knowledge come from a variety of religious backgrounds and often none at all. They are culturally and religiously diverse but united by varying degrees of commitment to the practice of Knowledge and their love and appreciation for Maharaji, who remains the central inspiration. Maharaji himself does not conform to any stereotype of a religious or spiritual leader but is highly committed to his conviction that Knowledge is effective and therefore he promotes its possibility to as many people around the world as are interested.

In order to promote the teachings, Maharaji pilots a leased executive jet himself. He will spend a few days in each place to which he is invited, speaking at locally organized events before flying on to the next venue. Elan Vital sponsors and supports these events and invites Maharaji to speak at these various locations. Maharaji utilizes modern technology extensively. All his speaking engagements are filmed and released as videos, and satellite technology allows Maharaji's discourses to be heard around the world. These ventures are supported by the donations of committed individuals who practise Knowledge and the work of volunteers. Elan Vital coordinates these activities but has only a few full-time staff. Individual practitioners of Knowledge remain in contact with Maharaji by attending his events live or by satellite, and watching videos.

Those interested in Maharaji's teachings are no longer confined to any one sector of society or any particular geographic location. After going through a major transformation, structurally and organizationally, Maharaji continues to promote the availability of Knowledge as in the heyday of the Divine Light Mission in the 1970s, but without the attendant Indian cultural accretions.

Adidam

James R. Lewis

Adidam was founded by Avatar Adi Da Samraj (Franklin Jones; b. 1939 in New York). He asserts that he was born into a state of perfect awareness of ultimate reality, but sacrificed that reality at the age of two in order to better understand the human condition. He began a spiritual quest in college that eventually led him to Swami Muktananda and other gurus in the Hindu tradition. Jones says that he reawakened to his true state in 1970. He renamed both himself and his group a number of times before settling on Adi Da and Adidam. He has also been known as Bubba Free John (1977), Da Free John (1979), Da Love-Ananda (1986), Jagad-Guru (1989) and Da Avabhasa (1991).

Adi Da claims that he has realized 'God' ('Truth' or 'Reality') and that he has the power to transmit that divine self-realization to others. All the traditional means of religious life are employed as a means of 'radical' understanding and devotional communion with Adi Da – meditation, study, ceremonial worship, community living and ethical observances.

Adi Da began to teach his path – a combination of self-analysis and devotion to the guru – in 1972, opening a small ashram (spiritual community) in Los Angeles. His method of working with his students was initially quite traditional. It soon became clear, however, that a different approach was needed, and he switched to a radical teaching style, based on Tibetan 'crazy wisdom', that was designed to shock devotees out of their complacent ways.

The institution of Adidam has an educational organization, the Laughing Man Institute, which is responsible for conducting courses all over the world. Additionally, the institution has a publishing mission, the Dawn Horse Press, which publishes books by and about Adi Da. The institution also publishes a number of magazines. Adidam maintains three ashrams, located in Fiji, Hawaii and northern California. The committed core of the movement numbers somewhat more than 1,000 people. For many years Adi Da lived in Fiji, but in recent years he has resided at the Mount of Attention in California.

The Santi Asoke Movement
Rory Mackenzie

'Santi' and 'Asoke' are two Pali words; together they can be translated 'peace without suffering'. The founder, now known as Bodhirak, was born in 1934 in north-east Thailand, and given the name Rak Rakphong. His mother died when he was a teenager, and he worked hard to support his six brothers and sisters. After graduating from a college of art in 1958 he began work at a Bangkok television station, in time becoming very well known as a songwriter and producer. Rak Rakphong became

interested in magic before turning to strict Buddhist practice. In 1970, he was ordained as a Buddhist monk and took the monastic name of Bodhirak. Not only was he strict in his monastic practice, he denounced his fellow monks for superstitious practices, smoking and eating meat. (Bodhirak had been a strict vegetarian for a number of years prior to being ordained.) Bodhirak's call to disciplined Buddhist practice struck a chord with some lay people but understandably drew fire from his fellow monks, who accused him of being divisive.

In 1973, Bodhirak set up his own religious centre. Two years later he informed the leader of the Thai *sangha* (monastic community) to deal directly with him, rather than through the monastic hierarchy. Bodhirak's refusal to line up with the two fraternities within the Thai *sangha* led in 1979 to a declaration by the *sangha* leadership that Santi Asoke was subversive. In 1990, Bodhirak and his followers were excommunicated from the Thai *sangha*. Continuous criticisms of the *sangha* leadership, departures from traditional Thai Buddhist practice, and apparent political involvement with the then governor of Bangkok, Chamlong Srimuang (a Santi Asoke lay member), were the key reasons leading to excommunication.

In March 2001, Santi Asoke had 9,929 registered members. However, there are also a large number, perhaps several thousand, who are in sympathy with the movement and follow its activities with interest. The seven religious centres are referred to as *phuthasathan* (stations of the Buddha) rather than the normal Thai term *wat* (temple). The 102 Santi Asoke monks do not use the mainstream Thai title of *Phra* (Venerable), but rather are referred to as *samana* (a Pali word for wandering religious ascetics). Asoke monks wear brown robes unlike the mainstream monks (who wear saffron-coloured robes). These differences serve to indicate that Santi Asoke differs from traditional Thai Buddhism.

There has never been an order of *bhikkiunii* (nuns) in Thai Buddhism. (*Mae chi*, female renounciates who wear white and shave their heads, are not the female equivalent of monks, and normally have a low status in Thai society.) In Santi Asoke there are 25 women who, after much rigorous training, have been ordained and have the same status as novice monks. The Santi Asoke term for such women is *sikkhamat* (a Pali term, which can be translated 'a mother who is studying'). The *sikkhamats* enjoy a high status in Santi Asoke. They are involved in teaching in the schools that are part of the Asoke communities, looking after the female residents of the centres, as well as teaching male and female adults.

Asoke members are strict vegetarians. They regard the eating of meat as a violation of the first of 'the five precepts' (to abstain from taking life). This perspective is not shared by mainstream Thai Buddhists, who correctly point out that the Buddha did not prohibit the eating of meat. Monastics, and laity who live in the centres, eat only one meal each day.

Another important Asoke belief is that traditional meditation practices do not lead to enlightenment. The Asoke approach is to strictly follow the middle (or noble eightfold) path. The practice of the first seven aspects will free the mind from the hindrances of sensual desire, ill will, laziness, remorse and uncertainty (also known as the training in higher morality). In practice, Asoke members will seek to have a correct outlook on and right attitude to life and keep the five precepts so they have good speech, conduct and occupation. They will work hard at developing the positive and eliminating the negative in their natures, and work hard at self-awareness. All this will lead to right concentration, the eighth aspect (also referred to as training in higher mentality). A concentrated mind will experience insight into reality, also known as enlightenment.

The Santi Asoke is a protest movement against all forms of greed, corruption and injustice, as well as what it perceives to be undisciplined and superstitious Buddhist practice. In its desire to help people to have 'peace without suffering' it seeks to bring society back to the basics of Buddhism. In doing so, it sees no need to remain with Thai (Theravadan) interpretations of Buddhism, and feels free to borrow Mahayana concepts. Excommunication has removed legitimacy from Santi Asoke, and the movement's ascetic message is hard for many fun-loving Thai to accept, yet the Asoke communities remain in good heart.

Lifewave

George D. Chryssides

Also known as 'Ishvara', Lifewave was originally founded in 1975 by John Yarr (b. 1947) as the Spiritual Organization for the Teachings of the Master (SOTM). This British group attracted a following of 500 at its height, but was disbanded in 1987, following allegations of sexual misconduct on the part of its leader. Yarr studied the occult extensively, as well as Eastern philosophy and meditative practices. He became a member of the Divine Light Mission (see *Elan Vital) in 1974, but founded his own organization the following year after claiming enlightenment. His spiritual name, *Ishvara*, means Lord of the Universe, and he claimed to be Kalki, the final avatar ('descent' of God).

Lifewave advocated a healthy lifestyle, free from recreational drugs, alcohol and tobacco, and recommended vegetarianism. It laid emphasis on family life and paid employment. Members sought the goal of liberation, in which they recognized their oneness with God. This was to be achieved principally through meditating on 'Light and Sound', which included the use of mantras given by Yarr. In addition to meditation, members were encouraged to pursue a study course, consisting of occultist material (such as *tarot, *astrology and *Kabbalism), and selected Eastern spiritual classics. There were four grades of progression within the organization: aspirant, initiate, second initiate and adept, the last of which consisted of those who recognized their essential divinity.

Following the disbanding of Lifewave, a few followers continued the practice, and some tried to revive the organization. One small group, known as The Path, existed in Leeds, Britain, for a short period.

The New Kadampa Tradition (NKT)
Christopher Partridge

The New Kadampa Tradition (often referred to as NKT) was founded by Venerable Geshe Kelsang Gyatso (also affectionately known as Geshe-la). Although, strictly speaking, Kadampa Buddhism can be traced back many centuries to the Buddhist teacher Tsongkhapa (1357–1419), it only established itself under the name NKT in 1991. Belonging within the Gelugpa tradition, it is a form of Tibetan Buddhism, although it does not acknowledge the Dalai Lama (Tenzin Gyatso) as its spiritual head. As with some other forms of Buddhism in the West, such as the *Friends of the Western Buddhist Order, the NKT is designed for and particularly appealing to westerners. Not only are the majority of followers and many of the teachers white British converts, but also in 1996 it was reportedly 'Britain's biggest, richest and fastest-growing religious sect'. It currently has over 5,000 supporters and over 400 centres in 36 countries around the world.

Born in Tibet in 1931, Kelsang Gyatso was ordained as a monk at the age of eight. He studied at Sera College (one of the principal monastic colleges near Lhasa) and, in 1959, travelled to India and spent many years meditating and teaching in the Himalayas. In 1976, his British followers established a centre, the Manjushri Institute (now Manjushri Centre), in Conishead Priory, Ulverston, Cumbria. A year later, fleeing from invading communists, Kelsang Gyatso travelled to England to teach Kadampa Buddhism to westerners. In 1979 he founded the Madhyamaka Centre in York and became its spiritual director. He has since established numerous centres and is revered as a great Buddhist master.

Unlike other forms of Buddhism popular in the West, the NKT seeks not to offer a westernized form of Buddhism, but rather to make traditional Gelugpa Buddhism accessible to westerners. Indeed, the NKT claims to practise a particularly pure form of Buddhism, possibly even purer than that taught by the Dalai Lama. This, of course, raises an issue that has brought the NKT to public attention in recent years, namely the split between the teaching of the NKT and that of the Dalai Lama. Most notably, in 1996, a widely reported controversy flared up over the NKT's worship of the deity Dorje Shugden. The history of Dorje Shugden worship within Buddhism is complex and has undergone several revivals, the most recent of which was led by Pabongka (1878–1943), the teacher of Trijang Rinpoche (1901–81) who was, in turn, the teacher of both the current Dalai Lama and Kelsang Gyatso. Pabongka believed Dorje Shugden worship to be a way of retaining the purity of the Gelugpa tradition. However, not only has the worship of this deity always been controversial within Buddhism, but it is particularly so today, because the current Dalai Lama explicitly rejects its validity as orthodox Buddhist practice. Indeed, believing Dorje Shugden to be an 'earthly deity' or even an evil spirit, the Dalai Lama has consistently spoken out against such worship since 1978 and, in 1996, issued an explicit ban. This resulted in the NKT taking the highly unusual step of organizing a protest against the Dalai Lama for restricting the religious freedom of Tibetan Buddhists. NKT members have even picketed the Buddhist Society headquarters during a visit of the Dalai Lama. They have formed the Shugden Supporters' Community and the Dorje Shugden Devotees' Charitable and Religious Society.

The Dhammakaya Foundation
Anonymous

The Dhammakaya Foundation, a Buddhist movement, is based at Wat Phra Dhammakaya in the province of Pathumthani, approximately one hour's drive north of Bangkok. The movement is founded on the meditation practice and teaching of Luang Phaw Sot (1885–1959), who served as abbot of Wat Paknam, Bangkok, for 43 years.

During a meditation session some 11 years after becoming a Buddhist monk, Luang Phaw Sot perceived a bright crystal sphere at the centre of his body (two fingers' breadth above his navel). He understood this to be the true spiritual nature of the *dharma* nature or body (hence the name *dhammakaya* in Pali, or *thammakaai* in Thai). In mainstream Theravada Buddhism, *dhammakaya* is understood to be the teachings and moral greatness that was the Buddha's, and which exists today in the teachings of the Buddha contained in the Pali canon. Luang Phaw Sot maintained that *dhammakaya* is the spiritual

Buddhist monks gather on steps outside Wat Phra Dhammakaya as part of the religious services honouring Earth Day in Thailand.

nature of the Buddha, which exists within everyone. He taught that the visualization of the *dhammakaya* was the meditative technique practised by the Buddha and his followers, that it had fallen into disuse and that he had discovered it.

In *dhammakaya* meditation, the meditator, through practice, is able to visualize a crystal sphere two fingers' breadth above the navel. As the meditator gains skills, bigger and clearer crystal spheres are visualized. As the meditator increases in ability, larger and brighter Buddha images are visualized instead of the spheres. According to one meditation teacher, when asked to describe the face of the visualized Buddha within, each meditator describes his or her own face without realizing it.

Dhammakaya meditation may be divided into ordinary and high-level meditation. The practice of low-level meditation brings success, contentment, and the moral power to overcome temptation. Ultimately it will lead to enlightenment. High-level meditation is extremely advanced. As it is practised, the meditator allegedly gains powers, such as clairvoyance, clairaudience and the ability to know his or her own past lives or those of others.

Luang Phaw Sot organized a group of high-level meditators to meditate in six-hour shifts around the clock. As these elite meditators focused on the clarity of their visualized image, the power generated was allegedly used to overcome evil, heal sickness and gain helpful insights into particular situations. The principal reason for high-level meditation, though, is to destroy the forces of darkness. This practice is not discussed with outsiders but continues at Wat Paknam and Wat Phra Dhammakaya.

After Luang Phaw Sot's death in 1959, one of his leading disciples, a woman named Khun Yai Chan (1909–2000), taught meditation to a group of students. In 1977, Wat Phra Dhammakaya was opened, and two of Khun Yai Chan's disciples were appointed as abbot and vice-abbot. There is much of which the Dhammakaya member (who always dresses in white while visiting the temple) can be proud. The temple stands on 800 acres of land and has a 40-acre assembly hall. Dhammakaya monks are usually very well educated. The first Sunday service of each month has over 20,000 in attendance. On important Buddhist holidays over 150,000 will attend, as the movement appeals to families. Often three generations of a family are seen sitting together during meditation at the temple. This is virtually unheard of in mainstream Thai Buddhism. The temple is clean and 'user-friendly'. The movement permits a prosperous lifestyle, yet provides participation in the 'spiritual' through chanting, meditation and listening to teaching. There are strong similarities between Dhammakaya and the Japanese Buddhist movement *Sôka Gakkai, in terms of excellent publicity and recruitment, intention for global expansion, and providing a sense of belonging for devotees.

Dhammakaya's style has been described as 'commodity Buddhism', that is, Buddha images are offered for sale and purchasing them secures a variety of benefits. The item, transaction and results are easily identifiable and measurable, rather than abstract. This is appealing to the hard-pressed business person, who is prepared to give to a cause he or she can relate to, especially if there is personal benefit involved.

Dhammakaya teaches that nirvana is a permanent, blissful realm where the Buddha and other enlightened ones reside after death. It is a physical place, which they refer to as *ayotnanibbana*. This forms a theoretical base for the ceremony of offering food to the Buddha in nirvana. This is conducted by the abbot of Wat Phra Dhammakaya on the first Sunday of every month at the temple. Such belief and practice is a significant departure from mainstream Buddhism, and lays

Dhammakaya open to charges of smuggling self into Buddhism.

Dhammakaya views its style of meditation as being suitable for people of all faiths, and one does not need to be Buddhist in order to practise it. Indeed, in the overseas context, Dhammakaya meditation is sometimes taught by teachers who have a minimum understanding of Buddhism. There are centres in Australia, Singapore, Hong Kong, Japan, Taiwan, France, Belgium, England and several in the United States.

Mata Amritanandamayi Mission
Maya Warrier

Mata Amritanandamayi (b. 1953), popularly known as Ammachi (mother), is an internationally renowned female guru from India, best known for her distinctive style of interacting with devotees. She bestows her blessings on devotees by hugging them individually. She belongs to the *bhakti* or devotionalist tradition of Hindu faith, marked by intense personalized devotion to a god or guru, in this case Ammachi herself. She was born in a tiny fishing village in Kerala in southern India. It is believed that she attained mystic union at the age of 21, first with the Hindu deity Krishna, and subsequently with Devi, the goddess. Among her most popular features today are her periodic appearances before devotees dressed in the regalia of the goddess, when she is believed to reveal her 'divine' aspect to them. Ammachi is believed to provide miraculous solutions to devotees' personal problems. She also offers them advice on ritual practice and spiritual seeking.

The Mata Amritanandamayi Math and the Mata Amritanandamayi Mission Trust were established in 1981 in order to spread Ammachi's spiritual message of service to all humanity. The organization's headquarters is in her native village in southern India, now renamed Amritapuri after her, and its largest centre abroad is located in North America in San Ramon, California. It has branches and networks across India, as well as in the United States, Britain, France, Italy, Germany, Spain, the Netherlands, Sweden, Finland, Singapore, Japan, Mauritius, the Reunion Islands and Australia. In India it owns and manages various charitable institutions, as well as educational and medical establishments. Ammachi tours her branches and centres in India and abroad every year, offering devotees a chance to see her and receive her 'divine' embrace.

Shambhala International
Lorne Dawson

Shambhala International is an umbrella organization founded in 1992 to unite the many different religious and cultural bodies created by the Buddhist teacher Chogyam Trungpa Rinpoche. Born in 1939, Trungpa was the 11th *tulku* (i.e. reincarnation of the abbot of the Surmang monastery) of the Karmapa sub-sect of the Kargyupa sect of Tibetan Buddhism. Forced to flee Tibet in 1959 after the Communist Chinese invasion, Trungpa learned English, studied at Oxford, and established one of the largest and most successful Tibetan Buddhist communities in the West. In 1968, after seeking guidance during a solitary retreat in Bhutan, and while recovering from a serious automobile accident, Trungpa decided to give up his monastic vows and dedicate himself to adapting his traditions to the needs of a Western audience. In 1970, he married a young British woman and moved to the United States, just in time to be carried into spiritual stardom by the tide of the youth counter-culture. He freely incorporated elements of other Buddhist traditions (e.g. Zen Buddhism), humanistic psychology, and Western pop culture into his lectures, many publications and programmes of meditative training. This unorthodox approach soon attracted thousands of followers. By 1974 he had founded several successful monasteries and training centres (e.g. Karme-Choling in Vermont), as well as the Naropa Institute in Boulder, Colorado, the first accredited Buddhist university in the United States. In 1983, fearing the growing influence of materialism in the United States, Trungpa controversially moved the international headquarters of his organization to Halifax, Nova Scotia, in Canada. Not long after, he built Gampo Abbey in a secluded part of Cape Breton Island. With training centres around the world, Shambhala today claims an active membership of approximately 6,000 people.

Trungpa attracted controversy as a practitioner of 'crazy wisdom', a form of Tibetan instruction designed to shock devotees out of their complacent ways. He drank, smoked, had affairs, and cajoled and bullied his students, while purposefully donning many different public faces. When he died of heart failure in 1987, considerable mystery surrounded this much admired and complex figure.

In the late 1970s, Trungpa began to create Shambhala Training, a supposedly secular programme of teachings and meditational practices. Under the leadership of his eldest son and successor, Sakyong Mipham Rinpoche, this training has become the central practice of the group. Shambhala training seeks to cultivate mindfulness: freeing our consciousness from the many distractions of this life, so we can become fully aware of the present moment, opening ourselves to the natural wisdom and basic goodness we all share. The metaphor of 'warriorship' is used by the group to express the disciplined pursuit of self-knowledge and self-acceptance through meditation. The followers of Shambhala can come from any walk of life, culture or religion, but the ideational base of the training remains Buddhist.

In Tibetan mythology, Shambhala is the name of a utopian community guided by gentleness and fearlessness, and Shambhala International is dedicated to societal renewal through the transformation of the consciousness of individuals. This orientation is well represented in their popular magazine, the *Shambhala Sun*, which discusses spirituality, contemplative practice in the arts, and contemporary social issues from a Buddhist perspective.

New Religions, Sects and Alternative Spiritualities with Roots in **The Religions of East Asia**

Confucius, from an 18th-century print.

RELIGIONS OF EAST ASIA
Christopher Partridge

There is an enormously rich diversity of religions and forms of religious expression in East Asia. However, because the aim of this introductory article is simply to provide background information for the new religions, sects and alternative spiritualities discussed in this section, the focus will be the principal religions of China, Japan and Korea, namely Confucianism, Daoism and Shinto. The other principal religion in East Asia, but one which has its roots in India, is Buddhism, which is covered in the introduction to the section on Indian Religions.

Chinese religions
Contemporary Chinese religion is sometimes understood to be the result of the confluence of three streams, namely Confucianism,

Daoism and Buddhism. However, while this is true to some extent, it is too much of a simplification to be an accurate description of Chinese religious practice. As with many other religious traditions, within popular forms of the religion one also finds evidence of early indigenous elements, such as *Shamanism, ancestor worship and nature worship. Indeed, while it has its origins outside China, Christianity has been in China for over 500 years and can now be considered a Chinese religion. In other words, there is a particular type of Christianity that is peculiarly Chinese, just as there is a particular

Tourists walk on the foot of Buddha Colossus – part of a 230-foot statue of the seated Buddha, carved out of the cliffs along the Yangzi River at Leshan, China. The statue was created to protect boatmen on the river.

form of Chinese Buddhism. Hence, while it was once popular to speak of the three principal streams of Chinese religion, Christianity, which is now as influential as Buddhism, should be considered as a significant stream of Chinese religion.

Much modern Chinese religious activity focuses on the celebration of rites of passage and the annual cycle of festivals. In other words, it is more cultural than theological. There is also a strong emphasis on social relationships and family values, much of which is the result of the strong influence of Confucianism.

Confucianism

It is often pointed out that Confucianism, the oldest school of Chinese thought, is less a 'religion' and more a philosophy of life and a code of conduct. Indeed, until the late 19th century, the term 'religion' (*tsung-chiao*) did not exist in the Chinese vocabulary.

Confucianism has its origins in the teachings of K'ung Tzu (K'ung Fu-tzu or Master K'ung; 551–479 BCE), known in the West as Confucius (a name devised by 17th-century Jesuit missionaries), who was arguably the most influential thinker in Chinese history. Although there are many legends about him, little is known of Confucius. We do know that he was born into a poor noble family in the state of Lu (now Shandong province) and that, at the age of 20, he began a career in the civil service as a keeper of the grain stores. Although most accounts of his life claim that he became a prominent government minister, this seems unlikely. However, at the age of 50 he left his position and became an itinerant teacher, wandering from state to state seeking to advise the various feudal rulers. He also managed to gather a large group of devoted disciples who, after his death, continued spreading his teachings and recorded his sayings. These sayings are collected in a book entitled *Conversations* or *Analects* (*Lun Yu*).

Confucius believed himself to be a teacher who had 'understood heaven's will'. His account of his spiritual journey reads as follows: 'At 15, I set my heart on learning [to be a sage]. At 30, I became firm. At 40, I had no more doubts. At 50, I understood heaven's will. At 60, my ears were attuned [to this will]. At 70, I could follow my heart's desires, without overstepping the line' (*Analects* 2.4). While this seems to suggest that Confucius was a man with a deeply religious spirit, in actual fact he was highly critical of much of the religion of his day and professed agnosticism regarding knowledge of the spiritual world. Living during a period of great turmoil in which traditional ideas and religious beliefs were being questioned, he contributed to this questioning and sought to develop an essentially humanist philosophy of how people should live and relate to each other. Also living at a time in which great importance was placed on social status and the correct ordering of society, he counselled individuals to live according to their place in the social order. Indeed, Confucius can be understood as a great moral teacher who sought to replace the old religious ideas with moral values. For Confucius, it is the latter and not the former that should form the basis of social and political life.

Central to Confucian thought are the principles of *jen* (or *ren*) and *li*. *Jen* is virtue, benevolence and being humane. One should, taught Confucius, 'regard everyone as a very important guest' and 'not do to others what you would not have them do to you' (*Analects* 15.23). *Li*, which traditionally meant simply 'ritual' (*Li Chi* is the *Book of Ritual*), is given a deeper meaning in Confucian thought. For Confucianism, *li* is akin to ethics. *Li* indicates not only the specific duties that are required for specific occasions, but, more generally, doing that which is appropriate – correct manners and protocol. *Li* sets out in great detail what an individual's duties are in society. Indeed, *li* is the outward expression of inner virtue and goodness (i.e. *jen*). *Li* makes the invisible visible. Hence, for Confucius, *jen*

and *li* belong together. Without *jen*, *li* is simply a formal carrying out of duty. *Jen*, however, needs *li* in order that the virtuous life may be lived correctly. When *jen* and *li* are properly related and fully implemented, they form the basis of the 'five relationships' of Confucianism, which, in turn, produce the good society.

The five relationships and their accompanying virtues, which it is believed are basic to human societies, are:

▪ the ruler should be benevolent and the subject loyal;

▪ the parent should be kind and the child should show filial devotion;

▪ the husband should be righteous and the wife obedient;

▪ the elder brother should act with gentility and the younger brother with humility;

▪ the older friend should be humane and the younger friend respond with due deference.

Within Chinese society the emphasis has consistently been on filial devotion. Children will often go to great lengths in their devotion in order to avoid dishonouring their parents. Indeed, this devotion is also extended to deceased parents. Bringing honour to one's parents is of paramount importance.

Daoism

Defining Daoism (Teachings of the Way) is not easy. The word *Dao* (often spelled *Tao*) simply means 'the Way' and is a word that appears throughout Chinese thought. Moreover, Daoism (or Taoism) is both a religion (*Dao chiao*) and a philosophy (*Dao chia*). Added to this, the beginnings of Daoism are shrouded in mystery and its influences are many and various. It is therefore difficult to trace exactly where many of the beliefs are drawn from.

Daoism emerged in the form of several distinct movements during the 2nd century CE, towards the end of the Later Han Dynasty (23–220 CE). A distinctively Chinese religion, it has had a massive influence on Chinese thought and history and is today practised by

During the New Year holiday, Daoists come to pray and make offerings at the Wong Tai Sin Temple in Kowloon, Hong Kong.

many Chinese people around the world. The earliest basic text of Daoism, an essentially philosophical work, is the *Daode Jing* (*Tao te Ching*), or *The Classic Way and Its Virtue*. This work is traditionally ascribed to Laoze (Lao-tzu) who, it is claimed, was a contemporary of Confucius – hence the text is sometimes simply referred to as the *Laoze* or *Lao-tzu*. However, this date seems unlikely and most scholars date it from about the 4th century BCE. The authorship is also uncertain as, indeed, is the existence of Laoze. This book, which has an increasingly wide following among westerners, contains all the main ideas of Daoism. The sayings of the *Daode Jing* are cryptic and therefore open to a variety of interpretations.

What is the *Dao*? The *Dao*, although meaning simply 'the way', and, more precisely, the way to be followed if one is to live in harmony with the cosmos, has another more profound meaning. It is the cosmic and controlling principle, according to which all nature functions. Things operate as they do because of the *Dao*. Indeed, it is the source of existence. Julia Ching, a scholar of Chinese religions, has pointed out that 'It has been used in translations of St John's Prologue – "In the beginning was the Tao" – and contains therefore echoes of the line "I am the Way, the Truth and the Life"... The Tao is thus described as existing before the universe came to be, an unchanging first principle, even as the ancestor of all things, that by which all things come to be.' The aim of the Daoist then, is to live naturally and spontaneously in accordance with the *Dao*. One should allow the *Dao* to determine the course of one's life. This is the way of self-control, a way that leads to harmony with others and harmony with nature. Indeed, one should simply go with the flow, so to speak, and live passively. In a very real sense, inactivity (*wu wei*), allowing nature to have full control, is the key to the harmonious life. Consequently Daoism is known for its emphasis on peacefulness, stillness and emphasis on oneness with the natural world. Indeed, Daoism cultivated a mystical, quietist form of religion in which an individual gains control of the body's appetites, longings and desires, stills the spirit, and seeks an inner union with the *Dao*. In other words, the successful Daoist will attain a oneness with the Eternal, harmony with that which is the source of all things and underlies all things.

Over time, Daoists have developed various techniques, similar to those found in yoga, in order to increase the effectiveness of their meditation and gain control over their mental and bodily processes. Unlike the dutiful activity encouraged by Confucianism, for the Daoist it is essential simply to quietly seek union with the *Dao*.

Also central to Daoism, and indeed all Chinese thought, are two further principles, indeed, opposites, namely the yin and the yang. This polarity of opposites has its origins very early in Chinese history. Yin is the female, passive cosmic principle, associated with wetness, darkness, cold, the moon and the earth. Yang, on the other hand, is the male, active cosmic principle, associated with light, heat, the daytime, the sun and the heavens. The shifting balance between these opposite, yet complementary forces, accounts for the cycle of seasons, and indeed for the whole progression of the natural world. Indeed, the existence of the world can be accounted for in this way, in that the dynamic interaction between these polarities gave rise to the five elements that make up the material world: fire, water, wood, metal and earth (each of which also represent cosmic forces). Moreover, many have understood the whole of human life – social, political, cultural, religious, ethical and personal – to be explicable in terms of changes in the yin–yang polarity. For example, the relationship between active Confucianism (yang) and passive Daoism (yin) has been understood in this way, in that the relative stability of the Chinese civilization is attributed to the interplay of these two necessary complementary forces. Again, bodily health and harmony in life, both of which are also central to much contemporary Western alternative spirituality, are the result of maintaining a proper balance of the yin and yang polarities.

Also central to Daoism, and much contemporary Western alternative spirituality, is *qi* (*ch'i*). *Qi* means air, breath, breath of life and, indeed, has been used by the Chinese theologian Chang Ch'un-shen to translate 'Holy Spirit'. *Qi* is a vital energy that permeates and animates the entire cosmos. From the perspective of personal health and longevity, seeking harmony within by harmonizing oneself with the external world (in accordance with the yin–yang theory) is related to the maintenance of *qi*. Important for ensuring harmony, facilitating the flow of *qi*, clearing the body of impurities and encouraging oneness with the *Dao* are meditation, breathing techniques, control of the body by means of disciplined exercises, and prescribed dietary habits. Perhaps the most well known and popular of such practices are *qigong* exercises, the aim of which is to enhance one's *qi* energies.

Daoism as a religion has, over many years, absorbed many 'folk' beliefs as well as aspects of Buddhism and Confucianism. Consequently, there is much to do with spirits, sorcery, exorcism, fortune-telling, the promotion of physical immortality, the use of magical amulets and talismans and geomancy. For example, a common form of geomancy that has, in recent years, become very popular in the West is *feng shui* (wind and water). The geomancer, who is able to assess the flow of cosmic currents and understand the implications of the natural features of earth and sky for buildings and living spaces, offers advice about the most propitious sites for burials, temples and residences in order to ensure the best possible happiness and success for the occupants and those who have died.

Shinto

Shinto forms the basis for Japanese religious life. It is a complex mixture of religious strands, which has, at times, merged with Buddhism. Indeed, many Japanese will consider themselves devotees of both Buddhism and Shinto, and it is common for both Buddhist temples and Shinto shrines to exist side by side at the same sacred site. Indeed, until the arrival of Christianity, religion in Japan was principally Shinto, Buddhist or a mixture of the two. Having said that, not only has Shinto

neither a founder, nor any sacred texts as such, but also many Japanese would not consider it to be a 'religion' at all, claiming that it is simply a collection of ancient civil customs and practices. Nevertheless, it did emerge out of early Japanese devotion to localized deities known as *kami*, and it still has a strong sense of the divine within nature, whether manifested simply as forces or as particular spirits and deities. Indeed, the very name 'Shinto', introduced in the 8th century to distinguish indigenous Japanese religion from Buddhism, is taken from the Chinese *shin dao* (way of the gods). However, it is important to understand, as the scholar David Miller has noted, that 'in Japanese thinking *kami* suggests something different from the Western concept of "god". *Kami* was used originally to refer to anything awe-inspiring in nature, and so trees, mountains, rivers and oceans may all be regarded as *kami*. It is very common throughout Japan, in any place of natural beauty to find a small shrine dedicated to the *kami* of that particular locality. Certain humans may also be regarded as *kami*, usually after they have died.'

While Shinto has no sacred texts as such, it does have two collections of myths and legends: the *Kojiki* (712 CE) and the *Nihongi* (720 CE). These myths concern, for example, the original creation of the cosmos out of chaos in the shape of an egg, the creation of the Japanese islands by the *kami*, and the establishment of the imperial family, descended from the sun goddess Amaterasu. In short, the basic Shinto myths stress the significance of the *kami* and outline the divine origins of Japan, the imperial line and the Japanese people. These ideas have served, in more recent times, as a focus for national unity. However, Miller points out that 'it was only during the period of intense Japanese nationalism, from the late 19th century until the end of the Second World War, that the emperor came to be regarded as a living *kami*. After the war, the link between Shinto and the state was broken, and the emperor is no longer held to be divine by the vast majority of Japanese. The concept of *ikigami* (living *kami*) does, however, still occur within some of the new religious movements that have their origin in Shinto.'

A monk takes part in a daily ritual at a Shinto temple on Mount Haguro, Japan.

The centre of Shinto worship is the shrine, which is entered via a distinctive arch (*torii*). Before approaching the shrine to pray, worshippers will purify themselves by rinsing their hands and mouth with water. Most Japanese will visit the shrine at least once a year, usually at New Year to offer the first prayer of the year (*hatsumode*) for security, health, and business and educational success. Some will write these prayers down on an *ema*

(small tablet) and hang it within the shrine. Some households will have miniature shrines (*kamidana*), in order that members of the household can regularly pray to the *kami* for the protection and the security of the home.

One notable feature of Shinto prayers is their lack of concern with 'eternal life' or spiritual salvation. (This is one of the reasons why many Japanese will also practise Buddhism and, for example, request a Buddhist funeral.)

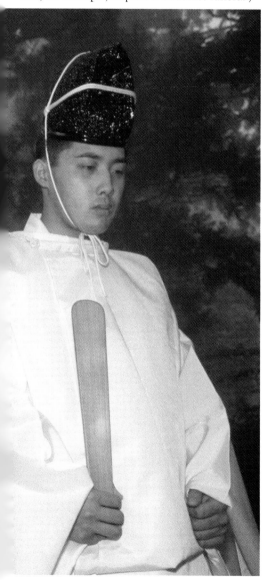

Shinto is principally concerned with material success and security, and the affairs of this world. Indeed, in modern Japan, although increasing numbers do not actually believe in the *kami*, many still practise Shinto as a way of confirming their commitment to Japan and expressing their Japanese identity. That said, Miller makes the important point that 'Shinto practice cannot be dismissed as a form of superstition or a traditional hangover from the past. Shinto has adapted remarkably well to contemporary "secular" Japan. The majority of those who leave *ema* at a shrine, for example, are young people. Companies often have a small shrine on the roof of their building. Construction projects begin with a Shinto ground-breaking ceremony. Many of the larger shrines even offer ceremonies of exorcism for newly purchased cars.'

Quan Zhen
Edward Irons

Quan Zhen (also spelled Chuan Chen), a long-standing Chinese religious tradition, is significant as one of the two living traditions of religious Daoism (also spelled Taoism). The other existing tradition, the Orthodox Single (Zheng Yi), is essentially a master–disciple tradition, not a communal religion. Quan Zhen, in contrast, is today a religious network of community-centred temples staffed by priests initiated through ceremonies passed down from Middle Ages China.

The sect traces its origins to the five immortals and seven patriarchs. Of the group of five, only Wang Congyang (1112–70), the last, was a historical figure. The others were legendary Daoists, the most important being Lyu Chunyang. Lyu today remains one of the most popular Daoist deities. His images are found in most Quan Zhen temples.

Of the seven patriarchs, the most influential figures were Ma Danyang (1122–83), a follower of Wang Congyang, and Qiu Changchun (1147–1227). With the Yuan Dynasty reunification in 1279, Quan Zhen merged with the southern internal alchemy school, a separate and older tradition. It then grouped into seven sub-sects or branches, including Long Men (Dragon Gate) under Qiu Changchun. Long Men is the dominant Quan Zhen branch today. Ordination certificates (*du die*) and daily rituals continue to mention the seven branches to this day.

Quan Zhen teachings are often characterized as a harmonization of the three teachings of Confucianism, Daoism and Buddhism. Harmonization means the three share the same origin and truth, they lead to the same result, and they can be learned together. In Quan Zhen thought, many concepts from the three traditional teachings are reinterpreted. For instance, nirvana, a Buddhist concept, is interpreted to mean release from the womb (*to tai*), a Daoist term.

The religion's name, Quan Zhen (Complete Perfection) is similarly given a multitude of interpretations. *Quan* means preservation, and *zhen* refers to the original perfection (i.e. the way to attain immortality). The original state is the state of simplicity, of being an infant. Fully regaining the original perfection – through the essence, the breath and the spirit – is the goal of Quan Zhen practice. In Buddhism, the term *quan zhen* refers to the state of awareness before conscious thought arises in the individual. And in Confucian terminology, *quan zhen* means 'the mind of heaven'.

Quan Zhen traditionally describes the pursuit of individual cultivation in Daoist terms, which emphasize internal visualizations and tours of the body's interior geography. Wang Congyang's *Congyang Zhenren Zhinguan Yuso Zhue* gives instructions on methods. Man must free the body from disease and impermanence through 'refining the five elements'. This means observing the precepts, abandoning the ten evil deeds, trying to save all sentient beings, being loyal to rulers, and respecting parents and teachers. Then one must recognize the correspondences between directions, ordinal numerals, the body, trigrams (the graphic figures composed of a series of broken and unbroken lines first listed in the *Yi Jing* [*I Ching*] or *Book of Changes*) and such chemical compounds as mercury and lead, and understand the flow and transformation of forces within the body. Semen and blood are the root of the original breath. The main concern is preservation of bodily life, especially fluids.

As Quan Zhen became a popular tradition, its emphasis shifted over the centuries to communal practices. Quan Zhen practitioners emphasized rituals of merit-gaining and contrition. Quan Zhen groups also began to practise spirit writing (*fuji*), in which deities are said to communicate with the living through an individual who writes out the message in a box filled with a thin layer of sand.

Today, the core ritual is the confession (*chan*), a Buddhist-inspired rite. Quan Zhen temples frequently hold three- or nine-day *fa hui* (communal rites).

The largest functioning Quan Zhen temple is probably Hong Kong's Qingsong Guan, which was founded in 1949 by Ho Qicong, a divination master from Guangzhou. The temple began to admit female disciples in 1970. From 1972 it was organized as a limited company. There are currently around 500 active disciples.

Nichiren Shôshû
David Miller

Nichiren Shôshû (Orthodox Nichiren School), is one of a number of Buddhist schools originating in the teachings of

Bamboo grows at the Nichiren Buddhist Myokenji Temple gardens in Kyoto, Japan.

Nichiren, the 13th-century Japanese Buddhist monk (1222–82). In 1253, Nichiren Shu (the Nichiren School) was begun. Byakuren Ajari Nikko, one of Nichiren's original six disciples, separated from the others and inaugurated Nichiren Shôshû, claiming to be the true upholder of Nichiren's teachings. In 1291, he established his headquarters at Taiseki-ji, the temple complex near Mount Fuji. For centuries it remained one of the smallest of the Nichiren Buddhist schools within Japan, themselves small in comparison with other Buddhist groups, but it grew significantly after the Second World War with the dramatic rise of *Sôka Gakkai, which began life as a lay movement within Nichiren Shôshû Buddhism.

The Lotus Sutra, a key text in Mahayana Buddhism, provides the core teaching of Nichiren Shôshû, namely that the historical Sakyamuni Buddha is a manifestation of the Eternal Buddha, the one who has been enlightened from the beginning. In Nichiren Shôshû teaching (and in other Nichiren groups), Nichiren himself is seen as the Eternal Buddha. This shift in focus from the historical Sakyamuni to Nichiren means that Nichiren Buddhism can be seen as a new, indigenous form of Japanese Buddhism. Nichiren's writings are regarded as the key source of doctrine for Nichiren Buddhism. Despite its Japanese origins and nationalistic emphasis, Nichiren Shôshû has been one of the Buddhist movements most active in proselytizing, both within Japan and internationally, through the activities of Sôka Gakkai.

There are three key elements – 'the three great laws' – in Nichiren Shôshû: the *kaidan*, a place of worship located at Taiseki-ji; the *gohonzon*, the sacred object of worship; and the *daimoku*, the title phrase of the Lotus Sutra.

Until the end of the Second World War, Taiseki-ji was in poor repair, but as membership of Sôka Gakkai increased into the millions, the complex was developed, becoming the centre of pilgrimage for

Nichiren Shôshû and Sôka Gakkai members. Until its destruction in 1999, the *Sho-hondo* (grand main temple) was the largest Buddhist temple in the world.

Taiseki-ji is also the home of the *Daigohonzon*. This is a mandala that, it is claimed, was inscribed by Nichiren himself. Unlike most mandalas it does not contain pictures, only phrases and names of various bodhisattvas and other spiritual beings, arrayed in a hierarchical order. Nichiren Shôshû claims that Nichiren intended the *gohonzon* at Taiseki-ji not just for an individual, but for all humankind. It is seen as the embodiment of Nichiren's presence, hence its significance as the focus of Nichiren Shôshû devotion.

The *daimoku* is the phrase 'namu-myoho-renge-kyo', the title phrase of the Lotus Sutra, and is chanted morning and evening by those seeking enlightenment and blessing. In the minds of many practitioners it is seen as the key to attaining health and happiness in the present age.

In 1991, Sôka Gakkai split acrimoniously from Nichiren Shôshû. In 1999, the Shôshû leadership demolished the *Sho-hondo* at Taiseki-ji. While Nichiren Shôshû and its new lay association, the Hokekyo, still function, it has lost much of the impetus that Sôka Gakkai brought to it.

Tenrikyô
David Miller

Tenrikyô (Religion of Heavenly Wisdom), founded in 1838, is one of the oldest of Japan's new religions. Nakayama Miki (1798–1887), a farmer's wife living near Nara became possessed by a spirit who announced that she had become the earthly residence of Tenri-O-no-Mikoto (the Lord of Heavenly Reason), usually referred to now as *Oyagami* (God the Parent). She also developed healing gifts, particularly for people with smallpox or

in the pains of childbirth. Those who came to her seeking wisdom began to see her as the focus of a new movement. Originally registered as a form of Sect Shinto (as opposed to State Shinto, the national ideology at the time), the movement was recognized as a distinct religion in 1970.

Tenrikyô has three main sacred texts: the *Mikagurauta* (Songs for Sacred Dance), the *Ofudesaki* (Tip of the Divine Writing Brush) and the *Osashizu* (Divine Directions). The essence of its teaching is the call for humankind to embrace the 'joyous life'. Ordinarily, 'spiritual dust' prevents the mind from being able to live this joyous life of service to others. This dust is removed through receiving divine grace (*osazuke*), and through personal striving to live harmoniously.

Tenrikyô's headquarters is in Tenri City near Nara. In the centre of its main sanctuary is the *kanrodai*, a hexagonal column from which it is believed sweet dew will one day flow, at which time Tenrikyô will become the religion of all humankind. Believers (known as *yoboku*) are the forerunners of a divine kingdom, timbers out of which this kingdom will be built. Tenrikyô claims over a million followers in Japan, but despite its missionary emphasis, it has had little impact outside Japan.

Cheondogyo
Jeong-Kyu Lee

Cheondogyo grew out of the Donghak (Eastern Learning) movement, which was founded by Cheu Choi (1824–64), the son of a Confucian scholar, in 1860. Cheondogyo was one of several sects derived from the Donghak movement, a sociocultural activity intended to change a decayed Confucian society and to improve the lot of commoners in the late 19th century, during the Korean Choson Kingdom. In 1905, the name Donghak was officially changed to

Cheondogyo (Religion of the Heavenly Way) to identify Donghak as a modern religious organization.

In order to commemorate the start of a new era, Cheondogyo needed to create a new ethical exemplar. As a result, Cheondogyo adopted 'Hanulnim' (God of Cheondogyo or the lord of heaven), in whom the Korean people have believed from ancient times, as the object of worship. Koreans regarded Hanulnim as the Totality or Great One, the Absolute or God. In regard to the relationship between human beings and God, belief in Hanulnim is arrived at through reason. Cheondogyo doctrine emphasizes the belief that the human being is of the same substance as Hanulnim, although both are not exactly the same.

In Cheondogyo's doctrine, each individual is capable of equality with Hanulnim and possesses the capacity to manifest the transcendent power of Hanulnim through spiritual self-cultivation or training. A self-cultivated person has harmonized their mind with the ultimate potency of Hanulnim; combined their will with Hanulnim's virtue; maintains Hanulnim's will in their mind; and attempts to know Hanulnim's way and wisdom.

Through self-cultivation, humans are able to achieve Cheondogyo's ultimate goal – the establishment of a paradise of heaven on earth (*Jisang-cheonkuk*). Accordingly, the concept of *Jisang-cheonkuk* focuses on improving the quality of human life rather than considering life after death. In other words, Cheondogyo has an emphasis on human virtue through which one seeks an ideal world in accordance with the wills of heaven and earth.

The two principal Cheondogyo scriptures are *Tongkyoung-Taejeon* (The Great Eastern Scripture) and *Yongdam-Yusa* (Memorial Songs of Yongdam), which include the works of the founder and the basic doctrines of Cheondogyo. In Cheondogyo's disciplines and ceremonies, *cheongsoo* (clean water), *shimko* ('swearing in mind') and *jumoon* (sacred incantation) are three significant disciplines. The *cheongsoo* ceremony is practised during the daily assembly for prayer at 9 p.m. In addition, Cheondogyo's ceremonies include ritual, daily prayer, Sunday services and Cheondogyo's anniversary days.

During the Japanese colonial period (1910–45), Cheondogyo was severely oppressed and persecuted by the Japanese government, as the organization played an active role in the anti-Japanese movement and independent enlightenment activities. Since the Second World War, Cheondogyo's influence has weakened in Korean society due to the rapid expansion of Christianity and Buddhism, but it remains an important force in promoting Korean culture and values. According to the assertion of the religious order, Cheondogyo was composed of 281 *kyodangs* (churches), 5,600 clergy and about 1.1 million believers in the mid-1990s.

Ômoto
Birgit Staemmler

Ômoto is one of Japan's most influential new religions. It was founded in 1892 by Deguchi Nao (1837–1918) and Ueda Kisaburô (1871–1948; later known as Deguchi Onisaburô). It claims 173,000 members in Japan and abroad, mainly in Brazil. Ômoto's religious centres are in Kameoka and Ayabe, both of which are sites near Kyoto closely linked to the lives of the founders.

Deguchi Nao, a poor and illiterate widow, experienced unsolicited spirit possession by the deity Ushitora no Konjin, commencing in 1892. She eventually became his prophetess, voicing prophecies and commands in a majestic voice. Deguchi Onisaburô had worked in various jobs and read widely on Buddhism, Shinto and Japanese Nativism. In 1898 he turned to religion after a week

☞ *continued on page 231*

JAPANESE NEW RELIGIONS

Ian Reader

The term 'new religion' (*shin shûkyô*) is a generic term used in Japan to refer to a broad category of religious movements that have developed there since the earlier part of the 19th century. 'New religions' stand in contrast to the established mainstream religions, Shinto and Buddhism, to which Japanese people have traditionally been affiliated through the normative social structures and through community and household ties. Traditionally the primary avenues of religious affiliation in Japan have centred around the established traditions through life cycle, household and community rituals and practices that build social bonds between the individual, family and community. Buddhism in such terms in Japan is primarily associated with dealing with death, funerals and caring for the spirits in household-centred rituals of memorialization, and Shinto with community rituals and festivals that tie households and individuals to the wider community. By contrast, new religions have developed outside these normative patterns, depending initially on individual conversion rather than inherited tradition as a means of gaining followers.

Often, too, their appeal has been because of their difference from established traditions, and their offer of new messages, teachings and promises of hope and salvation.

However, while the new religions are a departure from the normative mainstream parameters of Japanese religion, they have drawn extensively on the existing and established religious traditions for inspiration in terms of teachings, figures of worship, ritual structures and practices. A common way of classifying new religions relates to the tradition(s) from which they draw their primary inspiration: thus many of the early new religions, such as *Tenrikyô and Kurozumikyô, draw most extensively in ritual and conceptual terms on Shinto, and may thus be seen as Shinto-based new religions, while other movements such as *Risshô Kôseikai, *Reiyûkai, *Gedatsukai and *Agonshû, which draw inspiration from Buddhist texts and use Buddhist-inspired practices and rituals, are seen as Buddhist-derived new religions. Most, if not all, new religions also draw extensively from the folk religious traditions of Japan, particularly in terms of their use of spiritual healing and their interpretations of misfortunes (which are often attributed to the actions of

unhappy or angry spirits of the dead). Indeed, this ability to draw on, and utilize, elements of traditional cosmology, thought and practices has been a cardinal factor in the appeal of the new religions, which have been adept at reformulating traditional ideas and practices in ways that make them relevant to people in modern Japan. As such, while the new religions can be seen as manifestations of religious change and departures from normative Japanese socio-religious structures, they are also indicative of the continuities that exist in the Japanese religious world, and of the ways in which some of the basic parameters of Japanese religion can be reformulated in new ways relevant to the changing patterns of the modern world.

Numbers, historical patterns and social background

Accurate statistics on the membership levels of Japanese new religions are difficult to find. However, it is widely considered that as many as a quarter of the Japanese population (i.e. perhaps some 30 or so million people) either belong to one or other of the new religions or have at some stage been so affiliated. There are several hundred registered movements in Japan that are normally considered to be new religions: one authoritative Japanese dictionary of new religions lists over 300 movements in this category. They range immensely in size, from small movements with only a few hundred followers gathered around a particular spiritual leader and set of teachings, to massive organizations with millions of followers that have extensive publishing, educational and other interests and that carry some political influence. *Sôka Gakkai, for example, the largest new religion, has many million followers, publishes a daily newspaper, runs a university and has close links with one of Japan's main political parties. Other large new religions with in excess of 1 million followers include Risshô Kôseikai, Tenrikyô and *Shinnyoen.

Demographically, the new religions are stronger in urban rather than in rural areas where traditional community structures have been least deeply undermined by the forces of modernity. The larger movements, such as Sôka Gakkai and Risshô Kôseikai, are especially strong in Tokyo and Japan's other main cities. However, their constituencies extend across Japan and to all sections of the Japanese population: studies have shown that while many (especially the magically oriented new religions that have emerged

in late 20th-century Japan) have a high percentage of young followers, membership of the new religions overall comprises all age groups and social classes. Recent studies have shown that the education levels of the members of new religions is similar to that of the general Japanese population, while many of the most recent new religions, such as *Kôfuku no Kagaku, are widely noted for their ability to attract students and graduates from elite universities and for their successful recruiting campaigns on university campuses.

There is some differentiation between the Japanese new religions in terms of their eras of formation. The earliest of these can be dated to the early 19th century, when a number of movements appeared in rural Japan, such as Kurozumikyô and Konkôkyô, which emerged out of Shinto and centred around the revelations of creator deities to inspired religious figures who thus became their mouthpieces. Subsequent eras have seen the emergence of new waves of new religions, with, for example, a number of Buddhist-inspired new movements, such as Reiyûkai and Risshô Kôseikai, emerging in urban, industrial Japan in the 1920s and 1930s, and, most recently, a wave of

magically inspired, millennialist new movements, including Agonshû and Kôfuku no Kagaku, coming to the fore in the late 20th century.

The appeal of the new religions has been primarily centred in their ability to provide individuals of all ages and walks of life with a positive sense of hope in confronting the problems of everyday existence, and in providing spiritual inspiration and guidance that enables followers to find new meanings in life, to deal with personal problems and to develop hopes of spiritual salvation. It is also widely recognized that the state of Japanese society at various times in recent history has been especially conducive to the formation of new religions, which have particularly flourished at times of social crisis and unease. New religions have emerged to offer hope and promises of renewal and transformation at such periods of crises: indeed, the millennial promise of world transformation in which the existing material world would be swept aside to be replaced by a more spiritually pure and just society is a recurrent theme within the new religions of Japan.

Thus the earliest wave of new religions in the first half of the 19th century occurred at a time when the old feudal regime was collapsing and changing economic conditions had gravely affected the livelihoods and ways of life of rural Japanese, leading to immense social turbulence and unease. The movements that developed at this time generally appeared both to reaffirm traditional values (and hence provide a bulwark of emotional stability in a time of crisis) and

Namoro Shigomitso signs on behalf of Japan during formal surrender ceremonies on the USS Missouri in Tokyo Bay, 31 August 1945. After the war many new religious movements were formed in Japan.

promise a sense of world renewal, in which the injustices of the world, which were especially manifest at such times of crisis, would be eradicated, and the present world transformed and spiritually renewed. Similarly, in the 1920s and 1930s, a combination of rapid urban growth and mass industrialization was followed by economic depression. Amid this instability and turmoil various urban-based movements, such as Reiyûkai, grew quickly because of their ability to assuage the worries of the impoverished urban working classes and to offer them hope in a world of uncertainty.

The most dramatic period of rapid growth for the new religions, however, occurred in the period after Japan's defeat in the Second World War when it was in a state of ruin, its cities laid waste and the country occupied by the Allied Forces. This created a state of emotional and social crisis in which the older traditions of Shinto and Buddhism, which had been complicit in the war effort and with the regime that had led Japan to disaster, were incapable of providing emotional succour. By contrast, the new religions (some of which, such as Sôka Gakkai, had opposed the war and were thus freed from

negative associations with the past) appeared to offer a means of hope to a population seeking new ways forward in a time of adversity. The uncertainties of the immediate post-war period (and the upheavals caused by Japan's rapid modernization and the concomitant massive growth of its cities thereafter) thus gave rise to massive increases in recruitment to the new religions, and in the numbers of movements that appeared. Such was the growth that occurred in this period that one scholar coined the term the 'rush hour of the gods' to describe the situation.

A further period of rapid growth has occurred in the latter part of the 20th century, a period when Japan has apparently enjoyed major economic growth – but one also characterized by immense cultural uncertainty as the processes of modernization, rationalization and globalization eroded Japanese traditional culture, changed peoples' lifestyles and provoked a sense of identity crisis in the nation. In this period, new movements, such as *Mahikari, Agonshû and Kôfuku no Kagaku, which combine a ready acceptance of modern technology with an emphasis on spiritual healing, magic and esoteric religious practices, have attracted much attention and large followings as they appear to provide an alternative to the rationalizations of modern society.

Charisma, leadership, world renewal and individual transformation

Among the common characteristics that typify Japanese new religions, perhaps the most striking are those relating to the position and mission of their founders, and the ways that these relate to and provide messages and meanings for individual members and for the world at large. The new religions, with very few exceptions, have been formed around the activities of charismatic founding figures who become the focus of inspiration and authority in the movements they form and who are seen by their followers as conduits between the human and spiritual realms. This position enables them to provide their followers with spiritual healing and personal benefits as a result, while also transmitting to them new ethical codes through which to live.

The authority of such figures (who are often regarded as living deities in their lifetimes and who continue to be venerated in death by their followers) is normally based on their claims to have discovered new spiritual truths of vital significance for the world, coupled with their ability to demonstrate their power through such acts as spiritual healing. Such new truths, which may be discovered by the founder as a result of revelations transmitted by a deity, or through new understandings discovered by the founder in Buddhist texts and teachings, generally posit the necessity of world transformation through spiritual means, which will right the wrongs of this world.

They normally involve a potent critique of the materialistic foundations and orientations of society, and emphasize the importance of world renewal (*yonaoshi*), not so much in political or in social terms, but in spiritual terms. Thus, Nakayama Miki (1798–1887), the foundress of Tenrikyô, became spiritually possessed by a deity known as Tenri-O-no-Mikoto (translated by Tenrikyô as 'God the Parent', in English) who revealed himself as the initial creator of the universe. The world had subsequently fallen into corruption and ruin as a result of the greed of humanity, and hence God the Parent was returning (using Nakayama Miki as his mouthpiece) to transform the world and restore it to a spiritually pristine state. Buddhist-oriented new religions often have a similar dynamic: Agonshû, for example, believes it has a mission to restore 'true Buddhism' to, and thus spiritually transform, the world. Often such millennial missions assume a sense of urgency, with many of the more recent new religions such as Kôfuku no Kagaku and Agonshû speaking of imminent world destruction, whether through nuclear war, environmental pollution or similar catastrophic events that have been caused by the negative spiritual influences of materialism, and arguing that only through their messages and teachings can the world be transformed and saved.

Along with, and integral to, such promises of world transformation, the new religions also emphasize the importance of individual transformation: the individual is a microcosm of the universe and it is through personal spiritual transformation that the world at large may be saved. Here the role of the founder is crucial. It is common for the founders of new religions to assume such a position after having experienced personal spiritual crises that threatened their very existence. Kiriyama Seiyû (b. 1921) of Agonshû, for example, suffered a series of setbacks that took him to the brink of suicide before experiencing a revelation from the Buddhist figure Kannon, which caused him to turn to a religious way of life. Through austere spiritual practices he

overcame his own crisis (in Agonshû's terms, he 'cut his karma', i.e. eradicated or overcame the negative spiritual influences of the past) and acquired a sense of spiritual authority. His crisis was the spur that led him to religious awareness and to the attainment of spiritual power and authority. Thus his tribulations and his triumph over them both empowered him and served as an inspirational model for his followers, telling them that they, too, could 'cut their karma' and find solutions to their problems.

This transformation from suffering person to spiritual leader as seen in the case of Kiriyama is a prevalent one among the founders of new religions. It is usually accompanied by the practice of austerities that polish or cleanse the spirit and eradicate negative karma (a concept of immense importance among the new religions). The concept of karma, while derived initially from Buddhism, is found throughout the Japanese religious world, where it is seen as a basically negative force in which past deeds may have future spiritual repercussions. The physical world is affected by the spiritual: hence, personal misfortunes (such as illness) may be the result of bad karma, which may be manifest in the form of

a physical problem such as illness. Kiriyama's crisis was thus caused by his past misdeeds, which had to be dealt with spiritually before he could overcome his problems.

Hence, in order to solve problems, one has to confront the spiritual hindrances that have accrued from the past, whether from one's own misdeeds or from one's ancestors, who remain an important element in the Japanese religious world and whose influence on their living kin serves to emphasize the importance of the interdependence of the living and their deceased kin in the Japanese religious worldview. The eradication of negative karma, usually through accumulating spiritual merit via ritual practices, service to the new religion and wider community, and sometimes through ascetic practices, thus is a key element in the religious lives of the followers of the new religions. Many new religions also provide their followers with spiritual counselling, which enables them to confront and deal with personal problems and to identify and then deal with the potential spiritual causes of such problems. Such counselling generally emphasizes the importance of traditional morality and behavioural structures, in which followers are enjoined to respect their elders and ancestors, whose support is necessary for the maintenance of a healthy and happy life on this earth, and are taught the importance of maintaining good relations with, and respecting the position of, others. A notion found widely in the new religions is that 'other people are mirrors' (i.e. they reflect back on oneself the negative impulses one directs towards them). In other words, in order to deal with external problems, such as those relating to personal relationships, one must first reflect on one's own behaviour and make sure that this is in order and that one is treating others in an appropriate and correct manner.

When dealing with problems such as illness, followers may be encouraged to participate in the spiritual healing techniques practised widely in the new religions. Illness is not just based on physical causes (e.g. germs) but comes about through a combination of factors, including spiritual (i.e. karmic) causes, which need to be dealt with if a proper healing process is to be achieved. In some new religions (e.g. Tenrikyô), illness is thus seen as a result of misdeeds, and hence as a wake-up call extolling one to lead a more moral and spiritually aware life. Personal spiritual transformation thus may be every bit as important as medical treatment if one is to recover from illness. This emphasis on the spiritual aspects of healing in the new religions thus contains an implicit affirmation of traditional, folk-based Japanese healing practices over and above the Western-derived medicine that forms the basis of medical treatment in Japan today.

Such practices – along with the emphasis on eradicating negative karma – place the individual at the centre of any process of healing or other forms of problem solution. By emphasizing the individual, spiritual (i.e. karmic) aspects of illness, the individual thus becomes part of the process of solving the problem or illness. This effectively states that individuals can be in command of their own destiny if only they engage in appropriate spiritual activities. It also re-emphasizes the traditional family morality of pre-modern Japan, affirming the interdependence of people (especially in the notion that other people are mirrors), and hence serves as a conservative moral response to the increasing fragmentation of modern society. This, again, has proved highly efficacious in attracting followers inside Japan.

Structures and organization

Since Japanese new religions generally emanate from the teachings and activities of charismatically inspired leaders, it is normally the case that their words and writings become the basis of canonical authority in the movement, especially after the founder's demise. Thus, for example, Nakayama Miki's writings, collectively known as the *Ofudesaki*, have become central to Tenrikyô's subsequent teaching and doctrinal structures. Deceased leaders generally become viewed as protector figures watching over the movements they have founded, and commonly their tombs become important centres of worship in, and places of pilgrimage for, their movements.

This emphasis on the position of the founder has also resulted in a commonly followed pattern of succession to new religions, many of which have developed a pattern of inherited leadership based on family lineages. In *Ômoto, for example, titular leadership passes through the female line of descent from its foundress, Deguchi Nao, while in the Buddhist-oriented *Kôdô Kyôdan, leadership has passed from the founder Okano Shôdô to his son and grandson. Where a direct family heir may not be present, it is not uncommon for founders to adopt a devout disciple and make him or her their familial successor. The founder of Mahikari, Okada Kôtama, for instance, adopted a daughter who succeeded him on Okada's death.

This emphasis on the power of the founder and on inherited charisma means that the new religions in general have tended towards the conservative and hierarchic in organizational terms. At the same time, they have been innovative in that, unlike the established traditions, which are centred around ordained priests, the new religions have been lay-centred. Normally, it has been the ordinary followers of new religions who have formed the vanguard of the movement and who have been entrusted with the role of spreading its word to their fellows. Most commonly this is done through existing social structures: studies show that most members of new religions have been recruited by a family member, friend or workmate. Such recruitment activities are often the means by which members achieve advancement in the new religions, with most new religions developing hierarchical structures to this end, and with members acquiring a responsibility towards those they recruit (who may become their

'children' in organizational terms). As such, it is often the case that the organizational structures of new religions resemble extended family relationship structures of mutual interdependence between different followers, all of whom look up to the founder and/or his or her family and descendants as their spiritual 'parents'.

Japanese new religions outside Japan

Many Japanese new religions have sought to spread their message beyond Japan, initially and most successfully among Japanese immigrant communities in areas such as Peru, Brazil and Hawaii (areas to which many Japanese emigrated in the 19th and early 20th centuries), as well as, in the modern day, among Japanese expatriate communities involved in overseas business. However, they have not been especially successful in developing a following beyond the Japanese cultural milieu, largely because their message has been so closely tied to Japanese cultural traditions and arenas.

One or two new religions with Buddhist orientations have managed to attract some support beyond the Japanese cultural sphere, particularly Sôka Gakkai, which has developed a sound base of support in North

America, Europe and elsewhere, largely because of its positive, world-affirming messages that blend Buddhist concepts with ideas of self-improvement. Some movements with emphases on spiritual healing, such as Mahikari, have also attracted small followings in Africa and the Caribbean, as well as Europe and Australia. Overall, however, Japanese new religions have remained a rather ephemeral presence beyond Japanese boundaries. This stands in sharp contrast to their success and continuing presence in Japan, where they constitute probably the most striking religious phenomenon of the past century and a half, as well as one of the most vibrant and continuing aspects of Japan's contemporary religious culture.

of meditation and the experience of a journey of the soul. In 1899, he joined Deguchi Nao's budding religion as organizer and teacher. In January 1900, he married her youngest daughter, Sumi. Due to a ritual of spirit possession, vibrant millenarianism and mass media (its first magazine was published in 1909) Ômoto flourished during the 1910s. In 1921 the authorities considered it a potential threat and suppressed it in the 'First Ômoto Incident'. Ômoto recovered quickly, taught universal salvation, propagated Esperanto, conducted missions in Asia, Europe and Latin America, and developed into a nationalistic and politically very active organization, which was again regarded as a political threat resulting in the movement's suppression in 1935 (the 'Second Ômoto Incident'). With religious freedom after the end of the Second World War, Ômoto was re-established.

Today it is a rather inconspicuous, well-established movement concentrating on interreligious cooperation, Japanese arts and humanitarian activities. Ômoto's line of succession is matrilineal, its leaders being female descendants of Deguchi Nao, assisted by husbands adopted into the Deguchi family. Deguchi Kurenai (b. 1956) succeeded as the current leader in April 2001.

Deguchi Nao's *Fudesaki* (*From the Tip of the Writing Brush*), containing her revelations, and Deguchi Onisaburô's *Reikai monogatari* (*Stories from the Spirit World*), which describes his journey of the soul, constitute Ômoto's canon. However, writings by later leaders such as Deguchi Naohi (1902–90) or Deguchi Hidemaru (1897–1991) are equally treasured.

Ômoto draws heavily on Shinto's doctrine and pantheon. It adds that Ushitora no Konjin was the creator of the world and had taken possession of Deguchi Nao to save humankind from destruction by selfishness and materialism. Today, Ômoto's initially vigorous and political millenarianism, *yonaoshi*

(renewal of the world), has become more restrained and ethical: the true, good and beautiful future world will be effected through *kokoro naoshi* (renewal of the self). Art is regarded as the mother of religion and thus Japanese arts such as pottery, weaving, Noh theatre, the tea ceremony, music and poetry are practised and supported.

Jinrui Aizenkai, officially translated as 'Universal Love and Brotherhood Association', is Ômoto's volunteer organization founded in 1925. Its main activities today are development aid projects, the promotion of Esperanto, and campaigns for the abolition of nuclear weapons, organic agriculture, or against the acceptance of brain death, among other causes. Several founders of *Japanese new religions had formerly been members of Ômoto. Notable examples are Taniguchi Masaharu (see *Seichô no Ie), Okada Mokichi (see *Sekai Kyûseikyô), Tomokiyo Yoshisane (founder of Shindô Tenkôkyo), Nakano Yonosuke (see *Ananaikyô) and Asano Wasaburô (founder of Shinrei Kagaku Kenkyûkai).

Reiki
David Miller

Reiki, usually translated as 'Universal Life Force Energy', is a spiritual healing process with its origins in Japan. The Japanese word is made up of two characters meaning 'spirit' and 'energy'. It has grown considerably in popularity in the West since the 1980s, often as an element in the wider spread of New Age ideas. It was introduced into the West by Takata Hawayo, a Japanese-American, who had learned it from Hayashi Chujiro, who in turn claimed to be the recipient of the leadership mantle passed on to him by the founder of Reiki, Usui Makao (1865–1926). Traditionally Usui was said to be a Christian who, in seeking the source of Christ's healing power, had been drawn towards Buddhism. After a period of fasting on a sacred mountain, Mount Kurama, near Kyoto, a mystical experience led him to understand the meaning of healing symbols he had found in an old Buddhist text. On returning from the mountain, he placed his hands on a number of sick people who recovered, confirming to him that he had discovered the source of healing, the life energy of the universe. While Usui had been interested in spiritual healing since the 1890s, it is generally felt that his experience

A Reiki master plays an 'angel harp' on the abdomen of a client during a Reiki healing session. Reiki practitioners claim that the ancient Japanese technique can help people get in touch with their spirituality.

on Mount Kurama occurred around 1914, after which he began offering healing through Reiki.

Recent research has found no evidence that Usui was a Christian, nor that he intended the line of descent to pass through Hayashi and Takata. It seems possible that the Christian element was introduced into the story to increase its acceptance in the West. A number of Japanese groups practise Reiki, notably the Usui Reiki Ryoho Gakkai, though they do not recognize the transmission through Hayashi and Takata.

Reiki healing recognizes the existence of a universal energy (*ki*). This is similar to the Chinese idea of *qi*, the energy flow that underlies both acupuncture and *qigong*. When this flow of energy through the body is blocked, illness, both physical and emotional, results. Reiki practitioners seek to channel life-force energy into the body. This is done as the practitioner places their hands on, or lightly over, the person. It is also possible to give Reiki healing to oneself. In a full session, hands are laid on 12 different parts of the body. Some practitioners of Reiki have been influenced by Tibetan Buddhism, drawing on the concept of chakras, through which energy enters the body. This is an adaptation of original Reiki teaching that follows Chinese concepts.

People learn Reiki as much through practice as by instruction. There are three degrees of initiation, though one can give Reiki after the first stage. Some may go on to become masters after attaining the third stage. In the first two stages, practitioners receive 'attunements' to enable them to become more effective channels of energy, firstly for physical healing, and secondly for mental and emotional healing as well as healing at a distance. The third stage involves further development of healing powers, and the reception of a special healing symbol.

Usui also taught five core principles of

Reiki meditation: do not worry; do not get angry; honour your parents, teachers, elders and friends; earn your living honestly; and be thankful and respectful to every living thing.

Reiki practitioners would not call Reiki 'a religion', believing that it can be practised with or without a particular religious faith. Many Western practitioners see Reiki as part of the range of alternative techniques for healing, and for spiritual and self-development.

Perfect Liberty Kyôdan
Robert Kisala

Perfect Liberty Kyôdan traces its roots to the founding in 1924 of the Tokumitsu Church, a branch of the Ontake-kyo sect of Shinto, by Miki Tokuharu (1871–1938), a Buddhist monk of the Obaku Zen sect. Miki had been cured of asthma some years before by Kanada Tokumitsu and considered himself Kanada's successor. The name of the religion was changed to Hitonomichi Kyôdan in 1931, and the group was suppressed by the Japanese government in 1936 on charges of lese-majesty.

In the post-war period, the group was re-established under the name of PL Kyôdan, and later, Perfect Liberty Kyôdan, by the founder's son, Miki Tokuchika (1900–83). The main tenet of Perfect Liberty is that 'life is art', indicating that the believers should take charge of their lives and seize every moment as an opportunity for self-expression. The believers are exhorted to value sincerity and human relationships, to live humbly and with gratitude, to work hard and be uncomplaining – an ethic common to many *Japanese new religions.

Believers are encouraged to visit their local churches and participate in services on the 1st (for peace), the 11th (for the ancestors) and the 21st (in gratitude) of

every month, in addition to major services on New Year's Day, 1 August (commemorating the founder), 29 September (the foundation of the religion), and 2 December (the birthday of the present leader of the group). The group claims a membership of about 2 million and is active in North and South America, primarily among Japanese immigrant communities, with headquarters in Los Angeles, United States, and São Paulo, Brazil.

Reiyûkai
David Miller

Reiyûkai (the Spiritual Friendship Society) began life as a lay Buddhist group, strongly influenced by the teachings of *Nichiren Shôshû Buddhism. Like *Sôka Gakkai, it emphasizes recitation of the title of the Lotus Sutra (a key text in Mahayana Buddhism) or *daimoku* (namely the phrase *namu-myoho-renge-kyo*), and reverence for ancestors. However, unlike Sôka Gakkai, it has never been affiliated to any particular Nichiren sect, nor is it exclusivist, allowing members to remain part of their original Buddhist sect or, in the case of members outside Japan, in their original religious tradition.

Its founder, Kubo Kakutaro, grew up in Japan at the start of the 20th century. Japan was modernizing and urbanizing rapidly, while facing the accompanying problems of poverty and unemployment. Kubo saw in this an echo of the time of crisis in which Nichiren had emerged, and began to see himself as the Nichiren of his generation. He was also influenced by the shamanistic healing practices of Wakatsuki Chise, whom he met while studying at a temple in Nakayama, and the two of them decided to found their own lay Buddhist group. Initially unsuccessful, Reiyûkai, informally established in 1924, began to grow significantly when Kubo's sister-in-law, Kotani Kimi, became a member. This followed the healing of her husband, Kubo's brother, when she began chanting the *daimoku* and reverencing her ancestors. Kotani became an enthusiastic ambassador for the movement, giving herself in service to the urban poor of Tokyo, from whom the early followers all came. Kubo created the Blue Sutra, a collection of certain passages from the Lotus Sutra, and it became the group's key text.

Chanting the *daimoku* is seen as the key to self-development, though the movement also stresses the need to develop harmonious relationships with others. Following Kotani's example, there is a strong commitment to social involvement. Its other two key emphases are *senzo kuyo* (ancestor veneration) and *michibiki* (guiding others on the path of truth). In its ancestor practices, it continues Japanese tradition, but with some significant differences. Firstly, it encourages lay involvement, without the need for priests to be involved. Secondly, it encourages all members to participate, not just eldest sons. Thirdly, ancestors on both sides of the family, not just the father's side, are honoured, though they are not considered to be divine and are not worshipped. *Michibiki* (proselytism) consists of members guiding others in the practice of meditation and chanting. *Michibiki* is thought not just to help others but to help the members themselves in their path to spiritual development. Those guided into the movement become 'spiritual children' of those who guided them.

Practices of spiritual healing that have their roots in traditional Japanese shamanistic practices also feature, although this mystic power (*o-kuji*) is never described in print, and is passed on individually from spiritual parents to their spiritual children.

The movement claimed 3 million members in Japan in 1996 and 180,000 overseas. It has also seen a number of splinter movements emerge from it in Japan, the largest of which is *Risshô Kôseikai, claiming over 6 million members.

Cao Dai
David Burnett

Cao Dai is a syncretistic Vietnamese religious movement founded in 1926 by Ngo Van Chieu (1878–1932). Chieu was an official of the French colonial administration and was familiar with both Eastern and Western religions. He was especially interested in spiritism and during one seance in 1920 he

made contact with an apparition named Cao Dai ('High Tower', a Daoist epithet for the supreme God). The deity expressed certain fundamentals of its worship: universalism, vegetarianism and the image of an eye in a radiant circle. Chieu returned to Saigon in 1924 and began teaching what he had learned from Cao Dai. The following year, three of Chieu's friends were practising divination when a spirit introduced himself

and later revealed himself as Cao Dai come to bring teaching. Chieu was chosen as the leader of the new religion, but he preferred solitude, so Le Van Trung was selected to replace him as head of the movement (a

The Cao Dai temple in Tay Ninh province, Vietnam. Cao Dai worship is focused on elaborate festivals and daily rituals.

position frequently referred to as 'Pope'). To acquire legal recognition with the French authorities they signed the 'Declaration of the Founding of the Cao Dai Religion' on 7 October 1926, which listed 247 signatures of members.

Although the movement was initially resisted by Buddhists and French officials, it grew rapidly. By 1930 it had over 200,000 followers in a population of 8 million. It grew at a time when Roman Catholicism was the religion of the foreign rulers, Confucianism was associated with a social order that was passing away, and Buddhism in Vietnam was moribund. The success of Caodism is due in part to the popularity of spiritism and its ability to assimilate elements from the existing religions. It seeks to present itself as the unification of the religions of East and West. For example, it derived much of its social ethic from Confucianism, adopted the teaching of karma and rebirth from Buddhism, and borrowed many of its rituals from Daoism. Although the fundamental belief is in one God, the most high (Cao Dai), it acknowledges many intermediaries, including Joan of Arc, William Shakespeare and Lenin.

Cao Dai worship is focused on elaborate festivals and the rituals performed in temples four times a day. The rituals consist of prayers, chants and offerings of incense, tea and wine. Seances are held separately and are the method Cao Dai uses to transmit this new religion to humanity. A mechanical device is commonly used as a means of communication. Spiritual messages are received in the form of verses, providing an ever-expanding body of teaching. As a result, numerous sects have emerged. The *Thanh Ngon Hiep Tuyen* is a two-volume compilation of sacred messages received by Cao Dai leaders through seances.

The main headquarters of Cao Dai used to be in the sacred city of Tay Ninh, north-west of Ho Chi Minh City, where its main temple and the administrative offices were located.

Before unification of the country under communist rule in 1975, the movement controlled considerable agricultural land and businesses. It even had its own army until it was disbanded by President Ngo Dinh Diem in 1955. Although its allegiances changed with time, it was essentially nationalistic.

With the coming to power of the communist government, the movement was severely repressed. Land, property and businesses were confiscated and many priests arrested. Indeed the Cao Dai in Vietnam have now been shut down and their leadership dispersed. However, the movement has shown signs of renewed growth, especially among Vietnamese refugee communities around the world. It currently claims 6 million followers, and has major centres in Australia and particularly Canada, where its new international headquarters is located.

Gedatsukai
Birgit Staemmler

Gedatsukai (Enlightenment Society) is a Japanese new religion founded in 1929 by Okano Eizô (1881–1948), also known as Okano Seiken. It claims over 200,000 members, mostly in Japan, but also in the United States and Brazil. Gedatsukai's administrative headquarters is in central Tokyo and its central holy site is in Okano's home town, Kitamoto, about 30 miles (50 km) north-west of Tokyo.

Okano turned to religion after recovering from a near-fatal illness in 1925. On New Year's Day, 1929, he experienced a revelation that convinced him to found his own religious organization. Until religious freedom was granted in 1945, Gedatsukai was affiliated with Shingon Buddhism to avoid suppression.

Gedatsukai's doctrine is syncretistic, containing elements from Buddhism, Confucianism, Shinto and Japanese local religious traditions. The main objects of worship are *Gochi Nyorai* (the five Buddhas of Shingon Buddhism), *Tenjin Chiji Ogami* (Shinto deities of heaven and earth) and the founder himself, as a near-divine model person. Its focus is on gratitude and reverence to parents, ancestors and tutelary deities. Lack of these virtues is believed to be the ultimate cause of difficulties faced in this life.

Practices include yearly memorial ceremonies in Kitamoto and pilgrimage to three sites connected with the Japanese imperial family. Branch offices conduct monthly meetings, individual counselling, a form of meditation called *o-kiyome* and *gohô shugyô*, a ritual of mediation during which, under the guidance of a trained instructor, members are believed to receive messages from ancestors or deities. Daily individual practice should include *amacha kuyô*, a memorial rite involving sweet tea to pacify ancestral spirits and purify one's mind.

Seichô no Ie
Birgit Staemmler

Seichô no Ie, literally 'House of Growth', is a Japanese new religion founded in 1930 by Taniguchi Masaharu (1893–1985), a former member of *Ômoto. It claims about 850,000 members in Japan and nearly twice as many in Brazil, and has branches in many other countries as well. Its organizational headquarters is in Tokyo and its ceremonial headquarters in Nagasaki. Its current president is the founder's son-in-law, Taniguchi Seichô (b. 1919), whose son Taniguchi Masanobu (b. 1951) is vice-president and gradually taking over his father's responsibilities.

Seichô no Ie's central doctrinal text is Taniguchi Masaharu's 40-volume *Seimei no jissô*, officially translated as *Truth of Life*. Other books by the founder and succeeding leaders are also highly treasured. Seichô no Ie

publications also include a monthly newspaper (*Seishimei*) and four magazines aimed at men, women, young people and children respectively, with a combined monthly distribution of over 1.5 million copies.

Seichô no Ie's teaching is syncretic, containing elements of Shinto, Buddhist and Christian doctrine. Its key concept is that the world as we see it does not exist. It is only the reflection of divine reality distorted through the lens of the human mind, which is polluted because of vices and sins. If humans succeeded in ridding themselves of these vices and sins and concentrated on the divine reality they would perceive the divine truth, which is said to be harmonious, beautiful and complete. They would then also perceive themselves as the truly perfect, healthy and harmonious children of God and realize that illnesses and misfortune are just manifestations of their mistaken perceptions. A significant element of Seichô no Ie practice is, therefore, a form of meditation called *shinsôkan* in which practitioners strive to direct their thoughts at the supreme divinity in order to see its true form and become aware of their own true state of being.

Great emphasis is placed on the traditional role of the family, on parenting and on respect for the Japanese emperor. Other important practices thus include paying grateful reverence to one's ancestors and conducting rituals for still-born or aborted babies to apologize and ensure their well-being in the world beyond. This-worldly benefits, such as healing, financial improvement and harmony, are believed to be the results of faith, filial piety, a positive outlook on life and, in particular, gratitude. Religious practice also emphasizes the study of Seichô no Ie's publications by oneself, in informal meetings or through attending monthly or yearly lectures. An important element of Seichô no Ie's structure is local men's, women's or youth groups who meet regularly to study the doctrines, plan activities or informally discuss personal problems. Seichô no Ie also conducts regular so-called 'spiritual training seminars', which feature lectures, testimonials, hymns, *shinsôkan*-meditation, offerings and other rituals.

Sôka Gakkai
David Miller

Sôka Gakkai (Value-creating Society) was established in 1930 as a lay Buddhist organization of the *Nichiren Shôshû school of Buddhism. Its criticism of State Shinto meant that its leaders were imprisoned during the Second World War. Its founder, Makiguchi Tsunesaburo (1871–1944), died in prison. However, his assistant, Toda Josei, took over the leadership and, after his release from prison, set about establishing the organization.

During the 1950s, Sôka Gakkai grew rapidly. The movement's teaching that regular chanting of the *daimoku* (the phrase '*namu-myoho-renge-kyo*', which is the title phrase of the Lotus Sutra, a key text in Mahayana Buddhism) would lead to prosperity, health and happiness found great appeal in post-war Japan. The movement also practised a very aggressive style of proselytization, known as *shakubuku* (breaking down). This involved criticism of other religions and of other Buddhist groups, and very forceful attempts to convert people, resulting in many (sometimes rather reluctant) new members.

Toda died in 1958, and was succeeded by Ikeda Daisaku. In the 1960s, Sôka Gakkai entered politics through the Komeito, the 'Clean Government Party', which was at one time the third-largest party in Japanese politics, and has on occasions formed part of coalition governments.

However, public hostility to Sôka Gakkai grew in the 1960s, as a result of reaction against *shakubuku* and fears that its links with Komeito threatened the separation between religion and state, a fundamental part of the modern Japanese constitution. In 1970, Ikeda ended the formal link between Sôka Gakkai and Komeito. The movement also adopted less aggressive proselytism, emphasizing instead the benefits of involvement, especially regular chanting, and it continued to grow numerically.

Sôka Gakkai members hold to 'the three great laws' of Nichiren Shôshû. All members have their own *gohonzon*, a transcription of the Daigohonzon in Taiseki-ji, the mandala at the Nichiren Shôshû temple complex near Mount Fuji, which they keep in their own *kaidan* (altar) in their own home. They chant the *daimoku* daily before the *gohonzon*, and recite other sections from the Lotus Sutra. With its emphasis on personal Buddhist practice, and correspondingly less emphasis on the role of the priesthood, some observers see the movement as a kind of Protestant Buddhism.

As the movement grew larger, tension increased between Ikeda and the Nichiren Shôshû priesthood. In 1979, Ikeda resigned from the presidency of Sôka Gakkai and established Sôka Gakkai International (SGI), in order to concentrate on developing the movement outside Japan. However, tensions continued, and in 1991 the priesthood excommunicated all Sôka Gakkai members. The movement continued to function as a lay movement, and, with the transfer of allegiance of some Nichiren priests to SGI, it is able again to issue officially sanctioned *gohonzon* to its members.

It has also grown significantly overseas, and includes some high-profile converts, such as the singer Tina Turner. Ikeda has transformed the movement into one that focuses on issues of world peace and development, and it has become far less exclusivist and nationalistic.

☞ *continued on page 245*

CHINESE NEW RELIGIONS

Edward Irons

New religious groups with clear organizational identities and agendas form in all literate cultures, and China is no exception. Chinese culture has historically been a fecund source of religious creativity, from early official rites to Confucian moral systems to religious and philosophical Daoism. New religions have formed in all periods of Chinese history, a period extending back at least to the Shang Dynasty in the 2nd millennium BCE.

Historical study of new religious groups shows that they generally form in two ways. Firstly, they may come from outside cultural influences. In China's case, two obvious examples are the coming of Buddhism in the first centuries CE and the advent of Christianity in the late Ming Dynasty (1368–1644). Other common sources of new religious ideas are the many ethnic minorities existing within Chinese cultural space – there are today 56 officially recognized minority groups, most with distinct religious systems.

A second source of new religions is borrowing and adapting from existing cultural systems. The tradition's ideas and rituals are adapted to current realities, often under the direction of creative leaders. Groups formed in such conditions may be recognized as belonging to the original tradition, or they may be different enough that they are excluded from the tradition. They may, alternatively, see themselves as truly unique and 'new'. The claimed newness is almost always adaptation, however. An extreme example of cultural adaptation is syncretic borrowing from several traditions, often in an attempt to distil the essential truths from all competing traditions.

The Chinese new religions discussed here will show examples of both introduced and adapted religious ideas, and no truly indigenous creations. This may in fact be a universal phenomenon; humanity appears to excel at creative borrowing from what is at hand, with some occasional long-distance travel.

China's uniqueness

China's size and unbroken history give it several unique attributes, which influence how new religions are received. Firstly, its history has been a constant struggle between forces of centralization and regionalization. Although we often picture China as a central state, historically an empire, this received image is just as often refuted by strong regional tendencies and long lacunae in which regions exercised virtual independence. Geographic barriers – mountains, deserts, and impassable rivers and swamps – ensured the perpetuation of distinct cultural centres and languages. Large swathes of the south, west and north-east have almost always been frontier territories, spaces of cultural exchange. Minority groups frequently influenced dominant Han Chinese traditions.

With this background, the establishment of a unified and constantly redefined Chinese state is remarkable. The central governments throughout their many permutations have always been powerful forces in popular and literary consciousness, even in those areas in which they exerted little direct influence. Indeed, like the British Raj in India, the Chinese bureaucracy generally governed large areas with few officials and the threat of force rather than its actual engagement.

The apparatus of empire was consistently concerned with threats to its authority arising from the fringes of empire, or from popular disenchantment. Religious ideologies and leaderships have played roles in multiple uprisings in both Han and other ethnic group areas. Imperial governments have thus been suspicious of any independent religious teachings, and often took measures to stamp them out. For widespread, established religious systems, such as Buddhism or religious Daoism, the state generally worked towards an accommodation, which resulted in the de facto defusing of possible threats from such organizations.

A second key factor in China's background has been its literary tradition. While the vast majority of the populace has, until modern times, always been illiterate, the sheer bulk of China's refined literature has influenced perceptions at all levels. The written word has been given a status approaching the sacred. Oral traditions attain a special legitimacy once the teachings are written. Religious writings and the very paper upon which they are printed are accorded magical powers. While orality is a factor in the beginning of many new religions, they all tend to move in the direction of textual compilation and legitimation through texts, over time.

A third factor in China's background is its popular/official divide. Beyond officially sanctioned and sponsored state religious activities, such as annual ceremonies to certain deities, there is a vast region of religious life ignored by nearly all commentators up until modern times. Towns, villages and hamlets all hold such

popular celebrations as festivals, dramatic performances and processions that are replete with religious content. Such religious practices are not codified or separate, however; they remain embedded within the popular, local cultures. This phenomenon was clearly noted in C.K. Yang's writings on diffused religion. Yang noted that the concepts, practices and practitioners of traditional religious ideas were so thoroughly integrated into Chinese society that they required no separate institutional existence. In traditional life the social environment *as a whole* had a 'sacred atmosphere'. We cannot call these popular practices religions, since they lack organizational form or clear identity. Still, they are sufficient to refute any claims that Chinese culture is 'non-religious'. Chinese culture, like most others, has a deep awareness of religiosity. And, as a result of the profusion of popular, widely diffused practices throughout the culture, there is a huge repertoire of background content available for new religions to borrow.

Chinese new religions in the 19th century

Many 20th-century new religions derived directly from groups active in imperial times, especially in the Ming and Qing periods (1368–1911).

J.J.M. De Groot was the first writer to focus on non-mainstream religious groups – which he called 'sectarian' groups – active in the late 19th century.

De Groot noted such groups mentioned in Qing Dynasty legal proscriptions on sectarian groups as the Bagua Jiao (Eight Diagrams Sect) and the Fanxiang Jiao (Incense Burning Sect). He also left us with detailed fieldwork reports on two groups active in his city of residence on China's southern coast, the Long Hua (Dragon Flower) and the Xian Tian (Former Heaven). Such sectarian groups often built syncretic thought systems, usually attempting to combine Confucianism with Buddhism and Daoism. They also often promoted vegetarianism and worshipped the Unborn Ancient Mother, a popular deity widespread in the Ming period. Unborn Ancient Mother worship was in addition frequently combined with the cult of Maitreya, the Buddha of the Future. These sectarian groups segregated men and women in their activities, while at the same time allowing women a large measure of participation.

Chinese new religions from 1900 to 1950

The early decades of the 20th century saw the dissolution of the imperial system of government and education, and social order in general. While the political scene remained unstable, religious groups flourished with few hindrances, particularly during the 1920s and 1930s. Two groups that grew quickly in this period were *Yiguandao (Tian Dao) and the True Jesus Church, an independent church that is today found in many countries. Other sectarian groups active from the 1920s to the 1950s include Huangtian Dadao (Great Way of the Yellow Heaven) and Datong Hui (Society for Great Harmony).

Chinese new religions after 1950

Following the establishment of the People's Republic of China in 1949, new religious groups continued to crop up in Chinese cultural space, usually building on existing traditions. Developments in China and in areas of Chinese cultural zones on the periphery took different paths. Within China the government focused closely on controlling non-sanctioned organizations of all types, which meant that organized religious groups came under government control or were proscribed outright. Yiguandao was a major target, beginning in the 1950s.

Yiguandao has not been completely stamped out, however. Police reports from the 1980s mention several sectarian groups still active in China, with names such as Zhong Dao (Way of the Centre) and Pudu Dao (Way of Broad Conversion), many of which are pseudonyms for Yiguandao. In 1985, a government newspaper reported two men, who claimed to be the emperor and Maitreya, distributing photographs, conducting divination and appointing officials.

Since *Falun Gong's sudden rise to prominence in 1999, the central government has spared no efforts to crack down on this group's practitioners. Attention has also focused on the many Christian groups active in central China. A 2001 government publication lists the following 12 officially proscribed groups:

■ Huhan Pai (The Shouters): The Shouters is an offshoot of the Little Flock movement (Xiaoqun Pai), a congregational Christian movement that began in China in the 1920s. The Little Flock founder, Li Shuzu (1903–72; also written in some sources as Nee Shu-tsu and commonly referred to in the English literature as 'Watchman Nee'), was incarcerated by the Chinese government. His closest lieutenant, 'Witness Lee' (Li Changshou; 1905–97), moved to Taiwan just prior to the establishment of the communist state. He then relocated to southern California in 1962, where he established the Church of the Spirit, called in China 'the Shouters' because congregations are urged to shout. Some sources indicate members simply shout four words – 'O Lord, Amen, Hallelujah!' Witness Lee announced in 1979 that the focus of his movement's activities would thereafter shift to China. Lee's organization in fact stresses the local nature of each church, or assembly, which is probably one reason for its fast growth in China. Despite being banned in China from at least 1983, local Shouter assemblies have spread quickly in rural areas.

■ Beili Wang (The King Who Has Been Established): Founded by Wu Yangming of Anhui province in the late 1980s, the Beili Wang movement was an offshoot of the Shouters. The movement went underground when the Anhui police cracked down on the local Shouters. The Beili Wang group, which held its first meeting in 1993, was characterized by a strict stratification of ranks and titles and tight control over daily regimes. Meetings were held only at night and early departure from the meetings was forbidden. Wu exhorted his followers not to enter established churches or sing hymns. The sole object of devotion was to be the name 'Beili Wang'. Wu produced proselytization tapes, which substituted 'Beili Wang' for the name of Jesus, and he claimed to be the reincarnation of Christ. Wu was eventually arrested for rape and fraud in 1995, and was executed soon after.

■ Zhonghua Dalu Xingzhen Zhishi Zhan (Administrative Station of the Chinese Mainland): This offshoot of the Shouters appeared in 1994 and announced that it alone was responsible for administering all Shouter and underground churches in China. The group essentially promoted Witness Lee (Li Changshou) as the living Christ. Wang Yongmin, a Shouter leader, first established the Administrative Station in Anhui province. The group taught that the current government was associated with Satan and should be overthrown. The sect's leadership was eventually arrested in 1995. It is unlikely that the membership ever numbered more than a few thousand.

■ Zhushen Jiao (Religion of the Primary Deity): Liu Jiaguo started this Shouters offshoot in 1993 in Hunan province, in central China. Liu called himself the living

God and claimed powers to revive the dead, guarantee well-being and cure disease. By 1998, his group had spread into 23 provinces and numbered over 10,000, most of whom were middle-aged or young. Claiming that this world would end soon (in 1999), the Zhushen Jiao sought to establish a kingdom of God. The group had formal organization with an assembly that paralleled the national government's organization. Liu and his key followers were eventually arrested in 1998, and he was given the death sentence for rape and fraud.

■ Dami Xuanjiao Hui (Dami Mission Church): This Korean group's apocalyptic teachings entered China from 1991 and gained followers among China's sizeable Korean minority. Lee Jang Lim (in Chinese, Li Changlin) established the Church in Seoul in 1988. It had attracted over 100,000 followers worldwide by 1992. The fellowship foretold the return of Jesus on 28 October 1992, at which time a new era of calamities and retributions would begin. Jesus would return to heaven on that same day with the true believers. Finally, Jesus would return in 1999 to make the final judgement on the survivors. Human history would eventually cease in 2000. The group focused on expansion into China in the

months leading up to October 1992. Korean travellers often carried printed materials into China. The group's ministers held 'returning to heaven' training sessions throughout China. Group worship sessions were normally held at night, with intensive worship between midnight and 3.00 a.m. Most followers simply felt disappointed or cheated when the prophecies failed to materialize in October. However, many local governments remained alert to the threat of mass suicides after the disappointment. The danger of mass suicide is one reason given for keeping such apocalyptic groups under close observation in China today.

■ Children of God: This Christian group was first formed in the 1960s in the United States (now called *The Family). Members were first dispatched to Hong Kong and Macau in 1975, and first began travelling into China proper in 1980.

■ Xinyue Jiaohui (Congregation of the New Testament): This group was established and introduced into China by 1960s Hong Kong actress Mei Qi (Jian Duanyi). It spread first into Malaysia and Singapore. Following Mei's death, the movement was led by her daughter, Zhang Lidu, and moved to Taiwan. Additional branches were established by another leader, Hong Sanzi, and, from 1988, by another splinter group, the Complete Gospel Propagation Group of Jesus Christ's Blood and Water, under Zo Kun. There are currently 29 separate branch churches in Taiwan. In 1964, the headquarters was established at a location renamed Mount Zion in Gaoxiong, Taiwan. Since the 1980s, branches have been established in over 20 cities and provinces in the Chinese mainland. The group demands total obedience from members. It views most secular authorities with suspicion and has had run-ins with several of the governments in countries in which it is active, including the authorities in Taiwan. The group's activities and literature have been banned in China.

■ Lingxian Zhen Fozong (Immortal True Buddha): Lu Sengyan, a Chinese-American, established this group in 1979. It is headquartered at the Leizang Temple in Seattle, Washington, United States. Lu claimed to have attained enlightenment during meditation in 1971, and subsequently received instructions from Sakyamuni Buddha, Maitreya, and various Tibetan and Chinese Buddhist saints. Lu's

teachings blend Daoism with Tibetan Buddhism and emphasize transmission of a secret teaching, the Secret Dharma of the True Buddha. The group has been active in the larger cities in China since 1988. Lu has personally participated in Hong Kong memorial marches commemorating the 4 June 1989 Tiananmen incident.

■ Guanyin Famen (The Quanyin Method): The group centred on *Suma (Supreme Master) Ching Hai teaches the Quanyin (Guan Yin) method of attaining enlightenment. The Suma Ching Hai movement started in Taiwan and is now found throughout Southeast Asia and the United States. There are reportedly some adherents in mainland China and the group has been banned there.

■ Mentu Hui (Association of Disciples): The founder of this group, Li Sanbao, first gathered 12 disciples, hence its name. Because members are not allowed to enter churches and must meet in the open, the group is also known as Kuangye Jiao (Church of the Wilds). The movement has spread quickly throughout central China since 1989.

■ Quanyuanwei Jiaohui (Religion of the Complete Garden): This group, founded in 1984 in Henan, is also

known as the 'Criers' because members cry constantly at services. It is yet another offshoot of the Shouters. The founder, Xu Yongze, was arrested twice for participation in illegal religious activities.

■ Lingling Jiao (Teachings of the [Luminous] Spirit): Hua Xuehe founded this group in 1983 in Jiangsu, eastern China. Hua was a True Jesus Church member who was eventually expelled. Lingling Jiao remains active within Chinese Christianity.

All but two of the above religious groups are based on Christian teachings. This reflects the extent of interest in Christianity in contemporary China. And there are undoubtedly other new religions based on Christianity that are yet to be studied. For example, recent reports concern a new sectarian group known as Eastern Lightning (or the Church of Everlasting Foundation and Real God), which has reportedly kidnapped leaders from the China Gospel Fellowship, a larger underground church. Eastern Lightning, founded in Heilongjiang, in China's extreme north-east, contends that Jesus was reborn in 1990 in the person of a woman called 'Lightning'. From this example, it is apparent that Christian ideology mixes easily with popular practices. With a history of hundreds of years in China, Christianity should be seen as a deeply rooted, thoroughly Chinese religion.

Taiwan and Southeast Asia

Since 1950, Taiwan has seen the growth and, at the level of popular culture, partial dominance of Yiguandao groups. Like Yiguandao, followers of the Cihui Tang (Hall of Compassion) worship the Ancient Unborn Mother and practice divination. Similar groups exhibiting many of the syncretic trends seen in the pre-1950 period have been studied in Southeast Asian Chinese communities.

One notable development beyond Yiguandao and Christian groups has been the growth of lay Buddhist movements in Taiwan. These normally form around respected monks or nuns. Two of the largest groups, which now operate worldwide, are Foguang Shan (Mountain of the Buddha's Radiance) and Tzuchi (Great Compassion) Benevolent Society.

Prospects

Chinese religious culture continues to develop rapidly. The past hundred years have been tumultuous, and China still grapples with the extreme social dislocations accompanying modernity.

The degree to which the government attempts to control religious groups is an international issue today. Central government involvement in this arena is hardly new, however; as mentioned above, the government has, throughout Chinese history, often cast a suspicious eye on organized religious groups. Despite this, there are no indications that new religions will cease to form, or thrive, in contemporary China.

Current claims of around 15 million members in Japan, and over a million overseas may be overestimates. However, of all Japanese new religious movements, Sôka Gakkai has had the greatest success both inside and outside Japan.

Yiguandao (Tian Dao)
Edward Irons

Yiguandao (the Way of Pervading Harmony) is a religious tradition found in Chinese communities around the world. Most of its followers today use the term Tian Dao (the Way of Heaven) instead of Yiguandao, but outside commentators continue to use the older term.

Yiguandao as a distinct religious and moral movement took shape in the 1930s. At that time the mantle of leadership of a small sectarian movement in western Shangdong province, China, passed to Zhang Tianran (1889–1947). The small group he took over claimed descent from a distinguished line of cultural heroes (Confucius, the Yellow Emperor, the Buddha) and less well-known religious entrepreneurs stretching from the early Ming Dynasty (1368–1644) through the Qing Dynasty (1644–1911). It was one of a number of groups advocating vegetarianism, the worship of a central, feminine deity – the Unborn Ancient Mother (Wu Sheng Lao Mu) – and the imminent coming of a new age ruled by the Buddha Maitreya, her appointed emissary to the material world.

Zhang took this group, revised its foundation, reinterpreted its teachings, and repositioned it to appeal to many people

Flame of the Ancient Mother at Sun Moon Lake, Taiwan.

searching for security in modern China. He streamlined and fixed the ritual formulas, which remain in use to this day. He placed emphasis on recruiting new members by tying each member's progress to the number of new members introduced. And he elevated and standardized training for the transmission master (*dianchuanshi*), a key follower devoted to the group and authorized to initiate. By the time Zhang died in 1947, the movement had spread throughout urban areas and along the main commercial routes of China, to become what was arguably the largest Chinese religious grouping of the 1940s.

Yiguandao doctrine centres around the worship of the Ancient Mother. Ancient Mother veneration is a religious tradition that took shape in the mid-Ming Dynasty and spread throughout Chinese popular culture. The founding myth of all Ancient Mother groups depicts her as the creator of the universe who is at once omnipotent and ever-present, yet somehow still separated from her children, the wayward souls of humanity. Longing for their return to her side in heaven, and knowing that the universe will soon begin to unravel, she sends the Buddha Maitreya and all other dedicated bodhisattva figures to return to earth and assist humans to recover their lost birthright.

Already within this myth you can see the characteristic sense of urgency behind Yiguandao discourse. This is an apocalyptic view: the universe will end, and Maitreya offers us one last chance for salvation, which is obtaining *Dao* (the Way). Obtaining *Dao* is the single most significant ritual in Yiguandao. Through this act one's future in heaven is assured. In the ritual, the transmission master transmits the truth of *Dao* in three parts: the opening of the secret pass (*xuanguan*), a point on the forehead; the transmission of the secret hand contract (*shouyin*), a hand position used during rituals; and the teaching of the secret mantra (*kouzhue*), a five-syllable verbal formula useful in times of distress. The initiate is also led through a statement of faith and a long series of bow-salutes (*koushous*).

The *koushous* and veneration of deities are typical of Yiguandao ritual practice. Many deities are mentioned in Yiguandao rituals, often in long sequences of over 50 different figures. Each figure will receive from one to ten separate bows; the major deities Lao Mu and Maitreya may also receive up to 3,000 bows. Intense ritual activity was one aspect of the Yiguandao reconfiguration that harked back to deep roots in court practice during Chinese imperial periods. In fact many of Yiguandao's practices were borrowed directly from court ritual, with simplifications.

Unusually for a widespread religious movement in a highly literate culture, Yiguandao groups put relatively little emphasis on textual sources. Since all religious teachings are said to have their roots in a single reality, in principle the texts of all traditions are venerated. In practice, certain ideas and terms are borrowed from such Buddhist, Daoist and Confucian sources as the Maitreya Sutra, the Heart Sutra, the *Daode Jing*, and the *Analects* of Confucius (*Lun Yu*). Internal Yiguandao texts are limited to pamphlets, leaders' speeches, and, most importantly, revealed texts. In Yiguandao, the creation of revealed texts involves spirit writing on a sand-filled tray by a team of three selected members, often teenage girls. One of the team writes Chinese characters in the sand with a stylus as the second scrapes the sand smooth with a flat stick and recites what is written. The third team member then records what is written with pen and paper.

Yiguandao is significant as a typical Chinese religious group, one which, against the odds, has thrived under conditions of modernity. Yiguandao is representative of a host of non-mainstream religious groups. Its deities are inclusive and can expand to include any local deity figures. Yiguandao ritual practice harks back directly to imperial practice. Its moral teachings combine practical advice with urgings to respect parents, always a strong theme in Chinese culture. Yiguandao requirements are loose enough to appeal to many members busy in the business world.

Sekai Kyûseikyô
Robert Kisala

Sekai Kyûseikyô (Church of World Messianity) was founded by Okada Mokichi (1882–1955), a former member of *Ômoto, a religious group founded in the late 19th century that has had considerable influence on a number of other groups. The Japanese new religion has undergone a number of name changes: it was founded as the Dai Nihon Kannonkai in 1935, and later became the Dai Nihon Kenkô Kyôkai, Nihon Kannon Kyôdan, Nihon Miroku Kyôkai, and then Sekai Meshiyakyô, before the present name was adopted in 1957.

Okada taught a form of natural healing based on the power of light passed through the hand of the healer to the patient. He was opposed to modern medicine, believing that it not only hinders the natural healing powers of the body but also acts as a poison, making the patient's condition even worse. He believed that colds and fevers should be allowed to take their course, as they served as a means of purifying the body.

In addition to this healing activity, Sekai Kyûseikyô awaits the establishment of an earthly paradise, and has built several models of this paradise in Japan and Brazil. Okada was himself a collector of art, and the MOA (Mokichi Okada Association) Art Museum was established at the group's Atami compound in 1982, the 100th anniversary of Okada's birth. Sekai Kyûseikyô also promotes the practice of natural farming.

The church has been quite successful in attracting followers in Brazil, where it claims a following of 300,000. The membership in Japan is reported to be about 800,000. Sekai Kyûseikyô has spawned a number of break-away groups, and its healing practices in particular have influenced several other *Japanese new religions, including the *Mahikari churches.

Shinnyoen
Robert Kisala

Shinnyoen traces its establishment to 1936, when the founder, Itô Shinjô (1906–89), quit his job as an aeronautical engineer to devote himself full time to religious practices on the basis of a spiritual revelation received through his wife, Tomoji (1912–67). Itô, who had gathered a following through his use of fortune-telling, then established Shinchôji in 1938, a temple affiliated with the Buddhist Shingon Daigoji sect in Kyoto, later attaining the status of a high-ranking priest in that sect. In 1948, he established the independent Makoto Kyôdan, adopting the name Shinnyoen in 1951 following bad publicity regarding charges that he had attacked a former member of the group. The group maintains some ties with Daigoji and practises the Saito Homa, an open-air fire ceremony traditional to the Kyoto temple.

Shinnyoen recognizes the Nirvana Sutra as its basic scripture, and a large statue of the reclining Buddha, carved by the founder, can be found at its main temple and headquarters in Tachikawa, west of Tokyo. What is unique to Shinnyoen is the practice of *sesshin*, a form of spiritual guidance through a *reinôsha* (medium). The Itôs lost both their sons at an early age, and the group believes that the spirits of the two children guide the members

through the mediation of messages from the *shinnyo reikai*, or the spirit world, also identified with the Buddha realm. The members are encouraged to visit *reinôsha* regularly for guidance to grow in their spiritual lives. Special *sesshin* sessions can also be arranged for help with specific problems or needs. The rank of *reinôsha* is theoretically open to all the believers, and they are encouraged to develop their own spiritual potential through participation in three basic forms of activity: joyful giving (in the form of financial contributions to the organization), recruitment of new members and service to others.

Itô's wife died in 1967, and a split in the organization, accompanied by further bad publicity, occurred when his eldest daughter opposed his plans to remarry. Itô himself died in 1989. The organization is now led by Itô's third daughter, Shinsô. Shinsô was granted the rank of a high Buddhist priest by Daigoji in 1992, and in 1997 the Shinnyo Samaya Hall was dedicated to the memory of Itô Shinjô on the grounds of Daigoji in Kyoto. On that occasion, Shinsô became the first woman in the 1,100-year history of Daigoji to conduct a service in the main hall of the temple.

Shinnyoen has approximately 800,000 believers in Japan, and has been active in establishing branches in the United States, Europe, Australia and several countries in Asia. It has also been engaged in various social activities, such as supporting the restoration of Angkor Wat in Cambodia, research and care for the elderly in Japan, and education programmes in Sri Lanka, the United States and Japan.

Risshô Kôseikai
Ian Reader

This Nichiren Buddhist-based movement is generally regarded as the second-largest new religion in Japan, with several million followers, especially in Tokyo. It was founded

☞ *continued on page 250*

MARTIAL ARTS
David Miller

'Martial arts' is the overall term given to a range of fighting styles that have their origins in East or Southeast Asia. They include unarmed styles, such as judo or karate from Japan, taekwondo from Korea, Thai kick-boxing, and certain forms of Chinese *gong fu* (or kung fu), and other styles which involve the use of weapons, such as Japanese kendo (fencing) and *kyudo* (archery). T'ai chi would also be classed as a martial art. Commonly regarded as a system of personal exercises, its movements are actually fighting movements, and it is sometimes referred to as shadow boxing. Their significance is that the arts have a spiritual or mystical dimension to them. This explains the linguistic distinction between, for example, ju-jitsu (*jūjutsu*), where *jutsu* refers to the technique, and judo (*ju-do*), where *do* refers to the 'way', implying that the technical skill is part of a more holistic approach to life.

These martial arts trace their roots back to Buddhist teaching. The Shaolin style of *gong fu* claims to have originated in the Buddhist Shaolin temple in Henan, China, and some trace the arts back to Bodhidarma, the Indian monk who brought Ch'an (in Japanese, Zen)

Buddhism to East Asia. There is some debate as to the degree of connection with Buddhism. Some scholars detect the influence of Daoism on the development of the arts, and some question whether what is essentially a method of combat can be aligned with Buddhist ideals of compassion.

In Japan, however, in the Middle Ages the samurai were clear about their value as means of both personal and spiritual development,

embracing Zen Buddhism and martial arts together. They saw that the discipline the arts gave helped them to deal with the fear of death. Zen enlightenment, which freed the enlightened one to act naturally and unthinkingly, was seen as a part of the development of fighting skills. Takuan Soho, a Zen monk of the early 17th century, made the link in his book *The Unfettered Mind: Writings of a Zen Master to the Sword Master*. At the same time, the

concentration required in some of the martial arts was itself seen as an aid to enlightenment. The link between spiritual development and martial arts has also resulted at times in some practitioners making claims to possess mystical or magical powers against one's enemies.

Martial arts became popular in the West through films and TV dramas, such as those of Hong Kong stars Bruce Lee and Jackie Chan. These films initially emphasized the superior technical combat skills that martial arts taught, and thus appealed especially to young men who wanted to increase their own fighting ability. However, among those who studied them, in particular among those who went to China or Japan to train in earnest, interest increased in their spiritual aspects. This interest is found increasingly among those seeking forms of spirituality apart from organized religion. Often, however, this goes beyond Zen meditation, and embraces techniques such as the search for *kundalini* enlightenment, and other esoteric practices.

T'ai chi practitioners next to the Forbidden City in Beijing, China.

in the 1930s by Niwano Nikkyô (1906–99), a former businessman who, seeking to find a cure for his sick daughter, had joined *Reiyûkai, a lay Buddhist movement that venerates the Lotus Sutra (a key text in Mahayana Buddhism), and advocates the importance of the ancestors but that also engages in spiritual healing. His daughter's recovery led Niwano to become an ardent devotee of Reiyûkai, in which capacity he became a branch leader and an active proselytizer. However, disputes arose with the leadership of Reiyûkai as he began to formulate new interpretations of the Lotus Sutra, with the result that in 1938 Niwano broke away and formed his own movement, Risshô Kôseikai.

Among his early followers was Naganuma Myôkô (1889–1957) a woman with shamanic and divinatory powers, who became a de facto second leader of the movement. Risshô Kôseikai attained rapid success through the combination of Naganuma's spiritual powers, which spoke to followers' wishes to foretell the future and to interpret misfortune, and Niwano's lay-oriented interpretations of Buddhism, which provided a moral basis for practice and offered, according to Risshô Kôseikai, a path to the attainment of happiness in this life. The former aspect of its teaching has been largely downplayed since Naganuma's death, while the latter remains a main focus of the movement, which emphasizes what it terms 'basic Buddhism', centred on the 'four noble truths' of Buddhism, which members are enjoined to follow so as to achieve a harmonious existence in this world. Niwano, who stood down as leader of the movement in 1991 to be succeeded by his son Nichikô (b. 1938) and died in 1999, also emphasized social welfare and politically oriented activities. As a result, Risshô Kôseikai has been heavily involved in anti-nuclear campaigns and in the promotion of peace initiatives, and this remains one of its main areas of activity.

Kôdô Kyôdan

Ian Reader

This Buddhist-oriented Japanese new religion with some 400,000 followers was founded by Okano Shôdô (1900–77), a Buddhist believer and businessman who had suffered numerous misfortunes in his career. In 1935, Okano, who had close associations with the established Tendai Buddhist sect, joined the new religion *Reiyûkai, which based its teachings on the Lotus Sutra and emphasized the importance of venerating one's ancestors as a cardinal act of morality. Although Okano, assisted by his wife Kimiko, who claimed the ability to communicate with spirits, attained a position of influence in Reiyûkai, he was driven by a sense of mission that led him to develop his own movement. He left Reiyûkai in 1936 and officially founded Kôdô Kyôdan in 1939.

Okano wanted to serve the nation and sought to develop a movement that would do this while focusing on and following a spiritual path based on veneration of the Lotus Sutra, a key text in Mahayana Buddhism. In this he saw himself as following on from Buddhist teachers such as Saichô (767–822), the founder of the Tendai sect in Japan, whose form of nationalistic Buddhism linked Buddhism and state together through the teachings of the Lotus Sutra. Besides these nationalistic orientations, Kôdô Kyôdan's teachings were based in areas widely emphasized in the new religions, namely, the veneration of and emphasis on the importance of the ancestors, who serve as guardians of collective morality, and an emphasis on spiritual solutions to problems through spiritual healing. This latter practice was important to the movement while Kimiko was alive, although it was always viewed as secondary to Kôdô Kyôdan's focus on the Lotus Sutra and on ancestor worship, and it was largely abandoned after the deaths of Kimiko in 1976 and Okano in 1977.

东方红

毛主席是我們心中的紅太陽 68.9

Okano was succeeded by his son Okano Shôkan (b. 1925) who has systematically restructured the movement and strengthened its orientations as a lay Buddhist movement. Kôdô Kyôdan has developed close ties with the Tendai sect, and members of Kôdô Kyôdan make regular pilgrimages to the Tendai religious centre of Mount Hiei. The Tendai sect has bestowed various statues and Buddhist accoutrements on Kôdô Kyôdan, whose orientations as a new religion remain closely bound up with its identity as a Buddhist movement influenced by Tendai Buddhism.

The Cult of Mao and the Red Guards
Xinzhong Yao

Mao's reputation as a cultural hero started in the Long March during 1934–35, when the Red Army was forced to make a journey from south-east China to the north-west.

A 1960s propaganda poster of Mao Zedong with his Red Guards. Today 'Chairman Mao' is revered again by millions of Chinese people.

Ironically, the revolutionary movement that aimed at ridding all religious influences in China created the biggest religious-like fanaticism in Chinese history. From the 1940s to the late 1970s, Mao Zedong (Mao Yunzhi; 1893–1976) has been celebrated as 'the Red Sun' who brought life to all creatures, 'the Great Helmsman' who steered the ship of China from disaster to victory, and a saviour who rescued the Chinese from suppression and exploitation. The personal cult of Mao reached its peak during the Cultural Revolution (1966–76) and when he died in 1976 he was mourned sincerely by many people, who feared that China would again suffer without the great leader.

Zealous in making China a great nation in the world, Mao was impatient with slow progress in economic development in the late 1950s, and launched the so-called 'Great Leap Forward' movement, which not only destroyed the Chinese economy, but also led to criticism of him from within the Communist Party. Unsatisfied with his own position in the second line of leadership, unhappy with the popularity of the old tradition that was still evident in the arts, in literature, and in the Chinese way of life in general, and deeply worried about the recurrence of 'Russian revisionism' in China, Mao started criticizing the 'old' culture in 1965. This critique eventually assumed the aspect of a revolution in the summer of 1966. While the establishment of the Communist Party tried to cool it down, young high school and university students reacted fervently to the appeal of Mao and turned themselves into the 'Red Guards'. In their zeal for emancipation from the 'old ideas, old culture, old customs, and old habits', they attacked the establishment, education, arts, literature, the government and Communist leaders at various levels. With scarlet bands on their arms, badges of Mao's portrait on their breasts, and the 'little red books' of Mao's sayings in their hands, the Red Guards brought to every corner of China not only the newest instructions of Mao but also their love and devotion towards Mao. In the name of Mao they persecuted hundreds of thousands, who were branded as *hei bang* (black/sinister gangs). They also repeatedly confessed that they would die happily to protect Mao's ideas and to guard against any possible deviation from the path Mao had marked out.

Extremely hostile to religions and to 'old culture', the Red Guards unconsciously acted in a way that was clearly reminiscent of the religious enthusiasm and behaviour evident in traditional China. Their faith in Mao was like the traditional belief in the 'Son of Heaven', their trust of Mao's words was like traditional worship of 'the Sage' and his wisdom, and their demonstration and

propaganda were like religious processions to celebrate the festival of a god or goddess. The Red Guards movement ceased to be the main motivational power for the Cultural Revolution in 1969, and the Cultural Revolution itself formally concluded in 1976.

Traditional religious influences have demonstrated their power again in some people's attitudes towards Mao since the 1980s. The revival of traditional faiths has also changed the perception of Mao. Twenty years after his death, 'Chairman Mao' is again revered by thousands of people in China. Portraits of Mao are thought by many to have an effective function in warding off evil spirits or misfortune. Many no longer understand him to be simply a former leader of the Communist Party, but rather a deity who is able to protect devotees from disasters, to bless people, and even to help individuals make a fortune. For example, at the beginning of the 1990s many taxi drivers hung pictures of Mao in their cars, believing that his spirit would protect them. Temples or shrines dedicated to him and various miracles credited to him appear from time to time in rural areas. Such is the devotion to Mao that the Communist Party and the government have to issue orders to stop it.

Tenshô Kôtai Jingûkyô
Birgit Staemmler

Tenshô Kôtai Jingûkyô is a syncretistic, millenarian Japanese new religion founded by Kitamura Sayo (1900–67). The current leader is her granddaughter, Kitamura Kiyokazu (b. 1950). The organization claims approximately 450,000 followers, many of them living outside Japan, especially in Hawaii and South America. The headquarters of the movement is in Tabuse, a small town in south-west Japan where the foundress lived.

Kitamura claimed that since 1945 she had been possessed by the universe's ultimate god

(Tenshô Kôtai Jingû), an amalgamation of a masculine deity, Kôtaijin, and one of Japan's central deities, the sun goddess Amaterasu. Tenshô Kôtai Jingûkyô's aim is the construction of paradise on earth through purifying one's thoughts, words and deeds and thus realizing Kitamura's teaching of unselfishness and honesty in everyday life. The year 1946 is regarded as the beginning of the new era and counted as year 1.

Concerning religious practice, the emphasis is placed, not on rituals, but on everyday life. Thus, in a pun, the word *shinkô* (belief) is attributed different Chinese characters ('god' and 'go' instead of 'believe' and 'look up to') and thus is reinterpreted as 'actively going towards god'. Guidelines are the foundress's sermons, which were recorded and are now regularly replayed in Tabuse and regional centres. There is no system of religious instructors. Instead, followers meet locally for *tomo migaki* (to 'polish' one another) during which they discuss activities and experiences. The main prayer '*na-myô-hô-ren-ge-kyô*' was adapted from a popular Buddhist chant and aims at purifying evil spirits. Because of its *muga no mai* (dance of no-self), the Tenshô Kôtai Jingûkyô was nicknamed 'the dancing religion'. However, the dance is of minor importance today. It is performed as part of a monthly ceremony during which participants dance slowly with their eyes closed while an experienced member sings.

Bentenshû
Ian Reader

Bentenshû is a Japanese new religion that has emerged out of mainstream established Buddhism. It takes its name from the female Buddhist deity Benten, a deity associated with water and with wisdom and the arts, who manifested herself in revelations to Omori Kiyoko (1909–67) the wife of Omori Chijô

(1900–87), a priest of the esoteric Shingon Buddhist sect. She had been advised, in 1933, by a diviner to pray to Benten for relief from pains she was suffering, and so had begun to worship a statue of the deity that she found in the courtyard of her husband's temple at Gojo in Nara prefecture. Shortly afterwards, she began to receive spiritual messages from Benten, which led her to engage in spiritual healing and to start performing religious austerities. She also took on a new given name, Chiben (the wisdom of Benten), and, in 1940, became a recognized teacher in the Shingon Buddhist sect. Chiben's reputation as a teacher and healer began to grow, attracting increasing numbers of followers to her husband's temple. In 1948, her followers established a formal religious confraternity based on the worship of Benten. In 1952, the group was legally constituted as a religious organization, taking the name Bentenshû and centring its activities around Chiben's charismatic personality and teachings, and on the worship of Benten. It built a new head temple at Gojo and in 1964 constructed a new administrative headquarters at Ibaraki in Osaka prefecture. The movement estimated its membership at around 300,000 in the mid-1990s, although this figure may be on the high side.

Chiben's death in 1967 removed one of the prime elements within Bentenshû, and the movement lost some support as a result. Her presence and authority within the movement continued, however, as the movement followed a pattern common among *Japanese new religions by developing a cult of worship around its deceased founder. A mausoleum and founder's hall commemorating Chiben were built at Bentenshû's headquarters at Gojo, and these have since been a major focus of worship in the movement. Chiben's teachings, expressed in her book *Mizu no shô* (*The Essence of Water*), form the canonical basis of the movement, and emphasize the purity and healing powers of water, and hence

☞ *continued on page 256*

FENG SHUI
Sarah Lewis

Literally translated, *feng shui* means 'wind' and 'water' and refers to the art of living in harmony with the environment for health, wealth and happiness. The Daoist concept of yin and yang – the idea of a balance between forces – is central to *feng shui*. It teaches that the earth is covered with invisible, yet powerful energy lines, some auspicious, some inauspicious. The auspicious energy lines must be harnessed and the inauspicious ones avoided. *Feng shui* originated in China and has existed there as a tradition for thousands of years. In China it takes many years for a *feng shui* specialist to train, and this is done through working as an apprentice to an existing *feng shui* expert; the training in *feng shui* is a much longer and more serious process than is usually found in the West. In modern China, *feng shui* is usually limited as a practice to those who live in the countryside and who therefore have the space to adopt the principles. In the dense city areas, only wealthy people have the space, time and money to employ an expert and implement their proposals.

Good *feng shui* can only be created when there is balance and harmony between yin and yang, and this leads to harmonious relationships, prosperity, good health and success. *Feng shui* experts provide instructions for positioning homes and designing rooms in ways that promise to achieve this. Bad *feng shui*, created through a lack of balance, brings illness, disaster, accidents and financial loss.

Auspicious lines are *sheng chi*, or the dragon's cosmic breath. Inauspicious lines are *shar chi*, or killing breath, usually described as poison arrows. *Feng shui* experts warn against living and working in places that have poison arrows aimed at them. Compasses are used to investigate living and working spaces with respect to their orientation in the magnetic field of the earth and this locates the existence of particular elemental influences.

Killing breath is caused by the presence of sharp, pointed objects or structures through which bad *feng shui* can be channelled. People are harmed if these poison arrows are aimed at the front door of their house or their bed, for example. Poison arrow structures can also be a straight road, a tree standing alone, a protruding corner, or anything that has a threatening appearance. In the West, it is architecturally appealing to have a straight avenue leading directly to the entrance of an important building. In *feng shui* teaching, this means that poison arrows are pointing straight at the buildings and encouraging disaster for the occupants.

Good *feng shui* is associated with certain objects because of their shape or colour. Having pictures or ornaments of these will bring good fortune. For example, wealth is symbolized by the colour gold, antique coins and

waterfalls. Furthermore, different parts of a building symbolize different things. For example, the south-western part of the house is the marriage corner, so a toilet must not be fitted there as happiness will literally be flushed away.

The concept of *feng shui* has taken off in the West enormously over the last few years. Arguably, it is highly compatible with the Western 'quick-fix' mentality, with those involved rarely taking time to really study the faith. In addition to the many books and magazines published specifically on *feng shui*, general interest magazines often publish short articles on how a person can improve their lives rapidly with the simple relocation of furniture and the addition of certain accessories.

A businessman uses a feng shui *compass.*

of Benten, who, as has been noted, is closely associated with water.

Since Chiben's death, the movement has become known also for its use of *mizuko kuyô* – memorial services for fetuses (*mizuko*, a term that literally means 'water child') that die in the womb, usually through abortion. *Mizuko kuyô* has become a highly popular but controversial religious practice in modern Japan, and Bentenshû has been one of a number of movements that have engaged in it, constructing a large *mizuko kuyô* monument enshrining Benten for this purpose. The movement teaches that the spirits of those who die in the womb as *mizuko* are unfulfilled human beings who need to be consoled through memorial services that also assuage the feelings of their parents, and such teachings, and the ritual practices associated with them, have brought many people to its headquarters for this purpose. While Chiben's teachings did not mention *mizuko kuyô*, her successors have found a doctrinal connection for the practice through the medium of water (*mizu*), which formed a central element in her teaching and which is associated in Japanese with the aborted fetus around which the practice centres. Nowadays *mizuko kuyô* has become one of the movement's mainstays, along with the veneration of Benten and of Chiben.

Ananaikyô
Birgit Staemmler

Ananaikyô is a little-known Japanese new religion. It was founded in 1949 by Nakano Yonosuke (1887–1974) and claims about 10,000 members. Its head office is in Shimizu, Shizuoka prefecture. The current leader is Nakano Masamiya (b. 1950), the adopted daughter to Nakano's successor, Nakano Yoshiko (b. 1933). *Ananai* is said to be an archaic term for the rope attached to

shrine bells. Nakano Yonosuke had experienced a journey of the soul during a severe illness in 1926 and turned to religion. In 1929 he joined *Ômoto, where he was active as a missionary until the group's suppression in 1935. From 1932, Nakano studied *chinkon kishin*, a ritual of spirit possession, with the local Shinto scholar Nagasawa Katsutate (1858–1940). Particularly during the 1960s and 1970s, Ananaikyô was actively promoting interreligious cooperation.

Ananaikyô's doctrine is conservative, mainly of Shinto origin and heavily influenced by Ômoto. Its main scripture is Nakano's *Reikai de mita uchû* (*The Universe as Seen from the Spirits' World*). Proper veneration of ancestors is regarded as essential to ensure their well-being and protection. Because the universe's timeless and unfailing movements are respected as a model for those living on earth, Ananaikyô operates an astronomical observatory. Other practices include support for the arts, especially Japanese music and dance, a four-day seminar for new members and the *chinkon kishin* (spirit possession), which has since developed into a form of meditation.

In 1961, Nakano founded the Organization for Industrial, Spiritual and Cultural Advancement (OISCA), a non-governmental group that operates and supports development aid projects in many, mainly Asian, countries.

Byakkô Shinkôkai
Ian Reader

Byakkô Shinkôkai is a Japanese new religion founded by Goi Masahisa (1916–80). In 1940, he became a devotee of the new religion *Seichô no Ie, studying its spiritual healing and counselling practices and becoming a teacher in that movement. After profound religious experiences in which he felt a sense of union with the creator deity of the universe, and came to believe he was the mouthpiece on earth for that deity, he left Seichô no Ie to propound his own teachings. He founded Byakkô Shinkôkai, which was based especially in Goi's self-declared mission to bring peace to the world through prayer, in 1955.

Goi taught that humans are spiritual emanations of God, that they live on earth protected and watched over by guardian spirits from other realms, who exist in a relationship of mutual interdependence with this world, that the spiritual powers of God and these other realms can be harnessed to purify humans in this realm, and that the ultimate purpose of life is to bring peace to all humankind. Thus, while Byakkô Shinkôkai, like many *Japanese new religions, provides spiritual healing and counselling practices for followers to enable them to deal with their problems and misfortunes, its main focus – and the main activity of its practitioners – centres on its peace activities. Goi taught that peace came not from political but from spiritual activities, and as such initiated a variety of practices that adherents should follow to this end. These include the movement's 'world peace prayers', in which followers pray that each country on earth should fulfil its mission of peace, and the erection of 'peace poles' around the world. These 'peace poles', normally around two metres in height and bearing the words 'May Peace Prevail on Earth' in a number of languages (always including Japanese and English), are the most visible signs of Byakkô Shinkôkai's presence in global terms. They are a sign of the movement's belief that such direct actions (which remind people of the necessity of prayer) are essential to the realization of peace. The movement runs an organization known as the Society of Prayer for World Peace, which serves as its public face outside Japan. Accurate figures for the number of adherents are unknown.

Although Goi died in 1980, followers believe he remains spiritually connected to the movement. His successor, Saionji Masami, serves as his medium and mouthpiece on earth, while his spirit is believed to descend during Byakkô Shinkôkai's religious services, during which time his spiritual vibrations may be felt by followers.

Mahikari
Birgit Staemmler

Mahikari (true light) refers to two *Japanese new religions founded in 1959 by Okada Kôtama (1901–74): Sekai Mahikari Bunmei Kyôdan (SMBK; World Religious Organization of True Light Civilization) and Sûkyô Mahikari (Supra-Religion True Light).

Okada Yoshikazu, a former member of *Sekai Kyûseikyô, founded SMBK after hearing a divine command to found the movement, change his name to Kôtama, and save humankind from the impending end of the world. The new religion prospered, but after Okada's death a succession struggle ensued between his adopted daughter, Okada Keishu (b. 1929), and one of his most important followers, Sekiguchi Sakae (1909–94). In 1978, the Supreme Court of Japan ruled in Sekiguchi's favour and Okada Keishu, in the same year, founded Sûkyô Mahikari.

Sûkyô Mahikari claims nearly half a million members, SMBK around 100,000. Numbers of active members are probably much smaller. Both religions proselytize actively and are establishing branches worldwide. Both have large and conspicuous religious centres, Sûkyô Mahikari in Takayama, Gifu prefecture, and SMBK on the Itô peninsula near Tokyo. SMBK's current leader is Sekiguchi's oldest son, Katsutoshi (b. 1939). Sûkyô Mahikari and SMBK closely resemble each other in doctrine and practice.

Mahikari's doctrine is syncretistic, mainly Shinto, and supplemented with millenarianism. It teaches that the world consists of many layers of hells, and of physical, astral and spiritual worlds. At the apex is Su-god, assisted by several major deities. They believe that global warming and natural catastrophes demonstrate that the age of baptism by fire has recently begun, rousing humans from egoism and materialism and preparing them for the world's renewal.

The human body, it is believed, has three dimensions: the physical, the astral and the spiritual. Thus, most illnesses, misfortunes and financial or inter-personal problems are believed to be caused by either impurities accumulated within a person's spiritual body as a result of pollution, food additives, medicine or misdeeds, or, in some cases, by possession of the astral body by malevolent, often ancestral, spirits.

The central practice of Mahikaris is *okiyome* or *mahikari no waza*, a ritual of 'the laying on of hands'. Members, after a three-day introductory seminar, receive a pendant (*omitama*), which enables them to perform *okiyome* for humans, animals, plants, objects or spaces. During *okiyome*, divine light is believed to issue from the giver's hand and to stream through the receiver's body and there to melt away spiritual impurities and thus to eliminate their physical manifestations, such as illnesses. Consequently *okiyome* prepares humans for the world's renewal. It is stressed that *okiyome* does not heal illnesses, but resolves their underlying causes by purifying the patient's spiritual body.

Proper veneration of the ancestors is regarded as very important. Neglect or unseemly treatment of graves and ancestral home altars is believed to augment their suffering in the astral world and to cause them to inflict illnesses or misfortunes on their descendants.

GLA (God Light Association)
Ian Reader

GLA (God Light Association) is a Japanese new religion founded by the charismatic Takahashi Shinji (c. 1927–76). Takahashi's religious interests developed after a near-death experience when aged ten. He subsequently combined his religious interests with a successful career in business, but eventually his engagement in spiritual practices and his apparent ability to communicate with other realms attracted the attention of others. In the late 1960s, a group of followers began to meet at Takahashi's house to listen to his teachings, and in 1969 he established Shinkôkai (God Light Association), the name of which was changed to the acronym GLA in 1970. Its basic teachings draw on a variety of ideas extant in the Japanese religious world, including Buddhist and Confucian moral values relating to self-improvement through spiritual training, and beliefs about the interdependence between the living and the spirits of the dead. Takahashi taught that people are the children of the gods, and their role is to build a peaceful society on earth based on strict moral values and training, that one attains a rich and full life through self-reflection and spiritual training based on the Buddhist noble eightfold path of morality, and that one should always give thanks and be grateful for the benefits life brings, behaving compassionately towards all others and following the guidance of guardian spirits (such as one's ancestors) who watch over one and to whom the living should be devoted.

Takahashi's early death in 1976 was a severe blow to the movement. However, he had predicted his early demise and trained his daughter, Keiko, to take over his leadership role. Despite her continued espousal of his teachings the movement has never regained its early momentum and remains, at around

15,000 followers, a small new religion by Japanese standards. However, Takahashi's teachings have had a large impact on the development of other new religions in recent years, notably *Kôfuku no Kagaku. This movement, now one of Japan's largest new religions, was founded by Okawa Ryûhô (b. 1956), the son of a former follower of Takahashi, whose teachings provided an important basis for Okawa when he first established his movement.

Daesunjinrihoe
Jeong-Kyu Lee

The prototype of Daesunjinrihoe was founded in 1925 by Jeungsan Jo (Doju) (1896–1958), the son of a Korean nationalist, who formed a religious order called Mugeukdo. In 1969, Wudang Park (1918–96), who had received religious ordination from Doju, established a religious order called Daesunjinrihoe that aimed to build a utopia on earth. Daesunjinrihoe adopted the concept of Sangje (the Supreme Being) from Buddhism as the object of worship.

The symbol of unity is beaten during major ceremonies.

Daesunjinrihoe's principles are derived from the primitive sources of nature, the universe and *de Dao* (the Way), which include the connotations of *Daesun* (circulation of the universe) and *Jinri* (truth). The symbol of Daesunjinrihoe signifies *de Dao*, which contains Eastern religious and philosophical thought, and consists of three circles and the four letters of *Dae* in five colours (in Korean, *Dae* – meaning 'large' – has four letters in two concentric circles). Circles signify the origin and circulation of the universe. The three circles represent heaven, earth and humans. The four letters of *Dae* stand for the cardinal points (north, south, east and west), the seasons (spring, summer, autumn and winter), and the four human virtues (humanity, righteousness, propriety and wisdom). Five colours represent the yin–yang principle and the 'five elements' (wood, fire, metal, water and earth).

Daesunjinrihoe's scripture (*Kyungjeon*) contains the movement's basic doctrine, and guidance concerning faith, doctrine and ascetic discipline. According to the group's doctrine, adherents should pursue the following three main goals: to 'undeceive' oneself by opening or awakening the spirit; to realize the state of a *sinseon* (an ascetic hermit) by cultivating oneself; and to assist in the construction of a paradise on earth by restoring the universal conscience. In order for members to achieve these goals, Daesunjinrihoe emphasizes four tenets, four essential principles and three cardinal points.

The four tenets are: the integrated virtue of the yin and yang; the harmony between

Sangje and human beings; not holding grudges and living together peaceably; and mastering the truth of spirit and body. The four essential principles are: to shield one's mind from temptation and desire; to do the best for oneself without offending reason and courtesy; to respect Sangje as the Lord of Heaven; and to cultivate oneself by keeping the four tenets so as to serve Sangje. The three cardinal points are *seong* (sincerity), *kyung* (reverence) and *shin* (faith). According to Daesunjinrihoe's scriptures, sincerity is the state of mind willing to do its best; reverence is the state of mind in which you behave with respect for oneself and others; and faith is the state of mind firmly performing the precepts of Daesunjinrihoe (do not deceive; be courteous and merciful; do not bear animosity; live in acknowledgment of grace; and work for the welfare of others).

The organization not only conducts self-cultivation classes, religious education and propagation of the religion, but has carried out various kinds of socio-philanthropic work, such as social welfare, medical service and educational work. Under five *dojangs* (parishes), Daesunjinrihoe manages two hospitals, six secondary schools and one university.

There is no accurate official data on the number of believers and clergy. According to the assertion of the religious order's headquarters, the number of believers is estimated at approximately 2 million in South Korea, but this may be an overestimate.

Agonshû
Ian Reader

Agonshû is a Japanese new religion with around 300,000 followers that combines aspects of Buddhist esotericism, Japanese mountain religion, and practices such as yoga and meditation with many of the traditional themes found in *Japanese new religions, such as

spiritual healing and venerating the ancestors. Its founder, Kiriyama Seiyû (b. 1921), had suffered a series of personal crises (including a prison sentence) and failures in the 1940s and 1950s, before undergoing a conversion experience in which he believed he was saved by the Buddhist figure of mercy, Kannon. In gratitude, Kiriyama devoted himself to ascetic practices and established the Kannon Jikeikai, a religious group based on the veneration of Kannon, which was the precursor of Agonshû. In 1970, Kiriyama received a revelation from Kannon that he should cease his austerities because he had 'cut his karma' (a pivotal notion in Agonshû) and become spiritually liberated. His new task was to spread his teachings to a wider audience, and he embarked on successful proselytization campaigns from the 1970s, publishing numerous books and establishing Agonshû in 1978.

Kiriyama's teachings state that past deeds have a negative spiritual effect on the individual and their kin. Such negative karma is the cause of misfortune at individual and social levels. Karma, however, can be eradicated through the performance of good deeds and by spiritual activities such as meditation, and Agonshû has developed numerous rituals and practices to this end. In Agonshû, too, the spirits of the dead are extremely important. If they die before their negative karma has been eradicated or if the correct memorial services (which, according to Agonshû, can eradicate such karma) have not been performed for them, they are unable to attain liberation and will thus remain tied to this world and be a negative influence on it. Such accumulated negative influences had brought the world into a state of crisis, necessitating a spiritual transformation that, Agonshû preached, could be achieved through its teachings. This sense of mission, and its belief that it represents a new form of Buddhism for the modern age, are at the heart of Agonshû's contemporary activities.

Aum Shinrikyô
David Miller

Aum Shinrikyô, or Aum Supreme Truth Sect (Aum is one English transliteration of the Hindu mantra that signifies Ultimate Reality), sprang to public attention after it launched a sarin gas attack on the Tokyo subway system on 20 March 1995. Twelve people died and thousands were injured. This act, and other acts of violence committed by the group,

Victims of the sarin gas attack on the Tokyo subway in March 1995.

marks it out as significantly different from other Japanese new religious movements, and links it more closely with groups such as the *Branch Davidians and the *Order of the Solar Temple. At its peak it numbered around 10,000 members in Japan, with several thousand followers in Russia. Its significance lies not in its numerical size or its doctrines but in the impact its actions had on Japanese society.

Aum was founded by the almost blind Matsumoto Chizuo, who adopted the name Shoko Asahara. Having failed to gain entry to the prestigious University of Tokyo he set up a business selling Chinese medicines. He became increasingly interested in religion, in particular undertaking yoga practice with *Agonshû. He did not remain a member, and instead developed his own interpretations of early Buddhism. He also claimed to have the ability to levitate. For him, yoga, meditation and other forms of spiritual practices were for the purpose of gaining spiritual power.

In 1984, Asahara established his own yoga school in Tokyo. He began to make claims about his own messianic status, saying that the Hindu deity Shiva had appeared to him and had charged him with the task of creating a perfect society. In 1986, he established Aum Shinrikyô. That same year he travelled to the Himalayas, where he claimed to have received perfect enlightenment. As his teaching developed, he also began drawing on elements of Tibetan Buddhism, Hinduism and Christianity, and the prophecies of Nostradamus.

From Tibetan Buddhism came the idea of *poa*. Originally meaning 'the transference of consciousness to the Buddha world after death', Asahara claimed that it also allowed people to commit murder, because by doing so they were preventing the person being killed from accumulating bad karma. Thus the action brought benefit to the one carrying out the killing, since it was, in effect, an act of mercy. From Christianity (and Nostradamus) came the concept of Armageddon. He saw his own role increasingly in messianic terms, predicting in his 1989 book *Metsubo no Hi* (*Day of Destruction*) that there would be a major catastrophe by 1999 unless people began practising Aum's teachings. These two ideas laid the foundation for the violence that characterized much of the group's activities.

During this period the movement began to attract opposition within Japan. It failed to win any seats in the 1990 election. Complaints against its recruiting practices were also made by relatives of members. In 1990, Sakamoto Tsutsumi (a lawyer working on behalf of these relatives) and his family disappeared. It later transpired that they had been murdered by Aum members. Political failure and a feeling of national rejection led to increasing millenarianism. Asahara's teaching and writing now emphasized the inevitability of global destruction, the only hope of survival lying in developing superhuman qualities through Aum's spiritual techniques. Rather than saving the world, Aum had become a refuge for those who wanted to escape its destruction. Ominously, the group began to see itself as having a role in actually inaugurating Armageddon.

Its attacks on its critics continued, and it came under increasing police surveillance. It was initially thought the sarin gas attack in Tokyo was an attempt to inaugurate Armageddon, but it is also possible that it was an attempt to distract police from investigating the murder of the brother of an Aum member.

The attack horrified Japan, particularly because many of those involved were graduates of the country's top universities. Some attempted to explain the group's ability to attract such people by reference to mind-control techniques. Certainly the group's community life and isolation from outside sources of information, as well as the strong sense of loyalty to their leader and violence against dissident members, all played their

part. However, others see the movement as an extreme form of protest against the oppressive society Japan had become.

Japanese laws on religious freedom made it very difficult to ban the group altogether, though it was declared bankrupt and was no longer allowed to own property. Despite its reputation, it still functions under the name of Aleph, with an estimated 1,000 members. The group also runs successful computer companies, the profits from which it claims to pass on as compensation to the victims of the sarin gas attack. It has officially apologized for the attack, trying to distance itself from Asahara and others involved. It now presents itself as a group teaching meditative techniques for self-development, with a concern for world peace.

Kôfuku no Kagaku
Robert Kisala

Kôfuku no Kagaku (literally, 'the science of happiness', also known in English as the Institute for Research in Human Happiness) was founded in 1986 by Okawa Ryûhô (b. 1956), a graduate of the prestigious University of Tokyo, who had been employed by a major trading company before founding this religion. Born Nakagawa Takashi on the island of Shikoku, Okawa was influenced religiously by his father from an early age. The elder Nakagawa was a member of *GLA (God Light Association), a new religious group founded under the name Shinkokai in 1969 that preaches an elaborate cosmology incorporating various levels of spiritual existence. Okawa claims that he began to channel messages from the spirit world in 1981, and indeed it was from the spirit of Takahashi Shinji (c. 1927–76), the founder of GLA, that Okawa claims to have first received his vocation to found his own religious group.

Kôfuku no Kagaku is perhaps the clearest

example of the emphasis – seen broadly in contemporary religious movements – placed on the spread of religious ideas through popular publications. Early on, the criterion for membership was a test based on Okawa's writings, and although membership requirements have been loosened considerably in recent years, the emphasis placed on the founder's works remains high. Okawa has published at a prodigious rate, producing more than 200 titles, including a series of 'spiritual messages' channelled from various religious personalities that include prominent Japanese religious figures, such as Nichiren, as well as Moses, Confucius and Jesus Christ.

In addition to its elaborate cosmology, based on that of GLA, the group includes a mixture of Buddhist and Christian ideas, or perhaps more precisely Buddhist and Christian terminology, in its doctrine. The Buddhist 'four noble truths' for example, have been reformulated by Kôfuku no Kagaku as the 'four principles of happiness': love, wisdom, reflection and development. The attempt is to present a doctrine that both incorporates and transcends all religious truth, as we see in the explanation given for the principle of wisdom: knowledge of God's truth, as propounded in Moses' Ten Commandments, Jesus' teaching of love, and the Buddha's noble eightfold path.

Kôfuku no Kagaku was a rather prominent rival of *Aum Shinrikyô in the early 1990s, with the two groups having been founded at nearly the same time, heavily involved in the publication of their respective founders' works, and representatives squaring off rather sensationally on a popular television show. Kôfuku no Kagaku has always claimed a much larger following than Aum Shinrikyô, however, at one time claiming a membership in the millions. While reliable figures are hard to come by, the membership could be in the hundreds of thousands.

There are traces of nationalism in the doctrine of Kôfuku no Kagaku, and in the past, based on the Nostradamus prophecies, Okawa has predicted that Japan will re-emerge as a military power and conquer the world early in the 21st century, thus bringing about a golden age for humankind. The group has championed some conservative causes in Japan, largely revolving around public morality. Following an incident in which the group received negative publicity (later proven to be unfounded), the group has also been aggressive in pursuing redress for perceived slanders and attacks.

Suma Ching Hai
Edward Irons

The tightly knit religious group centred around the spiritual leader Suma (Supreme Master) Ching Hai (b. 1948) reflects in many ways the direction in which Chinese religions may develop in the era of globalization. Although the movement began in Taiwan and continues to attract ethnic Chinese recruits, it is today a multi-site, decentralized organization whose communication flows cover all continents. As a leader, the reclusive Ching Hai focuses less on doctrine or administration than on aesthetic and business issues. Most remarkable has been her easy transition from a traditionally garbed Buddhist nun into a flamboyant feminist who actively markets her own product lines of jewellery and garments. The movement can be dated to April 1990, when her magazine was first registered with the Taiwan government.

Ching Hai was born into an ethnic Chinese family from northern Vietnam, where she was exposed to Buddhism and Daoism, as well as Catholicism and Chinese medicine. She later worked as a Red Cross interpreter in Europe and married a German national. She studied many traditions and claims to have achieved enlightenment with the discovery of the Quan Yin (one lifetime) method of enlightenment, which she had first discovered mentioned in the *Surangama Sutra*, a classic text of Chinese Buddhism. Ching Hai later visited India and studied with Thakar Singh, a Runahi Satsang Sant Mat master. The Sant Mat tradition is centred on the use of sound vibrations – 'the *shabd* yoga of the sound current' – during meditation. Ching Hai next moved to Taiwan, where she received full ordination as a Buddhist nun. According to her own account, she was soon asked to lecture and guide disciples there, and although it was against her initial inclinations she acquiesced out of compassion for others.

The Suma Ching Hai Meditation Association today publishes monthly magazines, maintains websites, and sponsors large rallies at which members of the public are asked to join the group. The organization is also active in donating to disaster relief projects, most notably the Mount Pinatubo eruption in the Philippines and the boat people camps in Hong Kong. The core members live communally, mainly in a hilltop campsite in central Taiwan.

The key membership requirement is the *yin xin* (impress upon the heart) ritual in which a bond is created between the master, Ching Hai, and the initiate. Importantly, the *yin xin* technique involves transmission of a sound mantra, the *japa* yoga, an element introduced from the Sant Mat repertoire. Members are also required to adhere to the five precepts of Chinese Buddhism.

Adherents are urged to meditate daily for at least an hour and a half. They also constantly study Ching Hai's videotaped lectures, which range over common Chinese religious themes: the need for proper cultivation practice, compassion to other beings, and vegetarianism. The group practises a strict vegetarian regime, and has set up a network of vegetarian restaurants in many major cities. Despite some similarities to Buddhism, Ching Hai's teachings long ago

departed from the Buddhist tradition, and it is most accurate to see her religious thought as syncretic and international.

Ching Hai's organization came under pressure from tax authorities in Taiwan in 1998. There have also been several sensational television reports there concerning parents' efforts to get their children to leave the movement. Those who join her movement tend to be well-educated, young and idealistic men and women seeking a cause in life beyond the pursuit of money. There are no reliable figures on current membership, but it has been estimated at under 20,000

worldwide. There are probably fewer than 1,000 members in mainland China, where the group has been banned since 1999.

Falun Gong (Falun Dafa)
Edward Irons

The Chinese religious group called Falun Gong, or Falun Dafa (the Great *Dharma* of the Wheel of the Law), appeared on the worldwide scene in 1999 and has remained in the media spotlight since. Many aspects of Falun Gong remain enigmatic, from its organizational structure to its early history. Its tenacity and knack for self-publicity indicate it will remain in the spotlight for some time, although it is too early to forecast whether it will prove to be a long-lasting Chinese religion.

Falun Gong began as one of the many *qigong* (cultivation energy) groups that sprang up throughout China in the late 1980s.

Thousands of Falun Gong members protest peacefully in Beijing. From 1999 onwards the movement has been actively suppressed.

Qigong is a generic term for a type of physical/spiritual practice common in Chinese culture. Most *qigong* groups are loosely organized around an acknowledged master, usually a man who has practised for several years. Li Hongzhi (b. c. 1952), a former government official, first began public teaching in 1992, in particular through participation in an Oriental Health Fair in Beijing. He founded Falun Gong in the northeastern city of Changchun. Within several years, Li's group had expanded enormously and was prevalent in many parts of the countryside. Followers normally met in public parks each morning to practise the fixed set of five physical exercises (Buddha Showing a Thousand Hands, Falun Standing Stance, Penetrating the Two Cosmic Extremes, Falun Heavenly Circulation and Strengthening Divine Powers), while listening to a recording of Li's commands. There were also weekly meetings in member's homes, and larger convention-scale assemblies in cities. Its spread may have been promoted by the government at the time.

The Chinese government soon began to eye the movement suspiciously, however, and expressed concern that many government officials were members. Falun Gong's potential power as a social organization was vividly seen in April 1999, when some 10,000 members quietly assembled in Beijing and surrounded the national leadership's residential compound there in an expression of defiance over a disagreement in another city. The demonstration was peaceful yet unprecedented in communist China, and by July 1999 the movement was banned and actively suppressed in China. Association with Falun Gong is today a criminal act in China.

Li in the meantime had moved to the United States to lead a secretive, reclusive lifestyle. The movement continued to spread internationally, however, and groups today are active in most Asian countries as well as Europe and the United States. The movement's actual size is difficult to confirm; it once claimed to have 40 million adherents in China, but a reasonable estimate today would be far fewer than 1 million worldwide.

Li's teachings are concentrated in his major writings, *Zhuan Falun* (Turning of the *Dharma* Wheel) and *China Falun Gong*, as well as frequent messages disseminated over the internet. His message speaks to a perennial concern in Chinese religious groups: the urge to take up a cultivation practice (*xiu xing*). Li claims to be an advanced being, a Buddha, with higher powers not open to normal people. By taking up his teachings and practice each person is able to evolve to a higher realm of being. His writings are openly disdainful of competing teachings, which are said to be corrupted and not suitable for the current stage of history. He reserves his strongest criticism for secular ideology and belief in science and materiality.

As in all religious groups, some Falun Gong members join and soon lose interest. But there is clearly a dedicated core of adherents willing to make great sacrifices for the movement and Li. This religious enthusiasm can be seen in an attitude of quiet self-confidence, which may lead to acts of self-sacrifice. The depth of some adherents' convictions show Li's teachings strike a chord in contemporary Chinese society and, increasingly, in other modern cultures.

New
Religions,
Sects and
Alternative
Spiritualities
with Roots in
**Indigenous
and Pagan
Traditions**

*A sand painting of a yei god by a Native
American on the Navajo Reservation.*

INDIGENOUS AND PAGAN TRADITIONS

Christopher Partridge

There are fundamental discontinuities between indigenous religions and contemporary Western Paganism. That said, because many contemporary Pagans do seek to learn from indigenous cultures, there are also some (often tenuous) continuities between the two forms of religion. Hence, for example, while the *Shamanism practised in the West is distinct from that practised by the Tungus people of Siberia (from whom the term originates), or the Inuit, there are attempts being made to understand and follow indigenous Shamanism in a Western context.

Indigenous religions

From the Arctic to Australia, from Siberia to the Pacific Islands, from Southeast Asia to sub-Saharan Africa, indigenous religions can be found in small-scale societies. While a range of terms have been used, 'indigenous' is preferred to, for example, 'primitive', 'traditional', 'non-/pre-literate' and the more acceptable 'primal'. The reason for this preference is simply because earlier terms tend to be misleading in that they suggest simplicity, undeveloped antiquity, the archaic and, in some cases, homogeneity. In fact, these religions are often developed, highly complex, distinctive, literate and sometimes technologically aware.

PRINCIPAL BELIEFS AND PRACTICES

While it would be misleading to generalize about indigenous religions, and while, ideally, each indigenous religion should be studied alone in its context, there are certain common themes that can be identified. For example, there are fundamental continuities between the sacred and the secular. Although particular sacred spaces are recognized (e.g. shrines, rocks, trees, mountains), generally speaking, the environment and the whole of individual and communal life are invested with religious

significance. Likewise, it is commonly believed that all effects have personal causes, and that, consequently, all that happens is willed. Dreams, injuries, diseases, accidents, deaths, births all require consideration of spiritual forces.

As in some forms of contemporary Paganism, humans are believed to be outnumbered by numerous demons, deities, ancestor spirits and non-human persons. Transcending all of these is often a Supreme or High God, sometimes understood to be distant and relatively uninvolved in everyday affairs. As to how this High God is related to, there are various understandings: some communities believe that it can be directly related to; others believe that intermediaries (e.g. shamans or priests) are required; some direct prayers to lesser deities and spirits who may then intercede with the Supreme Being; and finally, there is a combination of these approaches. However, not all in the spirit world is personal. For example, many indigenous peoples recognize the presence of a spiritual power, sometimes termed

mana. This is an 'energy' that flows through the natural world, is concentrated in sacred places, amulets and charms, and can be manipulated for personal ends.

While not all indigenous worldviews are inherently 'green' (belief that they are is a common misconception), there is often a profound understanding of a spiritual relationship between humanity and nature. Because each plant, rock, stream and mountain is infused with spiritual energy or attached to a spiritual being, the natural world is accorded great reverence. This, of course, has immense religious implications. Walking through a river or sitting on a particular stone can be religiously meaningful. Similarly, activities such as hunting are commonly

saturated with religious significance and involve complex relationships between the hunter and the hunted. Consequently, they are never carried out recreationally.

Myths are central to indigenous (and Pagan) worldviews. All the big events and questions of life are expressed and given meaning by myths. Why is there evil in the world? Why is there a world at all? How do we relate to the gods? All indigenous cultures have narratives – which answer such questions and situate persons and groups within the world (cosmologies). Fundamentally related to myths, and equally as important, are rituals. Not only all significant life events, but also many everyday activities are interpreted and empowered by rituals.

Contemporary Paganism

The word 'pagan' (derived from the Latin term *pagus*, which literally means 'from the countryside' or 'rural') has, over the years, been used pejoratively by Christians to mean 'uncivilized', 'non-Christian' and even 'Satanic'. Indeed, the term 'pagan' was first used in a general religious sense by the early Christians to describe non-Christian, non-Jewish religions. 'Pagan' is now generally used to refer to a broad range of nature-venerating religious traditions. While the term 'neo-Paganism' is sometimes used by academics and even by some devotees, particularly in the United States (e.g. the *Church of All Worlds), practitioners seem to prefer the simpler term 'Paganism'.

PRINCIPAL BELIEFS AND PRACTICES

'Paganism' should not be understood as a synonym for *Satanism. For many Pagans such an association is offensive, being understood as one of the many ways Christians have historically sought to demonize indigenous, nature-venerating religions. Most contemporary Pagans will insist that, because Satan does not feature in the Pagan worldview, and because Satanists work with a perverted

The Devil's Marbles in Australia is an area sacred to the Aborigines. Aboriginal legend refers to these often precariously balanced boulders as the 'Eggs of the Rainbow Serpent'.

Men set off on a ritual pig killing in Papua New Guinea.

of God. Indeed, in common with some forms of *feminist and eco-feminist spirituality, there is a general opposition to patriarchal monotheisms and the depiction of God as solely male. Although Pagans do claim to seek a balance, and although many will teach that the masculine and the feminine are of equal importance, the emphasis is often placed very firmly on 'the Great Goddess' and the feminine. A variety of names are used, such as Isis, Diana, Astarte, Cerridwen, Sekhmet, Kali, Innanna, Hecate and the Lady. Similarly, the God, too, is referred to using a variety of names, such as Anubis, Bacchus, Pan, Zeus, Apollo, Odin, Herne, Cernunnos and the Lord.

In a similar way to indigenous religions, there is often a pantheistic deification of nature. An implication of this is the belief that humans are in some sense to be considered divine. That said, Pagans are usually more panentheistic than pantheistic in that they do recognize that, although inextricable, there is a conceptual distinction between the divine and the natural world.

Also important for Pagans are natural cycles: bodily, lunar and solar. For example, lunar cycles and seasonal festivals order the lives of most Pagans. In the Pagan calendar (the wheel of the year) there are eight major festivals: Samhain, Midwinter (also Yule or the winter solstice), Imbolc (also Oimelc or Candlemas), the spring equinox, Beltain, Midsummer (also summer solstice), Lammas (or Lughnasad) and the autumn equinox.

Finally, it is important to grasp the plurality within Paganism. Although there are many forms of Paganism, and while there are solitary and private practitioners, arguably there are three principal traditions: *Wicca (also called the Old Religion, witchcraft, wisecraft or simply the Craft), *Druidry and *Heathenism (also referred to simply as the 'Northern Tradition' or *Ásatrú*).

understanding of the Christian worldview, Satanists are not Pagans, but rather Christian heretics. Indeed, many Pagans will actively distance themselves from Satanists and Satanism. The Paganism–Satanism confusion, which probably stretches back to the Christian denunciation of Pagans as 'Devil worshippers', has been exacerbated in recent years by misrepresentations in films, horror novels and popular books dealing with the occult. Moreover, because Satanists themselves will use the names of Pagan gods (as well as the names of the gods of other faiths, e.g. Kali) to refer to Satan and the demonic pantheon, some have wrongly concluded that when Pagans refer to gods such as Hecate, Lilith, Pan and Set they are actually worshipping Satan. This, however, is not the case. Pagans do not think in terms of a cosmic struggle between the forces of good and the forces of darkness.

Many Pagans reject not only the concept of Satan, but also the Christian understanding

CARGO CULTS

Garry W. Trompf

With the impact of outsiders on traditional Pacific cultures – especially from the mid-19th century onwards and mostly through the influences of the Christian missionary message – various types of new religious movements arose in response, especially in Melanesia. These movements, frequently appearing as some kind of transition between traditionalism and a more settled indigenous Christianity, involved intercultural adjustments. Various descriptive epithets have been given to them:

■ protest movements and rebellions, where active force has been used by local peoples to oust intruding settlers;

■ revitalization movements, where groups have tended to break significantly enough with the past to attempt creating a more satisfying way of life;

■ nativist or neo-traditional movements, where groups have wanted to shore up or return to traditional ways when they perceive them to be under threat of destruction;

■ millenarian movements, where peoples have projected some radical transformation in the near future that will bring an end to the known order.

The Pacific has witnessed all these types of 'experiments in the face of change'. The most famous among them are the cargo cults, known especially in the south-west, where such activities have often been classified as millenarian movements (see *Apocalypticism and Millenarianism). More noticeable in recent years and across the region have been independent churches (or new churches inspired by breakaway indigenous leaders, some of them formerly cargo-cultist). The emergence of proto-nationalist political awareness out of collective anti-colonial religious sentiments has also been a crucial feature of modern Pacific history, cargo cults again providing impetus to such developments and resulting in political resistance.

This article concentrates on cargo cults as religious phenomena without forgetting their implications for other spheres of life and other related movements. In brief, a cult of cargo is one in which a group expects the supra-normal arrival of European-style (or internationally marketed) goods – or, in other words, such non-traditional commodities as tinned meat, matches and radios, and even cars and Western housing materials. These goods have usually been expected to arrive with the collective return of the dead ancestors, though sometimes also with the second coming of Jesus. When a final-looking cataclysmic event is anticipated, analytic reference to the 'millenarian' aspect is permissible, but otherwise we are dealing with more special or limited hopes for a miraculous transformation. The Iwa Islanders (Massim) of south-eastern Papua set up a coast watch from coconut palms during the 1950s, for example, to spot ancestor ships bringing tinned 'bully-beef' – not a very extravagant dream – whereas in 1941 the prophet Tagarab, of Madang in coastal New Guinea, proclaimed that the coming of cargo in great plenty, at the hands of the returning dead in the guise of Japanese servicemen, would be accompanied by cosmic catastrophes. The millenarian temperament, though, has hardly been confined to cargo movements, for apocalyptic ideas appealed to many earlier Christian converts and have left their mark on today's national churches throughout Melanesia, and on virtually all independent churches as well.

The presence of

technological marvels in the Pacific was bound to entice religious responses. Each isolated culture had a whole order of things that seemed to be potentially transformable. Perhaps the earliest signs of frenzied expectation are to be found in Polynesia: statues near the Rano Raraku quarry on Easter Island were apparently set up in a frenzy to face towards the sea (they normally face inland). Did the Spanish make a 16th-century landfall at Rapanui, and were the statues, one of which has a Spanish-looking galleon on it, hurriedly arranged to entice the Great Ancestors and their possessions back? Whether so or not, the earliest encounters of this more numinous kind among Polynesians and Micronesians soon took on a different aspect. Islanders tried a mixture of eager trading and acts of shore-line piracy in order to acquire highly prized European goods.

Melanesian manifestations

Cargoist expectations were hardly absent from Polynesia or Micronesia, yet were less obvious there. Why the distinctive 'cargo cults' came to be manifested more in Melanesia, especially during the first half of the 20th century, is due to a number of factors. In the wider Pacific, powerful chiefs, even monarchs, dominated the

flow of goods; in more egalitarian Melanesia, figures presaging drastic change could more readily rise up independently of social and structural constraints. The traditional religions of Melanesia were also more wealth-oriented than those of most other Pacific island complexes: the first priority of prophets in Polynesia and Micronesia was to establish their source of *mana* (spirit power) and heavenly authority (often as substitutes for Jesus), yet in Melanesia readier attention was to be had by predicting riches.

Time and space also had much to do with the differences. From the time that Ferdinand Magellan's fleet reached the shores of Guam in 1521 to the wider plotting of Pacific coastlines in the 1870s, European technological achievements became slowly yet steadily known to Micronesian and Polynesian societies, and items were relatively evenly distributed through the upper strata of quite homogeneous groupings. With most of Melanesia, by contrast, the missionizing (and colonizing) impacts come more suddenly towards the end of the 19th century, and from the time the first steel-bellied German ships docked in Rabaul harbour in the 1880s to the landing of the first jumbo jets at Port Moresby airport in the 1970s, the West had achieved

its highest pinnacle of technological achievements, with the appearance of one marvel after another. The greater cultural complexity of Melanesia, the larger land masses and the obvious isolation of so many groups meant that the distribution of new goods was sporadic and uneven. Moreover, from the great battles between chiefs on Tahiti in 1833 to the Chamorro Wars on Guam against the Spaniards in the 1890s, Micronesia and Polynesia had experienced a history of gun warfare. If Melanesia experienced this early enough on its edges (with wars of chiefly rivalry on Fiji in 1808), by the Second Industrial Revolution of the 1880s the Europeans had invented the quick-firing rifle. Such superior firepower meant that armed rebellions could be more quickly quelled with colonial punitive expeditions, and the local people therefore had to devise subtler means of protest.

Cargo cults were, after all, acts of protest as well as of high expectation. They were characteristically non-cooperative and altercatory. People grouped afresh to be independent from missions that presented the new faith in too foreign a fashion and from governments demanding head tax and productivity for international markets. The dream of the cargo cult is for

a transformation in which the disturbances caused by the intruders will be overcome or rendered irrelevant. Getting around colonial power arrangements, the new goods were to become accessible to all, with the local people regaining the power – total and 'sacro-political' – that they had lost. The outward forms of cargo-cultism, however, vary according to cultural context and take on different aspects in the passages of colonial and neo-colonial history.

The Vailala Madness

The most famous early cargo movement was dubbed the 'Vailala Madness', and this name was often used for comparable movements before the alliterative epithet 'cargo cult' was popularized by anthropologist Lucy Mair. Diary materials reveal that the Vailala movement began among the Elema (Papua Gulf) with villagers' gifts of money to the London Missionary Society at Orokolo station in 1917. The suggestion of entering into

Members of the Jon Frum movement on Tanna Island, Vanatu, perform the daily hoisting of the American flag. The American presence during World War II has had a profound effect on the cultists and led to a sense of identification with symbols of the superpower.

reciprocity with outsiders, combining spiritual and material goals, is strong. When hopes of better possibilities went unfulfilled, however, the heightened anticipations were diverted by one Evara, who orchestrated collective trance states and xenophobic behaviour, encouraged the destruction of native ceremonial items, claimed to be contacting the dead through a make-believe wireless, and allowed for hopes that a cargo ship manned by the ancestors would soon loom over the horizon. The autonomic bodily jerking and curious speech (*glossolalia*/speaking in tongues) convinced the government anthropologist F.E. Williams, who arrived late on the scene in 1920, that the situation was pathological. He missed the early desperation to achieve a meaningful reciprocity. The phenomena of trance and possession, moreover, so common in small-scale black religious traditions, eluded him. It was the popularization of these altered states that made the movement spread along the coast to the eastern Gulf.

The Vailala movement occurred during the First World War, which barely affected the Pacific (even if it involved the acquisition of German possessions there by Australian and New Zealand troops in 1914). The Second World War had many more

dramatic repercussions. Hawaii's Pearl Harbour, of course, was bombed by the Japanese to mark their entrance into the war in 1941, but Hawaii had already been experiencing rapid social change as a United States territory since 1900. In far-less-developed Melanesia, Japanese expansion towards Australia involved military incursions along the north coast of the large New Guinea island, through Manus and the Bismarck Archipelago and on into the Solomons as far as Guadalcanal. In the Solomon Islands and the New Guinea coastal and island areas especially, through the Allied and (most noticeably) the American repulsion of Japan's advance, various islands witnessed astounding, if short-term, manifestations of advanced technology. At Momote on Loniu Island in the Admiralty (or Manus) Islands alone, for instance, at least a million American servicemen passed through the airbase in one year (1944–45). Carrier ships disgorged large numbers of tanks and amphibious DUKWs, a four-lane highway was built down the centre of the island, and Manus experienced a sudden influx of American dollars. Other significant places with large camps included Saidor on the New Guinea coast east of Madang and Meokwundi

Island off Biak in Irian (Jaya). Interestingly, Madang, Biak and Manus all experienced cargo-cultist outbursts, and these were so substantial that they deserve comment.

Large cargo cult movements

Yali Singina of Sor (in the hinterland from Saidor, New Guinea) was an Australian-trained native coastwatcher and war hero who remained faithful to the Allied cause because he had been promised that the Australian government would radically improve the living conditions of his people after the war. He became the object of intense cargoist expectations, and, after becoming disillusioned with Catholic and Lutheran missionaries (who criticized his sexual laxities) and the post-war administration (which did not keep its promise), he began his own 'work'. The tentacles of his well-organized movement – held together through lieutenants and 'law bosses' – stretched from Manam Island in the west to the Huon peninsula in the east (a few Yali missionaries even operated near Goroka in the highlands). The cult came to be centred on a 'table ritual' in which Yali's bottled semen, collected by his 'flower girls', was ritually placed on cult tables. The rite was understood to multiply money, so that grandiose millenarian-looking yearnings became contained by weekly hopes focused on a Tuesday 'religious routine'. The movement splintered after Yali's death in 1975.

Among the Biak peoples in Irian or west New Guinea, we find a movement awaiting fulfilment of the promise of *koreri* (or 'eternal life' [of riches]) as projected in the teachings and healings of the Insumbabi islander prophetess Angganita. Her cause turned to magico-military action when the Japanese invaders kept her in custody. The 'AB' Army formed to secure her release, but was decimated by Japanese troops in October 1943 (and in any case Angganita had already been killed). Significantly, 'America Blanda' (the meaning of the Army's anagram), showed the high hopes pinned on the Americans as rumoured saviours, whose awesome forces came to Meokwindi Island – as it were miraculously – in 1944 and drove out Japan's forces, an event which reinforced this most popular of *koreri* movements for a further ten years.

Meanwhile, on Baluan Island, south of Manus, one Paliau Maloat returned from his time as chief of police in Rabaul, New Britain, under both Australian and Japanese rule. On this obscure outlier he began preaching a 'new fashion' of social organization

and thought, both deliberately opposed to government and mission. For the early post-war years, cargoist hopes were also pinned on Paliau, but he was more interested in building up a Manus trust fund (albeit for his own manipulations), setting up a local government and founding an independent church.

Cargo and churches

During the 1970s, many well-known cargo movements were actually in the process of becoming independent churches, and by then several of these churches had emerged without having much of a cargoist basis, but we find that, by 2002, ten of the 25-odd known new indigenous-originated small churches of Melanesia started with dreams of cargo. Naturally we find social rankings ('ministers' etc.), church buildings, altars, Bible-equivalents, service books, blackboards and written slogans from the world of the missions, showing a somewhat slavish imitation of Western appurtenances. For instance, the Peli Association, which was once connected with high millenarian expectations at Mount Hurun in the East Sepik region, is now a curious branch of the (Canadian) *New Apostolic Church. Of course, this imitative tendency, along with both

syncretism and quests for independence in such churches, is hardly confined to Melanesia; these tendencies have a wide history in the Pacific and beyond.

In all these cases and changes, important features to consider are the 'two faces' of response to the colonial order and its aftermath. On the one hand, cargo movements have a variable measure of resistance against the harbingers of change. They express an 'altercation' with the powers imposing themselves on village life: a statement of independence or opposition in terms of non-cooperation, making 'extravagant' moves, even on odd occasions resorting to violence (as with the 'AB' Army). On the other hand, cargo-cultists show an intense fascination for the new goods of the outsiders. During the history of the Jon Frum movement on Tanna Island (southern Vanuatu), followers have even had a special sense of identification with symbols of the great powers, marching with wooden 'rifles' and with GI painted on their chests, or ascribing a special leadership role to Prince Charles of Britain (especially in the 1980s). These cargoist movements are manifested in forms of negative 'payback' or reprisal, but they are also moves to enter into positive reciprocity with the powers that have brought wealth to the apparently miserly and unreciprocal colonials. If some cargo-cultists betray a very eager concern to learn about 'the whites', this is usually to uncover secrets from them that have too long been hidden, and the more typical actions of positive reciprocity are rituals, devised for the group to get direct access to the cargo and thus circumvent direct dealings with deceptive outsiders.

Cargo-cultism outside Melanesia

Most of the examples used here have been Melanesian. But one must still be on the lookout for some, if more occasional, cargo-cultist aspects in wider Oceania. In Polynesia, where prophet leaders characteristically confirm their power by establishing linkage with the sky/heavens there can be claims that goods will descend from on high. Such was the case with the so-called 'Nuipana Madness' on Rennell Island in 1936, when the priest Taupongi created the impression that he had sent off three messengers 'to heaven' to bring back calico for his supporters. And we can find a history of cargo cult activity on the fringes of Oceania, especially in Japan, and beyond that. Documentation of it in Japan goes back to the Ofube no Oshi movement of

the 7th century, on to the meditations for television sets and cars at the household shrines of the contemporary Namu-myoho-renge-kyo sect. On the opposite side of the Pacific Ocean, even tertiary students in California, that scene of supermarket religiosity, made use of this last-mentioned Japanese meditative technique in the hope of acquiring new gadgets.

Beyond Oceania, there are cases of cargo-cultism far and wide. Occasionally it was reported from the mission field in Asia. In 1923, for example, certain highland Burmese villagers packed up their (not unimpressive) wares and took off on an expedition following a prophet who said that money and new kinds of animals would be given to them in the high mountains, where Jesus was returning. Not long after (1925–27), the Mwana Leza movement erupted far away in equatorial Africa's Nyasaland, and it had the markings of a cargo cult even more clearly, with its prophet Tom Nyirenda announcing that 'the Redeemer would arrive in an aeroplane one day laden with motorcycles and bales of calico'. The story can be taken to our own time, with the popularity of the new Hindu goddess Santoshi Mata, to whom one prays for new-style commodity items, and with

the African-American Reverend Eikerokotter III's New York cinema, in which he has preached the Gospel of 'Green Power' (or of the all-problem-solving dollar). Some scholars (such as Marvin Harris and Jonathan Z. Smith) have concluded, in fact, that the general structure of attention lying behind cargo-cultism is endemic to all religion. This is not saying much that is vastly new, as almost all known traditional religions have celebrated fecundity, fertility or prosperity (see *Prosperity Spirituality); internationally marketed commodities have simply taken the hopes and possibilities of material security a step further. What may be called 'cargoism' is by now a global phenomenon – people feel much better about themselves when they have obtained some new comfort (such as a stove or refrigerator) or have marked themselves out as prestigious (with a sports car).

Druidry

Graham Harvey

Druidry has had many and various incarnations since the Iron Age. According to Greek and Roman authors, Druids in north-west European societies were ritual experts, philosophical mystics and advisors to rulers. In the centuries after the slaughter of the Druids on Anglesey by the Romans, they have been reinvented in literature and in practice many times. In the late 18th century in Wales and Cornwall, self-identified Druids established cultural and linguistic events, which were expected to encourage pride and self-determination. Almost all of these Druids were significant members of local Christian chapels and churches. A similar movement in Brittany was more radically polytheistic, reviving invocations of pre-Christian deities such as the solar hero Lugh. A parallel but more widespread trend blended spirituality with charity and led to the formation of various friendly societies, often with a Masonic flavour. These cultural/linguistic and charitable/mystical movements continue, and have inspired a considerable amount of poetry and mythology. However, in the 20th century a revival of pagan Druidry began and continues to generate new forms of contemporary spirituality. It is these pagan Druidries that will be the focus of the following discussion.

Druidry is now a significant part of the broader Pagan movement, celebrating seasonal festivals and honouring ancestral sacred sites. There are many different Druid groups or 'orders'. Some are large and international, networking through regular

Druids at Stonehenge, England, gather for the summer solstice over twenty years ago. Burning torches illuminate this sacred site, which has been a focus of celebration for over three millennia.

Dylan Apthium, Archdruid of the Insular Order of the Druids, prays for the clouds to disappear before the eclipse at St Michael's Mount, Penzance, Cornwall.

newsletters, websites and email; others are entirely local to particular places, such as Stonehenge or Glastonbury. However, the large orders have local groups, usually called 'Groves', in which people might meet more or less frequently. Some orders utilize historical references to 'Bards', 'Ovates' and 'Druids' to produce a system of grades through which one might progress with suitable training, experience and/or expertise. Others use these same labels to refer to roles that any member might fulfil at any time, and give equal respect and stress to all. Training schemes also vary from the systematic and structured distance-learning packages of some orders to the ad hoc or individualistic approach of others. Themes of importance in such training include a spectrum embracing ecology at one end and psychology at the other.

In some respects, Druidry differs little from witchcraft or *Wicca. Similar seasonal festivals are celebrated: the summer and winter solstices, the spring and autumn equinoxes, and the four 'quarter' days, usually known by Irish or Welsh names: Imbolc (1 February), Beltain (1 May), Lughnasad (1 August) and Samhain (1 November). These days mark the beginnings or middles of seasons. Ceremonies are typically conducted in circles, and usually commence with the greeting of the directions (east, south, west and north, but sometimes also including the above, below and within). Understandings drawn from folklore, ancient and historical literature, ecology, ceremonial magic, anthropology and imagination are blended into daily and ceremonial ways of life that are found to be satisfying and thought to be respectful of this world. In some orders, ceremonies are carefully crafted and require the participation of various role-players, equivalent to ritual experts or a priesthood. In other orders anyone present is free to participate in any way they see fit. Gender plays a minimal role in allocating roles or recognition of rank or ability in most contemporary Druid orders. Membership, too, seems fairly evenly balanced between men and women. There is diversity in the

invocation of deities: some orders speaking of and to a (seemingly) singular deity, usually 'the Goddess', others specifically addressing an expansive pantheon of largely Celtic origin.

Druids are more likely than witches to perform ceremonies in public – although many Druids also conduct private rituals, and witches do often participate in large open gatherings. It seems likely that a pervasive popular association of Druids with eccentricity and witches with malevolence is responsible for this difference of exposure. However, there is also a foundational difference between the two kinds of Paganism: witchcraft is a more initiatory tradition (akin to the ancient Mystery religions) while Druidry is a more inclusive mode of celebration. This is perhaps also made clear in archetypal ritual costuming: the white robes of Druids and the nudity of witches. While the robes mark Druids out as people who wish to be recognized as ritual celebrants, nudity occurs only in private rituals in which similarly initiated witches share understandings of equality. In fact, some Pagans are both Druids and witches, finding in one movement a powerful encounter with nature and in the other a powerful mode of self-discovery.

Two Druid chants illustrate issues of importance. The first is a widespread chant that is understood to evoke and resonate with a creative, sacred and inspirational force in the cosmos or locality. Such a force may be called *awen*, and may be understood to originate with the creator and imbue all that lives and all that exists. The three vowels, A-I-O, or the word Awen itself, may be chanted in a single long out-breath, and repeated three times. This is chanted in most Druid ceremonies and effectively unites the participants and may inspire them to be more attentive to the rest of the proceedings. A second common chant, or prayer, derives from Iolo Morganwg, whose creative writings (including outright forgeries) and energetic organizing were central to the earlier Welsh Druidic revival of 1792. With the alteration of 'God' to 'Goddess', 'Spirit' or 'God and Goddess' the prayer is often heard in open and ecumenical ceremonies. The original version read:

Grant O God, thy protection,
and in protection, strength,
and in strength, understanding,
and in understanding, knowledge,
and in knowledge, the knowledge of justice,
and in the knowledge of justice, the love of it,
and in the love of it, the love of all existences,
and in the love of all existences, the love of God
and all Goodness.

A stress on 'the love of all existences' conveys a strong interest in environmentalism, but Druidry is also deeply concerned with matters of justice, for example in direct action against road building and quarrying where these have been seen to be detrimental to eco-diversity, and in legal actions concerned with wider public access to Stonehenge and other sacred sites.

Santería (La Regla de Ocha)
Michael York

La Regla de Ocha is a form of the West African Yoruba religion that took root on the Caribbean island of Cuba with the slave trade of the 19th century. During the Cuban diaspora that began largely with the coup of Fidel Castro in 1959, this spiritual tradition came to the United States. Because of the secrecy traditionally involved with the practice of Afro-Latin spirituality, it is not possible to know the numbers of adherents involved. In the United States, it is known as Santería or Lucumí. While sharing a Native American intimacy with nature and the personification of natural fundamentals, Santería is more urban and less rural. It represents a Pagan desire to communicate with spirits through tangible objects. Colourful, organic and personally idiosyncratic shrines constitute some of the most salient and recognizable Afro-Caribbean spiritual features. Altars, prayers, songs, music, dance and costumes are part of an aesthetic assemblage designed both to inspire the worshipper and please the god. Dialogue with the otherworld is focused upon trance induction. The central sacred ceremony or *güemilere* involves the drum-and-dance *bembe* ritual.

Where contemporary Western Paganism largely represents an effort to re-establish a non-continuous tradition, Afro-Latin spiritism is both a direct and successful transplanting of an indigenous spirituality and one that crosses the ethnic divide. It escapes the controversy of appropriation found with the interest in Native American religious institutions by Euro-Americans. As a fluid

☞ continued on page 287

AFRICAN NEO-TRADITIONAL RELIGIONS

Elizabeth Isichei

It is now generally accepted by scholars that there is no such thing as 'African traditional religion'. Not only does each ethnic group have its own religious worldview, but also often a single religion differs from one town or village to the next. Again, specific religious cults are sometimes common to several ethnic groups. The sea god Olokun, for example, was a major divinity in Benin (the ancient southern Nigerian kingdom, not the modern nation) and among the coastal Yoruba people, but not, understandably enough, among the Yoruba who lived far inland. The Yoruba god of iron, Ogun, equates to the god Gu of their Fon neighbours. African 'traditional' religion is never static. Indeed, the process of change is well documented and communities often adopt elements of the religious practice of their neighbours, as well as their divinities.

Hence, problems emerge when anthropologists focus on the 'traditional' elements of life, including religion, with little or no explicit consideration of the winds of social change. For example, it was generally assumed that 'traditional' religions would die out as a result of the spread of world religions, such as Christianity and Islam, and the advance of Western education. While, statistically, there is truth in this assumption, the reality is often more complex. For example, a study of a small Yoruba town in Nigeria in 1981 showed that 50 per cent of its people were Christian, 40 per cent Muslim and 10 per cent 'traditional'. Similarly, the Niger Igbo town of Asaba (also in Nigeria) is overwhelmingly Christian and there is no longer an *orhene* (priest) of the river goddess, Onishe. While this would seem to indicate the virtual demise of 'traditional' religion, in fact people still speak of Onishe as a living presence. She is said to have appeared in the midst of a massacre of Asaba men, during the Nigerian civil war, and said, 'You are killing my children.' In any given 'traditional' religious universe some elements die out and others continue. Among the Yoruba, the cult of Ogun still flourishes, for he has become the patron of motor transport and of lorry and taxi drivers. A study of the changing 'traditional' religion of the Fipa of southern Tanzania shows that there is now only one divinity, Mungu, the God of Christianity. The nature spirits of the past, linked with mountains, lakes and so on, have disappeared, together with their shrines and sacred pythons. So have ancestor cults, traditional divination and spirit mediums. But there is still a lively belief in witchcraft. With the eradication of other possible agents (e.g. ancestors or divinities) it has, indeed, become a more important supernatural explanation of misfortune.

In a pioneering attempt to discern a pattern of religious change in black Africa, the anthropologist Robin Horton has suggested that local divinities, such as nature spirits, were suited to the microcosm of village life, but that as people became part of a wider world, a universal divinity seemed more appropriate. This explained not only the spread of Islam and Christianity in 20th-century Africa but also, for instance, the association, in the past, between long-distance trade and Islam. This is clearly evident in the history of the Aro. The Aro (Igbo traders of south-eastern Nigeria) brought clients from far away to the oracle of *Chukwu*, the supreme God. Horton's thesis (originally intended to explain conversion to Islam or Christianity) has been very influential. In many cases, the High God of 'traditional' religion has been equated with the God of Christianity. (This is true of *Chukwu*, among the Igbo.) It has also been suggested that the Nyakusa of Tanzania did not have a Supreme God before the 20th century. Missionary translators of the Bible tended to translate 'Satan' with the name of a local god. In the Yoruba Bible, Satan is Eshu, a trickster divinity who is far from wholly evil, and this equation has now entered general usage.

Any account of the core characteristics of African traditional religions as a whole is an invention. In the past, such books were typically written, not by anthropologists, but by theologians. An example is the Kenyan theologian John Mbiti's *African Religions and Philosophy* (1970). Studies of this kind were criticized, both for neglecting the many differences between local manifestations of 'traditional' religion, and, in some cases, for exaggerating the elements in it which seemed congruent with Christianity, rather than studying these religions in their own terms. In the words of one particularly influential critic (the Ugandan scholar Okot p'Bitek): 'They dress up African deities with Hellenic robes.'

While it is important to note the differences, there are of course real and striking continuities between the local manifestations of traditional religions, and we need some introduction to these if we are to understand the process of recent change.

Most African religious systems had a High God,

sometimes symbolically equated with the sun or the sky. This divinity is often understood to be withdrawn and distant. Hence, it is usually lesser gods, often nature spirits, who intervene in daily life and who are honoured with ritual and sacrifice, and who, in some instances, possess their devotees. However, having said that, the High God is not always and everywhere equally remote. Many Igbo personal names pay tribute to *Chukwu* (God) with names such as *Uchechukwuka* (God's wisdom is the highest), or *Chukwuemeka* (God has done well).

The number of divinities in a cosmology varied from one community to the next. There was a vast number in Yorubaland, but an individual typically worshipped only one of them. Complex pantheons are sometimes linked with large-scale political systems – hierarchies of divinities mirroring the complex hierarchies of Yoruba kingdoms. In the village democracies of Igboland, the sacred earth was of great importance, but daily religious life was typically dominated by the divinity of a local river. The Dinka of the southern Republic of Sudan had, in addition to a remote High God, Nhialic (Above), four major divinities, among them the rain god, Deng, and Macardit,

the source of suffering and misfortune. Garang was a recently introduced god, and Abuk, a goddess, was worshipped, but lacked shrines and a possession cult. The Dinka, like many African peoples, also had a system of totems, which have been called, in this context, 'clan divinities'.

The cult of ancestors was of great importance in the traditional worldview. A Nyakusa Christian hymn from the 1930s claimed that Christians worship Jesus, Europeans worship money, and traditionalists worship the dead. It was thought in many cultures that those who died a 'bad' death (among the Igbo, 'bad deaths' included deaths from leprosy, dropsy and suicide) and those whose descendants failed to honour them with sacrifices became angry ghosts who return to afflict the living. Those who died good deaths, and received the appropriate funerals and offerings, were benevolent guardians. The Yoruba practice of burying the dead beneath the floor of the house reflects this, as do the words of a Senegalese poet, Birago Diop:

Those who are dead have never gone away.
They are in the waters that sleep.
They are in the crowds. They are in the homestead.
The dead are never dead.

In recent years it has been increasingly apparent that 'traditional' religion still flourishes, and has often taken new forms in the colonial and post-colonial world.

The Cult of the Mermaid

Mami Wata is a water spirit. In a sense, she is a generalized form of a multitude of ancient water spirits who inhabit the rivers, lakes and deltas of West Africa, some of which are now also called Mami Wata. The spread of this cult can be seen as another example of Horton's thesis of enlargement of scale. Mami Wata is depicted as white (in the past, beings from the spirit world were often thought of as white, since the normal colour of humanity was black), often shown as a European, and her shrines are adorned with Western luxuries, such as bottles of Fanta, or scented talcum powder. In a sense, she is an invention of the West, reflecting both the longing of the poor for Western consumables, and, perhaps, an implicit critique of Western materialism. The name Mami Wata, however, can represent a number of different things. In West Africa, she is the focus of a cult of affliction; often those attracted to it are childless, or suffer from mental or physical health problems. To some of her worshippers (among whom women predominate) this is compatible with Christianity. For example, on the wall of a shrine run by a prophet in eastern Ghana is a mural showing Christ and Mami Wata side by side. To some evangelical Christians she is a very real demon.

In central Africa, particularly the Democratic Republic of Congo (formerly Zaire), she is not the object of a cult, but a motif in popular urban art who is depicted as a seductress in mermaid form, sometimes in explicit antithesis to Christianity. The earliest African image of the mermaid with a single fish tail is to be found in an African Portuguese ivory. African craftsmen for European patrons in Sierra Leone made these sculptures in the first phase of contact around 1500 CE. The mermaid was probably first seen on the prows of sailing ships, and thought to provide a telling demonstration of the reality of water spirits. In contemporary West Africa, however, she is typically presented in a different and distinct form as a woman, usually shown only above the waist, wreathed in snakes. The genesis of this image lies in the early 20th century in the Niger Delta (Nigeria)

A sculpture of a mermaid and a snake, a Mami Wata image, by Sierra Leone artist John Goba.

when a British official asked a local carver to copy a picture of a snake charmer. This icon is now found as far away as Senegal and Mali. It taps into a rich mythology of magical water serpents. Mami Wata devotees seek health and often children, but her image in wider culture is often that of a spirit who offers wealth instead of children. Where Mami Wata is the object of a cult of affliction, her devotees typically enter into a trance state called spirit possession.

Spirit-possession cults

The spread of these cults is one of the most striking aspects of neo-traditional religions. They are often dominated by women or by marginal men. Sometimes a devotee is possessed by a particular divinity, such as Mami Wata, or the Yoruba god of lighting, Shango. In some cultures, there is a whole parallel universe of possessing spirits. Belief in the Bori spirits of the Hausa spread widely in North Africa in the 19th century, taken there by the enslaved. The Bori cult is dominated by women, its spirits (conceptualized as *jinns*/spirits, here and elsewhere in a Muslim context), inhabit a spirit town. The cult of *zar* spirits is found in the Republic of Sudan and adjacent countries. Again, its members are mainly women who join it

seeking healing from particular kinds of sickness. *Zar* spirits include Dona Bey, an American doctor and big game hunter who shoots (and destroys) miniature antelope with an elephant gun. This is a telling example of the way in which spirit-possession cults depict and critique a changing world, in that Dona Bey is an indictment of the shortcomings and destructiveness of much Western technology.

In Zambia, the specific spirit-possession cults of local communities are now generally called *mashave*. In the course of this century, spirit-possession cults have spread in some communities where they were previously unknown. They have taken root among the Masai of Tanzania since 1960. Here, only women are affected, and spirit possession is seen as an illness that can be cured by the intervention of diviners from other ethnic groups or by Christian baptism. Some spirits are human (Masai, Europeans or members of neighbouring African ethnic groups) and others are animals. European spirits, who have much in common with Mami Wata, demand books, Western clothes or soap.

Hauka is a male spirit-possession cult that began in Niger and spread to Ghana (then the Gold Coast) by the 1930s. It is the subject of a famous, but much criticized,

ethnographic film made by Jean Rouch in 1953, *Les maîtres fous* (The Mad Masters), in which poor men acted out the roles of colonial authority, wearing sun helmets and carrying whips and rifles. An insightful and explicit indictment of the violence of colonial rule, it was, unsurprisingly, banned by the colonial government of the Gold Coast. At the time of colonial conquest, effective leadership in diverse resistance movements was often provided by prophetic figures, characteristically linked with the invention of new rituals. The great Shona and Ndebele revolt against British rule (1896–97) was at least partly organized by Shona spirit mediums. The Maji Maji revolt, which convulsed the southern part of German East Africa (now Tanzania) in 1905–06 derived its name from the sacred water (*maji*), which was thought to offer protection from bullets, but its founder, the prophet Kinjikilile, was the first casualty of the movement. It united 20 different ethnic groups. President Nyerere, the first president of independent Tanzania, claimed that the movement had successfully contributed to the problem of unity, albeit with an inadequate ideology. He felt that the challenge of independence was to find a more appropriate ideology which lay, he believed, in *ujamaa* (African socialism).

Prophetic leadership and reliance on neo-traditional rituals can also be found in independent Africa, in civil wars and revolts against African governments. A famous example is Alice Auma, often referred to as Alice Lakwena, founder of the Lord's Resistance Army in northern Uganda. She emerged in late 1986 and her leadership lasted only a year (she then fled to Kenya, where she was detained). It was believed that she was the medium of a spirit called Lakwena, who would overthrow the government of Uganda and cleanse the world of witchcraft and evil. Natural forces, such as bees and snakes, were thought to fight on the side of Lakwena's followers. It was believed that ritual means could protect soldiers against bullets. The movement survived after Alice's departure, and new leaders emerged. As with the Maji Maji, its continuance reflected the fact that it gave a focal point to strongly felt regional grievances.

Not all neo-traditional prophets called their people to war. In 1856, in South Africa, a movement sprang up which is remembered as the Xhosa cattle killing. Two young girls believed that they had received a message from two ancestors, telling them that if the Xhosa killed their cattle and destroyed their grain, the dead would return to life, bringing abundant food, and the Europeans would be swept into the sea. (The movement had elements in common with the Melanesian *cargo cults and the Native American Ghost Dance.) The Xhosa were divided in their response to this message, but the cattle killings that resulted led to famine.

The cult of Mumbo, a sea serpent of Lake Victoria, first recorded in 1913, was not dissimilar. Perhaps surprisingly, it lasted until the 1950s. The cult was clearly syncretistic, in that it merged the ideas of several cults and religions. Mumbo's followers did not fight against the colonial government but made a symbolic rejection of all things Western, including education and European dress. Mumbo, too, was said to have demanded the slaughter of livestock, and promised an abundant supply to emerge from the lake.

The changing face of witchcraft

It is generally agreed that the belief in witchcraft is one of the most enduring and pervasive elements of African traditional religion. The fear of witchcraft is found not only among the uneducated, but also among the highly westernized, who sometimes rationalize it as a fear of poison. It has often been suggested that witchcraft beliefs expanded in the colonial era because it was an 'age of anxiety'. Colonialism was imposed by violence, or the threat of violence, and accompanied by social dislocations and often, by natural disasters such as rinderpest pandemics. Because colonial governments outlawed witchcraft ordeals, it was widely felt that witches flourished undetected. The colonial era has been called an age of improvement and differentiation. Some welcomed new opportunities, but a growing gap between rich and poor intensified the resentments that fed witchcraft beliefs. Witchcraft ordeals were replaced by witchcraft eradication movements.

Among the most famous of these were the Atinga movement in western Nigeria, and *Mchape* or *Kamcape* (meaning 'Washing') in eastern and southern Africa. These movements sought to eradicate witchcraft in a community. People would drink a medicine that would, it was thought, kill them if they practised witchcraft in future. The cult leaders were typically young and Western-educated, and charged fees for this service. The evils witchcraft was thought to cause (death, infertility and disease) did not, of course, disappear, so that new witchcraft eradication movements tended to find a ready welcome. The 'traditional' concept of the witch was that of the 'soul eater' or 'astral cannibal'. It was widely believed that witches met in a coven and feasted on the life force of victims, which members took it in turns to provide. In Africa, as in early modern Europe, the typical witch was understood to be a woman – often an old and poor woman. In the colonial situation, successful entrepreneurs were regularly accused of being witches; certainly they feared this accusation. For example, the Bakweri, who live on the slopes of Mount Cameroon, were afraid to cultivate bananas lest the wealth this created led to witchcraft accusations. They solved the problem by importing, at considerable expense, a powerful anti-witchcraft mask. In Cameroon, an older concept of the witch as 'astral cannibal' was supplanted by a new idea – the witch who grows rich through the labour of zombie slaves. This concept, which emphasizes money rather than food, has also been recorded in Tanzania and South Africa. In the post-colonial era, the gap between rich and poor became much more extreme. In particular, the great wealth of many of independent Africa's rulers was thought to have been acquired by occult

means. An urban myth of blood magic suggests that helpless people – often women and children – are sometimes kidnapped and murdered, and their bodies used in magical money-making rituals by the rich and powerful.

Christian responses to neo-traditional worldviews

Foreign missionaries (and the churches they controlled) did not regard witchcraft as 'real' and therefore had little to contribute to witchcraft fears. In Zambia, Emmanuel Milingo, the Catholic archbishop of Lusaka from 1973 to 1982, embarked on a ministry that involved exorcizing possessing spirits and combating witchcraft. He won a huge popular following, but came into conflict with the church. In 1982 he was transferred to Rome, and in 1996 he was told to give up his public ministry. Pentecostals and evangelicals often regard spirits such as Mami Wata as 'real' demons. It has been said that, while many Africans have converted to Christianity and Islam, traditional religion in Africa lives on in the hearts of Christians and Muslims. While those who identify primarily or exclusively as traditionalists are a diminishing and ageing band, both individuals and communities in Africa create new forms of synthesis between old and new. One

of the great attractions of the independent prophetic churches (often called Aladura in Nigeria and Zionist in South Africa; see *African Independent Churches) was the fact that they regarded the traditional worldview with great seriousness. In the past, prophetic church members often destroyed traditional religious objects and attacked traditional shrines, because they believed that they were sources of real, if evil, power, in an apparent validation of traditional beliefs. Unlike traditional mission churches, they offered various forms of ritual protection against witchcraft, and, like traditional practitioners, their leaders often offered a ministry of healing for physical and mental ills. In this and other ways, they incorporated aspects of the traditional worldview – there was a strong emphasis on this-worldly benefits and protection. Prophetic churches often adopted complex prohibitions, which are similar to the ritual taboos of tradition, but are now often based on the book of Leviticus from the Christian Old Testament.

and highly adaptable Black African complex, it has increasingly developed into a signature of large sections of chiefly urban Latin American populations of European descent but is also becoming more and more popular among non-Hispanic peoples in the United States (especially within the gay community).

The versatility of African spirituality is a direct continuation of polytheistic understandings. In their homeland, the numbers of *orishas* or ancestor spirits range into the hundreds. There is a deity for every aspect of life. Some *orishas* fall out of favour, while others rise in popularity. In the New World, selective transformations have occurred. The number recognized in Cuba is 16. In the United States, on the other hand, a pantheon has emerged known as *Las Seite Potencias Africanas* (the Seven African Powers). Here, the religion has moved away from being one grounded in mythological origins to one based on psychological and ethical archetypes. The seven deities include the white god Obatala (the chief who is concerned with ethical purity), Changó (ruler of thunder and passion), Ogun (patron of iron and war), Orula (the god of divination), Eshu (the phallic trickster figure of passageways), Yemaya (the goddess of maternity and salt water) and Oshun (the goddess of life, love, marriage, gold and fresh water). Sometimes these *orishas* are considered to be manifestations of a ubiquitous divine force or supreme god but are more often understood as extraordinary ancestral human beings who were deified after death.

Another key aspect of Yoruba adaptability is the association made between African *orishas* and Roman Catholic saints. This was in large part a survival tactic, but it also represents an oppressed peoples' attempt to project empowerment and validation. While this leads to what is sometimes described as a syncretization between Catholicism and African spirituality, it appears that in the minds of most spiritists, the two religious systems are distinct and approached as separate.

Candomblé
Andrew Dawson

Established in Bahia, north-eastern Brazil, in the early 19th century, the first Candomblé temples (*terreiros*) were dedicated to an African pantheon earlier brought to Brazil by Yoruba (part of modern-day Nigeria) slaves. It was not until the latter part of the 20th century, however, that legal, demographic and cultural changes allowed Candomblé the social space in which to practise freely and subsequently flourish. Contemporary Candomblé comprises a well-developed cosmological bilingualism, as prolonged appropriation of popular Catholic imagery has resulted in Candomblé deities (*orixás*) serving simultaneously as 'African' god and Christian intercessor (e.g. the god Oxalá is taken to be Jesus, while Iansã doubles up as Saint Barbara).

Candomblé cosmology has the material arena of the earth (*aiê*) surrounded by a spiritual realm (*orun*) comprising nine semi-permeable concentric spheres. The outermost spheres are populated by the remote god Olórun and other foundational deities (the *Irumalé*). The souls of the dead (*eguns*) are dispersed throughout *orun*, their cosmological position in the spiritual hierarchy determined relative to their spiritual development when alive on earth. The spiritual spheres nearest the earth share a similar level of cosmic energy with it, thereby allowing the *orixás* most central to Candomblé practice to pass easily between the spiritual and the material.

Candomblé cultic practice revolves around a mutually advantageous exchange between *orixá* and adherent, facilitated by a ritually trained medium. Acting ostensibly as ambassadors of the higher deities, *orixás* possess their entranced hosts to enjoy temporarily the trappings of material existence. These trappings come chiefly in the form of food and clothing, with each deity having a very particular set of preferences corresponding usually to a particular range of powers. Possessing its medium at a set point in the Candomblé ceremony, and often working through divination, the *orixá* offers insight, guidance and encouragement to supplicants in exchange for a stipulated range of propitiatory gifts and thank-offerings.

Kardecism
Richard Hoskins

Kardecism is a Spiritist movement largely found in Brazil. It originated with, and derives its name from, the Frenchman Allan Kardec, an intellectual and academic whose real name was H. Leon Denizard Rivail (1804–69).

In 1854, Rivail first heard about a phenomenon of 'rapping' noises that had been heard in the United States, and then in Europe. Rivail began to investigate these phenomena, producing a notebook containing transcripts and journals of the alleged spirit communications who were causing the noises, and published it as *The Spirits' Book* (1857). Rivail became convinced of the truth of the spirits' communications. He wrote under the name of Allan Kardec in order to keep his academic and spiritist inclinations separate, the name of Kardec being one he believed he had held in a previous incarnation. He founded the Spiritist Society of Paris and established, and then edited, the journal *La Revue Spirite*.

The movement that sprang from Kardec's influence is most associated with Brazil. Children of wealthy Brazilians studying in France took Rivail's religious beliefs back with them to Brazil, where they were mixed with other African-derived and Latin American influences. In France itself Kardecism largely died out, but in Brazil it has flourished, often through transformation. One of the most important changes was that the movement took on an openly social, compassionate, approach to the world, seen practically in

work among the poor and in schools. Charitable work became a factor vital to the movement's growth among the poor and downtrodden in Brazil, marking quite a contrast to the intellectual and highly educated foundation of European and North American spiritism.

Kardecist meetings take place in spiritist centres, which may sometimes be in a private home. Group participation is usual before possession takes place. Specific songs and drumming come before the person acting as the channel for the spirit world is possessed by a spirit. Instructions and advice may then be given to the group through the person possessed.

It is easy to see how the views and practices of Kardecism could be mixed together with other influences in Brazil, even though their roots may appear to be very different. It is also important to recognize that while for scholars it may be neat to separate out religious beliefs, for the many followers such categories are meaningless. Indeed, arguably the fastest-growing religions in the world are those that evolve quickly. Thus many followers of Kardecism happily merge their beliefs with *Umbanda and Catholicism. Partly as a result of such adaptability, Kardecism has continued to be successful in Brazil, with some estimates putting the number of followers at 10 million.

Heathenism
Graham Harvey

Heathenism is one of several labels for a kind of contemporary Paganism that is rooted in Anglo-Saxon, Norse and Germanic traditions. Some Heathens distinguish between 'Heathenry' (being a Heathen) and Heathenism (the philosophy or theology). Heathens are inspired by medieval literature (including epics, sagas and poetry) and folklore in their search for worldviews and for ceremonial and other practices. Some, for example, adopt elements of ancestral costume for ceremonies and may identify themselves to others by wearing symbols representing Thor's hammer (*mjölnir*). Runes are not used primarily as everyday systems of writing, but as powerful symbols for meditative and magical use. Words from ancestral languages are part of the religious vocabulary of Heathenism, because elements of the Heathen understanding of the world are strongly rooted in tradition.

According to the 'lore' derived from respected sources and of importance to many Heathens, this world is one of nine linked by a vast 'World Tree' called Yggdrasil. Our world, Midgard (popularized by Tolkien as Middle Earth), can be presumed to be central to the other worlds. At the foot of the World Tree are the three Norns, who can be thought of as 'Past, Present and Future', who are spinners of *wyrd* (something like karma or fate – the result of action in obligatory action) in all the worlds and for all beings. *Wyrd* is sometimes also considered to be something like a web or a power that *is* the interconnection between all things, and some think it can be manipulated or followed as a guide to improve life and gain wisdom. Two groups of divinities exist: the Aesir and the Vanir, sometimes simplistically thought of respectively as deities of culture and fertility. In fact most deities are multi-talented and respected for actual deeds rather than symbolic associations. Both groups include goddesses and gods. For example, the god Thor and the goddess Sif are among the Aesir, while the god Freyr and goddess Freyja are among the Vanir. However, this is not a consistently systematized or dogmatic tradition: for example, Freyr and Freyja are usually considered to live among the Aesir, and in different areas different deities were considered most significant, and no complete list is available in ancient sources. This is typical of polytheistic religions, in which it is understood that there are a number of deities

but each person or family establishes close relationships with a particular divinity or perhaps a group of them.

Although some Heathens prefer to label their religion Ásatrú (faith in the deities), Heathens are rarely obsessed with worship of deities. They are also interested in encounters with wights (perhaps 'spirits') of place, ancestors and many other significant beings: the nine worlds are also populated by giants, elves, dwarves, trolls and so on. The fact that some movement is possible between the worlds has inspired great epics and much contemporary experimentation. An important development in Heathenism now is the development of particular forms of *Shamanism, for example *seidr* in which people induce trance to communicate more freely with ancestors and other important persons.

Heathenism is practised in a number of different ways, and different organizations are available to those it attracts. Some groups engage in more ceremonial than others; some are interested in Shamanism or magic; others in the re-enactment or re-creation of ancestral lifeways. In Iceland it is possible to register as a member of a Heathen organization for the purposes of paying the obligatory 'church tax'. Elsewhere, Heathen groups have varying degrees of recognition for charitable purposes but are generally happy, like other religionists, to receive only minimal attention from the state. Interest in strange ideas and ceremonies should not blind us to the important fact that Heathens and other polytheists find meaning and value in the varied ordinary lives of human and other-than-human persons. No great barrier exists between home and temple, the ordinary and the sacred. Deities do not primarily demand allegiance and worship but might instead return us to everyday life inspired to live it more fully, celebrate it more richly, and engage in it more respectfully. Finally, therefore, everyday life is valuable.

The Native American Church
John A. Saliba

The Native American Church (also known as the Peyote Church, the Peyote Way Church, or simply Peyotism) is one of the contemporary spiritual expressions found among Native Americans (often referred to as American-Indians). It was founded in 1918, but the use of the peyote cactus in a sacramental ritual can probably be traced back several thousand years. It is the largest religious organization among Native Americans in North America, comprising about 80 chapters, claiming a membership of about one quarter of a million adherents, and spread among many tribal groups or nations.

Like all modern Native American religions, the Native American Church combines religious beliefs and practices taken from the original pre-Christian religions of North America with Christian and New Age elements. Among its distinguishing marks are the close link between religion and the natural world, the tendency to ascribe supernatural significance to natural objects, and the belief that the presence of the sacred is to be found in various objects and locales.

The most obviously different feature of the Native American Church is its use of peyote (a hallucinogenic drug referred to as 'Father Peyote' by its members) as a sacramental ritual. Evidence suggests that peyote was originally used in divination in Mexico and that by 1630 it was widely spread throughout the south-west. The anthropologist James Mooney (1861–1921) was one of the earlier researchers of Peyotism and it was under his advice that the church was founded and obtained a legal charter to protect the religious freedom of its members.

The use of peyote is accompanied by ritual from its harvesting till its actual consumption during meetings where singing plays a prominent role. Those who go on a Peyote 'hunt' are like pilgrims; they prepare themselves with ritual confession and purification. In the mountains where the plant is found, the pilgrims pray for rain and fertility and listen to the shaman recite traditional stories and invoke protection on those assembled. Various rituals are observed

Episodes from the life of the Peyote Church, painted by the Kiowa artist Silver Horn.

while the peyote is prepared and ingested.

European settlers persecuted those who participated in the Peyote ritual, which was condemned as satanic and superstitious. In recent times, both local governments and religious groups have tried to suppress it either through legal means or by denouncing it as a non-Christian practice. Yet the Peyote cult has thrived and is now regarded by those who participate in it as both a divine medicine and a Christian sacrament. Some have even compared it to the body of Christ, the communion bread received by Christians, or even as the Holy Spirit sent by Christ to comfort people by its healing powers.

Scholars have observed that the revival of Peyotism occurred during a period of cultural disintegration. The success of the Peyote ritual may be interpreted as an alternative to the ancient tribal religions, which were in decline, and to Western versions of Christianity brought to Native Americans by Europeans. Several factors, such as the lack of federal restraint and tribal intermarriage, are said to have contributed to its rapid growth.

SHAMANISM
Elizabeth Puttick

The term 'shaman' is widely used to describe the role of the seer, medicine man or 'witch doctor' in traditional tribal societies. It originated with the Tungus tribe of eastern Siberia. The role has many names in different languages, but 'shaman' has become the international standard. Shamanism in some form is found among most indigenous peoples around the world, and is also growing rapidly as a new spiritual movement in many industrialized countries. It has been argued that shamans have certain general ways of operating that are universal, and similarities can be found in practice between traditions that could not possibly have had contact for tens of thousands of years, such as the Australian Aborigines and the arctic tribes. This view was most elaborately developed by the historian of religion Mircea Eliade in his book *Shamanism – Archaic Techniques of Ecstasy*, the first attempt to produce an in-depth overview of the subject, which after nearly 50 years remains the standard work. Eliade's account of Shamanism has its critics among contemporary anthropologists, who suggest that the differences between practitioners may be as important as the similarities.

There can be little doubt that Shamanism is very ancient; the oldest persuasive evidence is cave paintings in Europe and elsewhere that depict real and mythological animals, probably used for initiation ceremonies. These may have been re-enactments of a widespread belief in an underworld inhabited by animals and spirits, to which the shaman's disembodied spirit travelled to obtain healing or information. Some of these cave paintings have been dated to 30,000 BCE. This antiquity is part of the attraction of Shamanism to a growing number of adherents in countries that have not had a native tradition for many centuries.

What is a shaman? Eliade's term 'ecstasy' refers to soul flight, a religious experience, where the soul is believed to leave the body in order to experience another dimension, termed 'non-ordinary reality' by Carlos Castaneda, and more popularly as the 'otherworld'. This separation is achieved by going into a trance state, which can be attained by different methods. In Siberia, steady rhythmic drumming at around 180 beats a minute is the favoured way, while in South America, psychotropic plants are widely used. Western psychology has identified a range of similar phenomena, such as out-of-body experiences, near-death

experiences, and past life regressions, although not always accepting the idea of a soul, as this is contrary to the prevailing scientific worldview.

While out of his or her body, the shaman's spirit can travel to any or all of three identified realms – the upper world, the middle world or the lower world – each with its own geography and spirit denizens. Here, information, power or healing energy can be obtained, usually by negotiating with a spirit helper or ally, who has an ongoing relationship with the shaman. In the Native American tradition, these guides often take the form of 'power' or 'totem' animals, particularly the bear, coyote and eagle. The shaman then returns to his or her body, and can use the information gathered to achieve his or her aims, which usually are concerned with medicine, war, hunting, marriage brokering or agriculture.

Shamanism in the West
Shamanism is now a fast-growing new religion in industrialized countries. Good teachers are in high demand, and courses are usually full, whereas many other groups are experiencing a fall in demand. A number of influences have brought this about. Most importantly, the Carlos Casteneda books, purporting to be an account

of the teachings of a Yaqui (Mexican) shaman called Don Juan, had an enormous influence on the 1960s–1970s counter-culture. Don Juan's magical worldview was at complete odds with post-enlightenment rationalism, and this may have been a factor adding to their attraction.

At around the same time, an American anthropologist called Michael Harner was doing fieldwork in the rainforests of South America, and later he was to become a seminal figure in the Western shamanic revival. Harner was influenced by the Mircea Eliade view of a universal Shamanism with certain core features, which led him to develop a simplified practice that he called 'Core Shamanism'. He claims to teach the key common practices stripped of the cultural embellishments carried by tribal shamanism, and these are described in his book *The Way of the Shaman*. His school in California is now called the Foundation for Shamanic Studies, and offers a wide range of courses. Some of the teachers have become well known in their own right, particularly Sandra Ingerman who teaches soul retrieval, a shamanic technique for healing physical and psychological illness that is beginning to rival Western methods in its success rate. The majority of Western

shamanic teachers have been trained in Core Shamanism, which has spread worldwide. Core Shamanism has been criticized in some quarters as to the validity of its essentialist concept, and accused of disrespect towards living tribal traditions. However, sometimes called neo-Shamanism, it has become the largest, most influential and popular approach in the West.

Current trends

Other teachers, such as Terence McKenna, have experimented with South American psychotropic plants, and written widely read books on the subject (see *Psychedelic Spirituality). The combination of shamanic techniques, which are powerful tools, together with psychotropic plants, makes for a very high-octane spirituality. In a somewhat different vein, there is a movement or tendency called 'techno-Shamanism', which is connected with loud rock music and rave dancing, but which still seeks the trance state and a shamanic experience.

The current revival of Shamanism may be seen as a rebellion against organized religion, and against science and secularism. Its emphasis is on the human being as an embodied soul, living in a world where animals and even objects have souls or

spirits; the world itself is believed to have an *anima mundi* ('soul of the world'; a power believed to animate, organize and regulate the material world or universe). Further, the shamanic journey offers a way of enquiry into almost any issue or topic of significance in a person's life, without the usual religious constraints, or those of materialist secularism.

The modern shamanic movement, particularly Core Shamanism, has been accused by some members of Native American tribes of stealing and exploiting the cultural heritage of indigenous peoples. While there is undoubtedly truth in this, some Western practitioners do collaborate with tribal groups to conserve their heritage, and some native teachers are happy to share their wisdom with sympathetic westerners rather than see it die out through industrialization. It is also true that many (but not all) shamanic customs are so universal that they are in the 'public domain'.

Umbanda
Andrew Dawson

The origins of Umbanda are commonly dated to a series of visitations received by a practising adherent of *Kardecism, Zélio de Moraes (n.d.), during a prolonged illness in the early 1920s in Rio de Janeiro, Brazil. In these visitations, de Moraes was charged by the spirits of a Jesuit priest and an indigenous Amerindian to found a religion that might better meet the needs and aspirations of the Brazilian peoples (not least the emerging urban proletariat). This authentically Brazilian religion, to be called 'Umbanda', was principally to be centred around the worship and propitiation of two sets of spirits: *caboclos*, the spirits of deceased indigenous Amerindians, and *pretos velhos*, the spirits of dead Afro-Brazilian slaves. From its beginnings in the Niteroi district of Rio de Janeiro, Umbanda has spread to most major urban centres, with millions of Brazil's poorer citizens worshipping regularly at their nearest centre.

When formulating the central elements of this new religion, de Moraes and his co-founders borrowed heavily from the recently established Kardecist movement in Brazil (the importance of 'charity'), the long-established Roman Catholic faith (the centrality of saintly intercession) and the increasingly popular north-east Afro-Brazilian traditions, such as *Candomblé and Xangô (the ritual use of music, dance and dress). An eclectic dynamic was present from the beginning, and current Umbanda practitioners continue to appropriate elements of other religions (such as Indian religious and oriental mystical traditions) to augment and articulate their contemporary belief system.

Umbanda cosmology comprises a threefold hierarchy, with the earth (and its inhabitants) sandwiched between higher and lower spiritual planes. Occupied by a remote creator, the higher spiritual plane is populated by a complex assortment of lesser deities (most existing simultaneously as African gods and Catholic saints): *caboclos*, *pretos velhos* and numerous other spirits (e.g. *guias*). Excluding the realm of the creator, the higher spiritual plane is divided vertically into seven permeable lines (*as sête linhas de umbanda*), with each line itself divided horizontally into seven sub-sections. *Caboclos*, *pretos velhos* and *guias*, who figure most directly in Umbanda practice as mediators between the higher spirits and the earthly plane, occupy the lower lines that are most adjacent to our world.

Seeking to ascend (*evoluir*) the spiritual hierarchy by performing acts of charity, spirits temporarily possess ritually stipulated and cultically trained agents to offer insight and advice as to the cause and remedy of the particular ills besetting those who are seeking guidance. Although 'natural' causes and remedies are never ruled out, the origins of such ills are often attributed to the inhabitants of the lower spiritual plane or underworld (e.g. *exús*), who have visited the earthly realm (sometimes summoned by would-be enemies) to cause mischief and suffering through ill health, unemployment, family strife, unrequited love, and so forth.

Enacting the character traits, wearing the dress and performing the ritualistic expressions particular to the spirit whose possession he or she has induced, the medium serves as a conduit through which counsel is offered as to the most propitious means of remedying the supplicant's ills and staving off further spiritual assaults. Prescribed remedies range from spiritual cleansing through ritual exorcism, the making of placatory offerings and counter alliances with other spirits, to visiting a recommended doctor or adopting a more positive outlook on life. In rendering this counsel, the spirit is said to have performed an act of charity and thereby consolidated/enhanced its place in the Umbanda cosmic hierarchy. In acting as its conduit, the medium is considered to have faithfully served his or her adoptive spirit, furthering the likelihood of future success.

Wicca
Christopher Partridge

Also called 'the Old Religion', 'witchcraft', 'wisecraft' or simply 'the Craft', Wicca (from the Anglo-Saxon *wicce*, meaning 'witch' or 'wise woman') is possibly the most influential and certainly, largely because of the media, the most well-known form of Paganism. Needless to say, the popular media-perpetuated image of the witch – for example, the spooky old hags portrayed in William Shakespeare's *Macbeth* or Roald Dahl's children's book *The Witches* – is inaccurate. As with all Pagans, they are often very normal, unassuming people with ordinary lives across all age ranges, educational levels and occupations.

Wiccans meet regularly in small groups or 'covens' of like-minded people for social, religious and educational purposes. Sometimes during these meetings (and sometimes solitarily) they seek to practise magic, of which there are two forms – 'natural magic' and 'high magic' – both of which, it is stressed, should be directed towards good and healthy ends. Involving initiation and rituals, high magic (often spelled 'magick') aims at personal transformation through contact with the Divine. Natural magic, on the other hand, is more materialistic, in that, by means of herbs, crystals or other natural materials, it aims to harness what are believed to be natural (or sometimes supernatural) forces in order to effect changes in the physical world, from healing sick minds and bodies to influencing the weather. Needless to say, while some people become Wiccans out of a spiritual concern for the environment, or because they seek a radically feminist spirituality, or because they are attracted by non-dogmatic faith, many are drawn by the desire to practise magic. This is enormously attractive, not only because of the sense of power that it brings, but also because, particularly in high magic, there is a Gnostic-like sense of being initiated into a secret tradition, with secret knowledge and secret symbols.

Although there are many Wiccan paths, it is generally agreed that there are five principal ones: Gardnerian Wicca, Alexandrian Wicca, Hereditary Craft, Traditional Craft and Feminist Craft (a form of Gardnerian Wicca). Gardnerians base their religion on the techniques taught by Gerald Brosseau Gardner (1884–1964).

Gardner, who is arguably the most important figure in modern Wicca, zealously sought to make pre-Christian Paganism ('Wicca', as he called it) available and accessible. He claimed to have discovered and then, in 1939, been initiated into this 'Old Religion' by the enigmatic Dorothy Clutterbuck ('Old Dorothy'). However, this has been contested, and some have claimed that Gardner was actually the founder of contemporary Wicca. Indeed, academic historians have generally dismissed his claims to have been initiated into an existing ancient religion. If this is the case, where might Gardner have sourced his ideas? Gardner spent much of his life managing tea and rubber plantations in Ceylon, Borneo and Malaya, and later became an inspector in the Malay customs service. He had a great interest in the supernatural, a broad and detailed knowledge of the occult, and claimed to have gained experience of Buddhism and tribal magical practices, as well as *Spiritualism and *Freemasonry. It is also significant that he had a great interest in antiquarianism, an interest that led him to conduct pioneering work in Malay archaeology and folklore. In 1936 he retired to Britain, actively continued his interest in British and Near-Eastern archaeology, joined the Folklore Society, and, in 1938, became a member of the Rosicrucian Theatre and Fellowship (see *Rosicrucianism). Also important is Gardner's association with Margaret Murray, the author of the influential, but now discredited, 1921 study *The Witch-*

Wiccan rites are performed in Texas, USA.

Cult in Western Europe. Together, they produced a paper on what were believed to be relics of this ancient witch cult. However, while little can be proved, it is likely that these activities and interests contributed to his construction of contemporary Wicca. Some have argued that, whatever Gardner discovered, much contemporary Wicca is an eclectic mix of occult, Eastern, and indigenous beliefs and practices, influenced to some extent by Margaret Murray's work.

Following the 1951 repeal of the 1735 Witchcraft Act (which had forbidden witchcraft in England), Gardner published his influential *Witchcraft Today* in 1954. One of the most important Pagan figures to be initiated into Wicca by Gardner was Doreen Valiente (d. 1999) who, although far more private than Gardner, has remained an influential and revered figure, particularly in British Wicca.

Another influential, publicity-conscious Wiccan theoretician, who developed Gardner's ideas, was Alex Sanders, the leader of a coven near Manchester, England. Giving himself the title 'King of Witches', he established a rival form of Wicca – 'Alexandrian' Wicca. As to the difference between the Gardnerian and Alexandrian forms of witchcraft, Vivianne Crowley, a prominent British Wiccan scholar, puts it well: 'Loosely speaking, the Gardnerians are more Low Church and the Alexandrians more High Church. Alexandrian witches tend to be more interested in ritual magic than in folk Paganism.'

Hereditary Craft and Traditional Craft adherents argue that their beliefs and practices pre-date modern manifestations of the Craft and have been carefully preserved and passed down through the generations. The Hereditaries make the more specific claim that this knowledge has been handed down within particular families.

An increasingly popular Wiccan tendency should be mentioned, namely Hedge witchcraft. 'Hedge witch' is a term used by those practitioners who prefer to work on their own, rather than as a member of an organized coven.

Finally, greatly inspired by the book

The Spiral Dance: A Rebirth of the Ancient Religion of the Great Goddess (1979), written by the Californian witch Starhawk (Miriam Simos), many feminist and eco-feminist covens were established in the 1980s with several clear spiritual and political focuses: the worship of the Goddess, reverence for the earth/Gaia, the peace movement, the empowerment of women, and the eco-crisis (see *Feminist and Eco-feminist Spirituality). A particularly focused form of the Feminist Craft is Dianic witchcraft, which was developed in the United States by the Hungarian-born witch Zsuzsanna Budapest and Morgan McFarland. While, generally speaking, Wiccans (even feminist Wiccans) worship both the God and also the Goddess, Dianic covens tend to focus solely on the Goddess. Furthermore, the strong matriarchal focus of the Dianic Craft has led many covens to exclude men and restrict their worship to females only.

As with much Paganism, Wicca rejects patriarchal monotheisms and the depiction of God as solely male. Although the emphasis is often placed very firmly on 'the Great Goddess' and the feminine, generally speaking, Wicca does seek balance, teaching that the God and the Goddess are of equal importance. Most Wiccans (but, as we have seen, not all) would insist that, however the Divine is conceived, it must be conceived in such a way that both the masculine and the feminine are embraced.

A further variation of this inclusive understanding of deity is that of the Triple Goddess: 'the virgin', 'the mother' and 'the crone'. Often symbolized as the waxing moon (early life), full moon (prime of life) and waning moon (later life), the Triple Goddess affirms the equality of all the stages of womanhood. Moreover, this understanding of the Divine also affirms not just virginity, but also the sexual and the bodily; not just the young, but also the aged. Again, identifying the earth as 'the Great Mother'/Gaia, humans are understood to be her children. Mother Nature provides for her offspring and receives them back when they pass away. Similarly, as 'crone'/wise woman, the Goddess is understood to be a guardian and teacher of secret knowledge.

The many minor 'gods' and 'goddesses' of Wicca are often understood to be manifestations or representations of 'the Goddess' and 'the God' (or simply 'the Divine'). Hence, for some Pagans, these deities represent different facets of the Divine. There are warrior gods, fatherly gods, gods of fertility, virgin goddesses (e.g. Aradia), mother goddesses (e.g. Isis) and crone goddesses (e.g. Cerridwen).

Finally, as with other Pagans, some Wiccans will tend towards 'pantheism', in that they will understand the Divine to be, in some sense, identical with nature. The Goddess/God is the force that animates all living things. Having said that, most such Pagans are, arguably, more accurately defined as panentheists, in that, strictly speaking, they believe the Divine and the universe to be distinct. While the Divine *indwells* nature, is *immanent* within nature, and is *inseparable* from nature, there is also a sense in which the Goddess/God is distinct from nature. The Divine transcends, guides and cares for the natural world.

The Church of All Worlds
James R. Lewis

The Church of All Worlds (CAW) is a prominent neo-Pagan organization. CAW considers living in harmony with and understanding 'life' to be a religious act. While the community prescribes no particular dogma or creed, the commonality of the members lies in their reverence and connection with Nature (with a capital 'N'), viewing the earth as a living entity. Human beings are not only her children, but are also evolving cells in her body. CAW embraces philosophical concepts of immanent divinity and emergent evolution. As a neo-Pagan group, they are involved in efforts to reconstruct and revive ancient nature religions.

The Church of All Worlds grew out of a 'water-brotherhood' called 'Atl' formed by Tim Zell (now Oberon Zell-Ravenheart), Lance Christie, and their wives at Westminster College, Fulton, Missouri, United States, in 1962. The group continued at the University of Oklahoma in the mid-1960s. After Zell moved to St Louis, Missouri, in 1968, it was incorporated as the Church of All Worlds, a name derived from Robert Heinlein's novel *Stranger in a Strange Land*. Also in 1968, Zell began the *Green Egg* as the church's newsletter. In 1971, CAW became the first neo-Pagan group to win federal tax-exempt status, when the state ruling against it was overturned as unconstitutional.

Around 1970, Zell and the other members met Bobbie Kennedy, Carolyn Clark, and a few other Gardnerian-style witches. They began learning the Craft system, being initiated as witches, and combining the theology of *Wicca with Heinlein's libertarian philosophy. The resulting form of spirituality catapulted their newsletter, *Green Egg*, into national prominence as the major communication channel for the neo-Pagan movement between 1971 and 1976.

CAW and *Green Egg* continued to be a major force in the neo-Pagan movement until 1976, when Zell and his new wife, Morning Glory, moved to northern California, leaving administration and magazine editing in the hands of others. CAW became virtually moribund within a few months. However, several subsidiary or affiliated organizations (including Nemeton, Forever Forests, and several neo-Pagan covens) kept going during the late 1970s and early 1980s. In 1978, CAW merged with Nemeton, which had been founded by Alison Harlow and Thomas DeLong, on

whose land the Zells were living, and Nemeton became the publishing arm of CAW. In 1987, five years after DeLong's death, CAW, which had inherited his land, also absorbed Forever Forests, which had been overseen by several 'stewards'.

In 1988, Zell decided to revive *Green Egg*. The magazine grew rapidly and, consequently, CAW re-emerged as a major force in the neo-Pagan movement. Under the aggressive editorship of Diana Darling, *Green Egg* became a major national neo-Pagan journal, though financial problems forced the closure of the magazine in 2001. In 1988, CAW reported 100 members in six 'Nests' (local chapters). In 1993, membership was around 500 subscription-paying members nationally, in several dozen Nests and Protonests. There are also branches in Switzerland and Australia. The church is governed by a board of directors elected by the general membership at CAW's annual meeting. The Presidency must be held by a member of CAW's ordained clergy, which numbered ten persons in 1994.

The Covenant of the Goddess
Graham Harvey

The Covenant of the Goddess is an international but principally North American Pagan, specifically Wiccan (see *Wicca), organization. It describes itself as 'a confederation of covens and solitaries of various traditions, who share in the worship of the Goddess and the Old Gods and subscribe to a common code of ethics'. It was founded in 1975 in California in order to foster greater cooperation between witches and to seek their legal recognition and protection from harassment. It has tax-exempt status. People can join either as coven groups or as individuals. Criteria for membership include a theological and ceremonial focus on 'the worship of the

Goddess and the Old Gods (or Goddess alone)' and affirmation of a code of ethics built on the foundation of the phrase 'an it harm none, do as ye will'. Covens and individuals with the covenant remain autonomous and are expected to respect both the unity of the religion and the diversity of its modes of celebration and local expression. Covens are expected to have been established for some time before seeking membership of the covenant to be certain of their internal cohesion and individual character. The covenant does not define what a witch must be, or who is a witch. It not only recognizes and respects but expressly encourages the diversity and even anarchy (individual sovereignty) inherent throughout the Craft and other Paganisms.

The covenant has a central council in which each member coven has one vote and individual members form an 'Assembly of Solitaries' which also has one vote. Decision-making is by consensus following full discussion of issues. Local councils are also formed when there are sufficient member covens in a locality. The covenant requires that such councils contain covens from different traditions of the Craft (e.g. Gardnerian, Alexandrian, Dianic and so on). An annual festival changes location each year, provides an opportunity for members to meet and celebrate together, and includes educational workshops and stalls selling arts and crafts.

In addition to a members' newsletter, there is an informative website for both members and outsiders. It describes the purpose, function, structure and membership criteria of the covenant. While covenant membership, like that of most covens, is only open to those older than 18, the rise in youth interest has been considerable and requires some response. A part of the covenant's website is devoted to 'the next generation' or 'teen witches' and is among the clearest available statements of the nature of the Craft. The

Stela with sculpture of the goddess Diana.

following advice demonstrates that while the covenant is firmly rooted in initiatory Craft Paganism, it is also explicitly engaged in the celebration of nature: 'Spend as much time as you can outdoors. Learn the trees, the plants, the sky, the stars, the winds… you get the idea. The way to attune yourself to Nature is to experience it.' Finally, the website published an analysis of a census conducted in 1999, which includes an estimate that there are 768,400 Wiccans and Pagans in the United States and 1,219 in Canada.

The Fellowship of Isis
Hannah Sanders

The Fellowship of Isis was founded at Clonegal Castle in southern Ireland in 1976 by Olivia Robertson (b. 1917), a novelist, and her late brother and sister-in-law, Lawrence and Pamela Durdin-Robertson. The central aims of the fellowship, which were developed in 1976 and revised in 1999 by Olivia Robertson, are stated in a manifesto, inviting all who ally themselves with its principles to become members. Membership is organized on a democratic basis, without cultural, racial or religious exclusivity and without financial exchange. The principles of the manifesto outline the fellowship's dedication to honouring all religions of the Goddess through allegiance to the three 'divine principles' of love, beauty and truth, seeking to promote, as the manifesto states, 'friendliness, happiness, psychic gifts and compassion for all life'.

Over the past 30 years a body of liturgy has developed, detailing how these principles can be practised by interested members through establishing a relationship between self and deity. Members are encouraged to express this spiritual relationship by enacting rituals, prayers and meditations, as detailed in the liturgy. This liturgy is drawn from the ritual structures of contemporary paganisms, Goddess spirituality and diverse archaeological scholarship into religious experience in the ancient world.

The form and content of the work undertaken in any Fellowship of Isis group – known as a Lyceum or Iseum – or by a solitary member, is directed by the dedicatory deities chosen and the spiritual and secular interests of members. Therefore an innovative formulation of liturgy, inspiration and personal experience is encouraged in all aspects of the fellowship's spiritual teachings and exploration. Now spanning 96 countries and boasting a membership of over 21,000, the Fellowship of Isis continues to evolve. Independently and collectively, members create liturgy, ritual and other expressions of beauty, and embark on a range of global awareness campaigns, in order to develop dynamic ways of celebrating the immanence of the divine feminine.

Eco-Paganism: Protest Movement Spiritualities

Andy Letcher

The 1990s in Britain were punctuated by a series of dramatic environmental protests against the expansion of quarries and the construction of new roads and airport runways. Starting at Twyford Down (M3 motorway expansion) in 1992, the protest movement grew with camps being established across Britain. In all cases protesters used the same tactics: non-violent direct action, bodily obstructing construction work by 'digger diving', or locking themselves into tree houses or tunnels. Their idealistic aim was to prevent construction altogether, but more realistically they hoped to escalate costs to the extent that future projects would be rendered economically unviable. Media publicity peaked during the Newbury bypass campaign (at which there were 27 separate camps to be evicted), and, after the evictions at Fairmile in Devon, the then Conservative government capitulated by curtailing its road-building programme.

While by no means all protesters have religious inclinations, a Pagan sentiment suffuses the movement. Spiritualities found within protest, or DIY (do-it-yourself), culture are therefore labelled under the umbrella term 'Eco-Paganism', and are distinguished from other Paganisms by the importance placed upon the taking of direct action. Eco-Paganism includes two broad groups: initiated practitioners of existing Pagan faiths and the diverse spiritualities of protesters living more permanently at protest camps. The best example of the former is the Dragon Environmental Network (Dragon). Dragon was established by progressive Wiccans who sought to combine magical ritual with direct action, a practice they labelled 'eco-magick'. Eco-magick rests upon the notion of 'raising' supposed earth or 'dragon' energies to empower both a piece of threatened land and those attempting to protect it. They created a symbol, the 'dragon tree rune', which they 'charged' at a series of public rituals, often held at dance clubs and usually involving frenetic drumming. A tree daubed with the rune, or a protester wearing the rune, would benefit from the magical protection it offered. Dragon members often cite the saving of Oxleas Wood in London as an example of the efficacy of eco-magical practice.

The Eco-Paganism of the second group, that is the spiritualities of protesters living more permanently at protest camps, is harder to categorize owing to its elective nature: religion is regarded as a matter of personal choice, or 'what feels right'. This view is encouraged by the anarchist politics of DIY culture, in which there is a suspicion of authority and an emphasis on personal autonomy. These individualized Eco-Pagan spiritualities are principally influenced by the more established Pagan traditions of *Wicca, *Druidry and Goddess spirituality, but include elements drawn from the New Age, the *human potential movement and theosophy (see the *Theosophical Society); from Buddhism and neo-*Shamanism; from 1960s psychedelia and the hippie and Rainbow movements; and from British folklore. Christian, Islamic and Judaic influences are notably absent from Eco-Paganism. Protest camps are a melting pot for alternative ideas, and therefore enable such cross-fertilization.

Despite the individualized nature of this second Eco-Paganism, it is possible to describe broad patterns of belief and practice. In common with other Paganisms, practitioners hold a variety of perspectives regarding deities, but a duo-theistic perspective focusing on the 'God' and the 'Goddess' is common. The Goddess is typically perceived as the planet earth, or Gaia (as revealed by the protest slogan 'Gaia told me to do it'), while the God is understood in terms of the familiar horned god of Wicca. The 'universe', or 'universal mind', is also commonly referred to as a consciously guiding entity. Many practitioners hold pantheistic or animistic beliefs. Practitioners mark the eight Pagan festivals, full moons, and other celestial events, but in an ad hoc, and sometimes chaotic, manner – rituals tend to be spontaneous or to have very loose structures. Calendrical events are celebrated, and are often accompanied by the use of hallucinogenic substances (sometimes termed 'entheogens'), particularly indigenous hallucinogenic fungi (e.g. psilocybin/'magic mushrooms'). In part, the emphasis on celebration stems from the DIY culture's origins in the post-1960s rock and free festival scene, and the so-called 'new-age traveller' movements. Travellers moved between music festivals such as Glastonbury (organized) and Stonehenge (free) in an array of converted buses and caravans, regarding their itinerant lifestyle as anarchic and counter-cultural in and of itself. Because many protesters were originally travellers, Eco-Paganism exhibits what has been termed a 'new tribalism', the Dongas Tribe providing the best example. The Dongas formed at Twyford Down, from where they set out on the 'freedom trail', travelling on foot or by bicycle between the prehistoric sites of southern England, towing carts behind them. They identified themselves as the indigenous tribal nomads of Britain, and saw their gypsy-like lifestyle as being both ecologically and spiritually exemplary. They held several large ritual gatherings, including an earth-healing ceremony at Old Winchester Hill in Hampshire in 1996, designed to restore the 'dragon's head' cut off by the construction of the M3 motorway.

Eco-Paganism of both kinds stresses the importance of a bodily engagement with the natural world. Full-time Eco-Pagan protesters enjoy a closer relationship with nature than urban Pagans and often exhibit emotional ties with the land they are defending, or the tree in which they live. Likewise, a part of the philosophy of eco-magick is that practitioners should invest large amounts of time in the natural world, so as to build a relationship with the 'spirit of place' or *genius loci*. Furthermore, many Eco-Pagans maintain a belief in fairies as spirits of, or spirits dwelling within, a pristine nature. Occasional encounters with otherworldly beings (sometimes, but not always triggered by the use of hallucinogens) fuel the belief that practitioners have earned access to nature's secret realms, a reward for their self-sacrifice and spiritual and ecological example. Others maintain a symbolic identification with fairies. This maintains the belief that Eco-Pagans are somehow different, or set apart from mainstream culture. It also helps to justify the legal infractions of protesting, for practitioners believe that they are adhering to nature's morality rather than a 'corrupted' human ethic.

There is some evidence of similar practices occurring in Europe, there being, for example, active Dragon members in Germany. However, where it does occur in Europe, Eco-Paganism tends to be locally nuanced. Thus, for example, Heathen neo-shamans invoked the 'ice giants' of Norse mythology using *seidr* trance, so as to prevent residential construction outside Stockholm. Whatever its cause, the resulting freeze prevented work just long enough for the local government to be persuaded to abandon its plans. Again, in Iceland it seems that road-builders are implicitly Eco-Pagan, as there are regular reports of new roads being diverted specifically to avoid disturbing the land spirits or wights. While these accounts may be no more than modern myths, popular belief in the existence of wights remains commonplace in Iceland. Meanwhile Eco-Paganism seems to have made far less impact within the sizeable American environmental movement, being only one of an eclectic range of nature-based eco-spiritualities. Moreover, American radical environmentalists typically seek to emulate Native American, rather than European pre-Christian spiritual practices. Rightly or wrongly, Native American traditions are regarded as being ecologically exemplary.

As to the future of Eco-Paganism in Britain, the road-protests – by allowing practitioners to live outdoors and to exchange spiritual beliefs and practices – actually provided the spaces in which Eco-Paganism could flourish. As protesting has moved away from transport to issues of globalization and climate change (campaigns which do not require the establishment of camps), it is unclear how Eco-Paganism will be expressed in the future. Lacking the focus of the road protests it is currently in a dormant phase, but with the ever-pressing importance of environmental issues it may rise to be a significant religious movement once more.

New Religions, Sects and Alternative Spiritualities with Roots in **Western Esoteric and New Age Traditions**

Detail of illustration of zodiac signs from
The History and Doctrine of Buddhism
by Edward Upham, 1829.

WESTERN ESOTERICISM
Robert A. Gilbert

Esotericism is now the preferred term of use, among academics, for categorizing and describing a constellation of practices and belief systems that is a component of what has commonly been labelled 'occultism'. The term is not synonymous with occultism, for although it incorporates many of the occult arts and 'sciences', it excludes others and also takes in various initiatic systems that are often considered to be simply fraternal societies, together with schools of thought more usually placed within the confines of Western spirituality.

Esotericism, as a descriptive term, is also used by many of the practitioners and believers themselves as an alternative to another general label: the Western Mystery Tradition. For believers and academics alike, the term has similar boundaries, conveying the notion of something secret and of restricted areas of knowledge. It is also looked at as specifically 'Western', with roots in Graeco-Roman culture and Judaeo-Christian religion. Of course, academics and believers do not deny that there can be a parallel 'Eastern' esotericism, but this usually falls outside their areas of concern.

Those specific areas, the components of esotericism, are much the same for both groups, but their approaches to these components are very different. The academic sees them as legitimate areas of specialization within the general fields of cultural history and religious studies, and not so much an integrated whole as disparate parts related by common thematic elements, to be described, analysed and placed in structural and historical relationships with one another. For the believer they form parts of a larger whole, but his or her approach is less descriptive than prescriptive: the component parts of esotericism are closely related, forming parts of a continuing tradition and offering compatible guidelines of faith and morality, grounded in a common worldview,

albeit expressed in a variety of dialects. The two approaches can also be distinguished in other ways: that of the academic can be typified as external, objective and dispassionate, while the believer takes an internal, subjective stance. It does not follow, however, that the latter approach is necessarily uncritical.

The elements of esotericism

What, then, are the elements of esotericism and how are they interrelated? The essential underlying concept is that of 'gnosis': a saving knowledge accessible to humanity, once in possession of the right key, and involving an experiential element – illumination – that distinguishes it from simple faith. Gnosis is not simply a term descriptive of the faith and practices of the Gnostic sects of the early Christian era – it does not, for example, necessarily require a dualistic worldview in which good and evil are coequal – but it can be legitimately applied to the essential features of the Greek and Hellenistic Mysteries, and to their analogues down the ages. Among those features are the transcendental nature of this saving knowledge, thus requiring special training in order to comprehend it; its sacred nature, demanding that it be revealed only to those competent and spiritually worthy to receive it; and the existence of a class of enlightened teachers, uniquely able to transmit it to appropriate candidates in successive generations. From this it becomes clear why some initiatic systems and some schools of religious thought are considered to be components of esotericism.

Other key concepts are those of theosophy and hermeticism. The former, from '*Theosophia*' (wisdom of God), can be seen as a form of gnosis concerned not only with salvation, but also with the nature of God and of the created cosmos. For the theosopher, the natural world corresponds to the divine world, and has within it symbols of the divine that can be understood by means of divine revelation, which operates both through sacred scriptures and by way of personal illumination. A prime example of a theosopher, in this sense, is Jacob Boehme (1575–1624) whose work, which combines interpretations of the creation narrative in Genesis and of his personal mystical experiences, utilizes contemporary *Natur-philosophie*, alchemical symbolism and the traditions of medieval German mysticism.

At this point it should be made clear that this 'theosophy' has nothing to do with the ideas promoted by the *Theosophical Society, a still extant body founded in 1875 by Helena Petrovna Blavatsky (1831–91) to propagate her own versions of Buddhism and Hinduism. Nor should theosophy, or other elements of esotericism, be confused with mysticism. The goal of mysticism is the personal attainment of a direct experience of God, and while the discourse of mystics may make use of symbols also used in esoteric systems (e.g. alchemy), mystics neither lay claim to any higher, saving knowledge, nor espouse doctrines that are incompatible with the orthodoxy of their faith.

Jacob Boehme, c. 1605.

Hermeticism links the esoteric doctrines and practices of the Hellenistic period with those of the Renaissance and later periods. The pagan gnosis typified by the Greek Mysteries was first systematized in the *Corpus Hermeticum*, a collection of initiatic and revelatory texts ascribed to Hermes Trismegistus (the Greek form of the Egyptian god Thoth), which contained both Hellenistic and Egyptian elements dating from the first two centuries CE. When these texts were rediscovered in the 15th century they were perceived as foreshadowing the Christian revelation and offering secret but important insights into it. Seen in this light, they stimulated the production of commentaries and derivative texts of an esoteric nature.

From the time of the Renaissance, the term 'hermetic literature' has also been applied to alchemical texts, principally because they are considered to be ultimately inspired by Hermes – especially through the hermetic maxim, 'As above, so below', which neatly encapsulates the doctrine of correspondences between material and spiritual things that is central to alchemical theory. Also, the true interpretation of alchemical texts is usually concealed beneath a purely material surface meaning.

All the specific components of esotericism can be considered as sub-classes of these key concepts. Thus the kabbalah (see *Kabbalism), the codified Jewish mystical tradition, is also a form of gnosis, and, since the Renaissance, when it was perceived as containing concealed Christian doctrines, it has been treated as a significant element of Western esotericism. In like manner, the Rosicrucian manifestos, which contain alchemical – specifically Paracelsian – references, together with the vast body of secondary literature that they inspired, have been taken as either theosophical or hermetic in intent.

There are also other common themes in these related 'esoteric' texts. Understanding the concealed, inner meaning requires keys presented in the form of pictorial symbols, systems of numerical analysis, and the clear statement of the need for the reader to follow specific initiatory processes – accessible within the confines of one or another secret fraternity. Such processes usually involved both commonly known practices (natural magic and *astrology), and secret techniques such as those of 'spiritual' alchemy and theurgy (the invocation of angels). All of them, however, were directed towards the spiritual regeneration of the practitioner and were considered to be diametrically opposed to the self-seeking activities of the sorcerer or the avarice of the purely material alchemist.

Defining esotericism

This leads to a clear distinction, for their practitioners, between esotericism and occultism. Occultism is concerned with worldly gain and knowledge as a source of power in the material world. By contrast, the gnostic, the hermeticist and the theosopher seek knowledge that will set them on the path to God and lead them to salvation. To the modern mind the distinction may be less obvious without a careful and objective study of all the elements involved, and to this end the work of academic students of esotericism will be of great help. But pure academics are necessarily observers, and while academics can present a coherent historical and thematic picture of esotericism they will tend to miss some of the subtle doctrinal points, and, possibly, some of the major issues also.

An example of this is the inclusion within the general class of esotericism of initiatic fraternities without a careful consideration of their nature and purpose. Thus the Graeco-Roman Mysteries have an undoubted Gnostic content, just as 'Rosicrucian' groups – engaged in the invocation of angels or in the practice of Enochian magical evocation derived from the work of John Dee (1527–1608) – sought personal illumination. *Freemasonry, the best-known and most ubiquitous initiatic fraternity, is, by contrast, quite different. As an institution, Freemasonry is concerned with the moral improvement of its members and of society, not with the perfection or salvation of man. It is thus inappropriate, although a common practice, to include masonic initiation as an aspect of esotericism, even though some Freemasons, especially in the late 18th century, sought to associate it with *Rosicrucianism and magic.

In what may be termed esoteric initiation there is a perceived transmission from initiator to initiate of both knowledge and an understanding of the initiatic experience itself. There is also a clear salvific purpose, in that the initiate is set on the path towards spiritual regeneration and reintegration with God. Such terms are not found in a masonic context, but they are, for example, crucial to the initiatory processes of the 18th-century theosopher and kabbalist, Martines de Pasqually (1715–79). They, or equivalent terms, are also a universal feature of the essential components of esotericism.

Origins and purpose

It is unnecessary to list here every practice, symbol and motif associated with esotericism, whether by academics or practitioners, as such lists are widely given in the critical literature of the subject. What is desirable is to set out both the origins and the perceived purpose of the whole field of esotericism. As a preliminary it is necessary to recall its identity (for practitioners) with the Western Mystery Tradition, and to distinguish it from both occultism and the New Age, such as the Theosophical Society, that are Western offshoots of Eastern esotericism.

Both monotheism and the concept of a direct relationship between humanity and God emerged within the cultures of the eastern Mediterranean, and with them came the sense that we are separated from God – together with a desire to understand the nature of that separation, and to find a way of restoring the broken link between God and man. Official monotheism – Hebrew and Christian – offered repentance, obedience and trust in divine goodness as the way of reconciliation, but such a way was not considered adequate by all. In the Hellenistic world, two major strands of religious experience – the Greek and the Hebrew – had come together and united two

Detail of flagellation and a dancer from the Fresco Cycle at the Villa of the Mysteries depicting initiation into the Cult of Dionysus.

seemingly irreconcilable concepts of the Divine: the personal, intervening God of Christian and Jew, and the Unknown God of the Greek Mysteries. As a consequence of this fusion of the immanent and the transcendent God, it became possible to articulate intellectually the notion of saving knowledge (gnosis) and the exalted religious experience (illumination) with which it was associated. Of course, orthodox Christianity also posits a God who is both immanent and transcendent, but insists on faith as the path to salvation and this approach does not appeal to the gnostic temperament. In various forms 'esoteric' alternatives to orthodoxy have persisted to the present day.

Their common features are a conviction that humanity can discover an active way of reversing our separation from God (the Fall that was occasioned by human disobedience), and of returning to the divine presence; a recognition that such a way requires access to hidden knowledge; and that specific, secret techniques must be employed if this quest is to succeed. A necessary corollary of these is the notion that small groups of dedicated men and women continue to work secretly within orthodox religious traditions, preserving and transmitting the essence of both the theory and the practice of this gnostic way of return for the benefit of future generations.

Such practitioners, both past and present, have perceived their role as seeking to explore the paths that will lead to regeneration and reintegration with God both for themselves and for others. Inevitably they will see their particular aspect of esotericism as Christian, but this is a subjective viewpoint and it is, perhaps, ironic that it is the academic student of esotericism – who may have no religious faith, but whose task is to identify the various manifestations of this continuing tradition and to display their distinguishing features – who will determine whether or not the doctrines and practices of the practitioners are consonant with orthodoxy.

NEW AGE TRADITIONS
Michael York

New Age Traditions are religious and quasi-religious orientations that have been emerging as a self-conscious movement in the latter half of the 20th century. The major problem in developing a working understanding of New Age is that whatever might be said of it the opposite may also be true. In its general orientation, New Age represents a modern reformulation of Gnosticism, romanticism and theosophy. Even so, New Age is highly diversified and means many different things to different people. It is also fraught with internal tensions and unresolved dialectics, which only add to the New Age paradox. Consequently, for the student, the chief disadvantage in approaching New Age is that there is no adequate and comprehensive delineation of it.

A major difficulty with understanding New Age is that it does not conform to traditionally understood forms of religious organization. It is neither church, sect, cult or denomination. While the various forms of established religious models may apply to particular groups or organizations that identify with the movement, they remain unsuitable for describing the movement itself as a whole. Though this might be true for all religions, it is especially true of New Age. If we can identify the specific cultural or subcultural trends from which New Age descends, it is still a rapidly changing but complex mix of different movements and religions. Within the ephemeral coalitions and alliances of the New Age ebb-and-flow, there is no institutional mechanism for determining New Age membership or making judgements against individuals for not being 'properly New Age'. While there are many voices, there is no one who can speak for the movement as a whole. There is no list of New Age creeds and no registrar of membership. It is instead a loose series of networks between different groups or cells – some similar or even duplicates, others radically contrasting – while a constantly varying number of spokespeople, therapists and teachers who are in vogue at any given point in time move through its various circuits.

The fluid organization or even non-organization of New Age makes it actually more of a consumer phenomenon than anything that could be understood as traditionally religious. For the most part, people who identify with New Age are anti-institutional and claim to be 'spiritual' rather than 'religious'. It is, in fact, this non-institutional nature and marketing choice of New Age that appears to be its underlying appeal. The New Age is a spiritual consumer supermarket that is steadily superseding the appeal of traditional religion in the West through its affirmation and celebration of free spiritual choice. This in turn leads to severe accusations of cultural appropriation – especially from identity-endangered peoples, but New Age insists that the world's spiritual cultures are now public domain and available to everyone.

Origins of the New Age

The immediate origins of New Age lie with the emergence of humanistic psychology. One of the leading catalysts was the Jewish-German refugee Fritz Perls, who, in the 1960s, at the Esalen Institute in Big Sur, California, introduced his Group Gestalt Therapy, which emphasizes the value of immediate, authentic experience. Perls argues that the mind and body form a single, holistic organism. The *human potential movement developed from the work of Perls and his colleagues and, fusing with the American psychedelic heritage, spread quickly to spawn numerous self-help and psycho-physical therapeutic practices. In a sense, New Age represents the self-conscious spiritualization of the human potential movement. It grounds itself in the astrological consideration that we are leaving the obsolete Age of Pisces for the new Age of Aquarius. Taking its cue from the Maharishi Mahesh Yogi (the founder of *Transcendental Meditation),

the New Age is the expectation that spiritual development in sufficient numbers of individuals will eventually coalesce into a planetary quantum leap of collective consciousness.

Beneath its popular image, New Age derives from the spiritualist, New Thought and theosophical traditions of the 19th century. From these particular orientations, New Age inherits its practice of channelling spirits or entities from other dimensions, its belief that both illness and poverty are illusions or diseases of the mind, and its understandings of karma and reincarnation. These seminal traditions represent, in one way or another, non-mainstream spiritual and esoteric ideas imported from the East and blended with Western occult and Pagan notions. Within its eclectic mix, the bedrock New Age spiritual position is gnostic or transcendental and seeks divine truth as something that is masked by the physical phenomenal world. From this perspective, nature is considered ultimately an illusion and something that must be penetrated to gain access to 'higher understandings'.

Despite the great disparities of practice and pursuit encountered throughout the broad range of what can be labelled as New Age, we find certain common denominators or essential beliefs – that we have lived before, that we can communicate with discarnate forms of consciousness, that we can heal ourselves and are in charge of our lives, and that spiritual truth is something to be discovered within the sanctity of the self rather than in an external aid or tool. The attitude that our present life is not our first or only life is largely to be traced to Eastern ideas of reincarnation, which New Age inherited from theosophy. It is predicated upon the essentially gnostic belief that the cycle of rebirth is something to escape and transcend. In this sense, New Age contrasts strongly with contemporary forms of Western Paganism, which embrace the world as desirable and welcome reincarnation as offering a means for the return to earthly life. Terrestrial life for the New Ager typically represents an opportunity for learning and spiritual advance.

From its spiritualist legacy, on the other hand, New Age accepts that we can communicate with the dead. Once again, this possibility relates to the idea that this life is not all that there is. *Spiritualism insists that we can communicate with our deceased family members and loved ones for guidance, knowledge and confirmation. New Age has tended to take this further and, especially through its theosophical affinities, is less interested in the departed than in contacting spiritual masters or mahatmas, extraterrestrial beings or space-brethren, and extra-dimensional discarnates. New Age is not concerned with Spiritualism's desire to *prove* the existence of life after death but rather with the acquisition of 'higher wisdom' to assist one's spiritual development in the here and now.

From its origins in New Thought, New Age assumes that evil is an illusion of the mind. Since evil does not exist, New Age believes that the evolved individual can make both illness and poverty disappear. This possibility involves what New Age argues is the almost limitless power of the human brain and its relationship to ultimate universal energy. That we can heal ourselves is reflected in the many human potential therapies from Rolfing (Structural Integration), yoga, *Reiki, shiatsu, reflexology, t'ai chi (see *Martial Arts), gestalt, encounter groups, bio-energetics, iridology, *est* (*Landmark Forum), Zen, aikido, neo-*Shamanism, transactional analysis, to *Transcendental Meditation and more. These techniques aim to assist the spiritually aware person to remove the negative as a figment of the imagination.

The human potential aspect of New Age also relates directly to what we could identify as a fourth New Age belief. This holds that we are in charge of our lives and, along with its illusory understanding of evil and deprivation,

comprises the uniqueness of New Age: its insistence on the positive and utter denial of hindrance and negativity. In this sense alone, New Age is an affirmation that demands the world to be as it wishes. Concepts of retribution, original sin and punishment become completely alien in the New Age context, and, however naive and foolish such an attitude might be judged to be, New Age represents the affirmation of the power of positive thinking as a means to obtaining progressive ends. If there is one spiritual principle that distinguishes New Age from the world's major religions, it is probably this. To the degree that the 'negative is encountered', it is seen simply as providing an 'opportunity' for spiritual progress.

The fifth virtually ubiquitous and already mentioned New Age belief – spiritual truth comes from within – conforms with New Age's place in the gnostic lineage. Insight is not a product of revelation or external acquisition but one of inner development and discovery. In its complete exaltation of self-experience, New Age affirms its faith in both spiritual seeking and the validation of private experience. In this sense, New Age offers a new form of mysticism – not a mysticism of escape as we find in Hinduism and Buddhism, nor quite the mysticism of union with God that occurs with esoteric Christianity or Sufism, but a mysticism of *becoming* a god. This is a mysticism of self-empowerment. The ability to implement desired changes, along with authority and validity, belongs to the inner, private self. By internalizing the source of truth, New Age is at the forefront of a growing awareness that spirituality is about choice. This reflects Western society's increased valuing of the consumer and the right to make decisions that reflect personal needs and desires. The consumer of today is no longer expected automatically to follow the dictates of established authority. In a world of competing spiritualities, the consumer is 'persuaded' between the different offerings on hand. While part of the choice may be influenced by the marketing skills of the provider, the ultimate decision is still that of the individual and the particular resonance any spiritual commodity may have with the consumer's inner needs and stage of development.

Sociological profile of New Age adherents

But while the New Age displays an astonishing range of diversity, it also comprises different levels of commitment. At its 'core', we find the 'true' New Ager – the person who believes that a New Age is dawning. It is this core New Age individual who sees the future as a collective shift in humanity's spiritual understanding of the world. A larger group is comprised of 'spiritual seekers'. Here we have those who are not as committed but who are 'surfing' the spiritual alternatives in their personal searches for truth. These are the experimenters, and while they might eventually arrive at a position of belief in the New Age as something that is or is about to happen, they are in general more often committed to the search as an end in itself. For these people, it is the quest that is important rather than what lies at the end of the road.

An even wider and more diffuse group than either the core believer or the spiritual seeker consists of those who are looking for themselves. For these people, authenticity is central. While they experience the alternative expressions of human potential, their main concern is to be themselves, to be whoever they authentically are. In other words, the pursuit of the experiential is considered to be the most authentic activity – one which has perhaps developed from American spiritual teacher Ram Dass' injunction to 'be here now'. These 'expressionists' usually themselves coalesce from the largest New Age 'group' – those that can be designated simply as 'clients'. This majority comprises the casual consumer – the person who may try some yoga, take a workshop in visualization, consult a homeopath, train in *neuro-linguistic programming, attend a lecture on spiritual ecology or enrol for a sexual alchemy retreat. These people are the least committed to New Age per se but usually have a specific problem or concern that they endeavour to address – whether it be a desire for greater professional confidence, to save a failing relationship, to eliminate debt or to deal with an ailment. While most New Age clients remain more peripheral within the full New Age arena, some develop into self-searching expressionists. From these last, the spiritual seeker may emerge, and some of these 'questers' may come to affirm belief fully in the imminence of an Age of Aquarius of radical evolution. Consequently, while New Age displays a vast range of 'horizontal' expression, it also comprises a 'vertical' continuum from casual association to deep commitment.

Orientations of the New Age

Finally, from an analytical perspective, New Age may be broken down into three distinguishable, though often overlapping, orientations: occult, spiritual and social. Occult or esoteric New Agers are those who accept the supernatural as a real, intervening force in human and terrestrial affairs (e.g. Benjamin Crème [see the *Share International Foundation], Shirley MacLaine, José Arguëlles). In this orientation there is often an expectation of violent, even apocalyptic, earth changes (earthquakes, storms, famine, pole shift, plagues) and these will constitute the transition into the new era (as predicted by Ruth Montgomery, Edgar Cayce, Elizabeth Clare Prophet [see the *Church Universal and Triumphant] and others). There is general acceptance of an external or divine intervention as the instigator if not designer of collective consciousness. By contrast, and unlike the media-promoted occult side of New Age, with its associations of spirit guides, channelling, crystal meditation and appropriation of symbols from different cultures, the spiritual and social dimensions of New Age place their emphasis on human effort rather than supernatural intervention. The former stresses spiritual development of the individual – whether through meditation, yogic practice, Shamanism, personal discipline, human potential and/or psycho-physical therapy (e.g. the *Osho movement, the *Meher Baba movement, spiritual realization teacher Guru Maharaji, popular New Age writer Terry Cole-Whittaker, self-help author Shakti Gawain and *A Course in Miracles). The rationale is based on the belief that, as individuals develop and transform, so, too, will global society and the human biosphere. Personal enlightenment in enough numbers will bring about collective enlightenment, that is, a new age. The social dimension of New Age, on the other hand, is epitomized in Marilyn Ferguson's Aquarian Conspiracy (1980). Here the emphasis is on social service and pragmatic work in the areas of educational, institutional, environmental and remedial change (e.g. Ram Dass, Ma Jaya Bhagavati, Jean Houston). The concern is neither with the self nor with transcendental or magical assistance but with concrete work that brings about empirical transformation. The social-service wing of New Age preoccupies itself with charity work and both humanitarian and ecological reform.

But while these three orientations may be distinguished analytically, in actuality most New Age practices are a blend of at least two of these, if not all three. Nevertheless, the many critics of New Age accuse it of being shallow, self-indulgent, escapist and superstitious – offering little more than a potpourri equivalent of snake-oil cures. New Age is described as cheaply false, spiritually kitsch, a mumbo-jumbo mash that is pastel-coloured, lavender-scented and simply a faddish attempt to make money from the gullible. But despite receiving attack for narcissism and cultural theft, New Age is an attempt to use the currently popular to explore, test and digest each religion's symbols, images, objects and 'spiritual truths'. While to date much of this pursuit can accurately be labelled uncritical and insensitive, New Age's insistence on the undemanding and pleasant is largely a reflection of present-day consumer society. The critic accuses New Age of adopting the position that 'anything goes', but the reality of New Age experimentation is that everything is tried and sampled. There are no restrictions. This is the way it seeks to uncover meaning and value within a religious framework that applies as much to the individual as it might also to various collectivities, communities, society or the planet.

Rosicrucianism
Robert A. Gilbert

Over the course of some 400 years the popular view of the doctrines and practices set out in the Rosicrucian manifestos of the early 17th century – the *Fama* (1614), *Confessio Fraternitatis* and *Chymische Hochzeit Christiani Rosencreutz* (*Chemical Wedding*) – has changed radically. At the time of publication the manifestos were perceived, correctly, as allegories containing a call to a new Reformation, but their sectarian nature (they are markedly anti-Catholic) and claims about a mysterious religious order privy to the secrets of nature, ensured that continuing controversy would surround them.

The manifestos were the work of a group of Lutheran 'spiritual reformers', but only one of them, Johann Valentin Andreae, the author of the *Chymische Hochzeit*, can be identified with certainty. Their principal aim was to encourage the expansion of a reinvigorated Protestantism, but they also

Image of the man in the moon, from a 17th-century Venetian alchemical manuscript.

sought to promote the transformation and spiritual renewal of man. Each of the three texts approaches its tasks in a different manner, but utilizes the common thread of the mythical Christian Rosencreutz. His life story is told in the *Fama*; the aims and doctrines of his followers are presented in polemic fashion in the *Confessio*; and he is the narrator of the humorous alchemical allegory, the *Chymische Hochzeit*.

In the *Fama*, Christian Rosencreutz is presented as a young pilgrim who travels to the Holy Land to receive instruction from wise men in Arabia, Egypt and Morocco before returning to his native Germany. He then founds a select religious community dedicated to philosophical speculation and healing the sick. After his death, in 1484, he is buried in a seven-sided vault that is opened after 120 years, when his uncorrupted body is found within an altar covered, as is the whole of the vault, with symbolic designs and inscriptions. Their essence is subsumed in the final inscription, which reads: 'We are born of God, we die in Jesus, we live again through the Holy Spirit.' Both the *Fama* and the *Confessio* also emphasize the need for a true understanding of the Bible and the peril of

pursuing material alchemy – as opposed to spiritual alchemy, which is concerned with human regeneration and is the central theme of the *Chymische Hochzeit*.

The essential Christian content of the manifestos is beyond dispute – the *Fama* can justly be seen as an allegory of the life of Christ, and the putative Rosicrucian Fraternity as a Protestant alternative to the Jesuits – but by the early 18th century the Rosicrucians had become synonymous with unorthodox spirituality and the pursuit of physical alchemy. Throughout the following centuries, a variety of 'Rosicrucian' orders and societies have been founded, some of which still survive. All of them accept, in some sense, the historical reality of a fraternity that never existed, but they are Rosicrucian in name only: their members perceive themselves not as reformers, but as alchemists, kabbalists (see *Kabbalism), esoteric Freemasons (see *Freemasonry) or advanced occultists.

Among the most prominent of such bodies active today are the Ancient and Mystical Order Rosae Crucis (AMORC), an eclectic body offering the wisdom of Atlantis, Egypt and Tibet; the Rosicrucian Fellowship, deriving from followers of Rudolf Steiner and principally concerned with *astrology; and the Lectorium Rosicrucianum, which is essentially neo-gnostic in character. If they have characteristics in common, they are an overt elitism and a rejection of orthodox Christianity. None of them can be considered as representative in any way of the Rosicrucianism of the authors of the manifestos.

Grail Spirituality
Seán O'Callaghan

The largely medieval symbol of the Grail has been imported into modern popular consciousness in recent times by the publication of a range of books dealing with supposed esoteric mysteries. Indeed, the theme of the Grail is also to be found in fantasy historic adventure films, such as *Indiana Jones and the Last Crusade*. This recent resurgence of interest in the Grail as a symbol of mystery and spiritual searching is the popular manifestation of a much deeper appreciation of the Grail in esoteric and occult circles, which has been particularly strong since the 18th-century Romantic revival sparked a renewed interest in Templarism and related areas.

A greater awareness of the Knights Templars – a military order founded in 1118 ostensibly to protect pilgrims on the way to Jerusalem, and which was controversially suppressed for heresy in 1307 – and the belief that they guarded a great secret, has led to many organizations claiming lineage back to that order, and incorporating Grail mythology into their own belief systems. Members of many esoteric and occult groups, particularly *neo-Templar orders, regard the Grail as being, among other things, the archetype of the symbolic object in which each individual can encapsulate the goal of his or her personal spiritual quest. The Grail itself is understood on many different levels. The most influential recent interpretation to excite public interest was published by Baigent, Leigh and Lincoln in the book *Holy Blood, Holy Grail* (1982). The central premise of the book is that the Grail should be understood as a 'sacred bloodline', which perpetuates the lineage of Jesus and Mary Magdalene. However, perhaps the most popular image of the Grail is based on ancient legends in which it is the cup that held the blood of Christ.

These are not the only interpretations of the Grail. Indeed, when the Grail made its first appearance in European literature between 1180 and 1190, in Chrétien de Troyes' unfinished story, *Le Conte del Graal*, it was presented as a receptacle of sorts with no religious connotations. Chrétien's story caused a sensation and many attempts were made to finish the tale, leading to further developments with Christian and Celtic elements attached to them. One version, *Perlesvaus*, written around 1200, introduced Templar symbolism into the legend. However, perhaps the most influential of the versions was Wolfram von Eschenbach's *Parzival*, written around 1220. Von Eschenbach's version clearly links the Grail with the Knights Templars, whose task it was to guard the 'Grail castle'. The Grail itself is understood by Von Eschenbach to be a powerful stone.

In the modern period, the Grail has been appropriated by many esoteric belief systems, both as a symbol and also as an object of veneration. Many ascribe an alchemical power to the Grail, believing that it is through the quest for the Grail that spiritual transformation can occur. The Grail quest, then, is an allegory for the spiritual journey undertaken by an individual who is seeking both the truth and a way of spiritual development.

While there is no single Grail movement per se, the idea of 'the Grail' is a common element, holding different degrees of significance for a variety of groups. Although it is particularly important for neo-Templar organizations, its influence is widespread.

Freemasonry
Robert A. Gilbert

Because there is no universally accepted theory of its origins, and because its nature and purpose have been given such widely divergent interpretations, a concise, adequate definition of Freemasonry remains elusive. What is, perhaps, the most effective attempt at a definition is that given by the United Grand Lodge of England (UGLE), the controlling body of English Freemasonry:

[Freemasonry is] one of the world's oldest secular fraternal societies... a society of men concerned with spiritual values. Its members are taught its precepts by a series of ritual dramas, which follow ancient forms and use stonemasons' customs and tools as allegorical guides. The essential qualification for admission and continuing membership is belief in a Supreme Being. Membership is open to men of any race or religion who can fulfil this essential qualification and are of good repute.

Even this statement must be expanded. Although its members must believe in God, Freemasonry is not a religion, nor a substitute for religion. The masonic precepts are simply those of public and private morality, based on the principles of brotherly love, relief (in the sense of charity) and truth. It is also necessary to emphasize that Freemasonry does not engage in political, economic or legal coercion. The UGLE is restricted to men, but there are organizations for women freemasons and others that admit both male and female members. These are not recognized as 'regular' by UGLE or any other Grand Lodge, but there is no hostility towards them.

Having defined the nature of the institution, other questions about Freemasonry remain: when and how did it originate, how did it develop, how is it structured and what is the nature of masonic ceremonies? In other words, what do Freemasons do?

The traditional view of the origin of Freemasonry is that it descended in a direct line from a presumed governing body of operative stonemasons. There is, however, no firm evidence to support this view. In England, no organization of operative or working masons survived the Reformation, and there are only a few instances of non-working masons being admitted to masonic lodges during the 17th century – probably with the aim of creating meeting places for those who sought to promote religious and political tolerance in an intolerant age. Honorary members were also admitted to operative masonic lodges in Scotland, but there is no evidence that such lodges employed ceremonies of initiation or engaged in philosophical discussion.

Truly speculative Masonry can be certainly dated only to 1717, when four lodges in London united to form a Grand Lodge as a governing body of English Freemasonry. The number of lodges under the premier Grand Lodge increased rapidly, and by 1723 their rules and regulations had been codified in the first publication of the *Constitutions*.

By the 1730s, Freemasonry had been established in most European countries, North America, the West Indies and India, but its membership was neither numerically nor politically significant. Its social composition, however, was subject to considerable variation. In England, Freemasons were mostly tradesmen and members of the professions and the landed gentry, with a smattering of the nobility and, from the 1740s, an increasing number of artisans. Until the later 18th century the composition of European Freemasonry was quite different, being drawn largely from the nobility with a smaller number of professional men. As a consequence, the ethos of continental Freemasonry was quite distinct from that of the English-speaking world: European masons strove to emulate the old chivalric orders and to introduce esotericism into their lodges – matters quite alien to the basic principles.

The first setback to Freemasonry came in 1738 when Pope Clement XII, alarmed at its perceived universalist nature, condemned it in *In Eminenti*. Except in fervently Catholic countries this was observed more in the breach and Freemasonry continued to expand despite further papal edicts. But, as it grew, so the divisions increased. Not only were increasing numbers of Grand Lodges established, each claiming jurisdiction over lodges in its territory, but newly invented forms of Masonry required new governing bodies, and, by the end of the Napoleonic era, some 2,000 different masonic degrees, rites and orders had been created, mostly short-lived and many existing only on paper. Some of them, however, survived and prospered.

English Freemasonry suffered a schism in the 1750s with the setting up of a rival Grand Lodge in London, and the breach was not healed until 1813 and the establishment of a United Grand Lodge. Subsequently, English Freemasonry became an eminently respectable pillar of the establishment, enjoying royal favour with a succession of royal Grand Masters. The progress of Freemasonry in other parts of the world has been more chequered. Wars, political upheavals and oppressive regimes have frequently led to its temporary or permanent disappearance in many countries, and even in democratic nations it has been made the scapegoat for perceived evils in society. An

The Annual General Meeting of English Freemasons in 1992. Members enjoy the camaraderie and ceremonial of Freemasonry.

anti-masonic movement in the United States
in the 1820s – based on false allegations of
masonic murder – led to a 30-year decline in
membership; Freemasonry was blamed for
Germany's defeat in the First World War; and
both the Roman Catholic Church and some
Protestant denominations have condemned
Freemasonry as anti-Christian. Most of these
attacks have centred on a misunderstanding
of masonic ceremonial – especially that of the
so-called 'Additional Degrees'.

The three basic degrees of Freemasonry –
Entered Apprentice, Fellowcraft and Master
Mason – involve a linked series of initiatory

ceremonies loosely based on the legendary
building of King Solomon's Temple. These
'Craft' degrees constitute the essence of
Freemasonry and in the course of working them
the basic moral precepts are conveyed to the
new Freemason. There is no esoteric content.

There are, in addition, many other degrees,
often with impressive titles and colourful
ceremonies, the purpose of which is to
increase or deepen understanding of the
precepts of the Craft degrees. In Britain, the
majority of Freemasons do not enter these
degrees, but they are extremely popular in the
United States, where they are incorporated
into the structure of the York Rite and the
Ancient and Accepted Scottish Rite.

Despite the attacks and misunderstanding,
and with the problems of disengagement
faced by all fraternal bodies, Freemasonry has
managed to survive, drawing in men who
enjoy both its camaraderie and its ceremonies,
while supporting its moral stance. Current
masonic membership, worldwide, is
approaching 3 million, of whom some
2 million are in the United States and
450,000 in the British Isles.

Neo-Templar Orders
Seán O'Callaghan

The neo-Templar orders are chivalric orders,
which either claim to have revived the
spiritual legacy of the medieval Knights
Templars, or have recreated and adapted that
legacy. The original Knights Templars were
soldiers of a military monastic order founded
in 1118 by Hugh de Payens and Geoffrey de
Saint-Omer, the aim of which was the
protection of pilgrims travelling from Europe
to Jerusalem. They thus gained the support
of the famous Cistercian abbot, Bernard of
Clairvaux, as well as the pope and the reputed
king of Jerusalem. However, over the years the
Knights Templars accumulated great wealth
and power and also, as a result, many enemies.

A *Palm Sunday procession of the Knights Templar in Jerusalem. The knights' robes are decorated with the Jerusalem Cross.*

Pope Clement V and King Philip IV of France eventually suppressed them in 1307. They were formally disbanded as an order in 1312.

In the 19th century, Templar-type movements experienced a revival, not least because of the rising interest in Romanticism. Various groups and individuals claimed to have discovered an unbroken lineage of Templar Grand Masters, a lineage that had continued in secret since the death of the last Grand Master, Jacques de Molay, in 1314. The principal figure in this early revival of Templarism was Bernard-Raymond Fabré-Palaprat (1773–1838) who reconstituted the order, claiming that he himself was a Grand Master. In more recent times, the French esotericist, Jacques Breyer (1922–96), following a mystical experience at the chateau of Arginy in France on 12 June 1952 – usually referred to as the 'Arginy Renaissance' – was instrumental in the foundation of the Sovereign Order of the Solar Temple (OSTS)

on the instigation, he claimed, of certain 'Masters of the Temple', whom he considered to be the spirits of elite Knights Templars. Breyer was a major figure in contemporary neo-Templarism and exercised much influence over the various groupings that emerged around that time and subsequently. Generally regarded as a spiritual mentor, he moved in the same circles as Julien Origas (1920–83), the founder of the Renewed Order of the Temple (ORT) and Jo Di Mambro (1924–94), a major figure within the *Order of the Solar Temple (OTS). Attempts were made in 1981 to merge the OSTS and the ORT, but, following the death of Origas in 1983, the ORT descended into schism and one faction, led by Luc Jouret (1947–94), split off to eventually form the OTS. The OTS gained considerable notoriety in October 1994 when it was discovered that 53 people had committed suicide (or possibly been killed) in Switzerland and Quebec. Similar events took place in France in December 1995 and again in Quebec in March 1997.

This idea of the secret continuation of the Knights Templars is a very prevalent one in the historiography of current neo-Templar organizations. Moreover, the symbolism and mythologies of neo-Templarism are important in that they have influenced and have in turn been influenced by significant esoteric movements such as *Freemasonry and *Rosicrucianism.

Neo-Templar groups are far from homogenous in their beliefs and practices and there is a very wide degree of variation in their different spiritualities. Many of the neo-Templar orders exist to promote extreme and arcane magical-esoteric agendas; some, but not all, of these being strongly linked with a belief in extraterrestrial beings and 'Ascended Masters'. These groups generally exercise secrecy in their operations and require initiation into the 'mysteries' of Templarism by means of ritual. Other groupings are no more than social clubs, which exist primarily for 'romantic' and ceremonial reasons, enabling members to dress up in Templar robes and attend social functions, while subscribing to medieval views of chivalry. Some groups exist as a means to grant titles and privileges in return for financial outlay on the part of members, who then benefit in terms of status from the use of such titles. There are also many very reputable orders, which subscribe to an overtly Christian outlook and seek to emulate what they see as the Christ-like qualities of the original Templars, engaging in charitable works and promoting Christian and chivalric values. Many of these would not view themselves as neo-Templar, being nervous of an identification with the more fringe and cultic esoteric groups, but would consider themselves to be 'revived' orders within wider Templarism.

Spiritualism
Nigel Scotland

Spiritualism includes a variety of differing networks and groups, some of which hold some specifically Christian beliefs and others of which are almost totally devoid of any religious dogma at all. They all, however, share one central concept – communication with the spirit realm through gifted or psychic individuals. Spiritualists always speak of the 'departed' rather than the 'dead'. Worldwide, Spiritualism is a predominantly secular phenomenon.

Early Spiritualism would very largely be understood today as 'physical mediumship' in which the 'spirit' operates on a physical level, perhaps lifting or turning tables, levitating objects or creating audible rappings. It also includes manifestations of ectoplasm, which is thought to be a viscous substance that sometimes appears to exude from the body during a sitting. Physical mediumship is associated with 'trance mediumship', where the medium passes into an unconscious state and is then 'possessed' by a spirit who communicates with the 'sitters' or people attending the seance.

The later 19th century witnessed the emergence of mediumship in which the medium remains in a state of full awareness and either sees in a parapsychological way (is clairvoyant) or hears (is clairaudient) and then passes on the information to the sitters. The mediumship practised in most spiritualist churches is almost exclusively clairvoyant.

The origins of Spiritualism stretch back into the ancient world of the Middle East. In more recent times, Emanuel Swedenborg (1688–1772), who had a remarkable gift of clairvoyance, sowed the seeds of spiritualist thought (see the *New Church). In the following century, two sisters, Katie and Margaret Fox, were the first people on record to have reputedly held a conversation with a spirit. This took place on 31 March 1848 at Hydesville in New York State. The resulting publicity stirred hundreds, perhaps thousands, of ordinary people to investigate the possibility of communicating with the dead. In the United States, Spiritualism is fostered by the National Spiritualist Association of Churches (NSAC), an undogmatic organization, which was founded in 1893 with its present headquarters at Lily Dale, New York.

Spiritualism took root in England through individuals, such as the socialist entrepreneur Robert Owen (1771–1858), and the first spiritualist church was established in England at Keighley in Yorkshire in 1853. In the 20th century, two main umbrella organizations emerged: the Spiritualist National Union (SNU), constituted in 1902, and the Greater World Christian Spiritualist League, formed in May 1931. This latter group, which subsequently changed its name to the Greater World Christian Spiritualist Association, emerged from the secularist SNU, partly through the influence of Sir Arthur Conan Doyle. 'The Greater World Belief and Pledge' invites members to 'accept the leadership of Jesus Christ' and makes reference to his 'redemptive power', but is nevertheless a long way removed from apostolic, creedal Christianity.

Most Christian spiritualist churches hold several services a week. Divine worship on a Sunday normally includes clairvoyance and sometimes a short service of healing follows. Some Christian spiritualist churches also hold services of Holy Communion, which have much the same appearance as those in the denominational churches. The Spiritualist National Union, which has its registered office at Stansted Hall in Essex, is an altogether larger organization, with some 382 affiliated churches and a total membership in 1996 of 20,267.

All spiritualists, whether they adhere to a semblance of Christian belief or not, are united in the conviction that after death the spirit is set free from the individual's body. It is then free to roam and can either choose to go on to a higher spiritual level, or reincarnate or become a spirit guide to the living. The major business of Spiritualism is about helping to put congregational members in touch with spirit guides who will then be of assistance to them in life.

The Theosophical Society
Kevin Tingay

The Theosophical Society was founded in 1875 in New York by Helena Petrovna Blavatsky (1831–91), a Russian, and Henry Steel Olcott (1832–1907), an American. The founders soon moved to India where the headquarters of the movement was established at Adyar, now a suburb of Chennai (Madras). The objects of the society were: to form a nucleus of the Universal Brotherhood of Humanity without distinction of race, creed, sex, caste or colour; to encourage the study of comparative religion, philosophy and science; and to investigate unexplained laws of nature and the powers latent in man.

Behind these objects lay Blavatsky's belief that in journeys through Asia she had discovered the existence of a secret wisdom tradition, which was the source and origin of religion. She averred that behind the beliefs and practices of the great world faiths there was an esoteric or hidden body of doctrine. This had been preserved through the ages by a succession of adepts or 'Masters of the Wisdom'. Two of those masters had, she claimed, selected her to present these teachings to the Western world, where they had long been suppressed by the Christian church, and to the adherents of the faiths of Asia, who had forgotten them. Blavatsky published two major works – *Isis Unveiled* (1877) and *The Secret Doctrine* (1888) – as well as a number of more accessible books (c.g. *The Key to Theosophy* and *The Voice of the Silence*) and a very great number of contributions to theosophical and other periodicals. Her writings have been kept in print until the present time and have enjoyed a sale far beyond the membership of the theosophical movement.

Though Blavatsky had been the prime impulse behind the establishment of the society, the president from the start had been Olcott, whose administrative gifts complemented the fiery and eccentric Blavatsky. Her teachings were accompanied by psychic manifestations, which were alleged to be fraudulent by an investigator from the Society for Psychical Research. Theosophists have always challenged this and, on reinvestigation, the Society for Psychical Research has acknowledged that the original report was flawed.

Fraud or not, Blavatsky attracted a great deal of attention both in India and in the drawing rooms of late 19th-century Europe. Among converts to the movement was the charismatic Annie Besant (1847–1933). The estranged wife of an Anglican clergyman, Besant had espoused secularism, socialism, trade unionism and the rights of women. She joined the Theosophical Society after reading *The Secret Doctrine* and rapidly took over the intellectual leadership of the movement after Blavatsky's death. Upon Olcott's death in 1907, Besant was elected president and threw her remarkable energies into the development of the society. Its worldwide membership rose from 15,000 when she took office to a peak of over 40,000 in 1929. She encouraged the members of the society to social action in such fields as women's suffrage, vegetarianism, alternative medicine, progressive education and the Garden City movement. She became an active supporter of independence for India, where she made her home. The dominance of her personality, and that of her associate C.W. Leadbeater, led to disputes over the interpretation of theosophy and to the formation of other groups. The Theosophical Society (Point Loma, later Pasadena) and the United Lodge of Theosophists claimed to preserve the original teachings of Blavatsky. Alice Bailey (see the

Helena Petrovna Blavatsky, c. 1880.

*Arcane School) claimed further communications from a Master of the Wisdom. Rudolf Steiner, who led the Theosophical Society in Germany, seceded in 1912 and founded the Anthroposophical Society (see the *Anthroposophical Movement). His actions were prompted in part by Besant's proclamation of the figure of the young Krishnamurti (see *Krishnamurti and the Krishnamurti Foundation) as a potential world spiritual teacher. In 1929, Krishnamurti left the theosophical movement and the membership declined. Since 1945, the society's membership has continued to drop in the Western world but has continued to be of some significance in India, where it might be seen as a universalist reform movement within Hinduism.

The doctrines of theosophy teach a scheme of spiritual evolution that underlies physical evolution. Human beings are seen as the embodiments of sparks of the Divine, which journey back to their origin through a series of incarnations. The law of karma is the mechanism that controls the circumstances of each successive life. Among those who reach a high stage of moral and spiritual development are those masters who attempt to assist their 'younger brethren' through the work of the Theosophical Society and other movements. Theosophists are enjoined to follow a disciplined life of meditation, with vegetarianism and abstention from alcohol and drugs being held up as ideals. The society stresses, however, that membership is open to all who can subscribe to the three objects noted above, and that no doctrines or beliefs are binding upon members.

The Theosophical Society had a profound

influence on the popularization of both esoteric thought and the basic teachings of Hinduism and Buddhism in the Western world. Much of the thought and practice of the contemporary New Age can be traced back to its activities in the period from 1875 to 1925. Some of its members were active in social reform movements of various kinds, and its teachings had an influence on the development of abstract art in Europe. The writings of Blavatsky, and to a lesser extent Besant, Leadbeater and others, continue to be used as source material by contemporary esoteric writers. A hundred years ago, theosophical books and periodicals included articles on yoga, meditation, *astrology, chakras, the human aura, crystals, past lives, spiritual healing, angels and fairies, symbolism, folklore, the mystery religions of antiquity, and the esoteric interpretation of the scriptures of the world religions.

The Theosophical Society has suffered the fate of many pioneering movements in that its aims and ideals have been taken up by others in succeeding generations, leaving the parent body behind.

The Hermetic Order of the Golden Dawn
Robert A. Gilbert

The Hermetic Order of the Golden Dawn is the paradigm of an esoteric order, conforming precisely to the definition given by Dion Fortune (see the *Society of the Inner Light):

[a fraternity] wherein a secret wisdom, unknown to the generality of mankind might be learned, and to which admission was obtained by means of an initiation in which tests and ritual played their part.

As such, the order encapsulates the essence of Western esotericism in both its theoretical and practical aspects.

The order was founded in 1888 by a London coroner, William Wynn Westcott (1848–1925), who based its administration and its graded system of initiatic ceremonies on that of a masonic Rosicrucian body, the Societas Rosicruciana in Anglia, which had been established in 1867 and of which he was secretary-general. Westcott was inspired by a series of enciphered ritual texts that he had found among the papers of their author, a fellow masonic Rosicrucian, Kenneth Mackenzie (1833–86). These 'cipher manuscripts', which were easily translated, gave only the outlines of the ceremonies and Westcott developed them into workable form with the aid of Dr W.R. Woodman, the head of the Societas Rosicruciana in Anglia, and Samuel Liddell Mathers (1854–1918), another prominent member of the society.

Legitimacy was given to the order with the aid of a spurious history, provided by Westcott, and by a series of forged letters from a fictitious German adept, 'Anna Sprengel', purporting to authorize Westcott to establish temples of the Golden Dawn in England. The first of these, named Isis-Urania, was set up in London in March 1888, followed rapidly by Osiris, at the seaside resort of Weston-Super-Mare, and Horus, at Bradford in Yorkshire.

Candidates for admission were drawn from a variety of esoteric bodies, for the Golden Dawn was not restricted to Freemasons and admitted both sexes. Within a year, 51 men and 9 women had entered the order, all of them willing to undergo the discipline of a symbolic ceremonial progress through the stages of the kabbalistic Tree of Life (see *Kabbalism), to take on a motto as an official name in the order, and to accept the authority of the three chiefs (Westcott, Mathers and Woodman). As the Golden Dawn grew, further temples were established – Amen Ra in Edinburgh and Ahathoor in Paris – and the proportion of female members increased. By the end of 1897, 331 men and women (in a ratio of roughly three to two) – including prominent figures such as W.B. Yeats, William Crookes and Constance Wilde – had been initiated as Neophytes, but of these some 25 per cent did not remain as members.

Those who did stay progressed from the grade of Neophyte through those of Zelator, Theoricus, Practicus and Philosophus, which corresponded to the lower four *sefiroth*, or stages, of the kabbalistic Tree of Life. Beyond this lay the Second, or Inner Order: the *Rosae Rubeae et Aureae Crucis*, which was Rosicrucian in its ethos and consisted of three further grades – Adeptus Minor, Adeptus Major and Adeptus Exemptus – corresponding to the next three *sefiroth*. The final three *sefiroth* were considered to be unattainable by human beings still in the flesh.

The ceremonies associated with each grade were highly original and highly effective. They followed the pattern of all initiatory ceremonies, in that they were designed to produce a powerful psychospiritual impact on the candidate, and by an inventive use of language and an eclectic mix of esoteric and religious symbols, they successfully inculcated the essentials of Western esotericism. Members were also required to follow prescribed courses of study and to learn certain basic ceremonial techniques. Those who progressed to the Second Order, some 40 per cent of the total, were required to gain a much deeper knowledge of esotericism and to become proficient in the theory and practice of magic. At this level there was a very demanding curriculum and only a small number advanced beyond the Grade of Adeptus Minor, but all members of the Second Order tended to be of independent mind, and this inevitably led to conflicts in such a rigidly hierarchical body as the Golden Dawn.

Although Westcott was the creator of the Golden Dawn, Mathers became the dominant figure in the order after Woodman's death in 1891. The members were in some awe of him – he had devised the rituals for the Second Order and set up a 'Vault of the Adepts', within which the ceremonial and magical work took place – but they resented his dictatorial manner. In the early years the need for discipline had been recognized and generally accepted, but as Mathers' behaviour became increasingly autocratic, so signs of discontent appeared within the order.

They first surfaced in 1896, in reaction to his cavalier treatment of Annie Horniman, one of the most active members of the Golden Dawn, better known for her work in the theatre, whom he unjustly expelled from the order when she withdrew the financial support she had been providing for Mathers and his wife, Mina Bergson. Four years later, he told another prominent member (the actress Florence Farr) that the letters giving authority to establish the order had been forged by Westcott, but Mathers refused to offer proof of this claim and, when he demanded unquestioning obedience from the members, open rebellion broke out.

After a farcical episode in which Aleister Crowley, who was briefly a member from 1898 to 1900, attempted, unsuccessfully, to seize control of the Vault of the Adepts on Mathers' behalf, the members in London expelled Mathers and set up a new hierarchy. Further problems arose between those who supported W.B. Yeats and wished to maintain a strict curriculum with examinations, and those around Florence Farr, who favoured the development of unofficial magical ceremonies. No compromise was reached and in 1903 the old Golden Dawn disintegrated.

The Isis-Urania Temple continued under A.E. Waite, the writer on esoteric subjects, who took it in a wholly mystical direction, eventually transforming it into a new body, the Fellowship of the Rosy Cross. Mathers continued to work his tiny remnant of the order in the Ahathoor Temple in Paris until his death in 1918, after which it was continued for a further ten years by his widow, while the magical faction of the Golden Dawn reformed themselves as the Stella Matutina. Against the odds, the Stella Matutina survived. It was ruled by Dr R.W. Felkin, who established a temple in New Zealand while maintaining others at London and Bristol. In 1933, the Bristol temple, Hermes, admitted a young American, Francis Israel Regardie (1907–85), and in so doing ensured the survival of the order.

Regardie came to believe that the rituals and teachings of the Golden Dawn should be made available to all, and between 1937 and 1940 he published the bulk of them. His texts have been frequently reprinted since 1969 and their wide distribution has resulted in the creation of a number of new Golden Dawn temples, mostly in the United States. Some of these still survive, and although they are descendants of the original order in name only, they have perpetuated its rituals and ensured the wide dissemination of many aspects of Western esotericism.

Ordo Templi Orientis (OTO)
Seán O'Callaghan

The Ordo Templi Orientis (Order of the Temple of the Orient), more commonly known simply as OTO, is a magical order, and is, perhaps, the largest and most influential of the occult orders, with lodges in Britain, the United States, Europe and Australasia. Strongly influenced at its inception by the German occult revival, the order is generally claimed to have been founded in Germany between 1902 and 1904 by Karl Kellner (1851–1905), a wealthy Austrian industrialist. Kellner had originally intended to found OTO in the middle of the 1890s, but those he wanted to start it with were, at that time, involved in the unsuccessful attempt to set up another

occult order, the Order of the Illuminati.

The early development of OTO was shaped by the thought of Kellner and Theodore Reuss, both of whom were prominent in the German occult movement, Kellner being particularly significant within *Freemasonry. Later, the controversial magician Aleister Crowley (1875–1947) would become its most prolific and public exponent. Crowley came from a Plymouth Brethren family and became a source of great dissension within the fledgling OTO, emerging as a major figure within the order and taking over as Grand Master within the British jurisdiction. OTO drew on the traditions of Indian tantrism and certain historical Western secret societies, particularly the Knights Templars, from whom it claimed spiritual descent.

One of the most important elements

Aleister Crowley, who liked to be known as 'the great beast' and 'the wickedest man alive'. Certainly many who associated with him died tragically, including his wife and child.

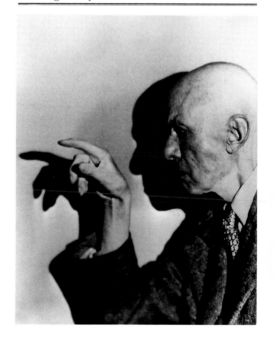

within OTO teaching is concerned with the power of sexual magic, that is the use of sex to orientate and empower magical practices. Sexual magic is regarded as the key that opens up all masonic and hermetic secrets. Crowley developed his own brand of 'magick', spelt with a 'k' to distinguish it from conjuring trickery, and arguably to denote a particular sexual focus. Thelemic magick, also a form of sex magick developed by Crowley, is particularly concerned with the specific role of the individual's 'will', his famous dictum being, '"Do what thou wilt" shall be the whole of the law.' Not surprisingly, therefore, OTO worship (the Gnostic mass) has a central female focus. Indeed, Christian Gnosticism as a whole is a central idea within OTO.

The Anthroposophical Movement
Kevin Tingay

The Anthroposophical movement describes a range of organizations and activities that follow the teachings of the Austrian philosopher Rudolf Steiner (1861–1925). A gifted and visionary child, Steiner went to study at the Institute of Technology in Vienna at the age of 18, but felt a deep sense of revulsion at the materialism inherent in his scientific and technical studies. In 1883 he found employment as an editor of the works of Goethe, and also worked as a tutor to a mentally disabled child. In 1919 he was invited to set up a school for the children of workers in the Waldorf-Astoria cigarette factory in Stuttgart.

In 1900 he was invited to lecture at the Berlin branch of the *Theosophical Society and soon was invited to lead that organization in Germany. His writings during this period reflect the topics that were of interest in theosophical circles and his published books included *Reincarnation*, *How Karma Works*, *Theosophy: An Introduction to the Supersensible*

Knowledge of the World and the Destination of Man, *Atlantis and Lemuria* and *Occult Science: An Outline*. He lectured energetically for the movement in the German-speaking parts of Europe not only on these topics but also on his esoteric interpretations of the Christian Gospels. This was in contrast to other theosophical speakers who, for the most part, concentrated on Asiatic texts.

In theory, the Theosophical Society allowed its members complete freedom of expression in their religious and philosophical views, but Steiner's growing insistence on the centrality of Christ in the cosmic scheme caused tensions between his followers and those of the wider movement. (His Christology, however, was unorthodox and never accepted by any of the mainstream Christian traditions. A number of Lutheran ministers were later instrumental in setting up the Christian Community, which gives expression to Steiner's specifically Christian theology.) In 1912, after disagreements with Annie Besant, the president of the Theosophical Society, he (with a large proportion of the German membership) withdrew from it and set up the Anthroposophical Society to propagate spiritual teachings based on his own insights rather than those of Helena Petrovna Blavatsky and other theosophical leaders. Steiner held that it was possible for human beings to have a direct perception of the spiritual realities that were the basis of the evolution of individual human consciousness, and the development of human society as expressed through economic, political or cultural activity.

Steiner's death in 1925 at the age of 64 meant that his direct perceptions were no longer available to the movement he founded, and none of his followers seemed to have claimed to continue them with similar authority. His influence has, however, continued. The Anthroposophical Society

*Austrian social philosopher and educationalist,
Rudolf Steiner, c. 1910.*

and the School of Spiritual Science (a group
following particular spiritual disciplines within
the society) have continued to propagate
his wider philosophy and scheme of spiritual
training. Steiner's pedagogical experience
had led him to produce a complex theory of
education for children. Waldorf Schools have
enjoyed a reputation of helping children with
disabilities over the years since Steiner's
death. The Camp Hill communities in
Britain, and related activities in other
countries, provide for the lifetime care of
people with learning difficulties. He also
inspired systems of bio-dynamic agriculture,
anthroposophical medicine, architecture and
economics. These continue to be practised
by a small but significant body of followers,
particularly in the German-speaking nations.
These effective practical expressions of
Steiner's philosophy have meant that Steiner

is regarded as a more significant figure than
others in the Western esoteric tradition.

Steiner wrote many books during his
lifetime, but much of his teaching was
delivered through a large number of lectures
in the period between 1912 and his death.
These have been subsequently published
in German and in translation, and many of
them are kept in print by anthroposophical
publishing houses.

The Society of the Inner Light
Kevin Tingay

The society came into being in 1922 as the
Fraternity of the Inner Light, being founded
in London by Dion Fortune (1891–1946).
Fortune was born Violet Mary Firth, but
generally used her pen name in all her public
work. The name Dion Fortune was taken
from her family motto, *Deo, non Fortuna*
(By God, not by chance). A member both of
the *Theosophical Society and the *Hermetic
Order of the Golden Dawn, she developed
her own interpretation of the Western
esoteric tradition. Her teachings were
expressed in her two major books *The
Mystical Kabbalah* and *The Cosmic Doctrine*.
She wrote a number of other books, including
novels on occult themes, which have
remained in print over many years. The
Society of the Inner Light facilitated both
Dion Fortune's teachings and their expression
through ritual magic. After her death in 1946,
the society worked quietly in its own way to
continue the tradition they had inherited.
From the 1960s onward, its work seems to
have been overtaken by other groups, which
claim to perpetuate the Golden Dawn
tradition but present a less retiring face to the
outside world. Membership has never totalled
more than a few hundred adherents, most of
whom were British.

Although they have changed over the
years, the teachings of its founder have

always been central to the beliefs and practices of the organization. Most of Fortune's teachings can be found in her 24 books (six of which are occult novels). While the society advertises itself as 'a registered charity based on the Christian religion', it also belongs within the Western esoteric tradition. For example, taken from theosophy, there is an emphasis on secret spiritual masters, including Jesus and Comte de Saint Germain, both of whom Fortune claims to have met. There is also an emphasis on the kabbalah (see *Kabbalism) and Celtic mythology.

A member of the society can follow three paths: the Mystic Path – the disciplined individual seeks to purge the mind of all that hinders progress towards the goal of union with God; the Path of the Green Ray – the individual seeks God in the natural world and in what can be known through the senses; the Hermetic Path – the advanced individual finds a mediating position between the other two paths, holding in balance the sensual and the spiritual.

Gurdjieff and Ouspensky Groups
Elizabeth Puttick

Georgi Ivanovitch Gurdjieff (c. 1866–1949) was one of the founding fathers of non-traditional spirituality in the West. His influence has been extensive, and his teachings have inspired and informed many new movements, both religious and secular. Much of this impact is due to his most famous follower, Pyotr Ouspensky (1878–1947), who systematized 'the Work' by writing several books and disseminating it as a teacher.

Gurdjieff was born in Russian Armenia and spent many years travelling and learning from 'mystery schools' in Tibet, Afghanistan, Egypt and India. However, it should be noted that we have only his own accounts of this period, which are clearly somewhat self-mythologizing. The sources of his philosophy remain largely unknown but include Sufi mystics. By the time he moved to Russia (St Petersburg and Moscow) he had a nucleus of students; one of the earliest was Ouspensky, who had previously been studying theosophy. In 1922, Ouspensky and Gurdjieff parted company acrimoniously, after the former was exposed to considerable difficulties and apparently futile tasks by his teacher.

Gurdjieff then moved to France, where he set up the now-defunct Institute for the Harmonious Development of Man (1922) at Fontainebleau on the estate of an old priory. Many of his pupils came here for instruction; some were famous and influential, including the architect Frank Lloyd Wright, the novelist Katherine Mansfield, the occultist Aleister Crowley, and other musical and literary figures from Europe and the United States. Later, Gurdjieff moved to Paris and continued teaching throughout the Second World War, supporting himself and a whole community of elderly people by wheeling and dealing on the black market.

The essence of Gurdjieff's philosophy (the Work) is the idea that man is asleep, and needs to wake up – hence the title of his Work: 'the war against sleep'. The key technique for achieving awakening is 'self-remembering': a process of close observation of inner states, especially negative personal traits, in order to attain higher states of consciousness and self-awareness. This was often accomplished through movement, including sacred dances, which were occasionally publicly performed to great acclaim. The Work was intentionally hard and demanding, and students typically note and accept how little progress has been made in relation to the amount of effort required. Gurdjieff's teaching style was highly idiosyncratic; for example, he would order students to perform tasks inappropriate to their social position, such as menial labour, under the supervision of someone with an abrasive personality. Alternatively, he might make vegetarians eat meat or teetotallers drunk, in order to 'wake them up'. He would 'hold court' at the evening meal and during these sessions he sometimes made devastating pronouncements about people – including Aleister Crowley, who had come to him for help with a drug habit.

Gurdjieff was heavily criticized in his day by the media, in similar vein to contemporary gurus. He often demanded free labour and money of his students, wielding seemingly hypnotic influence over them. It is also clear that he had sexual relations with some female followers. His public behaviour and statements could be outrageous. It is interesting to see that one or two contemporary, high-minded Gurdjieff groups include in their publicity material guidelines for avoiding 'false teachers', telling people to steer clear of gurus who do any or all of the above, which presumably means that they would not have approved of their founder. And yet, Gurdjieff rises above all of this, and is widely acclaimed as one of the greatest teachers of modern times.

The main systematizer of Gurdjieff's extensive and often inaccessible teaching was Ouspensky, whose books remain an important part of the canon. However, it was Jeanne de Salzmann, a music teacher who became one of Gurdjieff's closest students, who was most influential in spreading the teaching by setting up many branches of the Gurdjieff Foundation around the world. Other students wrote books describing their time with the teacher, which are invaluable sources. Contemporary Gurdjieff schools and groups generally claim direct lineage from the founder, even though they are now several generations distant. This is very important, as Gurdjieff always insisted that real psychospiritual progress was only possible by working with, and submitting to, a competent teacher in a group of like-minded students. Indian and other Asian religious traditions have for many centuries followed this rule, but it is one that the West has difficulties with, since one is expected to be self-reliant and responsible for one's own personal development, unless following an established religion.

Gurdjieff schools sometimes call themselves the 'Fourth Way', an alternative to the old paths of the monk (emotional), the fakir (physical) and the yogi (intellectual). The Fourth Way claims to integrate and exceed these, thus offering a comprehensive, multidimensional system for self-awareness. 'The Work' nowadays is less dependent on the spontaneous insights of the teacher, less physically demanding, more routinized, but still maintains the essential features of the original. Normally, great emphasis is placed

George Ivanovitch Gurdjieff, one of the founding fathers of non-traditional spirituality in the West, c. 1931.

on verification of what is taught, so that students can confirm for themselves the validity and reliability of the information. Faith, doctrine and belief have little or no part in the Fourth Way, and this may well be a part of its attraction in a sceptical age, whose boundaries are defined by the prevailing scientific method, which has itself rejected dogma.

Among the many movements that have been influenced directly or indirectly by the Gurdjieff–Ouspensky teachings are the *School of Economic Science and *Transcendental Meditation. The Indian guru Osho (formerly Bhagwan Shree Rajneesh; see the *Osho Movement) replicated elements of Gurdjieff's methods at his ashram in India, including the performance of 'pointless' tasks and the appointment of aggressive personalities as supervisors. Gurdjieff has also been influential on New Age divination systems, including the Enneagram, a complex personality typology developed by Oscar Ichazo but apparently first used by Gurdjieff and Ouspensky. Another interesting modern development is a system of self-development in the United States known as 'the Michael teachings', which is purportedly channelled from a discarnate entity known as 'Michael'. It is a highly complex and sophisticated system that has grown rapidly in recent years and contains many elements from Gurdjieff's work – plus a great deal more in the same vein that he did not cover.

The Arcane School
Kevin Tingay

The Arcane School exists to disseminate the teachings of Alice A. Bailey (1880–1949). Born Alice La Trobe-Bateman in England, Bailey was brought up in an evangelical Christian environment and worked in India as a welfare worker for British troops. After the breakdown of her first marriage she moved to the United States and became associated with the *Theosophical Society. That movement claimed to be inspired by hidden adepts or 'Masters of the Wisdom', some of whom lived in Tibet. Bailey's claim to have received communications from one of these adepts, who used the name Djwal Khul, led to her break with the theosophists. In 1923, she established her own group, the Arcane School, to propagate the teachings she received.

The esoteric teachings generally followed those promulgated by the founder of the Theosophical Society, Helena Petrovna Blavatsky. They centred on the development of the human spirit through reincarnation and the existence of an ancient but concealed wisdom tradition. Bailey attempted to avoid the development of a movement centred around her personality and laid stress on the practice of meditation, the study of the teachings, and on their practical application in the world though service. Her second husband, Foster Bailey, assisted in the management of the work. The teaching work of the group went on under the title of the Arcane School, while public service activities use the name 'World Goodwill'. The group is widespread in the Western world and membership is probably a few thousand people worldwide.

From the early 1920s to the end of her life, Bailey produced a steady stream of books dictated to her by Djwal Khul, including *Initiation Human and Solar*, *A Treatise on the Seven Rays*, *A Treatise on White Magic*, *A Treatise on Cosmic Fire* and *Discipleship in the New Age*. These books have remained in print to the present day through the publishing activities of the Lucis Trust, and have been translated into several European languages. They have been influential, along with other texts in the theosophical tradition, on the development of the New Age from the 1960s.

The Emissaries of Divine Light
Sarah Lewis

According to their own website, the Emissaries of Divine Light (EDL) is an international network of people whose primary purpose is to encourage the experience and expression of divine identity: 'We… believe that the world is transformed when people know and live in alignment with their innate divinity.'

Although his work had begun some years previously, the group was initiated in 1932 in the United States by Lloyd Meeker (1907–54), who wrote under the name Uranda. The first community was established at the Sunrise Ranch near Loveland, Colorado, in 1945 'as a way of demonstrating practical spirituality'. Today there are several small communities, mainly in the United States, Canada and Britain.

Emissaries believe that the psychological and emotional obstacles created by a materialistic world have led individuals to forget their inner divinity. It is the role of EDL to enable individuals to clarify and deepen their connection with the Source (the individual's sacred core) through vibrational alignment and healing.

The group supports and sponsors seminars and workshops that nurture spiritual awakening and expression. The 'Opening' is designed as an immersion experience introducing participants to the foundational principles of the art and science of living. The 'Quickening' is an individual journey, a sequence of carefully directed processes designed to connect individuals with the Source.

EDL offers correspondence courses, runs 'EmNet', which is a global electronic network of Emissaries, and publishes *The Emissaries International Monthly*. The group is attracting an increasing number of younger members, which is perhaps due to their concern with environmental issues.

The 'I AM' Religious Activity
Christopher Partridge

Founded in 1934 by Guy Ballard (1878–1939) and Edna Ballard (1886–1971), the 'I AM' Religious Activity has its roots in theosophy and is one of the most significant forerunners of New Age spirituality, particularly that of Elizabeth Clare Prophet (see the *Church Universal and Triumphant).

As with theosophical teaching and many of the groups that have their roots in theosophy, there is a core belief in the existence of 'Ascended Masters' (called 'Masters of the Wisdom' by theosophists). Originating in the writings of the co-founder of the *Theosophical Society, Helena Petrovna Blavatsky, the Ascended Masters are a hierarchy of supernatural beings. (Interestingly, along with a host of exotic-sounding figures such as Koot Hoomi/Kuthumi, El Morya and Comte de Saint Germain, the list of masters often includes Abraham, Moses, Solomon, Mary and Jesus.) The masters (sometimes also referred to as the Illuminati or the Great White Brotherhood), are enlightened beings who, it is claimed, having escaped the cycle of reincarnation, are benevolently seeking to guide humanity from their exalted position by communicating through specially sensitive individuals (e.g. Blavatsky, Ballard and now Elizabeth Clare Prophet). Guy Ballard, while on a walking holiday on Mount Shasta in California, claimed to have met the Ascended Master, Comte de Saint Germain. It is claimed that, after hundreds of years of searching for someone to impart the 'Great Laws of Life', he eventually found that person in Guy Ballard.

Following the setting up of the 'I AM' Religious Activity in 1934, the Ballards founded a publishing house (Saint Germain Press) in order to make their works on 'I AM' available. They also began training teachers to propagate their particular brand of theosophical spirituality. However, while the group quickly attracted interest, it

☞ *continued on page 332*

THE TAROT
John Drane

The tarot consists of 78 cards, 22 in the major arcana (trump cards) and the remainder divided between the four suits of wands, cups, swords and pentacles. The tarot was invented in Italy in the 14th century, to be used as ordinary playing cards, but by the 18th century it was being given esoteric meanings by Western European mystics, especially in France. They claimed it was of more ancient origin, going back to classical Babylon or Egypt and containing secret wisdom that would be accessible only to those with special understanding and insights.

This wisdom was associated with many different movements and ideas, including the legendary Egyptian *Book of Thoth* and the Jewish kabbalah (see *Kabbalism), while others claimed they contained the secret spirituality of the Romany people, handed on from one generation to another.

In post-revolutionary France, this was all part of a concerted effort by the aristocratic intelligentsia to maintain their privileged position. They claimed that, though their political and economic power base had vanished, they were still elite because of their access to these spiritual secrets. But the tarot was subsequently used more widely for fortune-telling and occult purposes. There are many different packs, the classic tarot being the Rider-Waite deck, compiled by English mystic Arthur Waite in about 1910. Most of its images depict Bible stories, with the cards organized around themes that have many similarities with the archetypes of Jungian psychology. This explains the development of the tarot as a therapeutic tool, which is probably its most common use today.

Tarot cards are largely associated today with therapy and fortune-telling.

equally speedily ran into a series of unfortunate problems. Firstly, although Guy Ballard's writings spoke about the power of disciplined, positive thought over death, he unexpectedly suffered a stroke and, in 1939, died. Secondly, some devotees of the group became disillusioned and critical of the wealth the Ballards had accumulated. Thirdly, the movement was challenged by members, who claimed that it was breaking the law by using the United States postal service to distribute material that fraudulently sought to obtain monies for a religion which was, in fact, 'a false religion'. Although these claims were challenged in the courts over a period of 12 years, it was a period during which the movement was denied use of the postal service. However, eventually the courts upheld the 'I AM' Religious Activity's claim to be 'a religion' and in 1957 the movement was granted tax-exempt status.

As to the teachings of the Ballards, the name 'I AM' refers to the name of God revealed in Exodus 3:14. However, in Ballard's thought, 'I AM' is not simply a name to be uttered by God, but it belongs just as much on the lips of every human being. There is a 'spark' of the Divine Flame (a 'Christ Self') within all of us and followers of the movement are encouraged to focus on this belief and affirm it as a reality. By 'affirming' or 'decreeing' something to be the case, an individual, through the power of 'positive thinking', is enabled to truly experience it. Indeed, it is possible, by means of such affirmations and decrees, to bring a state of affairs into being. The 'I AM' movement claimed to be able to release this power of positive thought in devoted individuals, but taught that, because it is powerful, it must always be used wisely, in love, and for good ends.

On the death of Edna Ballard in 1971, the leadership of 'I AM' passed to a board of directors.

The School of Economic Science
Christopher Partridge

Founded in Britain in 1937 by Andrew MacLaren (1883–1975), an Independent Labour Party member of Parliament, the School of Economic Science (SES) was originally a political organization that focused on the study of economics and philosophy. However, under the leadership of MacLaren's son, Leon (1910–94), a Labour politician, the focus of the group gradually shifted. While Leon continued to emphasize the importance of economics, particularly social justice and tax reform, he became increasingly convinced that economic problems could only be fundamentally changed if the nature of humanity was transformed.

Believing that philosophy held the key to this transformation and the course it should follow, his studies eventually led him to the teachings of Giorgi Ivanovitch Gurdjieff and his disciple, the Russian intellectual, Pyotr Ouspensky (see *Gurdjieff and Ouspensky Groups). The philosophy of these thinkers is still central to SES belief and practice. As with Gurdjieff's and Ouspensky's thought, there is a belief in an ancient tradition of knowledge communicated through a series of esoteric schools. This knowledge is nothing less than a formula that enables individuals to leave behind the suffering of the world and achieve immortality. Put simply, the process involves disciplining appetites and desires in order to find the inner self, which is understood to be part of 'the Absolute'.

A practice encouraged by the SES is the concentration of the mind on a particular task – a practice very similar to 'the Work' in Gurdjieffian teaching. For example, individuals might attempt to draw a perfect circle freehand, a task which clearly requires massive and disciplined concentration, a blocking out of the external world, and full control of one's body and senses.

Another shaping influence on the SES,

possibly the key influence, is Hindu philosophy. After meeting with Maharishi Mahesh Yogi (the founder of *Transcendental Meditation) in 1960, Leon MacLaren travelled to India where he met Shantananda Saraswati (often referred to as Shankaracharya). The thought of both of these men, particularly the latter, has been significant. Indeed, Leon MacLaren regularly sought guidance from Shankaracharya and, from 1965, travelled to India every two years to meet with him. Consequently, much SES thought is indebted to Vedantic Hinduism, particularly the famous tradition of Hindu philosophy known as Advaita Vedanta, which teaches a form of absolute monism. Meaning 'non-dual', it teaches that the human self (the *atman*) is identical with the Divine Absolute (*Brahman*); the individual self/*atman* of each person, is identical with the Absolute Self/*Paramatman*/*Brahman*. The teachings and practices of the SES, many of which are drawn from the ancient Hindu scriptures, the *Upanishads* (which members are encouraged to study), are aimed at leading individuals to an understanding of this 'truth' and to removing distorted understandings of reality.

Reflecting both Advaita Vedanta and Gurdjieff's thought, the SES encourages a disciplined life of meditation and carefully regulated activities. For example, it is important that devotees know when to sleep, rise, fast, eat, work and rest. The life of the wise SES student is 'measured'. Students rise early, meditate daily (often for fairly lengthy periods), undertake periods of manual labour (some of which has little obvious point), and follow a disciplined vegetarian diet.

The SES has branches throughout the Western world. It is perhaps important to understand that members do not understand the SES to be 'a religion' as such, but rather a philosophy that enables one to live a disciplined life. Hence, there is no sense that one has to convert to it. SES members, for example, may well be committed members of mainstream churches. Often people become interested in the SES as a result of attending local evening classes advertised as 'philosophy' courses, which, it is claimed, 'take students through an exploration of how daily life can be informed and governed by the love of wisdom'.

The SES attracted attention after it became the subject of a sensational book entitled *The Secret Cult* (1985) which was advertised as 'a full exposé of a strange and destructive organization that is penetrating the corridors of power'. The book, written by the investigative journalists Peter Hounam and Andrew Hogg, despite a lack of scholarly objectivity in places and some controversial claims, is still the best study of the SES.

In 1994 Leon MacLaren died, having appointed Donald Lambie his successor as Senior Tutor.

The Church Universal and Triumphant (Summit Lighthouse)
James R. Lewis

The Church Universal and Triumphant (CUT) is a theosophically inspired, Montana-based New Age church. A descendant of the *'I AM' Religious Activity, it began as Mark L. Prophet's Summit Lighthouse. The 'I AM' Religious Activity, founded by Guy Ballard and his wife Edna Ballard, is a popularized form of theosophy that views the Ascended Masters (called 'Masters of the Wisdom' by theosophists), especially the Comte de Saint Germain, as leading the world towards a New Age of light and truth. These fairly standard theosophical teachings are mixed with patriotism and the practice of 'decreeing', a modified version of New Thought affirmations.

Mark Prophet had been active in two 'I AM' splinter groups, the Bridge to Freedom (now the New Age Church of Truth) and the Lighthouse of Freedom. He eventually founded his own group, the Summit Lighthouse, in Washington, DC, in 1958. The orientation of Prophet's new group was the publication and dissemination of the masters' teachings. In the theosophical tradition, the spiritual evolution of the planet is conceived of as being in the hands of a group of divinely illumined beings – Jesus, the Buddha, and other advanced souls. Like earlier theosophical leaders, Mark Prophet viewed himself as serving as the mouthpiece for these Ascended Masters.

Elizabeth Clare Wulf joined the group in 1961, eventually marrying Mark Prophet. Over the course of their marriage, Elizabeth Clare Prophet also became a messenger. After Mark's death in 1973, Elizabeth took over his role as the primary mouthpiece for the masters, as well as spiritual leadership of the organization. (As a corporation, CUT is run by a board of directors.)

The headquarters of Summit Lighthouse moved to Colorado Springs in 1966. In 1974, CUT was incorporated, taking over ministerial and liturgical activities, retaining Summit Lighthouse as the publishing wing of the organization. After several moves within southern California, the church headquarters was finally established on the Royal Teton Ranch in Montana, just north of Yellowstone Park, in 1986. In addition to its teaching and publishing activity, the church also established an international community of several thousand people in the surrounding area.

Membership in the church is flexible. Church outreach around the globe is primarily accomplished through study groups – groups with which spiritual seekers can become informally affiliated. In 1962, the Keepers of the Flame Fraternity was established. Keepers vow to keep the flame of life and liberty alive, and receive monthly graded instruction. After they have

advanced to a certain stage, Keepers of the Flame may choose to become communicants. These full members are formally baptized, subscribe to certain church tenets, and tithe.

Following a series of crises and controversies in the early and mid-1990s, CUT seemed to rebound, but then went into a decline. Part of the problem was that Elizabeth Clare Prophet was suffering from a debilitating illness that was making her a progressively less effective organizational leader. She eventually stepped down from her role as the corporate head of the church. The church was then able to reorganize, sell off some of its holdings, and effectively stop what had threatened to be a gradual dissolution. From an estimated high of approximately 10,000 core participants, membership appears to have fallen off sharply in the wake of these events.

The Findhorn Foundation

John Drane

The small village of Findhorn, located just to the east of Inverness on Scotland's Moray Firth, is home to one of the largest and most influential spiritual communities in the Western world. Though it originally described itself as New Age, it now prefers to see itself as a place where many different spiritual traditions can be explored without its members needing to have a common mind on what the life of the spirit might be like, or indeed what 'God' might mean.

The Findhorn Foundation began in a small way in 1962, through the work of Peter and Eileen Caddy, along with their friend Dorothy Maclean. Peter had a long-standing association with *Rosicrucianism, and Eileen had developed an ability to receive messages from what she recognized as the voice of God. Guided by such spiritual revelations, they developed a garden at the caravan site where they lived, which attracted publicity not only for its beauty and prolific growth, but because Eileen believed it was inhabited by nature spirits (*devas*) who brought wisdom that would empower those who took them seriously to develop a better world. Spiritually concerned people began making pilgrimages to Findhorn from around the world. One of them, the American David Spangler, already had a similar vision for the future, and settled at Findhorn for an extended period during which he wrote several influential books that helped to

Sacred dance is part of community life at Findhorn.

publicize what was going on at Findhorn, as well as providing an intellectual foundation that influenced much of the subsequent development of Findhorn itself.

In the late 1970s, Findhorn was caught up with the kind of esoteric practices that then characterized much New Age thinking: magic, crystals, arcane techniques for personal development, machines claiming to deliver altered states of consciousness, messages from extraterrestrials, and much more besides. While some members are still interested in such things, Findhorn generally emphasizes more serious concerns, especially through its broadly based educational programme, which offers seminars exploring the spirituality of many different traditions. First-time visitors begin with the 'Experience Week', which provides an in-depth opportunity for participants to reflect on their lifestyle and worldview, with the intention of becoming more closely attuned to the spiritual forces believed to undergird all aspects of the universe. Sacred dance, the study of spiritual texts from many different sources, and exploration of the meaning of community all play a major part in this reorientation process. Elements of the same thinking are also available through the distance-learning course, *The Quest*. Most workshops take place in the Universal Hall, a magnificent five-sided structure built on a point that is said to mark the convergence of many ley lines.

Findhorn has also established itself as a leading centre for alternative technologies, with a variety of businesses organized on agreed spiritual principles, including ecological housing, computing, waste disposal, electricity generation, pottery and publishing. The community also operates a Steiner School, as well as Cluny College, a large residential facility (formerly a hotel) in the nearby town of Forres.

Satanism
Christopher Partridge

Satanism, sometimes referred to as 'Devil-worship', should not be confused with *Wicca/witchcraft or any other form of Paganism/neo-Paganism. As Pagans will point out, Paganism is essentially a nature religion in which the biblical figure of Satan has no part. Although some confusion is sometimes caused by Satanists who refer to themselves as Pagans, generally speaking, Pagans distance themselves from Satanism and belief in the Devil.

Satanism is popularly understood as a 'cult of opposition', in that it seems to be a religion based on opposition to a particular religion and culture, in this case Western Christian religion and culture. However, many Satanists claim that their religion is not simply an inversion of Christianity. It is rather a 'self-religion', which encourages egocentricity and personal development, and has little interest in actively opposing Christian doctrine and practice. Nevertheless, for whatever reason, Satanists often do vehemently oppose Christian doctrine, symbolism and practice, judging Christian civilization to be corrupt and hypocritical.

Partly because of the secretive nature of some Satanist groups and partly because there is a paucity of serious academic research in this area, there is no consensus regarding the numbers involved in Satanism. While those who are convinced of the existence of a massive underground network of organized satanic groups permeating all levels of society are almost certainly mistaken, it does seem clear that, although the numbers are small, it is a growing phenomenon. Even if those who belong to particular groups, such as the Church of Satan and the Temple of Set, are still relatively small (Graham Harvey, for example, estimates that, in Britain, 'There are six groups who between them have less than 100

☞ *continued on page 340*

ASTROLOGY
James R. Lewis

The most widespread aspect of the modern renewal of interest in things occult has been the growth of interest in astrology. There are probably more than 10,000 professional astrologers in the English-speaking world, serving more than 20 million clients, aside from those who read astrology magazines and the astrology column in almost every daily newspaper. Astrologers write syndicated advice columns for the national news services. The fact that computers are now universally used to carry out the calculations needed to erect a chart has added to the modern popularity of astrology.

'Astrology' literally means the 'study' (or the 'science' – depending on how one translates the Greek word *logos*) of the 'stars' (*astron*). Most people are familiar with only a tiny area of this subject, namely the 12 signs of the zodiac as they relate to the personality of individuals and the use of astrology for the purposes of divination. The zodiac (literally the 'circle of animals') is the belt constituted by the 12 signs: Aries, Taurus, Gemini, Cancer, Leo, Virgo, Libra, Scorpio, Sagittarius, Capricorn, Aquarius and Pisces.

The notion of the zodiac is very ancient, with roots in the early cultures of Mesopotamia. The first 12-sign zodiacs were named after the gods of these cultures. The Greeks adopted astrology from the Babylonians, and the Romans, in turn, adopted astrology from the Greeks. These peoples renamed the signs of the Mesopotamian zodiac in terms of their own mythologies, which is why the familiar zodiac of the contemporary West bears names from Mediterranean mythology.

Astrology in the modern world

Astrology occupies a peculiar position in the modern world. Since at least the Enlightenment, the Western world has been home to certain self-appointed guardians of human rationality who have railed against religion and anything else that suggested the human being was anything more than a physical organism. Astrology was lumped into the category of irrational superstition. Derided as medieval superstition, it nevertheless continues to exercise a fascination over the human mind. Indeed, polls indicate that its popularity is growing rather than waning.

To understand the attraction of this 'superstition' for the typical citizen of modern, industrialized societies, one explanation might be that for many people, everyday life – that is, life as it is experienced on a day-to-day basis – appears to be empty of significance. Many people will feel themselves to be at the mercy of social, economic and political forces that they often cannot understand, much less predict. Though, to the outsider, astrology appears to be unappealing because of its apparently fatalistic determinism, it does allow people to comprehend events in their lives as part of a meaningful, predictive system over which they can gain a certain amount of control. Furthermore, even the most mundane life acquires cosmic significance when viewed through the lens of astrology, in the sense that the system portrays humans as beings that are basically 'at home' in the universe.

Two approaches to the zodiac

Approaches to explaining how astrology 'works' move between two poles. On the one hand, it is stressed that the study of the stars is a natural science (and that, consequently, it should be distanced from occultism). On the other hand, while often referring to astrology as a science, the spiritual or occult dimension of the study of planetary influences is emphasized. The former

The sun is surrounded by the twelve signs in this illustration of zodiac signs from The History and Doctrine of Buddhism *by Edward Upham, 1829.*

correspondence explanation.

The cosmic interconnectedness that the second approach tends to see as fundamental to understanding astrological influence implies a kind of monistic view of the universe related to the worldview held in common by most strands of the West's metaphysical/occult subculture. This link is the primary reason why astrology has been severely criticized by militant secularists as well as by conservative Christians.

The metaphysical/occult subculture

The metaphysical/occult community is a loose-knit subculture. Its most distinctive institution is the metaphysical/occult bookstore, although there are also many metaphysical organizations. The largest of these organizations, such as the various theosophical societies and spiritualist churches, were formed in the 19th century. The metaphysical community was relatively small until the late 20th century. As the counter-culture of the 1960s faded away in the early 1970s, many former hippies found themselves embarking on a spiritual quest – one that, in many cases, departed from the Judaeo-Christian mainstream. These new seekers swelled the ranks of the metaphysical subculture until it became a significant social force.

perspective, using the natural science model, tends to conceive of astrological influences in terms of natural forces, analogous to the forces of gravity and magnetism, which are actually 'radiated' by the planets. The latter perspective, while often speaking in terms of 'occult forces', usually emphasizes that correlations between celestial and earthly spheres result from a kind of pre-arranged harmony that is built into the very structure of the cosmos. In other words, the various correspondences that astrology studies are a result of 'synchronicity' (to use Carl Gustav Jung's term), rather than a result of straightforward cause and effect. Moreover, a large number of astrologers attempt to adhere, simultaneously, to both a force and a

One important manifestation of this subculture was the so-called 'New Age movement'. Despite its continuities with the older metaphysical community, the New Age departed from tradition in certain ways. Of particular importance for the practice of astrology, the New Age blended metaphysics with certain other, distinct movements, such as the *human potential movement and humanistic psychology. As a consequence, the significance of such familiar occult practices as astrology and *tarot were altered. Under the impact of the human potential movement and humanistic psychology, astrology, tarot and so forth were no longer regarded as mere fortune-telling devices, but became tools for self-transformation. The net result of this on the contemporary practice of astrology is that at least two kinds of astrologers can be distinguished: astrologers who (like Joan Quigley, the astrologer to the former United States President Ronald Reagan and his wife) primarily predict events and advise clients on when to perform certain actions; and astrologers who primarily see themselves as quasi-therapists, leading their clients to deeper understandings of themselves. Most contemporary astrologers would, of course, fall somewhere between these two extremes.

Eastern zodiacs

Outside the West, the two most significant schools of astrology are Chinese astrology and Vedic astrology. The latter tradition, perhaps better known as Hindu astrology, is referred to as *jyotish* by its practitioners. Like Western astrology, Vedic astrology is ultimately rooted in Mesopotamian astrology, and thus shares a family resemblance with Western astrology. Like the Western tradition, *jyotish* casts a natal chart in which the influences of the planets are determined according to their placement in the 12 signs of the zodiac. Furthermore, the traditional Indian zodiac is basically the same as the West, the primary difference being that, *jyotish* uses the 'sidereal' or 'fixed' zodiac in contrast to the 'tropical' or 'moving' zodiac favoured by Western astrologers. A unique feature of *jyotish* is the practice of dividing one's life into specific periods during which different planets exercise more influence over the individual.

In much the same way that popular astrology in the West is confined to a knowledge of the 12 monthly sun signs, most people's awareness of Chinese astrology is confined to the 12 animal 'year signs'. The Chinese were one of the few cultures to develop a sophisticated system of astrology entirely independent of Mesopotamian influences. One result of this is that the Chinese group the stars into quite different constellations. Also, the Chinese traditionally gave primary importance to the Moon's placement in the daily lunar mansions (a kind of 28-sign lunar zodiac). Finally, the Chinese assigned meanings to the general appearance of a planet as modified by earth's atmosphere, meaning that, unlike Western astrologers, who examine the stars only indirectly through tables, traditional Chinese astrologers maintain a continual watch of the heavens.

members'), there are larger and increasing numbers of solitary practitioners who consider themselves Satanists and make use of the writings of LaVey and Aquino (see below).

The figure of Satan is drawn from the Bible. Consequently, some Satanists are unhappy with the term 'Satan', preferring, for example, the name 'Set' instead. Such 'Setians' will claim that the concept of Satan was simply invented by the Christian church in order to frighten followers into submission and to justify Christianity's existence. This is, they claim, not the deity they follow. However, generally speaking, most Satanists are happy to work with the concept of Satan.

According to a 1995 survey by Graham Harvey, Set/Satan is understood in various ways by contemporary Satanists: 'Some say that Set is a "real being", "an incorporeal entity", "a metaphysical reality"… "Lord of this world"… Others consider Set to be "the archetypal rebel", "the ultimate male principle", "a figure representing pride, self-interest and self-gratification"… "the driving force in human evolution".' However, although some view Set/Satan as being a rebellious, self-serving being, rather paradoxically they rarely view him in the sinister way that Christians do, believing him to be a deity who can be 'approached as a friend' and who (sometimes with reference to the serpent in Genesis 3) dispenses knowledge (the black flame) to those who strive for it.

Other Satanist groups, while they sometimes speak in terms of a personal being called Satan, do not require belief in such an entity. Satan is understood more in terms of a useful icon that encourages self-interest and individualism, and promotes opposition to institutional religion and the dominant culture. Indeed, in this sense, Satanism is essentially a self-religion or *human potential movement, which utilizes the rebellious, offensive and provocative symbolism the figure of Satan provides.

Although it may be true that few of the Satanists who belong to organized groups would claim to actually worship the Devil of the Bible, there are a growing number of individuals (usually adolescents) inspired by, for example, gothic imagery, horror films and certain rock musicians who, because they very clearly define themselves by their opposition to Christianity (symbolized by the wearing of inverted crucifixes), do claim to worship the Devil. Although in many cases this may be little more than youthful rebellion, it has led to, for example, the desecration of churches and criminal activity.

There are perhaps two identifiable streams of what might be called Satanism: groups that have a systematic set of Satanic teachings and practices, and those that don't have a systematic belief system, but use Satanic imagery, icons and general occult beliefs and paraphernalia to justify extreme, antisocial behaviour, such as grave robbing, sexual abuse, sadomasochism and even, in a few cases, murder.

Although several Satanist groups have proved to be short-lived, usually because of the small numbers involved (e.g. the Process-Church of the Final Judgement), there are nevertheless several active Satanist groups in the West (e.g. Dark Lily, the Order of the Nine Angles and the Church of Satanic Liberation) some of which are very secretive and about which little is known. However, within contemporary Satanism, the following two rival groups – the Church of Satan and the Temple of Set – are clearly the most important.

On the evening of 30 April 1966, Anton Szandor LaVey (who died in October 1997) declared the arrival of 'the Age of Satan'. Declaring himself to be 'the black pope', in that year he founded the Church of Satan in California, perhaps the most well-known and influential Satanist organization. It wasn't too long before the charismatic LaVey was gaining considerable publicity by performing satanic weddings for celebrities and the satanic baptisms of children.

LaVey's *The Satanic Bible* (1969) – which has been translated into Swedish, Danish and Spanish – and *The Satanic Rituals* (1972) remain key texts for many Satanists (whether they belong to the Church of Satan or not).

Central to the beliefs of the Church of Satan is an emphasis on the 'animal' or physical appetites of humans, which are to be indulged rather than denied. LaVey is particularly critical of Christianity for suppressing this side of humanity by labelling it 'sinful'. Indeed, *The Satanic Bible* contains an assault upon Christianity and, while LaVey denies that he worships an actual entity called Satan (the Satanist's object of worship being the self), he argues that Satan is nevertheless a powerful symbol of opposition to Christianity. Indeed, this rebellion is not directed solely against Christianity, but against all authority. Having said that, according to Jean La Fontaine, a former professor of anthropology in the London School of Economics who was commissioned by the British government to carry out research into claims of Satanic abuse, LaVey was 'a firm believer in order and observing the rule of law, which appears somewhat inconsistent with rebellion against authority'. Indeed, although some Satanists will use drugs in their rituals (following Aleister Crowley, a notorious and influential British occultist), the Church of Satan has maintained a strong opposition to the use of drugs (apart from alcohol). Also inconsistent with their stance against authority, was the centralized, hierarchical ordering of the church into local 'grottoes', overseen by the 'central grotto' run by LaVey. However, in 1975 the church was decentralized. The hierarchy was dismantled and individual grottoes were given independence. As a result, many small

groups have emerged with different names, some with little connection to the Church of Satan.

As with many forms of Satanism, the implications of LaVey's social Darwinism are brutal. For the Church of Satan, a principal law by which life should be lived is survival of the fittest. The human is understood to be an animal that should strive to overcome the weak. Such 'human garbage' should be pushed aside in the interests of attaining one's own potential. Indeed, Satanists are encouraged to distance themselves from 'the common herd'.

According to La Fontaine, there has been 'only one defection from the church: it became Michael Aquino's Temple of Set, which, although much smaller, is the Church of Satan's main rival and is never mentioned by name'. Michael Aquino (a former United States army officer) left the Church of Satan in 1975 and founded the Temple of Set. Although it shares some beliefs with the Church of Satan, the Temple of Set is arguably a more intellectual form of Satanism. Whereas the Church of Satan stresses the continuity between animals and humans, and emphasizes evolutionary development, the Temple of Set insists that humans are distinct from animals by virtue of their intellect and that this enquiring intellect is not simply the result of evolution, but is rather the gift of Set/Satan to humanity. The Temple of Set seeks to exercise this gift, symbolized as the black flame. The black flame is, according to La Fontaine, 'the symbol of knowledge and scepticism towards the received wisdom of established religions'. The increase in knowledge leads, in a gnostic-like way, to self-development and spiritual progress: 'As Set was, we are; as Set is, we will be.' The aim is, therefore, not to worship Set, but rather to learn from him and eventually become like him. As noted above, the Temple of Set seems to take the figure of Set/Satan far more seriously than the Church of Satan, in that he is understood to be a real, personal being.

As with many Satanists (who, in many respects, follow the practices and theories of Crowley), there is an emphasis on ritual and ceremonial magick (spelt with a 'k' to distinguish it from conjuring trickery). Of particular note is the distinction made by Satanists between the 'objective universe' (the natural world) and the 'subjective universe' (one's personal perspective). Essentially, one is able to effect changes in the objective universe by the application of the will. Ceremonial magick, particularly 'Black Magick' – as described in Aquino's book, *Black Magic in Theory and Practice* (1992) – has an impact upon the subjective universe, 'raising power' within the individual, and thereby increasing the effect of the will upon the 'objective universe'.

The Temple of Set is hierarchically ordered: the ruling body is called 'the Council of Nine' and the smaller groups are known as 'Pylons'. In a way which again reminds one of gnostic initiation, there are six 'degrees' (levels) of members. Beginning with the lowest, these are: Setian; Adept (the status of most members); Priest/Priestess; Magister/Magistra Templi; Magus/Maga; and Ipsissimus/Ipsissima.

Anton LaVey, founder of the Church of Satan, declared himself to be 'the black pope'. Here he stands in front of his distinctive inverted pentagram, which incorporates an image of a goat.

The Movement of Spiritual Inner Awareness

James R. Lewis

The Movement of Spiritual Inner Awareness (MSIA) was founded in the United States in 1971 by John-Roger Hinkins, generally called John-Roger, or, more informally, 'J-R' (b. 1934). With headquarters in Los Angeles, MSIA has approximately 5,000 active members worldwide, the majority of whom live in the United States. Although sometimes characterized as a New Age spirituality, the basic MSIA worldview is closer to that of the north Indian Sant Mat

lineage, as embodied in the north Indian *Radhasoami Tradition.

In common with both Sant Mat and neo-platonism, MSIA pictures the cosmos as composed of many different levels. At the point of creation, these levels sequentially emerged from God along a vibratory 'stream' until creation reached its densest manifestation in the physical world. MSIA teaches that individuals can be linked to God's creative energy, and that this stream of energy will carry their consciousness back to God. The Mystical Traveller Consciousness – which was formerly manifested in John-Roger and has since been anchored in John Morton, his co-leader –

accomplishes this link-up during initiation. However, it is important that, after their initiation, individuals appropriate and utilize the link through the practice of special meditation techniques referred to as spiritual exercises.

In the late 1970s, MSIA developed its own training seminars – Insight Training Seminars – comparable to est (Erhard Seminar Training; now *Landmark Forum) and Lifespring. MSIA also gave birth to the University of Santa Monica which, like Insight, has since developed into a separate institution. A second educational institution, Peace Theological Seminary (PTS), was formed later, and has become an integral part of MSIA's outreach.

The Servants of the Light (SOL)
Christopher Partridge

Based in Jersey, founded in 1972 by W.E. Butler (1898–1978), and currently led by Dolores and Michael Ashcroft-Nowicki, the Servants of the Light (often simply known as SOL) is an esoteric organization that claims to have approximately 2,600 students in 23 countries. Butler, who was a former member of Dion Fortune's *Society of the Inner Light and an authority on Western esotericism, founded what appears to be a typical esoteric organization. That is to say, while it is certainly distinctive in some respects, as with other esoteric schools it has outer and inner levels and a standard hierarchical structure, which requires that individuals enter as novices and progress upwards. For example, a novice will begin with a 50-lesson course, which includes Jewish kabbalistic material and also lessons based on the teachings of Israel Regardie, a former member of the *Hermetic Order of the Golden Dawn. After perhaps 12 lessons, if progress is satisfactory, the novice will be considered to have completed the First Degree and will

become a 'Fellow' of the Servants of the Light. The Second Degree brings with it the title of 'Frater' or 'Soror'. Following this there is also a Third Degree which, unlike the first two degrees, can only be entered by invitation. By this time, the individual will have been studying and working within the Servants of the Light for some years.

As with many occult groups, it is only when an individual has passed through the outer levels (the first two degrees) and has entered into the inner levels, that they are considered to have access to the real power of 'the overshadowing Hierarchy on the Inner Planes'. Also, in a similar way to other occult and 'magical' New Age organizations, this process can only be understood with reference to their particular interpretation of the kabbalah (see *Kabbalism), which provides a sort of symbolic route map through the different levels identified by the Servants of the Light.

As with the Society of the Inner Light, so members of the Servants of the Light are encouraged to study mythology in order to gain an understanding of the religious thought world of the ancient past. Of particular import, it would seem, are the legends surrounding King Arthur and the Holy Grail.

As with many esoteric movements, the kabbalah (often spelled 'qabalah' in Western esoteric texts) is central to the philosophy of the Servants of the Light. Meaning 'that which has been received/handed down', the kabbalah is a system of Jewish mystical thought, originally transmitted orally. It was developed along two lines, the practical and the theoretical or speculative, the latter of which developed special methods of interpretation to uncover secret doctrines in the Jewish scriptures (particularly the first five books of the Bible – 'the Books of Moses'). The core of Jewish kabbalistic philosophy is written down in the *Sefer ha-Zohar* or *Book of Splendour* (usually referred to simply as 'the *Zohar*'), a text discovered in Spain in the late 13th century. Said to be the mystical teachings of Rabbi Simeon bar Yochai and his followers who had lived in Palestine in the 2nd and 3rd centuries CE, it is essentially a commentary on 'the Books of Moses'. However, while the history of Western kabbalistic occultism has its roots in this text, kabbalism became distinctive once loosed from its Jewish moorings and reinterpreted by non-Jewish esoteric scholars and practitioners. Of particular significance for the development of Western esotericism is the emphasis placed on a diagram or glyph, known as the 'Tree of Life', that emerged from kabbalistic exegesis. As Gareth Knight, a former member of the Society of the Inner Light, puts it, the Tree of Life 'was to form the backbone for most later magical theory and practice'. This glyph, which is understood by many occultists to unlock hidden knowledge and provide access to realms of spiritual power, has ten circles/spheres arranged in three columns, and 22 paths connecting them. The circles represent *sefiroth*, which are, according to Jewish kabbalism, the ten ways God (the Unknowable) has chosen to reveal himself. The *sefiroth* are, in other words, the faces or aspects of God. In truly knowing the *sefiroth* we truly know God. In kabbalistic thought God is usually referred to in non-personal terms as the *Ein Sof* (the Unlimited and the Undefined) or *Ein Sof Aur* (the Limitless Light) – an understanding which, again, has had an influence on Western esoteric thought.

While different interpretations are provided and different magical groups claim to have the key to unlocking the secrets of the Tree of Life, essentially the glyph is understood to be a representation of the relationship between humanity and God, who is the Source of all and permeates all. Consequently, everything in the physical world has its source in, and a fundamental connection with, the world of the *sefiroth*. Indeed, what happens in this world mirrors what happens in the world of the *sefiroth*: 'as above, so below'.

Included in the glyph are often Hebrew letters which (according to a Jewish philosophy known as *gematria*) can be given numerical value and esoteric meanings and thus take on magical significance. However, the point is that the kabbalistic Tree of Life is understood by many to be a complex and powerful spiritual tool which, when correctly understood, can provide enlightenment as to the true nature of the universe and can be used as a blueprint for magical rituals. Once one understands the levels and the ordering of the spiritual world, one can, through ritual, through meditation, and, sometimes, with the guidance of angels and higher beings, explore the paths connecting the *sefiroth* (which are essentially doors to higher levels of reality and power – bearing in mind that what happens in this world is reflected in the physical world). This exploratory practice is an esoteric technique of guided meditation often termed 'pathworking'.

While the early non-Jewish kabbalists were often Christians who sought to interpret kabbalistic thought from a Trinitarian theological perspective, others developed more occultic interpretations. Particularly in the 19th century, the kabbalah had a significant influence on the occultist movement. Key groups, such as the Hermetic Order of the Golden Dawn and, later, the Fraternity/Society of the Inner Light developed a distinctively magical kabbalism. It is this type of thought, as found in Dion Fortune's influential book *The Mystical Qabalah* and Gareth King's *Practical Guide to Qabalistic Symbolism*, that has shaped the occultism of the Servants of the Light. For example, developed by Dolores Ashcroft-Nowicki, the Servants of the Light have a set of *tarot cards that is influenced by their understanding of kabbalah, which is, in turn, informed by Gareth Knight's *Practical Guide to Qabalistic Symbolism*. For the Servants of the Light, tarot is an important spiritual tool for the group, in that it assists them in their 'pathworking'.

The Share International Foundation
Michael York

Following the theosophical tradition of Helena Petrovna Blavatsky (see the *Theosophical Society) and Alice Bailey (see the *Arcane School), British painter Benjamin Crème (b. 1922) began to receive telepathic messages in 1959 from the 'Ascended Masters' (called 'Masters of the Wisdom' by theosophists) foretelling the arrival of the future Buddha Maitreya as the head of their collectivity, known as the Great White Brotherhood. Crème announced in 1972 that the arrival of Maitreya/Christ was to occur shortly. In 1974, Crème claimed to have been 'overshadowed' by Maitreya when the Master began dictating messages concerning the preparation of a *mayavirupa* or 'body of manifestation' through which he would then visit the earth. Although Maitreya did not appear to the world in 1982 as had been predicted, Crème has continued to insist in public talks that Maitreya is at present living among the Indian community of London and will manifest himself shortly to the world as a whole.

Through Crème's mediumship, Maitreya has promised that when the world is ready by its own free will to share and take the first steps into right human relationships, he will come with a tangible group of Ascended Masters. On the Day of Declaration, Maitreya will present himself on television and radio to the entire world – speaking telepathically in everyone's own language. Crème's own organization, formerly the Tara Center (Los Angeles) and the Tara Press (London), is now known as the Share International Foundation. It promotes Maitreya's basic message: 'Share and save the world... Take your brother's need as the measure for your action and solve the problems of the world. There is no other course.'

The Universal Christian Gnostic Church
Andrew Dawson

The Universal Christian Gnostic Church was founded in 1972, in Mexico, by the Venerable Master Samael Aun Weor, originally of Bogotá, Colombia. Born Victor Manuel Gómez Rodríguez in 1917, the title of 'Bodhisattva of the Venerable Master Samael Aun Weor' was adopted subsequent to a series of visions and spiritual experiences. These mystical experiences started in 1948 upon the death of his mentor in Gnosticism, Master Huiracocha (Arnold Krumm-Heller) and culminated in 1954 with Weor's completion of the 'Five Great Initiations' at an underground temple in Santa Marta, Colombia. Charged with the threefold mission of 'forming a new culture', 'forging a new civilization' and 'creating the gnostic movement', Weor declared the commencement of the Age of Aquarius on 4 February 1962. Weor died ('abandoned his physical body') on 24 December 1977, and is believed now to be a member of the Secret Government of the World that rules from Tibet. Weor bequeathed the title of Gnostic Patriarch to Gargha Kuichines who, upon his 'disincarnation', was succeeded by the Third Gnostic Patriarch Igassan Bindu (subsequently stripped of his title in September 2002 in light of alleged sexual impropriety). Although strongest in South America, the Universal Christian Gnostic Church has institutional branches, adherents and affiliated organizations all over the world.

The doctrinal core of the Gnostic Church is founded upon a number of authoritative sources. The Coptic (Egyptian) and Greek writings of the early Gnostic communities (e.g. Nag Hammadi codices, Valentinian writings and hermetic texts) are of import, furnishing much of the Gnostic Church's cosmology. Chief among the early Gnostic corpus is the 3rd-/4th-century text *Pistis Sophia* (Faith-Wisdom; known formally as Codex Askewianus). Among other things, *Pistis Sophia* contains a lengthy account of the post-ascension Jesus returning to instruct his disciples in the esoteric interpretation of his revealed teaching (i.e. parables, sayings etc.) and in the previously unrevealed knowledge (*gnosis*) of the origins, structure and destiny of the universe. The modern writings of Weor (over 60 books in total) complement these historical texts to form the basis of the contemporary Gnostic Church's belief and practice. Highly eclectic in character, Weor's writings draw upon a very wide variety of sources, chief among which are the theosophical reflections of Helena Petrovna Blavatsky (particularly *The Secret Doctrine*; see the *Theosophical Society), the Eastern mystical teachings of Krishnamurti (see *Krishnamurti and the Krishnamurti Foundation) and the work of Swiss psychotherapist Carl Gustav Jung. In addition to the primary authoritative resources of Weor and early Gnosticism, the Gnostic Church draws freely upon Christian and Indian scriptures (e.g. the *Rig Veda* and *Bhagavadgita*), not to mention a broad range of contemporary occultist and New Age sources.

Gnostic cosmology divides 'Reality' hierarchically into five planes, each inhabited by an assortment of beings whose substance correlates with their particular sphere of existence. The first and most important plane is that of pure immateriality, the Divine sphere of Absolute, Ineffable Mystery. Gnostics believe that the universe originated in the ordering activity of the Absolute upon chaotic primordial matter, giving rise to (emanating) the subsequent planes of the created order (*Pleroma*). Emanating from the Absolute in order of relative immateriality, these planes are: the Divine, the Spiritual (Treasure of Light), the Mental (Psychic), the Astral (Planetary), and the Material (Physical). Each plane is ordered internally (from 'right' to 'left'), again according to a hierarchy of relative immateriality.

Humankind is located in the 'middle' sector of the basest (i.e. most physical) plane, the Material. Despite our base materiality, consciousness, itself an element (spark) of the Divine Mind, permits us to participate and grow (evolve) spiritually relative to our place in the Eternal Order. Party to the inner workings of the cosmic hierarchy, the Universal Christian Gnostic Church regards itself as charged with the task of communicating what is necessary (i.e. 'New Gnosis') to enlighten humankind as to its latent spiritual potential. This enlightenment comes in the form of theoretical content as to the nature of Reality and practical material concerning those exercises most suited to enhancing consciousness by limiting the stultifying effects of the body upon its proper functioning. Conceptual content about the inner workings of the *Pleroma* is drawn chiefly from received Gnostic wisdom (particularly *Pistis Sophia*), whereas practical instruction draws heavily upon Eastern yogic and tantric mystical traditions. Oscillating seamlessly between literal assertion and allegorical allusion, contemporary Gnosticism substantiates the spiritual efficacy of its teaching through frequent reference to Jungian psychology. Ancient esotericism, Eastern mysticism and modern psychology thereby combine to instruct, cosmically orientate and spiritually liberate the 'divine spark' that is human consciousness.

The Order of the Solar Temple
Jean-François Mayer

The Order of the Solar Temple is a generic name for a series of groups that have had a variety of names, but were all led (directly or indirectly) by a French citizen, Jo Di Mambro (1924–94). The movement became famous under the name 'Order of the Solar Temple' in October 1994, when it was discovered that 53 people, including the leaders of the group, had either committed suicide or been killed in Switzerland and Quebec. Subsequent events took the lives of 16 more people in France in December 1995 and 5 in Quebec in March 1997.

Jo Di Mambro used to be a member of the Ancient and Mystical Order Rosae Crucis (AMORC) in France between 1956 and the late 1960s. He then founded a group of his own, the Centre for the Preparation of the New Age, in 1973, and subsequently a community called 'The Pyramid'. As with many other groups in the Western esoteric tradition, Egypt played a significant role in their thought. The reference to the Knights Templars and to *Rosicrucianism proved crucial as well. The idea of the entrance into the Age of Aquarius was strongly associated

Members of the Order of the Solar Temple. In the 1990s many followers either committed suicide or were killed.

with increasingly apocalyptic views, partly borrowed from the works of French esotericist Jacques Breyer (1922–96). He had initiated a Templar resurgence in France in 1952, from which several *neo-Templar orders derived. The apocalyptic orientation was at first survivalist: the group even attempted to set up 'survival centres' in order to allow its members to go unscathed through apocalyptic turmoils; in the 1990s it led to escapism and to the idea that the only way left for the elect was to abandon this world.

In 1978, the nascent movement established its headquarters in an attractive property in Geneva, Switzerland. During the 1980s, it came to develop a quite intense public activity through lectures and clubs, which served as recruiting tools and front organizations for the esoteric side of the movement. Instrumental in the propagation of the message of the movement was a Belgian homeopathic physician, Luc Jouret (1947–94). A charismatic speaker, Jouret attracted large audiences in French-speaking countries, but few of his listeners enrolled in the group: the order apparently never gathered more than 500 to 600 members at the same time.

From the early 1990s, the movement went through several crises, and a number of members who used to belong to the core group leading a communitarian life defected, including Di Mambro's own son. They had concluded that the supernatural phenomena and apparitions that allegedly took place during secret ceremonies had been counterfeited. They were also sceptical of Di Mambro's claims to be the representative of a secret hierarchy of hidden masters.

There are reasons to believe that those manifestations of internal dissent played an important role in persuading Di Mambro and a group of close followers that there was no other option left than to quit this world – and to suppress at the same time the threatening voices of some dissenters, since the leaders of the group wanted to leave a legend behind them. However, the fact that several more members chose the same way to die (i.e. 'transit' to another world, as they euphemistically described their deaths) at a later time demonstrates how strong the doctrinal justification had succeeded in becoming in the eyes of some followers. Indeed, there are still former members who remain convinced that the miraculous apparitions and phenomena were not faked, but the movement itself has ceased to exist.

A Course in Miracles
Ruth Bradby

A Course in Miracles, a channelled text, is a self-study curriculum that leads its students to a disciplined spirituality by confronting all negative obstacles to the mind's awareness of love. Since its publication in 1976, the Course, as it is popularly called, has become one of the best-known texts of contemporary spirituality. Over 1 million English copies have been sold and it has been translated into many languages, including German, French, Spanish, Portuguese, Chinese, Russian, Italian and Hebrew. Its principles may have influenced millions more through their use in best-selling, spiritual self-help books.

The Course consists of 1,200 pages divided into a main text, a workbook with an exercise for each day of the year, and a manual for teachers. Although no author is listed, the text implies that it was channelled from Jesus Christ, and its monistic teaching is couched in biblical vocabulary. Christian concepts, such as resurrection, atonement and forgiveness, are given new meanings. The miracles referred to in the title are not external acts: they refer to the perception that nothing exists that is separate from God. This core belief echoes the non-dualistic Advaita Vedanta of the 8th-century Hindu philosopher Shankara. The denial of the possibility of evil makes connections with *Christian Science, and its uncompromising otherworldliness links it with Gnosticism.

A *Course in Miracles* came from the collaboration of Dr Helen Schucman (1909–81), research psychologist at Columbia-Presbyterian Medical Center in New York, and her department director, Dr William Thetford. In 1965, Dr Schucman, an atheist who did not believe in paranormal phenomena, began to hear an inner voice and was encouraged by Thetford to transcribe the messages from this voice. Over the next seven years, Schucman wrote the Course in shorthand, then read it to Thetford, who typed it. Although Schucman transcribed the inner dictation, she refused to admit authorship and claimed to be ambivalent about its message until her death in 1981.

At first the Course was distributed by photocopies to friends of Schucman and Thetford. As the Course's fame spread by word of mouth, demand outstripped supply. In 1975, Kenneth Wapnick edited the material for publication, and the Foundation for Inner Peace (FIP) was founded by Judith Skutch to publish it. Annual sales rose to 60,000 by 1985 and the Course became a perennial bestseller. In 1996, the copyright for the Course was given to Viking Penguin, and the Foundation for *A Course in Miracles* (FACIM) was established by Kenneth and Gloria Wapnick as the official teaching organization of the original publisher.

By the turn of the millennium, the copyright of the Course had returned to FACIM and there were over 2,000 Course study groups in more than a dozen countries, as well as several online Course forums and websites used by students from the United States, Britain, Europe, Australia, Japan, Singapore and South Africa. More recently FACIM's protection of the copyright of the Course has brought strife to the community of Course groups. Some Course leaders have accused Kenneth Wapnick of imposing a religious orthodoxy that is contrary to the Course's own teaching. However, Wapnick responds that he has never insisted that students adhere to a single understanding of Course principles, only that standard copyright laws apply, that excerpts of the Course not be published and that the three parts of the Course (text, workbook and manual for teachers) should not be published separately from each other as they were 'conceived as part of an integrated thought system'. In spite of copyright controversies, large numbers of people continue to be influenced by the Course and new study groups are emerging in many parts of the world. New Age scholar Wouter Hanegraaff has referred to the Course as 'the "one single text" which might be said to function as "sacred scripture" in the New Age network of spiritualities'.

Damanhur
Christopher Partridge

Damanhur is a spiritual community (with connections to New Age and esoteric thought) which, in accordance with the community's belief that the planet is a living being, seeks to foster an environmentally friendly, sustainable lifestyle. Situated in the Valchiusella Valley, northern Italy, Damanhur was founded in 1977 by Oberto Airaudi (b. 1950) as a centre for spiritual research. Damanhur is now a federation of communities which, according to its own description, 'numbers over 500 resident citizens and 370 others who live nearby and take part in its activities. Damanhur offers different kinds of citizenship, according to the level of involvement each person decides upon… The homes and the companies of the Federation are not concentrated in one single area, but are scattered all over the Valchiusella Valley. They include 200 hectares of woods, 200 hectares of urban surface, 60 hectares of farmland, and over 800 buildings, including private homes, studios, laboratories and farms.'

In his youth, Airaudi had contact with spiritual healers and some interest in *Spiritualism and Theosophy (see the *Theosophical Society). He also claimed to possess paranormal powers. In 1974 he gathered a small group of people around him and founded the Horus Centre in Turin to run courses based on his teaching. Soon Airaudi began expounding a specific set of ideas he called 'meditation'. During this time, Airaudi showed his group of disciples a map, on which were drawn strange lines which he claimed to have researched. The 'synchronic lines' he had discovered were lines of energy that could be found all over the planet – lines which could be understood as the earth's nervous system. There were two significant places where these lines converged: Tibet and a location near the village of Baldissero in the Piedmont valley of Valchiusella, just north of Turin. Hence, the group searched for and found property there and, in 1977, began to build Damanhur.

Central to the Damanhur community are the 'Temples of Humankind', a vast underground network of sanctuaries constructed by Damanhur citizens and considered by devotees to be the eighth wonder of the world: 'The Temples of Humankind follow the flow of the [synchronic] lines and are an initiation path, the reproduction of the inner rooms of every human being. Walking through the halls and corridors is an immersion inside

oneself, a path towards the reawakening of the human being.' Although work on the temple had begun in 1977, its location was not publicly known until 1992 when an ex-member, Filippo Maria Cerutti, disclosed details.

Damanhur philosophy teaches that humans share an original divine nature. Through a series of reincarnations, and now through the philosophy of Damanhur, individuals are progressing towards enlightenment. They are being reawakened to their true nature and to their potential as a divine self. This is done not only through spiritual exercises, but also through experimentation with group dynamics, art, and various other activities. In particular, it is taught that the divine within can be awakened by continuous interaction with others. Indeed, this emphasis on spiritual growth as a community, rather than solitarily as individuals, has led Damanhur to create what they believe will be a new human people group, 'the Spiritual People': 'The Spiritual People was born to realize in concrete terms the liberation and reawakening of Humankind as a divine, spiritual and material principle, to create a model for a self-sufficient way of life based upon shared living and love; to reach a harmonious integration and collaboration with all the Forces connected to the evolution of Humanity.'

Fiat Lux

Andreas Grünschloss

Fiat Lux is a small religious community in Germany's southern Black Forest, with centres in Ibach and Strittmatt (near Waldshut-Tiengen). The community perceives itself as a 'religious order' that was founded in 1980 directly 'by Jesus Christ through his speaking-tube Uriella'. Despite its rather small size, with an 'inner circle' of

135 full-time members (Ordensträger/-innen) and roughly 800 followers (and some 2,000 sympathizers), Fiat Lux has become relatively well known in Germany today – mainly because of some media attention during previous years (especially court trials concerning toll or tax avoidance and the sale of spiritual medicaments and fluids with alleged healing powers). The charismatic leadership is in the hands of Uriella, the 'spiritual name' of Erika Bertschinger Eike (b. 1927), who is the primary 'medium' for privileged information and revelation from heavenly reigns. In 1970, the former secretary and interpreter, born in Zürich, Switzerland, became involved with spiritual healing and natural cures. Claiming to be endowed with divine gifts such as clairvoyance, remote hearing and similar paranormal faculties, she presents herself as God's sole 'channel', 'full trance medium' and 'speaking-tube' for today, receiving her esoteric messages directly from Jesus (and sometimes Mary).

Important religious events are the Sunday services with Uriella's public 'full trance-revelations', delivered as long speeches (by Jesus) addressed to the assembly, with various spiritual healings to follow in separate sessions. Uriella's 'messages' and 'visions' are collected and printed and thus form a cumulative body of new revelations, which are the primary source of information. In this bright 'Fiat Lux castle', members gain access to a privileged 'panorama', since Uriella opens all the relevant 'windows' onto the machinations of the fallen world. The lifestyle is strictly regulated and monastic: devotees are given new ritual names, there are prescribed times for prayer, white (shining) clothes are worn, and other rules for 'pure' conduct are adhered to, including celibacy and vegetarianism. Furthermore, the order runs a small humanitarian help project called Adsum.

The faith is syncretistic and apocalyptic in outlook, and includes many assumptions typical of contemporary esoteric ufologies (e.g. reincarnation and ascension of the soul) (see *Ufology and UFO-related Movements): Humanity is now living in the end-times; parts of the earth are going to be destroyed by huge tidal waves, asteroids, volcanic eruptions, earthquakes, and a terrible world war (including Nazi-UFOs currently hidden in the Antarctic). Only one third of humanity will survive this great tribulation during the 'three dark days'. But benevolent interplanetary beings under the command of Jesus Christ will help to evacuate the chosen few in small spherical spaceships descending from giant spherical 'mother ships' (however, access will be denied to the spiritually unprepared). This evacuation will last for three weeks; a spiritual awakening and purification of

Erika Bertschinger Eike in court in Mannheim, Germany, for tax evasion in 1998.

earthly souls will take place on the mother ships, and earth is going to be transformed into a new paradisiacal entity called Amora (with a return of the ancient sunken continents, mild climate, new fauna and flora etc.). A millennial era of peace, harmony and unity with all creation is going to follow on Amora: Christ will return, Mary will reign, yin and yang will be in balance, and there will be visible contact with angels and other spiritual beings. Creative powers will prevail and new energies and solely 'green' technologies are going to be employed.

Originally, it was announced that this 'final phase' would commence in 1998. But in the course of that year Uriella revealed that, due to immense praying energies, God had granted a 'temporary postponement' or 'time of grace'. In the future Uriella may pronounce other concrete deadlines, stressing the apocalyptic tension again. The other option would be that the millenarian events are increasingly spiritualized or deferred (as in the case of other esoteric ufologies that concentrate more on 'light work' and 'ascension') – and some of the order's current publications seem to indicate this. However, at present Fiat Lux's religious theory and practice is still devoted to a world-and-society-renouncing strategy of religious 'coping', which mediates new meaning to participants' lives by focusing solely on the imminent 'Golden Age' foretold by the charismatic leader, and on a purification of the soul within a supportive enclave of the chosen few.

The Impersonal Enlightenment Foundation

James R. Lewis

The Impersonal Enlightenment Foundation (formerly the Moksha Foundation) is a spiritual group founded by Andrew Cohen

(b. 1955). Cohen was born in New York, where he spent his childhood, but in early adolescence he travelled abroad to complete his education before returning to New York in his early twenties. Unable to forget a spontaneous spiritual experience that occurred when he was 16, Cohen decided to abandon all other aspirations and, at the age of 22, became a serious spiritual seeker. After pursing many different spiritual paths, his search led him to India where, in 1986, he met a little-known teacher, H.W.L. Punja. This meeting was a catalyst for a spiritual awakening that transformed his life. Almost immediately afterwards, Cohen began to draw students to him.

Cohen has continued to travel and teach around the world. In addition to giving over 100 public talks each year, he holds retreats and many shorter intensive seminars. In 1988 he returned to the United States and established a group in Cambridge, Massachusetts. A year later he moved to Marin County, California, to join a small communal group founded by some of his followers. In 1997, the group moved its headquarters once again to Lenox, Massachusetts. The group had several names, but finally became known as the Impersonal Enlightenment Foundation in the late 1990s. Communities of students dedicated to his teachings have also formed in New York, Boston, Europe and Australia. Cohen devotes much time and energy to these communities.

Cohen is the founder and editor of *What is Enlightenment?* magazine, a biannual publication devoted to promoting significant spiritual enquiry. He is also the author of a number of books, including *An Unconditional Relationship to Life, Autobiography of an Awakening, My Master is My Self* and *Enlightenment is a Secret.*

The Temple of the Vampire

Christopher Partridge

The Temple of the Vampire was founded by Lucas Martel and is, it claims, 'the only authentic international church in the world devoted to and uniquely authorized by the Vampire religion and its immortal leaders'. It has clear similarities to *Satanism and is happy to be associated particularly with the Church of Satan. It can officially be dated to 1989 when it published *The Vampire Bible* and was legally registered with the United States government. Since 1989, it appears to have grown considerably (precise figures are hard to determine). Beginning as a relatively small new religion based in the United States, it now claims to have 'cabals' (local Temple groups) throughout the world. Essentially, the organization oversees a network of cabals – 'the Vampire Connection' – and when memberships are registered over the internet, the individual's email address is forwarded to the nearest cabal. Hence, it would seem that email accounts and the internet are crucial tools for members. Temple members are given their own password, a red lifetime membership card (which is used for identification at official rituals and functions) and access to a monthly newsletter, *Lifeforce*.

The Vampire religion is explicitly elitist, in that it is solely the religion of those who believe themselves to be 'born to the Blood' (i.e. vampires). As to how an individual knows whether he or she is a vampire, this is essentially intuitive. Just as one is, or becomes aware of one's own sexual orientation, so, in a similar manner, one becomes aware that one is a member of the vampire race. Do you 'feel the draw of the night'? Do you feel 'different from the herd of humanity and glory in that difference'? Are you attracted to vampire religion and culture? A positive answer to such questions

indicates the possibility of vampire blood. It is the Temple's mission 'to find those who are of the Blood but have been unaware of their true heritage'.

The key elements of the religion are explained in *The Vampire Bible*. Along with this slim volume (51 pages), there are four other bibles, *The Vampire Predator Bible*, *The Vampire Priesthood Bible*, *The Vampire Sorcery Bible* and *The Vampire Adept Bible*. While all of these bibles used to be available for purchase by any interested individual, since 1 January 2003, only *The Vampire Bible* is available to the public. The four 'higher bibles' are now only made available to members. At each of the five 'circles' or levels through which a member of the Temple progresses, a particular bible is used, beginning at the first level with *The Vampire Bible*. At the end of this process, the individual becomes a 'Master Adept' who understands and applies the information contained in the five bibles. The member may also become a vampire sorcerer who, working at an advanced level, is able to manipulate the external world.

The Temple of the Vampire, in a similar way to the Church of Satan, teaches the following core beliefs (most of which are summarized in a short 'Vampire Creed'): members do not belong to the common 'herd' of humanity, in that they are, in some sense, higher beings; members should worship their own egos; one's individual 'lifeforce', the self, is divine; reason is paramount and no member should hold beliefs that cannot pass the test of their own rational scrutiny; 'survival is the highest law'; 'the Powers of Darkness' are natural laws to be understood and utilized; heaven and hell do not exist. Again, like the Church of Satan, it prohibits members from harming humans and from any form of criminal behaviour. There are also specific vampire beliefs. For example, there will be a 'Final Harvest' of humankind when 'the

Undead Gods', who function at 'a Higher Level beyond the human', return to power, taking their rightful place as the rulers of the world. As in the vampire stories of popular culture, 'the Undead' are those powerful individual vampires who are not subject to death and decay, unlike mortal humans. These beings are the focus of Temple worship, in that they are called upon to empower members and to transform them from 'mortal life', thereby ensuring their eternal life.

Jasmuheen and the Breatharians
Lynne Hume

All the major world religions are represented in Australia and while the majority of the population is nominally Christian, a plethora of alternative religions and new spiritualities exist, their numbers and diversity having increased in the last three decades. Many of these new religions place great emphasis on positive living and on the health and healing aspects of spirituality.

One of the lesser-known groups to emerge in Australia in recent years was known previously as the Breatharians, and later established as the Self Empowerment Academy (SEA) in 1994 in Brisbane. SEA's founder is Jasmuheen (Ellen Greve; b. 1957). Jasmuheen claimed that it was possible to exist solely on 'pranic nourishment' (living on Light), without having to eat food; hence the term Breatharians. Not only was this possible, she said, but she herself had done so for several years after she had met the Ascended Masters (called 'Masters of the Wisdom' by theosophists) and undergone a sacred 'Prana Initiation' in 1993. This involved connecting with the 'Divine One Within' (referred to as 'DOW'). She wrote of her experiences in two of several books she has published:

Living on Light: Nutrition for the New Millennium and *Ambassadors of Light: Living on Light*.

Jasmuheen gained some notoriety in the 1990s when media reports highlighted this claim after three people died attempting to simulate Jasmuheen's practice. In response to the media attention, Jasmuheen insisted that she did not advocate this method for everyone and warned against people attempting to do so if they were not fully prepared. However, she does say that 'living on Light' is the future direction for the new millennium, one that will answer the problems of world hunger, and that all people have the inherent powers to make it possible, as well as the ability to develop clairvoyance and clairaudience.

Jasmuheen receives her teachings telepathically from deceased master alchemists whom she refers to as the Ascended Masters or the Ascended Ones who, in the past, have incarnated on planet earth as (among others) Jesus, Mary, Buddha, Krishna, Muhammad, Comte de Saint Germain and Kwan Yin (a Chinese feminine deity). The principal message is 'positive personal and planetary progress', which can be aided by an eight-step programme she calls the 'Luscious Lifestyle Programme' consisting of the following: daily meditation, daily prayer, mind mastery (thoughts create reality), a vegetarian diet (although Jasmuheen herself lives on Light, she realizes that most people are unable to do this), regular daily exercise, selfless service to others, spending time in nature and singing devotional songs daily and/or mantras that focus on the Divine One Within. The benefits from this eight-step programme are the attainment of personal paradise for the practitioner, which will then lead to global paradise.

The Cosmic Internet Academy (CIA) was instigated in 1996 and is almost solely run by Jasmuheen herself. She also founded the

SEA and the Movement of an Awakened and Positive Society (MAPS). As the MAPS ambassador, Jasmuheen is nourished by Light and is a servant to the Divine, the one she calls OH–OM (One Heart–One Mind) and which others refer to as God, Allah, Brahma or the Supreme Intelligence.

Jasmuheen travels worldwide, giving lectures and workshops with titles such as 'Luscious Lifestyles', 'Living on Light', 'Warriors and Wizards' and 'The Game of Divine Alchemy'. She also channels messages from the Ascended Masters. Jasmuheen works from a post office address in Brisbane, and an internet site, the CIA, from which she propounds her philosophy of life and her own view of metaphysics. The CIA is open to anyone interested in, and committed to, 'positive personal and planetary transformation'.

The Celestine Prophecy
John Drane

The Celestine Prophecy by James Redfield, published in 1994, is a novel set in Peru that focuses on the discovery of some previously unknown Mayan texts, containing nine 'insights' that explain the meaning of life. Briefly summarized, the message of the book is that we can find true fulfilment by recognizing that we are interconnected not only with other people, but also with an underlying cosmic energy source. If we fully engage with one another in the light of that knowledge, we can change the world and empower humanity to undergo the final stage in evolution. This will end the familiar cycle of birth and death, as our bodies themselves are transformed into the higher energy field that as yet is only accessible after death. James Redfield published two further 'insights' subsequently, highlighting the spiritual disciplines necessary for this, and a twelfth 'insight' has been promised.

The fact that these 'insights' address everyday issues of relationships almost guaranteed that the book would become a source of spiritual direction for many people. It has a large worldwide following, and has given rise to several websites. Its attraction lies in its claim to give access to hidden ancient wisdom, which (in contrast to conventional Western scientific thinking) can heal rather than destroy the planet and its inhabitants. It also instills confidence in ordinary people to believe that they really can make a difference because the future is in their own hands.

The Company of Heaven
George D. Chryssides

The Company of Heaven is an arm, currently in the process of formation, of the *Hermetic Order of the Golden Dawn, and affiliated to Argentium Astrum ('Silver Star' – an order founded by magician Aleister Crowley in 1907). The organization's activities are as yet unspecified, but its 11 articles of association affirm its openness to all Thelemites – that is to say, to those who subscribe to the dictum '"Do what thou wilt" shall be the whole of the law.' The organization thus respects the free will of its members, and is committed to tolerance. It looks forward to a period of truth and justice, affirming the interrelationship of all life forms (human, 'extra-human' and 'praeter-human'), which can be furthered by greater ecological responsibility. Membership can be gained simply by affirming the 11 articles and sending these to its Clearing House in London.

It should also be noted that, unrelated to the above, the expression 'Company of Heaven', although originating within mainstream Christianity, has been increasingly used within the New Age network. It originally referred to the angelic hosts, the saints, martyrs and other faithful departed ones who reign with Christ in heaven. Within the New Age, however, there has been less interest in institutional Christianity and its formal definitions of such concepts, and the expression tends to refer to the angelic presences that are felt, but not systematically defined. Angelic presences are typically regarded as guiding, healing and (particularly in the case of guardian angels) protecting.

New Religions, Sects and Alternative Spiritualities with Roots in **Modern Western Cultures**

Marilyn Monroe *by Andy Warhol, 1967.*

THE MODERN WESTERN WORLD

Christopher Partridge

During the previous century, particularly in the years after the Second World War, the religious landscape in the West dramatically changed. For example, individuals and families, for a variety of reasons, travelled from the countries in which they were born and settled in other countries and cultures. This has led to a situation in which many people in the world, certainly the Western world, live in religiously plural societies. Moreover, not only do modern methods of travel mean that the world's cultures are only a few hours away, but, thanks to radio, television and the internet, fewer and fewer people are able to avoid learning about other cultures and religious communities. As a result, contemporary westerners are increasingly aware of, and influenced by, not only other faiths but also the very fact of religious plurality. Whereas the majority of westerners at the beginning of the 20th century knew very little about non-Christian faiths and often regarded their devotees as deluded and possibly backward, generally speaking this is not the case nowadays. Not only are westerners much more tolerant of and interested in the religious beliefs of others, but, in some cases, they adopt those beliefs in preference to the dominant beliefs in their own culture.

Secularization

Although Western societies are increasingly characterized by religious plurality, it is often pointed out that in most industrial societies there has been a decline, not only of the social significance of religion, but also of its appeal. The process by which a society becomes increasingly secular (non-religious) has been termed 'secularization'. Although aspects of the secularization thesis are debated, looking back over the past couple of centuries it would seem to be overwhelmingly evident that religious beliefs, practices and symbols are gradually being abandoned at all levels of modern society. Whereas a more scientifically educated, less credulous, and even cynical public is an important factor in the process of secularization, it is not the only, or even the principal, factor. Rather, the reasons for religious decline are primarily social not intellectual. Secularization is intrinsically related to modernization, in that modern societies inhibit the growth of traditional, institutional religion. For example, commerce and industrialization have led to the division of labour and thereby to the break-up of modern societies. Small closely knit, family-based communities with the church at the centre have been eroded. Over the past few centuries, religious authorities have lost their grip on the reins of economic power. Gradually, education, economic production, health care and a host of other activities have shifted from the control of the church to secular institutions. Consequently, religious influence has gradually weakened to the point at which it is all but absent.

Central to this apparent decline of religion is religious pluralism. Communities in which people shared the same religious beliefs and morality and within which an individual's material, intellectual and spiritual sustenance was provided, are rapidly disappearing. Unlike earlier communities in which a single religion was dominant and permeated all areas of community life, in modern societies there are few shared values to which one can appeal. Believers are constantly aware that their faith is *chosen* from a spectrum of beliefs on offer. Consequently, beliefs that were once taken for granted as exclusively and absolutely true seem increasingly implausible. This is further encouraged by contemporary consumer cultures, which are driven by an insistence on variety and individual choice. Religion is increasingly a private, rather than a public matter. It is not that religion disappears, but rather that it is relegated from the social to the private sphere. For example, a consequence of this shift in modern democracies has been a series of laws that have repealed certain sanctions in order to ensure the equality of most forms of religious expression. Hence, in Britain, the 1951 repeal of the 1735 Witchcraft Act was not an attempt to promote witchcraft, but rather a logical step in a modern, secular democracy. There are no longer any acceptable reasons for defending the rights of one set of religious beliefs over another. As religion is simply a matter of personal preference, and since there is little evidence to establish the validity of one choice over another, or indeed to establish the validity of any of the choices, there are few reasons to limit choice.

Re-enchantment?

While there is undoubtedly truth in the above analysis, in that traditional institutional religion is on the decline in the West, it is not the whole picture. Throughout the West there has been a subtle growth of new and alternative forms of spirituality, which seem particularly suited to contemporary Western culture. Moreover, while many of these draw on occult, New Age or Eastern traditions, there are others that seem to be peculiarly Western, in that they have emerged directly out of Western cultural movements and interests, such as the UFO movement (see *Ufology and UFO-related Movements), psychotherapy or contemporary dance culture. Indeed, it is difficult to avoid the conclusion that the weight of evidence seems to favour the general thesis that religion is so psychologically and socially bound up with the human condition that it is unlikely ever to disappear. However dire the situation might be, however hostile to religion a culture might seem, spiritualities evolve and flourish. It is significant that Peter Berger, an important sociologist and one of the principal architects of the secularization thesis, has

recently changed his mind and predicted that the world of the 21st century will be no less religious than it is today. The 'religious impulse,' he writes, 'the quest for meaning that transcends the restricted space of empirical existence in this world, has been a perennial feature of humanity... It would require something close to a mutation of the species to extinguish this impulse for good.' Consequently, spirituality is being explored in some unexpected areas of Western life (such as the world of business) and may incorporate a range of beliefs informed by anything from the world religions to ideas about UFOs and dolphins. Indeed, one of the principal characteristics of contemporary Western spirituality is that it is *not* a return to previous ways of being religious, but rather the emergence of new ways of being religious that are often directly influenced by trends in Western culture.

The significance of the self

For example, a notable feature of the contemporary West is the 'turn to the self'. Traditionally, authorities have been external, in the sense that authority has resided in institutions and various social hierarchies. The priest, or the doctor, or the teacher, or the government, knows best. The point is that things have changed. Even in the last 30 years there has been a massive decline in deference to traditional authorities. In the modern Western world, not only are people less respectful of traditional authorities, but, as we have seen, increasingly authority is located in the individual, understood primarily as a consumer. We *decide* what is true for us; we *decide* what is good for us; we *decide* according to our own desires, conscience and reason. This shift has influenced the way people understand and practise religion in the West. Increasingly religious authority is understood to be located, not in a clerical hierarchy, nor in an institution, nor even in a transcendent God, but in the individual self. If you want to encounter the divine, *go within*. Self-spirituality tends to treat religions, and a lot else besides, as resources for a personal DIY spirituality.

Celebrities

Another feature of modern Western culture has been the cult of the celebrity. This, too, has led directly into *celebrity-centric spirituality. Notable in this respect was Diana, Princess of Wales. The public reaction to her death was an unprecedented global phenomenon. Not only did the events and grieving surrounding her funeral have distinctly religious overtones, but within a short space of time Diana the media icon became Diana the religious icon. People began praying to her, a Church of Diana was formed and a book claiming to contain channelled messages from the celestial Diana was published: *The Celestial Voice of Diana: Her Spiritual Guidance to Finding Love*.

While several typically Western forms of spirituality are discussed in the previous section, the primary focus of this section is spiritualities that are directly the product of modern Western cultural trends and ideas. Whether we think of consumerism, technology, issues concerning the body and gender, the tension between faith and modernity, or the challenge of postmodernism and postmodern culture, particular forms of spirituality have emerged which, although they may contain elements from the world religions, have their roots in the modern West.

Celebrity-centric Spirituality
John Drane

People have always loved celebrities. Many ancient stories reported the deeds of heroes with superhuman qualities, and offered them as inspiring models for ordinary people. The trend continued through the stories of Christian saints – people who not only displayed exemplary devotion to God, but also had the power to affect human lives long after their death, by offering healing miracles or appearing in visions at times of special need or hardship.

Medieval people were fascinated by the post-mortem deeds of saints, and travelled long distances to worship at their tombs or come into contact with their relics. Saints fulfilled much the same function as celebrities do today. On the one hand, they were ordinary people who therefore understood the rigours of everyday life. But on the other hand, they had triumphed over their own circumstances, often through sudden death, and because of their fortitude or moral achievements were believed to be closer to God than other mortals could ever hope to be.

The modern phenomenon can be traced back to the 19th century, when Prince Albert, husband to Queen Victoria, was venerated after his death by pilgrims who made frequent visits to London's Albert Memorial. When the British prime minister W.E. Gladstone died in 1898, his death provoked a mass outpouring of grief on the streets, including the writing of notes to him and about him, and the spontaneous creation of shrines by ordinary people. The trend continued throughout the

Diana, Princess of Wales, with a young girl during a visit to Shaukat Khanum Memorial Hospital in Pakistan. Since her death in 1997, Diana has become the focus for spiritual devotion and a permanent pilgrimage site has been created in her memory.

☞ *continued on page 365*

POSTMODERN SPIRITUALITY

Jeremy R. Carrette

The meaning of the term 'postmodern' is much debated and the idea of 'postmodern spirituality' is even more contentious, and, for some, a contradiction in terms. Nonetheless, it is possible to identify a number of ways in which these terms function in the contemporary world. It is first necessary to make a distinction between postmoder*nity* and postmoder*nism*. Postmodernity is seen to refer to the developments of late capitalistic society, such as

mass urbanization, architectural diversity, information technology, the World Wide Web, cyberspace, mass media and the global economy. In this sense, postmodernity is a cultural and social phenomenon, reflecting technological developments in the Western world. Some would argue that this is 'late' modern not postmodern, but either way there is a sense that the social world has gone through some revolutionary changes since the Second World War, which in turn challenge and change religious thought and practice.

Postmodernity or postmodernism?

Postmodernity can be regarded as distinct from postmodernism, which is seen as a collection of ideas challenging the philosophical assumptions of Western thought. Postmodernism is a challenge to the project of the Enlightenment (the rational and scientific understanding of the world emerging from 17th-century Europe). Postmodernism is

Singer and performer Madonna on The Virgin Tour Live, 1985. She has been described as the perfect postmodern icon.

often used to refer to a set of critical ideas, often unrelated and extremely divergent, emerging out of post-war Europe and, more specifically, from post-1968 France. In the light of the machines of mass destruction, Nazi Germany and the Holocaust, postmodern thought questions the idea that rationality and science is progressive and somehow improving the world. The horrors of mass destruction bring into question the idea of progress in history and put so-called 'rational' enquiry under suspicion. The postmodern questioning of progress highlights a contradiction in the term 'postmodern', in so far as it assumes a period of time 'after' modernity and thus paradoxically adopts a linear progression of time characteristic of modernity. Modernity is an equally difficult term, but can be used to refer to the social order emerging from the Enlightenment, particularly the industrialization and rationalization of society.

Postmodernism questions the basis of this modern world, not necessarily by giving up rationality, but by questioning the nature of rationality and its hidden assumptions. It is in this sense that the postmodern is also seen as 'reflexive' or self-questioning modernity. Postmodernism also questions

'grand narratives', Jean-François Lyotard's term for the great explanations of life (religious ideas and science); it questions the certainties of knowledge. Knowledge is no longer regarded as neutral but politically motivated and socially conditioned.

Postmodern or post-structuralist?

As the term 'postmodern' is used to classify a whole range of thinkers it can be useful to make a distinction between 'post-structuralist' and 'postmodernist' thinkers (often both classified as simply postmodern). Post-structuralist thinkers (e.g. Michel Foucault and Jacques Derrida) challenge the given structures behind history, texts and ideas. They demonstrate the hidden social, political, philosophical and historical conditions of knowledge. This is slightly different from postmodern thinkers (e.g. Jean Baudrillard and Jean-François Lyotard) who tend to be more playful and relativistic in their attempts to show the dominance of technology and the mass media in Western society. It should be noted that most thinkers classified as postmodern would reject the title and it is often the case that thinkers are grouped in this way by critics who wish to dismiss a set of ideas. Some also believe the term 'postmodern' is

deliberately vague and ambiguous in order to be disruptive to any system of clear, rational thought, but such responses are often used to avoid the hard work of dealing with the difficult texts of such writers. On the whole, the postmodern marks out a space within, or after, modernity, which reflects powerful changes in society, politics, culture, aesthetics and philosophy.

What is postmodern spirituality?

Postmodern spirituality is the religious response to and the engagement with postmodernity and postmodernism. Postmodern spirituality is, therefore, a reflection of the changing cultural context and a critique of Modern philosophical assumptions. Such a challenge brings into question the boundaries between religious tradition, space, community and the body. In postmodern spirituality there is an anxiety about, and questioning of, the boundaries between past and present, sacred and profane, self and other, and body and mind. The pre-modern and modern order is suspended and a crisis of identity emerges. There are two distinct responses in postmodern spirituality to this questioning of the Modern. Firstly, a reaffirmation of the pre-modern world and tradition, as in the academic Christian theology of Radical Orthodoxy and forms of religious fundamentalism; and, secondly, a re-evaluation of tradition, space, community and the body, as in New Age groups and forms of individualized or private spirituality. Postmodern spirituality can be seen as both a conservative reaction against the Modern or radical liberation from the Modern. Both are responses to the fragmentation and collapse of Modernity as a unifying and cohesive system of ideas. However, the term 'spirituality' tends to be associated more with non-institutional forms of practice and a radical rethinking of tradition, space, community and the body. In this sense, postmodern spirituality reflects the collapse of religious authority and institutional practice.

Tradition, technology and popular culture

Postmodern spirituality transforms tradition into something important for the present, rather than seeing tradition as something imposed from the past; the so-called 'New' Age is a classic example of this reworking and adaptation of traditions for present concerns. Tradition is perceived as a rich resource entangled in the politics of transmission and recognized

as serving the interests of race, class and gender. Postmodern spirituality suspends the notion of a 'pure' tradition and celebrates the diversity of interpretations. Religious spaces are also radically transformed in postmodern spirituality. The sacred space is no longer delimited simply by institutional power, but is rather contested and relocated according to the politics of individual experience (supported by shared values). Postmodern spirituality can be equally found in club cultures, the music industry and cinemas, as well as on mountain tops and in private homes. Postmodern spirituality also questions the traditional religious space and assumes a 'spacelessness' as it flows along information highways and becomes a cyber-reality. The spiritual community is in turn transformed by the values of individualism, as tradition and space become fragmented into commodities to be purchased in the spiritual supermarket. In postmodernity, various spiritual identities can be purchased; by simply signing a cheque you can have the book, the T-shirt and the film. In postmodern spirituality, the body is acknowledged as the key site (and sight) of religious knowledge, something given but not outwardly celebrated

in the Modern period. In postmodern spirituality, the body and sexuality are celebrated as potentially positive forces for spiritual renewal, not least seen in the advancement of alternative therapies, such as acupuncture, aromatherapy and body massage. Sexuality is also rescued in postmodern Christian spirituality and in the development of Eastern tantric rituals. The importance of the body is a reflection of how postmodern spiritualities question the division between the transcendent and the immanent. In postmodern spirituality the transcendent is either seen as present in the immanent or as a false division, making creation divine. In postmodern spirituality, the old religious certainties are dissolved and rediscovered in the cinema, the shopping mall and the music of Madonna. Some would argue that this reflects the domination of capitalism; others, that the mass-produced and the material have taken on important spiritual value.

20th century in many different countries. Indeed, as commitment to traditional religious faiths has weakened in the West, so devotion to celebrities has strengthened and increased in importance. Well-known individuals who have become the focus for this kind of spiritual devotion include Marilyn Monroe (d. 1962), John F. Kennedy (d. 1963), John Lennon (d. 1980), Che Guevara (d. 1967), and other more local celebrities. But the most famous of them all must be Elvis Presley (d. 1977) and Diana, Princess of Wales (d. 1997) – both of whom not only live on in popular memory, but also have their own permanent pilgrimage sites. In a remarkable parallel with the medieval saints, they not only died in tragic circumstances, but have also become the object of much myth-making, especially in relation to whether or not they are really dead at all, or whether they might still live on in some way that is either physical or mystical, or both.

Elvis's former home, Graceland, in Memphis, Tennessee, attracts enormous numbers of visitors from all around the world. What they find when they get there is much the same as what medieval pilgrims encountered at the tombs of saints and martyrs. The constant speculation about whether Elvis is actually dead merely serves to enhance his status. It certainly makes it seem perfectly natural to pray to him, as if he continues to be a bridge between the pain and anguish of this world and the spiritual perfection of some other world. At the same time, Elvis is rarely regarded as divine in himself, and one of the most striking features about Graceland is the way in which overtly Christian symbolism appears everywhere, not only in the displays but also on the persons of most pilgrims. For those who visit, Elvis seems to fulfil the kind of role ascribed to John the Baptist in the New Testament, pointing to Jesus as being more important than himself, but still retaining an enigmatic fascination because of his lifestyle and, more especially, his death. It should be no surprise that this has happened with Elvis, for during his life he continually raised spiritual questions through his music, no doubt reflecting his own origins in the Assemblies of God Pentecostal Church.

It is more surprising that a similar phenomenon should have appeared in connection with Diana, Princess of Wales, especially at a time when the popularity of the British royal family (and the aristocracy generally) was at an all-time low. It was inevitable that, at the time of her death, there would be speculation about what had 'really' happened, but it has continued, partly facilitated by the fact that, like Elvis, her grave has also become a permanent pilgrimage site. One of the key features there is a plaque with a sentence from one of her speeches: 'Whenever you call to me, I will come to your aid.' When she said this, it can hardly have been intended to have any transcendent implications – but in the context of her ancestral home at Althorp, it naturally evokes images of immortality, if not divinity. That view is certainly promoted more overtly in the many websites devoted to Diana, not to mention books of spiritual wisdom that claim to have been communicated from her in the next world.

Why is this kind of celebrity-centric spirituality still popular? One answer is that historic conventions rarely disappear altogether, and if our forebears were reverencing their celebrities centuries ago, why should we be surprised if we still do it? But there are other factors operating. For, unlike the saints, today's heroes are not perfect, and we would not regard them highly if they were. Elvis struggled with alcoholism, Diana with bulimia, and both of them had relationship difficulties. Yet they also brought much happiness into people's lives. They showed that it is still possible for people who are imperfect to do good. In that sense, they were already spiritual role models while they were alive: their attractiveness has only been enhanced through death. By way of contrast, traditional religions generally offer 'perfect' role models. In the past, people aspired to that perfection for themselves, but today we are more likely to acknowledge that we are not perfect, and never will be. We settle for being the best we can, and in that context flawed celebrities can seem to offer more realistic spiritual prospects than individuals who appear to have done everything right, whether they be Mahatma Gandhi, Jesus Christ or a medieval saint.

Transpersonal Psychologies
Michael Daniels

The word 'transpersonal' means beyond (or through) the personal. It refers to experiences in which there is an expansion of our ordinary limiting sense of self and a feeling of connection to a larger, more meaningful reality. Religious or spiritual experience is often seen as central to the transpersonal agenda, although the transpersonal can also be about extending our concern for (or our sense of identification with) other people, humankind, life, the planet or nature.

The first true transpersonal psychology was arguably born in 1901–02, when the American psychologist William James delivered the Gifford Lectures at the University of Edinburgh. In these lectures (published in 1902 as *The Varieties of Religious Experience*), James approached religion through the study of individual people's direct personal experience. Religious experience, he argued, is the legitimate subject matter of psychology and may be investigated using empirical, scientific methods. William James (brother of the novelist Henry James) was also a pioneer of psychical research, and his interest in religious experiences was further informed by his acquaintance with the doctrines of Emanuel Swedenborg (see the *New Church), American transcendentalism, the *Theosophical Society, Christian

mysticism, Sufism, Buddhism, Vedanta and yoga, as well as by his own experiments with mind-altering drugs. James is the first person known to have used the English term 'transpersonal' (1905). He argued that our ordinary waking consciousness was a special and limited case and that a thin veil separated this from a whole range of other types and possibilities of mystical and extraordinary experience.

The year 1901 also saw the publication of *Cosmic Consciousness* – a seminal and highly influential book about exalted and joyous experiences of the whole universe as a living and ordered Presence, written by the Canadian psychiatrist Richard M. Bucke. The investigation and systematization of mystical experiences, pioneered by James and Bucke, was later refined and developed by writers such as Evelyn Underhill in *Mysticism* (1911) and Marghanita Laski in *Ecstasy* (1961). It has since become a major area of research interest, as represented in the work of American psychologist Charles T. Tart and also of the Religious Experience Research Unit (now Centre) established by the distinguished British scientist Sir Alister Hardy in 1969.

Another important impetus in the development of transpersonal psychologies came from the psychoanalytic movement. Like William James, the Swiss analytical psychologist Carl Gustav Jung (1875–1961) was very interested in paranormal and religious experiences. At one time a close associate of Sigmund Freud, Jung became highly critical of Freud's uncompromising dismissal of the 'occult', and his belief that religion was a form of neurosis. Instead of immature and unhealthy psychological projections, Jung viewed the religious impulse as the manifestation and projection of spiritual archetypes (universal patterns of human experience) that exist within our 'transpersonal' collective unconscious. Jung saw the goal of human life as individuation –

essentially a spiritual quest for full humanness and psychological integration, or the realization of the archetype of the Self. He believed that individuation could be facilitated by working creatively and imaginatively with dream images, symbols and myths, which represent the process of spiritual transformation.

The Italian psychiatrist Roberto Assagioli was a student of raja yoga and also of the esotericist Alice Bailey (see the *Arcane School). Assagioli developed a theoretical and practical system of therapy and psychological development called 'psychosynthesis', which incorporates and emphasizes the spiritual dimensions of human experience. He argued that Jung's concept of the collective unconscious does not adequately distinguish between 'higher', 'middle' and 'lower' realms of the unconscious. For Assagioli, psychological development involves the exploration and integration (synthesis) of all three realms. In exploring and working with the higher unconscious, Assagioli believed that we make contact with the higher Self (or transpersonal Self). In learning to express and manifest the higher Self, we move beyond personal psychosynthesis to spiritual or transpersonal psychosynthesis. As a psychological system, psychosynthesis advocates various practical techniques, including meditation and visualization, as aids to transpersonal exploration and integration.

The American psychologist Abraham Maslow is best known as the founder of humanistic psychology (see the *human potential movement), which he saw as the 'third force' in psychology (the first two being behaviourism and psychoanalysis). Humanistic psychology emphasizes human rationality, agency, consciousness, positive mental health, realization of individual potential and self-actualization. It also seeks to recognize and study the 'higher' human experiences, which are generally ignored or neglected by mainstream psychology. These include love, empathy, creativity, intuition, mystical experience, altruism and compassion. Maslow found that many self-actualizing people report experiences of transcendence (e.g. self-forgetting, 'peak' or ecstatic experiences, and metamotivation or the desire to actualize universal values). Maslow interpreted these transcendent experiences as expressions of our common (essentially biological) human nature. Because of their undoubted reality and significance, he suggested that a psychology should be developed to investigate these phenomena. In the late 1960s, together with his colleagues Stanislav Grof, Anthony Sutich and others, he proposed the term 'transpersonal psychology' for this 'fourth force'. In 1969, the *Journal of Transpersonal Psychology* was launched, under the editorship of Anthony Sutich, and in 1972 the Association for Transpersonal Psychology was established.

Social changes in the 1960s had also contributed to the development of transpersonal psychologies. These included the widespread use of psychedelic drugs among the youth of the United States and Europe. Although this was often little more than a recreational activity, or a way of confirming an anti-establishment alternative lifestyle and identity, LSD and mescaline were viewed by some as facilitating valid states of spiritual consciousness (see *Psychedelic Spirituality). In *The Doors of Perception* (1954), the British writer Aldous Huxley had argued that mescaline could be a valuable aid in expanding human consciousness. Also in the 1960s, the Czech psychiatrist Stanislav Grof had pioneered the clinical use of LSD. Grof found that, especially with high doses, people would often report an extraordinary variety of unusual experiences in which the sense of time, space and self was drastically altered. Grof believed that LSD enabled people to experience 'transpersonal' realities normally hidden from our everyday consciousness. When LSD use was prohibited, Grof found that similar experiences could be induced using a technique he developed called 'holotropic breathwork', which involves lengthy sessions of altered breathing combined with music.

Around this time, there was also an explosion of interest in Eastern religions (especially Hinduism and Buddhism) and in meditation. Eastern teachings were seen by many westerners as both practical and psychologically sophisticated. They offered the promise of direct spiritual experience often lacking in traditional occidental religions. These philosophies were not only absorbed into the popular counter-culture of the time, but also increasingly came to dominate academic transpersonal psychology through the influence of writers such as Alan Watts, D.T. Suzuki, Sri Aurobindo (see *Auroville) and Chogyam Trungpa Rinpoche (see *Shambhala International). Although Hinduism and Buddhism have had the clearest impact on theory and research in transpersonal psychology, other religious-mystical teachings have also been influential. These include *Kabbalism, Christian mysticism, Gurdjieff's teachings (see *Gurdjieff and Ouspensky Groups), *Shamanism, Sufism, Daoism, theosophy and *Wicca.

At this point it should be noted that, despite being influenced by religious ideas and practices, transpersonal psychology is essentially an applied science and not a religion. It is also rather different from most traditional approaches to the psychology of religion. As well as including a concern with 'non-religious' phenomena, such as dreaming, transpersonal psychology is distinct in emphasizing *experience* (rather than beliefs,

Carl Jung, who believed human life is a spiritual quest for full humanness and psychological integration.

attitudes or social behaviours) and its insistence that the psychologist must *participate* in (rather than simply observe) the spiritual-transformational process. In this way, personal spiritual experience and practice serve to inform, ground and enrich the transpersonal psychologist's research.

Transpersonal psychology is also to be distinguished from parapsychology and psychical research, although they share many important interests (e.g. in lucid dreaming, out-of-body and near-death experiences, reincarnation, mediumistic phenomena and telepathy). The emphasis in parapsychology and psychical research is upon seeking objective evidence for the reality of paranormal phenomena, whereas transpersonal psychology is more interested in the subjective meaning that these experiences have for the individual, and in their capacity for promoting psychological and spiritual transformation.

From the early 1960s, meditation and other methods of personal transformation such as encounter groups, yoga, psychodrama, gestalt therapy, holotropic breathwork and body work, came to be taught at avant-garde 'growth centres' such as the Esalen Institute, which was established at Big Sur, California, in 1962. These centres became the focus of the human potential movement – a diffuse, rich, eclectic mix of transformational approaches and technologies that in many ways represents the practical and experientially orientated wing of humanistic and transpersonal psychology.

A number of important developments have occurred in transpersonal psychology since its academic foundation in 1969. These include extensive research on altered states of consciousness and into the physiological and psychological effects of meditation. Transpersonal psychology has also attempted to define itself more carefully, to develop epistemologies and research methodologies that are more appropriate to its subject matter, to create intelligible theoretical models of transpersonal states and processes, and to provide effective methods and practical guidance for people seeking to explore the transpersonal. It has also sought acknowledgment and acceptance from the psychological establishment and, in 1996, the British Psychological Society became the first professional psychological association to approve the formation of an academic section in transpersonal psychology.

The most influential (and controversial) contemporary theorist in academic transpersonal psychology is the American philosopher Ken Wilber, who now prefers to describe his own psychological approach as 'integral'. In a series of brilliant books and articles, beginning with *The Spectrum of Consciousness* (1977), Wilber has developed a conceptual framework of extraordinary breadth, sophistication and wide-ranging application. Wilber's theories are based upon Aldous Huxley's *Perennial Philosophy* (1947), or the belief that all religions share a common doctrinal and experiential deep structure. For Wilber, the perennial philosophy teaches the *Great Chain of Being* – the evolutionary interconnectedness of matter, mind and spirit. In psychological development, this evolutionary chain manifests as a progression from *prepersonal* consciousness (where there is no sense of self, or a very rudimentary physical one), through *personal* consciousness (involving a strong mental-egoic personality) to *transpersonal* consciousness (involving the expansion of identity beyond the personal, mental-egoic realm). Wilber also identifies successive stages at the transpersonal level. Transpersonal development, he argues, involves movement from *subtle* consciousness

(identification with nature, or experiencing imaginal, archetypal forms) through *causal* consciousness (formless experience, or transcendent witnessing) to *ultimate* consciousness (in which the world of form reappears, but is now *directly experienced* as the play or projection of mind/spirit). Wilber's model of transpersonal development has been criticized by some for being too heavily based on Eastern philosophies, especially Advaita Vedanta, Zen and Tibetan Buddhism, and for its failure to account adequately for theistic religious experience. Some feminists and transpersonal ecologists have also denounced Wilber for what they see as his patriarchal and hierarchical assumptions, and for seeming to devalue nature mysticism.

Although academic transpersonal psychology has developed within the domain of scientific psychology, it has always recognized the value of other disciplines in contributing to our understanding of the transpersonal. In this way, transpersonal psychology is sometimes seen as part of a larger, interdisciplinary *transpersonal movement* that incorporates, for example, transpersonal approaches within anthropology, business, counselling, ecology, education, medicine, neuroscience, pharmacology, philosophy, politics, psychiatry, religious studies and sociology. This broad transpersonal movement is generally understood to represent not only an approach to knowledge, but also a commitment to spiritual transformation in the individual, social, cultural and political spheres.

For people wishing to study transpersonal psychologies, academic courses are taught at several universities (mainly in the United States and Britain). There are also training programmes in transpersonal counselling and psychotherapy offered by various independent organizations, including those based on Buddhist and psychosynthesis approaches. Consistent with the general transpersonal ethic, an important feature of both academic study and professional training in transpersonal psychology is the way in which courses typically include an emphasis on students' own experiential learning and personal transformation.

URANTIA
Lorne Dawson

The URANTIA movement is based on the study of *The URANTIA Book*, a collection of papers (2,097 pages) first published in 1935. This book contains the revelations of numerous alien beings about the true nature of the universe, the history of planet earth (called URANTIA) and the life of Jesus. The messages were channelled by a person while sleeping and recorded by Dr William Samuel Sadler (1875–1969), a respected psychiatrist at the University of Chicago and lecturer at McCormick Theological Seminary. The book describes a startlingly complex universe of multiple dimensions containing thousands of inhabited worlds ruled over by thousands of gods of varying ranks with diverse duties. At the highest level is the 'I AM' who resides in Paradise. The last part of the book contains many new claims about the childhood, travels, ministry, death and resurrection of Jesus. Jesus is identified as but one of 700,000 Creator Sons incarnated on various worlds, and he will return to earth once humanity is transformed by this new set of revelations. It is believed that a 'thought adjuster' dwells in each of us, seeking to direct our lives to the truth. Upon death our souls will enter into a deep sleep and be taken to other worlds to begin an endless journey of self-discovery culminating in admission to Paradise. The sole activity of the membership is to study the book, often in groups. There are no clergy or churches. Disagreements over the legal ownership of the book, its interpretation, and the reception of new

revelations, have led to many struggles and schisms in the movement. However, these appear to have now been settled to the satisfaction of most members.

Psychedelic Spirituality
Christopher Partridge

Psychedelic spirituality is a form of spirituality in which hallucinogens are central. Hallucinogens are substances which, when taken in small doses, cause a chemical reaction in the brain, the effect of which is an alteration in the user's perception, mood and thought processes. However, unlike some drugs, people under the influence of hallucinogens will often (not always) be aware of what is going on and will be able to reflect, usually in detail, on the experience after it has passed. Generally speaking, there is a heightened sense of awareness and a belief that one's perception is sharper, deeper and more responsive to the material and spiritual environment. Reflecting what is often felt to be a spiritual experience, psychedelic drugs are sometimes termed 'entheogens' because they are thought to engender a sense of 'god within'.

Throughout religious history there are examples of the use of hallucinogens. For example, in the earliest sacred text of Hinduism, the *Rig Veda* (c. 1200–900 BCE), 120 hymns are devoted to soma, a psychoactive plant also visualized as a deity. Soma seems to have been given its privileged position in Vedic spirituality because of its powerful hallucinogenic properties and it is not difficult to find evidence of this attitude to hallucinogens in many human societies.

Although drug-related spirituality has a long history, the modern Western psychedelic story can be said to have begun in 1938, when Albert Hofmann, a research chemist working for Sandoz Pharmaceutical Laboratories in Switzerland, produced LSD-25. More significantly (as far as modern psychedelic spirituality is concerned), Humphrey Osmond, a British psychiatrist working in Canada who had used LSD to treat alcoholics, introduced Aldous Huxley (1894–1963) to the use of mescaline. Huxley became convinced that the altered states of consciousness produced were in fact mystical states and that drugs provided a gateway to a larger, truer grasp of reality. Indeed, the term 'psychedelic' (which means 'soul- or mind-manifesting') was coined by Osmond to indicate the mystical and visionary potential of hallucinogens. However, if Osmond coined the key term, Huxley produced the most influential text of psychedelia: *The Doors of Perception* (1954). The revealing title of the book is taken from William Blake's *Marriage of Heaven and Hell*: 'If the doors of perception were cleansed, everything would appear to man as it really is – infinite.' When the doors of perception were cleansed for Huxley in Los Angeles, on the morning of 6 May 1953 after ingesting 300 mg of mescaline, he was literally lost for words and awed by what he felt and saw. It wasn't simply that he was struck by the rainbow brilliance of the world he had entered, but, more profoundly, he was moved by his sense of oneness with reality, a reality which, he perceived, was essentially divine. That he perceived this is not coincidental, in that, arguably, mescaline simply allowed him to experience the type of Indian-influenced mysticism explored in his earlier book *The Perennial Philosophy* (1946).

One of Huxley's principal claims was that psychedelic experience is directly analogous to those experiences claimed by mystics in the world's religions, but that psychedelics provide those experiences instantly: 'Training in mysticism can be speeded up and made more effective by a judicious use of the physically harmless psychedelics now available.' Indeed, he believed that mescaline had introduced him to the Beatific Vision which, he argued, was to be identified with the experience of *sat chit ananda* (Being-Awareness-Bliss) in Indian religious tradition. However, not only are there problems with this identification, but R.C. Zaehner, a scholar of Eastern religions, has argued that it betrays muddled thinking rather than any profound mystical experience. Nevertheless, similar claims are regularly made by those who practise psychedelic spirituality.

It is difficult to underestimate the significance of Huxley for the development of psychedelic spirituality in the West. Certainly psychedelic religious experience gained a kudos that would have been denied it had it not been for Huxley. His ideas, set forth in eloquent and informed prose, found their way into the minds of those who would not normally have considered psychedelic spirituality worthy of critical scrutiny.

The psychedelia of the 1950s tended to be the elitist philosophy of several prominent intellectuals who wanted to avoid damaging publicity, stress respectable research and develop psychedelic esoteric thought. Elitism was hardly true of the man Allen Ginsberg called 'a hero of American consciousness… faced with the task of a Messiah', namely, Timothy Leary (1920–96).

Motivated by Leary's drive and

Aldous Huxley, caricatured by Sir Max Beerbohm.

☞ *continued on page 377*

UFOLOGY AND UFO-RELATED MOVEMENTS

Andreas Grünschloss

In March 1997, there was a mass suicide in San Diego, California, when 39 members of *Heaven's Gate decided to leave 'this world' in expectation of a better ufological future, as previously announced on their website:

RED ALERT! HALE-BOPP brings closure to HEAVEN'S GATE. As was promised, the keys to Heaven's Gate are here again in Ti and Do (the UFO Two) as they were in Jesus and his Father 2,000 years ago. Whether Hale-Bopp has a 'companion' or not is irrelevant from our perspective. However, its arrival is joyously very significant to us at 'Heaven's Gate'. The joy is that our Older Member in the Evolutionary Level Above Human (the 'Kingdom of Heaven') has made it clear to us that Hale-Bopp's approach is the 'marker' we've been waiting for – the time for the arrival of the spacecraft from the Level Above Human to take us home to 'Their World' – in the literal heavens. Our 22 years of classroom here on planet earth is finally coming to conclusion – 'graduation' from the Human Evolutionary Level. We are happily prepared to leave 'this world' and go with Ti's crew.

Mostly members of long-standing, they did not wait for some alien technology or a dawning millennium on this planet, but rather staged their own collective apocalypse supported with biblical references, esoteric 'ascension' metaphors and technological terminology: they hoped to 'discarnate' their fleshly 'containers' while their 'soul-software' would be 'saved' to a numinous spacecraft of the 'Higher Level'.

Origins of modern ufology

Heaven's Gate is part of a new phenomenon in modern religious history, which, although largely unnoticed by the wider public, has gradually surfaced during the last 50 years, namely, the rise of prophets and more or less organized religious groups claiming to be in contact with space aliens, either from other planets in our solar system or from remote galaxies. Following the North American UFO sightings that began in 1947 (especially famous cases such as the sightings by Kenneth Arnold and the Roswell incident of a supposed crashed spacecraft and the recovery of aliens in New Mexico), several people began to receive telepathic 'messages' from spiritually and technologically advanced 'star brothers', and some of them even reported 'close encounters' with these beings and alleged flights in their interplanetary space crafts. It wasn't long before books with titles such as *Inside the Space Ships* and *I Rode a Flying Saucer* began to appear.

While ufology is, generally speaking, a fairly recent phenomenon, there are several notable forerunners. For example, John Ballou Newbrough, a medical doctor and spiritualist (1828–91), reported esoteric revelations concerning the spiritual universe and its celestial angels (ashars), who travel the skies with ethereal 'ships'. Similarly, Charles Fort's *The Book of the Damned* (1919, followed by three further volumes) reported all kinds of strange 'sightings' that had been 'excluded' and 'damned' by modern science. In his book he propagated the general idea that we are the property of some extraterrestrial force. Fort inspired many science fiction and fantasy writers (e.g. H.P. Lovecraft), as well as popular authors like Robert Charroux and Erich von Däniken, who initiated the modern 'ancient astronauts' theories and related attempts to collect archaeological and mythological evidence for the belief that, in Von Däniken's words, 'the gods of antiquity were alien astronauts – nothing else'. Indeed, in terms of particular religious ideas, there is a great deal of continuity with 19th-century esoteric and occult traditions. Strictly speaking, however, the founding fathers of modern religious ufologies were more recent individuals. Of particular note are George Adamski, George Van Tassel, Orfeo Angelucci and Daniel Fry, all of whom reported their extraterrestrial 'contacts' back in the early 1950s and thereby inspired a new tradition and the increasingly popular phenomenon of the 'contactee'.

Early messages

Most messages from the 'star people' agree that the members of the Galactic Federation, Star Brotherhood (etc.) are highly alarmed because of humankind's recent access to atomic energy. Consequently, they give spiritual advice and warn that, unless their advice is heeded, the earth is doomed to a great disaster. The main problem seems to be that humans – who are technologically advanced – are spiritually underdeveloped and therefore not in a position to handle their new power. In the final analysis, the risk is that the planet will be destroyed (as depicted in the film *Abyss* in 1989). This can be illustrated by the following quotation from an early message to the American contactee George Van Tassel (July 1952):

Hail to you beings of Shan [i.e. earth], I greet you in love and peace, my identity is Ashtar, commandant quadra sector,

patrol station Schare, all projections, all waves. Greetings, through the Council of the Seven Lights, you have been brought here inspired with the inner light to help your fellow man. You are mortals and other mortals can only understand that which their fellow man can understand. The purpose of this organization is, in a sense, to save mankind from himself. Some years ago your time, your nuclear physicists penetrated the 'Book of Knowledge'; they discovered how to explode the atom. Disgusting as the results have been, that this force should be used for destruction, it is not compared to that which can be... Our missions are peaceful, but this condition occurred before in this solar system and the planet Lucifer was torn to bits. We are determined that it shall not happen again... Your purpose here has been to build a receptivity that we could communicate with your planet, for by the attraction of light substances atoms, we patrol your universe. To your government and to your people and through them to all governments and all people on the planet of Shan, accept the warning as a blessing that mankind may survive. My light, we shall remain in touch here at this cone of receptivity. My love, I am Ashtar.

A closer investigation of the religious content of these extraterrestrial messages, however, shows striking family resemblances to rather well-known earthly strands of modern theosophical or esoteric traditions. Indeed, the same holds true for most of the later ufological channellings up to the present day. Figures from earlier esoteric beliefs (e.g. the Ascended Masters, or the Great White Brotherhood) reappear in 'space age' outfits. This is certainly true of the prominent enlightened being Ashtar, who is supposed to serve as a space commander of a huge star fleet with millions of 'ships of light'. (The very word 'ashtar' appears already in Helena P. Blavatsky's *The Secret Doctrine* of 1888.) The spiritual teachings (e.g. the books by Adamski, Angelucci or Paulsen) simply reformulate the basic faith beliefs common to esoteric and theosophical views on reincarnation, ascension of the eternal soul, 'resonating frequencies', the renunciation of the world and matter and the desire to be transported to higher 'spiritual' spheres. Often they incorporate the idea of sunken continents (Atlantis, Mu) and apply Eastern meditation techniques and concepts of the *atman* (self).

Ufology and apocalypticism

As in the famous (and first) socio-psychological study of an early ufological group by Leon Festinger, Henry

Reichen and Stanley Schachter, *When Prophecy Fails* (1956), some of these messages are very apocalyptic in tone and content, and many religious UFO groups await an imminent 'Big Beam' onto the waiting ships of the 'Star Brotherhood' before the earth's destruction, cleansing or ultimate restoration to a paradisiacal state. This millenarian strand of ufology has contributed much to the formation of some new religious movements. For example, several loosely organized groups belong to the worldwide network of the so-called 'Ashtar Command'. Instead of the early references to a nuclear holocaust or 'cleansing' of earth, it is now anticipated that 'the cosmic being' (earth), is severely suffering from human pollution and will soon undergo a 'Great Tribulation' of earthquakes, volcanic eruptions, polar shifts and tidal waves. Before this, a great 'evacuation' and 'lift off' to the space ships will be organized by Ashtar and his celestial crew, which has to be anticipated by a chosen 'ground crew' of human disseminators. Aboard the ships, human beings will be trained with new technologies and spiritual means in order to 'ascend' to higher resonating frequencies, resulting in spiritual liberation and paranormal states of consciousness. Earth will then be turned into a perfect garden, and the spiritually transformed will return to live in a millennium of peace, happiness and light. The apocalyptic scenario described here is disseminated by a variety of Ashtar-related web-pages, brochures and books – some of them having already become 'classics', like E.P. Hill's *Ashtar: In Days to Come* (1955) or T.B. Terrel's *Project World-Evacuation* (1982). The same ideas are expressed by other groups, for example, *Fiat Lux, the North American Ground Crew and the Planetary Activation Organization. The idea of spiritual ascension and the hope for higher stages of consciousness is mostly blended with the advent of superior alien 'cargo' with incredible new technologies and ecologically harmless energies (especially so-called 'free energies'). With regard to this combined vision of perfect technology and spiritual (and cosmological) perfection, many millenarian versions of UFO faith can indeed be perceived as a Western parallel to the Melanesian *cargo cults.

Non-apocalyptic ufology

Not all religious ufologies share the apocalyptic tension described above. The *Church of Scientology, for example, nowadays has to be placed within a non-millenarian ufological strand of modern religious history. That said, Scientology shares a basic ancient astronauts myth and conceives of earthly human beings primarily as (extraterrestrial) 'thetans' who have to access their 'bridge to freedom' – a belief about the soul that has strong similarities with typical ufological notions of 'star seeds' or 'walk-ins' who had been planted in this earthly 'garden' for spiritual growth. According to Scientology's secret mythology, a fierce intergalactic ruler named 'Xenu' carried the thetans to earth. Interestingly, L. Ron Hubbard, the founder of Scientology and a science fiction author, has written a book called *Revolt in the Stars* (so far unpublished, but unofficially disseminated on the internet), in which he explores this story of the ancient ruler Xenu. The *Aetherius Society, founded by George King (1919–97) is another group in which the idea of 'religious technology', so dominant in Scientology, also finds many striking expressions. For example, 'prayer energy' is supposed to be 'accumulated' in crystal 'batteries', which can be used to charge certain earthly places with good energy. Here, one can also find a strong reception and application of yoga meditation, which is combined with the ufological cosmology.

Some movements, on the other hand, have changed their eschatological attitude over time. For example, the Californian Solar Logos Foundation (previously the Sunburst Community or Brotherhood of the Sun), which was founded by Norman Paulsen, a student of Yogananda (see the *Self-Realization Fellowship), had strong millennial expectations in the 1970s, but now this small community seems to have resorted to a rather calm application of Paulsen's meditation technique in order to enlighten the human soul with the 'Solar Logos' – quite similar to other esoteric 'ascension' and 'light work' programmes.

Religious aspects and undercurrents can also be detected in the so-called 'paleo-SETI' discourses of Erich von Däniken and similar authors. 'SETI' is an established acronym for 'Search for Extraterrestrial Intelligence', whereas 'paleo-SETI' denotes a focus on antiquity. An international network for paleo-SETI discussions is provided by the Research Association for Archaeology, Astronautics and SETI (originally called the Ancient Astronaut Society). Various magazines are devoted to discussion of paleo-SETI-related issues, such as *Ancient Skies* and *Sagenhafte Zeiten*. In the writings of Von Däniken and

others, diverse myths, archaeological remnants and sacred scriptures are interpreted as factual accounts of alien interventions in ancient human history. Instead of turning to 'eschatology' (end-times), here the focus is on 'protology' (origins): creation, the origins of human life and other paradigmatic events in the past. While the whole paleo-SETI enterprise describes itself as alternative historical/scientific research, it has to be said that the relationship to contemporary science and history is rather tenuous: without referring carefully to the original contexts, religious myths are taken primarily at face value in order to 'prove' the belief that our ancestors had encounters with superior alien technologies.

To the student of religion, these ideological reconstructions must appear as a 'neo-mythic' activity, a mythic 'foundation' of the modern worldview: technological explanations, projected back into the past, serve as a disenchantment of old mythic accounts (i.e. the supernatural is 'explained' in technical terms), but at the same time the myths are retained as basically 'true', although reinterpreted in terms of the 'ancient astronaut' hypothesis. These modern myths about the ancient astronaut gods

reappear in contemporary science fiction films such as *Stargate* or *Mission to Mars*, and they are sometimes fully incorporated into contactee versions of UFO faith or other esoteric reconstructions of humanity's religious history. The most prominent example of this is the *Raëlian religion of Claude 'Raël' Vorilhon, one of the most consolidated UFO groups internationally active today (with important centres in Quebec). French-born Vorilhon published a story of his encounter with a returned ancient astronaut named 'Jahwe' in 1973 near Clermont Ferrand in France. The interpretations of biblical events disclosed to him by the aliens are strikingly similar to the theories of Von Däniken and Charroux published a few years previously. For example, he claims that he was informed that, originally, the ancient extraterrestrial Elohim (a biblical Hebrew word for God/Gods) created humanity in their image by genetic manipulation. Moreover, many other religious texts witness to these alien interventions. However, with Raël's election as human contactee for the Elohim (he claims to be a son of Jahwe), a new phase in human history has begun, as the end-time, when 'science replaces religion', is near. Eternal life is to be gained, not by spiritual salvation, but rather through genetic science: 'Then, we wake up after death in a brand new body just like after a good night's sleep.' So states the homepage of 'Clonaid', Raël's prestige cloning project and subject of many media reports during the last few years. The internet, in general, has become the place where most of these groups and their ufologies are internationally disseminated.

Prominent themes in religious ufologies

Despite their differences in detail, religious ufologies express a common theme, namely, the search for an integral vision, a 'synthesis of science and religion'. This ufological view of the 'unity of reality' attempts to be in accordance with the modern scientific and technological worldview (especially the space age) with its inherent ideas of progress, perfection and easy utilization, and, at the same time, propagates a mythological re-enchantment of heaven with (in most cases, benevolent) celestial beings (humanoid 'astronaut gods' or 'angels in space suits') and reconstructs personal and cosmic life in profoundly 'religious' ways (reincarnation, ascension of the soul, millennial paradise, return of the sunken continents etc.). Obviously, it is this language of technology

and of scientific 'explanation' and 'proof' (of particular note is the popular series *The X-Files*, which has popularized the phrases 'the truth is out there' and 'I want to believe') that makes inherited religious ideas appear more plausible and compatible with the modern world than the traditional religious language employed in established religious traditions.

Not all contemporary ufologies are 'religious' in nature. There are many ufological discourses that merely concentrate on cumulative research and publications (in print, as well as on the internet) on modern UFO sightings, varying in degree from strong enthusiasm to sharp critique (e.g. organizations like NICAP, CUFOS, MUFON, MUFON-CES, CENAP, GEP and many more). The religious ufologies are treated with special disregard by such critical UFO investigators. For example, the famous 'photographs' of alleged alien spacecrafts – flying saucers ('scouts') and cigar-shaped 'mother ships' – by contactee George Adamski have long been the target of severe criticism, as well as the pictures by contactee Eduard 'Billy' Meier (founder of the Swiss FIGU: Free Community of Interests in Fringe and Spiritual Sciences and Ufological Studies), who

reported various UFO contacts and meetings with star people from the Pleiades (especially religious instructions by the space girl 'Semjase'), and others. As becomes apparent (not only to outside observers) the history of modern ufology is in some respects also a history of fraud and manipulation.

This is also apparent in the 'abductee' version of UFO faith, which forms a topic in itself. Inaugurated by a variety of alien abduction reports, the experiences of supposed abductees have already become a distinct genre of modern folklore. Some have sought to provide psychological explanations for these accounts, or have made comparisons with the gnomes, dwarfs and fairies of traditional folklore; the manipulative and sometimes erotic activities of the legendary 'little green men' from Mars or outer space seem to share several aspects of older stories about the 'little people' in Europe's rural traditions. So, despite their apparently 'modern' and technological garments, many ufologies seem to represent older strands of alternative religiosity – *Spiritualism, theosophic/esoteric faith or folk traditions – but in a contemporary space age outfit.

Timothy Leary, 'a hero of American consciousness' according to Allen Ginsberg.

charismatic personality, the 1960s psychedelic revolution quickly became a large and influential subculture. The term 'psychedelic' rapidly expanded to include all forms of culture that were thought to inspire, or to be inspired by, the use of hallucinogens. A great deal of time and creative energy was invested in the production of music and art that would encourage successful psychedelic 'spiritual' experiences, much of which reflected the impact of Huxley's and Leary's thought. As is evident in writings from the period, it was clearly believed that humanity was on the verge of a new age of drug-provoked, Indian-influenced, expanded consciousness. The 1960s beatnik culture had turned East, enthusiastically converted to psychedelia, and, for the most part, accepted Leary's philosophy of 'turn on, tune in and drop out' – the new psychedelic mantra.

It is not difficult to trace the continuity between the psychedelic hippie culture of the 1960s and the rave culture of the 1980s and 1990s. That said, while Buddhist and Hindu beliefs were central to much earlier

psychedelic mystical experience, and although their influence is still important, contemporary psychedelia tends to be more eclectic and certainly more Pagan in orientation. A good example of this type of essentially neo-Pagan psychedelia is that developed by the late Terence McKenna, probably the most important recent exponent of psychedelics. Essentially McKenna's spirituality is based on the belief that the evolution of human spirituality and rationality was kick-started by the ingestion of hallucinogenic mushrooms. Indeed, he claims that humans have a very basic and important relationship with mushrooms. Our existence as rational, spiritual beings, is a consequence of our early ancestors eating hallucinogenic mushrooms. McKenna's basic thesis is simply that psychedelic spirituality takes us back to our roots. Hence, the drug-induced feeling of oneness with nature is by no means coincidental. Hallucinogenic plants encourage the re-emergence of a Gaia consciousness, which is, he argues, the archaic consciousness of primal peoples who recognize humanity's connectedness to the planet.

What is the appeal of psychedelic spirituality? The increasing desire in Western consumer culture for instant experience makes psychedelic spirituality particularly appealing. The ingestion of natural hallucinogens (psilocybin mushrooms etc.), which increase the user's perception of oneness with the earth, is attractive in a culture with a heightening sensitivity to environmental issues and a consequent emphasis on humanity's interdependence with the natural world. The current appeal of primal cultures, which are considered to be more in tune with the earth, has led to a rise of interest in the religious use of hallucinogens in these cultures as an aid to a more nature-centric spirituality. Because hallucinogens tend to engender experiences of a monistic or pantheistic nature, psychedelic spirituality is attractive to the increasing numbers of westerners sympathetic to Buddhist, Hindu and Daoist worldviews. Finally, it should be noted that many psychedelics and 'dance drugs', such as 'ecstasy' (MDMA), are now illegal in Western countries and are so because they have proved not to be as harmless as Huxley and others believed them to be.

Silva Mind Control
John A. Saliba

Silva Mind Control (or the Silva Method) is a self-help organization created by Jose Silva (1914–99). Developed as early as 1944, it went public in 1966 and since then has grown into a worldwide organization, offering its techniques in 107 countries and in 29 languages. Though membership statistics are not available, it is reckoned that millions of men and women have taken the basic course. The methods of self-improvement can be found in its basic manual, *The Silva Mind Control Method*, which describes the techniques. This was later expanded to include practical applications for solving human problems.

The basic lecture series is made up of four main courses. The first, 'Controlled Meditation', teaches the student how to relax physically, mentally and emotionally through various exercises and hypnosis. The second, 'General Self-Improvement', uses the expanded awareness acquired in the first course to solve specific problems. Memory techniques, habit control and the enhancement of the powers of visualization and the imagination to make it clearer are among the goals pursued at this stage. The third course, 'Effective Memory Projection', is directed towards increasing students' awareness and enabling them to use their intuitive faculty to solve problems dealing

with work, health, love and money. In the final course, 'Applied Effective Sensory Projection', students learn to function at the alpha level of the mind (normally associated with the dream state) and thus to further the betterment both of themselves and society.

It is unclear to what extent the Silva Method can be called 'religious' and the group would prefer not to be called a religion. It appears to be largely a *human potential movement that applies psychological and psychic techniques to enhance the capabilities of the mind. There are no initiation rituals, no specific beliefs or dogmas, and no regular ceremonies characteristic of religious organizations. Yet its use of meditation and psychic methods, its claim to teach its members supernatural skills, and the similarities of its spiritual goals to those of the New Age has led some to classify it as a 'quasi-religious' movement. Such a conclusion is supported by the fact that spiritual presuppositions and teachings that are accepted on faith undergird the movement. Moreover, statements in the Silva Method literature that the method is 'god-oriented' and that its members seek to attain 'Christ consciousness' suggest that there is an underlying, albeit undeveloped, theology behind the movement.

Most of the negative reactions to the Silva Method have come from evangelical Christians who argue that Silva's theology, especially regarding Christ, the nature of sin, and the need for salvation, are at odds with orthodox Christianity. The major scientific critique of the Silva Method has been that it is a rather subjective process that is difficult to test and impossible to prove. Yet Silva Mind Control has been a very successful programme for helping many people in their daily problems and it is likely to continue as an option for those who are in search of self-improvement and solutions to the problems that beset human life.

FEMINIST AND ECO-FEMINIST SPIRITUALITY
Ursula King

Both 'feminism' and 'spirituality' are evocative terms raising significant questions. How different is feminist spirituality from other spiritualities? How is eco-feminist spirituality related to feminist spirituality? I will first deal with the general meaning of spirituality in its more inclusive, universal sense, then discuss the specific meanings of feminist and eco-feminist spirituality.

'Spirituality' has its origin in the Christian tradition but is no longer an exclusively Christian or even exclusively religious term. Originally derived from the biblical *pneumatikos* or 'spiritual', referring to what was under the Spirit of God, it was later applied to the interior life of Christians. For many centuries, spirituality held a special place in Christian theology and practice; especially linked to the human search for holiness and inner perfection, it meant above all the search for God. Today the concept of spirituality has been cut loose from its Christian theological roots and is now applied universally across different religious traditions, even though many non-Western languages possess no strictly

corresponding concept to that of 'spirituality'. Instead of relating it to particular theological doctrines, spirituality is now primarily understood anthropologically as the exploration into what is involved in becoming fully human. Thus spirituality is seen as intrinsic to the human subject as such, as an inner dimension relating to a general search for meaning, wholeness, self-transcendence and connectedness with others. In this sense, spirituality can function in multiple secular contexts and can be postulated as a potential dimension latently present within every human being, whether young or old, or of whatever social and cultural background.

Today much spiritual experimentation is taking place within and across different religious traditions, within new religious movements, and outside religions altogether. From a historical and comparative perspective, there exists no single permanent spirituality, but only the living dynamic of different 'spiritualities' linked to particular times, places and cultures. The contemporary revisioning of spirituality seeks holiness through wholeness and integration by reconnecting all forms of life and by transforming traditional attitudes to gender, work, the environment and many

other aspects of personal and social experience.

Spirituality can be understood in three ways:

■ as lived experience and praxis/discipline;

■ as the spiritual teachings that grow out of such praxis (e.g. counsels on how to lead a good life; on finding liberation or salvation; or how to gain holiness and perfection);

■ as the systematic, comparative and critical study of spiritual experiences and teachings.

This is a fast-growing new field of study, dealing with specific spiritualities of different religions or groups – comparative spirituality, women's spirituality, ecological spirituality and so on – and global spirituality based on the spiritual heritage of the whole of humankind.

Contemporary spirituality shows signs of extraordinary cultural creativity. One of the most important new developments is the worldwide growth in women's spirituality, especially feminist spirituality, whereas others concern native spiritual traditions and the spiritual heritage of indigenous peoples and cultures. Their inherent reverence for life and nature, especially their belief in the sacredness of the earth, is one of the important sources for eco-feminist spirituality.

Spirituality is a process of inner growth in awareness and sensitivity linked to reflection and transformation, which results in a growing sense of well-being, wholeness and trust, a feeling of joy and graciousness, of reverence and gratitude for the wonders of creation and the mystery of life. These new understandings capture the dynamic, transformative quality of spirituality as lived experience, as a great adventure of body, mind and soul, seeking the goodness and abundance of life, a life sustained and nurtured by the ever-present powers of the spirit.

Feminist spirituality

In its widest sense 'feminist spirituality' can be understood as the spiritual quest and creativity of contemporary women, pursued in diverse traditional and non-traditional ways. In a more specific sense, feminist spirituality refers to a new spiritual movement that has arisen out of 'second wave feminism' (see below) and exists outside traditional religious boundaries and institutions. Feminist spirituality is the reclaiming by women of the reality and power designated by 'spirit', but it is also a reclaiming of female power, of women's partaking in the Divine, and their right to participate in shaping the realm of spirit by fully taking part in religion and culture.

Feminist spirituality is rooted in and oriented towards women's experience and bonding among women; it believes in the inherent goodness of matter, body and the world, thrives on ecological sensitivity, and creatively re-imagines the Divine. It has created new rituals and liturgies drawn from *Wicca and folk traditions celebrating especially life and nature cycles, but is also based on the imaginative reinterpretation of traditional religious rites and texts.

Contemporary women's interest in spirituality is sometimes referred to as the 'womanspirit movement', or as 'spiritual' or 'metaphysical feminism'. Some radical feminist activists reject this as a soft option, while others proclaim spirituality a

The Goddess Isis. The rediscovery of ancient goddess traditions is a significant feature of feminist spirituality.

necessity beyond political and social activism: ultimately only a spiritual orientation can inspire and sustain practical advocacy and engagement. The whole women's movement itself has been described as a spiritual revolution, and it can be argued that contemporary feminism possesses in fact an implicit spiritual dimension besides the explicit developments of women's spirituality. The feminist search for liberation, equality, peace, justice and the full humanity of women is ultimately not only linked to social, political and economic goals, but to spiritual ones as well.

In the past, spirituality was developed by particular social and religious elites (ascetics, monastics, yogis, *pirs*, holy men and women) who possessed the necessary leisure and aptitude for pursuing paths of spiritual excellence and attainment. Although ultimately gender-transcendent, spiritual ideals are not gender-neutral, but are shaped by deeply embedded patriarchal structures and androcentric (male-centred) thought that have affected all traditional spiritual practices and teachings. On the face of it, spiritual advice seems to be addressed to apparently asexual spiritual seekers, but on closer examination it often turns out to be anti-body,

anti-woman and anti-world. Male models of holiness often imply not only a contempt for the body in general, but especially for women's bodies. The worldwide history of renunciation and asceticism, which remains still to be written, is certainly responsible for a great deal of misogyny and sexism.

Feminist insights critically call into question many traditional forms of spirituality, rejecting spiritual ideals of the past that hold little attraction for contemporary women. Countless women seek alternative patterns of a new, more embodied and immanent spirituality, more attuned to their own experience, but they also draw on the spiritual heritage of women of past ages who, in spite of difficult conditions and numerous social obstacles, struggled to follow their own spiritual quest within the particular religious and cultural contexts of their times. Contemporary women are discovering a rich spiritual heritage in the women saints and mystics of the past, and in the female imagery and symbolism of the world's religions. However, with a new consciousness and sense of identity, and an awareness of new possibilities for transformation, many women today can no longer practise a form of spirituality simply handed down from the past, but must develop their own.

Yet, at the same time, they can draw strength and inspiration from innumerable 'women of spirit' from different religions and times, from ancient cultures to the Middle Ages, the early modern period, and the 19th and 20th centuries.

Key themes and figures in feminist spirituality

Key themes of feminist spirituality include women's discovery of their own self and agency, the experience of bonding and power-sharing, the new awareness of empowerment from within to effect personal, social and political changes, the creative re-imaging and renaming of the sacred, and a growth in sensitivity to the interdependent connectedness and sacredness of all forms of life, and to a special earth-human relationship. Many of these themes are reflected in contemporary women's culture, which, through the literary forms of poetry and fiction, through songs, music, film, art and theatre, explore different aspects of women's spiritual quest, their experience of loss and pain, oppression and freedom, intimacy and mutuality with others, and the multiple connections between sexuality and spirituality.

Interest in feminist spirituality began to appear in second wave feminism during the 1970s in the United

States, and in Europe during the 1980s. A ground-breaking publication was Carol Christ's and Judith Plaskow's *Womanspirit Rising: A Feminist Reader in Religion* (1979), followed a decade later by their *Weaving the Visions: New Patterns in Feminist Spirituality* (1989). Equally influential was Charlene Spretnak's collection on *The Politics of Women's Spirituality* (1982) with essays by many founding mothers of feminist spirituality. The contributors show that women's search for wholeness and integration is based on radically transforming traditional patriarchal attitudes to gender, sexuality, work and society, so this profoundly empowering spirituality has important political implications.

Following women's spiritual quest and seeking to meet women's spiritual needs is linked to the growing recognition of where to find spiritual resources. Many, but not all, can come from women's own experience, their inner power and strength. But contemporary women are now also discovering the rich spiritual heritage of women in different world religions, where countless female saints and mystics provide inspiring examples for today. Much feminist theological writing also helps to uncover the rich female imagery and symbolism in different world

faiths, which is often profoundly ambivalent, however. The greatest efforts go into re-imaging the Divine and developing more inclusive images and metaphors for God. Central to this is the recognition of the power of the Goddess and the rediscovery of many very ancient goddess traditions around the world. Yet, however powerful, these do not necessarily have a direct bearing on the status of women in society. Some women prefer an androgynous or monistic conceptualization of divine reality over either a matriarchal or patriarchal expression.

The rediscovery of 'the Goddess' is probably the most significant feature of contemporary feminist spirituality, so much so that the latter is sometimes simply equated with 'Goddess spirituality'. This spirituality draws on both traditional and non-traditional religious sources and has led to new religious rituals and practices. The Great Goddess, manifest in myriad historical and cultural forms, is seen as immanent rather than transcendent, and is strongly connected with body and earth. Thus she can be experienced within ourselves, within other human beings and within nature. One of the most powerful symbols of the Goddess is the moon, which is linked to women's

monthly cycles of bleeding and fertility.

Systematic reflections on the Goddess have been called by Naomi Goldenberg 'thealogy' in order to distinguish it from traditional 'theology', which is primarily concerned with God-talk in male terms. The rediscovery of the Goddess has produced a vibrant Goddess thealogy grounded in embodiment and linked to the reaffirmation of female sacrality. This new approach to 'ultimate reality', using female images and metaphors, has largely drawn on historical scholarship about goddesses of the ancient Mediterranean world, but has focused much less on goddesses in other cultural and religious traditions, such as Hinduism for example. Hinduism is one of the historically richest traditions regarding feminine perceptions and embodiments of the Divine and probably possesses the most vibrant living goddess worship in the contemporary world. But women must critically investigate the relationship between female symbolism of the Divine and the real lives of women, for religions with goddesses do not necessarily affirm and enhance women's actual lives.

The greatest contribution of thealogy probably consists in the reaffirmation of female sacrality by seeing the life-giving powers of women's bodies linked to divine creative activity. This has led to a new 'spiritual feminism', which has significantly contributed to contemporary transformations of religious practice. The theme of a 'divine feminine' and a new female symbolic order has also been developed by French feminist philosophers, especially Luce Irigaray and Julia Kristeva, who have exercised a wide influence on the intellectual discussions of religious feminists, but are less significant in the development of new spiritual and ritual practices.

The rediscovery of the Goddess is also linked to women's reclamation of witchcraft and the practice of *wicca* (meaning both 'wisdom' and 'witch'). Wicca religion is not a discrete religion within thealogy, but it is a Goddess-centred religion that represents a distinct grouping within the wider Goddess-worshipping community. It is organized in covens, which can consist of both women and men. Followers of Wicca have created their own rituals, dances and chants, and they sacralize their own space through a sacred circle or by creating an altar in their own home. One of the most influential practitioners and theoreticians of feminist witchcraft is Starhawk (originally Miriam Simos, from a Jewish background; b. 1950), sometimes described

as the high priestess of the modern witchcraft movement. Her book *The Spiral Dance* (1979) is a classic of feminist spirituality, containing many exercises, invocations, chants, blessings and spells. As an active teacher, Starhawk has set up workshops and covens that have created a distinct community, especially the 'Reclaiming Collective' in and around San Francisco, whose priestesses, rituals and spirituality have been studied in great detail by Jone Salomonsen in her book *Enchanted Feminism* (2002).

Other approaches include Rosemary Radford Ruether's suggestion to describe the deity as 'God/dess', claiming that by using this term women can appropriate all that is true of what has been traditionally said about God, while at the same time rejecting the patriarchal and 'masculinizing' deformation of that tradition. Another way of doing this consists in the feminine personification of the Divine as 'Holy Wisdom'.

Contemporary feminist spirituality is also influenced by psychological writings about the Goddess, primarily linked to the archetypal theory of Carl Jung about the feminine and masculine within every human being. However his theory, formulated from a predominantly male perspective, is linked to

traditional sexual stereotypes, which can reinforce established gender hierarchies.

Women working with existing religious traditions have created their own rites and liturgies, so that new symbols, prayers, songs and festivals have come into being. Different aspects of feminist spirituality and the womanspirit movement have been disseminated globally, but these developments have occurred everywhere mainly at the margins of or outside religious institutions; they represent the invention of new religious traditions or the radical transformation of old ones.

Changes in religious practice also include the adoption of gender-inclusive language in religious readings and prayers, and institutional changes that give women access to official religious positions, such as admission to the priesthood in many Christian churches around the world (except in Roman Catholicism and Eastern Orthodoxy), or women's new opportunities to take up traditional paths of renunciation in Hinduism and become gurus in their own right, or the reclaiming of full ordination for Buddhist nuns in Sri Lanka.

Women's spirituality groups have created new symbols, prayers, songs, and feasts; they also use special blessings, silence and meditation, and some work with crystals to energize and balance the subtle centres of the human body.

Eco-feminist spirituality

The thealogical discourse on the Goddess has wide ethical, ecological and social implications, as it opens up new religious and political possibilities and relates to the perspectives of eco-feminist spirituality. Eco-feminist spirituality shares many similar themes with feminist spirituality, but has a more explicit focus on ecological issues and a far stronger emphasis on women's connection with the earth and all forms of life.

Eco-feminist spirituality grew out of eco-feminism, a word first coined in 1974 to describe a new movement based on the close connection between ecology, especially 'deep ecology' and feminism. Deep ecology examines the symbolic, psychological and ethical patterns of destructive relations of humans with nature, whereas one of the principal eco-feminist insights consists in the belief that the oppressive exploitations of women and nature are closely related and equally destructive to the wholeness of life and the peace of the earth. There exists a disconnection between ourselves, the earth and the Divine – a deep split which

eco-feminists insist must be healed. Women can make an essential contribution to this 'earth-healing', for earth and women are linked through their birthing activities, in weaving the fabric of life through continuous renewal, creating a multi-stranded web of which we are all part. This is a very creation-centred spirituality, where nature itself is experienced as 'hierophany' (revealing the presence and beauty of spirit). The world is seen as the body of God/dess, as Gaia (the Greek earth goddess) and therefore the earth must be revered. The women's movement is needed for the required environmental changes in order for all people to live in peace with each other and all living beings.

Eco-feminism thus has a strong orientation towards the sacred. It seeks to revisit traditional religions through the development of new eco-feminist spiritualities, but also draws on alternative religions and spiritualities as well as on the spirituality of the land found among indigenous and native peoples. Significant themes of eco-feminist spirituality are the connections between the bodies of women and the earth, the alignment with the seasons of nature, the dynamism and energy of life, and the inter-connectedness of the web of life. This spirituality aims at

an alternative culture that is peace-loving and non-hierarchical and breaks down the boundaries between nature and culture. The spiritual dimension of the eco-feminist movement is well expressed by Mary Daly's description of the 'cosmic covenant of sisterhood', which embraces our 'sister earth' and all her non-human inhabitants.

Like eco-feminism, eco-feminist spirituality is also a form of global activism. It involves advocacy of and commitment to global planetary and social change, which cannot happen without a spiritual change nor without the indispensable, essential contribution of women from all parts of the world. As Rosemary Radford Ruether has commented, 'women healing earth' is an integral part of the activism of many women's groups in the so-called Third World. Women and their spirituality are necessary to promote sustainable development, ecological integrity, and a just and peaceful world. This is also affirmed in the *Earth Charter*, launched in The Hague in 2000.

The Church of Scientology
George D. Chryssides

Scientology is one of the few new religious movements (NRMs) that have no obvious antecedents, being very much the creation of its founder-leader Lafayette Ron Hubbard (1911–86).

Hubbard was born in Tilden, Nebraska, in the United States. It is difficult to find firm corroboration for the details of his life, but Scientologists aver that he was a precocious child, and that he travelled widely as an adolescent, acquainting himself with Beijing magicians, Tibetan lamas, Mongolian bandits, Pygmy huntsmen and shamans from Borneo. Hubbard returned to the United States in 1929, when he completed his school education and was accepted by George Washington University as a student of mathematics and engineering. He also claimed to have studied psychology under one of Freud's own students. Unsatisfied with psychologists' understanding of the human mind, he left university and pursued his own independent researches.

Scientologists credit Hubbard with mastery of no less than 29 areas of expertise, regarding him primarily as a philosopher and an authority on the human mind, but also as an anthropologist, educator, humanitarian, artist, film director, horticulturalist, musician, aircraft pilot, writer, poet and photographer. Hubbard certainly wrote prolifically, his earliest publications being in the realm of science fiction. He authored *Battlefield Earth* in 1981, which became a bestseller.

Hubbard's ideas on the human mind gained public attention in 1950 with the publication of *Dianetics: The Modern Science of Mental Health*, which sold over a million copies within a very short period of time. This text remains the recommended basic introduction to the subject, and is still widely used by Scientologists. Dianetics is the prerequisite for the study of Scientology:

Scientologists do not regard Dianetics as a religion, although they insist that Scientology is one. The Church of Scientology was founded in 1954. Dianetics offers an analysis of the human self, which Hubbard called the 'thetan' (pronounced *thaytan*). The thetan is distinct from both the mind and body, and is the true immortal godlike self.

The body consists of matter, energy, space and time (MEST), all of which lack independent reality, and depend on the thetan. Much modern philosophy, psychology and psychiatry, however, have mistakenly come to regard matter as the sole true reality, and hence have denied the essentially spiritual nature of humanity. Men and women need to attain freedom from MEST.

The mind consists of two entities: the analytical mind and the reactive mind. The analytical mind is rational, being able to analyse, calculate and recognize distinctions. The reactive mind, by contrast, is irrational: it draws extensively on MEST, and stores memories of unpleasant events, which reappear to cause pain, irrational fears and mental blocks. These effects are known as 'engrams', and require to be eliminated. When this is achieved, the reactive mind disappears altogether and the student is declared 'clear'.

To become clear, the 'pre-clear' must undergo a process of 'auditing'. This is a form of counselling in which the pre-clear is invited to recall all the details of unpleasant past incidents, thus identifying and removing engrams. Auditing is normally done by trained auditors within the Church of Scientology, which requires payment for such services. However, it is permissible for students to work in pairs, using Hubbard's *Dianetics*. Since most humans have many engrams, the attainment of 'clear' is a lengthy process, normally taking years, and many active Scientologists still remain pre-clear. During auditing, use is made of the 'E-meter' (electropsychometer), a device that measures galvanic skin response.

The E-meter is placed so that only the auditor can see its dial, thus enabling him or her to recognize the incidents that need to be addressed within the auditing session.

Scientologists believe that toxins in one's body impede the process of becoming clear. Pre-clears are encouraged to take a 'Purification Rundown' course, which involves physical exercise, vitamins and frequent saunas, the aim of which is to sweat the toxins out of one's body. Scientologists are opposed to recreational drugs, although caffeine and nicotine are permitted, since these are believed to stimulate rather than dull the mind. Scientology's Narconon programme – offered to the society in general – aims to wean drug users off their addiction. Alcohol is allowed, but it can interfere with the auditing process, and must be avoided for 24 hours before an auditing session. Scientologists have actively campaigned against the use of drugs to control psychiatric conditions, arguing that this treats the self as a physical rather than a spiritual entity.

Although Scientology has sometimes been labelled a 'self religion', Scientologists point out that the 'self' is only one of eight 'dynamics' that Scientology addresses. The other dynamics are 'creativity', 'group survival', 'species', 'life forms', the 'physical universe', the 'spiritual dynamic' and 'infinity'. Scientology particularly addresses the spiritual aspects of the thetan, and enables the clear to make spiritual progress through a number of levels of 'operating thetan' (OT). The OT material is strictly confidential, and, it is said, can cause mental or even physical harm if it is divulged to those who are unauthorized to receive it. Some lapsed Scientologists ('subversives') claim to have placed OT material on the internet, but Scientologists insist that such material is a mere travesty. From official Scientology literature, however, it seems likely that OT material relates to 'body thetans' – the remains of thetans who lost their bodies many millions of years ago as a result of a gargantuan explosion. These beings, devoid of

An exhibition devoted to the founder of Scientology, Ron Hubbard.

physical bodies, continue to latch on to the physical bodies of others, and it is incumbent on those who progress through OT levels to help to release them from this situation.

Scientology is often criticized for being expensive. There can be no doubt that many Scientologists have spent a great deal of money on courses, although those who remain in the organization typically claim that this has been worth it. The Church of Scientology points out that monies for Dianetics and Scientology courses are its main source of income, and that members are not required to make donations or to engage in fund-raising activities. There are around 5.6 million practising Scientologists worldwide.

The Aetherius Society
John A. Saliba

Founded in 1954 by George King (1919–97), the Aetherius Society is a spiritual organization that centres its ideology and ritual practice around the belief that the Ascended Masters, who in their view are inhabitants of other planets, are helping human beings to bring in the New Age of peace and enlightenment. King was chosen to be the human channel through whom these extraterrestrial beings communicated various messages called 'cosmic transmissions'. With two headquarters, one in Hollywood, California, the other in London, England, the society has members on different continents. Contact with its widespread membership is maintained through many publications, including a newsletter.

Among the basic tenets of the society are the belief in the law of karma and reincarnation, the conviction that intelligent life is found throughout the universe, the insistence that Mother Earth is a living organism (Gaia theory), the acknowledgment that service to others is essential for human progress, and the principle that spiritual

energy can be manipulated to heal people. A new master is awaited shortly to initiate the New Age, but no details are given about the time and place of his arrival, though it is said that he will come 'only when the time is right'. The society also believes that the earth faces periodic disasters from both internal and external sources (such as the misuse of nuclear power and attacks from alien evil beings). Its literature, for example, contains accounts of several assaults on earth made by evil extraterrestrial forces, assaults warded off by King with the help of those aliens who are interested in the well-being and development of the human race.

The religious rituals of the society are held in a temple weekly and on special commemorative occasions. Weekly services include a prayer meeting that comprises of the following: a short period of meditation; the recitation of various prayers and petitions for the healing of those not present; a service dedicated to Operation Prayer Power; a private healing service; and a regular Sunday service during which taped lectures of George King and/or messages from various planetary beings are played. The practice of yoga and meditation and the recitation of mantras are also encouraged.

Unique to the society are various operations or missions started by George King with the help of extraterrestrial intelligences: Operation Starlight, which charged 19 selected mountains with spiritual energy (completed between 1958 and 1961); Operation Space Power, which involves the radiation of spiritual energy to earth when a large satellite takes up its position several times during the year; Operation Blue Water, which lessens the harm done to the earth's magnetic field through atomic tests and the negative thoughts and actions of human beings; Operation Sunbeam, which restores the spiritual energy taken from the earth by human beings; and Operation Prayer Power, which stores spiritual energy accumulated

☞ *continued on page 396*

APOCALYPTICISM AND MILLENARIANISM
Daniel Wojcik

Apocalyptic beliefs about the catastrophic destruction of the world are a central feature of numerous new and alternative religious movements, and such ideas have had an enduring appeal throughout human history. In nearly every society, people have held beliefs and told narratives about worldly cataclysm and the creation of a terrestrial paradise by deities or divine forces. Apocalyptic beliefs have been an important feature in the founding of numerous religious traditions, including Christianity, Islam, the *Bahá'í Faith, *Rastafarianism, the *Church of Jesus Christ of Latter-Day Saints and the *Jehovah's Witnesses, and have played an important role in the development of the *cargo cults of Oceania, Pure Land Buddhist traditions, Native American Ghost Dance movements, the Taiping rebellion (1850–64) in China, the Xhosa cattle-killing movement in South Africa (see *African Neo-traditional Religions), and medieval millenarian groups, such as the Ranters and the Brethren of the Free Spirit. In contemporary societies, apocalyptic ideas have been embraced by religious movements that express

dissatisfaction with the current social order and yearn for its destruction and transformation.

The terms of apocalypse
The word 'apocalypse' (from the Greek *apokalypsis*), means revelation or unveiling, and the term came into theological use in the 2nd century to designate a specific type of early Jewish and Christian literature characterized by mysterious revelations communicated by a supernatural figure, such as an angel. These visions reveal a divine plan for history involving the ultimate defeat of evil, the destruction and judgement of the current world, and the creation of a new heaven and a new earth – ideas that are similar to those of a wide range of new religious movements. The terms 'millenarianism' and 'millennialism' are usually applied to the study of apocalyptic beliefs. They refer to the expectation of imminent world transformation, collective salvation, and the establishment of a perfect, new world of harmony and justice to be brought about by otherworldly beings acting in accordance with a divine or superhuman plan. In Christian traditions, this perfect age is associated with the return of Christ and a predicted 1,000-year period

of peace and prosperity – the millennium.

Millenarian ideas associated with new religions often include the belief that the transformation of the present world will be cataclysmic; this worldview (referred to variously as catastrophic millennialism, apocalypticism or premillennialism), expresses a pessimistic view of humanity, maintaining that the world is fatally flawed and unredeemable by human effort, and that only a divinely ordained world cataclysm can usher in a millennial age of peace and prosperity. Groups such as the *Branch Davidians, *Aum Shinriykô and the *Peoples Temple exemplify catastrophic millenarian views. Yet not all millenarian beliefs emphasize a scenario involving worldly destruction; some groups, including various Christian, New Age and UFO religious movements, hold 'progressive millenarian' beliefs (also referred to as postmillennialism), which assert that collective salvation and a golden age will be brought about gradually and non-catastrophically by human beings acting according to a divine plan that will transform the world.

Like previous millenarian worldviews, the catastrophic and non-catastrophic traditions of belief embraced by recent religious movements provide systems of meaning for understanding human existence and assure followers that the universe is ordered, that evil will be eliminated, and that an age of justice will be established. Similar to creation myths, which awaken the desire for a lost paradise that once existed in a primordial time, apocalyptic beliefs, whether ancient or emergent, frequently appeal to a sense of loss and alienation, inspiring a yearning for a perfect world that is free from suffering and evil. For a number of new religious movements, the imagined millennial realm is the antithesis of current society, with its overwhelming suffering, evil and injustice, none of which can be remedied by the established political, social and religious institutions. In apocalyptic systems of belief, fatalism about the current society is reinforced by faith in its inevitable destruction and redemption by divine forces. Recent apocalyptic traditions thus offer religious solutions for both suffering and injustice by promising the destruction of an evil and oppressive old order, and the establishment of a morally just millennial kingdom of peace and harmony.

'Doomsday cults' and violence

Historically, most millenarian movements have not been violent, yet the stereotype of the dangerous 'doomsday cult' pervades the public discourse about millenarian movements and new religious groups. For this reason, it is important to understand the negative connotations of the word 'cult' (see the Introduction on the use of the word 'cult') and the recent apocalyptic groups that have been involved in episodes of violence: the Peoples Temple, the Movement for the Restoration of the Ten Commandments of God, the Branch Davidians, Aum Shinriykô, the *Order of the Solar Temple and *Heaven's Gate. These groups are not necessarily typical of other millenarian movements, nor are they representative of new and alternative religious movements in general, the majority of which do not embrace apocalyptic worldviews.

Of the various apocalyptic groups in recent history, the Peoples Temple led by the Reverend Jim Jones has been depicted as the epitome of a 'doomsday cult' and is often regarded as representative of apocalyptic movements in general. Jones' millennial community ended tragically on 18 November 1978, with the mass suicide of more than 900 people. The Peoples

Temple was initially praised for its humanitarian work, but Jones later embraced more apocalyptic beliefs, condemning the world as corrupt and dehumanizing. Claiming to be an end-times prophet, Jones attempted to establish a socialist millennial kingdom, called Jonestown, in Guyana. As Jones grew progressively more paranoid he became convinced that his opponents were out to destroy his community. Jones had a visiting congressman killed, and then encouraged members to commit collective suicide. This final 'revolutionary act' was regarded as a protest against the cruel conditions of an inhumane world, proof of commitment to the group, and a means of attaining a higher spiritual level of existence.

Another tragedy comparable to Jonestown occurred in the year 2000, when more than 900 members of the Movement for the Restoration of the Ten Commandments of God (MRTC) were killed. This group, located in Kanungu (south-western Uganda), centred around the visions of Credonia Mwerinde, who declared that she communicated messages from the Virgin Mary. Mwerinde's visions caught the attention of other disaffected Roman Catholics in a region torn by war, plague, genocide and oppression. The leaders of the group saw 31 December 1999 as the day the world would end and the faithful would be saved by God or the Virgin Mary. When the date passed uneventfully, a significant number of followers lost faith in the leaders and threatened to leave the group, demanding the return of the money and property that they had donated. Authorities believe that the leaders responded to this crisis by murdering the dissidents and then attempting to end the movement through the mass murder of the other followers. Like the Peoples Temple, the MRTC was an authoritarian, separatist movement with a radically dualistic view of good and evil; when the community was threatened by defections and criticism, the leaders resorted to violence and self-destruction.

Another millennialist group that met a violent end was the Branch Davidian movement, a splinter group from mainstream Seventh-day Adventists. The group's leader, David Koresh, believed that he had been chosen to interpret the meaning of various passages in the book of Revelation, and he claimed that biblical prophecies about the apocalyptic opening of the 'seven seals' were being fulfilled, and that the Davidians had a chosen role to play in the end-times plan.

The group separated from the broader society and armed itself in anticipation of a final battle with the forces of evil. Federal agents, in search of illegal weapons, attempted a raid on the group's wooden compound in Waco, Texas, on 28 February 1993, and a number of agents and Davidians were killed. After a 51-day stand-off, Koresh and more than 70 of his followers died in a fiery conflagration. Although the Davidians frequently have been depicted as brainwashed cultists whose deaths were the inevitable result of mindless fanaticism, numerous scholars have argued that the entire tragedy might have been averted if government officials had attempted to better understand the Davidians' beliefs.

An apocalyptic group that attempted an assault on broader society was Aum Shinrikyô (Supreme Truth), a Japanese movement. In March 1995, its members staged a nerve gas attack in the subways of Tokyo that killed 12 people and resulted in more than 5,000 others being hospitalized. The group's scientists were researching and experimenting with various forms of weaponry in order to fulfil their leader's prophecies of an apocalyptic scenario that would destroy a world overwhelmed by evil. The

Aum movement initially was optimistic in its millennialist vision, believing that members could save the world from evil and bring about a peaceful transition into a more spiritual age. The views of the group became more apocalyptic after conflicts with parents of some group members and confrontations with authorities and police. Shoko Asahara, the group's leader, subsequently believed that he was being persecuted and the world was not worthy of salvation. He became more authoritarian, acts of violence within the group increased, and followers believed that the movement was the victim of a massive conspiracy; they regarded their attacks on the broader society as part of a cosmic battle between the forces of good and evil.

Another syncretistic apocalyptic group was the Order of the Solar Temple. The group's leader, Luc Jouret, believed that the apocalypse foretold in the book of Revelation predicts an ecological catastrophe that will soon destroy the world. He maintained that members of the order would first be purified by this disaster and then be transformed into solar beings who would dwell in another celestial realm. In September 1994, three members of the group were ritually murdered in Canada. Soon after, the bodies of 53 members of the group were found in three separate incidents in Switzerland and Quebec. Since that time 21 other members of the order have died, as the result of the belief that death is a means to reach another spiritual dimension and escape the suffering and destruction of the world. Like Aum Shinrikyô, the Solar Temple initially embraced an optimistic millennial view of worldly transformation, but the beliefs of the group became increasingly pessimistic, and were characterized by conspiracy theories and extreme feelings of alienation. External pressures on the group in the form of lawsuits, police investigations, internal strife and defections added to followers' feelings of persecution, a loss of faith in humanity and the desire for planetary escape.

A similar fatalism for the future of the world motivated the collective suicide of 39 members of the UFO group known as Heaven's Gate, who killed themselves on 23–25 March 1997 in Rancho Santa Fe, near San Diego, California. A primary belief was that by overcoming human attachments and living an ascetic lifestyle, the faithful could escape from a corrupt and doomed world and ultimately be transported by a UFO to a higher realm. The secretive group, formed

in the 1970s, disappeared from public view until 27 May 1993, when it placed an ad in *USA Today* entitled 'UFO Cult Resurfaces with Final Offer', which declared that societal institutions and mainstream religions are controlled by an evil conspiracy, and that the earth would soon be destroyed. Group members interpreted the criticism and ridicule of their beliefs as a form of persecution and further proof that the world was corrupt and could not be saved. The passing of Comet Hale-Bopp in late March 1997 was embraced as a final prophetic sign. Followers believed that the comet was being trailed by a gigantic spacecraft that would transport them to the 'Evolutionary Level Above Human'. Like the Peoples Temple and the Solar Temple, members of the group viewed the world as irredeemably evil, and suicide was embraced as a means of evacuating a doomed world.

The groups mentioned above differ in their doctrines, but aspects of their belief systems share certain common ideas, such as a rigid dualism, a totalistic worldview, a sense of fatalism for a world regarded as evil and doomed, and a desire for planetary escape and salvation. These movements epitomize the notion of 'fragile millennial groups', which engage in violence in

order to preserve the religious ideals and goals of the group. Most of these groups were experiencing internal conflicts (either caused by the leader or related to strife within the group), and all of them experienced external pressures, whether in the form of investigations or assault by government and law enforcement agencies, negative news reports, or criticisms by defectors and concerned relatives. Because of the fragile and volatile nature of these groups and their conspiratorial worldviews, when threatened they responded with acts of violence against themselves or against critics, dissidents or the larger society. In addition to a profound sense of paranoia and persecution (real or imagined), these groups were led by authoritarian and dominating leaders who claimed to have sole access to the source of ultimate knowledge, and who attempted to closely control the behaviour of members, using weapons to enforce their authoritarian control or to attack perceived enemies.

Contemporary Christian millenarian groups
Although many mainline religious organizations de-emphasize apocalyptic prophecy or reject outright the concepts of an apocalypse and/or a millennial kingdom on earth, belief in apocalyptic

prophecy is integral to the worldviews of numerous denominations of Protestantism, particularly evangelical, Pentecostal and charismatic groups. Members of these movements assert that recent wars, plagues, famines and earthquakes are proof that doomsday is imminent; some maintain that the world will experience a seven-year period of misery and tribulation, but that Christians will be physically lifted up from the earth in 'the Rapture' and delivered from the terrors of worldly destruction. Such beliefs are not confined to Western societies, but are embraced by evangelical groups throughout the world. In South Korea, for instance, more than a million people believe in end-time prophecies; one well-known apocalyptic group, the Mission for the Coming Days (the Tami Church), claimed 20,000 members who expected the Rapture to occur on 28 October 1992.

Adventism is another Protestant branch that holds millennialist views, and which grew out of the Millerite movement, named after its founder William Miller, who predicted that the world would end by 1843 or 1844. After his predictions failed, some disenchanted Millerites were attracted to other millenarian movements, such as the Seventh-day Adventists. According to Adventist belief, Miller's predictions were accurate, and an 'invisible' or spiritual apocalypse was initiated in 1844 with the 'cleansing of heaven', and it would soon be followed by the destructive cleansing of earth. Adventist belief stresses prophetic interpretations of the present and future, maintaining that various apocalyptic predictions have been fulfilled and that Christ will return in the near future.

The Jehovah's Witnesses, another group formed from the Millerite movement, assert that the spiritual, invisible second coming of Christ occurred in 1874 in the 'upper air' and that Christ's invisible reign started in 1914. According to the group's founder, Charles Taze Russell, the fulfilment of Christ's millennial kingdom would only be completed after the foreordained destruction of nations, governments, churches and world leaders, all of which Russell considered represented Satan's rule. Rejecting formal religious and governmental organizations, the Witnesses developed the practice of door-to-door evangelism in an attempt to convert non-believers as the apocalypse approaches.

Millennial beliefs are also an important part of the theology of the *Church of Jesus Christ of Latter-Day Saints. The religion was founded by Joseph Smith Jr in 1830. Smith had various apocalyptic revelations and was informed by an angel in a vision that Christ's second coming was imminent; Smith believed that he had been chosen to gather together the saints in the last days and prepare humanity for the millennium. According to Smith's visions, the millennial kingdom is destined to be established in the United States. Although millenarianism has been de-emphasized by the church in recent years, apocalyptic prophecy beliefs continue to thrive at the level of 'folk' tradition, with many Latter-Day Saints stockpiling a year's supply of food and provisions in preparation for an apocalyptic period of tribulation.

Apocalyptic beliefs often exist at a grass-roots level as a form of 'folk' or 'popular' belief – vernacular religious ideas and personal expressions of alternative spirituality that exist apart from the sanction of formal religious institutions. For instance, popular interest in the apocalyptic predictions of Nostradamus, a 16th-century French physician and astrologer, or the end-time prophecies associated with visions of the Virgin Mary (see the *Global Network of Divergent Marian Devotion), are familiar to millions of people worldwide, yet exist apart from the approval of institutional religion.

Recent varieties of millenarian belief

Ideas about earthly destruction and transformation have been an aspect of the worldviews of other diverse contemporary religious movements, such as the *Family Federation for World Peace and Unification (the Unification Church), Christian youth movements originating in the 1960s (such as *The Family), the *Lubavitch movement, the Israelites of the New Universal Covenant (an indigenous Peruvian messianic movement), the *Osho movement, Islamic fundamentalist and Mahdist movements, and various Bahá'í organizations, as well as other new religious movements based on non-Western traditions that envision a golden age of spiritual awakening and planetary transformation, such as *Transcendental Meditation and *ISKCON (the International Society for Krishna Consciousness).

Millenarian ideas have been emphasized to varying degrees within Black Nationalist groups (e.g. the *Nation of Islam and the Nation of Yahweh) and back-to-Africa movements in Western societies. Rastafarianism, which arose

in the 1930s on the island of Jamaica, began as an indigenous millenarian response to British rule, poverty and oppression, and draws upon Christian apocalyptic prophecies promising the destruction of Babylon (regarded as the evil forces in the world that oppress people of African heritage). Ideas about a millennial return to Zion, interpreted as the African homeland, are central as well.

Millenarianism and the New Age

Millenarian ideas associated with the New Age exemplify the ways that eschatological beliefs exist as a form of alternative spirituality apart from institutional religion. New Age ideas about the transformation of the world range from beliefs about catastrophic earth changes to ideas concerning a gradual shift in global consciousness and spirituality that will lead to a golden age. The eclectic nature of New Age prophetic beliefs was epitomized by the Harmonic Convergence, which was organized around a cross-cultural melange of prophecy traditions, the cycles of the Aztec and Mayan Calendars and the configuration of the planets in the solar system. The event was celebrated by tens of thousands of people throughout the world on 16–17 August 1987, dates

interpreted as a critical juncture that would help determine the future destruction or salvation of the planet.

New Age beliefs tend to offer a kinder and gentler apocalypse, emphasizing a progressive millenarian view that involves the gradual evolution into a new age of harmony and peace. For example, the Star-Borne or '11:11 Doorway' movement, led by the American channeller Solara Antara Amaa-ra, asserts that humanity has entered a 20-year 'doorway' of opportunity to eliminate evil, attain higher consciousness and transform the world. However, catastrophic millenarianism does exist among some New Agers, such as spirit channeller J.Z. Knight (the Ramtha School of Enlightenment) and the *Church Universal and Triumphant, who predict cataclysmic disasters and have advocated a survivalist response among followers. Like other New Age groups, the doctrines of these movements are a synthesis of varied religious beliefs, including Christianity, Eastern religions and esoteric traditions, with an emphasis on apocalyptic warnings from Ascended Masters, who are believed to be helping humanity fulfil its destiny of spiritual evolution on earth.

A group that shifted its

emphasis from progressive to catastrophic millenarianism is the *Holy Order of MANS, which was founded in the late 1960s. The group initially anticipated planetary and spiritual transformation resulting in a new millennial realm, but later became more apocalyptic in response to the cultural and political upheavals in the early 1970s, and particularly because of negative events directed at the group – death threats against its leader Earl W. Blighton, a firebombing of Blighton's residence and negative publicity in the press about the group. After Blighton's death, the group changed its emphasis once again, due in part to the anti-cult milieu of the late 1970s, and transformed itself into a sectarian offshoot of the Greek Orthodox Church in order to fit within an established Christian tradition. The changing millennial views of the group illustrate the adaptability of apocalyptic belief systems and their relation to particular cultural, social and individual contexts.

Millenarian UFO religions

The variable and vernacular nature of emergent traditions of apocalypticism in the 20th century is epitomized by UFO religious movements, which are comprised of a synthesis of earlier mythologies, religious traditions, occult teachings, scientific discourse and ideas inspired by science fiction literature and popular films (see *Ufology and UFO-related Movements). For more than 50 years, beliefs about UFOs have been characterized by expectations of imminent worldly destruction and the belief that extraterrestrials will rescue human beings from catastrophe or help humanity transform the world and usher in a new age of peace and enlightenment. These popular UFO beliefs have concerns in common with other millenarian traditions and express similar yearnings for collective salvation and earthly transformation by otherworldly beings.

Although Heaven's Gate is the best-known UFO group to embrace a theology of imminent apocalypse and planetary escape, numerous other movements espouse similar notions. *Chen Tao consisted of about 150 Taiwanese members who relocated to Garland, Texas, in 1997, where they waited for God's flying saucers to rescue them from nuclear annihilation and other disasters. The Guardian Action International organization anticipates a spaceship landing by the Ashtar Command, in which Jesus and other space beings will evacuate the chosen ones prior to worldly catastrophe, and later return them to

repopulate the planet. The *United Nuwaubian Nation of Moors also predicts the arrival of UFOs to evacuate the chosen ones, who are believed to be people of African origin or dark skin.

Like other millenarian movements, numerous UFO groups assert that humanity has become increasingly evil and that worldly disasters are imminent, but that apocalypse may be avoided if people follow the advice of otherworldly beings or a cosmic plan. This view is exemplified by the *Aetherius Society, which has claimed for decades that planetary catastrophes may be averted and that worldly redemption is possible through the promotion of the metaphysical teachings of the Ascended Masters, as well as through the use of 'Spiritual Energy Batteries' that harness and amplify the society's prayers for world salvation.

The belief that a complete transformation of the human race is required to avert disaster and attain a golden age finds full expression in the cosmology of the Raëlian movement (see the *Raëlian religion). The Raëlians attempt to help humanity make a leap to a new planetary consciousness and prepare the world for the arrival of the extraterrestrials, who they believe created human beings through a synthesis of DNA in their laboratories. Unlike many other UFO groups, the Raëlians do not emphasize planetary escape in the form of their physical bodies, but rather the perfection of life on earth and a type of immortality achieved through a process of cosmic cloning. By attaining spiritual perfection, the Raëlians believe that they will alter and perfect their DNA; they hope that duplicates of themselves will be cloned by the extraterrestrials for future space travel and settlement on other planets. The group has become well-known for its human cloning research, known as 'Clonaid', and the movement's views on improving the human species through genetic engineering reflects the millenarian yearning for human perfection and a golden age on earth.

The progressive millenarian vision of the attainment of a utopia on earth without an apocalyptic scenario is exemplified by the *Unarius Academy of Science in El Cajon, near San Diego, California. The group, in existence since the 1950s, predicts a space fleet landing in the near future, with each space ship carrying a thousand intelligent beings who will work with humanity to save the world and spiritually transform the earth. In contrast to apocalyptic beliefs that express a pessimistic view of the world as irredeemably evil, the Unariuns regard current problems as conquerable by human beings working in harmony with superhuman beings and cosmic forces. Unlike dualistic apocalyptic worldviews, which emphasize salvation for the righteous and destruction for the evil 'others', the progressive millenarianism of the Unariuns and other UFO groups tends to accept all humanity in its inclusive millennial embrace.

The persistence of apocalyptic belief

As this survey of apocalyptic beliefs and millenarian visions indicates, ideas about the destruction and transformation of the world are tremendously diverse and reflect current fears, hopes and concerns. Although apocalyptic ideas are often demonized or dismissed as irrational, such beliefs have an enduring appeal in a world threatened by nuclear weapons, environmental destruction, chemical and biological warfare, deadly viruses and other possible forms of extinction. Apocalyptic beliefs address issues of ultimate concern, such as the reasons for suffering and injustice, the nature of good and evil, the fear of collective death, the desire for salvation and the assurance that a divine plan underlies history.

Apocalypticism is a complex and adaptable worldview that many people find deeply meaningful. In some cases, such beliefs may reinforce feelings of helplessness and encourage a fatalistic acceptance of human-made crises by asserting that the world can be saved only by otherworldly beings; on rare occasions, apocalyptic ideas may result in acts of violence and self-destruction; and in other instances, such beliefs may be an incentive for societal transformation, inspiring people to confront current crises or situations of oppression. Beliefs about worldly destruction and redemption are a significant part of numerous new and alternative religious movements, and, considering the appeal and dynamic nature of apocalyptic traditions, there is no doubt that such ideas will continue to thrive and be transformed in the years ahead.

through the prayers of the members and then periodically releases them to alleviate human suffering.

Some scholars find many similarities between the teachings of the Aetherius Society and theosophy. While the belief in Ascended Masters (which theosophists call Masters of the Wisdom; see the *Theosophical Society) is similar to both organizations, the Aetherius Society has placed the belief in extraterrestrials at the heart of its ideology and has developed practices which make it a unique UFO religion.

The Unarius Academy of Science
Diana Tumminia

In 1954, Ernest L. Norman (1904–71) founded the Unarius Science of Life with the help of his new wife, Ruth (1900–93). A channeller who envisioned life on spiritual planets, Ernest Norman's first publication was the *Voice of Venus* (1954). The couple maintained their organization by doing psychic readings and by producing new books with lessons in their 'fourth-dimensional science'. The Normans acquired a small following by advising 'students' about their past lives. After Ernest's death, Ruth renamed herself Archangel Uriel, and with the help of her students she established a centre in El Cajon, California, where meetings and classes could be held. In the persona of Uriel, Ruth Norman costumed herself as a glittering goddess for publicity interviews or for films that were aired on public-access television.

In the 1970s, the group claimed to have contacted the so-called 'Space Brothers', who reportedly promised a mass spaceship landing that would initiate a New Age of Peace. Uriel announced that 33 ships (pictured as flying saucers) would arrive to form a towering university that would teach the Unariun Science. In the 1980s, an additional ship from the Planet Myton was prophesied to arrive first

in order to initiate the preparation for the others. Every October, members celebrate the advent of this Interplanetary Confederation with a parade and other festivities. Although the space fleet was predicted to arrive in 2001, members still cling to the prophecy despite its disconfirmation. Since Ruth Norman's death, devoted students have managed the centre by giving classes in past-life therapy and by keeping alive the memory of Uriel.

Unarius has about 40 local members and thousands of people on its mailing list, of which only a small fraction actively identifies with the group. A few cities support satellite study groups in North Carolina, Canada and Nigeria.

The Synanon Church
Richard Kyle

Originally established in 1958 by Charles (Chuck) Dederich (1914–97) as the Synanon Foundation (and referred to simply as Synanon), the Synanon Church was initially a psychotherapy group, which then evolved into a religion. It evidenced four stages of evolution: beginning as a voluntary association, it became a therapeutic community, then a social movement and eventually a religion. Dederich began the movement in California as a self-help organization for alcoholics and drug abusers. From its base in Santa Monica in the United States, Synanon communities first formed along the West Coast and then spread to the Midwest, the East and Puerto Rico.

In the treatment of alcoholics and addicts, Dederich used harsh dictatorial tactics focusing on manual labor and group support systems. His seminars, which became known as the Synanon Game, consisted of techniques designed to strip down a person's defence mechanisms and uncover the real person. For this treatment, Synanon received many contributions and government grants and developed into a multimillion-dollar

☞ *continued on page 399*

IMPLICIT RELIGION

Edward Bailey

Although earlier use of the expression 'implicit religion' has occasionally been found elsewhere, its widespread current usage dates from 1969, when the term was chosen in preference to 'secular religion'. It refers to those phenomena in secular life that seem to be religious in some way. They may express a recognized religion; for instance, helping a little old lady across the road could be seen as putting Christ's commandment to 'love your neighbour as yourself' into practice. Often, however, they seem to express a religiosity that is independent of any recognized religious system. Such behaviour (or beliefs, or feelings) are frequently remarked upon. 'Devotion' in the spheres of sport, politics, warfare and the arts is often described as 'worship' or 'sacrifice', or as 'religious', and their 'stars' compared to 'gods'.

The concept was originally formulated in order to direct attention to this aspect of human life, in the belief that Religious Studies had so far neglected this dimension of 'secular' behaviour, and that its study would be a helpful addition to the insights provided by the other social sciences. At that time the suggestion seemed to strike academics (and clerics) as self-contradictory: it was widely assumed that religion was bound to disappear, because it was 'really' something else (class interest or wishful thinking). However, in the 1980s and 1990s, the growing acceptance of the reality and relevance of the 'spiritual', outside the sphere of organized religion, had made the concept of 'implicit religion', in this primary sense of secular spirituality and faith, seem almost commonplace. In this respect, the 'intelligentsia' had 'caught up with' ordinary speech. The 'man in the street' had always said, for instance, 'I read the papers religiously,' counting as truly 'religious' only those commitments that formed the core of everyday living. Although he understood the word 'secular', he did not see it as different *in kind* from 'religious': it expressed either an official religion – or an unofficial one.

Devotion to soccer is often likened to religious worship. Here England fans in Trafalgar Square, London, celebrate a world cup goal by Michael Owen against Brazil in June 2002.

Defining implicit religion

The expression was understood from the first as capable of three definitions: *commitments, integrating focuses* and *intensive concerns with extensive effects*. Each may be seen as focusing on a different aspect of the reality to which they all try to point. *Commitments* suggests a subjective attitude, which may be conscious or unconscious, inherited or chosen. *Integrating focuses* suggests that the 'body' that has the implicit religion may be an individual or a group (of any size from a family to a nation or the species). *Intensive concerns with extensive effects* suggests that a commitment, however fervent, must be expressed in wider ways if it is to qualify as an implicit religion and not just as a hobby (or hobby horse!). If it does not interface with the rest of life, a belief or practice regarding, for example, the number 13 is merely a superstition or fetish.

Probably no expression is perfect in saying all that should be said and leaving no room for misunderstanding. In this case it should be explained that the 'religion' that is discerned may sometimes be made explicit, in word or in deed, and it may even be seen as a sort of religion by its carrier; but it is not usually seen as expressing one of the recognized religions. It may also be worth adding that possession

of (or possession by) any implicit religion does not suggest any value judgement: as with the recognized religions, any instance must be judged (if at all) on its own merits. Likewise, the concept carefully avoids any suggestion as to whether (any form of) implicit religion is either anterior or posterior to (any particular form of) explicit religion. Such developmental sequences are highly suitable subjects for empirical study (historical, psychological or social), but should never be assumed.

The sociologist Thomas Luckmann's 'invisible religion' is almost identical in meaning to 'implicit religion'. Apart from the change of metaphor (from speech to sight), the main difference lies in the empirical testing, both academic and pastoral, that 'implicit religion' received before its publication. Sociologist Robert Bellah's 'civil religion' is a fine reflection on a particular form of implicit religion: in particular, the theology espoused by the Inaugural Addresses of American Presidents. However, this meant it began life rather as 'civic theology' than as 'civil religion'. The Protestant theologian Paul Tillich's 'ultimate concern' is likewise a more particular instance, in this case, of an existential and cultural kind, more suited to student

seminars than everyday praxis.

All three definitions avoid assuming that people have a religion that is internally integrated and comprehensively all-embracing – in other words, that they only have one religion. That possibility is not excluded. No doubt some would suggest that Jesus, the Buddha or Muhammad and so on were individuals whose own internal integrity was matched by their external integration with their surroundings – whose inner identity was matched by their identification with their environment. Such a statement of faith would, no doubt, be an extrapolation, based upon an assessment of the available evidence. However, the definitions allow for the possibility that (until the evidence suggests otherwise) human behaviour is generally characterized by mixed motives, incomplete understandings and even contradictory intentions. The 'single-ness' of the three great monotheistic faiths, Judaism, Christianity and Islam, may speak of a 'consummation' that is 'devoutly to be desired'; but the heuristically East Asian model of Religious Studies (which assumes that individuals may belong to more than one religion) may be more enlightening.

organization. But the group's structure gradually changed. Outsiders who had no addictions were attracted to Synanon because of its communal, non-violent and disciplined lifestyle. They joined Synanon, bringing many skills and financial assets, which they gave to the community.

The organization could not formally be called a religion, as many people being helped by Synanon had rejected religion. But this gradually changed. The religious nature of Synanon could not be denied, so the articles of organization were changed in 1975, incorporating religion into its mission. In 1980, the name 'The Synanon Church' was formally adopted.

The religious dimension of Synanon could be seen in its behavioral characteristics and its theology. Synanon began to develop traits resembling a religious cult. Leaving the community was seen as the unpardonable sin and force was allegedly used to keep people in the group. Dederich took on the character of a secular god, wearing priest's robes and becoming quite dictatorial, and his wife declared herself to be the group's high priestess. Members were required to surrender the right to bear children, to swap spouses and to participate in physical fitness programmes. As Synanon failed to substantiate its therapeutic claims, the occult and mysticism became more prevalent, for example the use of Ouija boards and messages from the dead.

Theologically, Synanon drew its perspective from Eastern thought (Buddhism and Daoism) and from Western mystics who had adopted a significant Asian religious perspective into their teachings (e.g. Ralph Waldo Emerson and Aldous Huxley). In its communal emphasis, Synanon sought to demonstrate the basic principles of oneness within themselves and in their relations with others. The Synanon Game, the group's chief sacrament, was the primary tool used to achieve this unity. Similar to encounter groups, this game allowed people to express intense emotional feelings and led to confession and repentance.

Synanon was surrounded by controversy from its inception. Its enemies accused the organization of various crimes. In one case Synanon won a libel suit, but a number of people associated with Synanon were indicted for crimes. None of these cases reached trial, either because of lack of evidence or because Synanon pleaded no contest.

For a variety of interrelated, overlapping personal, social and organizational reasons the Synanon Church has now officially disbanded, but similar organizations, such as the Amity Foundation, are run by former Synanon members.

The Human Potential Movement
Elizabeth Puttick

The human potential movement (HPM) originated in the 1960s as a counter-cultural rebellion against mainstream psychology and organized religion. It is not in itself a religion, new or otherwise, but a psychological philosophy and framework, including a set of values that have made it one of the most significant and influential forces in modern Western society. Under its broad umbrella, a variety of psychological theories, approaches and movements are clustered; most self-development groups are offshoots from it, and it has shaped many New Age and alternative spiritualities. It has also influenced Eastern-based new religious movements and liberal Christianity as well as many secular movements and institutions. The explorations and advances of the HPM trailblazed the now widespread interest of mainstream society in personal development, the quality of relationships, emotional literacy, human values in the workplace, and the replacement of hard political causes with softer issues such as environmentalism. The plethora of popular

Humanistic psychologist, Abraham Maslow.

self-help books highlight and encourage the growing acceptance of these values.

The HPM developed out of humanistic psychology, which was created by Abraham Maslow (1908–70) in the 1940s and 1950s as a 'third force' in response to the limitations of psychoanalysis and behaviourism. His most solid and influential theory on the HPM was the 'hierarchy of needs', which explains how once the basic survival needs of a healthy, fully functioning person are met, higher needs for individuation emerge, culminating in the need for 'self-actualization', which drives one 'to become everything that one is capable of becoming'. Maslow believed that mystics were the most likely group to be self-actualized and have 'peak experiences' of ecstasy and union. He thus paved the way for the later spiritualization of psychotherapy.

HPM philosophy was adapted and developed into a number of major schools of humanistic psychology and psychotherapy, in particular Carl Rogers's person-centred counselling, Fritz Perls's gestalt therapy, Eric Berne's transactional analysis and Will Schutz's encounter groups. Another important influence on the HPM was the German psychologist Wilhelm Reich, particularly through his book *The Function of the Orgasm* (1927). Reich identified the root cause of neurosis as repression, imprinted in the body in the form of 'character armour', leading to many psychosomatic disorders and sociopolitical problems, including fascism. The common approach of these psychotherapists was the exploration of the affective domain of feelings and relationships. The result was the demystification and destigmatization of therapy, which was now seen as a path for 'normal neurotics' to explore the full range of human potential. In the 1960s, these techniques were further developed by counter-cultural 'growth centres', of which the largest and best known is Esalen, founded in California in 1962 by Michael Murphy and Richard Price, which now offers over 400 courses and programmes covering not just bodywork and spiritual therapies but health, philosophy, ecology, gender issues, arts, business and professional training. Nowadays there are hundreds of different kinds of counselling and psychotherapy available, and thousands of training organizations, leading to a proliferation of therapy and self-development centres worldwide.

The 1970s were labelled pejoratively by Tom Wolfe as the 'Me Decade', and the HPM has been criticized as narcissistic and lacking social conscience. Self-development is perhaps inevitably a self-centred process, and the movement may have overreacted to a perceived overemphasis on service and self-sacrifice in Christianity. A core HPM belief is that self-love is the precondition for real love of others – altruism – and that awareness (or insight) is essential for effective social action. It has also been argued that, as with magical practice in Paganism, self-development is a response to powerlessness: the individual cannot change the world but at least one can change oneself.

Yet there was a growing feeling during the 1970s that the full potential implied in self-actualization had not been realized: self-improvement had indeed happened, but not radical transformation. Many of the therapists and their clients thought of themselves as seekers, and began to look for broader perspectives and deeper solutions in spirituality. At this time Christianity was widely perceived within the counter-culture (and outside) as arid, authoritarian, hypocritical and out of touch. Eastern mysticism, on the other hand, exerted a magnetic attraction with its sophisticated praxis based on meditation, seen by some thinkers as compensating for the spiritual emptiness of the Protestant ethic. Whereas psychotherapy offered, at best, methods for improved mental health and social adaptation, spiritual praxis based on meditation can lead to self-transcendence and ultimately enlightenment. Seekers therefore began to explore Hindu and Buddhist spirituality and visit the ashrams of Indian gurus, who were perceived to be superior to psychotherapists as guides to the inner world.

Some psychologists, such as Carl Gustav Jung and Erich Fromm, had made theoretical connections with Eastern philosophy, but it was within the practical, experiential approach of psychotherapy that a living synthesis was created. Therapists of the HPM were utilizing meditation as an adjunct to 'growth' and experimenting with it in their groups, particularly at Esalen. The most significant developments happened in the *Osho movement, which attracted many of the leading HPM therapists, including Michael Barnett, founder of the movement 'People Not Psychiatry'. Rajneesh therapy was created at their growth centres in London during the early 1970s and further developed at the Osho ashram into a synthesis of humanistic psychology, tantra, Reichian and Buddhist breathing techniques, and meditation.

Initially, other Eastern-based new religious movements tended to ignore or disparage psychotherapy, particularly in Britain, although in the United States the two movements were seen as compatible and mutually enriching, particularly by Buddhist psychologists such as Jack Kornfield. This more positive attitude towards the benefits of psychotherapy is now also pervading British Buddhism. Outside religion, the psychologist Ken Wilber was utilizing Eastern philosophy to create *transpersonal psychology, and Roberto Assagioli did much the same thing with psychosynthesis. Within Western alternative spirituality, most of the groups and movements loosely classified as New Age can also be fitted under the HPM umbrella, as can many of the Pagan and shamanic groups. Self-development and empowerment are key concepts in magical ritual. Reciprocally, some shamanic healing techniques have been taken up by psychotherapists, although shamans interpret spirits and the 'non-ordinary reality' in which they are encountered as ontologically more 'real' than the material world, whereas psychologists tend to interpret these experiences as elements of the personal psyche or archetypes.

Nowadays the HPM has expanded from the margins into mainstream society, and has become quasi-institutionalized in representative councils and associations such as the Association of Humanistic Psychology and hundreds of training organizations. It has also had a major impact on social attitudes through the adoption of its methods in teacher-training colleges, academic courses, and, above all, in management training programmes. The most interesting and significant secular development of the HPM is its impact on business philosophy, practice and training. Personnel and management training is increasingly focused on the affective domain, utilizing frameworks such as transactional analysis and techniques including sensitivity training, interpersonal skills development, role play, feedback and group dynamics. Business philosophy is increasingly influenced by 'soft' HPM values, such as the widespread emphasis on stress management as an alternative to rampant ambition and competition.

Despite the HPM's emphasis on personal development extending into spiritual growth, it has usually been largely pro-business and entrepreneurial. For example, many of its practitioners have amassed large personal fortunes and founded successful commercial organizations. This is also often the case with some of the self-development groups who become involved in business consultancy and management training, such as *Landmark Forum (formerly *est*), the *Church of Scientology's subsidiaries WISE and Sterling Management, Programmes Ltd, Lifespring, *Silva Mind Control and the Insight Training Seminars run by the *Movement of Spiritual Inner Awareness. Most of these groups were founded for personal development, but often the founders and most of their clientele were drawn from the sales and business world. These organizations are sometimes classified sociologically as new religions, though they tend to describe themselves in secular terms.

Most of these trainings do not focus on spirituality directly, though the values may be implicit, but there are attempts to worship God and mammon simultaneously, as expressed by the futurist (and former *Transcendental Meditation leader) Peter Russell: 'My aim is to get all IBM's managers to experience themselves as God.' Business leaders are themselves becoming interested in spirituality, and inculcating these values into their organizations. Richard Barrett, an executive of the World Bank, is also founder of the World Bank's Spiritual Unfoldment Society, whose members discuss personal development,

meditation and reincarnation. He believes that spirituality can improve the bottom line of companies and even the health of national economies. Hundreds of Japanese companies have implemented corporate meditation programmes through the Maharishi Corporate Development International, which has several multinational corporations as clients, as does the Osho movement's Centre for Consciousness in Organizations. Conversely, therapy and spiritual centres regularly present events and workshops on prosperity consciousness and other approaches to money and spirituality, including Esalen and London's Alternatives centre.

Whether business, personal development and spirituality can combine as easily and smoothly as some of these experiments might suggest has yet to be seen. The ethic of self-improvement points in two directions: outwards towards the world, success and the 'ripening' of the ego, which a well-known Tibetan lama, the late Chogyam Trungpa Rinpoche (see *Shambhala International) termed 'spiritual materialism'. Simultaneously, it points inwards towards spiritual growth culminating in enlightenment, which implies the destruction or transcendence of the ego. The more holistic philosophies within the HPM and New Age see these positions as compatible: the ego as a fruit that has to ripen (through the fulfilment of desires and ambitions) before falling in the blaze of light of meditation, which reveals its illusory nature and leads us to true self-realization.

Neuro-Linguistic Programming
David Major

Neuro-linguistic programming (NLP) may be best thought of as a system of psychology concerned with the self-development of human beings. It claims to provide a set of skills and techniques that enable its practitioners to achieve competence and excellence in any field. Although it also claims that its techniques provide a way of relating to the spiritual side of human experience, it is essentially neutral with regard to religion. Its origins lie in the United States in the 1970s and among its earliest exponents are Richard Bandler and John Grinder with their ideas of self-improvement through studying, and then modelling, the behaviours of people who excel in their respective spheres of operation. By so doing, it is argued, individuals can achieve the same degree of excellence for themselves.

The term 'neuro-linguistic programming' is designed to embrace three ideas: all behaviour starts from the neurological processes; we use language to organize our thinking and to communicate with others; and we can choose to 'programme' our behaviour to achieve the results we desire.

The justification for an entry on NLP in this volume is that it may be seen that the linchpin of NLP is the area of belief. Within NLP's system of logical levels (that is, their identification of different facets of being human), belief occupies a midway position between, on the one hand, capability, behaviour and environment (which, in one way or another, *express* belief), and identity and spirituality, on the other (which *inform* belief). What is important in NLP is an understanding of the power of belief. Beliefs can both empower and disempower an individual; they can be both enabling and disabling. It is, therefore, crucial that the beliefs a person holds are examined and, if they are shown to be limiting or dysfunctional, ways and means of changing them are employed so that the individual can achieve his or her true potential. A key understanding in NLP is that human beings do have the ability to change their beliefs and to make themselves what they want to be, and that they can achieve this through the techniques offered by NLP.

Beliefs, however, are complex and may exist at a variety of levels. Many of our beliefs are held unconsciously, deriving, as they do, from culture and our innate spirituality. They are largely unexamined and unquestioned and are probably not particularly negotiable or susceptible to change. Other beliefs may be those we share with others within a group context but are not held by the community at large. At this level may be placed religious, political and other ideological positions. The consciously held beliefs of members of such groups may be challenged frequently by outsiders but not (or less so) by those within the group and, although there may be some movement of members in and out of a group, the majority remain secure in the group beliefs they have made their own. It is arguable that NLP techniques have neither the potential nor the direct intention to bring about belief change at the higher levels of belief. Although it may be the case that NLP leaves itself open to use by unscrupulous religious sects who may operate its techniques in order to bring about change in those they seek to convert, NLP proper has the positive intention of self-development and, unless a religious belief was proving to be limiting or dysfunctional in some way in the life of an individual, NLP would not normally focus on that area.

The level of belief with which NLP is most directly concerned is that of personal belief and, principally, self-belief. For most people, beliefs of this type are much less securely held and may be subject to challenge in all sorts of ways. Such beliefs are held mainly consciously (though some, for various reasons, may be suppressed) and with varying degrees of certainty. Beliefs at this level may also be much more to do with normal everyday operation and functioning and may be more susceptible to change anyway in the light of experience and feedback. A precondition of belief change at any level is, of course, the desire of the subject to be free from a limiting belief in order for the therapy to have a positive outcome.

The principal concern of NLP is with

psychology and with the function of belief rather than with its nature and, therefore, it raises concerns for philosophy and theology alike, especially with its claims that we are free to choose the beliefs we hold and that, in some respects, it does not matter whether a belief is true or false but, more importantly, whether it is empowering or disempowering. NLP's focus on subjective experience and its view that we cannot comprehend objective reality means that it fits well as an example of postmodern thought. Along with the theory of the social construction of reality of modern-day sociology and psychology, of critical theory in philosophy, and of reader-response theories in literature, we have, in NLP, a system of self-development that, to a large degree, focuses on individual subjectivity.

Emin
Sarah Lewis

Emin was founded in London in 1973, and based on the ideas of Raymond Armin (b. 1924), known to members as Leo. His teachings developed largely out of chance encounters with people who were similarly searching for answers to the fundamental questions of purpose and existence. It is one of the few movements of this type to be indigenous to Britain. According to their website:

Emin is a natural, living philosophy... a human journey... opening up the vast panorama of human capabilities in original, exciting and very practical ways... Its appeal cuts across all boundaries... The philosophy has no dogma or fixed agenda, but is rather a cutting edge exploration into the fundamentals of how things actually work... and how this can be useful in the improvement of a person's life...

The aim of Emin is for practitioners to abandon the trappings of materialism in order to find what is important in life and the purpose of life: 'The motive... is the discovery of truth, at core, and to proceed from this as a guiding template for personal decision making and behaviour.' This is ideally a group activity, with ideas being bounced from person to person, but still upholding 'the freedom of each individual to choose and experience and come to their own understandings'. Those involved in Emin are to live the beliefs and show a passion for life.

Emin places emphasis on the importance of the planet, with practitioners involved in ecological awareness, village community development, building design, world trends, human evolution, behavioural sciences, art and music. Ideas are spread through meetings, lectures, workshops and charitable activities.

Emin is established in 15 countries worldwide, each group reflecting the nature of not only the particular country but also of the individual members. Membership comprises possibly only a couple of thousand people.

The Raëlian Religion
George D. Chryssides

The Raëlian religion is a UFO religion founded by Claude Vorilhon (b. 1946), a French motor-racing journalist and a singer, known to his followers as Raël. In 1973 in Clermont-Ferrand, France, he claimed to have seen a flying saucer, and conversed with a space alien. Much of Raëlian teaching, disseminated in writing from 1974 onwards, purports to be biblical, bearing some affinities with Erich von Däniken's earlier work, *Chariots of the Gods?* (1968).

Raël's encounters with the extraterrestrials, together with their teachings, were initially recorded in two books: *The Book Which Tells the Truth* (1974) and *Extraterrestrials Took Me to Their Planet* (1975), both published in French, and brought together in 1978 as a

Raël, formerly known as Claude Vorilhon, poses with a model of the spaceship he claims to have encountered in 1973.

single volume, subsequently entitled *The Message Given to Me by Extraterrestrials: They Took Me to Their Planet.* The book teaches that biblical history is an account of the interaction between humanity and the Elohim. Raël notes that the word 'Elohim', conventionally translated as 'God', is a plural noun, and hence refers to a multiplicity of extraterrestrial beings, who were responsible for the creation of the world and of humankind (initially created as an artificial life form).

One group of extraterrestrial creators, called the Nephilim in the Bible (Genesis 9:1), engaged in sexual relationships with the human race, and thus produced a race of people with superior intelligence. This race is held to be the Jewish people. Jesus of Nazareth is believed to have been born as a result of sexual union between his human mother, Mary, and one of the Elohim, and in recent times Raël has affirmed that he also is the offspring of a human–extraterrestrial relationship. Raëlians have established their own calendar, whose years are counted from Raël's birth.

Raël is regarded as the new Messiah, whose role is to prepare humanity for the arrival of the Elohim on earth. The Elohim will come in peace, but must be received voluntarily by the human race. Their purpose is to establish a new world government, which will be controlled by a geniocracy: only those whose intelligence is 50 per cent higher than the human average will be eligible for public office. The new government will promote scientific and technological advancement, creating material prosperity and increased leisure; robots, for example, will be developed to perform menial tasks, thus enabling human beings to enjoy an enhanced lifestyle.

In order to receive the extraterrestrials, an embassy must be built. The Raëlian preference is for a site in Jerusalem, but their attempts to procure land have so far been unsuccessful. Anticipating that the Jews may once again reject their Messiah (that is, Raël), Raëlians have contingency plans to construct their embassy elsewhere.

The creators offer human beings the prospect of immortality. This is not an automatic right, but will only be afforded to those whose actions merit it. After one's death the Grand Council of the Eternals will determine whether a human should be recreated by means of cloning. Cell banks will be held inside the embassy and used for this purpose. Those who are ineligible for cloning will normally experience oblivion, but there are occasions where humans might be recreated for other purposes than immortal life. Following the terrorist attacks on New York and Washington on 11 September 2001, Raëlians suggested that cloning could be used to bring disaster victims back to life (with erasure of traumatic memories), and criminals such as suicide bombers could be recreated to experience appropriate punishment. In 1997, Raël set up an organization called 'Clonaid', headed by Dr Brigitte Boisselier, a Raëlian 'bishop'; in December 2002, Boisselier announced that the group had successfully cloned the first human baby.

Heaven's Gate
James R. Lewis

Heaven's Gate was founded by Marshall Herff Applewhite (1931–97) and Bonnie Lu Nettles (1955–97). In 1973, they had an experience that convinced them they were the two witnesses mentioned in Revelation 11. Preaching an unusual synthesis of occult spirituality and UFO soteriology, they began recruiting in New Age circles in the spring of 1975. Followers abandoned friends and family,

detached themselves completely from human emotions, as well as material possessions, and focused exclusively on perfecting themselves in preparation for a physical transition to the next kingdom (in the form of a flying saucer). For followers, the focus of day-to-day life was following a disciplined regime referred to as 'the overcoming process' or, simply, 'the process'. The goal of this process was to overcome such human weaknesses as sexual desires.

In the early phase of their movement, Applewhite and Nettles taught that the goal of the process they were teaching their followers was to prepare them to be physically taken aboard the spacecraft, where they would enter a cocoon-like state, eventually being reborn in transformed physical bodies. They also taught that heaven was the literal, physical heavens, and those few people chosen to depart with them would, after their physical transformation, become crew members aboard UFOs.

Later, the idea that the group might depart via suicide emerged in Applewhite's thinking. In contrast to his earlier idea of physical ascension, he rethought his teaching and adopted the view that Heaven's Gate members would ascend together spiritually rather than physically. The arrival of the Hale-Bopp comet was interpreted as an indication that the long-awaited pick-up of the group by aliens was finally about to take place. This precipitated the suicide of all 39 members of the group, whose bodies were found in a mansion outside San Diego on 26 March 1997.

Landmark Forum (*est*)
Elizabeth Puttick

The Landmark Forum is a direct descendant, with substantial changes, of *est (Erhard Seminar Training). est* was one of the most successful manifestations of the *human potential movement (HPM), and was founded in the 1960s by Werner Erhard (originally John Paul Rosenberg; b. 1935) in San Francisco. It provided short, highly intensive programmes lasting a few days, which were described by participants as emotionally intense, confrontational and verbally abusive. However, they also had a significant philosophical ethos behind them. The central idea was to challenge the effects of social conditioning on the ability of a person to take charge of their own lives. Up to three-quarters of a million people underwent the *est* seminar training, and many gave glowing testimonials to their transformative quality. *est* graduates have founded several spin-off organizations, of which the best known was Exegesis, which had around 7,000 graduates. However in 1984, perhaps largely owing to the criticisms of an English member of Parliament, David Mellor, Exegesis folded and was relaunched as a telesales company, Programmes Ltd, which no longer offers public courses.

Landmark Forum was founded in 1985 by a group of people who purchased the training methods and materials ('the technology') from Werner Erhard, and modified these into the softer, more didactic techniques still in use. Interestingly, the change from hard to soft occurred at a time (the mid-1980s) when other group leaders in the HPM were doing much the same thing. This period was a watershed between the hard 'encounter' style groups so widespread in the 1970s, and the more sophisticated later approaches. The reasons for this probably lay in the risk of litigation in the United States and elsewhere, but there were other more commercial factors, such as desire to reach a wider public.

Werner Erhard's brother Harry became the chief executive of Landmark Forum, but their official position is that there is virtually no continuity between their seminars and the *est* seminars. They are also adamant that Landmark Forum is not a religious movement, or a sect of any kind, but that they are solely an educational foundation. A central theme of the training is for a person to be free from their personal history, including events, education or influences, and instead to look to the future as their main reference point. There are undertones of Eastern philosophies, particularly in the aim of looking at the familiar in new ways, but participants emphasize goals of success and self-improvement rather than spirituality. Landmark Forum is significant in being a profitable business (figures of US$50 million per year are quoted), and claims a client group mainly in their thirties and forties who are 'already very successful in their lives'. Their publicity material promotes the theme that the seminars add value by opening up unexpected possibilities for these people, and quotes their own surveys.

Both *est* and Landmark Forum could be classified as LGATs (large group awareness trainings), a sociological grouping that includes *neuro-linguistic programming, Insight Training Seminars (see the *Movement of Spiritual Inner Awareness) and a whole plethora of sales and motivational courses. The LGAT format can have advantages, mainly in terms of affordability and the powerful support of being in a crowd of like-minded people. However, they have their critics, who say that they offer a 'one-size-fits-all' approach, where the group leaders make assumptions about clients' problems, and have an excessive focus on defining interpersonal relationships as the central objective in life.

Thee Church ov MOO

Lorne Dawson

Thee Church ov MOO is an exemplar of a new type of religious phenomenon: an online religion. While some of its members have gathered occasionally for ritual and social purposes, the community was originally formed on the internet (on a 'bulletin board' in Ottawa, Canada, in the early 1990s), and it operates primarily in cyberspace. A MOO is a multiple-user object domain. It is a place in cyberspace where participants can interact in a shared and self-created fantasy environment, most often for the purpose of playing a game. The founders of the church have engaged in an elaborate and self-conscious act of social construction: creating a purposefully postmodern, relativist, irreverent and humorous system of religious ideas. Their site offers hundreds of pages of material ranging from fabricated mythologies of MOOism, through blueprints for ritual practices, to pseudo-academic essays on a variety of spiritual and social themes. The 'religion' is broadly neo-Pagan in character, but it is subject to constant change (as is the address and content of the website). As the homepage states, the central premise is that 'paradox and radical self-contradiction are… the most reasonable way to approach the Absolute'. It is difficult to determine if MOOism is a 'religious' movement or just a sophisticated hoax. Certainly the objective is to have fun with religion. But the substantial and ongoing investment of time and energy suggest a more serious and significant underlying impulse of spiritual experimentation in response to an ever more sceptical and sophisticated social context.

Chen Tao (God's Salvation Church)
Daniel Wojcik

Chen Tao ('True Way', pronounced 'jun dao') is a small religious movement in the United States that attracted extensive media attention in the late 1990s for its doomsday predictions and belief that the faithful would be rescued by flying saucers. The group consisted of about 150 members from Taiwan, who relocated to San Dimas, California, in 1995, and then moved to Garland, Texas, in 1997, after the leader of the group, Hon-Ming Chen (b. 1955; then 42 years of age and known as Teacher Chen), received a prophecy from God (Chen noted that Garland, when pronounced quickly, sounds like 'God's Land'). The Chen Tao belief system involves a blend of Buddhism, Christian apocalypticism, Taiwanese folk beliefs and popular science, with an emphasis on the omnipresence of demonic forces and the redemptive role of flying saucers in human history. Members of the group dressed in white clothing as an expression of purity, and many wore cowboy boots and white cowboy hats after they moved to Texas, which quickly caught the attention of the media.

Established in 1993, Chen Tao has its origins in the 1950s, in a southern Taiwanese organization called the Research Group for the Study of Soul Light, which emphasized the development and study of spiritual energy or 'soul light'. The current leader of the group, Teacher Chen, taught at the Chianan College of Pharmacology and Science when he joined the organization in 1993. Chen declared that he had psychic and healing powers and, later, prophetic abilities, and he began predicting various apocalyptic scenarios. Like various other flying saucer religious movements, such as the Raëlians (see the *Raëlian religion), the *Unarius Academy of Science, the *Aetherius Society and *Heaven's Gate, the group attracted primarily educated people and professionals who were dissatisfied with traditional religions, and who found the movement's syncretism of scientific discourse and alternative spirituality especially appealing. Chen's teachings not only promise planetary escape on flying saucers prior to worldly catastrophe, but also

☞ *continued on page 415*

FUNDAMENTALISMS

Harriet A. Harris

'Fundamentalism' is a heavily loaded and often dangerous word. It has now become a term of vilification, and is increasingly used to justify attacking people, destroying property and holy sites, overturning governments or taking lives. But at the same time, there are many who do want to call themselves 'fundamentalists'. They choose the term as a rallying cry to call people to particular standards of belief or practice that they believe to be the hallmarks of true religion. They then regard those who do not subscribe to these standards as failing to be true adherents of the faith. Typically fundamentalists aim to cleanse 'false believers' from their midst, or to separate themselves from them. This is why fundamentalism sometimes leads to violence and usually leads to schism.

Origins of the term

Since the late 1970s, the term 'fundamentalism' has most commonly been used of politically active religious groups who are often militant in their message and sometimes also in their actions. It was not always so. Curtis Lee Laws, the man who coined the term

in 1920, was relatively mild-mannered, and he carefully chose a new word so as to avoid the more reactionary and exclusivist connotations of the word 'conservative'. Ironically 'fundamentalist' soon acquired these very connotations to an extreme degree. Laws was a member of the Northern Baptist Convention in the United States. He was concerned about the influence of theological modernism in his denomination, and he rallied like-minded believers to defend supernaturalist understandings of particular doctrines, such as the virgin birth and the resurrection of Christ. He suggested that 'those who still cling to the great fundamentals' of the faith and 'who mean to do battle royal for the fundamentals' call themselves 'fundamentalist'. Talk of the 'fundamentals' had been around in the preceding decades, and most particularly in a series of pamphlets known as *The Fundamentals*, produced in Chicago between 1909 and 1915 and containing articles by a range of evangelical theologians and ministers from North America and Europe. The crucial issue in these booklets was to defend the authority of God in scripture in relation to the authority of modern

science and new forms of biblical criticism.

The development of fundamentalism

To Laws' dismay, fundamentalists within his own and other denominations (notably the Presbyterians) soon showed militant and schismatic tendencies. During the 'fundamentalist–modernist' controversies that raged in the northern states in the 1920s, fundamentalists first tried to drive modernists out of their denominations, and failing that many of them formed breakaway churches. Soon the doctrine of biblical inerrancy became the watershed issue between fundamentalists and modernists. This doctrine was classically formulated in 1881 by A.A. Hodge and B.B. Warfield, biblical scholars at Princeton Theological Seminary. It holds that the Bible contains no errors, but is a perfectly reliable source of revelation from God. The doctrine goes hand-in-hand with belief in plenary verbal inspiration: that the biblical writers were inspired word for word so that not only is the Bible the Word of God, but that all of its words are God's chosen words. Since God cannot err, the Bible must be free from error. This notion of scriptural inspiration is closer to the Islamic view of the Qur'an than to traditional Christian views of the Bible. Laws himself was not a biblical inerrantist, though inerrancy quickly became a hallmark of fundamentalism and now characterizes fundamentalist notions of biblical authority.

Premillennialism – believing in the imminent return of Christ and his 1,000-year reign – was an important doctrine in the early fundamentalist movement. Premillennialists studied the 'signs of the times', looking for fulfilment of biblical prophecies that would signify Christ's return. Significantly, this made many American fundamentalists inactive politically, for if Christ is about to come again it would be a misuse of resources to spend one's time and energy trying to change the world when one should be saving souls. Laws was not a premillennialist. Nor was he a six-day creationist. In fact, few of the early fundamentalist spokesmen (for they were mostly men) were anti-evolutionists. There were large-scale crusades against Darwinism in the southern United States, culminating in the notorious 'Scopes Monkey Trial' of 1925 in Dayton, Tennessee, when a schoolteacher was tried for teaching evolution. But fundamentalism had begun in the north, mostly in the university cities of Boston, Chicago and New York, and northern fundamentalists were embarrassed by the

Scopes Monkey Trial spectacle. Creation science, which attempts a scientific defence of six-day creation, has grown since the 1960s and is making increasing inroads into Protestant fundamentalist culture.

By fundamentalist standards today, the man who first proposed the label 'fundamentalist' was fairly moderate and not much like the separatist fundamentalist Bob Jones or the politicized fundamentalist Jerry Falwell, both famous in the world of American Protestant fundamentalism. He would have born little resemblance to the Ayatollah Khomeini, and even less to Osama bin Laden. Nonetheless, fundamentalists soon gained a militant reputation. Some developed the separatist tendencies of the *Exclusive Brethren, who refuse to mix with unbelievers or with Christians unlike themselves. Such separatist fundamentalists remain a real presence in American life. They regard the more irenic evangelicals, including the evangelist Billy Graham, as 'fallen brethren' because they cooperate with diverse Christians for the sake of mission. On similar grounds they criticize the politicized fundamentalists who have fuelled the New Christian Right in America since the 1970s. Bob Jones attacked the Moral Majority for being

'unequally yoked' with 'Catholics, Jews, Protestants of every stripe, [and] Mormons'.

Fundamentalism across the world faiths

For most of the 20th century, fundamentalism was understood to be a Protestant Christian phenomenon existing mostly in the United States and the 'Anglo-Saxon' world. But in 1979 something happened within American fundamentalism that seemed to be paralleled in the Muslim world. The political lobbying group known as the Moral Majority was formed by the televangelist Jerry Falwell, and this coincided with the revolution in Iran and the return of the Ayatollah Khomeini from exile. The concept of fundamentalism was rapidly applied to the Muslim context.

The founding of the Moral Majority signified a turnaround for American fundamentalists, who had been politically withdrawn for most of the 20th century. Khomeini rejected the fundamentalist label precisely because he associated it with the apolitical otherworldliness that had more usually characterized American fundamentalism. Nonetheless the term was quickly extended to a range of Islamizing movements, many of which had been in existence since early in the 20th century as reactionary movements against Western colonialism. It was then extended to Judaizing movements, and scholars suggested that the Abrahamic, monotheistic faiths particularly fostered fundamentalist tendencies by encouraging exclusivism and absolute claims to truth.

Notably, these three religions are 'religions of the Book'. If their scriptures are accorded absolute status, as happens when they are held to be either inerrant or absolutely legally binding, then people who do not adhere to scriptural teaching – as fundamentalists understand it – are deemed to be false believers. Even so, Christian, Islamic and Jewish groups are not fundamentalist about scripture in exactly the same ways. Protestant fundamentalists police people's doctrinal beliefs more than their religious practice, whereas Islamizing and Judaizing groups primarily call people back to the observance of scriptural laws. In Muslim contexts this has often meant the state reintroducing shariah law (divine law), including amputating hands in cases of theft and stoning women caught in adultery. Moreover, Protestant fundamentalists believe they are going back to the 'plain sense' of the text and that interpretation interferes with the immediacy of the divine revelation. By contrast, all Muslims and Jews consciously interpret their sacred writings in the light of particular traditions. Hence Khomeini insisted that the Qur'an cannot be understood outside 11 centuries of Shiite scholarship. Jewish traditions follow the authority of rabbinic commentary, which diversifies rather than closes down interpretative possibilities.

It took longer before *Hindutva* (Hinduness) groups, and Buddhist and Sikh activists were called fundamentalist, and longer still for Far Eastern religions to be given this label. But once the label had extended this far, scripturalism could no longer be held as essential to fundamentalism. Unlike the religions of the book, Hinduism and Buddhism reject an exhaustive and one-off revelation and stress periodic revelations suited to the requirements of different *yugas* or historical epochs. Hinduness groups have tried to define *Hindutva*, the essence of a Hindu, but they have been able to say only that a true Hindu is one who looks upon the land of India as his or her *pitrubhumi* (fatherland) and *punyabhumi* (a sacred or holy land). On this definition, Indian Christians, Buddhists and Muslims could qualify as 'true' Hindus if they have the right attitude to the holy land of India. The Bharatiya Janata Party, widely referred to as a Hindu fundamentalist party and a major force in Indian politics, maintains that its argument is not with all Muslims in India, but only with those whose greater allegiance is towards Pakistan.

Hindu and Buddhist fundamentalisms could be said to promote cultural and national purity, rather than scriptural, doctrinal or legal purity. Buddhist fundamentalists who fight against the Tamils in Sri Lanka aim to defend the Buddhist purity of that island. This fight is now against Hindus but it began in the late 19th century against Western colonialism: 'The sweet gentle Aryan children of an ancient historic race are sacrificed at the altar of the whiskey-drinking, beef-eating belly god of heathenism [Christianity]. How long, oh! how long will unrighteousness last in Lanka?' asked the Buddhist activist Anagarika Dharmapala (d. 1933). He founded the Mahabodhi Society of Colombo (1891) for the renaissance of Buddhism and the rescue of Buddhist sites.

IDENTIFYING FUNDAMENTALIST CHARACTERISTICS

None of these groups in Islamic, Jewish, Hindu or Buddhist contexts fully exhibit the Protestant fundamentalist approach to scripture or the emphasis on right belief. A single core definition of fundamentalism is not possible now that the term is applied so diversely. But the groups we call 'fundamentalist' do overlap with each other in various respects. Jewish 'fundamentalists' share Muslim 'fundamentalist' devotion to scriptural law,

Muslim women demonstrate in Iran. The Iranian revolution and the Ayatollah Khomeini's return from exile saw the term 'fundamentalism' applied in a Muslim context for the first time.

and some share the desire to build a religious state. Like Hindu fundamentalists in India and Buddhist fundamentalists in Sri Lanka, Jewish fundamentalists identify their people by the preservation of religious rituals and by religio-historical links to a particular land. The Fundamentalism Project, based at the University of Chicago between 1988 and 1993, identified nine characteristics that recur in fundamentalist groups (but which may not all be found in any one group). The first five are ideological characteristics,

and the remaining four are organizational:

■ reactivity to the marginalization of religion;

■ selectivity with regard to the traditions and writings of one's religion;

■ moral dualism;

■ absolutism and inerrancy;

■ millennialism and messianism;

■ elect membership;

- sharp boundaries;

- charismatic and authoritarian leadership;

- behavioural requirements.

The project suggested that groups that score highly against this list are fundamentalist, while groups that manifest some but not many of the characteristics are non-fundamentalist or 'fundamentalist-like'. The project concluded that many of the Abrahamic movements they looked at were fundamentalist, while Hindu and Buddhist extremists were fundamentalist-like. Sikh radicals were judged to be fundamentalist because Sikhism 'acquired Abrahamic qualities' via Islam. The project came to define fundamentalism in shorthand as 'religiously motivated political activism'. A primary reason why the Hindu and Buddhist groups were not regarded as fundamentalist was because they reversed the priority of religion to politics. Ulster Protestants were not regarded as fundamentalist for the same reason.

A suggested use of the label

However, we can point to more than overlapping resemblances in explaining why so many disparate and seemingly unconnected movements are called 'fundamentalist'. All of these movements are absolutist in that they require some fixed truths upon which to build their religious system, and they behave in a threatened manner if their absolutes are called into question. This understanding of 'fundamentalism' is not inherently religious and could also apply to non-religious movements.

What religious fundamentalisms fix as their absolutely true foundation varies according to the religious, political and cultural context. It may be an inerrant Bible, or a command to safeguard the purity of a land, or a particular understanding of divine law. But there is always an attempt to get back to some original teaching, claim or insight, and to strip away accretions in the development of the religious tradition that have clouded unconditioned truth. It is in this sense that fundamentalists are selective with regard to their religious traditions. So Protestant fundamentalists go 'back to the Bible' and bypass elements of tradition they believe obscure or deviate from the plain truth contained in scripture.

Fundamentalism (as absolutism) is more at home in some religions than others. It fits the Protestant context best. Not only did it originate there, but its thought-patterns are those prevalent in the post-Reformation, and especially post-Enlightenment, Christian West. They reflect a non-contextual, non-developmental notion of truth, and a conviction that one needs a reliable foundation (one that is satisfying to reason) upon which to rest faith.

In other religions, fundamentalism ironically betrays some influence from Western patterns of thought. For example, Hindu and Buddhist movements that attempt to uncover pure 'ancient wisdom' have been influenced by the Western *Theosophical Society of the 19th century. Theosophy was an American and British movement claiming that Asian religions were ethically and metaphysically superior to Christianity. *Hindutva* ideology embodies an interesting tension in celebrating plurality and the absence of essentials as essential to Hinduism. For many Eastern religious groups, the assertion of self-identifying essentials against the encroachment of Western culture itself manifests some encroachment from the West.

On this suggested usage, fundamentalisms are movements with absolutist belief structures which can, but may not, engender political activism. If they are politically active, they may or may not be revolutionary, and may or may not be violent.

Fundamentalism and politics

It is religious-political resurgence that people most commonly think of as 'fundamentalist', but we should not lose sight of the diversity of fundamentalist groups on the matter of political engagement. As with Protestant Christians, Islamic and Jewish groups range from politically quietist to militantly activist. When activist they are more revolutionary (more opposed to secularism) than their Protestant counterparts, who want to uphold the separation of church and state. Some Islamizing groups regard the establishment of Islam as a personal, private matter; others hold that it requires governmental, legal and social reform based on Qur'anic principles. The Tablighi Jama'at (Association for the Propagation of Islam, established in 1926) proselytizes Muslims within both Muslim and Western countries, and shuns politics. By contrast, the Muslim Brotherhood, founded in Egypt in 1927 by Hassan al-Banna and now bearing an influence over much of the Sunni Muslim world, called for the establishment of an Islamic state governed by shariah, as opposed to the secular Arab states governed

by European laws. They are now criticized by more radical groups for operating in mainstream politics. These groups include Jama'a Islamia (al-Gama'at al-Islamiyya; Islamic Group or IG), Egypt's largest militant group, active since the 1970s, who were involved in the 1993 World Trade Center bombing and Osama bin Laden's fatwa of February 1998 calling for attacks on the United States, and Jemaah Islamiah (known as IJ), who are active in Southeast Asia and have links to Osama bin Laden. Several offshoots from the Muslim Brotherhood, such as Hamas in Palestine, have become separate entities. Muslim 'fundamentalist' ideology, especially as influenced by the Pakistani revolutionary, Abul Ala Maududi, has promoted a pan-Islamic vision, but some groups seek to create individual Muslim nation-states.

Jewish 'fundamentalisms' disagree over the relation between the political state of Israel and the biblical 'Land of Israel' (Eretz Israel). Haredim, Jews who are self-proclaimed 'zealots', are usually anti-Zionist or opposed to the state of Israel. The Neturei Karta (Guardians of the City) emerging in the 1930s, are the most prominent group among them. They believe the Land of Israel will be created by the Messiah, until

which time Jews are spiritually exiled from God. In Israel they form enclosed communities, condemn the Zionist compromise with non-Jews, and challenge the religious leadership verbally and through the destruction of property. They do not take up arms. By contrast, settler groups, notably Kach and *Gush Emunim (established in 1974), believe that the Zionist return to Israel will herald the coming of the Messiah. They sometimes violently defend the territories disputed between Israel and Palestine.

We have already mentioned the politicized Buddhist fundamentalists in Sri Lanka, but there are also politically quietist forms of Buddhism that have attracted the fundamentalist label. The Western Buddhist Order (established in 1968 by Sangharakshita; see *Friends of the Western Buddhist Order) is purist in accusing other forms of Buddhism of elevating matters of secondary importance over the primary act of 'going for refuge'. The order claims to develop a Buddhism for people living in the modern world, and has been described as 'Protestant Buddhist' for containing deeply ingrained Western assumptions about returning to the essence or fundamentals of faith.

offer a means of escaping the karmic cycles of life and death, a way to attain nirvana, and a return to God and the Buddha through spiritual exercises, meditation and good works.

In his treatise, *God's Descending in Clouds (Flying Saucers) on Earth to Save People* (1997), Chen states that nuclear catastrophe and other disasters would begin in Asia in August 1999, but that believers would be safe in the United States, where they eventually would be evacuated by God's flying saucers, disguised as clouds. According to Chen, the world has suffered four great periods of tribulation, each of which has ended in nuclear war. In the past, a few human beings escaped from the nuclear cataclysms in flying saucers, and then later returned to live underground until the radiation dissipated. Chen announced that God would soon warn humanity of an impending nuclear apocalypse that would destroy most of the world, by appearing at Chen's home on 31 March 1998 at 10:00 a.m. and entering into Chen's body. Six days prior to that, on 25 March, God would make a public announcement of his arrival, which would be seen on every television set in the world by tuning into Channel 18. Chen also declared that, as proof of God's presence at his home on 31 March, he would perform three miracles (turn invisible, make duplicates of his body to greet people simultaneously, and communicate with all visitors in their native language).

As the prophetic dates approached, the media speculated about the possibility of a mass suicide or a violent outcome if God did not appear as predicted, similar to the Heaven's Gate tragedy, even though Chen condemned suicide as a demonic act. When 25 March arrived, and God did not appear on Channel 18, Chen acknowledged his miscalculation, stating that his second prediction about God materializing in his

home could be considered 'nonsense'. Then, on 31 March, Chen offered a symbolic interpretation of his prophecy about God's appearance at his home – God was in fact present among everyone in attendance, since God is within everyone. Chen also announced that the presence of hundreds of news reporters on the scene was a miracle in itself, God's way of spreading his message of salvation to millions of people throughout the world. Although Chen acknowledged that aspects of his prophetic timetable were wrong, he continued to assert that worldly cataclysm is imminent and that God will rescue the chosen ones in flying saucers.

After the failed prophecies, more than half of the group's members returned to Taiwan because of visa problems, but a core group of Chen's followers remained convinced of his prophetic and healing abilities, and moved with him to Lockport, New York, in May 1998, where they continued to anticipate the end of the world and the arrival of God's spaceships. In 1999, when apocalypse did not occur as predicted, Chen explained that God had postponed the catastrophe to allow human beings the chance to convert their bodies from the normal 3 per cent of divine material to a complete 100 per cent, which will occur only if people take responsibility for their karmic debts and realize the evils of materialism. Recently, Chen has emphasized the idea that the collective health of the planet is in danger, and that the earth's immune system is being destroyed, resulting in natural disasters and diseases like AIDS and cancer.

Chen Tao has opened a new branch in Brooklyn, New York, where a counselling centre has been established, and Chen and his followers regularly gather in Central Park, now said to be God's main base to help humanity, where they share their views about worldly destruction and salvation and offer daily services to heal people from cancer and AIDS.

Doofs and Raves in Australia
Lynne Hume

Australia is host to many new religious movements and alternative spiritualities, including the amorphous New Age. New religious movements vary from those that are almost indistinguishable from the predominantly Christian groups, to those whose ideas differ significantly. Some groups are highly coercive and totalitarian, while others allow their followers enormous freedom of ideas and expression.

Alternative communities are prolific throughout the country, especially along the more populated eastern and southern coastline and its hinterland, and have created a popular calendar of annual events, such as the Woodford Folk Festival (formerly the Maleny Folk Festival), held in Queensland, which draws thousands of people from all over Australia and beyond. Mind, Body, Spirit festivals that provide information on all aspects of spiritual healing, alternative medicines and New Age ideas are also annual occasions in most Australian cities. Such events represent the increasing importance contemporary Australians place on healing, the environment and alternative spiritualities that emphasize personal growth and individualism.

In the 1996 government census, a significant number of Australians were identified under the loose rubric of 'New Age' religion, which included a diverse range of smaller groups such as *Spiritualism, nature religion and neo-Pagan/Pagan groups, such as *Wicca. What was not included in the census information was any mention of a rapidly increasing interest among Australian youth in what is called, interchangeably, 'dance parties', 'bush parties', 'raves' or 'doofs'.

The 'rave' began as a British phenomenon and was first reported in Australia in Melbourne in 1988. Raves subsequently

infiltrated the night-time underground of Australian capitals, especially Sydney and Melbourne, between the late 1980s and 1992. With its rejection of state-imposed structures, clandestine raves were largely underground affairs conducted in empty city warehouses and industrial estates. Initially, they drew relatively small crowds, but by 1997/8 one New Year celebratory rave event hosted around 10,000 people.

The mild Australian climate lends itself well to outdoor celebrations, and dance parties are now held in the desert, on the beaches, and in the bush, as well as their original locations in inner-city warehouses. In spite of the enormous difficulties of moving sizeable technical music equipment long distances, the move to more remote hinterland bush locales has increasingly incorporated an ecological component. While the aim is essentially one of pleasure through dance, sound, music and the use of hallucinogenic drugs, there is a sociopolitical component to these events. Participants talk of the failure of government and the Australian people in general to address the traumatizing legacies of colonialism, such as its effects on Aborigines and the destruction of the environment.

The spiritual yearnings of Australian youth are incorporated into the social and community aspects of the bush dances, where their needs for self-expression, affiliation with Aboriginal causes and their own sense of ethics are combined with a mixture of pleasure and spirituality in the pursuit of a re-enchanted world.

This new youth subculture turns the outback into a dance floor, where participants can 'stomp' all night to the pulse beats of a DJ and the sounds and visions of digital

A rave in Melbourne. In 1997/8 one New Year celebratory event in Australia attracted around 10,000 people.

technology. The term 'doof' describes the bass-driven kick drum that provides the 'doof-doof-doof' sound of the music and has become a synonym for youth cultural dissonance. The northern coast of New South Wales, especially around Lismore, Nimbin and Byron Bay, is a focal point for alternative lifestyles and was significant in the emergence of doofs. The doof has been described as a post-rave phenomenon with bohemian origins and as such has been welcomed in areas that attract alternative lifestyles, such as Nimbin in northern New South Wales, home to a hippie population since the 1960s.

Doofs are said to be rituals of communion with other participants that provide mystical bonds with nature. Participants are keen to explore alternative states of consciousness in a stimulating environment that incorporates loud music from mobile sound systems, fireworks, physical theatre, performance troupes, gigantic sculptured figures and flashing lights – and to dance their way into trance. The trance dance becomes a portal to other states of consciousness, often with the aid of 'entheogens' (see *Psychedelic Spirituality). Doofs are part of an anarchic and anti-corporate movement that is non-hierarchical, youth-community oriented, and youth-instigated and directed.

Affiliation with Aboriginal Australian causes is one of the political aspects of this youth subculture, proponents of which deem dance raves to be 'anarcho-mysticism'. Indeed, some events are described as 'psychorroborees', implying association with Aboriginal inter-tribal gatherings (corroborees). A biannual alternative cultural event 'ConFest' (conference festival) held in New South Wales draws in over one thousand gesticulating trance dancers, both Aboriginal and non-Aboriginal, to its outdoor dance odyssey. A New Year's Eve 2000/01 celebration called Coexistdance, held at Lake Tyres in Victoria, was attended by local Aboriginal rights activist Robbie Thorpe, and about a third of the attendees (200 people) were Aboriginal people, including some Aboriginal elders.

One rave celebration held at an electronic dance music village at Tocumwal, New South Wales, during Easter 1996, was called 'Rainbow Dreaming' and billed as a 'trance-dance' event. According to its principal organizer, DJ Krusty, the purpose was to create a sacred space for people to find their own sacred dance for healing themselves and the planet. The promotional literature included references to a putative pagan past, the valorization of indigenous practices and reverence for nature. Advanced audio, lighting and visual technologies generated an all-night dance odyssey that peaked at sunrise. Participants moved into a trance dance and were collectively invited to revere their natural surroundings and question their separation from the natural world. Paradoxically, the emphasis on spirituality and nature seems dependent upon the incorporation of advanced technology.

List of Contributors

General Editor

Christopher Partridge is Professor of Contemporary Religion at University College Chester, England. His research and writing focuses on new religions and alternative spiritualities in the West. He has published research in the areas of both contemporary Christian theology and also Western alternative spiritualities. He is the editor of *Fundamentalisms* (2001), *Mysticisms East and West: Studies in Mystical Experience* (with Theodore Gabriel, 2003) and *UFO Religions* (2003). He is the author of *H.H. Farmer's Theological Interpretation of Religion: Towards a Personalist Theology of Religions* (1998) and edited H.H. Farmer's second series of 1951 Gifford Lectures, *Reconciliation and Religion* (1998).

Contributors

Ariel Abel is Rabbi at the Independent Orthodox Waltham Forest Hebrew Congregation, London, England.

Allan Anderson is Senior Lecturer in the Graduate Institute for Theology and Religion at the University of Birmingham, England. He is also the Director of the Research Unit for Pentecostal Studies at the same university. His numerous publications include *Pentecostals After a Century* (ed., with Walter J. Hollenweger, 1999), *Zion and Pentecost: The Spirituality and Experience of Pentecostals and Zionists/Apostolics in South Africa* (2000) and *African Reformation: African Initiated Christianity in the 20th Century* (2001).

Edward Bailey is Visiting Professor in Implicit Religion at Middlesex University, England, having started its study in 1968. He is the founding Director of the Centre for the Study of Implicit Religion and Contemporary Spirituality, and has been Rector of Winterbourne, Bristol, since 1970. He has written numerous articles on 'implicit religion' and is the author of *Implicit Religion: An Introduction* (1998) and *The Secular Faith Controversy* (2001). He also edits the journal *Implicit Religion*.

Ruth Bradby lived and taught in India for 20 years. She is currently carrying out doctoral research into alternative spiritualities and popular self-help literature at Chester College, England. She has published articles on aspects of Hinduism and on alternative spirituality.

Ian Bradley is a Church of Scotland minister and Reader in Practical Theology in the School of Divinity at the University of St Andrews, Scotland. He is the author of more than 25 books, including four on Celtic Christianity, of which the most recent is *Colonies of Heaven: Celtic Models for Today's Church* (2000). His most recent book is *God Save the Queen: The Spiritual Dimension of Monarchy* (2002).

David Burnett is Director of Studies at All Nations Christian College, Ware, Hertfordshire, England, and a Fellow of the Royal Anthropological Institute. He is the author of several books and articles, including *The Spirit of Hinduism* (1992) and *The Spirit of Buddhism* (1996).

Jeremy R. Carrette is Senior Lecturer in Religious Studies at the University of Stirling, Scotland. He teaches in the psychology of religion and social theory and religion. He is editor of *Religion and Culture by Michel Foucault* (1999) and the author of *Foucault and Religion: Spiritual Corporality and Political Spirituality* (2000).

Eric Christianson is Senior Lecturer in Hebrew Bible and Judaism at Chester College, England. He has published in the areas of Holocaust studies, Bible and film, and wisdom literature in the Hebrew Bible. He is the author of *A Time to Tell: Narrative Strategies in Ecclesiastes* (1999).

George D. Chryssides studied philosophy and religion at the universities of Glasgow and Oxford. He has taught in several British universities, and is currently Senior Lecturer in Religious Studies at the University of Wolverhampton, England. His main research interest is new religious movements and recent publications include *Exploring New Religions* (1999) and the *Historical Dictionary of New Religious Movements* (2001).

Dan Cohn-Sherbok is Professor of Judaism at the University of Wales, Lampeter. He is the author and editor of over 60 books, including *The Jewish Heritage* (1988), *Issues in Contemporary Judaism* (1991), *Israel: The History of an Idea* (1992), *The Jewish Faith* (1993), *Atlas of Jewish History* (1994), *God and the Holocaust* (1996) and *The Jewish Messiah* (1997).

Michael Daniels is Senior Lecturer in Psychology at Liverpool John Moores University, England, where he is also Co-Director of the Consciousness and Transpersonal Psychology Research Unit, and joint programme leader for the MSc in Consciousness and Transpersonal Psychology. He has published research on self-actualization, moral development, Jungian psychology, conceptual issues in transpersonal psychology, the transpersonal shadow, the psychology of evil and parapsychology.

Douglas J. Davies is Professor in the Study of Religion in the Department of Theology at Durham University, England. He has been Professor of Religious Studies at Nottingham University and has studied at the universities of both Durham and Oxford. He was awarded an honorary doctoral degree by the University of Uppsala, Sweden. His research interests are reflected in his major publications, which include *Meaning and Salvation in Religious Studies* (1984), *Latter-Day Saints in Wales and Zion* (1987), *Mormon Identities in*

Transition (ed., 1996), *The Mormon Culture of Salvation* (2000), *Anthropology and Theology* (2002) and *Death, Ritual and Belief* (2002).

Andrew Dawson is Senior Lecturer in Theology and Religious Studies at Chester College, England. He researches in the area of religion and society in South America and is the author of *The Birth and Impact of the Base Ecclesial Communities and Liberative Theological Discourse in Brazil* (1998).

Lorne Dawson is Chair of the Religious Studies Department and an Associate Professor of Sociology at the University of Waterloo, Ontario, Canada. He is the author of *Comprehending Cults* (1998) and the editor of *Cults and New Religious Movements: A Reader* (2003). He has published many articles about the study of new religions and his current research is focused on religion and the internet and the cultural significance of new religious movements in late modern society.

John Drane teaches in Practical Theology at the University of Aberdeen, Scotland, and also at Fuller Seminary, Pasadena, California. His numerous publications include *What is the New Age Still Saying to the Church?* (1999) and *Beyond Prediction: The Tarot and your Spirituality* (co-authored with Ross Clifford and Philip Johnson, 2001).

Gavin Flood is Professor of Religious Studies in the Religious Studies Department at Stirling University, Scotland. He has published in the areas of Hinduism and method and theory in the study of religion. His publications include *An Introduction to Hinduism* (1996) and *Beyond Phenomenology: Rethinking the Study of Religion* (1999).

Theodore Gabriel trained in anthropology and religious studies at the University of Aberdeen, Scotland. He was Senior Lecturer in Religious Studies at the University of Gloucestershire, England, until 2000, and is currently Honorary Research Fellow at the same university. He has

carried out research into Islam and Hinduism in Kerala, Lakshadweep and Malaysia, and has published articles on both Islam and Hinduism. Recent publications include *Christian-Muslim Relations: A Case Study of Sarawak, East Malaysia* (1996), *Hindu-Muslim Relations in North Malabar* (1996), *Hindu and Muslim Inter-Religious Relations in Malaysia* (2000) and *Islam in the Contemporary World* (ed., 2000).

Ron Geaves is Senior Lecturer in Religious Studies in the Department of Theology and Religious Studies, Chester College, England, where he teaches Islam, Sikhism, religious ethnography and new forms of religion. He was formerly Head of the Study of Religion at University College, Chichester. Although most of his published work, including his latest book *The Sufis of Britain* (2000), has been in the field of Islam, he has a long association with Sikhism arising from personal contact and his ethnographic work in South Asian diaspora communities in Britain.

Robert A. Gilbert is an antiquarian bookseller, a recognized authority on the 'occult revival' of the Victorian era, and has lectured extensively in Britain and the United States. He is the author of three books on the Hermetic Order of the Golden Dawn, and of both a biography and a bibliography of the esoteric author, A.E. Waite. He has been an active member of the Churches' Fellowship for Psychical and Spiritual Studies for 30 years, and is a lay preacher in the New Church.

Tim Grass is an Associate Lecturer at Spurgeon's College, London, England, and also teaches in Eastern Europe. He has published several historical articles, edited *Evangelicalism and the Orthodox Church* (2001) and is currently working on a history of the Brethren movement.

Andreas Grünschloss is Professor of Religionswissenschaft at the University of Göttingen, Germany. He has carried out research into new

religious movements, Buddhism, the study of religion and interreligious relations. His publications include *Religionswissenschaft als Welt-Theologie: Wilfred Cantwell Smith's religionstheologisches Programm* (1994) and *Wenn die Götter landen…Religiöse Dimensionen des UFO-Glaubens* (2000).

Harriet A. Harris is Chaplain of Wadham College, Oxford, England, and Honorary Fellow of the University of Exeter, where she was formerly Lecturer in Theology. She has written extensively on both fundamentalism and the philosophy of religion, including the book *Fundamentalism and Evangelicals* (1998).

Graham Harvey is Reader in Religious Studies at King Alfred's College, Winchester, England. His research considers the construction and presentation of identities among ancient Jews and early Christians, contemporary Pagans, indigenous people and shamans. His publications include *The True Israel* (1996), *Listening People, Speaking Earth: Contemporary Paganism* (1997), *Indigenous Religions* (2000) and *Shamanism* (2002).

Almut Hintze is Zartoshty Lecturer in Zoroastrianism at the School of Oriental and African Studies, University of London. She has published on Indo-Iranian philology and Zoroastrian literature and religion. Her publications include *Der Zamyad Yasht*, an edition of the Avestan Zamyad Yasht (1994) and *Lohn im Indoiranischen*, a study of the words for reward and retribution in Vedic Sanskrit and Avestan (2000).

Richard Hoskins is Senior Lecturer in the Study of Religions at Bath Spa University College, England. After working in the Congo for six years, Richard studied theology at Oxford University and then completed a PhD in the theology and religious studies department at King's College, London. He specializes in African religions, Christianity and contemporary spiritualities. He is currently writing a book on the

Kimbanguists and is the author of *The Doctrine of the Trinity in the Works of John Richardson Illingworth and William Temple* (2000) and several articles. He continues to travel to Africa regularly.

Lynne Hume is an anthropologist and Lecturer in Religious Studies at the Department of Studies in Religion, University of Queensland, Brisbane, Australia. She has travelled widely and carried out fieldwork in the South Pacific, Canada and Australia. She has written studies of Australian Paganism, Aboriginal Christianity, various new religions and women in religion. She is the author of *Witchcraft and Paganism in Australia* (1997) and *Ancestral Power: The Dreaming, Consciousness and Aboriginal Australians* (2002).

Edward Irons is Director of the Hong Kong Institute for Culture, Commerce and Religion, a private research centre studying social change in Hong Kong and China. His research focuses on Chinese new religions.

Elizabeth Isichei is Professor of Religious Studies at the University of Otago, Dunedin, New Zealand. She worked for 16 years in Africa, and was Professor of History at the University of Jos, Nigeria, for nine years. She has written many books on African history and religion, among them *A History of Christianity in Africa* (1995) and *Voices of the Poor in Africa* (2002), which discusses the changing symbolic universe of neo-traditional religion.

William Kay is Senior Lecturer in Theology Education at King's College, London, England, and Director of the Centre for Pentecostal and Charismatic Studies, University of Wales, Bangor. He has doctorates in theology and education. His many publications include *Drift from the Churches: Attitudes Towards Christianity During Childhood and Adolescence* (with L. Francis, 1996) and *Religion in Education* (ed. with L. Francis, 1997).

Ursula King is Emerita Professor in Theology and Religious Studies, University of Bristol, England. She

was Visiting Professor of Feminist Theology at the University of Oslo (1998–2001) and has lectured in many countries of the world. She is the author of numerous books and articles, including *Women and Spirituality: Voices of Protest and Promise* (1993) and *Christian Mystics: Their Lives and Legacies throughout the Ages* (2001). She works on comparative studies of spirituality, feminism and interfaith dialogue, and wider issues of religion and gender.

Robert Kisala is a Permanent Fellow of the Institute for Religion and Culture at Nanzan University, Nagoya, Japan. He is the author of *Prophets of Peace: Pacifism and Cultural Identity in Japan's New Religions* (1999) and co-editor of *Religion and Social Crisis in Japan: Understanding Japanese Society through the Aum Affair* (with Mark Mullins, 2001).

Richard Kyle is Professor of History and Religion at Tabor College, Hillsboro, Kansas, United States. His publications include *The Religious Fringe: A History of Alternative Religions in America* (1993), *The New Age Movement in American Culture* (1995) and *Awaiting the Millennium: A History of End-time Thinking* (1998).

Jeong-Kyu Lee graduated from Korean Union College in Seoul, South Korea and the University of Montana, United States, and carried out doctoral research in higher education administration at the University of Texas, Austin, United States. He is currently Research Fellow at the Korean Educational Development Institute, Seoul, and Joint Professor at Hongik University, Seoul. He has written several books and articles in the areas of Korean religion and higher education, a number of which have been translated into English, French and Spanish. His recent publications include *Historic Factors Influencing Korean Higher Education* (2000), *Impact of Confucian Concepts of Feelings on Organizational Culture in*

Korean Higher Education (2001) and *Korean Higher Education: A Confucian Perspective* (2002).

Andy Letcher carried out doctoral research into Bardic performance within contemporary Paganism at King Alfred's College, Winchester, England. Previously he was involved in direct action as a road protester and was a member of the band, Jabberwocky.

James R. Lewis is Lecturer at the University of Wisconsin, Stevens Point, United States. He is a recognized authority on non-traditional religions and the author and editor of several dozen books in the field, including *Perspectives on the New Age* (with J. Gordon Melton, 1992), *The Gods Have Landed: New Religions from Other Worlds* (1995), *Magical Religion and Modern Witchcraft* (1996) and *UFOs and Popular Culture* (2000).

Sarah Lewis is Teaching Fellow in the Department of Theology and Religious Studies at the University of Wales, Lampeter, specializing in new religious movements and New Age. She has written a doctoral thesis on the theology of the Unification Church.

Shirley Lucass has a BA in Theology and Religions from Liverpool Hope University College, England, and an MA in Jewish Studies from Manchester University, England. She is currently carrying out doctoral research at the University of Manchester into the concept of Messiah in Judaism and its implications for Jewish-Christian relations.

Rory Mackenzie is Lecturer in Practical Theology at the International Christian College, Glasgow, Scotland, where he also teaches Buddhism. He formerly worked in Thailand for ten years with the Christian community and is currently carrying out research at the University of Sunderland into the teaching and practice of new religious movements within Thai Buddhism.

Duncan MacLaren is Chaplain of St Edmund Hall, Oxford, England. He is currently engaged in doctoral research in the sociology of religion at King's College, London.

Michael McMullen is Associate Professor of Sociology at the University of Houston, Clear Lake, Texas, United States. His publications include *The Bahá'í: The Religious Construction of a Global Identity* (2000). As well as continuing to research the American Bahá'í community, he also works more generally in the areas of the sociology of religion, organizational development and change, and conflict resolution and mediation.

David Major is Director of the Centre for Work Related Studies at Chester College of Higher Education, England, and a former Lecturer in Theology and Religious Studies at the same college. As well as articles on neuro-linguistic programming, his publications include *Witness in a Gentile World: A Study of Luke's Gospel* (with E. Johns, 1991) and *Shaping the Tools: Study Skills in Theology* (with R. Ackroyd, 1999).

Peter Jan Margry is Director of the Department of Ethnology at the Meertens Institute, a research centre of the Royal Netherlands Academy of Arts and Sciences, Amsterdam. His research focuses on contemporary religious culture in the Netherlands and Europe and on the popular (religious) culture of the 19th and 20th centuries. He has published numerous books and articles on pilgrimage, rituality, sanctity and devotions.

Jean-François Mayer is Lecturer in Religious Studies in the Study of Religions Department at the University of Fribourg, Switzerland. He is known internationally for his expertise in the area of new religious movements and has authored several books and articles on related topics, including religion on the internet.

J. Gordon Melton is an international expert on new religions, Founder/ Director of the Institute for the Study of American Religion in Santa

Barbara, California, and a research specialist for the Department of Religious Studies at the University of California–Santa Barbara.

David Miller is Lecturer in Mission Studies at the International Christian College, Glasgow, Scotland. Between 1986 and 1996 he and his wife worked in Japan. For some of that time they were staff members with Kirisutosha Gakusei Kai, the Japanese Christian Students Association. He is now pursuing postgraduate study at Lancaster University looking at conversion among Japanese, comparing those who convert to Christianity with those who convert to Japanese new religious movements.

Robert Morrison was Visiting Numata Professor in the Department of Religious Studies at McGill University, Montreal, Canada, and is currently Associate Lecturer in Religious Studies at Cardiff University, Wales, and Honorary Fellow in the Department of Philosophy at the University of Liverpool, England. He has published numerous articles on Buddhism and philosophy and *Nietzsche and Buddhism: A Study in Nihilism and Ironic Affinities* (1997).

Malory Nye is Professor of Religious Studies at the Al-Maktoum Institute for Arabic and Islamic Studies, University of Abertay, Dundee, Scotland. He has conducted research on various Hindu communities in Britain, including ISKCON in London, and has published *A Place for Our Gods: A Hindu Temple Community in Edinburgh* (1996), *Multiculturalism and Minority Religions: Krishna Consciousness, Religious Freedom and the Politics of Location* (2001) and *Religion: The Basics* (2003).

Seán O'Callaghan is an ordained Pentecostal minister and has degrees from the National University of Ireland (History) and Chester College, England (Theology and Religious Studies). He has been Visiting Lecturer in Theology at Regents Theological College,

Nantwich, England, and is currently carrying out doctoral research at Chester College. He has a research interest in contemporary esoteric and occult movements.

Elizabeth Puttick completed a PhD in the sociology of religion at King's College, London, England. Her current research interests are business and spirituality, personal development, New Age, Shamanism and women's spirituality. She is now a literary agent and teaches in London at the City University and at the American College of Liberal Arts. She is the author of *Women in New Religions: In Search of Community, Sexuality and Spiritual Power* (1997).

Ian Reader is Professor of Religious Studies at Lancaster University, England. He has previously worked at academic institutions in Japan, Denmark, Scotland and Hawaii. He specializes in the study of religion in Japan, and has written widely in this area as well as on millennialism, religion and violence. Among his books are *Religion in Contemporary Japan* (1991), *Practically Religious: Worldly Benefits and the Common Religion of Japan* (with George J. Tanabe, 1998) and *Religious Violence in Contemporary Japan: The Case of Aum Shinrikyô* (2000).

John A. Saliba studied philosophy and theology at Heythrop College, London, England, and has a diploma in anthropology from Oxford University, and a doctorate in religious studies from the Catholic University of America, Washington, United States. Since 1970 he has been Professor of Religious Studies in the Department of Religious Studies at the University of Detroit, Mercy, Michigan, United States. For many years his principal area of research has been new religious movements. Among his recent publications are *Perspectives on New Religious Movements* (1995) and *Christian Responses to the New Age Movement* (1999).

Hannah Sanders is currently completing doctoral research into media culture and teenage witchcraft in contemporary Britain at the Norwich School of Art and Design, England.

Nigel Scotland is Field Chair in the School of Theology and Religious Studies at the University of Gloucestershire, England. His most recent publications include *Sectarian Religion in Contemporary Britain* (2000), *Good and Proper Men: Lord Palmerston and the Bench of Bishops* (2000), *Charismatics and the New Millennium* (2000) and *Evangelical Anglicans in a Revolutionary Age 1789–1900* (2003).

Birgit Staemmler studied for her BA in Japanese at the School of Oriental and African Studies, University of London, England, for her MA in Japanese and Anthropology at the University of Heidelberg, Germany, and received a PhD from the Tübingen University, Germany, for her work on Japanese new religions: 'Chinkon Kishin: Mediated Spirit in Japanese New Religions'. She has also been involved in a research project on Japanese religions on the internet.

Bronislaw Szerszynski is Lecturer in Environment and Culture at the Institute for Environment, Philosophy and Public Policy, Lancaster University, England. He is the co-editor of *Re-Ordering Nature: Theology, Society and the New Genetics* (with C. Deane-Drummond and R. Grove-White, 2003) and author of *The Sacralization of Nature: Nature and the Sacred in the Global Age* (2004).

Kevin Tingay is Rector of Camerton in Somerset, England, and Inter-Faith Advisor in the Diocese of Bath and Wells. He has a particular interest in the contemporary New Age and its precursors. He has published articles and carried out doctoral research on the nature and impact of the Theosophical movement.

Garry W. Trompf is Professor in the History of Ideas in the Department of Studies in Religion at the University of Sydney, Australia. He

was formerly Professor of History at the University of Papua New Guinea. He is the author of *Cargo Cults and Millenarian Movements: Transoceanic Comparisons of New Religious Movements* (1990), *Melanesian Religion* (1991) and *Payback: The Logic of Retribution in Melanesian Religions* (1994).

Diana Tumminia studied ethnography at UCLA, United States, where she received her doctorate in 1995. She now teaches social psychology, race relations and gender at California State University, Sacramento. Her publications range from advice on teaching to the social history of millenarian groups, including several studies of Unarius.

Maya Warrier is Lecturer in Hinduism and the Anthropology of Religion at the University of Wales, Lampeter. For her doctoral thesis, she conducted extensive fieldwork-based research in India and Britain on Mata Amritanandamayi and her devotees, and she has published an article in the area.

Frank Whaling is Professor Emeritus of the Study of Religion at Edinburgh University, Scotland, where he has taught since 1973. He has doctorates from Cambridge University and Harvard University. He has written over 100 papers and over 150 reviews, and is the author or editor of 14 books in the areas of the Hindu tradition, comparative religion, history and phenomenology of religion, methodology, dialogue, theology and spirituality.

Daniel Wojcik is Associate Professor of English and Folklore Studies at the University of Oregon, United States. He is the author of *Punk and Neo-Tribal Body Art* (1995), *The End of the World As We Know It: Faith, Fatalism and Apocalypse in America* (1997) and articles on apocalyptic beliefs, vernacular religion, self-taught artists and visionary art.

Xinzhong Yao is Professor of Religion and Ethics in the Department of Theology and Religious Studies at the University of Wales, Lampeter. He has been

teaching courses on Chinese religions and philosophy, and comparative ethics in Wales since 1991. Dr Yao has published widely in the area of Chinese religions and comparative studies of religion. His recent English publications include *An Introduction to Confucianism* (2000) and *Confucianism and Christianity* (1996), the Chinese translation of which has been published by China Social Science Publishing House, Beijing (2002).

Michael York is Principal Lecturer in Cultural Astronomy and Astrology as well as Director of the Sophia Centre at Bath Spa University College, England, where he also teaches at the Department for the Study of Religions and coordinates the New Age and Pagan Studies Programme. He also directs the Bath Archive for Contemporary Religious Affairs. He is the author of *The Emerging Network: A Sociology of the New Age and Neo-Pagan Movements* (1995), *The Divine Versus the Asurian: An Interpretation of Indo-European Cult and Myth* (1996) and *Pagan Theology: Paganism as a World Religion* (2003).

Select Bibliography

Please note: An extensive bibliography, including primary and secondary sources and relevant website addresses, is available on the publisher's website (see address on page 4).

M. Adler, *Drawing Down the Moon: Witches, Druids, Goddess-Worshippers, and Other Pagans in America Today.* Boston: Beacon Press, 1986.

E. Arweck & Peter B. Clarke, *New Religious Movements in Western Europe: An Annotated Bibliography.* Westport: Greenwood Press, 1997.

R.D. Baird (ed.), *Religion in Modern India.* New York: South Asia Publications, 1989.

E. Barker (ed.), *New Religious Movements: A Perspective for Understanding Society.* Lewiston: Edwin Mellen, 1982.

D.V. Barrett, *The New Believers: Sects, 'Cults', and Alternative Religions.* London: Cassell, 2001.

John Bowker (ed.), *Oxford Dictionary of World Religions.* Oxford: Oxford University Press, 1997.

D.G. Bromley & J.G. Melton (eds.), *Cults, Religion and Violence.* Cambridge: Cambridge University Press, 2002.

S. Bruce, *God is Dead: Secularization in the West.* Oxford: Blackwell, 2002.

G.D. Chryssides, *Exploring New Religions.* London: Cassell, 1999.

G.D. Chryssides, *Historical Dictionary of New Religious Movements.* Metuchen: Scarecrow Press, 2001.

P.B. Clarke (ed.), *The New Evangelists: Recruitment, Methods and Aims of New Religious Movements.* London: Ethnographica, 1987.

P.B. Clarke (ed.), *New Developments in the World of Islam.* London: Luzac Oriental, 1998.

L.L. Dawson, *Comprehending Cults: the Sociology of New Religious Movements.* New York: Oxford University Press, 1999.

L.L. Dawson, *Cults and New Religious Movements: A Reader.* Oxford: Blackwell, 2003.

J.J.M. De Groot, *Sectarianism and Religious Persecution in China.* New York: Barnes and Noble, 1972.

C. Eller, *Living in the Lap of the Goddess: the Feminist Spirituality Movement in America.* New York: Crossroad, 1993.

R.S. Ellwood, *The Sixties Spiritual Awakening: American Religion Moving from Modern to Postmodern.* New Brunswick: Rutgers University Press, 1994.

M.P. Fisher, *Religions Today: An Introduction.* London: Routledge, 2001.

J.R. Hall, *Apocalypse Observed: Religious Movements and Violence in North America, Europe, and Japan.* London: Routledge, 2000.

O. Hammer, *Claiming Knowledge: Strategies of Epistemology from Theosophy to the New Age.* Leiden: Brill, 2001.

W.J. Hanegraaff, *New Age Religion and Western Culture: Esotericism in the Mirror of Secular Thought.* Leiden: Brill, 1996.

H. Hardacre, *Kurozumikyô and the New Religions of Japan.* Princeton: Princeton University Press, 1986.

G. Harvey, *Listening People, Speaking Earth: Contemporary Paganism.* London: Hurst & Company, 1997.

G. Harvey, *Indigenous Religions: A Companion.* London: Cassell, 2000.

P. Heelas, *The New Age Movement: The Celebration of the Self and the Sacralization of Modernity.* Oxford: Blackwell, 1986.

P. Heelas (ed.), *Religion, Modernity and Postmodernity.* Oxford: Blackwell, 1998.

I. Hexham & K. Poewe, *New Religions as Global Cultures: Making the Human Sacred.* Boulder: Westview Press, 1997.

S. Hunt, *Alternative Religions: A Sociological Introduction.* Aldershot: Ashgate, 2003.

E. Isichei, *Voices of the Poor: a History of Imagination in Africa.* University of Rochester, 2002.

R. Kisala & M. Mullins (eds), *Religion and Social Crisis in Japan: Understanding Japanese Society through the Aum Affair.* Basingstoke: Palgrave, 2001.

R. Landes (ed.), *Encyclopedia of Millennialism and Millennial Movements.* New York: Routledge, 2000.

J.R. Lewis, *Legitimating New Religions.* New Brunswick: Rutgers University Press, 2003.

D. Lyon, *Jesus in Disneyland: Religion in Postmodern Times.* Cambridge: Polity, 2000.

M.E. Marty & R.S. Appleby (eds), *Fundamentalisms Comprehended.* Chicago: University of Chicago Press, 1995.

J.G. Melton, *New Age Almanac.* New York: Visible Ink, 1991.

J.G. Melton, *Encyclopedia of American Religions*, 6th edition. Detroit: Gale Research, 2001.

J.G. Melton, *Encyclopedic Handbook of Cults in America.* New York: Garland, 1992.

T. Miller (ed.), *America's Alternative Religions.* Albany:

State University of New York Press, 1995.

S. Palmer, *Moon Sisters, Krishna Mothers, Rajneesh Lovers: Women's Roles in New Religions*. New York: Syracuse University Press, 1995.

S. Palmer & C. Hardman (eds), *Children in New Religions*. New Brunswick: Rutgers University Press, 1999.

C. Partridge (ed.), *Dictionary of Contemporary Religion in the Western World*. Leicester: IVP, 2002.

C. Partridge (ed.), *Fundamentalisms*. Carlisle: Paternoster, 2002.

C. Partridge (ed.), *UFO Religions*. London: Routledge, 2003.

J. Pearson (ed.), *Belief Beyond Boundaries: Wicca, Celtic Spirituality and the New Age*. Milton Keynes & Altershot: Open University & Ashgate, 2002.

E. Puttick, *Women in New Religions*. London: Macmillan, 1997.

A. Rawlinson, *The Book of Enlightened Masters: Western Teachers in Eastern Traditions*. Chicago: Open Court, 1997.

I. Reader, *Religion in Contemporary Japan*. Basingstoke & Honolulu: Macmillan and University of Hawaii Press, 1991.

T. Robbins & S. Palmer (eds), *Millennium, Messiahs, and Mayhem: Contemporary Apocalyptic Movements*. New York: Routledge, 1997.

M. Rothstein (ed.), *New Age Religion and Globalization*. Aarhus: Aarhus University Press, 2001.

J.A. Saliba, *Perspectives on New Religious Movements*. London: Geoffrey Chapman, 1995.

J.A. Saliba, *Christian Responses to the New Age Movement*. London: Cassell, 1999.

N. Scotland, *Sectarian Religion in Contemporary Britain*. Carlisle: Paternoster, 2000.

A. Sharma (ed.), *Today's Woman in World Religions*. Albany: State University of New York Press, 1994.

J.R. Stone, *Expecting Armageddon: Essential Readings in Failed Prophecy*. London: Routledge, 2000.

S. Sutcliffe & M. Bowman (eds), *Beyond New Age: Exploring Alternative Spirituality*. Edinburgh: Edinburgh University Press, 2000.

T. Swain & G. Trompf, *The Religions of Oceania*. London: Routledge, 1995.

G.W. Trompf (ed.), *Cargo Cults and Millenarian Movements: Transoceanic Comparisons of New Religious Movements*. Berlin: Mouton de Gruyter, 1990.

P.H. Van Ness, *Spirituality and the Secular Quest*. London: SCM, 1996.

C. Wessinger (ed.), *Millennialism, Persecution, and Violence: Historical Cases*, New York: Syracuse University Press, 2000.

B. Wilson & J. Cresswell (eds), *New Religious Movements: Challenge and Response*. London: Routledge, 1999.

D. Wojcik, *The End of the World As We Know It: Faith, Fatalism, and Apocalypse in America*. New York & London: New York University Press, 1997.

L. Woodhead, P. Fletcher, H. Kawanami & D. Smith (eds), *Religions in the Modern World*. London: Routledge, 2002.

L. Woodhead & P. Heelas (eds), *Religion in Modern Times: An Interpretive Anthology*. Oxford: Blackwell, 2000.

C.K. Yang, *Religion in Chinese Society*. Taipei: SMC, 1994.

Index

Acknowledgments

My work as editor has been greatly assisted by the careful scholarship and professionalism of the contributors. More than that, I have, as ever, learned a great deal from reading their excellent articles. To them all, I am deeply indebted.

In particular, I should like to thank Dr J. Gordon Melton for his support for the project, for reading through the entire manuscript, for his invaluable advice and for writing the Foreword. I am also indebted to Dr George D. Chryssides for his much-appreciated readiness to discuss material and for his always-sound comments. Many thanks too to Professor Paul Heelas for being so willing to look through the final manuscript and offer comment. Thanks are also due to Professor Gavin Flood, Professor Andreas Grünschloss, Dr Almut Hintze, Dr Richard Hoskins, Dr William Kay, Dr Robert Kisala, Professor James R. Lewis, Dr Jean-François Mayer, Dr Jaakko Närvä, Professor Ian Reader, Professor Mikael Rothstein and Dr Birgit Staemmler, all of whom offered nuggets, sometimes very large nuggets, of advice and assistance at various stages of the project.

Finally, I am enormously grateful both to Morag Reeve, the Commissioning Editor at Lion Publishing, for her patience over the last couple of years, helpful comments and continuous enthusiasm for the project, and also to Angela Handley, the superb copy editor, whose insightful comments and attention to detail made this volume far better than it otherwise would have been.

Picture Acknowledgments

Picture research by Zooid Pictures Limited

AAP (Australian Associated Press): pp. 416–17

Associated Press: pp. 87; 15, Pier Paolo Cito; 109, Mike Ablans; 143, Ric Feld; 206–207, Apichart Weerawong; 232, Kathy Willens

Auroville Outreach: pp. 196–97

Copyright © Bibliotheca Philosophica Hermetica/J.R. Ritman Library, Amsterdam: p. 114

Bridgeman Art Library: pp. 103, Private Collection/Rubin Museum; 125, Louvre, Paris, France

Corbis UK Ltd.: pp. 4, 41, 171, 194–95, 290–91; 2-3, 234–35, Owen Franken; 5, Phil Schermeister; 18–19, 123, 334–35, Sandro Vannini; 25, 31, 211, 299, Archivo Iconografico, S.A.; 28–29, 277, Adam Woolfitt; 39, 72–73, 77, 92, 140, 226, 313, 321, 342, 362, 368, 371, 377, 400, Bettmann; 60–61, Daniel Lainé; 63, Alain Le Garsmeur; 66, Richard Hamilton Smith; 78, Roger Ressmeyer; 79, Greg Smith SABA; 82, Kevin Schafer; 85, Ed Eckstein; 106–107, Annie Griffiths Belt; 133, George W. Wright; 157, Ted Streshinsky; 159, Ric Ergenbright; 160–61, Blaine Harrington III; 164–65, David Samuel Robbins; 167, 186, Lindsay Hebberd; 169, 361, Tim Graham/Sygma; 179, Chris Lisle; 212, Dean Conger; 214–15, Kevin Fleming; 218–19, Chris Rainier; 221, Michael S. Yamashita; 248–49, Wolfgang Kaehler; 251, Swim Ink; 254–55, Yang Liu; 264–65, Touhig Sion/Sygma; 267, Buddy Mays; 268–269, Michael & Patricia Fogden; 270, Charles & Josette Lenars; 273, Anders Ryman; 283, Contemporary African Art Collection Limited; 296, Rebecca McEntee/Sygma; 303, 338, Historical Picture Archive; 307, Mimmo Jodice; 316–17, Zen Icknow; 318, Dave Bartruff; 324, Hulton-Deutsch Collection; 331, Geray Sweeney; 357, Burstein Collection; 380, Gianni Dagli Orti; 386, Schifres Lucas/Sygma

Eckankar. p. 190

Dr Theodore Gabriel: p. 180

Gamma/Katz Pictures: p. 412

Hulton|Archive/Getty Images: pp. 36, 305, 326, 328

Magnum Photos: pp. 45, Abbas; 120–21, Leonard Freed; 192–93, Raghu Rai

Dr Peter Jan Margry: p. 99

Network: pp. 33, 34, Robert Huber/Lookat; 48, Jodi

Bieber; 65, Mike Goldwater

Bury Peerless: pp. 145, 151, 154

Photo Oikoumene/World Council of Churches: p. 57, John Taylor

PictureNet Africa: pp. 52–53, Nadine Hutton

Press Association: pp. 37; 136, EPA European Press Agency; 278–79, Toby Melville

Raël: p. 405

Rex Features: pp. 115, Ralph Merlino; 128–29, 261, Sipa Press; 183, Henry Grossman/ TimePix; 188, Geoff Dowen; 347, John Pickering; 351, Action Press; 397, Alex Woods

Trip & Art Directors Photo Library: pp. 148, Ibrahim; 176, Dinodia; 245, H. Rogers; 259, A. Deutsch

Lion Publishing

Commissioning editor: Morag Reeve

Editors: Angela Handley, Jenni Dutton, Olwen Turchetta

Jacket designer: Jonathan Roberts

Book designer: Nicholas Rous

Production manager: Kylie Ord